4-18-03

Software Engineering and Computer Games

We work with leading authors to develop the
strongest educational materials in Computing,
bringing cutting-edge thinking and best
learning practice to a global market.

Under a range of well-known imprints, including
Addison-Wesley, we craft high quality print and
electronic publications which help readers to understand
and apply their content, whether studying or at work.

To find out more about the complete range of our
publishing, please visit us on the World Wide Web at:
www.pearsoneduc.com

Software Engineering and Computer Games

Rudy Rucker

San Jose, California State University

ADDISON-WESLEY

An imprint of Pearson Education

Harlow, England • London • New York • Boston • San Francisco • Toronto • Sydney • Singapore • Hong Kong
Tokyo • Seoul • Taipei • New Delhi • Cape Town • Madrid • Mexico City • Amsterdam • Munich • Paris • Milan

Pearson Education Limited
Edinburgh Gate
Harlow
Essex CM20 2JE
United Kingdom

and Associated Companies throughout the world

Visit us on the World Wide Web at:
www.pearsoneduc.com

First published 2003

The programs in this book have been included for their instructional value. They have been
tested with care but are not guaranteed for any particular purpose. The publisher does not
offer any warranties or representations nor does it accept any liabilities with respect to the
programs.

Many of the designations used by manufacturers and sellers to distinguish their products are
claimed as trademarks. Pearson Education has made every attempt to supply trademark
information about manufacturers and their products mentioned in this book. A list of the
trademark designations and their owners appears on page xxiii.

ISBN 0201 767910

British Library Cataloguing-in-Publication Data
A catalogue record for this book is available from the British Library

Library of Congress Cataloging-in-Publication Data
Rucker, Rudy v. B. (Rudy von Bitter), 1946–
    Software engineering and computer games / Rudy Rucker.
        p. cm.
    Includes bibliographical references and index.
    ISBN 0-201-76791-0 (alk. paper)
    1. Software engineering. 2. Computer games—Programming.   I. Title.
QA76.758 .R83   2002
005.1—dc21   2002074649

10   9   8   7   6   5   4   3   2   1
07   06   05   04   03

Typeset in 9/12pt Stone Serif by 35
Printed in Great Britain by Henry Ling Limited, at the Dorset Press, Dorchester, DT1 1HD

Brief contents

Contents

Foreword

Rudy Rucker. You may know him as a science fiction author, mathematician, or technologist who dreams of worlds inhabited by living machines, two-dimensional creatures, or numbers with names. Or, you may know him as the guy giving you a test today in your Computer Science class! That's where I started . . .

It was some time in the mid 80's that I first met Rudy, or back then Dr. Rucker. I was a freshman attending San José State University, triple majoring in Math, Computer Science, and Electrical Engineering. I had enrolled in an assembly language class or something similar that he was teaching. I remember arguing with Dr. Rucker about not getting full credit for a program I had written that multiplied two numbers together really fast in 8-bit assembly language. Dr. Rucker didn't really look at the program closely and assumed I was wrong since the technique I used was very subtle and very advanced, a standard trick of a game programmer, but to the untrained eye it couldn't possibly work . . . So I went into his office and I convinced him to really look closely at it, and he did. When he was complete with his analysis, he smiled and said something like, *'André you're right'*. From that point on, we spoke more frequently and I told him about my development of video games. Rudy was very interested in something that I too had a love for, which was artificial intelligence, emergent behavior, and cellular automata, all of which began his obsession with ants and little creepy crawling things that pervade all of his work (and mine).

Back in those days we were all exploring new worlds – we didn't have a plan – just looking around and seeing what happened. Out of all the professors I encountered, only two made an impression on me and Dr. Rucker was one of them. Of course, his lectures always seemed to be a little from the 'hip', or maybe a better word 'organic'. I rarely took notes, I listened for the meaning between the lines, the things he was thinking, but couldn't really say in a class-room setting. Crazy things like the possibility of living machines, computers that have sex, anti-time, and many other concepts that could get you hanged in these parts. In the end, I confirmed that there are other people that have the same crazy ideas I do, and that was important.

Time passed, I graduated, and Rudy and I kept in touch. Every now and then I would ask him something, or vice versa. I would read one of his sci-fi books once in a while, his name would come up in conversations about William

Gibson's work, or AI, and people couldn't believe I knew him! They would ask what he was like, and so forth. Rudy Rucker had a huge cult following based on his sci-fi work which was really cool, and a part of his personality I never knew about in detail.

But, the only thing I ever wondered was why he had never written a serious technical book about computer science? Make no mistake, he is a brilliant mathematician, but only now did he finally have time or the subject matter to write a computer science book that really interested him. At least that's what I think.

In any case, *Software Engineering and Computer Games* is a very important book: it's the first time that anyone has even attempted to try and make heads or tails of the software engineering paradigm as applied to the development of video games. As far as I am concerned, this book should be a requirement of anyone that wants to write games – period. Every game book I have ever read, or written for that matter, explains techniques to develop games, graphics, AI, networking, whatever, but no one ever really explains how to 'software engineer' a game.

After reading Rudy's book, I was really excited: all the techniques that I had been using and developing over the years, he had put into a nice, complete package for others to read and learn from. Additionally, he made a science of game development. Game programmers are gods, that's without a doubt, but this book shows why! Rudy has step-by-step created a game programming framework which he calls 'Pop' (I will let him tell you why) that allows you to create 2D and 3D games without worrying about all the low level details. So what, you might ask? Well, the point is that he shows the entire thought process, and software engineering cycle of this framework, from UML diagrams to implementation. This is something I guarantee even the guys that wrote HALO didn't do!

Point being, after reading this book you will be a better coder, software engineer, and game programmer all in one. Not to mention that the book is all inclusive. It covers object oriented programming, physics, 2D, 3D, C++ techniques, MFC (yuck!), and contains numerous complete projects to illustrate various techniques.

But, here's a secret . . . come close . . . read between the lines. In these pages is a story, a story about something that today we are seeing the first baby steps of – if you look carefully you will find it. So take advantage of this rare glimpse of such a fascinating and brilliant personality as Rudy Rucker applied to this very technical matter of game development and software engineering.

André LaMothe
Computer Scientist/Author

April 2002

Trademark Notice

The following designations are trademarks or registered trademarks of the organizations whose names follow in brackets: 3D Studio Max (Autodesk, Inc.); Ada95 (Kempe Software Capital Enterprises); Age of Empires, AppWizard, DirectX, DirectX Sound, Internet Explorer, Microsoft C#, Microsoft Foundation Classes, Microsoft Office, Microsoft PowerPoint, Microsoft Project, Microsoft SourceSafe, Microsoft Visual Basic, Microsoft Visual Studio, Microsoft Windows, Microsoft Word, Windows Explorer, Windiff, WordPad (Microsoft Corporation); APL (International Business Machines Corporated); Asteroids, Breakout, Centipede, Missile Command, Pong (Atari, Inc.); Defender (Williams Electronics, Inc.); Director, DreamWeaver, Flash, Shockwave (Macromedia, Inc.); Doom, Quake (Id Software, Inc.); Fortran (Compaq); Galaga, Pac Man (Namco Ltd.); Gauntlet (Midway Games West, Inc.); Half-Life, King's Quest (Sierra On-Line, Inc.); Java, Modula (Sun Microsystems, Inc.); KaZaA (Sharman Networks); Linux (Linus Torvalds); MAME (The MAME Team); Mario, Nintendo GameBoy (Nintendo of America, Inc.); MIDI (Midi Manufacturers Association, Inc.); Napster (Napster, Inc.); Netscape (Netscape Communications Corporation); Photoshop, PostScript (Adobe Systems, Inc.); Rubik's Cube (Seven Towns Limited); SimCity (Maxis Corporation); SmallTalk (Xerox Corporation); Space Invaders (Taito America Corporation); StairMaster (StairMaster Sports/Medical Products, Inc.); WinZip (WinZip Computing).

Abbreviations

AFX	Application Frameworks
API	Appication Program Interface
CAD	Computer Aided Design
GUI	graphic user interface
GDI	Graphics Device Interface
IDE	Integrated Development Environment
MFC	Microsoft Foundation Classes
MDI	Multiple Document Interface
MAME	Multiple Arcade Machine Emulator
OOP	object-oriented programming
OOD	object-oriented design
OOA	object-oriented analysis
QA	quality analysis
RAD	requirements and design
RCS	Revision Control Software
RTF	rich text format
ROP	raster operation
SDI	Single Document Interface
SAD	specification and design
UML	Unified Modelling Language

Acknowledgements

Special thanks to those of my students whose games I mention in Chapter 19.
Student games marked with a ∗ appear on the book cover; the biggest cover image is from the 3D Jewel Hunter game.

Fall, 1999	Scott Choi, N. Yen, J. C. Wang	Body Defense
	Paul Sumares, Jake Woodhams, Puneet Dhaliwal	Brick Bugs
	Vladi Sankin, Pasha Sadri, Vu Hwang	Garden∗
	Sue Wilner, Theresa Nguyen, Jean Schundler	Grammar
	Joe Bond, Keith Shum, Vinh Vu	Lunatic
	Minh, Sean, Norman	Olympod
	Supriya, Shimali, Raymond	Paratrooper
	Wei Zhang, Ramya Parasuram, Chris Feliton	Safari
	Kelvin Shum, Ken Shitamoto, Tam Minh	Shepherd Boy
Spring, 2000	Bryan, Minh, Norman	Airstrike
	Harry Fu, Kerry Goodman, Rosanna Tse	Amazing Mouse
	Mark Anderson, Raymond Ochoa, Rina Desai	BB Rampage
	Bobby Tse, Douglas Andersen, Sarah Levantine	Deer's Revenge∗
	Karissa Huang, Karen-Hoa Do, Kendra Ladeau	Pixie Quest∗
	Naheed Himmati, Smita Joshi, Sunita Gupta	Treasure Hunt
Fall, 2000	Chi-Ping Chang, Wyley Dai, Chung Vong	City Hunter
	Michael Moore, David Dong, Karno Halim, Martina Mesic	Climber
	Allan Wong, Chetan Jhaveri, Tuan Vu	Dash 2000
	Sudhir Srikanth, Thu Nguyen, Jason Ngai	Four Pieces of Fate
	Wen Jin Mei, Stanley Chen, Myat Min	LifeSaver
	Hung Dinh, Nam Lam, Thanh Phan	Pinball
	Jeremy Dittrich, Gerry Girard, Nisha Ahluwalia	Robonator
	Gary Chin, Chi Chan, Uri Rayzberg	Soccer
Spring, 2001	Marvin, Alex, Phuoc	Alien Invaders
	Jimmy Huang, Tony Xu, Duy Nguyen	Footsball
	Craig Clark, Cherry Yang, Jason Peng	Labyrinth Roller
	Lee Lacanlale, Andrew Nguyen, Kiminori Inagaki	Lost Crown
	Dipti Bhatt, Donna Portacio	Triangle Stacker
Fall, 2001	Chi Chan, Wyley Dai, Madhuri Potu	3D Blaster
	Giavinh Pham, Charlie Tran, Thuy Bui	3D Jewel Hunter∗∗
	Randolph Schmidt, Jose Rivera, Bharat Joshi	AntiVirus∗
	Andy Wu, Sam Wu, Anthony Tu, Nhut Hyunh	Bermuda
	Don Bernal, Wallun Chan, Frank Chang	Ghostcastle
	Isabel Zhang, Karen Chow, Yisi Lau	GoFishing
	Lee Gong, Rich Prillinger, Joseph Cheng	TequilaWorm
Spring, 2002	Kwok Wing Tang, Minh Dang, Thuy Nguyen	3D Bug
	Chiao-Kai Yang, Raymond Chan, Doug Simmons	3D Rat Race
	Jim Cheung, Nithin Reddy, Joko Sutomo	JumpSport
	Doug Uno, Kenny Moy, Haitham Halloum	KillTime∗
	Kenji Tan, Bao Mai, Rui Chen, Dung Luc	Pop Rally
	Darrian Hale, David Wong, Ken Pao	Smart Cat∗

Introduction

In developing *Software Engineering and Computer Games* and its accompanying software framework I had four broad goals.

- To teach a lively style of object-oriented software engineering.
- To show how to bring a complete program to the level of a commercial release.
- To provide a 'game engine' framework of linked classes for game development.
- To create programs that are interactive, rapidly executing, and visually beautiful.

Software Engineering and Computer Games was originally developed for use as the primary textbook in my undergraduate software engineering and graduate software projects courses in the Department of Computer Science at San José State University (SJSU for short). In these classes we cover the topics of software engineering in the context of having student teams design and implement computer games. Depending on the nature of the course, lesser or greater emphasis can be placed on the student projects.

The book is also meant to be suitable for self-study. Readers are encouraged to use the book to create their own games. *Software Engineering and Computer Games* is specifically designed so as to allow would-be game developers to get their own games running easily and rapidly.

In order to make it feasible for readers of this book to carry out a game project without getting lost in endless details, I've created an open source C++ software framework for developing computer games; this is the 'Pop Framework,' with source code available for free download from the book's website:

www.rudyrucker.com/computergames

As well as working as a software engineering text or as a self-study guide for budding game-developers, *Software Engineering and Computer Games* can also serve as the text for a course on computer games such as the Computer Game Design and Programming one we have at SJSU. The idea of having university Computer Science departments teach computer game programming is a fairly new idea. *Software Engineering and Computer Games* should serve to show that a course of this nature can be taught in a sound and academically respectable fashion.

Software Engineering and Computer Games uses the Windows platform. Why Windows? Although the death of Windows is regularly predicted, it remains the most popular operating system on personal computers. Windows is a strong, mature platform for writing graphics-intensive and/or computation-intensive programs to run on a desktop machine. By using Windows we get, essentially for free, a lot of goodies that can otherwise be hard to implement: things like menus, toolbars, cursor tools, resizable windows, multiple document interface, cutting and pasting and file handling. Certainly the Java environment can implement these features, but the process is somewhat easier with the Microsoft Visual Studio development environment. And in terms of job-hunting, it's very nice to have a solid Windows computer game project of one's own to demo.

As at most other universities, SJSU has no formal Windows programming prerequisite for the software engineering or software projects courses; in fact we've recently switched our introductory courses to Java. But it's valuable to study Windows programs in some upper-division courses so that the students can gain experience with full-featured real-world desktop projects. *Software Engineering and Computer Games* is designed so as to be self-contained, with no prior knowledge of Windows programming required. A familiarity with C++ is recommended, but we have a C++ review chapter for those starting with only a knowledge of Java.

The book has two parts. *Part I: Software Engineering and Computer Games* is the essential lecture material to be covered in the course, and *Part II: Software Engineering and Computer Games Reference* contains detailed reference information about topics essential to fully understanding Part I.

My procedure in using this book as a textbook is to lecture during the first half of the course and during the second half of the course to help the students spend the classroom time working on projects in three-person teams. We try and cover most of the Part I material during the lectures, and the students read from the Part II material on their own as needed. If using the book for self-study, you might expect to read through most of Part I and to occasionally refer to Part II. If your immediate goal is simply to get going on making working games, you can skip right to Chapter 3, do the exercises at the end to get a first game working, and then study Chapters 7–17 to see how to make more complicated games.

The necessity of breaking the book into two parts arises from the dilemma of wanting to teach Windows-based software engineering to people who might not know Windows programming. Part II covers topics such as the advanced features of C++, Windows programming, the Microsoft Foundation Classes (MFC), and the use of Microsoft Visual Studio – which is indeed the standard tool used by many computer game designers.

The book touches on nine topics.

- Basic *software engineering* principles and techniques.
- How to organize and complete a substantial software *project*.
- Practical examples of *object-oriented* design and programming.
- The design of *computer games*.

- *Simulating physics* inside our computer-generated worlds.
- *Artificial life*, or how to simulate live creatures inside a computer program.
- Using two- and three-dimensional *Computer graphics* to create a virtual reality.
- *Windows* programming using the MFC application framework.
- How to develop a project using Microsoft *Visual Studio*.

The code accompanying the book is called the Pop Framework. The Pop Framework consists of C++ implementations of a few dozen classes that are useful for constructing two- and three-dimensional computer games. *Software Engineering and Computer Games* starts with the basics of software engineering, and then presents the user with the Pop program, built with the Pop framework to have a number of different game modes. The game modes include an Asteroids-style Spacewar, a Picknpop game of picking and popping bubbles, an Airhockey game, a three-dimensional shooting game, a free-play game called Dambuilder, a side-scroller stub called Ballworld, and a few more. Each of the games can be run in two-dimensional or three-dimensional graphics.

The name 'Pop' for the framework was chosen in memory of my beloved father, not that he was at all interested in computers, but what the heck. This is for you, Pop!

At the writing of this introduction nearly 100 different student projects have been built using the Pop Framework, with the result that the code has become

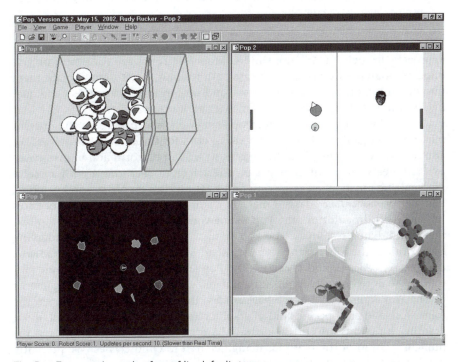

The Pop Framework running four of its default games

quite solid and easy to extend. In *Software Engineering and Computer Games*, the workings of the Pop code is explained within the general context of software engineering, and the user is guided into extending one of the game modes to create his or her own computer game.

Why teach something so seemingly frivolous as computer game programming and design in an upper-division computer science class?

- *Breadth*. Computer games integrate techniques and code from the whole spectrum of computer science: software engineering, graphics, artificial intelligence, and user interface design.

- *Depth*. Developing a computer game involves many different levels of skills, from low-level algorithm implementation to high-level object-oriented design. Completing a computer game project requires a deep, sustained effort.

- *Excitement*. The visual and interactive nature of computer game projects can deeply engage a student's interest. Because it's fairly easy to tell if a game works well, the goal is satisfyingly clear-cut and challenging.

- *Simulation applications*. Writing a computer game involves creating an object-oriented real-time simulation of a certain kind of toy world. The skills and techniques can be transferred to simulating a wide range of other systems.

- *Career preparation*. A completed computer game is an impressive program for students to demonstrate to prospective employers, whatever the nature of the job. In addition, a number of students are interested in getting jobs specifically as game developers.

Software Engineering and Computer Games uses C++ and an object-oriented approach throughout. We use Unified Modeling Language (UML) for object-oriented analysis, we discuss software patterns and how to incorporate them into our object-oriented design process, and we consistently use the techniques of object-oriented programming to implement our classes.

Among the special classes in the Pop Framework is a *cCritter* class to represent our computer game 'critters,' and a *cGame* class for the games themselves. We also develop some reusable utility classes such as a polygonal and bitmap-based *cSprite* objects for putting images on the screen, a *cRandomizer* with a useful randomizing function, a *cVector* class and a *cMatrix* class for physics and graphics, and a *cPerformanceTimer* class to make our animations real-time and processor-independent. In addition, the Pop Framework includes some sound, toolbar, menu and dialog resources. The Pop Framework is built upon the underying framework of the MFC, using some standard MFC classes: *CPopApp*, *CMainFrame*, *CChildFrame*, *CPopDoc*, and *CPopView*. The Pop Framework's MFC classes are customized so as to be easily usable for animated simulations or computer games.

The Pop Framework has a *cGraphics* class that acts as a bridge between the framework and any specific kind of graphics implementation. That is, all of our graphics functions are in the abstract base class *cGraphics*, with the specific implementation of the methods being deferred to child classes. We presently have *cGraphicsMFC* and *cGraphicsOpenGL* implementations.

The *cGraphicsMFC* uses standard Windows API graphics calls. These calls have an undeserved reputation for being slow; the Pop Framework's speed is in fact more than adequate for typical computer games, easily achieving update rates far in excess of the minimal 30 frames per second that one typically needs. The key trick is to assemble each new frame in an offscreen *cMemoryDC* object provided by the Pop Framework, and to then rapidly block copy this image to the screen. The *cGraphicsMFC* is optimal for two-dimensional games including sprites and graphics, but doesn't have adequate support for fully three-dimensional games.

The *cGraphicsOpenGL* provides support for three-dimensional graphics, with z-buffering, lighting effects, and so on. On modern machines with graphics cards that have hardware OpenGL support, the *cGraphicsOpenGL* gives acceptable animation frame rates. As well as supporting polygons, we support bitmap textures in OpenGL.

Software Engineering and Computer Games was developed through nearly a dozen draft versions for use in my undergraduate software engineering and graduate software projects courses over the past 15 years. Above and beyond covering the syllabi for these courses, my agenda is always the same: to teach the students to write complete, visually interesting programs that seem to come alive.

Being a programmer – or a computer science professor – is a little like living on a Stairmaster. Your field never stops changing; your old knowledge is continually being swept into oblivion. *Software Engineering and Computer Games* and the Pop Framework undergo updates and upgrades every semester. It's never really finished; there are always more features one could add. The Pop Framework has many good starting points for further projects, ranging in level from a homework assignment to a Master's Degree thesis.

Software Engineering and Computer Games is designed for the latest flavors of Windows and C++. As of 2003, the flavors of Windows we support are Windows 95, Windows 98, Windows Millennium Edition, Windows NT 4.0, Windows 2000, and Windows XP. The current Pop Framework was developed using the C++ compiler and integrated development environment that are part of the development product called Microsoft Visual Studio. Strictly speaking, the part of Visual Studio that we use is called Visual C++, but in this book we will use the more general 'Visual Studio' to refer specifically to the Microsoft C++ compiler and development environment.

There are two versions of Visual Studio in current use, the older Visual Studio, Version 6.0, and the more recent Visual Studio.NET, which is also known as Visual Studio, Version 7.0. With regard to our task of building C++ programs, the two products are quite similar, although there are some minor differences in the layouts of the controls. When necessary, we distinguish between the two products by calling them Visual Studio 6.0 and Visual Studio 7.0.

Although most of the Pop Framework was developed while using Visual Studio 6.0, the most recent builds have been created using Visual Studio 7.0. The framework code builds with no warnings in either environment. We supply both Version 6.0 and Version 7.0 project files with the code.

When the text mentions specific control sequences for Visual Studio interface, we will, where necessary, describe both the Version 7.0 [and the Version 6.0] controls, using square brackets around the Version 6.0 controls. Certainly most readers will be moving to Visual Studio 7.0 soon, but at this point, Visual Studio 6.0 is still very widespread. Also it may be that some programmers will prefer to stick with the battle-tested Version 6.0 until more service packs for Version 7.0 have been released.

We provide a convenient Appendix C to summarize for both versions the specific Visual Studio control sequences which we discuss. Any problems or fixes involving the code will be discussed on the book's web-site **www.rudyrucker.com/ computergames**. This is also the place to check for new upgrades to the Pop Framework and for examples of student projects.

Software Engineering and Computer Games will also be useful to individual readers who are looking for a quick path into Windows MFC programming. Let's stress again that you do not need to know any Windows programming before using *Software Engineering and Computer Games*. A familiarity with C++ is recommended, but *Software Engineering and Computer Games* does include discussions of all the key C++ topics that we use.

A note on notation. We've tried to consistently use some special fonts for different purposes.

- **C++ Language reserved words, Windows API functions, Windows Data types, built-in MFC classes and their methods**

- *Special purpose classes and methods defined for our project*

- Names of directories and names of files

- **Menu item selections or dialog box controls**

- `Examples of C++ code`

There are already some very good books on many of the coding topics we treat. For a more traditional software engineering course, it may be appropriate to accompany the use of *Software Engineering and Computer Games* with a book such as Steve McConnell, *Software Project Survival Kit* (Microsoft Press, 1997). It's worth mentioning that Steve McConnell's other books, *Code Complete* (Microsoft Press, 1993) and *Rapid Development* (Microsoft Press, 1996), are wonderful sources of information about, respectively, program-level and project-level practices to use for efficient software engineering.

Perhaps the most popular older surveys of the field of software engineering are Roger Pressman, *Software Engineering: A Practitioner's Approach* (McGraw-Hill, 2000) and Ian Somerville, *Software Engineering* (Addison-Wesley, 2001). And there is much to recommend in the more recent book, D. Hamlet and J. Maybee, *The Engineering of Software* (Addison-Wesley, 2001). Software engineering texts range from being very code-oriented to being very process-oriented. Viewed as a software engineering text, my *Software Engineering and Computer Games* is further towards the code-oriented end of the spectrum than the other software engineering books mentioned.

Ideally, a computer science curriculum might have two software engineering courses: a broad-based process-oriented course, and an in-depth software project course using a book like *Software Engineering and Computer Games*. It would seem that the two courses could be taken in either order, as each would shed light on the other. On the one hand, it's nice to have studied the software engineering process before attempting a big project; on the other hand, it's much easier to appreciate the purpose and importance of the software engineering process after you've actually gone through the experience of building at least one substantial project.

Two good C++ books are those by Cay Horstmann: *Mastering C++* (John Wiley, 1991), and *Practical Object-Oriented Development in C++ and Java* (Wiley, 1997). Charles Petzold, *Programming Windows 95* (Microsoft Press, 1996) is a classic general reference for non-MFC Windows programming. The successive editions of *Inside Visual Studio* (Microsoft Press, 1997), by David Kruglinski and others, have good overviews of the Microsoft Visual Studio Developer's Studio with many short examples. Alan Feuer's rich and knowledgeable *MFC Programming* (Addison-Wesley, 1997) is an excellent book about MFC. George Shepherd and Scot Wingo, *MFC Internals: Inside the Microsoft Foundation Class Architecture* (Addison-Wesley, 1996), gives a valuable low-level guide to the workings of MFC, including some material which can't be found in the official documentation or in any other books.

Kendall Scott and Martin Fowler, *UML Distilled* (Addison-Wesley, 2000) is a very nice little book covering the basics of the Unified Modeling Language. The standard book on design patterns is the well-written and inspiring book, Erich Gamma, Richard Helm, Ralph Johnson, and John Vlissides, *Design Patterns: Elements of Reusable Object-Oriented Software* (Addison-Wesley, 1995).

Regarding OpenGL programming, the so-called 'Red, Blue, and White' books (named after the main colors of their otherwise identical covers) are canonical. These are, respectively, Jason Woo, Jackie Neider, Tom Davis, and Dave Shreiner, *OpenGL Programming Guide* (Addison-Wesley, 1999), Renate Kempf and Chris Frazier, eds, *OpenGL Reference Manual* (Addison-Wesley, 1999), and Ron Fosner, *OpenGL Programming for Windows 95 and Windows NT* (Addison-Wesley, 1997). These books can also be found on-line. A recent link to the Red Book, for instance, is **http://fly.cc.fer.hr/~unreal/theredbook/about.html**.

Finally, let's mention some recent books on computer game design and programming. Andre LaMothe, *Tricks of the Windows Game Programming Gurus* (Sams, 2001), is an excellent, wide-ranging book on writing games. LaMothe has written a number of other useful books as well. David Bourg, *Physics for Game Developers* (O'Reilly, 2001), is quite interesting. Ian Parberry, *Learn Computer Game Programming with DirectX* (Wordware, 2000), gets the user up and running with a simple DirectX game framework. Also of interest are David Astle, *OpenGL Game Programming* (Prima Tech, 2000); Rouse, Ogden, and Rybczyk, *Game Design: Theory and Practice* (Wordware, 2001); Andrew Rollings, *Game Architecture and Design* (Coriolis, 1999); and Mark DeLoura, *Game Programming Gems 1 & 2* (Charles River Media, 2001).

You are free to use the Pop Framework in developing your own programs. The Pop Framework source code is explicitly placed in the public domain. This means that you can freely use any or all of the source code for any purpose, including commercial products or inclusion in other texts. You do not need a separate permission from the author or his publishers to do this, and you are not required to acknowledge any use of the code (although a public line of thanks is always nice!). You are free to place your own copyright notice on works which include the source code, with the understanding that the author accepts no liability for problems caused, and with the stipulation that all of the author's code remains in the public domain and may be further re-used by others.

Let's say a few words about some possible future extensions of the Pop Framework.

A feasible near-term enhancement of the Pop Framework is an implementation of a *cGraphicsDirectX* class which might make faster three-dimensional animations than *cGraphicsOpenGL*.

As support for three-dimensional games was only developed in late 2001, there was not time to develop classes for three-dimensional geometrical objects, classes to represent complex three-dimensional worlds, or strong examples of three-dimensional games. This is an area that some of my students will be working on in the near future. Any useful new code may be incorporated into new releases of the Pop Framework available on the book's website.

A less obvious future improvement might be to extend the framework to support four-dimensional computer games (e.g. a HyperPacMan in a four-dimensional maze or a four-dimensional Space Invaders). This could open some interesting new ground. The fourth dimension is a topic dear to my heart.

Networking is lacking from the current Pop Framework. Although the framework supports multiple players, it doesn't support multiple players on different machines. Perhaps a *cListenerSocket* child of the *cListener* class could to be implemented for this. And one would need to research the existing work on architectures and programming idioms that can keep two game sessions sufficiently in synch with each other. As future versions of the Pop framework are tailored to take advantage of Visual Studio.NET, it may turn out that we can get networking features fairly easily via the use of .NET methods.

Experienced gamers will think of many other enhancements that could be made. The Pop Framework presently has no support for scripting, for joysticks, for DirectX Sound, or for loading meshes and skins. As the code is open source and the architecture is resolutely object-oriented, adding these kinds of enhancements is quite feasible. I gladly offer up these tasks to the more adventurous readers. As time goes by, the book's website will post the source and documentation for any significant improvements to the Pop Framework.

The Pop Framework is written in C++, and it makes essential use of the Microsoft Foundation Classes for its document-view architecture. Some will wonder about porting it to Java. The port is feasible, given that: (a) the Pop Framework classes use solid principles of object-oriented design, (b) most of the classes are independent of any specific features of C++, Windows, or MFC, and (c) the class members are, by and large, either primitives or *pointers to other class objects* (as opposed to *instances of other classes*, which Java does not allow). Regarding Java, the speed of Java applets does seems to be acceptable for game play; see for instance the prototype Java applet Asteroids game at **www.rudyrucker.com/computergames/java**. Nevertheless, there are some disincentives to porting the Pop Framework to Java. Among the disincentives would be that the Java language standard is something of a moving target, that existing Java development environments don't seem as powerful and solid as Microsoft Visual Studio, that deploying a Java package across many platforms is a 'write once, debug everywhere' experience, and the fear that Java may yet be marginalized. A C++ port might be a liklier opton.

In closing, I'd like to thank my colleagues Jon Pearce, Cay Horstmann, and Michael Beeson, with whom I've had so many useful discussions about the practical and theoretical sides of computer science. Thanks also to John Sutherland and to John Foster who read a final draft of the book and made many useful suggestions. Any errors that remain are my own.

Special thanks go to the programmers I learned real-world software engineering with at Autodesk, Inc., in the early 1990s: John Walker, Eric Lyons, Josh Gordon, Bob Holt, Steve Demopoulos, Eric Gullichsen, Marc LeBrun, and John Castellucci. Thanks to my wife Sylvia for her patience and support during the seemingly endless hours of work this project took. And thanks to my many students, without whom *Software Engineering and Computer Games* truly could not have been written.

Rudy Rucker

San Jose, California
August 12, 2002

Part I
Software Engineering and Computer Games

Overview

The goal of this course is for you to learn some principles of software engineering and to use these techniques to design and build a Windows-based computer game. Part I contains the main text. Part II is a reference section containing a number of secondary topics that you may need to look at from time to time.

Projects and games
1

In this book you'll learn about software engineering in the context of working on a computer game project of your own. The purpose of this chapter is to get you to start thinking about your game project.

Software engineering is the set of techniques used to produce computer programs which people are willing to buy. In a single phrase, the software engineer's goal is: 'Ship it!' Although shipping a product used to mean putting a disk and a manual in a shrink-wrapped box, these days it can equally well mean making a program available for download from the web.

Although there is only one goal, there are many different aspects to software engineering. If you go into a large computer bookstore and look at the section on software engineering, you'll find an extraordinary range of books.

In this book we are going to focus on software engineering as something that *programmers* do, as opposed to something that *managers* do. Managers can motivate and orchestrate the process – but they are not doing the kind of software engineering that we're going to focus on. Here we think of a software engineer more as a programmer, as the kind of person a business is looking for when they advertise, 'we are looking for programmers who have shipped an application.' This book will show you how to make a certain kind of shippable application.

What kinds of applications? We're going to focus on using C++ and the Microsoft Foundation Classes (MFC) to create Windows applications for personal computers. And the kinds of programs we look at will be computer games of various kinds.

All you really need in order to use this book is to have a solid knowledge of C++ or, at the very least, Java or C. You'll learn about Windows and MFC programming as we go along. If you already know some Windows programming, so much the better!

1.1 Features of a successful program

Here are two reasonable criteria for a successful program. Does it make money? Is it beautiful?

A program you write can make money in a direct way if it is so attractive that people are willing to pay to use it. Indirectly, a program can make money for you if it is good enough to convince someone to hire you for a good job.

It's also important for a program to be beautiful. Beautiful things don't always make money, but they do have their own value. In trying to make a program that is profitable and beautiful, there are four areas to bear in mind.

• Basic concept.
• Interface.
• Documentation.
• Stability.

Let's say a few words about each of these.

Concept

This is the hard one. If your program is to make money, people need some reason to want it. Your program must do something which people value, and it should do it better than competing programs. If your program is to be beautiful, it must be based on an original and interesting idea – and these aren't easy to come by.

If you look at the kinds of programs people buy, you'll notice that they fall into a few main categories: tools, games, education, and content.

Tool programs are things like word-processors, spreadsheets, paint programs, compilers, web browsers, Computer Aided Design packages, and so on. These are large programs with lots of code and are usually created by big teams of software engineers. Tool programs are probably the hardest to create and the hardest to market, and for this reason the author's manager at Autodesk used to say, 'Apps good, tools bad.' *App* is short for *application*, which is what executable programs are usually called in the Windows world. And a really good app is often called a *killer app*.

Game programs range from simple solitaire time-wasters up to interactive virtual realities. And the web has opened up a lot of interesting possibilities for shared-world games. As with tools, the key to a really massive success is to think of a completely new kind of game. But even a fairly standard kind of game can sell well if it is based on an original graphical concept and is soundly executed. It's worth noting that games and tools are about the only kinds of software that people are still willing to actually buy in a shrink-wrapped box.

A game that you play on the screen of a wireless device like a cell phone will be tiny, but commercially successful console and computer games are huge. As well as including game-engine code, a game will use lots of data files with things like sounds, bitmaps and level designs. Some contemporary games are said to take over 100 person-years of work. The projects in *Software Engineering and Computer Games* will focus on smaller games, of a complexity at about the level of a classic arcade game.

Educational programs cover a wide range. The largest part of educational software consists of very low-end programs to teach readin', ritin', and 'rithmitic. Simple educational programs can involve even less code than games; indeed these are usually developed in a high-level programming environment such as Microsoft Visual Basic or a Macromedia product such as Director or Flash.

More sophisticated education programs often illustrate scientific concepts with computer simulations. *Simulation programs* can model abstract mathematical ideas like fractals and chaos theory, for instance, or they might model biological systems using the techniques known as artificial life. The style of programs known as cellular automata simulate real and imaginary kinds of physics. Artificial life programs show creatures moving about as if they were little pets inside a toy world. Higher dimensional programs display objects that can't fit into the confines of three-dimensional space. These are some examples of beautiful calculations that computers are good at doing, but which would be absolutely impossible to perform by hand.

Content programs are multimedia packages of text, pictures, video, and sound clips with a computer interface. A content program might be an encyclopedia or a travel guide. It's common to have a huge number of support files, including bitmaps, sounds, and animations. Many programs are in fact small engines whose main purpose is to navigate through the contents of a data base. Encyclopedia and reference programs are examples of this. A modern commercial computer game often includes enough media resources to be a kind of content program on its own, by the way, with the content presentation driven by the play of the game.

Although there's no money in them, it's worth mentioning that you can also create programs which are art. The best known examples of art programs are screensavers. These programs create images that people like to look at. A really good artistic program can produce such a variety of interesting outputs that people are mesmerized.

In this book, the programs we focus on will be computer games whose agents, or critters, have behavior driven by an underlying physics simulation. (We'll use the Wild-West word 'critter' throughout this book for the creatures in our computer games.) In that the critters are more or less autonomous, the programs are a simple form of the scientific computer programming known as artificial life.

We focus on computer games because they're interesting. To work hard on a program, it has to be attractive to you in the first place, and to finish a program, you have to want to see it in action. Just as you need something to write about in order to learn how to write, you need something to program about to learn how to program. Games are a rich source of inspiration.

Interface

Hardly anyone is happy with a program that is to be run from a command-line prompt and controlled by special keyboard combinations. Any serious program must run in graphical windows, support the mouse and include menus and dialog boxes. One great virtue of developing for Windows using MFC is that in this programming environment it's very easy to implement a rich graphic user interface.

Of course a good graphic user interface, called GUI for short, takes a lot of thought. You usually need to try out several interfaces till you get it right.

Drawing sketches of the interface before you build it is a very good idea. There are some commonly agreed upon principles of Windows interface design, but getting a really nice and easy-to-use design is an art in itself.

> In a nutshell, to develop a good set of controls and menu selections: test, watch, pay attention, revise, revise, revise.

It may be that you can envision several different ways in which someone might want to use your program. In this case it's a good idea to make the interface user-customizable. That is, you might have menu selections that change the program's response to certain kinds of mouse or keyboard controls. Or you might have menu selections to control the kind of view that the program displays.

In addition to the user controls, you might also regard the selection of your games graphics and sound media files as being a part of the interface design. Of course if you plan to work primarily as a programmer, there's a good chance that you yourself won't be responsible for interface design. Nevertheless, in the projects we do in *Software Engineering and Computer Games*, you will be developing the entire package: code, interface, media files, and documentation. It's good to have some hands-on experience with interfaces, so that you have a clear idea both of what kinds of interface are possible, and also of how to provide code hooks to work with various kinds of interface controls.

A final interface-related feature is file-handling. If you can support file-handling, you allow the user to save and reload the current state of the program, including all of the current parameter values. Alternately, file-handling can be used as a way to extend user-customizability, perhaps by allowing the user to load different graphics backgrounds or sound files into your program. Depending on what files get loaded, your program can behave in very different ways. It's worth mentioning that bug-free file-handling can be tricky to maintain, so programs often settle for simplified kinds of saving and loading.

Documentation

This is often the last thing that software engineers think about. But you should really think about it right from the start, and in this book we'll stress the importance of working on your User's Guide at the same time as you work on your code.

You should keep in mind that the important thing about your documentation is that it has useful and accurate information, not that it has a whiz-bang web-like interface. The user cares more about real information than about the exact way in which the topic windows are indexed and linked. Programmers tend sometimes to get lost in the maze of help file design.

The User's Guide should include an explanation of why your program is interesting, a guide to installation and quick start, and a feature by feature explanation of all of the menu and dialog controls.

The User's Guide is both the printed manual and the online help file. These two are normally based on the same document. Your work, once again, is in making this a good document, rather than worrying about giving it an intricate interface. As it turns out, there is a tool called the Help Workshop that makes it quite easy to convert your documentation file into an online Windows help file to distribute with your program. With a certain amount of additional work, you can eventually give your help file a wide range of hypertext features.

It's worth mentioning too that you should also put a lot of documentation into your code in the form of comments to help future programmers who might work on your project – or to help you when you come back to the code in six months and have forgotten why you made some of the choices that you did.

Stability

It goes without saying that your program shouldn't crash. Its behavior should be stable and consistent no matter what the user does. Attaining this goal means putting energy into testing and debugging. Of course every program has bugs. Keeping them down to a manageable level takes a sustained effort on the part of the software engineer. Bug management has several parts: coding defensively, inspecting and testing the code to find existing bugs, and fixing those bugs.

Another aspect of stability means that you, as a programmer, should be willing to leave out a flaky feature that always causes trouble. The tendency to include unnecessarily complicated features is sometimes known as 'developer gold-plating.' You have to have the willpower and big-heartedness to disable or comment out the flaky code when you ship.

1.2 Game design

Many programmers have at some point in their lives been obsessed with computer games. Programming itself is the 'big game', the meta-game, a game made the more enticing by the fact that the points you score can be real-world fame and fortune. Programming has a lot of the elements of gaming at its best. Why settle for gaming when you can *program*?

Of course when you're programming, you need something to program *about*, and this is where computer games are useful in another way. Not only do computer games get you started with the computer, they are in and of themselves interesting things to try and program. Even a simple game program is reasonably challenging, and it's very easy to tell if a simple game works or not. And once you get started with game programming, you have the possibility of building up your program until it becomes something quite large and impressive. Another plus is that it's often possible to get your friends and family to play with your games, which is rewarding.

Computer games are especially interesting as programming projects because they draw on such a wide range of skills, including the following.

- Computer graphics – to get the game on the screen.
- Physical simulation – to make the objects move realistically.
- Artificial intelligence – to make your virtual enemies worthy opponents.
- Computer art – to provide beautiful images.
- Computer sound – to provide effects and background music.
- Interface design – to make the game interesting and intuitive to use.
- Code optimization – to make the runspeed high enough.

Another good thing about computer games is that the lessons that we learn from designing games can be carried over into our non-game programs. So let's make some games!

A fresh look at the dimensionality of games

Ordinarily people speak of games being either two-dimensional, three-dimensional or two-and-a-half-dimensional. The first two are fairly easy to explain: the older arcade games with flat shapes moving in a plane are two-dimensional, while the newer console and computer games where the player moves about in a virtual reality are three-dimensional. The 2.5-dimensional case refers to those games that view a three-dimensional world from a fixed direction – popular examples of this are the Maxis games SimCity and The Sims. We don't regard these games as fully three-dimensional because we aren't able, for instance, to move our viewpoint down into the streets of SimCity and look up at the buildings as we could in a truly three-dimensional game. From a programming point of view, 2.5-dimensional games are closer to being two-dimensional than to being three-dimensional; one builds up a 2.5-dimensional game by drawing a limited number of two-dimensional layers.

But now, for the rest of this subsection, we want to use a quite different and somewhat idiosyncratic way of talking about the dimensionality of games. Temporarily set aside your usual ideas about game dimensionality and get ready to look at things in a novel way. What we will do here is to talk about three separate dimensionalities: the player motion, the world motion, and the viewer motion.

Just to make sure we're in synch here, recall that a dimension is a degree of freedom. The motion of a barnacle on a rock is zero-dimensional, it never moves. A car on a road or a bug crawling along a thin twig is moving one-dimensionally, it can go forward or backwards and that's all. A horse galloping across a prairie enjoys two-dimensional motion, and birds and fish move three-dimensionally. A person's motion upon the surface of the earth is largely two-dimensional, although at small length scales you do have three-dimensional freedom: you can jump up and down, and you can zoom your hands around.

All computer games have two key elements: the player and the world. In many games the player is in some way represented on the screen: as a cursor tool, as a moving figure, or as a hand holding a weapon. The world is the scenery and objects that you see on the screen. We can try and classify games in terms of

Table 1.1 The dimensionalities of some familiar kinds of games.

Games	Dimensionality of player's motion	Dimensionality of the world motions	Dimensionality of the viewer motion
Shooting gallery type	0	1	0
Space Invaders	1	1.1	0
Centipede	1	1.5	0
Galaga	1	1.5	1
Defender	2	1.25	1
Slot Car Race	1.25	1.25	0
Atari Rally Race	1.75	1.1	1.75
Pong, Breakout	1	2	0
Asteroids	2	2	0
PacMan	1.25	1.25	0
Tetris	2	1	0
Mario	1.5	1.5	1
King's Quest	2	2	2
Gauntlet	2	2.5	2
SimCity, The Sims, Age of Empires	2.5	2.5	2.5
Doom, Quake, Half-Life	3	3	3
Flight simulators	3	2.5	3

the dimensionality of the player's motion, the dimensionality of the motions of other objects in the world and the dimensionality of the viewpoint motion.

Table 1.1 gives the names of some games and numbers for the three kinds of dimensionality for each. In some cases we've used a fractional dimension to suggest the idea of being in between two dimensions. If you happen to have heard of the mathematical shapes called 'fractals,' you might wonder if the fractional dimensions in this table are meant to be like fractal dimensions in the mathematical sense – and the answer would be no. The fractional dimension numbers are used here in a somewhat loose and metaphorical fashion. Thus a motion dimension of 1.25 is used here to refer to a two-dimensional motion which is in some way constrained to be close to straight-line motion, and a motion dimension of 1.5 is used to mean a two-dimensional motion that's a bit less constrained.

Harking back to the notion of '2.5-dimensional' games mentioned at the start of this subsection, we can see that this fits in with our new usage, if we regard a 2.5-dimensional world as a three-dimensional world in which the inhabitants are constrained to move in certain orderly ways, being mostly limited to moving in a particular plane.

In looking at the table and reading the discussion, keep in mind that if there are some number values you disagree with, it's possible that you're right. The point is to get you to start thinking about computer games in a novel way, not to pronounce certain number values as being true once and for all.

We will sometimes speak of a game whose dimensionalities are, respectively, a, b, and c as having an (a, b, c) 'dimension signature'.

The most rudimentary games are the shooting gallery type in which the user controls a little gun sitting still at the bottom of the screen. A row of targets – things like bullseyes and ducks – moves across the middle of the screen. The user presses a key to shoot bullets up at the objects. The user's motion is zero-dimensional, for the gun never moves. And if all that the targets do is move along a steady line from right to left, we can think of the world as being essentially one-dimensional. Admittedly there is a two-dimensional element here because the gun's bullets do move vertically, unlike the horizontally moving targets. But, this is hardly a motion at all really, for the only thing the bullet's motion does is to establish a fixed time-lag between when the user presses the shoot key and when the target might explode.

Like most of the early computer games, the shooting gallery type has a zero-dimensional viewer motion, which is just another way of saying that the user has no control over the viewpoint. In the early games one simply sits above the world, looking at all of it at once.

In a variation on the shooting gallery game that was called Missile Command, the user was allowed to rotate the barrel of the gun so that it shoots in different directions. In a typical game like this, the user might be firing missiles at plane-shaped targets. We can think of the gun rotation as a degree of freedom, so for these games it would make sense to say the user's motions are one-dimensional.

In a Space Invaders style game, the user has a gun at the bottom of the screen, but now the gun can move back and forth. And instead of moving across the screen, the objects are now moving steadily downward. The player is trying to shoot the objects before they touch the bottom. In non-violent variations of this game, the user is 'catching' the falling objects rather than shooting them.

Note that if the gun can move back and forth it usually can't rotate. This is because giving a user too many degrees of freedom in the controls can make the game confusing to play.

In classic Space Invaders, the steady, unrelenting downwards-only motion of the game objects is just a shade above one-dimensional. This is because the enemies jiggle back and forth in synch with a sound the game makes. But the jiggling is quite restrained; thus one might call the motion 1.1-dimensional.

More advanced offshoots of the Space Invaders game, such as Centipede, have target objects which swoop wildly back and forth as they move down. This isn't a true two-dimensional motion, since the objects always do move downwards, so let's put 1.5 in the table. Centipede also had the fresh feature of having the dead creatures leave obstacles on the screen.

Galaga was a game of the Space Invaders family in which the enemies swooped about quite wildly. As an additional point of interest, this game had a visually scrolling background, with new targets emerging from the top of the screen and disappearing at the bottom, giving an effect that one is looking down at a player object which is continually flying upward through space. Although the user can't directly control the viewpoint motion, the visual effect is of a viewpoint that moves with one degree of freedom.

Defender was a game in which the player is limited to the left half of the screen, but is free to move a bit forward and backwards as well as up and down. The enemies come in from the right with slight variations in their motions. The background scrolls to the left.

How about a game that doesn't involve shooting? A common kind of game is Slot Car Race. In a game like this, you look down on a race-track from a fixed aerial view, seeing the whole track at once. The player and some rivals are little cars that race around the curves of the track. You control the player by turning a bit to the left and the right, by speeding up and slowing down. It would be an exaggeration to say you have two-dimensional motion, as you have to stay on the track. 1.25 dimensional motion is more like it, with the rivals having about as much freedom as the player.

There's another way to make a car-racing game, and this is to try and immerse the player in a three-dimensional world. In a very early Atari car Rally Race game, there is a player which is a car near the center of the screen, near the bottom of a triangle that represents a road. Little rectangles flick past on either side; these are fence posts along the road. You move left and right from one side of the 'road' to another to avoid obstacles that appear; this is one dimension of your motion. Your second dimension of freedom is how fast you drive forward. Although this is nominally a three-dimensional world, you can't hop up and down, so you don't get any use out of the third dimension. The world is effectively a plane that you are looking at from the side. And, as in Slot Car Race, you can't drive off the track. Even so, there's a more dimensional feeling in this game, so let's call it 1.75. That might seem too stingy, really, given that the world is, in principle a three-dimensional one. But if you look at your degrees of freedom, the number does seem pretty low.

Most of the obstacles in the Rally Race world appear and move down the screen towards you as predictably as the monsters in Space Invaders, with only a small amount of oscillation, so let's call their motions 1.1-dimensional. (Note that we're well into a debatable gray zone here; remember that the purpose of this discussion is to get the gears turning in your head, not to lay down any absolute facts.)

In the Rally Race game the viewpoint is attached to the player's car. The viewpoint shares in the dimensional motion of the player. It's worth mentioning here that in almost all games which begin to try and show three-dimensional space, player motion, the viewer and the player are attached.

The Tetris game is an interesting non-violent game which is a kind of variation on the Space Invaders style game. Here objects are falling, but rather than being a gun or a basket at the bottom of the screen, the player is essentially a controller that sits upon each block as it falls. The player is able to move the block he or she is on back and forth and in addition can rotate the block. So we can think of the player as having two degrees of freedom, with the understanding that the second degree is rotation rather than motion.

Pong and Breakout were the first kinds of games with truly two-dimensional world motions. Here something like a ball is moving around on the screen, and the user moves a paddle back and forth along the bottom or side of the screen to keep the ball from escaping there. Note that the player motions are one-dimensional and the viewer, which sees the whole world, is still zero-dimensional.

Asteroids was the first game with two-dimensional player motion. The asteroids move along two-dimensional paths, and the user's ship moves two-dimensionally as well. What makes the controls for Asteroids intriguing is that rather than directly moving the ship with left/right up/down controls, the user moves the ship via a pair of controls affecting the strength of the ship's rocket and the direction the rocket is pointing in. Unlike any previous games, Asteroids uses a little bit of physics: the ship has inertia, and tends to keep moving in the same direction until you rotate it and send a pulse of rocket energy the opposite way. The ship is also able to shoot bullets; these always travel along the same direction as the ship's rocket currently points.

PacMan was the first great maze game. Here the user and the objects move somewhat two-dimensionally, but they are constrained to move around inside a maze. So we speak of the motions as 1.25-dimensional. We use a number so close to 1 because the maze branches very little, and there aren't all that many places where the user does indeed have two degrees of freedom in the motion choice. Programming a maze game takes a little extra work because you need to put in the maze-wall objects and arrange for your moving objects to notice the walls.

Historically, the next big advance after PacMan was the Nintendo family of 'side-scrolling' games like Mario. In these games, the player's figure moves across a landscape that runs indefinitely along to the left and right. The player

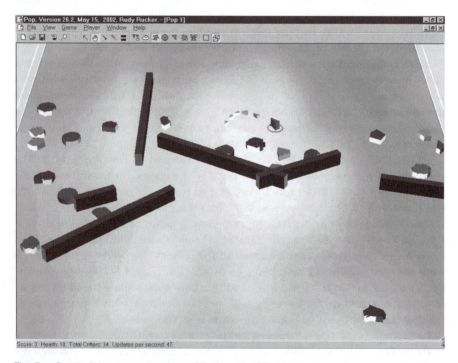

The Pop Dambuilder game showing a 3D view of a 2D game

can jump up and down a little bit, so we think of the player's motion as, say, 1.5-dimensional. Most of the objects in the landscape move pretty much one-dimensionally, but a few of them hop up and down a bit too. What made this game unique was that here we had a moving viewpoint that mattered. Unlike the scrolling star fields of Galaga and Defender, we move through a world with interesting new features (though parts of the backgrounds do repeat).

We mentioned before that in games with a moving viewpoint, the motion is normally attached to the player. In a side-scroller like Mario, the viewpoint moves along through the world with the player. The next advance in games was to look down on a big world in which the viewpoint moves two-dimensionally. King's Quest and Gauntlet were examples of this. In both of these games, the viewpoint is set to always keep the player in view. That is, the viewpoint won't actually move till the player bumps into an edge of the screen; at that point the viewpoint will scroll (or jump) so as to keep the player onscreen.

King's Quest was a room-based or tile-based game; that is, the player moves in jumps from one screen to the other by passing across the edges. As mentioned above, we say a game has an (a, b, c) dimension signature if the player has a degrees of freedom, the world's motions are b-dimensional, and the viewer motions are c-dimensional. In and of itself, each screen of King's Quest has a (2,2,0) dimension signature; that is the player and world objects move two-dimensionally and the viewpoint doesn't move. The twitching of the viewpoint from room to room gives the game as a whole its (2,2,2) dimension signature.

In Gauntlet we have a more distant view of the world, we see several rooms at once, and the viewpoint scrolls when the player touches the edge rather than jumping. An additional aspect of the Gauntlet game is that here we begin to use a two-and-a-half-dimensional view of the game world. Rather than being shown as a flat pattern seen from above, the world is drawn as if seen from a fixed angle a bit to one side in space. This kind of view is also known as 'isometric'.

SimCity and Age of Empires are games that take the two-and-a-half dimensional view and run with it. In these games the user can design huge cities or even civilizations. In a sense there is no onscreen player, as the gamer is the all-pervasive 'creator' of these worlds. This said, the user can at times have the experience of an embedded player by temporarily taking control of one of the world creatures or, in SimCity, by controlling a cursor that acts as the 'Finger of God'. Although these games are isometric view, they give something almost like an effective third dimension of viewer motion by allowing the user to zoom in on close-up views.

The next wave of games were 'first-person shooters' like Doom, Quake and Half-Life. In some ways these games are like three-dimensional PacMan. The player moves through a three-dimensional maze of rooms, hallways and staircases, enjoying a motion that we might call 2.5-dimensional (although once in a while in these games you get a chance to swim underwater and you have something like pure three-dimensional motion). The motions of the objects appear truly three-dimensional; they sometimes bounce around all over the rooms.

Although the viewpoint location is attached to the player in the first-person shooters, we have additional extra freedom in the viewpoint because we have two degrees of freedom in controlling which way the player looks – which is the direction in which the player's weapon gets aimed as well.

It's often said that first-person shooter games are excessively violent. Certainly it would be interesting to see more games like this in which you did something other than shoot everything that moves. An aspect of the first-person shooter games that seems a little sad is that the image of the player is generally nothing more than a hand holding some kind of gun. There are, however, other immersive three-dimensional games that are not primarily about shooting things.

We haven't talked about flight simulators yet. In principle the idea of a flight simulator seems very promising: you're going to fly around in three-dimensional space. But there are two big problems. First of all, the space that you fly around in often doesn't feel three-dimensional at all. In the lower-end simulators, you're always way up in the 'sky' looking down at a map. It feels like you're in a two-dimensional map world with a weak third degree of freedom that involves magnifying the map. A second problem with flight simulators is that they tend to be so closely coupled to the mechanics of how airplanes actually fly. Rather than just getting out there and enjoying pure bird-like flight, you're worrying about complicated machine-age technology like ailerons, rudders, and stall speeds. But some players enjoy mastering this. In some of the newer computer games, the flight is more natural and less mechanical: you're flying through all sorts of interesting objects, like a fish in a reef or a bird in a forest, and you're flying as naturally and as effortlessly as you fly in your dreams.

Have we reached the end of the dimensions with three? Not necessarily. In mathematics there is such a thing as a fourth dimension, a dimension perpendicular to every direction of our space. One way in which we think about the fourth dimension is via analogy based on the notion of a two-dimensional world called Flatland. The fourth dimension is to us as the third dimension would be to Flatland. But there's not room to say more about the fourth dimension here. Suffice it to say that it would be really cool to write a four-dimensional PacMan game or a four-dimensional Asteroids. To get some ideas about how to start, you can download the Hyperspace 98 program from the author's home page. The Pop Framework is in fact designed in such a way that it would be relatively easy to extend it to four-dimensional space; more on this topic can be found in the comments at the start of the **vectortransformation.h** header file, and any progress in this direction will be posted on the book's website.

Looking back over this section, what can we conclude about the dimensionality of the games that we should try and design? Certainly more dimensions tend to make a game more interesting. The risk in adding too many dimensions is that a game can become confusing and hard to use. Another cost of more dimensions is that you need to provide more furniture to put into your world.

When proposing a project, be sure and think about what dimensionalities you plan to use for the motions of your player, his or her opponents, and the viewpoint. In this author's courses, shooting gallery or Space Invader game projects aren't acceptable for term projects as they're too easy and too dull. (Later we'll do Space Invaders as an introductory exercise.) What's wrong with choosing a really easy project? In grading a projects course, it's reasonable for the professor to base at least part of the grade for a project on the difficulty. This is an instance of how it is important to get good feedback during requirements gathering. The very best student projects not only create a challenging game, but also implement some new classes to make the game work.

The intelligence of games

A really well-designed game like Tetris forces the player to behave intelligently. In Tetris you need to think ahead about which block to place where, keeping in mind which blocks are coming. A game like Space Invaders requires very little intelligence. You simply shoot everything you can as fast as you can.

It is exceedingly difficult to design a game which incorporates an inherently challenging puzzle. The whole trick in a game of this nature is to give the user several possible courses of action at all times, and to balance the consequences of the actions so that there is some real difficulty in deciding which strategy to use. Games are highly sensitive to very small tweaks in their play parameters, and it's a long-drawn-out process to get the values just right. But, you should try.

A simpler way to make your games intelligent is to give your game's creatures various kinds of behavior. In a shooting game like Asteroids, for instance, you can have the asteroids check the player's location and make a point of heading towards the player. Or you can let the asteroids access the locations of the bullets you shoot, and allow them to try and move out of the bullets' way. (The asteroids in the Pop Spacewar game do both.)

We're not talking about a huge amount of intelligence here, we're simply talking about giving your game creatures some rudimentary abilities to gather and use information about the player's activities. Of course you can't make the enemies impossible to beat, as then there's no game.

A good design trick might be to let the enemies do annoying things like chasing the player and avoiding the bullets, but to have an enemy's abilities differ in a random fashion from one to the other. You might even have some 'dumb and clumsy' enemies who do exactly the wrong thing; these guys might head towards bullets, for instance. This way the player is unable to be sure what will happen when a new enemy is attacked.

Requirements for playable games

It goes almost without saying that a game should be attractive to look at, that it shouldn't run too fast or too slow. A game should also be relatively platform-independent, that is, it should be able to behave well at different screen resolutions and processor speeds.

Here are some less obvious principles that we might also keep in mind.

- The game needs a good *interface*.
- The user should get instant visual *feedback* from game actions, with sound feedback for major events.

- The user should have a *score* or some other way of keeping track of how well he or she is doing overall.

- There should be clear *goals* for the game and a clear *termination* point.

- There have to be *advances and setbacks*.

- Doing well should involve *strategy* as well as manual dexterity and quick reactions.

- You may want to give the user the possibility of using different *tools*.

- Things should happen at a *human pace*, that is, not too slow or not too fast. In particular, things shouldn't change instantaneously.

The issue of good *interface* can't be stressed enough. Most of all, the interface must be simple. As a developer, you tend to want to put in lots of controls. The Pop Framework games, in particular, are loaded with tons of menu selections. These selections are really just present to help you look at some of the different ways that the games might be configured. When you actually complete and distribute a game, almost all of the menu selections should go away. In the words of the game developer Will Wright (designer of SimCity, SimAnt and The Sims), 'A user interface isn't done until there's nothing left to remove.'

The most important part of the user interface relates to the actual game controls rather than to the more or less rarely used menu selections. People can only handle a few controls. Generally you shouldn't expect to use more than these: mouse moves, mouse clicks, arrow keys and the space bar. And maybe not even all of those.

Regarding sound, it's worth mentioning that sound can be used to set an emotional tone, to signal critical events, and to speak clues and information. In a pure Windows program, we're limited to playing sounds that are stored in the ***.wav** file format, as described in Chapter 30: Sound. It is, however, possible to make a fairly simple extension of the Pop Framework to use the more powerful sound capabilities of the DirectX library.

Any significant game event should be accompanied by visual or audio *feedback*. At the barest minimum, you maintain some health and score numbers in the status bar where the user can see them. But really the feedback should occur directly within the game world. If you damage a critter, the critter should blink, or send out fragments, and there should be a sound as well. When you gain some health or score points there ought to be a sound, or perhaps a brief change in your player icon.

The *score* is an all-important feedback to the user about their overall performance. Once you have a specific score number to work with, you can tell if you're getting 'better' at a game, and you can compete at the game with your peers. The point of a game is to make the users feel good, so you don't want to be stingy with your score numbers, though you don't necessarily have to go overboard and start dishing out scores in the billions. Another point to note is that the more aspects of the game that affect the score, the better. Try and find a way to award scores for each of the interesting kinds of things that a skilled player can do.

Another issue relating to the interface is raised by Bruce Shelley (designer of Age of Empires). You should evolve your game by *playing* it. Shelley suggests that you play, test, and adjust your game daily while it's being developed, and that you use your own instinct as a gamer for guidance. When we discuss an 'Inventor' software lifecycle model for developing our game projects, we'll factor in the notion that in the early part of the project you will be repeatedly testing and revising your game.

Regarding *goals*, a fully engaging game will have a hierarchy of goals. There will be cycles of success or failure applicable to different levels of time: say the ten second level, the one minute level and, in advanced games, the one hour or even one day or one week level. In order to make a game really successful, you need to have users be interested in it for a fairly long period of time; an 'infectious' period longer than a week is necessary if you hope for your users to recruit new users.

Let's say a bit about *advances and setbacks*. One of the things that makes an activity a game is that there has to be some sort of conflict. There need to be advances and there need to be setbacks. The classic board game 'Chutes and Ladders' is a really simple example of this. Some actions move you forward, others drag you back. Playing roulette or craps has the same kind of rhythm, you alternate between gaining and losing. In Asteroids you blow up an asteroid, but then something hits you and you lose one of your lives. We need to make it possible for the user to do 'bad' things as well as 'good' things. The game should be geared so that the player should be able to do well. He or she should sweat, but in the end, the player should win.

Regarding *strategy*, a game is more involving if the changes depend on things you do. In an arcade 'twitch game', the issue is simply to react fast enough so as to do the right things rather than the wrong things. In a turn-based strategy game like chess, the issue is to figure out the right thing to do. The best kinds of games involve some physical skill and some thought. If a user has a choice, there should be something good about both possibilities, rather than some-thing bad about both possibilities. A decision shouldn't be trivial in the sense of there being only one right answer, nor should it be random in the sense of it not really making a difference which option you choose.

Will Wright remarks that it makes the decisions in a game fun if you allow the player an occasional chance to be subversive, to go against what might seem like the official and correct way to play the game. He gives the example of allowing players in SimCity to remove buildings with their virtual bulldozers.

Regarding the pace and strategy of a game, Bruce Shelley remarks that in a game, the player should be the one having the fun, not the programmer or the computer! The player should feel like the hero.

One type of strategy decision is to let the user choose different kind of *tools* for his or her onscreen player. The simplest example is in a shooting game, where the user selects which kind of gun to blaze away with. In adventure games, the player may pick up or acquire all sorts of health packs and weapons that can then be strategically deployed.

The issue of having things happen at a *human pace* ties in with the notion of feedback and playability. The player needs to see things happen at a reasonable, comprehensible rate.

All this said, none of the simple games we work on in this introductory book are likely to rise to these high levels of design finesse. But it's good to be aware of what we'd really like achieve.

1.3 The Pop Framework

There are a zillion different projects that people can dream of. In *Software Engineering and Computer Games*, we're only going to help you do a few specific kinds of projects. The book describes a framework called the Pop Framework which will make it easy for you to build programs suitable for computer games or for other kinds of simulations.

If you want to get a quick idea of what the Pop Framework can do, download the Pop program from the book website, start up the Pop program and look at some of the different game modes you can choose with the Game menu. A recent version of the Pop help file is printed out as Appendix B, should you wish to spend some time with it right now.

It turns out that the code for the Pop demo program is the same as the code that we call the Pop Framework. Though getting a program to run is hard, it's even harder to design your code so that it is extensible enough to warrant being called a framework.

You can call the code for a particular program a framework in the case where the code has been designed to be very easy to extend to different types of programs. Ordinarily, a framework is a set of files that make up a complete, buildable project. The files contain implementations of some classes that are reasonably easy to tweak and/or extend so as to make the program do different things. The Pop Framework files are based on a 'document view' framework generated by Microsoft Visual Studio. We'll call this underlying framework the MFC framework.

The Pop Framework is actually a bit more than just a collection of new classes, it's the notion of arranging these classes according to certain kinds of patterns. By the same token, the MFC framework is both a collection of new classes, and a certain way of arranging these classes. The special arrangement of MFC classes is called the AFX framework, where the 'AFX' stands for *application frameworks*. Instead of just speaking of the MFC framework, people sometimes speak of the AFX/MFC framework. But for simplicity we'll stick to just saying 'MFC framework'.

Terminology aside, the idea for your project is simple. You build it on top of the Pop Framework, which is in turn built upon the MFC framework (see Figure 1.1).

The complexity of the kinds of programs people want keeps getting higher. In order to stay afloat, software engineers are continually devising ways to work at higher levels, and to spend less time on low-level tasks. The use of

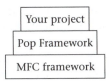

Figure 1.1 Building on frameworks

object-oriented methods is one way to work at a higher level; instead of designing the same kinds of structures over and over, we encapsulate them into reusable classes. Learning how to apply software design patterns is another way to work at a higher level; instead of reinventing ways of making your classes relate to each other, you arrange your classes into a familiar pattern. Finally, the use of frameworks provides software engineers with a huge amount of leverage. A framework comes with a number of classes already organized into useful patterns. Frequently you use a framework simply by deriving off a few child classes from the basic classes it comes with; this is in fact what you'll do to make your computer game project with the Pop Framework.

To introduce you to the Pop Framework, let's list the basic requirements it was designed to satisfy.

(1) We want to be able to open more than one window within the program. The different windows can correspond either to different game sessions or to different views of the same session. A Windows way of putting this is that we will use the multiple document interface (MDI for short) rather than the single document interface (SDI for short).

Strictly speaking it's not really that necessary to have multiple windows for most games. But as the MFC framework gives us this pretty much for free, we're going to use it so as to make our framework as powerful as possible.

So as not to confuse the users unnecessarily, the Pop Framework's default behavior is to show a single maximized view that fills the main window. It will automatically tile additional views into the main window.

Another feature of the MDI is that we use a *document-view architecture*. This means that we conceptually break the program into three main pieces: the application, the document, and the view. These will be represented by classes called, respectively, *CPopApp*, *CPopDoc*, and *CPopView*. The application is the thing in charge of running your executable program. The document holds the data involved in your game: things like the characteristics and positions of the game pieces. The view is the graphical object in charge of displaying your window on the screen.

(2) The graphics objects in a window must be stable and persistent, that is, they shouldn't disappear if we resize the window or temporarily cover it with another window. This is a standard expectation, but it turns out to be something you have to do a little bit of work to make happen. You *don't* get this for free. One way to achieve visual persistence is to maintain

an array that holds information about the appearance of your objects. This array lives inside your document, and it is used whenever you need to refresh the appearance of your view.

We use templates for our arrays so that they'll be resizeable. Rather than using the C++ Standard Template Library (STL) array templates, we'll use a special Microsoft MFC array template called **CArray**.

(3) We should have menu and toolbar commands for changing program parameters and controlling the program flow. Once you have menu commands in place, making them into toolbar buttons is quite easy with Visual Studio.

An MFC program handles messages by putting message-handler functions into some of its classes. As it turns out, a message can be handled either by the app, by the document, or by the view. Generally we try and partition out the responsibilities in a reasonable manner. Thus, a program-wide switch for turning the sound off would be handled in the app, a command for restarting a game would be handled by the doc, and a command for switching between solid and wire-frame graphics would be handled by the view.

(4) We'll support mouse and keyboard input. These inputs normally go directly to the view, but we pass them on from there to the game and the game objects. Most people expect to use arrow keys to control computer games. But for more complicated game play we'll use the mouse and have the option of changing the 'cursor tool' and appropriately changing the action of the mouse.

(5) We want to have flexibility in the set of function calls that we use to put our graphics onscreen. The Pop Framework is developed in a somewhat graphics-neutral fashion, so that it can use standard Windows graphics calls or OpenGL graphics calls, with the option of eventually adding support for DirectX graphics calls.

(6) We want the graphic images to be independent of the window size and the screen resolution, that is, we want to see the same kind of pattern in the window no matter what size it is. This is a somewhat non-standard notion. There are many computer games that take over the whole screen, throw it into some fixed resolution and don't allow you to use resizable windows at all. In effect these kinds of programs are making your Windows machine behave like a dedicated arcade-station or like an old DOS machine.

Many full-screen programs of this type give you a range of possible resolutions you can choose from, but even so, once the game starts the resolution is no longer adjustable.

The author's feeling in designing the Pop Framework was that it's more elegant to have the game run in a well-behaved standard window on your desktop, a viewport window with graphics that adjust to fit the size of the window. We do this by saving our objects' positions in terms of real-number-valued vectors which we'll convert into pixel positions depending on the size of the viewport. We write the tools for this con-version in Windows graphics; we get it pretty much for free in OpenGL graphics.

(7) We want to have the option of displaying either 2D or 3D game worlds. Note that the Windows graphics of the Pop Framework supports only the 2D worlds, and to see the 3D worlds, you need to use the OpenGL option.

(8) The objects in the program should move around on their own even when you're just sitting there watching, that is, we should have real-time animation. We want to have an animation speed of at least 20 frames per second.

(9) The animation should be flicker-free. This is a less obvious requirement than some of the others, but it takes a special effort to keep a graphics program from flickering. The technique used is often called 'double buffering', meaning that as well as writing to the videocard buffer (which is what a normal graphics call does), you also make use of a memory-based video buffer. In the case of Windows graphics, it is the framework's job to construct and maintain this memory buffer; in the case of OpenGL graphics, the buffering happens more or less automatically.

(10) The apparent speed of the game objects' motions should be independent of the number of frames per second that are being displayed by the par-ticular combination of processor and videocard. Like being flicker-free, this is a less obvious requirement that takes a certain amount of work. The trick is to link the simulated motion per frame to the actual real-world time elapsed between frames.

(11) We want to be able to save and to load files that contain the current state of the game or process being shown. This is fairly easy to do in MFC, by making use of an overridden **Serialize** function.

(12) We want to have character sprites based on geometric objects like polygons and polyhedra. These objects should be able to change dynamically, that is, rotate, change size, flex, etc.

(13) We also want to have character sprites which are based on bitmaps in addition to objects that are based on geometrics such as polygons and polyhedra. It should be possible to flip through sequences of bitmaps to achieve character animation.

(14) Our objects should have easily alterable virtual functions controlling their behavior. This way we can give them virtual personalities that are easy to customize.

(15) We should handle collisions between moving objects in a physically reasonable way.

(16) We should try and develop code which is as reusable as possible. This means encapsulating our code into classes with the proper function calls for making the classes fit together in an easily usable framework.

(17) Finally, and most difficult of all, we would like to make playable games.

1.4 Your project

As mentioned before, the best way to learn programming is to have some project that you yourself want to work on. Read through this section and then take a look at the exercises at the end of the chapter. Exercise 1.1 is designed to get you into a mind-set where you're thinking about things you might possibly do, and Exercise 1.2 encourages you to take the initial step towards specifying a game project you can build with the Pop Framework. It would be a good idea to actually write out your answers, especially to Exercise 1.2.

Once you've come up with some ideas about what you might want to do for your project, remember to keep thinking.

Don't lock in on a particular project idea too early. Keep an open mind. You should plan on getting feedback and revising your project idea several times before you finalize anything. This iterative process is an example of what's called *requirements gathering*. Here are some suggestions for your requirements gathering.

First of all, you'll want to become familiar with the Pop code we're using so as to get an idea of what kinds of technical things will be easy to do.

Secondly, you'll need to make sure you find a project of the right level of difficulty. You don't want a project that's trivially easy, on the other hand you don't want a project that's too hard to finish within the available time. Given the realities of software development, it's wiser to pick something on the easy side, as software projects always take longer than you first expect them to. Your professor can help you gauge this.

Thirdly, you may be using this book in a course where you're expected to work with a team, and you're going to need to have a project that all of the team members can commit to.

Fourth, don't plan for your game to be an exact clone of an existing game such as one of the Nintendo games, and don't plan on using bitmaps or character names from any commercial games or other media sources such as Disney or Warner Brothers. Although you may want to use the basic design and play of an existing game, you *must* come up with your own, independently developed name and graphics theme. Otherwise you will be (a) violating copyright or trademark and (b) writing an 'imitation' game that is going to forever look second-rate compared to the 'real' version of it. Regarding the copyright issue, you might feel that a big game company wouldn't bother to come after a student project – and you're probably right. But what if your project turns out really well and you want to put it up on the web for free download? At this point you actually do stand a chance of running afoul of a corporate webcrawler. Regarding the issue of being second-rate, students sometimes feel that using a commercial game's graphics will make their game seem better. The opposite is true. Reminding users of a real Nintendo game when they play your game is only going to make your game look weak! Your game needs to stand or fall on its own qualities, not on the borrowed glamour of some other work.

A fifth thing to keep in mind is that sometimes it only takes one good concept to really make a game interesting. Try and think of an original concept that is fresh and not over-familiar. Don't be afraid to be inventive or even downright weird! Even an easy project can seem fresh and new if it has a good concept.

Take, for instance, our Spacewar game. This is more or less a copy of the familiar Asteroids game. It has nice code in it, but the appearance isn't fresh. Perhaps the simplest kind of projects that students do is to take Spacewar and to add something to make it seem new. One might, for instance, have the player be a fairy with a wand, and have the enemies be bees. Or one might have the player be a swimmer with a harpoon and have the enemies be sharks. Or have the player be a photographer with a camera and have the 'enemies' be wild animals seen on a photo-safari. Or have the player be a deer who's shooting at hunters. Or have the player be a shepherd who's chasing away wolves. In each case, you'd still be using the same guns-and-bullets code of Spacewar, but you'd be clothing the program in a concept that made it look a little fresher.

A more powerful notion than redecorating an existing game is to come up with some wholly new elements in the game. You might, for instance, have a game like Spacewar, but specify that, to start with, the enemies are all inside a box and the player is outside the box. And then have the enemies come tunneling out one by one. Or have a treasure that the player has to pick up as well having to shoot enemies. Or have your player racing the enemies through a maze or around a track.

Also keep in mind that a game doesn't have to be like Spacewar at all. There are several other examples of games in the Pop program, and you may think of still more.

The best of all is if you can think of some completely new idea. If you look at the range of commercial games for arcade machines, game consoles and personal computers, you'll notice that there are a handful of games totally different from the others. These are the killer apps, the ones that nobody's thought of before.

A final suggestion is that you should take a look at some of the descriptions of past student projects in the Hall of Fame section of Chapter 19: More Ideas for Games.

Review questions

A   What are the features of successful programs?

B   What are the three kinds of dimensions used to describe a computer game? What are the values of these dimensionalities for Space Invaders? For Pong? For PacMan? For Quake?

C   What are some of the basic principles of good game design?

D   What is a software framework?

E   What is the Pop Framework?

Exercises

Exercise 1.1: Beginning to think about your project

In the following series of questions, you begin trying to work out what level of project you might do.

(a) What are two computer programs you really like? Say what it is that you like about them. These can be any kind of program at all.

(b) What is a 'dream' program you would like to write if you were the world's best programmer and had all the time in the world? Write out some of the great features you'd like for this program to have. If you have ideas for several different dream programs put them all down.

(c) What are some areas of programming you think you'd need to learn about to write some really great programs? Try to be as specific as you can.

(d) What is an easy program you're fairly sure you might be able to do, assuming that you got a little help along the way? If you have several ideas put them all down.

(e) What are some features you could add to an easy program to make it more like a great dream program? If you have several ideas put them all down.

Exercise 1.2: First specification sketch for your game

Spend a half hour running the Pop program. Assume that you're going to build a project by extending this code. Now write up an idea for a game project you think you might like to do. This document will be what we call a specification sketch. It should have four parts: (a) explain the concept of the game, (b) draw a picture of how you think your game screen might look, (c) say how the user controls might work, and (d) describe how the play of the game will run. Don't forget to draw a picture, no matter how rough it looks; pictures are all-important in the early stages of conceptualizing a game.

Basics of software engineering

2

Before talking any further about your specific project, let's look at some basic software engineering issues. How should you organize your effort and your time? How do big programs get written?

In this chapter we lay out some of the basic software engineering principles and tools that you need to carry out the goal of the course, which is to produce a fairly large and complete computer game program based on an existing object-oriented framework.

Software Engineering and Computer Games focuses on showing you how to carry out one particular kind of software project. We are not going to give you a complete or advanced treatment of the whole field of software engineering here. Rather than attempting a broad-based survey, we are out to give you the tools to carry out one kind of task in depth. And while discussing this task we'll also show you some things about the practice of object-oriented software engineering.

Hopefully the lessons you learn here will give you a better insight into the more theoretical principles of software engineering when you encounter them in some other context. If this chapter gives you an appetite to learn more about software engineering, consult some of the books suggested in the Introduction.

2.1 The Constraint Triangle

If there's one single thing you should know about software engineering it's the Constraint Triangle (see Figure 2.1).

Cost is the measure of how many programmers are hired to be on your team. *Time* is the measure of how long you have to finish the project. *Quality* is the measure of how many features your software will include and of how extensively it will be tested.

Controlling time, cost, and quality are all important goals. You want to manage time so that your project will be ready by its deadline. You want to control development costs so that the project will be affordable and even profitable. And you want the quality of the software to be good enough to make the software attractive to users.

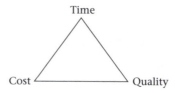

Figure 2.1 The Constraint Triangle

In a fantasy world, we'd like for our projects to be done instantly, to cost nothing, and to be of infinitely good quality. But in the real world, we have to compromise. The reality is that in order to change one of the time, cost or quality goals we need to provide some slack by adjusting one of the other goals.

- You can decrease the time needed for your project, but to do so means increasing the cost by hiring more programmers and/or reducing the quality by eliminating features and perhaps cutting corners on the product testing.

- You can reduce the cost of your project by using fewer programmers, but this means you'll need more time and/or to reduce the quality.

- You can opt for a very high level of quality, but this means your project must take more time and/or cost more.

Any change to one goal must be compensated for by a change to one or both of the other goals.

If you let your customer (or your manager) arbitrarily specify all three corners of the Constraint Triangle, your project is doomed to fail. Any change to one corner must be balanced off by changes to the other corners.

The moral is that if your project is to be successful, you must be permitted to make a realistic assessment of cost, time, and quality, and you must be permitted to make the necessary adjustments to at least one of the goals. Unless you are allowed to realistically adjust at least one corner of the Constraint Triangle, your project will fail.

In the 1990s, NASA briefly adopted the slogan: 'Faster, cheaper, better.' This was followed by a series of unsuccessful projects – and then they abandoned the slogan. It's important to realize that, pushed to the limit, the 'Faster, cheaper, better' slogan is impossible to satisfy. It's as absurd a statement as 'I can fly' or 'I can turn rocks into gold.' There's a saying among software engineers that a *correct* statement of NASA's praiseworthy but impossible goal is this: 'Faster, cheaper, better: pick two out of three.'

At some point in your career you're likely to be saddled with a manager who thinks a rah-rah, can-do attitude is enough to get things done. Always speak up and protest if you hear anything like 'faster, cheaper, better.' Don't accept it if your manager suddenly decides to halve the cost, halve the time, or double the quality without making any compensatory changes to the other corners of the Constraint Triangle. If you let so foolish a plan stand, it will come back to haunt you. Mention the Constraint Triangle and draw a picture of it. Explain that it is a simple impossibility to arbitrarily specify all three corners.

Unless you are in a fairly powerful position, you usually don't have much control over the time and cost corners. In particular, if you're a student doing a team software project in a course, you aren't going to have any control over the time you have to do the project, and you aren't going to have much to say about how many programmers you get to have on your team. The only corner of the Constraint Triangle that you have control over is the quality corner.

The way to economize on the quality corner is not to say, 'Well, I'll write a program with lots of bugs and I won't fix them.' The idea is, rather, to say, 'we're going to strictly limit the number of features that our program will have.'

In limiting features, we need to avoid gold-plating, which is the mistake of accepting overly strong requirements for the program. In addition, we need to avoid feature creep, which is the tendency to keep adding cool new features as the program goes on.

2.2   Requirements and specifications

Requirements

The development of a software product begins with a *requirement* for a certain kind of program and a brief *specification* for what such a program might be. The requirement is a little like a question and the specification is like an answer. Put a little differently, the requirement is like a request and the specification is a proposed solution.

The usage of the words 'requirement' and 'specification' is somewhat fluid, and you will find different conventions in different books on software engineering. In *Software Engineering and Computer Games*, we treat the requirement as a request for a certain kind of software and a specification as a proposed description of the software. And we stress that there is considerable interplay between the requirement and the specification. During this *requirements gathering* process, the stakeholders in the project try to converge on coming up with a requirement and a specification that match each other. The stakeholders might include corporate customers, investors, the managers, the programmers and perhaps a sampling of eventual users.

So, once again, a software requirement says what the target program is supposed to do. A requirement might be something as clear-cut as, 'Write a program which displays our inventory data in an attractive format,' or something less precise like, 'Write a Web browser that runs on cell phones,' or something open-ended like, 'Write a really nice game.' At the preliminary level, the initial requirement can also be called a *vision* or a *software concept*.

As well as saying what the program is supposed to do, a requirement may list some specific features that the program is expected to have. Sometimes a software requirement starts out very detailed, but more often it will be brief.

In industry, another aspect of a software requirement is that it will include some ideas about the marketability of the intended product. An industrial software requirement will say why the program is worth doing and why people will want to have it. Managerial types have a very persistent way of asking, 'What is the intended market?' So usually a software requirement will address this question as well as the question of what the program will do.

UML diagrams

In recent years there's been a movement to consolidate the different kinds of ways that software engineers talk about what they do. The result is a loosely defined set of names and conventions called the Unified Modeling Language, or UML. UML is primarily used as a methodology for drawing diagrams relating to the creating of programs. The fact that it is 'unified' means that UML includes the contributions of many different computer scientists, to the point where it is a bit of a catch-all. There are at least nine different kinds of UML diagram: use case, class, object, activity, statechart, sequence, collaboration, component, and deployment. We should also mention that much, though not all, of the UML assumes that you are using an object-oriented style of software engineering like we'll be discussing in this book.

In *Software Engineering and Computer Games* we'll discuss only these five kinds of UML diagrams.

- Use case diagrams for software requirements.
- Component diagrams for the dependencies of the source-code files.
- Activity diagrams for program execution flowcharts.
- Class diagrams for the high-level structure.
- Sequence diagrams for interactions of program objects.

A basic thing to remember about UML diagrams is that they're meant to be quite simple. The primary purpose of UML diagrams is to make it easy for a project's various stakeholders to communicate with each other about the project. Keep in mind that a number of the stakeholders are likely to be non-technical. There's nothing like putting some UML diagrams on a white-board to get a discussion going. UML use case diagrams are of particular value during requirements gathering.

Another purpose of UML diagrams is for what is called *forward engineering*, where we move from a concept towards actual code. UML class diagrams are particularly useful when you are in the stage of working out the high-level design for your program. The UML activity diagrams are useful for understanding the overall program flow. And the UML sequence diagrams are good for working out the details of how your objects interact.

A third purpose of UML diagrams is for *reverse engineering*, that is, for understanding how an existing program works. This is in fact the situation that the readers of *Software Engineering and Computer Games* are in. In order to use the Pop Framework to build a new game, you need to have some understanding of the Pop program's design structure and running behavior. This is also the situation that you're usually in when you start working for a big company. They have some large body of code in place, and you're supposed to start maintaining or extending it. UML diagrams are a perfect tool for getting started with the process.

A use case diagram can help you understand what the program is supposed to do. A component diagram lays out the interdependencies of the source-code files. An activity diagram shows the overall program flow. Class diagrams show you the interrelationships between the kinds of objects the program uses. And sequence diagrams can clarify the details of how the objects interact.

Use case diagrams

In a UML use case diagram, you represent your program as a big rectangle. Outside the program you put one or more stick-figures corresponding to the *actors*, that is, the people or other programs who might make requests to your program. Inside the program box you put ovals corresponding to *use cases*, which are things the actors might ask the program to do. You may also draw relationship lines from actors to use cases to indicate which kinds of actors get involved with which kinds of use case.

Even more than other UML diagrams, use case diagrams are exceedingly simple. The stick-figures are a low-tech bit of psychology to make you to feel more engaged with what is really little more than a list of requirements.

A use case diagram for the Pop Framework code might look like Figure 2.2.

Since Pop is both a program and a framework, its use case diagram mentions two kinds of actors: the users who play the Pop games and the programmers who use the Pop Framework to build new games.

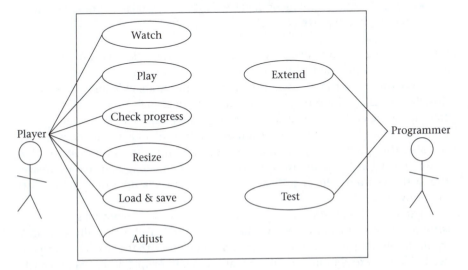

Figure 2.2 A use case diagram for the Pop Framework

Rather than going into a high level of detail about how we will display our graphics, we simply have the 'watch' use case to express the idea that the game should be pleasant to look at. The 'resize' case expresses the requirement that the game should be resolution independent. The 'adjust' use case expresses the fact that we require an ability to be able to do things like selecting game levels or resetting the game. The 'check progress' use case leads to a requirement that the game should display the current score, player health, and so on.

On the programmer side of things, we mention an 'extend' use case and a 'test' use case. Requirements coming out of the 'extend' case are that the code should have clear, easily extended classes, and that the various numerical parameters should be easy to find and easy to change. Requirements arising from the 'test' use case might be that the framework should have methods for randomizing parameters for so-called black-box testing, as well as an autorun mode in which the game 'plays by itself'.

Requirements gathering

A software requirement is a more or less detailed *request* for a certain kind of program. A requirement asks, 'Will you write a program to do such and such which appeals to so and so and runs on the following platforms?'

A software specification is a more or less detailed *description* of a program. A specification arises as an answer to the question posed by a requirement. A specification answers a requirement by saying, 'I can write a program with the following features, and its appearance and behavior will be something like this.'

As mentioned before, the key thing to realize is that – like so many aspects of software engineering – arriving at a final requirement and specification is an *iterative process*. This is the process we call requirements gathering.

> It is essential to spend a good amount of time on requirements gathering before writing a single line of code!

Without enough requirements gathering you run the risk of spending a lot of energy writing a program that your customer doesn't want.

In order to discuss requirements gathering a bit more, let's think of a simple situation where you are the lead software engineer planning to create a program for some customer. The customer proposes a requirement, you propose a specification and show it to the customer, the customer alters the requirement, you alter the specification, and the process is continued until the customer has figured out what he or she really wants, and you have figured out an answer which the customer finds satisfactory. This is an example of requirements gathering.

What about the situation where you are developing a program on speculation, without any investors or corporate clients involved? Well, you really shouldn't try to develop a program for an imaginary customer that exists only in your head. You need to get out and talk to real people, to people other than yourself. If you're developing for the mass market, your 'customer' might be possible users. If you're well-funded, you might have a formal focus-group of users. If you're upgrading an existing product, your users might be your customer base. If you're pretty much on your own, your sample users might be whatever friends or family you can find who are interested in what you're doing.

In most situations there are project stakeholders other than customers. If you're starting a company, one of your stakeholders might be a venture capitalist. If you're an executive of a company, a key stakeholder might be an executive at another company that's contracting for you to write a specific program. If you're a low-level employee at a company, your most important stakeholder is your boss. If you're a student in a software projects class, your stakeholders are your professor, the other members of your team, and any sample users you can manage to talk to.

In each case one of the stakeholders proposes some more or less vague requirements and it's up to you to come up with a specification of a program such that (a) all the stakeholders agree that the specification satisfies the requirement and (b) you feel you can complete the program given the existing time, cost, and quality constraints.

Condition (b) means that in the requirements gathering phase you need to keep the Constraint Triangle well in mind. It's a mistake to 'gold-plate' the requirement and insist that you will be able to include a huge list of fancy features. Always remember the Constraint Triangle of cost, time, and quality. If there are some absolutely necessary fancy features which are bulking up the quality corner, you need to make sure you get allowances to the cost and/or time corners to compensate. If your customer, or your boss, or your marketing department, won't accept a realistic feature set, you should quietly start looking for a new customer or a new job. It's too stressful to work on a project that's doomed from the outset by unrealistic estimates.

The specification sketch

It's a bad idea to code without having any written plan at all. If you have a written plan, looking at it can keep you from going off on tangents that may not be crucial. And a short written plan makes a good starting point for discussions with others. So you really do need to write up a specification before starting to code.

What should a specification look like? We distinguish between two kinds of specifications: a short, casual one called a *specification sketch*, and a longer, cleaner, more formal one called a *full specification.*

An ideal full specification might consist of your class header files and a complete User's Guide for the program. Realistically, you usually aren't in a position to correctly write a full specification until your program's nearly done! That's why, to start with, we settle for a specification sketch. Better a sketch than nothing.

It's liberating to accept that it's unreasonable to want to write out a *full* specification before you write a line of code. In the real world, it helps to play with some code while you're thinking and to try a few things out so that you have some idea of what your possibilities are.

This is where the notion of a specification sketch comes in. If you feel like the only possible specification you can write up is a full specification, you're going to be tempted to not make any kind of specification at all and just start right in on coding. But if all you have to write up is a one or two page specification sketch, the process feels more like a helper than like an obstacle.

As your program evolves, your specification will gain more and more detail. Some aspects of the specification may not be worked out until you've written several builds of the code.

The specification sketch should describe four basic areas: (S1) the concept, (S2) the appearance, (S3) the controls and (S4) the behavior of the program.

- (S1) Concept. The *concept* states what the program is about, and describes the unifying theme of the program.

- (S2) Appearance. The *appearance* should be specified by a few drawings of what you expect the screens of your program to look like. For a very large project you might go so far as to make software mockups of sample screens, creating these either as paint program bitmaps or as outputs of a quick and dirty prototype program. But for a small project, a pencil drawing on a piece of paper may be enough.

- (S3) Controls. The *controls* should be specified by saying how the keyboard, mouse, and more important menu controls will work.

- (S4) Behavior. The description of the *behavior* should mention the main features of the program. It's often useful to step through how the program would respond to user actions in a typical use case scenario. Also describe how a typical user will get started with the program, and mention some expected tips for successfully using the program.

Suppose that your requirement is to write a computer game. A proposed specification sketch might be based on, for instance, the concept for a game resembling the PacMan game. (S1) The sketch's concept would also need to include an idea for a coherent graphical theme distinct from the graphics of PacMan. (S2) The sketch would include a drawing of the screen of your game. (S3) The controls are simply the arrow keys. (S4) Regarding the behavior, the sketch would have some details about how many enemies there will be, what the score for eating a power pellet will be, what the shape of the maze will be, and how the successive levels of the game might differ.

Of course the customer's response to such a specification might be, 'I want a new kind of computer game, not a clone of an existing game.' And then you'd need to find a way to make your PacMan specification more original, and continue on through the next cycle of requirements gathering.

2.3 The software engineering process

A software project consists of both the *code* and the *process* by which you develop the code. It is important to formalize the process that you use. This means that you should have a set of documents describing your process, and that you should frequently look at and revise the documents while the project is underway.

There are many ways to separate out the different aspects of the software development process (as distinct from writing, testing, and debugging the code). Here we'll view the process as having four pieces.

- Requirement and specification.
- Schedule.
- Design.
- Project documents.

We already discussed requirements and specifications. Now let's say a bit about the next three areas.

Schedule

We put a number of things under the category of schedule: lifecycle, milestones, task list, QA plan, and risk management.

A software *lifecycle* is plan for what to do when, i.e. what order to carry things out in. Different projects use different kinds of lifecycle models. The lifecycle is a large enough topic that we'll devote a whole section to it a little later on in this chapter, eventually focusing on the Inventor lifecycle that you will use for your game project.

Setting *milestones* means (a) figuring out some definite, identifiable stages to reach, and (b) setting dates for when you plan to hit these milestones. As well as the finish-line milestone of shrink-wrap (or of posting your package on the Web), you have many preliminary milestones.

In a typical classroom project, your main milestones might be these.

- Preliminary specification sketch (followed by requirements gathering).
- PowerPoint presentation of an approved specification sketch and a UML class diagram for the design.
- Classroom demo of an alpha build.
- Classroom demo of a beta build.
- Final demo.

Several times during the semester, you and the professor (the project stakeholders) need to make out a list of your remaining class meeting dates and figure out reasonable delivery dates for the milestones.

If you're using this book for self-study, pretty much the same kind of schedule might apply – with the difference that you'll want to find friends or relatives to discuss the specifications with you and to view and test your demos.

One thing to realize about the milestones and the schedule is that they need to be continually revised – like everything else in software engineering. Managers often make use of the Microsoft Project software to keep track of their schedule and their milestones.

As well as the main milestones, you may also want to think in terms of smaller milestones. In the case of a PacMan style game, getting to a presentable alpha build would involve, for instance, the milestone of creating a *cMaze* class or writing a method that simply builds such a maze out of *cCritterWall* objects.

When thinking about how to fit the smaller kinds of milestones into your schedule, it's useful to have a *task list*. This would be a list of all the things you need to do before the project is done. Particularly on your first few projects, you tend to underestimate the number of little extra tasks you're going to have to do near the project's end. These might include getting the bitmaps or art ready, making demonstration files, checking the help file against the program, and so on.

In making a schedule it's also important to allocate time for testing the program and testing how well the documentation matches the behavior. This is why software projects are usually divided into an alpha phase and a beta phase. The beta phase is when the testing and debugging takes place.

The process of testing is called QA, for quality assurance. It's important to allocate sufficient time to this, and to accept that you really need to retest after each new beta build. It's not unusual for a bug fix in one spot to break something somewhere else. In making out the schedule you need to consciously plan in enough time for sufficient QA. We'll say more about the testing process in Section 2.3: The Software Lifecycle.

As mentioned above, when you manage a software project you have to keep going back over your schedule and making sure that it matches the reality of what you've currently done. The process of *risk management* means looking ahead and trying to anticipate some of the possible ways in which you may go off schedule.

There are two main parts to risk management: monitoring and recovery. Monitoring means that you have to honestly admit what the most dangerous problems are so that you will immediately recognize them if and when they start to happen. If your program hinges on your being able to integrate a certain kind of image file into your code, there is a risk that you're not going to be able to do it. Monitoring means facing the fact that the worst can happen – and persistently asking if it's happened yet. The risk of not being able to use a type of image remains until it's been demonstrated that it can be done. Because this task is a risk, it is not left until the very last minute.

The recovery aspect of risk assessment means formulating a Plan B, an alternate strategy to pursue if a given fear comes true. If, say, such and such a team member is unable to integrate *.gif image files into your code by the second alpha build, then you will reduce the risk by using, say, only *.bmp image files. If the team member who was supposed to provide your enemy creature's behavior algorithm stops coming to class or answering email, then someone else better start working on it, and if no one can, then you better figure out how to have a game in which the enemies simply use a default framework behavior algorithm.

Risk assessment monitoring is about having your team be honest with yourselves and not hiding your heads in the sand. Risk assessment recovery is about formulating Plan B, and, to mix up the metaphors, being willing to throw the stove and food out of your balloon basket if that's what it takes to stay aloft.

Design

Design breaks into two levels: the *high-level design* and the *detailed design*. The high-level design is also known as the *architecture*, which tends to sound a bit more impressive.

The architecture or high-level design involves specifying the program's 'nouns' and its 'verbs', that is, the program's classes and the program's runtime behavior. The detailed design involves getting more specific about the classes and beginning to write out prototype code for them.

When we are doing the high-level design, we use a process known as *object-oriented analysis* to help figure out what classes we should use. This is a matter of singling out the key concepts used by your problem, and thinking about how best to represent the concepts as classes. Once you've decided which classes to use, the process known as *object-oriented design* helps you find the best way to make your classes work together.

Recall that we use 'UML' to stand for 'Unified Modeling Language'. A good way to talk about your class design is to use a UML class diagram, which is a bunch of rectangles representing classes, with lines showing the relationships among the classes. Drawing a class diagram is a good way to get a useful discussion going about the spec, and can be helpful in moving from the architecture to the detailed design. A class diagram on a whiteboard makes a focus for a group discussion of class design, and provides a non-technical channel by which coders and managers can usefully interact. Look ahead at the class diagrams of the Pop Framework in Chapter 3: The Pop Framework (Figures 3.4 and 3.10).

Describing the program's runtime behavior means figuring out the order in which things happen. How, for instance, does an animation program update itself? When a user clicks the mouse, what is the sequence of events we expect to have? UML sequence diagrams are very useful for sketching this out. Look at, for instance, some of the sequence diagrams in Chapter 6: Animation, for instance Figure 6.3 showing the sequence diagram of how our Pop programs animate the creatures onscreen.

The detailed design for your program states what members and methods your classes will have. In C++, the detailed design can consist of explicit definitions of the classes you will use; a good way to be precise about your classes is to go ahead and start writing up the formal class definitions as ***.h** header files. You can postpone the ***.cpp** implementation of the class methods for a little while. But you will find, once you do get into implementing a class's method, that you often need to rethink the original class design. This kind of back and forth is one of the enjoyable parts of object-oriented design. We say more about this in Chapter 4: Object-Oriented Software Engineering.

Project documents

The most visible project document is the User's Guide, whether in printed or in help file form. For now suffice it to say that the User's Guide might typically include sections called Overview, Getting Started, Things to Try, and Controls,

Table 2.1 Documents for software development.

Specification	Revised requirement document
	Specification sketch with concept, appearance, controls, behavior
Scheduling	Calendar with 'milestones'
	Risk list
Design	UML class diagram
	UML sequence diagrams
	Class headers
Documentation	All of the above, plus User's Guide

where the last section exhaustively describes the effect of each control found in the user interface.

Looking back over the first three parts of our project process, we can imagine making a document (or set of documents) for each of them, that is a specification document, a schedule document, and a design document – all these in addition to the User's Guide document.

Table 2.1 lists software process stages and some of the documents that might accompany them.

All documents should be visible to all the stakeholders involved in the project: the managers, the coders, and the customers. On a really well-run project, one might put all four pieces up on a website, possibly an intranet site or password-mandatory site rather than a public one.

None of these documents is set in stone. We expect that each of them is going to change somewhat during the project lifecycle, although there will normally be a 'feature freeze' date after which no further changes to the specification documents are allowed. But, up until that point, we are going to learn more about our project from the code, from the early builds, and from the way we see the schedule unfolding, so it's reasonable to keep changing things.

There are various models for how to update the documents. Either one person is in charge of maintaining each document, or they are changed during group meetings, or stakeholders might be allowed to 'check out' a copy of the document for revision, with the earlier versions being preserved.

2.4 The software lifecycle

Whether you're working alone or working as part of a large team, there will be a plan of action for how to design, code, test, debug, and document the software. A plan like this is usually called a *software lifecycle*. In this next section we'll discuss a couple of possible lifecyles and then describe an Inventor lifecycle to use for the kind of exploratory, time-constrained project that we'll do in this book.

If you do not consciously choose a particular software lifecycle, you end up in fact using a scenario known as 'code and fix.' It means making no plan at all,

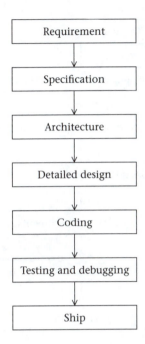

Figure 2.3 The Waterfall lifecycle

but instead simply diving in, writing code, and trying to fix each new problem as it develops. Code and fix is considered one of the most inefficient ways of developing software.

You should always take some time before starting a project to try and figure out what you are going to do. A good rule of thumb is to estimate how much time you should spend planning – and then plan for three times this long. One well-spent hour of planning can save hundreds of hours in coding and fixing further down the line. When you have a really clear vision of what you want to do, writing the code to do it does not in fact take all that long. The hard part is in getting the vision.

There are a number of tried and true software lifecycles which involve a good measure of planning. The most traditional model is called the 'Waterfall' software lifecycle. This model describes a straight-through process: completely plan what you want, specify how the program will behave, nail down the architecture, work out the detailed design, and only then begin coding, finally testing and debugging. The stages of the Waterfall are given in Figure 2.3.

In practice, people tend not to use a pure Waterfall approach, because it is difficult if not impossible to completely specify and plan your program in advance of writing any code. It's more common to see a lifecycle that resembles the linear Waterfall approach but which allows for the possibility of 'swimming upstream' and revisiting the earlier stages. It would be quite reasonable, in other words, to draw additional upwards arrows from the specification, architecture, detailed design, coding, and testing and debugging boxes.

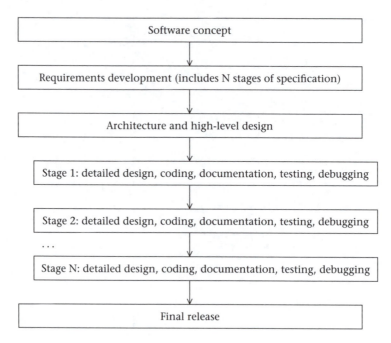

Figure 2.4 The Staged Delivery lifecycle

Another popular lifecycle is known as the Staged Delivery model. In this life-cycle we organize the requirement phase so as to break the program into several stages of functionality. The plan is that at the end of each stage the program should be fully releasable. But stage one might include only basic functionality, stage two a richer set of features, and perhaps stage three will have lots of bells and whistles, while stage four will be incredibly deluxe. So as to be sure of being able to deliver some kind of product when the time runs out, the Staged Delivery method completely finishes stage one, then stage two, and so on. The sketch for this lifecycle is given in Figure 2.4. Note that here we try and fix the architecture early in the process, but we allow for changing the detailed design at each stage. Note also that we try and figure out all of the features that we want right at the start so that then our architecture will be roomy enough to accommodate all of our planned functionality.

Names and descriptions for many other software lifecycles can be found, for instance, in Steve McConnell, *Rapid Development* (Microsoft Press, 1996), from which our description of the Staged Delivery model is taken.

In this book we're going to use a somewhat exploratory software develop-ment process where we tend to be occasionally groping in the dark. For this we'll use a model which is a linear process with two repetitive loops in the middle. Just to have a name for it, we call it the Inventor lifecycle, to suggest that it's a reasonable lifecycle to use when you're exploring an area that's new to you and are planning to discover new things about how to use your tools and your framework, possibly developing some entirely new features as

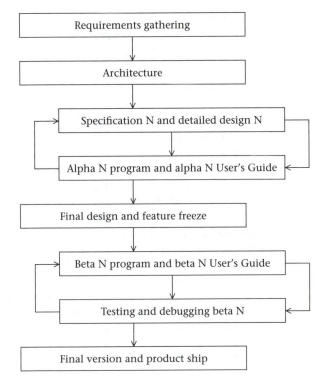

Figure 2.5 The Inventor lifecycle

well. The name isn't meant to rule out the possibility that you might use the Inventor lifecycle to make a highly polished final product. The Inventor lifecycle goes as shown in Figure 2.5.

We expect to develop our program though a number of builds. The builds break into the alpha and the beta stage. In the alpha stage we still don't know exactly what features we're going to have, so we allow for the possibility of changing our specification several times. When we see our deadline coming into sight, we switch into beta mode by freezing our feature set and focusing on testing, and debugging.

Now let's discuss each stage of our Inventor lifecycle.

Requirements gathering

As discussed above, in the requirement phase you start with one or more software concepts and try them out on the other stakeholders, who will be your professor and your other team members in a classroom situation. If you're using this book for self-study, you might try and involve at least two other people as stakeholders – if only in the role of interested on-lookers. After several cycles of requirements gathering you arrive at a basic plan for how the program will behave. You get a specification sketch describing the program and including some drawings of how the screens will look. The specification sketch should have the four components (S1) concept, (S2) appearance, (S3) controls, and (S4) behavior.

Architecture

Before doing any coding, you need to figure out what classes you are going to use. It is likely that your class structures will change somewhat as time goes on, but it is important at the outset to make an honest effort to separate out your classes and, above all, to think about how they will inherit from existing classes. The most common design mistake that beginning programmers make is to *block copy* an existing class's code for a new class when it would be so much cleaner and easier to have the new class be a *child* of the existing class. UML class diagrams are a good tool for working out the high-level design.

Once you have a high-level design and a specification that's been honed by requirements gathering, you can put these together into a document sometimes called the 'RAD' for 'requirements and design'. (Presumably by the end of the requirements gathering, the requirement and the specification match.) Of course, in an exploratory classroom or individual project, we can expect the specification to get more detailed and feature-rich as time goes on.

Specification N

Once your requirement and basic architecture has the go-ahead, you need to figure out what members and methods go into your classes. You will also need to work out a more detailed draft of the User's Guide so that you know exactly what you want your program to do.

The specification N is a list of the features you expect the program to have, and the detailed design includes all the methods you need to implement them. When you get into the low-level design, what you will often be doing is to write out C++ headers for your classes. You can start the process informally, but given that you must eventually write the code, it's not a bad idea to simply do the low-level design by actually writing real headers. New inspirations will come as you try and implement the methods, get them to compile, and make them work in the program.

As time goes by, you will of course think of new features to add to your program – and this is why we talk about specification N and detailed design 'N', where N is a number that starts at 1 and usually ranges between ten and several hundred. In practice you will end up cycling through steps specification and detailed design N and alpha N many times. As you develop your program, more and more new features will suggest themselves, and it would be foolish not to include the good ones simply because they aren't on some list you made up before you really knew what you were doing. Conversely, you may also find that some features you'd planned to include will be too difficult or time-consuming; reduce your risk by throwing them out.

It seems odd to admit that it's not possible to fully control the development process, but this is a reality of contemporary software development. There seems to be no way around it. A completed program is such a large and complex object that it's impossible to fully predict the form of the finished object when you start. It seems likely that software engineering is intrinsically *chaotic* in the formal sense of not being entirely predictable. It's entirely possible that software engineering never will become an exact science. [There's an interesting book about this notion: David Olson, *Exploiting Chaos: Closing in on the Realities of Software Development* (Van Nostrand Reinhold, 1993).]

This fact leads some people to question if we should really call it *engineering*. If you ask a mechanical engineer to build a bridge, he or she can tell you precisely how long it will take, how much it will cost, and what the finished bridge will look like; but thanks to the chaos of complex systems, it's hard to make firm predictions about a software project. Of course your managers will ask for predictions anyway. Try and buy yourself as much time as you can, and if there's still not enough time, remember the Constraint Triangle, and negotiate to reduce the feature set or to add programmers to your team.

Alpha N program

The nearly-finished version of a program is usually called the *beta* version, and the *alpha* versions are the ones that come before that. An alpha version of a program is normally somewhat rough and unfinished.

The very first version of the program – the *alpha 1* – is sometimes more of a 'prototype', which is a quick and dirty version of the program simply to prove that your concepts will work. Very commonly there will be some existing program that you use as a kind of 'seed' or 'starter dough' to get your program going. These are prototypes of a kind. But for your real alpha 1, you need to make the program show at least some minimal functionality in implementing your required features. If there are several possible approaches, you will sometimes want to prototype all of them so that you can compare. So in some situations you may have several competing alpha 1 programs. But, by the time you get to alpha 2, there should be only one version of the program.

As mentioned above, you can expect to run through at least ten or 20, and more typically over 100 alpha versions of your program while developing it. One thing to be careful about is that you don't get stuck with some sloppy design that happened to get into the alpha 1. During the early stages of alpha development you should keep thinking about your class structures. If anything is crude or awkward, now is the time to fix it, before the program goes on and gets a lot more complicated.

Usually you'll run through two or three alphas before going back and changing the design, so it's more like you'll do a specification and detailed design step, a couple of alpha programs, then another specification and detailed design, then a few alpha programs, and so on.

The most important practical thing of all when doing multiple versions of a program is to keep the versions straight. There is so much to say about this issue that there is a File Names and Directory Structure section in Chapter 21: Tools for Software Engineering.

Alpha N User's Guide

Just as there is a distinction between a detailed design and actual code, there is a distinction between a specification and actual User's Guide documentation. While doing new versions of the program, be sure and keep your documentation current. Put your documentation in a handy text file, and every time you change a feature in your program, write this change down in your documentation. At the early stages, you do *not* want to be involved with a technical writer or an expensive technical publications division. The alpha documentations should be quick and light, preferably written by the programmers. The alpha documentation doesn't need to be anything fancy, but it does need to clearly state what the controls are and what the ranges of the control parameters are. Otherwise you're likely to forget. This is particularly important if some of your controls are still in the popup or hot-key stage. In a way, the ongoing documentation acts as notes for the next specification. It's also a good idea to keep a separate document listing known bugs and desired features.

The User's Guide should include an explanation of why your program is interesting, a guide to installation and quick start, and a feature by feature explanation of all of the menu and dialog controls. Often working on the documentation will give you ideas on how to improve the user interface.

You should make your documentation as tight and neat as your code. Use good clear English sentences, and always be sure to use a spell-checker on your documentation. Avoid repeating obvious things over and over, and avoid uninformative statements like 'The Change Size control changes the size.' Instead explain what size is being changed, what the allowable range of size values is, why someone might want to change size, and give examples of relevant behavior at the lower and higher ends of the range.

As well as the User's Guide, there is another kind of documentation which you can create: the programmer's documentation. Most of the programmer's documentation appears inside your code: as dated logs at the beginning of the main program files, as short comments on individual lines of code, and as extensive comments next to the 'tricky' parts of the code. In addition there might be a short overview document that explains to a new programmer how all of your project files fit together.

Final design and feature freeze

In developing software, you are usually faced with some kind of temporal deadline. You can't go on changing and adding to the program forever if you are going to hit your ship date. Polishing up the program and getting the final bugs out is usually going to take more time than you expected. In fact there's a saying among software engineers: 'The first 90% of the program takes the first 90% of the time, and the last 10% takes the second 90% of the time.'

The final design has a set-in-concrete nature that the alpha N designs do not. Once you get to this point, this is what you are going to finish, and nothing more or less. 'Feature freeze' means, of course, that you are not going to be adding any more features, no matter how enticing they may seem.

Regarding how long it takes add things to a program, the author often thinks of a fractal such as a coastline. Standing on one rocky outcropping of a coast, you might look along the coast towards the next promontory and think it's an easy walk. But coasts and programs are fractals, and you're likely to find inlets blocking your way, inlets with further smaller inlets along them.

Beta N Program and Beta N User's Guide

At this point you know exactly what the program is supposed to do. The problem is to make this really true. So now you alternate making new versions of the beta N release with testing and debugging the release. This phase is also when you get really serious about your User's Guide.

In software companies, the creation of the documentation is often farmed out to a technical writing division within the company. The final specification and detailed design acts as a good starting point for the tech writers; although it is easier for them if you have been dutiful about your alpha N documentations. In general it is *not* a good idea to let the tech writers get started before you have done your feature freeze and gotten your final design together, otherwise they may waste a lot of time working on documentation for features which are still subject to change.

What's wrong with that? The problem is that your company will account the cost of the tech writers' time as part of your project's expense, making your work appear much less cost-effective.

Testing Beta N

It's hard to anticipate all of the bugs that a program may contain. The more people you can get testing it the better. Often the writers working on the documentation function as a kind of testing staff; they try writing down what the specification says the program does, and they see if this is true as they write it.

While testing your program, always run it in debug mode (by pressing the F5 key) so that if and when it crashes, you will be able to use the debugger information.

It's a good idea to develop an 'autorun' mode for your program under which it will run and do things without any user input. This is a type of automated testing that can be pushed pretty far; you can, for instance, have your automated test periodically change values of the program parameters as if a user were doing things.

Larger companies will have a special group devoted to testing the software; this is sometimes called the QA group. The fact is, developers don't want their code to break. Whether consciously or not, they know which kinds of tests to avoid. Only a dispassionate QA tester can really find the problems in your code. By way of testing the Pop program, the author has let successive waves of students try to find bugs in it, with extra homework points going to those who succeed.

If a lot of people are interested in your program, you may be able to hand out beta versions to them and have them try the program out.

As with the sequential alpha versions, you need to be careful to keep the successive beta versions distinct. Another issue is that of bug tracking. You should have a big document (or data base file) which includes a brief description of each bug and how to reproduce the bug, along with a record of what has been done to fix the bug. For the purposes of a student project, a simple text document with a name like **bugs.txt** can do the job. You might keep such a file in with your source code and revise it as time goes on.

Debugging Beta N

There are a lot of special techniques software engineers use to try and keep bugs out of their code.

Using the object-oriented language C++ instead of C is one good way for avoiding bugs. C++ allows you to encapsulate closely related variables and functions into the special kinds of types we call *classes*. (The instances of your classes are your *objects*.) With the object-oriented approach, your code becomes simpler to read and to understand, and this means it is less likely to have major bugs in its logic. The use of 'operator overloading', for instance, enables you to write something like a = b + c to stand for, say, vector addition just like you would want it to.

Another good thing about object-oriented programming (called OOP for short) is that it allows you to code up some frequently used routine only once, and to provide interfaces so this same piece of code can be used over and over. It is much easier to perfect and maintain a piece of code if it lives only in one place instead of having variant versions copied all over the place. OOP also provides a kind of access-protection for the member variables of objects, which makes it harder to carelessly alter a variable without taking into account the side-effects that this change may have. Instead of arbitrarily changing member variables, you use special 'mutator' functions that you have written so as (hopefully) to nail down all side-effects once and for all.

Still another gain from OOP is the use of constructor and destructor functions. These functions, which you write yourself for each class you define, take care of initializing the fields of your objects to default values, allocating necessary memory and resources for your objects, and freeing up memory and resources when you are through with an object.

A final benefit to C++ is the availability of template libraries which include, for instance, templates which encapsulate the notion of a linked list, a map (also known as a hash table) and an array. The MFC templates for these useful classes are called **CList**, **CMap**, and **CArray**, respectively. A **CArray** template class, for instance, takes care of the memory management issues involved with allocating and deallocating space for an array.

It should go without saying that learning how to use the debugger is all-important. Beginning and intermediate programmers tend to avoid the debugger, as it seems too confusing. But really and truly, *the debugger is your friend*. While developing a program you should primarily be building the *'Debug'* version of the program as opposed to the *'Release'* version – there is a switch for selecting between the two in the Microsoft Visual Studio compiler (see Appendix C for the control sequence). See Chapter 21: Tools for Software Engineering in Part II for more detailed information about using the debugger.

Final version and product ship

Putting together the final version can involve figuring out things like how to fit it all on the required number of disks, and how the users are going to install the software from the disks. Lots of issues relating to the documentation will arise as well. Often you will want to provide screen-shots for use in the documentation.

In a truly Staged Delivery cycle, it's conceivable that after you reach this level you jump all the way back to the specification and detailed design N stage, and implement a new layer of features. Note, however, that this is time-consuming, as once you start adding new features, you need to take them through the repeated alphas to get them working, and then take them through multiple betas to get them tested and debugged.

Trying to add new features late in the lifecycle is risky, but sometimes the pressure is irresistible. The urge is known as *feature creep*. Unless you know that you're going to have enough time to fully test the new features after implementing them, resist feature creep.

The development spiral

We mentioned above that there's a kind of software lifecycle known as the Spiral lifecycle. This means thinking in terms of spiraling clockwise around and around through four stages: analysis, design, implementation, and maintenance.

Analysis	Design
Maintenance	Implementation

The *analysis* phase involves figuring out what you want the program to do. This is similar to making a software requirement. In reality, we don't immediately know all the things we want the software to do, so actually we pass back through this stage numerous times.

The *design* phase involves several things. One part is the object-oriented design: figuring out which classes to use, and what the class methods should be. Another part is the program design, figuring out how to break your code into modules, and how to hook the modules together with global variables and function calls. A third part of the design means figuring out your user interface. All this is too much to do at once; what you do is to keep extending and improving the designs as you pass through the design phase over and over.

The *implementation* phase means writing the code. As with design there are at least three types of coding you need to do: the class method coding, the program flow code, and the user interface code.

As used here, the *maintenance* phase includes the debugging and tweaking that goes into the program to make it work properly. The first time you implement something it rarely works just as you wanted it to. You may need to fix a bug, alter a function's behavior, or change a dialog box design.

After each cycle through the four phases, you look at what you have and try and document it. The documentation is itself a kind of analysis, and as you get a deeper understanding of your program you're ready to alter the design, implement the new design, do some maintenance on the new implementation, analyze what you've done, and so on.

Like most lifecycles, our Inventor lifecyle is a kind of cross between the Waterfall and the Spiral lifecyles.

Some students are disappointed when they take a course in software engineering. They had hoped to learn a clear and simple series of steps to follow so as to build a program. But the process turns out to be neither clear nor simple. Like it or not, software engineering is a fuzzy discipline which involves a certain amount of creativity.

A main design methodology we're going to be using in this book is the object-oriented approach described in Chapter 4: Object-Oriented Software Engineering. To begin with, we're using the object-oriented language C++, but we need to do more than write in C++ to make our design and our code truly object-oriented. More than anything else, doing object-oriented software engineering involves iteration and successive levels of refinement.

Here's a relevant passage from a classic book on object-oriented software engineering:

B. Curtis studied the work of professional software developers by videotaping them in action and then by analyzing the different activities they undertook (analysis, design, implementation, etc.) and when. From these studies he concluded that 'software design appears to be a collection of interleaved, iterative, loosely-ordered processes under opportunistic control . . . Top-down balanced development appears to be a special case occurring when a relevant design schema is available or the problem is small . . . Good designers work at multiple levels of abstraction and detail simultaneously.'

Most software systems are highly unique, and therefore their developers have only a restricted basis of experience from which to draw. In such circumstances, the best we can do during the design process is to take a stab at the design, step back and analyze it, then return to the products of the design and make improvements based upon our new understanding. We repeat this process until we are confident about the correctness and completeness of the overall design.

[Grady Booch, *Object-Oriented Design* (Benjamin/Cummings, 1991), p. 189]

2.5   Managing your project

Remember to regularly pause from your team's mad programming frenzy to put your heads up and think about the lifecycle and the schedule of your project. What build are you on, is it an alpha or a beta, when's your next demo, how much time is left, who's doing what now, and what are the major risks to finishing your project on time?

At the beginning of the project your team (possibly a team of one, if you're working alone!) is in the prototype phase; this is the phase when you barely know what you're doing and are still trying things out. Later on you're in the alpha phase where you're got a basic handle on things and you're adding neat features to the program as fast as you can. And then the team has something you can show people, and that's your alpha 1. Then you incorporate feedback from your demos, add more features, clean it up a bit and get to alpha 2. And so on. Eventually your team gets to the beta phase where you're not allowed to change things anymore and you have to focus on getting everything to work in the nicest possible way.

In the early stages of a software project you have to keep going back over it to make your design cleaner and simpler. When you first add some features, you're likely to do this in a messy, hurried fashion. As soon as you see that they work, you want to go back and clean them up. If your team leaves anything messy in your program it's going to cause you trouble later on after the program grows – maybe a lot of trouble.

In a simpler world, perhaps we would know what our programs are going to do before writing any code at all. But this is impossible when you're in a process of learning new programming tools and exploring new intellectual concepts. And, given the rapidly changing nature of the software business, a programmer is *always* in the process of learning new programming tools. The new features never stop, and it's a shame not to learn how to use them. Remember that process and project-management can be something you do to make things easier. Don't let it be an empty ritual done only to appease a boss.

Tracking the builds

Let's say a bit about how to describe the build you're currently on. How can you tell the difference between alpha and beta builds? Entering beta means that you've frozen your features and are now focusing on polishing and debugging. So before that you're in alpha phase. Is each new build an alpha? It's really just a matter of taste. Some software engineers call each successive build an alpha build.

It's more common to call a build a new alpha only if you plan to show it to people outside your group, that is, only if the build is in some sense a big deal, a rounding off point. In this way of thinking, the first true alpha of a program would be the first version that has the program's basic functionality and architecture in place.

Of course for a programmer what really matters is which version number of the program is being built. You start with version 1, and you go on from there, and you never ever mix up the code from different versions. Given the fractal nature of software development (remember the crinkled coastline), you sometimes will do a number of builds without changing the version number – in these cases be sure to add a date to the caption bar of the program and to the name of the directory where the code lives. It's worth the small extra organizational effort to avoid losing track of which is the latest build.

A formal name like 'the alpha 1 build' has more to do with your relationship to society than it does with your relationship to the code. That is, if you're in a software projects class, the professor is going to want you to hand in an 'alpha 1' build of your program, so whatever build you have done by that date is perforce your alpha 1. If you're writing a program for fun, the first build that's good enough for you to feel like showing it to your friends is your alpha 1. If you're working in a company, and there's going to be a little demo for a key manager, the program you get working for that first demo is your alpha 1. The boundary line between your prototypes and your alphas is hazy. It can very well happen that the 'alpha 1' is 'build 5' of your program.

By the same token, you will probably develop a bunch of intermediate builds between your official alpha 1 and your official alpha 2. If your professor wants an alpha 2 version of your project, that doesn't mean you're only supposed to rebuild the program *once* after the alpha 1! And of course in a business environment, the expectation is that the alpha 1 is going to be a springboard that suggests all kinds of improvements you can still make before the alpha 2. It might happen that you have two, three, or more version builds in between your official alphas.

No matter whether you call a build an alpha or a beta, it's extremely important to be *fanatically, obsessively, compulsively organized* about which files belong to which version of your program. By far the best strategy is to assign numbers and dates to the successive versions of your program, and to keep the code for the separate versions in separate directories whose names include the version number and the calendar date of the most recent build. Generally, before starting to make extensive new changes, you should copy the directory of the most recent successful build and change the directory name to include the new date. That way, if something goes wrong, you haven't thrown out the last good build.

A modern way to handle this is to use a revision control tool like Microsoft SourceSafe or the RCS (Revision Control Software) commonly used on Linux systems. A complicating factor with using a revision control tool is that there needs to be one master server directory which all team members use for checking out and checking in their code. Since a laboratory course will often involve teams of students working at home on disparate machines and without access to a single server site, Chapter 21: Tools for Software Engineering in Part II presents a cruder form of 'manual' directory-based revision control. But once you get more serious about software engineering, you will definitely want to learn how to use something like SourceSafe.

Commenting your code

Always try and construct the code so that it's easy for you or other programmers to understand it, and to tweak it. In this subsection we'll first give some very specific suggestions and then some more general ones.

It's a lot easier to read code that's properly indented. A good way to enforce this is to always use tabs for your indents, and never use spaces, the reason being that it's easier to be inconsistent with spaces for indents, you might easily vary between using three, four, or five spaces. In its default setting, the Visual Studio editor will muddy the water by sneaking and replacing tabs by spaces. To block this behavior, use **Tools** | **Options** dialog, go to the **Tabs** tab, check **Keep Tabs** instead of **Insert Spaces**. Regarding the **Auto Indent** selection below that, it's not a bad idea to work with it set to **None** so that you have full control over your tab indents. The basic principle is simple: each new block level is indented one more tab. When lines run off the right of the page you break them with an Enter, and add another indent to the typed lines.

As a rule, comments should be indented one tab more than the lines they are commenting on; it should be easy to scan down some code and see where the actual lines are. Every now and then, for a really long comment, particularly at the start of a block of code, you can bring it over to the leftmost margin. Indenting the comments is a little bit of work because as you edit a comment, say by adding a long phrase in the middle of a paragraph, you'll mess up the line breaks and have to keep going through them and reorganizing the tabs and Enters. Code editors like Visual Studio don't do automatic line-wrap like a text-processor.

Where should you comment? It's easy to tell someone to comment everything, but that's neither helpful nor practical. One useful rule of thumb is to comment the 'intense' parts of your code. If your heart actually beats faster when you are writing some code, this is definitely a spot where you should add a comment. Common coding emotions are confusion, pride, and anxiety.

When you're confused you're kind of feeling around in the dark, and the comment will be helpful if you need to change what you tried. If you're proud, it means you thought of some cool trick that needs some explanation. Or this might be a place where it took you a while to get things to work right, and now you've finally gotten out the bugs. Tell about it, so that others can learn. When you're anxious, it means you've gotten something to work that you or somebody else could easily break again, so you should explain what not to do.

2.6 Working in teams

Communication

Make sure to exchange email addresses and phone numbers at the earliest opportunity. Make an address alias in your email program including the addresses of all the team members. Try sending a message to the whole team at least once per week, and preferably at least once between each class meeting. To supplement email, you can also bring copies of printed texts to team meetings to make double sure that everyone gets the message.

Practice doing code hand-off. The idea is to (a) clean out the unnecessary files from your source directory (we supply a **clean.bat** batch file for doing this), (b) use the well-known WinZip utility to make a ***.zip** file, being sure to include all files needed for a successful build, and (c) hand off the code by emailing it as an attachment or putting it on a disk. Doing this right takes a little practice, so make sure before handing off your zip that you can in fact build the executable from the unzipped files. Take the time to test it. We discuss this a little more in Chapter 21: Tools for Software Engineering.

Don't overdo the sending of attachments. It can be a burden to get a large ***.zip** file over email. It's also possible to exchange your new files in class, bringing them in on disk, or copying them across the lab's high-speed local network.

In exchanging informational documents, remember that you can just paste the document into the email instead of making it a Word attachment. Due to macro viruses, people are increasingly uneasy about opening attached text documents. It's easy to do an **Edit | Select All** on a text document, followed by an **Edit | Copy** in the document and then an **Edit | Paste** in the email document. If you do get a Word document you're uncomfortable in opening, use **Windows | Programs | Accessories | WordPad** to open it, as this app doesn't support macros.

Merging code

Unless you happen to be working completely alone, other people are going to be working on other code modules at the same time you work on the modules you're responsible for. Every day, or every few days, you'll have to merge the modules. That is, you put all the updated modules into one directory and try and build the program from there. Usually you'll have to fix a few things to get all of the new modules to build together. When working in a group it is especially useful to maintain a 'log' section of comments at the beginning of the modules you are changing.

Merging the code is a bit tricky when two people have worked on the same module, but sometimes that can't be avoided – it might be, for instance, that they've added new functions to their own modules, and these functions need to be called from the main module. In this case the two developers will each have changes to the main module. When two people have changes to the same module, someone needs to use a utility program which can locate the lines where similar files differ. Chapter 21: Tools for Software Engineering describes how to use the Microsoft Windiff utility.

Team roles

There are a number of separate tasks involved in making a complete program. Seven of the main tasks are the following.

- Coming up with the design.
- Writing and debugging the code.
- Integrating the code and building the executable.
- Testing the code.
- Creating the written documentation and the help files.
- Creating images and sounds to be used in the program, or finding public domain ones that you can copy.
- Giving public demonstrations of the product.

In a company, these roles might be filled by seven completely different departments. Management might come up with the program design, the technical department might write and debug the code, the so-called 'build' or 'development' group would integrate the files and build the executables, the quality assurance or 'QA' department would test for bugs, the technical publications department would create the documentation, the multimedia department would provide bitmaps and sound files for use in the program, and marketing would go out and give demos of the program.

On a small team of students a more typical situation is that the group jointly arrives at a design they all can agree on. And then each of the students might write some of the code. From week to week, it's necessary to integrate the code. It's important to have one single individual in charge of the code integration each week, as otherwise there will be uncertainty about which is the 'real' new build. Let's call this person the 'builder'. It is the responsibility of the builder to bring in the executable for the current class presentation or professor evaluation. If the builder fouls up and doesn't do his or her job, the team can get a poor grade. Remember to do code hand-off when it's time to change builders.

As well as being a position of responsibility, being the builder is a position of some power, as it's up to the builder to decide which pieces of the code to put in, and which pieces to change or to leave out. For this reason, it's a good idea to let the position of 'builder' change from one student to another every couple of weeks, so that each student has the experience of being the builder.

Another key role during the project is the 'documenter.' It's the documenter's responsibility to produce the written User's Guide and (later on) the help files. As the periodic project evaluations are based on the current executable and the current documentation, it's the builder and the documenter who determine the team's grades. As with the 'builder', it's a good idea to let the 'documenter' role change every couple of weeks.

A third element in the project evaluation is the 'presenter', that is, the student who stands up in front of the class and explains the current state of the program. Each student should be the 'presenter' at least once.

At this level, it's not always useful to think of any one student as being a 'team leader'. All the students are still learning, and it's a good idea to try and let everyone have a go at a variety of roles. If anyone is really the 'leader' it's probably the 'builder,' which is why it is important to let this role shift from student to student every few weeks.

In parceling out the coding duties, the fact that we'll be using object-oriented design is helpful. Once the team agrees on a class's members, it is (theoretically) possible to have someone implement the class members separately from someone who's writing code to use the class. In practice, though, these tasks need to be done hand-in-hand, as you always find that the way you plan to use a class will change your ideas about what the class's methods should be. And it's not really practical to write code that uses a class without having the class already implemented so you can test it.

An easier kind of coding division is between the program and its interface. Sometimes it is practical to have one person working on the way the program runs while having someone else work on the menus and the dialog boxes.

A common pattern is that two students get very involved in the coding, while the other one or two members do not. The students who write less code should try and do more in the other areas: the documentation, the testing, and the art.

By the time you get down to the project's end and the last build, you'll have a good idea of which individual is going to do the best job at the final coding push, and this will be the person the team should pick for the final builder. By the same token, there will be a person who works best with the documentation, and that person should handle the final documentation. Finally there will be a student who's going to be your best candidate for the presenter. For the final version of your program, use the most appropriate team member for each role.

Inevitably the members of the team are going to be better at different things. It's important for each member to find some area that he or she 'owns' and is responsible for during the final push. For fairness, nobody should do everything, and everybody should do something.

In order to try and balance the contributions of team members, the author usually groups together students who have accumulated similar cumulative point totals on the assignments and tests given before the teams are assigned.

Although a reasonable standard policy is to give the same grade on a project to each member of the team there can occasionally be some variations within the team's grades based on the individual contribution.

2.7 Giving a presentation

As a software engineer you can expect to have to give two kinds of presentations. First there are presentations in which you might discuss the concept, specification, and design of your program. These days, presentations of this sort are almost universally made into a series of PowerPoint slides. Second, there are the presentations in which you show a live, running demonstration of your program in its current state.

The two most important rules for either kind of presentation are these.

- Face the audience. Resist the tendency to turn your back to the audience and stare at the screen. This is a particular risk when you're presenting a software demo. For software demos you really need one person to be at the computer running the demo while another person talks.

- Speak loudly, clearly, and not too fast. Speaking loud to a group can be psychologically difficult if you've never done it before. It's said that fear of having to speak to a group is one of the most widespread phobias. Practice with your family or friends in advance if you get a chance. And when you make your presentation, try and think of the group as not being hostile or judgmental. Think of them as friends.

PowerPoint

Here are a few basic rules to remember about a PowerPoint style demonstration.

- Content, not graphics. You can be sure that your audience has seen Power-Point presentations before. What is going to impress them is the content of your material, not the fancy themes or colors that you use. Work the content out first, and think about the graphics frills second – or not at all.
- Make the slides have good contrast. Yes, black text on white background seems boring when there are so many other possibilities. But the person in the last row is going to be unable to read your slides if they're green on beige or some such. PowerPoint is simply a medium for getting your words across. Don't let it get in the way. If you'd rather be different and use white text on black background, that's okay, but you'll need to make the font a bit larger, as this color-scheme is slightly harder to read.
- Use a big font. You shouldn't try to squeeze more than three or four lines of text onto a slide. Even if the font is still readable, too much information on a slide loses your audience. When necessary, split a thought into two or three subthoughts, start with a 'contents' slide listing the two or three thoughts you're about to discuss, show a slide for each thought, and when you're done come back to the contents slide to summarize.
- Supplement with paper handouts. It's often not possible to fit a complicated UML diagram onto a slide and still have it legible. You can break the UML up into small pieces or, if this doesn't seem to communicate the pattern properly, you can print out copies of the full UML and hand it out. People like getting a few paper handouts at presentations. It gives them something to make notes on, and it reminds them of what you said.

Software demo

Software engineers refer to something called the 'demo effect'. This is a weird force which sometimes makes your wonderful program turn into a buggy piece of junk in front of a large audience. Here's a little law, gleaned from some years of experience:

> The strength of the demo effect is directly proportional to the size of the audience times the importance of the demo to your career.

The ideal method is to bring your demo on a laptop, but sometimes you won't be allowed to do this. In a course using this book, it's reasonable to require the students to use a classroom machine which is hooked up to the classroom computer projector. If you build your project on an individual self-study basis, you might eventually take it to a friendly gamers' group and show it on a projector there.

If you have to bring your demo in portable form, there is the issue of getting it to fit onto a disk. Floppy disks have a 1.44 Meg maximum size. If your game includes a lot of bitmaps, it may well be larger than this size. But if the exe itself is less than 1.44 Meg, put it alone on a floppy and put any support files like *.hlp or parameter files or sample source code on another disk.

If you can't fit your exe on a floppy, you can consider using a compress utility like WinZip, or burning a CD or even DVD with your game on it.

Theoretically you can use the old-style DOS Backup utility to back a file up onto two disks, but it can be tricky to get the command prompts for this right, especially in a stressed situation. There are also other backup utilities that one can download from various software sites on the internet, but they're not much easier to use. Forget backup utilities.

A typical sequence on demo day in a classroom might be that the students bring their disks up, the professor gets all the executables copied or unzipped from the floppies (or other types of disks), and puts them all into a directory on a network drive, and then the students come up in teams and run the executables on the classroom machine. If you're doing a demo at a conference or a meeting, it's more likely that you yourself would be responsible for plugging in your own laptop or for copying your software to the demo machine.

Here's a list of tips for avoiding the demo effect, starting with our two principles of scale and speed independence.

- Write your program so its behavior is independent of the resolution of the display.

- Write your program so its behavior is independent of the speed of the machine.

- Bring your program on your laptop if you can. But do keep in mind that there's a real chance that for some reason you won't be able to use your laptop; it's not uncommon for people to have a problem in connecting their laptop to a computer projector. Any task can become surprisingly hard in a stressed situation with people watching you and giving you advice. If at all possible, test your laptop with the projector during a break before your demo.

- Understand that your demo machine may well be a randomly configured rental machine with no Internet hookup that was delivered to completely non-technical people (who are likely as not Windows-hating Mac-lovers) five minutes before you go on.

- Before the demo be sure and test your program on a variety of machines. Carry a disk with your *.exe around and try to run it other machines. If you're running it on someone else's machine, you should ask permission and, if possible, run the program from your floppy rather than cluttering up their hard drive. Note by the way that WinZip actually lets you double-click on a zipped executable and run it without formally unzipping the file.

- Bring your program to the demo in more than one medium: laptop, floppy disk, CD ROM, on the Web for download, etc. For a really challenging event – like if you are flying to another country to do your demo – give yourself some insurance by bringing transparencies of some sample screens. If all else fails you can show the slides with an old-fashioned overhead projector.

- If you bring your program on a floppy disk, bring an extra copy of the floppy in case the floppy goes bad. All floppies die, sooner or later. On the same theme, use a *new* floppy for your big demo.

- If you do bring your program in compressed *.zip form, bring a disk with an unzipping utility program on it, just in case you need to install the utility on the spot. If the demo is important enough, the demo machine (a) will not have an unzip utility and (b) will not have an Internet hookup that would let you download one.

- If it's at all possible, get a half an hour of 'quality time' alone with the demo machine and projector so you can properly install your program.

- Remember that what you see on the screen is not necessarily the same as what goes over the computer projector. Projectors often don't like high resolutions. You can set the demo machine to a lower screen resolution by right-clicking on the desktop and going to **Properties | Settings**.

- In the case of a Pop Framework program, remember that, as a last measure, there is a **File | Run Speed...** dialog that might possibly help if your demo machine goes too slow or too fast.

- Imagine the most horrible scenarios you can conceive, and then expect something worse!

- Don't cry or lose your temper. How you look and act and talk is as important as anything your audience sees, or doesn't see, on the screen.

Review questions

A What is the Constraint Triangle?

B What is the relationship between requirements and specifications?

C What does 'UML' stand for? What are some kinds of UML diagrams?

D What is requirements gathering?

E What should a specification sketch include?

F What are some examples of project milestones?

G What is risk assessment?

H   What are high-level and low-level design?

I   What are some documents that will be associated with your project?

J   Diagram the three software lifecycles: Waterfall, Staged Delivery, and Inventor.

K   What stage separates the alpha builds from the beta builds?

L   At what point in the software lifecycle should you start work on the User's Guide?

M   Draw a picture of the development spiral.

N   What sort of name should you use for the directory where your most recent build lives? What are some other ways to keep track of your build version?

O   What are the steps of code hand-off?

P   What are the two most important rules for giving a presentation?

Q   What are some steps you can take to help ensure a successful software demo?

Exercises

Exercise 2.1: Use case diagram

Suppose that you had a requirement for an online concert-ticket-ordering service. The requirement might go like this.

A client can visit the server and search a schedule for a concert. A concert specifies a performer, a venue and a date. After selecting a concert, the client sees a list of some available tickets, specifying seat and price. The client can view a map to see where the seats are located. The client can select tickets and add them to his or her order. The client can buy the order by filling in an address form and giving credit card information.

Draw a use case diagram indicating some of the possible scenarios.

Exercise 2.2: Scheduling

If you are using this book as the text in a projects class, make out a preliminary schedule for your project, indicating target dates for the following milestones: initial specification sketch, completion of requirements gathering, high-level design (architecture), detailed design and first build, alpha demo, beta demo, final demo.

Exercise 2.3: Specification sketch

Write a preliminary draft of a specification sketch for a game project based on the Pop Framework. Show it to friends, fellow students, and/or your teacher in order to get started on your requirements gathering.

The Pop Framework

3

3.1 Object-oriented simulations

One of the reasons why computer games are a good kind of programming project is that writing computer games gives you some experience with creating computer simulations of something like real-world processes. Simulation is one of the most important things that we can do with a computer. In a simulation, we set up a model of some real-world system we are interested in. By watching the behavior of the simulation we can gain insights about the real world.

Things that have been simulated include factories, industrial machinery, the stock market, people's buying behavior, automobile traffic, the formation of stars, nuclear weapons explosions, the spread of disease, the solar system, organic molecules like human DNA, and games like golf and tennis. The entire business of computer aided design, or CAD, is about simulating the appearance of physical objects in mathematical space, and these days nearly everything that is manufactured is first modeled in some CAD program.

Even something like a telephone or Internet control system is a kind of simulation, insofar as the users and routes are being represented as data structures which the program manipulates. Payroll programs are again a kind of simulation, with data fields standing in for dollars and employees. Spreadsheets are one of the oldest kind of simulation programs; the power of a spreadsheet lies in the fact that you can alter a single entry and automatically simulate the changes that propagate out from it.

Object-oriented design (OOD) lends itself very well to simulation. The reason is that when we have a system to simulate, the system tends to naturally break into interacting objects, each object with its properties and behaviors. A class is a very natural kind of model for an object of this kind. One of the big differences between C++ and C is that while in C we can have **struct** objects to hold collections of data, in C++ we can have **class** objects that not only hold data but also hold specific methods that act on the data. This is *encapsulation*.

Another good thing about OOD is that it makes it easy to give your simulation objects a uniform behavior, such as is enforced by physical laws. Let's explain this a bit more. If you are modeling physics, all of the objects should obey Newton's laws of motion. By using the OOD mechanism of *inheritance* we can avoid having to reprogram Newton's laws over and over and over. Instead, we define a base class with, say, a *move(dt)* method embodying Newton's laws, and then we derive all of our simulation classes from the base class. Thanks to inheritance, the child objects will all obey the same laws of motion as the parent class.

The OOD technique of *polymorphism* is useful for expressing the fact that, although real-world objects tend to group themselves into classes of similar objects, it's also the case that there will be subclasses that have their own distinctive behaviors. And each object knows on its own how to behave. By using polymorphism, we're free to think abstractly, and say something like 'let each of the objects move a time increment step now,' and be able to trust our individual objects to know to use their own specialized styles of motion. Thanks to polymorphism we can ignore the differences between objects when working at a high level – as when we form an array of them – and still be sure that on the low, individual, level, the objects will be 'smart' enough not to exhibit simple generic behaviors.

In our discussions, we are going to focus on depth rather than breadth. Instead of talking about a wide range of processes to simulate, we'll concentrate on simulating one particular kind of thing: material objects moving around according to the laws of physics. And we are going to place these objects into the context of computer games built with the Pop Framework.

3.2   Running and testing the Pop program

At this point, the reader should get familiar with the sample Pop program that we have built using our Pop Framework of classes. Read through the Pop help file while running the Pop program, so as to get an idea of the code we're going to be working with. While you're doing this, you can also get some experience with software testing. Write out some answers to Exercise 3.1.

Before starting work, make sure that you have downloaded the very latest version of the Pop program and help file from the course website. Even if two builds have the same version number, it may be that their build dates differ; compare the build date in your executable's caption bar to the build date given for the latest version of the downloadable program.

If you don't like reading help files onscreen, we've also printed a version of the help file as Appendix B, although this printed form will inevitably become outdated at some point; compare the dates in the printed help file and in the online help file. Note that when you open an electronic help file, you can use File | Print to make a hard copy of it.

3.3   The Pop source code

Pop is a program built using the files listed below. In the first group we have C++ files for each of which there is a *.h header file and a *.cpp implementation file. To save space, we simply list each of these file names once, with the understanding that each name represents two files, the *.h and the *.cpp.

We can roughly group these files according to their purpose. The MFC Class files control things having to do with the program's standard Windows appearance. The Game files describe the different game modes that the Pop program allows. The Critter files specify the moving objects in the game programs and the Sprite files describe the appearances of these objects. The Physics files implement classes used to define the shape and the physics of the world. The catch-all category of Utility files includes a number of specially crafted files used, among other things, to make graphical animations run smoothly. There is no significance to the fact that some of the file names happen to be capitalized and some are not. This is simply an accident resulting from the ways the author typed in the new file names over the years. The Visual Studio compiler ignores the case of file names.

MFC Class files
childfrm
mainfrm
pop
PopDoc
popview
stdafx

Game files
game
gameairhockey
gameballworld
gamedambuilder
gamepicknpop
GameSpacewar
gamestub
gamestub3d

Critter files
biota
critter
critterarmed
critterwall
critterviewer

Sprite files
sprite
spritebubble
spriteicon
spritepolygon
spritemultiicon

Physics files
VectorTransformation
realbox
force

Utility files
controller
listener
metric
Randomizer
timer

Graphics files
graphics
graphicsMFC
graphicsOpenGL
memorydc
RealPixelConverter
texture
glshapes

Dialog file
SpeedDialog

We also have a few files used for holding certain constants and parameters. These files do not appear in both the ***.h** and ***.cpp** format.

Parameter-holding files
static.cpp (and NO **static.h**)
graphicsconstants.h (and NO **graphicsconstants.cpp**)
RealNumber.h (and NO **RealNumber.cpp**)

In addition we have the Project files, which tell Visual Studio which files to compile and how to link them together.

Project and resource files

In order to build an executable file from a collection of source code and resource files, we need a *Project* file to orchestrate how the files are to be combined. A Visual Studio project is described by two levels of files, a primary higher-level project file called a Workspace or Solution file, and one or more secondary lower-level files simply called project files. Generically any or all of these kinds of files may occasionally be termed 'project files.'

Microsoft changed the standard file extensions for their project files when they replaced the older Visual Studio, Version 6.0, by the newer Visual Studio.NET, also known as Version 7.0.

Table 3.1 will clarify the situation.

Table 3.1 The old and new Visual Studio names for project files.

Version of Visual Studio	High-level main project file extension, and name	Lower-level project file extension, and name
.NET Version 7.0	*.sln, Solution file	*.vcproj, Project file
Version 6.0	*.dsw, Workspace file	*.dsp, Project file

Another essential part of the source code is the Resource files. In a Windows program, a 'resource' can be, among other things, a menu, a toolbar, a dialog box, a bitmap, an icon, a cursor icon, or a sound. **resource.h** and **Pop.rc** describe which resources to use, and the **res** subdirectory holds the digital information used in the resources themselves.

Don't forget that you need to keep the **res** subdirectory in order to be able to rebuild your executable; you *must* include it when you hand-off your source code to someone else.

Resource files
resource.h
Pop.rc
*.bmp Bitmap files, ***.ico** Icon files, ***.cur** Cursor files, ***.wav** Sound files, etc.
[Note that these last files are located in the **res** subdirectory.]

One final file that we usually include with our source code is **pop.clw**, where CLW stands for 'CLass Wizard'. This file keeps track of the names of all your classes, and the class members and methods. You don't really have to keep this file, as Visual Studio can rebuild it if necessary. But it saves time to keep it around.

A component diagram for the build process

A UML component diagram shows the dependencies among a set of the physical components involved with your program build. In this section, we'll use 'physical component' to simply mean a file (or group of files) on your hard drive.

In a component diagram we draw nodes for different kinds of components and we draw dotted arrow-lines to indicate a dependency. An arrow from node A to node B means that *A depends on B*.

If you look at Chapter 20: Using Microsoft Visual Studio, you'll find quite a bit of detail about how the different kinds of files are combined to build an **exe** file. We can summarize some of that information with a component diagram (Figure 3.1) that shows how different kinds of files depend on each other when we build an **exe** file. In this figure, all the little names are kinds of file extensions.

The way we use these files is that we open the main Project file (sometimes called a Solution or a Workspace file) with the IDE (integrated development

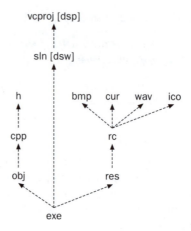

Figure 3.1   Component diagram for file types used in a Windows build

environment) program such as Visual Studio, use the IDE to edit the h and cpp files like text files, use the IDE to edit the rc file in a WYSIWYG fashion, and possibly create or import some additional resources of the types bmp, cur, and the like. If we like, we can use the IDE to change the build parameters of the Project files. Part of the Project file information is stored in a subsidiary Project file, though this is not something we normally notice.

As shown in Table 3.1 above, the extensions and names of the main and subsidiary 'project' files differ between Visual Studio Version 6.0 and Visual Studio.NET, also known as Version 7.0.

When you compile, the **h** and **cpp** are pulled together into **obj** files and the **rc** and resource files are combined into a **res** file. The linker wraps the **obj** together into an exe and then binds the **res** into the **exe** as well.

Another point to make about this diagram is that all of the files from **cpp** and **rc** up are *text files*, that is, simple ASCII files that we can edit with a simple text editor. (By the way if you ever happen to edit one of these files with a word-processor, be careful to save it in text-only format and make sure the file name gets the proper extension.) The **obj**, **res** and **exe** files, on the other hand, are *binary files* consisting of raw zeroes and ones.

3.4   The essential Pop classes

To help organize this discussion, let's start with a UML class diagram of some of the main classes involved in the Pop Framework. We'll give a more detailed explanation of how to 'read' UML class diagrams in Section 3.5. For this initial diagram, we use three conventions.

First, we represent a class by the class name inside a rectangle. Second, we represent the class relationship of *composition* by a line with a diamond at one end. The composition relationship means that a class object of the type at the diamond end owns or has as members class objects of the type at the other end. You can think of the diamond as a 'socket' where we 'plug in' one or more instances of the class at the other end of the composition line. We express the composition relationship by the phrase 'has a' (see Figure 3.2).

Figure 3.2   Composition. Read as 'a *cCritter* has a *cSprite*'

Third, we put a star at the end of a composition line to indicate that the 'owner' class may have more than one instance of the other class. We express this relationship by the phrase 'has a number of'. See Figure 3.3.

Figure 3.3   Multiple composition. Read as 'a *cGame* has a number of *cCritters*'

Okay, so now here's a class diagram (Figure 3.4) of some of the main classes involved in the Pop Framework.

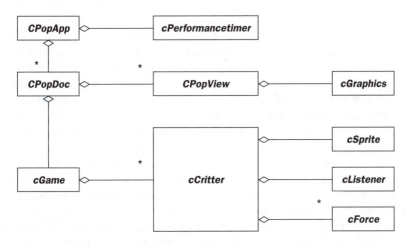

Figure 3.4   Class diagram for Pop Framework classes

The most central class is the *cCritter* class. *cCritter* objects are our game pieces: players, enemies, bullets, furniture, and even the camera through which we look at the world. The word 'critter' is a colloquial Wild-West variation on the word 'creature,' chosen for no better reason than that it's fun to say. We often use the word 'critter' to stand for '*cCritter* object'.

We have quite a number of child classes derived from *cCritter*, specifying different kinds of critters. These classes include *cCritterArmed*, *cCritterBullet*, *cCritterArmedPlayer*, *cCritterArmedRobot*, *cCritterWall*, *cCritterViewer*, etc. (These child classes are not shown in Figure 3.4.)

A unifying notion behind the critters is that they are implemented in such a way that their motions obey a reasonable simulation of physical laws. Why should our game objects move like physical objects? In order for a game to engage the user's attention it needs to feel in some way realistic. You want the user to feel immersed within the world of the game. Given how accustomed we are to the laws of physics, a game whose motions approximate physics is going to be easier to relate to. Keep in mind that we are going to allow ourselves to be fairly arbitrary about the kinds of interactions and 'force fields' that we put into our worlds, so the use of some basic physically-inspired laws of motion is not going to be a drastic limitation. We'll talk about the physics of *cCritter* objects in Chapter 7: Simulating Physics.

One of the principles of OO is to not make one class do too much. In line with this principle, we let a separate *cSprite* class be responsible for a critter's appearance.

The most important method of the *cSprite* class is its *draw* method, which is overridden in various ways for the different *cSprite* child classes. The child classes include *cPolygon*, *cSpriteIcon*, *cSpriteDirectional*, *cSpriteLoop*, *cSpriteCircle*, *cSpriteBubble*, etc. We often speak of '*cSprite* objects' simply as *sprites*.

Each *cCritter* will have a pointer to a *cSprite* object. We say that a critter *delegates* the task of drawing to its sprite. Delegation is a very useful technique in OO. Rather than having a class be responsible for a given task, you use composition to give it a *member* class that handles the task.

One of the advantages of the delegation approach to drawing critters is that after we develop a critter's behavior, we can change its appearance without having to create a new class. It would be tedious, for instance, to develop a *cCritterArmedRobot* and to then have to derive off *cCritterArmedRobotWithBitmapSprite* and a *cCritterArmedRobotWithPolygonSprite*. Since we've delegated the drawing task to a *cSprite* member, we define a single *cCritterArmedRobot* class and then, according to the needs of the game we're writing, we put either a `cPolygon*` or a `cSpriteIcon*` into the `_psprite` field of our *cCritterArmedRobot* objects.

A computer game, or other kind of simulated world, will contain a number of critters, each with its own sprite. We have a *cGame* class which holds a special array of critters. The *cGame* class has several important duties. A game initializes the critters of its game world. A game carries out repeated updates of the critter simulations, and makes calls to display the updated critters on the screen. A game keeps track of the critters' status and displays information about the status of the game. The game method that updates the world is called *step(dt)*; it takes a real number argument *dt* that represents how big a slice of time is to be simulated in this update.

We attain resolution independence and the possibility of simulating physics by having all of our critter and game data stored in terms of real numbers. The game exists in a two- or three-dimensional mathematical plane or space. We have a class called *cVector* to specify the points or vectors in the world. *cVector* is equipped with a wealth of methods and overloaded operators. There is a related *cMatrix* class that's heavily used for three-dimensional graphics. As class members of this type are so all-pervasive we don't include them in Figure 3.4.

In line with simulating physics, we allow for each *cCritter* to be influenced by any number of *cForce* objects, or *forces*. Rather than making a force an essential part of a critter's implementation, we delegate out the forces, so that we can 'plug in' whatever forces we like to each critter. Examples of our child class forces include *cForceGravity*, *cForceDrag*, *cForceObjectSpringRod*, *cForceObjectSeek*, *cForceEvadeBullet*, etc.

We also delegate out the task of listening to the user's input from mouse and keyboard. At each update, each critter's *cListener* member, called simply a listener, is given access to the current mouse and key state, and is allowed to change the critter's motion or other states. The default listener does nothing, usually we attach meaningful listeners to only two of our critters: firstly the critter that the *cGame* recognizes as the 'player' to represent the user on the screen, and secondly the *cCritterViewer* object that acts as a camera to determine the active window's point of view. Listener child classes include *cListenerArrow*, *cListenerScooter*, *cListenerCursor*, *cListenerViewerRide*, etc.

We also use some MFC class files that were defined automatically by the Visual Studio AppWizard when the original Pop application was created. Over time, of course, the files for these classes have been edited so as to override and alter the behaviors of the base classes.

The *CPopApp* is an *application object* or simply the running instance of the program. It has an overridden **OnIdle** method that the system calls whenever the program has no other tasks to do. We use the **OnIdle** call as the 'pump' to drive our animation; our *CPopApp::OnIdle* uses an instance of our *cPerformanceTimer* class to find the time *dt* elapsed since our previous update and then sets off a cascade of calls that lead to invoking the *cGame step(dt)* method.

The *CPopDoc* *document* holds the data associated with your windows. The document serves to hold the data about the game you are running.

The *CPopView* is a *view* that controls how your data is displayed in an onscreen window and also does the initial processing on user input with mouse and keyboard. We'll say more about the Document and View pattern in Chapter 5: Software Design Patterns.

The *CPopView* delegates the details of drawing graphics to a *cGraphics* class object. The *cGraphics* class embodies a kind of software pattern known as the Bridge, which means that it can work as a stand-in for such widely varying kinds of graphics implementations as standard Windows graphics and OpenGL. These are embodied in the *cGraphics* child classes *cGraphicsMFC* and *cGraphicsOpenGL*.

3.5   UML class diagrams

As we've mentioned before, a UML class diagram is a good way to think about a program's class structure. Now that we have some familiarity with the classes of our Pop Framework, we can use the relations between these classes as the basis for a more detailed discussion of UML class diagrams.

Keep in mind that UML diagrams are meant as visual tools to be used to clarify the structure of your program. They are not formal, precise objects like pieces of code. The vagueness – or even, horrors!, the downright sloppiness – of a UML diagram is a reality that you simply have to get used to. It's a bit inimical to a programmer's usual way of thinking. This is because UML is meant to be a communication channel that non-programmers (like customers and managers and computer-science theorists) can use as well as programmers. Always keep in mind that the point of drawing one of these diagrams is to clear things up. The point is *not* to show every possible detail. And remember that, unlike code, there is not, and never will be, any objective standard for being a truly *correct* UML diagram. Code either compiles and runs or it doesn't – but a UML diagram is simply a springboard for thought and discussion.

There are, by the way, a number of programs which will automatically generate UML diagrams from a directory containing your C++ (or, for that matter, Java) code. But often a hand-drawn and custom-designed UML diagram is more informative.

The basic principles of drawing a UML class diagram are pretty simple. First you write down the names of the most important classes in your program, drawing rectangles around them. One way to find out the names of all the classes in an existing Visual Studio project is to take a look at the Class View, using **View/Class View** (Version 7) [or **View/Workspace/Class View** (Version 6.0)]. And then you draw lines among your classes expressing their relationships. Of course if you haven't written the program yet, then you need to first give some thought to what classes you might need to use – we'll say more about this process of 'object-oriented analysis' in Chapter 4: Object-Oriented Software Engineering.

There are three main kinds of relationships that classes can have with each other: *inheritance*, *composition*, and *association*.

Inheritance lines

Say ClassA and ClassB are classes. If I say ClassB inherits from ClassA, this means that ClassB has the same members and methods as ClassA plus some possible new members and methods. It's also possible that ClassB overrides some of the ClassA methods to implement them differently. When ClassB inherits from ClassA, we also say that ClassB is derived from ClassA, or that ClassB is a child class of ClassA. Most concisely, if ClassB inherits from ClassA, we say that 'ClassB *is a* ClassA.'

In a UML class diagram, we use a single line with a big hollow triangle-arrow at one end to express the relationship of inheritance. If ClassB is a child of ClassA, we draw a line with an arrow pointing from ClassB to ClassA. In other words the arrow points at the parent; this is a kind of 'ancestor worship' situation in which the parent is pointed out rather than the child! In the case where we have a number of child classes beneath a single parent, we use a horizontal bar to combine the three inheritance arrows into one, thus cleaning up the picture a little bit.

Figure 3.5 is a picture of some of the classes that are used by the *cGameStub* class.

One thing you'll notice is that we are allowed to 'fork' an inheritance line. That is, in order to reduce clutter, if ClassB and ClassC both inherit from ClassA,

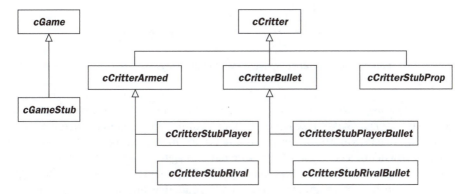

Figure 3.5 UML diagram of some Game Stub classes

we can draw a single hollow-triangle-headed arrow to ClassA and have the arrow's shaft fork in two to have two tails, one ending at ClassB, one ending at ClassC.

Just to make sense out of what these classes refer to, you might want to run the Pop program and choose the **Game | 2DStub** option to see these classes game in action. The *cGameStub* itself inherits from the base class *cGame*. If you look at the game onscreen, you'll see a variety of moving critter objects. The triangular critter that you move with the arrow keys is a *cCritterStubPlayer* object, and it shoots *cCritterPlayerBullet* objects. The critters that look like bitmaps are the *cCritterStubRival* objects, that is, your enemies. They are shooting *cCritterStubRivalBullet* objects at you. The polygonal critters are *cCritterStubProp* objects, and they are not shooting anything, since they inherit from *cCritter* and not from *cCritterArmed*.

Composition lines

We use the word *composition* to refer to the situation where ClassA has a ClassB object as one of its members. The operative phrase here is 'ClassA *has a* ClassB.' In this situation we often say that a ClassA object *owns* a ClassB object. And if you have a ClassA objectA with a ClassB objectB member, the objectB can say that objectA is its *owner*.

Regarding composition, note that there are two different ways in which a ClassA can have a ClassB member: either ClassA has a ClassB object, or ClassA has a pointer to a ClassB object. That is, either ClassA has a member field ClassB _bmember or it has a ClassB* _pbmember. (In C++ we very commonly start our member field names with an underscore _.) The former kind of ClassB member is called an embedded member or an *instance member* of ClassA, while the second kind of ClassB member is called a pointer member or a *reference member*. If the ClassB *_pbmember is truly related to ClassA by composition, we expect that (a) the ClassB constructor will initialize _pbmember with a **new** call and (b) the ClassB destructor will destroy _pbmember with a **delete** call. Condition (b) is sometimes expressed by saying the ClassB reference member of ClassA satisfies the 'cascading delete' condition.

Figure 3.6   *cGame* and *cCritter* composition with multiplicity

The word *aggregation* is used for a weaker version of composition where ClassA may have a class ClassB reference member without this member satisfying the cascading delete condition. That is, if a reference member object is not deleted when its owner object is deleted, then we have an aggregation relationship rather than a composition relationship. Making such fine distinctions when discussing class relationships can sometimes be counter-productive, and we are not going to say much more about the difference between composition and aggregation.

We draw a composition line with a diamond at one end – which we might as well call the tail. This is used to mean that the class object at the diamond end owns or has as members the class objects at the other end. As mentioned before, you can think of the diamond as a 'socket' where we 'plug in' one or more instances of the class at the other end of the composition line.

Another enhancement to the composition line is to write a little numerical symbol like 1, 2, or * at the head (the non-diamond end) of a composition line to indicate either how many different ClassB objects might belong to a given ClassA object. The '*' symbol stands for any number from one on up. A *cGame* can own any number of *cCritter* objects, so we put a * by *cCritter* (see Figure 3.6).

If we don't put multiplicities on a composition line, we will usually mean that there's meant to be only a single member object at the head, although it's also permissible in UML to take a lack of numbers to mean that you simply don't feel like mentioning (or haven't thought about) the number of members.

Some UML experts like to graphically distinguish between the composition relationship and the weaker aggregation relationship by filling in the diamond with solid black for composition and leaving it hollow for aggregation. But we won't do this here, we'll use the hollow diamond to stand for (usually) composition or (rarely) aggregation. In a nutshell, the diamond-headed line means 'has a' or, if there is a star at the end, 'has several.'

A final thing to mention about composition lines is it is not considered acceptable to 'fork' a composition line in analogy to the way we can fork an inheritance line.

Association lines with navigation

The notion of being related by *association* generalizes the notion of composition. If two classes are related by composition, we can also say they're related by association, but we can use the association relationship more broadly than that. We might say ClassA and ClassB are associated in any of the following cases. ClassA and ClassB are associated if (a) each ClassA object has a ClassB object as an explicit member (the same as composition); or if (b) ClassA has a method that returns a ClassB object. Working the other way around, we also say ClassA

Figure 3.7 *cGame* and *cCritter* association

and ClassB are associated if (c) each ClassB object has a ClassA object as an explicit member (the same as composition), or if (d) ClassB has a method that returns a ClassA object.

In speaking of association, we don't distinguish between actual objects and pointers to objects; that is, we think of case (a), for instance, as true regardless of whether the ClassB member is an instance member or a reference member.

We use a plain line to indicate the association relationship (Figure 3.7). It's pretty clear that a *cGame* object is associated with *cCritter* objects.

Occasionally people will even speak of ClassA and ClassB as being associated if one of the ClassA methods takes a ClassB as an argument, or the other way around.

Given how easy it is for two classes to be thought of as associated, you might fear that UML diagrams would turn into spider-web diagrams very much like what's known in graph theory as a 'complete graph', in which every node is connected to every other node. But in practice we don't draw every conceivable association line.

Part of the job in drawing class diagrams is knowing what to leave out. It's usually better to have three or four small, simple class diagrams instead of one large, complicated one.

As well as the hollow-triangle-headed inheritance lines, the diamond-tailed composition lines and the plain association lines, UML class diagrams also have navigation lines. A navigation line is an association line that has been decorated with barbed arrow heads at one or both ends. If a barbed arrow points from ClassA to ClassB, this means that ClassA has a way of 'navigating' to some specific ClassB objects. This would be the situation in cases (a) and (b) mentioned above: ClassA has a ClassB member or has access to a method that returns a ClassB object. We'd put an arrow pointing from ClassB to ClassA in the cases (c) and (d) mentioned above.

To 'navigate' to an object might mean being able to get a copy of the object or get a pointer to it. Or, in a broader sense, to 'navigate' to an object might just mean being able to do something to it, perhaps by calling some kind of mutator method.

In the Pop Framework, a *cGame* owns an array that lists all of its member *cCritter* objects, and each *cCritter* actually has an accessor that returns a pointer to the *cGame* that owns the *cCritter*. So we can navigate in both directions (see Figure 3.8).

As with the composition line, we can put multiplicities on association or navigation lines. Here we can put multiplicities at either end to indicate either how many different ClassA objects might associate with the same ClassB object or how many ClassB objects might associate with a given ClassA object (see Figure 3.9).

Figure 3.8 *cGame* and *cCritter* navigation

Figure 3.9   *cGame* and *cCritter* navigation with multiplicity

In true composition cases with cascading delete, it only make sense for a ClassB object to belong to one single ClassA object, so we assume by default that the multiplicity at the diamond tail of a composition line is 1. So we will often see lines in which there is a diamond at one end and a star at the other, as Figure 3.10, indicating that a given class is composed with multiple instances of another class.

Figure 3.10   *cGame* and *cCritter* with composition and navigation

If we don't put multiplicities on an association line, we will usually mean that it's a 1 to 1 association, although it's also permissible in UML to take a lack of numbers to mean that you simply don't feel like mentioning (or haven't thought about) the multiplicities. Always keep in mind the UML is meant to be a fairly loose way of expressing things, and not a precise language like computer code.

It's not considered good form to draw an arrow on a line with a diamond at one end, so if we want to show the composition relationship along with the navigation from *cCritter* to *cGame* we draw a diamond line for the composition and an arrow line for the navigation as in Figure 3.10.

Now let's draw a big UML diagram showing the relationships among our custom Pop Framework classes and the MFC-generated classes *CPopDoc* and *CPopView*. This is given as Figure 3.11.

Regarding Figure 3.11, note that the author had to redraw it a number of times to try and make it as useful as possible. If your UML diagram makes things seem more confusing, then you need to keep working on it. It usually takes a few tries to get a UML class diagram into its most useful form. A typical thing that happens, for instance, is that you have lines crossing each other, and then you will, if possible, want to rearrange the locations of the classes so that the lines don't cross. Or you might leave out some of the less important associations. Or you might split the diagram into several pieces. In this case, we split off the standard MFC part of the diagram from the computer game-oriented Pop Framework part of the diagram that is shown here. The MFC part is shown in Figure 5.14.

With an eye to the diagram, let's say a bit more about how the Pop Framework works. Once again, the moving objects one sees in the game are *cCritter* objects. Each *CPopDoc* document holds a single `cGame* _pgame` pointer. A *cGame* holds an array of pointers to all the active *cCritter* objects. The actual appearance of a *cCritter* is separated off into a separate object called a *cSprite*; each *cCritter* holds a `cSprite* _psprite`.

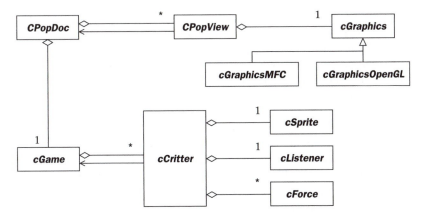

Figure 3.11   Class diagram for Pop Framework classes using navigation arrows

The motions of the critters are affected by user input, which is often fed in from a *cListener*, and also by various simulated physics forces. Each critter has an array of *cForce* objects. The sprites, listeners, and forces don't need to maintain a pointer to their owner critter. (We do in fact pass a pointer to the owner as a function argument when we call the listen and force functions of the *cListener* and the *cForce*, so a case could be made for having navigation arrows go from *cListener* and *cForce* back to *cCritter*.)

The display of the game objects is the responsibility of the *CPopView*. A *cGraphics* object is used to convert the critters' real-valued positions into pixel-valued positions within the visible window of the *CPopView*. We have two kinds of *cGraphics* implementations, the *cGraphicsMFC* and the *cGraphicsOpenGL*.

3.6   Using the Pop Framework

In this section we'll talk about how to use the Pop Framework to make a game of your own. To be quite concrete, we'll work through the steps necessary to use the Pop Framework to make a version of one of the simplest and oldest arcade games, the Space Invaders game of the early 1980s.

Extending the Pop Framework

To use the Pop Framework to create a computer game, you take over all of the **Pop** code and then make some changes to it: either by changing some of the files, by adding some new files of your own, or both.

The fact that this is fairly easy to do means that the **Pop** code is actually a *framework*, where a framework is, once again, a collection of powerful code that is written in such a way that it is easy to tailor it to your needs.

By way of making the Pop code into a usable framework, the code is designed so that a fairly complete description of a game can be fitted into a single class extending our basic *cGame* class. Thus, if you were to make a game called, say, Space Invaders, you might do this by creating a new *cGameSpaceInvaders* class which extends *cGame*. The class declaration for *cGameSpaceInvaders* would live in a new file called **gamespaceinvaders.h**, and the implementation of the class methods would be in a file called **gamespaceinvaders.cpp**.

With good planning and object-oriented design, your project need not involve much more new code than is found in, for example, the two **gamespacewar** files. How will you add files to the project? An easy way is to use copy-and-paste in Windows Explorer to copy some existing similar files, then rename the files, then edit them using the Visual Studio editor, and then use the Visual Studio **Project/Add Existing Item...** dialog [or **Project | Add to Project | Files...** dialog (Version 6.0)] to add your new files to the project. If your game is very similar to, say, the Pop Framework's Spacewar, you might use the **gamespacewar** files as the ones to copy and rename, otherwise you might use one of our other sample pairs of game files such as **gamedambuilder**, **gamestub**, or **gamestub3d**.

What other new code might you need? You may need some new kind of behaviors for the moving objects onscreen. This involves extending the *cCritter* class. So as to make your code easier to work with, it's usually a good idea to define your new kinds of critters within your two game class files; that way you still only have two files to open and close.

Another area that you will eventually change in building your game is the appearance of the bitmaps and the background, not to mention the menus and the toolbar. These are all resources that live in the **res** directory.

The Game Stub classes

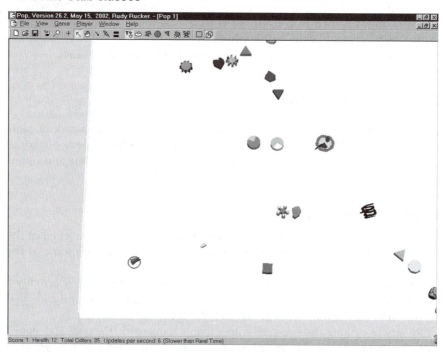

Game stub with solid background, Open GL view, and mixed sprites

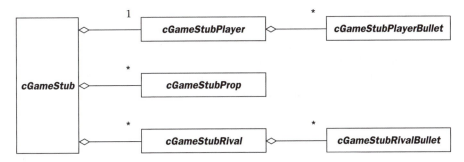

Figure 3.12   UML diagram of the Game Stub classes

In the exercises at the end of this chapter, you will actually carry out a series of changes to the Game Stub classes that turn it into a Space Invaders game. For reference, let's get an overview of what the Game Stub classes are. To begin with, Figure 3.12 shows a UML diagram of the important Game Stub classes.

Each class has its own constructor, of course. This is where we internally set the characteristic features of the object, such as its behavior and its appearance.

The *cCritter* child classes generally override *damage*, *collide*, *update* and sometimes in the case of a player critter the *reset* method. The *cCritterBullet* children often don't need to override anything, but will sometimes override the *initialize(cCritterArmed *pshooter)* method that gets called right after the bullet's constructor. The *cGame* child class overrides a few more methods; the most important ones will turn out to be *seedCritters* and *adjustGameParameters*. This is illustrated in Table 3.2.

Table 3.2   The special classes used in the Game Stub code.

Parent class	Child classes	Overrides
cGame	*cGameStub*	constructor
		Serialize
		reset
		seedCritters
		adjustGameParameters
		statusMessage
		InitializeView
		collide
cCritter	*cCritterStubPlayer*	constructor
	cCritterStubRival	*damage*
	cCritterStubProp	*collide*
		update
		reset
cCritterBullet	*cCritterStubPlayerBullet*	constructor
	cCritterStubRivalBullet	*initialize*

Just for example, here's what two of the class prototypes look like in a recent version of Pop. Note that our UML diagram (Figure 3.12) wasn't fully detailed. There is actually an intermediate Pop Framework class called ***cCritterArmedPlayer*** between ***cCritterStubPlayer*** and ***cCritterArmed***; and ***cCritterRivalBullet*** derives from a special kind of Pop Framework bullet called ***cCritterBulletSilver***. You can find more information in the **gamestub.h** file.

```
class cCritterStubPlayer : public cCritterArmedPlayer //Our player.
{
DECLARE_SERIAL(cCritterStubPlayer);
public:
    cCritterStubPlayer();
//overrides
    virtual void reset();
    virtual int damage(int hitstrength);
    virtual BOOL collide(cCritter *pcritter);
    virtual void update(CPopView *pactiveview, Realdt);
    virtual cCritterBullet* shoot();
};

class cGameStub : public cGame
{
DECLARE_SERIAL(cGameStub);
//Name your statics here
static int PLAYERHEALTH;
static int DEFAULTRIVALCOUNT;
static int DEFAULTSEEDCOUNT;
private:
    int _rivalcount;
public:
    cGameStub();
//overrides
    virtual void Serialize(CArchive& ar); /*Override for
        _rivalcount */
    virtual void reset();
    virtual void adjustGameParameters();
    virtual CString statusMessage();
    virtual void initializeView(CPopView *pview);
    virtual void initializeCritterViewer(cCritterViewer *pviewer);
        //To change the default view direction.
    virtual void seedCritters();
    virtual BOOL collide(cCritter *pcriti, cCritter *pcritj);
};
```

Review questions

A   Why is an object-oriented approach useful for simulation?

B   What are some of the different game modes that the Pop program runs in?

C   What is the difference between a *.h file and a *.cpp file?

D   What do the *.res file and the *.sln or *.dsw file do?

E   Draw the component diagram of the Windows build process.

F   Draw a class diagram for the Pop Framework.

G   What is the relationship between *cGame*, *cCritter*, and *cSprite*?

H   What is the difference between composition and inheritance?

I   How many files do you need to edit to write a game with the Pop Framework? How do you get started?

Exercises

Exercise 3.1: Testing the Pop program

Any large program's code is likely to have bugs in it, and it's even more likely that there are places where the documentation is out of sync with the actual behavior of the program. While going through the help file and testing the Pop program, look for these three kinds of problems.

Bugs. A bug is when the program does something that seems wrong. Crashing is the extreme case, but other kinds of odd behavior can be bugs as well. For a useful bug report, explain exactly how to reproduce the bug. Note that it possible that something the tester thinks of as a bug may be what the programmer thinks of as a feature.

Bad features. Features of the program that you find bad or confusing or which look like bugs. Explain what you don't like. If many testers have the impression that a feature is a bug, then the feature needs be changed or, at the very least, better documented.

Bad documentation. Find cases where the help file description does not seem to match the behavior of the program. Also note cases where some program feature is not well-explained.

Exercise 3.2: First build

Install Visual Studio. Put the Pop code onto your hard drive, find the pop.sln file (Version 7.0) [or pop.dsw file (Version 6.0)] file in the Windows Explorer and double-click on it to open up the project in Visual Studio. Press **Ctrl+Shift+B** (Version 7.0) [or **F7** (Version 6.0)] to build the Pop program, watching the messages that go by in the Output pane that can be found at the bottom of the Visual Studio window. If you get a successful build, press **F5** to run the Pop program inside the Visual Studio debugger. If you have any problems or questions check Chapter 20: Using Microsoft Visual Studio for more information. After the build, use Windows Explorer to see what kinds of files have been added to your disk by the build.

Exercise 3.3: Code hand-off

First clean your Pop code directory by closing Visual Studio, using Windows Explorer to navigate into the directory, and clicking on **clean.bat**. After clean.bat runs, use Windows Explorer to see if there are any ***.exe** still in the directory. If there are, delete them so as to minimize your directory size.

If you don't have WinZip on your machine, go to **www.winzip.com** and download and install a free evaluation copy. Choose the 'Classic' settings as your preferred WinZip default.

Right-click on your Pop code directory and select **WinZip** from the context menu to zip it up.

Note these considerations about the WinZip settings. Let's assume you are running WinZip in the 'Classic' interface mode and that you are using the current (as of Spring, 2002) Version 8.1. WinZip will save your directory name, which is good, as the directory name will probably have version and date information. Also WinZip automatically saves your directories subdirectories, which is good, as you need the **res** subdirectory to be able to rebuild the code.

In the **Options** field of the **Add** dialog box, don't check **Save Extra Folder Info**. You don't want to check **Save Extra Folder Info** because, for portability, you don't want to include the full path to directory where your files live. Even if this isn't checked, WinZip *will* save the name of the directory you are zipping.

Choose the name **mypop1.zip** for your zip file and save it somewhere where you can find it, perhaps in the C:\Temp directory. Don't save it in with the same code that you're zipping. After its been zipped, find **mypop1.zip** and unzip it (not into the same location as the original Pop code that you were working with). Open its **pop.dsw** with Visual Studio and see if it will build. If this works, try sending **mypop1.zip** to yourself as an email attachment, see if you can then unzip it and build it. Practice these steps until you can do them all.

Exercise 3.4: Changing the date information for your build

Set the date of your Pop build to match the current date in three places. (a) Put a version number and a build date into the name of your executable file. In Visual Studio, Version 7.0, first make sure that you have **View | Project Explorer** open and that you have clicked on the Pop node, and then use **View | Property Pages | Linker | General | Output File**. If another node is active, **Property Pages** will open up a different dialog. [In Version 6.0, you can always simply use the **Program | Settings | Link | General | Output File Name**.] Change the name of the executable both for the Release build and the Debug build. You switch between them in either Version 6.0 or 7.0 by using the **settings for** control in the upper left-hand corner of the dialog box with which you are editing the output file name. (b) Open the Resource view. You can do this in Version 7.0 with **View | Resource | View**. [In Version 6.0, use **View | Workspace | Res**, where you'll find the 'Res' as a tab at the bottom of the Workspace window.] Click on the **String Table** resource in Resource View and then click on IDR_MAINFRAME to use this string to include the build number and the date; this string is what appears in the caption bar of your *.exe. (c) Change the name of the directory where you code lives by highlighting the the directory name in Explorer and pressing F2 so you can edit it.

Exercise 3.5: Look at some Pop code files

With the Pop project in Visual Studio, use **File | Open** to open the **gamespacewar.h** and **gamespacewar.cpp** files to get an idea of how much code goes into a game definition. You'll see that it's not all that much, as you only need to mention the methods that you plan to override. Now look at the **game.h** and **game.cpp** files to get an idea of what kinds of methods *cGameSpacewar* inherits from *cGame*.

Now take a brief look at the **critter.*** and **critterarmed.*** files. This code is fairly gnarly (in the sense of 'complex'), but we'll explain a lot of it later on. For now just scan over **critter.h** to get an idea of what the *cCritter* methods are.

Exercise 3.6: Look at the Pop resources

Open the Pop project in Visual Studio and then open the Resource View. You can do this in Version 7.0 with **View | Resource View**. [In Version 6.0, use **View | Workspace | Res**, where you'll find the 'Res' as a tab at the bottom of the Workspace window.] Now click on the various items in the Resource view to view them – the way this works is that anything with a + next to it is like a directory to be opened up. Click down through the things with + till you get some bottom level things like bitmaps, menus, etc. Find the IDB_BACKGROUND bitmap and the IDR_POPTYPE menu. Note that the Resource view of the menu is 'live,' that is, you can open up the menu selections and edit them. This is useful as, later, when you want to turn **Pop** into a single game, you can simply remove the menu references to the other game modes so that the users won't have the possibility of going into them.

Exercise 3.7: Renaming a game

Changing the names of a game that appear in copies of existing files is a little tricky. In this problem we ask you to practice. In Windows Explorer, select the **gamestub *.h** and ***.cpp** files, and use **Ctrl+C** and **Ctrl+V** to copy them. Highlight the file names one by one, press F2 and change the names to, say, **gamemyproject.h** and **gamemyproject.cpp**. Now open up the Pop Framework in Visual Studio and use the **Project | Add Existing Item...** dialog (Version 7.0) [or **Project | Add to Project | Files...** dialog (Version 6.0)] dialog to add your new files to the project. Edit the files in Visual Studio to replace every instance of the phrase 'Stub' by the phrase 'MyProject,' being sensitive to upper and lower case. That is, you must replace 'Stub' by 'MyProject', 'stub' by 'myproject' and 'STUB' by 'MYPROJECT'. You can do this by using **Ctrl+H** to do a search and replace several times in each file, with the **Match Case** checkbox turned on. Now see if you can get the altered project to compile. This may take a couple of tries, especially if you weren't careful about case sensitivity in the search and replaces. If you've totally messed things up (always easy to do when starting out!) make fresh copies of the files and start over. Once it compiles, edit the *CPopDoc* constructor in the **popdoc.cpp** file so that the default start up game class is *cGameMyProject*. You'll have to add a line #include "gamemyproject.h" to popdoc.cpp so this will compile. If you want to do a bit more, look at Chapter 27: Menus and Toolbars and figure out how to add and implement a **My Project** option on the Game menu.

Exercise 3.8: Expanding a UML diagram

The UML diagram given for the *cGameStub* in this chapter is missing the classes *cCritterArmedPlayer*, *cCritterArmedRobot*, and *cCritterBulletSilver*. Redraw the picture, with these intermediate classes squeezed into the tree of inheritance.

Exercise 3.9: Writing a Space Invaders game

The rest of the problems on this chapter have to do with converting the Game Stub game into a Space Invaders game.

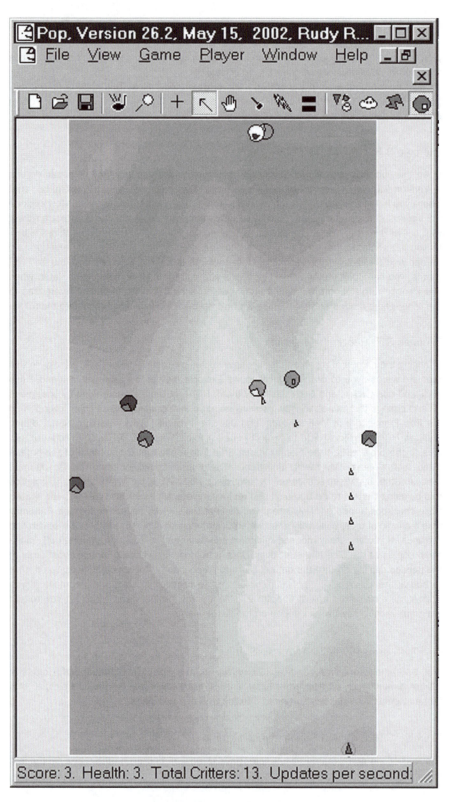

Game stub modified to resemble a Space Invaders game

Rather than carrying out the slightly tricky task of changing all the names in the **gamestub**.* files, let's just use these files as is, and make some changes in them. You might want to save off reference copies of these files called **gamestubold**.* in case you want to get the old code back after a while. Or simply make sure that you do your work in a fresh copy of the whole Pop source directory.

The following exercises describe a specific series of changes to make to the files. The purpose is simply to have you get a feel for how you might make your own game out of the Pop code. Don't feel you need to be able to understand all of the code you see, just go ahead and carry out the following steps to see how you might work with it.

Just in case you've never seen a Space Invaders game, the idea is that the player controls an upwards-pointing critter that can be moved left and right along the bottom of the screen with the arrow keys. The critter shoots a bullet upwards when the spacebar is pressed. Falling down from the top of the screen are enemy critters. Shooting enemies gives the player score points, and each time an enemy survives to touch the bottom of the screen, the player loses a health point. Whenever all the falling creatures have been shot, a new wave of them appears; alternately we can bring in new enemies as fast we kill them off. Typically the player starts with three or maybe five health points and plays until he or she loses them all. The new waves of enemies move faster than the earlier waves, so that as time goes on, the game gets harder and harder to play, inevitably ending in the player's death. The score points accumulated are a measure of how long the player managed to stay alive.

A Space Invaders style game is generally *not* considered to be an acceptable project for a course taught with the *Software Engineering and Computer Games* textbook. The reason is that (a) this project is too easy and (b) the one-dimensionality of the Space Invaders game player motion makes the game pretty boring. Once you finish the Space Invaders game in this section, you should set it aside and make a fresh start for your real course project.

Exercise 3.10.1: Change the default game. Beware the wrong-directory-gotcha

When you get into tweaking one particular game mode, it saves time to have the Pop program start up in the game mode that you want to play with. The way to control this is to edit the **CPopDoc** constructor in **popdoc.cpp**. Simply comment in exactly the one **setGameClass** line corresponding to the game you want to play. If you make a new game class, add a line for it. For the following exercises, have your startup game be **cGameStub**.

```
CPopDoc::CPopDoc():
_pgame(NULL)
{
/* Choose the type of game you want at startup by commenting in ONE
setGameClass line. The setGameClass sets brandnewgameflag to TRUE. */

//   setGameClass(RUNTIME_CLASS(cGameSpacewar));
//   setGameClass(RUNTIME_CLASS(cGameAirhockey));
//   setGameClass(RUNTIME_CLASS(cGameBallworld));
//   setGameClass(RUNTIME_CLASS(cGameDambuilder));
//   setGameClass(RUNTIME_CLASS(cGamePickNPop));
//   setGameClass(RUNTIME_CLASS(cGameWorms));
     setGameClass(RUNTIME_CLASS(cGameStub));
//   setGameClass(RUNTIME_CLASS(cGameStub3D));
//   setGameClass(RUNTIME_CLASS(cGameDefender3D));
}
```

If you do this exercise and the game still starts up in the original Spacewar Game mode, it's very likely that you edited the wrong copy of **popdoc.cpp**. One of the gotchas of Visual Studio is that when you use the **File | Open** command, the file selection dialog doesn't make it clear which directory you are in. Visual Studio has a certain persistence of state, and if you open a file in DirectoryA, the next time you open a file the dialog is likely to search in DirectoryA again, even if you are now working on a project in DirectoryB. One often has multiple copies of the Pop Framework code on one's disk, and it is easy to be editing a file in the wrong directory.

A sure sign that you're editing the wrong files is if (a) your program always compiles and runs with no warnings or error messages and (b) the appearance of the executable looks the same after each 'build.'

How to avoid this gotcha? If you see signs of (a) and (b), close all your files, close your project, reopen your project in your desired directory, and then open your file, only this time use the **File | Open** dialog to back a step or two up the directory tree to find out what directory you're really in, and then go back down into the correct directory.

Exercise 3.10.2: Change the *cGameStub* world

We edit some of the *cGameStub* methods in the gamestub.cpp file to change the appearance of the game world.

(a) Our goal here is to make a simple Space Invaders game. Let's not use the *cCritterStubRival* at all, let's just have dumb non-shooting *cCritterSpaceInvadersProp* falling down on us. We can do this by changing the two static critter count numbers that are used in the *cGameStub* constructor to initialize _rivalcount and _seedcount. The statics are defined right before the *cGameStub::cGameStub()* constructor. Change the lines to read:

```
int cGameStub::DEFAULTSEEDCOUNT = 8;
int cGameStub::DEFAULTRIVALCOUNT = 0;
```

(b) Let's make our world tall and thin. We can do this by changing a line in the *cGamestub::cGamestub* constructor. Take the line _border.set(60.0, 40.0), and change it to _border.set(20.0, 40.0).

(c) We don't want to start out zoomed in on the world. Find the code for the void cGameStub::initializeViewpoint(cCritterViewer *pviewer) method and comment out two lines.

```
//pviewer->zoom(4.0);
```

and

```
//pviewer->zoom(2.0);
```

(d) We don't want the view to move with the player, so find the void cGameStub::initializeView(CPopView *pview) code and comment out a line.

```
//pview->pviewpointcritter()->setTrackplayer(TRUE);
```

Exercise 3.10.3: Change the *cCritterStubPlayer*

(a) Before changing the constructor, change the value of a static variable used in the constructor. At the start of the **gamestub.cpp** file, change the PLAYERHEALTH line to this.

```
int cGameStub::PLAYERHEALTH = 3;
```

Now we're going to add some code to the end of the cCritterStubPlayer::cCritterStubPlayer(cGame *pownergame) code in **gamestub.cpp**.

(b) We want to use the arrow keys to move our player. Either add this line to the end of the constructor, or alternately use it to replace the existing setListener line with this line.

```
setListener(new cListenerArrow());
```

(c) To make the arrow key motion a little peppier, give the player a higher maximum speed (which is the speed the arrow moves it at). Add this line.

```
setMaxspeed(30.0); // Careful not to write setMaxSpeed
```

(d) Limit the player to moving back and forth along the bottom of the screen. This means we want to change the player's cRealBox _movebox field.
   We do this in the player's constructor. Our framework is set up so that in this code block you can assume that the player's _movebox has already been set to match the game's _border box. We now want to use **setMoveBox** to change the _movebox.
   The **setMoveBox** call takes a **cRealBox** as argument. The **cRealBox** constructor we use here takes **cVector** specifying two opposite corners as arguments, the lower left front corner and the upper right back corner. Add this block of code to the end of the constructor code. What we're doing here is to move the 'high corner' down almost to the bottom of the _border box.

```
/* At this point the player's _movebox matches the _border it got
from pownergame.
Now we want to make the _movebox just be the bottom edge
of the world. */
    setMoveBox(cRealBox(
        _movebox.locorner(),
        _movebox.hicorner() -
        //Move high corner almost to the bottom of world.
        (_movebox.ysize()-2*radius())* cVector::YAXIS
        ));
```

(e) Another aspect of a Space Invaders game is that the player's gun always points straight up. We'll make this change in the **cCritterStubPlayer** constructor. Change the old **cCritterStubPlayer** constructor by adding these lines to the bottom of it.

```
setAttitudeToMotionLock(FALSE);
    /* The default for _attitude motion lock is TRUE, which means
that by default a critter turns its heading to match its direction
of motion. We turn this behavior off so the player can always
point up. */
setAttitudeTangent(cVector::YAXIS); /* Call this AFTER turning off
the lock setAimVector(cVector::YAXIS); */
```

Exercise 3.10.4: Change the *cCritterStubProp* constructor

Now we make some changes to the bottom of the cCritterStubProp::cCritterStubProp(cGame *pownergame) code in gamestub.cpp.

(a) Let's have the props automatically be positioned up near the top of the world. Since the **cCritterStubProp** constructor uses a **cGame** argument, its base class constructor will have set its _movebox to match the game's _border. To move the critters up to the top of the world, add these lines.

```
randomizePosition(cRealBox(
    _movebox.locorner() +
        (_movebox.ysize() - 2*radius()) * cVector::YAXIS,
    _movebox.hicorner()
    ));
```

(b) Let's put a force of gravity on the **cCritterStubProp** critters. Usually when you have gravity, it's a good idea to put in some 'air friction' as well. Add these lines to the end of the constructor code.

```
addForce(new cForceGravity());
addForce(new cForceDrag());
```

(c) Let's soup up the game by allowing the critters to fall a bit faster. Add this line. You might find the value 8.0 to be a shade too low or high.

```
setMaxspeed(8.0); //Careful not to write setMaxSpeed
```

(d) Now let's try having the **cCritterStubProp** critters run away from the bullets. Try adding a line like this. You may not like the effect of this, so it's optional.

```
addForce(new cForceClassEvade(4.0, 1.0,
    RUNTIME_CLASS(cCritterStubPlayerBullet)));
```

Exercise 3.10.5: Change *cCritterStubProp::update*

Each critter has an `int` `_outcode` field that is an **OR** combination of bit flags telling you which, if any, edge of its `cRealBox` `_movebox` the critter touched during its last move. The bit flags, which are defined in the **realbox.h** file, have simple names like `BOX_LOY`. We will use the `_outcode` to take action when a *cCritterStubProp* hits the bottom or the top of the screen.

When one of the *cCritterStubProp* critters hits the bottom of the screen, we want to kill off the critter and reduce the player's health by calling its *damage* method.

If you have called `setWrapflag(cCritter::WRAP)`, then the *cCritterStubProp* might get to the bottom by going around the top. When our *cCritterStubProp* run away from bullets they might sometimes do this. It would unfairly punish the player if we let the *cCritterStubProps* get away with that, as then they would be in a position to cross back and the game might think they landed on the bottom. Therefore if a *cCritterStubProp* hits the top of the world we kill it off without charging the player a damage point.

We do all this by changing the *cCritterStubProp* update method to look like this.

```
void cCritterStubProp::update(CPopView *pactiveview, Realdt)
{
    cCritter::update(pactiveview, dt); //Always call this first
    if (_outcode & BOX_LOY) //Landing damages me
    {
        pplayer()->damage(1);
        die();
    }
    if (_outcode & BOX_HIY) //So they don't sneak around over the top.
        die();
}
```

Exercise 3.10.6: Change *cCritterStubPlayer::collide*

Let's eliminate the feature of *cGameStub* which rewards the player for bumping into a *cCritterStubProp* critter. This means you should comment out this line from within the lines from the `cCritterStubPlayer::collide(cCritter *pcritter)` code.

```
//    setHealth(health() + 1);
```

Exercise 3.10.7: Change *cCritterStubPlayer::shoot*, and the *cCritterStubPlayerBullet* behavior

(a) In the **gamestub.cpp** file, try giving yourself prop-seeking missiles for your bullets. Change the code of the `cCritterStubPlayer::shoot()` as follows.

That is, give your bullets a *cForceObjectSeek* so they turn into smart missiles that hunt down whichever critter was closest to the line you aimed along. If you think it makes the game too easy or too hard, leave it out or perhaps use a smaller value for the argument 50.0 passed to the *cForceObjectSeek* constructor.

```
cCritterBullet* cCritterStubPlayer::shoot()
{
    cCritterBullet *pbullet = cCritterArmedPlayer::shoot();
    cCritter* paimtarget =
```

```
            pgame()->pbiota()->pickClosestAhead (cLine(position(),
                aimvector()), this);
            /* Find the critter closest to your aiming line. Including
                "this" as the second argument means to exclude
                yourself from consideration as the closest critter.
                Note that you can use additional params with
                pickClosestAhead to narrow the angle the critter
                "sees" and also to limit the possible targets to
                certain kinds of critters, see biota.h for details. */
        pbullet->addForce(new cForceObjectSeek(paimtarget, 50.0));
        return pbullet;
    }
```

(b)   You may now find the game is now hard to play because your bullets die at the screen edges and sometimes do this before hitting a prop. Fix this by adding this line to the **cCritterStubPlayerBullet::cCritterStubPlayerBullet()** constructor.

```
_dieatedges = FALSE;
```

(c)   A downside of (b) is that you'll now notice that some silly bullets bounce off the top and get confused and bumble around on the bottom of the world. To fix this, you have to override the void cCritterStubPlayerBullet::update(CPopView *pactiveview, Real dt) as follows.
      Add this line to the prototype in **gamestub.h**.

```
virtual void update(CPopView *pactiveview, Realdt);
```

Add this code to **gamestub.cpp**.

```
void cCritterStubPlayerBullet::update(CPopView *pactiveview, Realdt)
{
    cCritterBullet::update(pactiveview, dt);
        //Always call base update first
    if (_outcode & BOX_LOY || _outcode & BOX_HIY)
        //Landing damages me
    die();
}
```

Exercise 3.10.8: Change the **cGameStub::adjustGameParameters**

(a)   To make this more of a game, it's better to have the action be non-stop. As it presently stands, you can kill off all the attackers. We fix it so each time you kill an attacker, some new ones come in. We do this by adding this code to the bottom of the cGameStub::adjustGameParameters code.

```
int propcrittercount =
    pbiota()->count(RUNTIME_CLASS(cCritterStubProp));
if (propcrittercount < _seedcount)
    new cCritterStubProp(this);
        //The constructor automatically adds the critter to the game.
```

Note that if you've killed, say, three *cCritterStubProps* all at once, it will take the game three steps of calling `adjustGameParameters` to restore the full *cCritterStubProp* count. This is fine, as visually it's just as well not to change the game too rapidly.

(b)   What about making the game get harder as you play it? This step is optional.

You could keep track of the *cGame::score()*, and each time this gets larger than some increment size, make the game harder in some way, perhaps by increasing the size of _seedcount.

Or you could add a *cCritterStubRival* whenever the score passes a certain size, similar to how the Spacewar game adds *cCritterUFO*. To make this effective you might need to tweak the *cCritterStubRival* methods a bit.

Exercise 3.11: Hand in a Space Invaders project

This is an assignment the author usually gives his classes fairly early in the semester. Typically, the credit assigned for the three parts of this problem is in a 25%, 50%, 25% ratio for, respectively, mechanics, basics and improvements.

Even if you're studying this book on your own, you will find it worthwhile to carry through the mechanics steps so as to have experience in putting your code into a form that can be handed off.

Mechanics. Hand in the following: (1) A sheet of paper with a little 'User's Guide' describing the controls of your game and listing any special features you added. (2) Two floppy disks: one disk with a release build of the executable in the root directory, and another disk with clean, minimal-sized, buildable source code. Label the disks with your name and with a word to indicate if this is the EXE or the SOURCE disk. You will probably need to WinZip your source and probably your executable to fit onto floppies. If the *.zip is larger than 1 Meg you probably haven't cleaned your source directory properly (or you've included a lot of extra big sounds and bitmap files). Another option is to write the information onto a CD-ROM. Emailing your homework to the professor as a gigundo attachment is forbidden! (3) Put disks and paper in a two-pocket folder with your name on it. (4) Put your name on the program caption bar. To change the caption bar, see Section 23.9 of this book.

Basics. Carry out the steps outlined in the series of Space Invaders exercises 3.10.1–3.10.8 just above. You don't necessarily need to use all the exact same parameter values suggested. Get the program working so that the critters are neither too hard nor too easy to hit, the game itself should be neither too hard nor too easy. You may need to tweak some parameters to get it right.

Improvements. Possibilities: change the background, use different kinds of sprites, add code to make the game use levels that get progressively harder, change the code so that the enemies jiggle back and forth like in the traditional Space Invaders rather than running away from bullets. Add sound effects. Have some enemies that shoot at you. Have the enemies change appearance when you hit them before disappearing, maybe have them shatter or show a *cSpriteIcon* or *cSpriteLoop* explosion bitmap for a few seconds. Looking at the **gamespacewar.cpp** or the **gamedefender3d.cpp** files may provide inspiration.

Object-oriented software engineering

4

4.1 OO is the way

As computer science continues to evolve, our programs get more and more powerful, using larger and larger amounts of code. The Pop program has some 10,000 lines of code, and if we were to take into account the code for the underlying Windows functions, we'd be looking at hundreds of thousands of lines more. How can we deal with such large programs?

Our only hope is to continually move to higher levels. We learn to design and program in higher-level and more abstract ways. In the earliest days, software engineers worked very close to the hardware writing microcode to directly control the processor chip. Machine language is a step up from this, consisting of coded instructions that the processor can read and execute. Assembly language is human-readable code quite close to the machine language level, but which allows the programmer a few higher-level constructs like macro statements to abbreviate having to write out repetitive blocks of code.

Assembly language gave way to a range of high-level languages designed to be something much closer to something a human can read. Some of the earlier languages were Fortran, APL, Modula and Pascal. Eventually these converged on C, which is still something of an industry standard. Libraries of C functions are available so that programmers don't continually have to reinvent the wheel. With the advent of object-oriented languages like C++ and Java, computer science moved to a new still-higher level of programming and design. There's no turning back. An object-oriented approach (OO for short) is the way.

We can draw a UML dependency diagram to illustrate the progress, with the arrows indicating that the higher levels depend on the lower levels (see Figure 4.1).

Simply using C++ or Java doesn't guarantee that you are doing object-oriented software engineering. Object-oriented techniques can be used at a variety of levels. Software engineers often distinguish among three kinds of OO: object-oriented analysis (OOA), object-oriented design (OOD), and object-oriented programming (OOP).

The idea behind OO software engineering is to break your programs up into independent self-sufficient objects. If you don't plan to alter an object's behavior, you don't need to worry about how its code works. All you need to know is

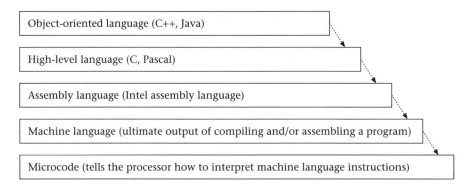

Figure 4.1 Levels of language

what the object does. The object becomes like a black box with input/output jacks. You feed things into it and you get things out, and you don't worry about what's inside.

The objects of OO are instances of data structures called classes. A class is like a C structure, except that it has functions, or *methods*, inside it as well as *data fields* (see Figure 4.2). A class is like a high-level data type. And an object is an instance of a class. To make the distinction between class and object quite clear, you might compare a class to a type like int, and an object to a specific integer like 2.

There is some variability in the language that people use to talk about classes. The data fields of a class can also be called class attributes. And the methods of a class can also be called the class's functions or its operations.

The OO approach suggests that instead of trying to analyze a problem in terms of a zillion small tasks, we look at the problem in terms of a few high-level classes. Figuring out which classes to use for your program is the process of OOA. Deciding what members and methods your classes should have is a matter of OOD. And actually implementing the code for the classes is the work of OOP.

The three stages do blend together a bit, so if we list the expected outcomes of the OOA, OOD, and OOP processes, it makes sense to list some outcomes in two lines.

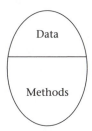

Figure 4.2 A class has data and methods

Table 4.1   Three stages of the OO process, with expected outcomes.

OOA	Which classes? UML diagrams
OOD	UML diagrams, *.h header
OOP	*.h header, *.cpp implementation

A preliminary way of describing the stages is to say that OOA involves looking at a problem with the aim of understanding it. OOD means defining and designing an appropriate solution. And OOP is building that solution. These three steps are really part of any reasonable approach to problem solving (see Table 4.1). Now let's look into what we do to make the steps object-oriented.

The OOA stage is a high-level design phase in which we figure out which classes to use and what data and methods to put into them. Initially you might simply write out class names and key data and methods. But after a bit, you want to actually start moving down towards the detailed design phase and writing out correct C++ class headers.

The OOA phase shades into the OOD phase when we begin thinking in some detail about what to put into the classes. The OOD phase of the process continues through the writing of the ***.h** header files, while the OOP part kicks in when you write the ***.cpp** files where the implementation of the methods lives. You shouldn't think that first you finish the OOA and OOD, and then you move into OOP without ever coming back to OOA and OOD again.

The reason you can't just finish one stage off completely and then start on the next stage is that it's so hard to design a program. You're rarely going to nail it right off the bat. Of course you do need a design to get started, but every time you finish a new alpha build, you should step back and take a long look at your design. A good place to start is by looking at the ugliest, most complicated parts of your code, the parts that you feel most uneasy about. Ask yourself how this could be made simpler. And, as long as you're revisiting your design, think about what features you want to add to your program next, so that you can lay the groundwork for them.

OOA is about figuring out how to arrange a collection of classes that does a good job of representing your real-world problem in a format which a computer program finds easy to deal with. OOD is about what kinds of data and methods go into your classes and about how the classes relate to each other in terms of inheritance, membership and function calls. OOP is about making the class implementations work. The three go hand in hand. You need to do some OOA and OOD before you OOP, and after you OOP you learn enough new things about your program to go back and improve the OOA and OOD. Like so many other things in the software engineering process, it's a feedback loop that you can run through as many iterations as your schedule allows. And, again like other things in software engineering, the precise boundaries between OOA, OOD and OOP can be somewhat fuzzy.

A useful terminology that people sometimes use is to speak of a distinction between 'top-down' design and 'bottom-up' design. In our present context, we're thinking of OOA and OOD as a top-down process where you use some high-level abstract thinking to figure out which classes to use and how to design them. And then you move down into the details. This describes a top-down movement from OOA to OOD into OOP.

The bottom-up part of the process comes about like this. When you go about implementing a design you find out a lot of things about it that you hadn't anticipated – some things work out easier than you'd hoped, and a few things turn out to be harder. So then you change your design to make the hard things work better. This describes a bottom-up movement from OOP into OOD and OOA.

The OOD expert Grady Booch puts it like this.

> Our experience indicates that design is neither strictly top-down, nor strictly bottom-up. Instead . . . well-structured complex systems are best created through the use of 'round-trip gestalt design.' This style of design emphasizes the incremental and iterative development of a system through the refinement of different yet consistent logical and physical views of the system as a whole . . . Object-oriented design may seem to be a terribly unconstrained and fuzzy process. We do not deny it. However, we must also point out that one cannot dictate creativity by the mere definition of a few steps to follow or products to create.

[Grady Booch, *Object-Oriented Design* (Benjamin/Cummings, 1991), p. 188]

4.2 Object-oriented analysis

The first part of the OOA stage is figuring out what classes you will use and what some of their main methods might be. How might this work? Suppose that you have completed the requirements-gathering stage, and you've come up with a written summary of what the software is supposed to do. A good way to start the OOA process is to review a printed copy of the requirement summary and mark it up. Circle the noun and noun phrases in one color ink and circle the actions in another color ink – or use boxes and circles. The nouns are likely to be either classes or member fields of classes. The verbs are likely to be class methods.

In keeping with our book's theme of being a case study about software engineering a computer game framework, let's look at a requirement for this.

Requirement: a framework for computer games with moving critters. The critters are drawn as polygons, bitmaps, or animated loops of bitmaps. The critters update themselves on the basis of the world around them. The world may include forces like gravity and friction. The critters listen to mouse-keyboard controls. The critters can shoot bullets. It is possible to open more than one view of the game. The games can use 2D or 3D graphics.

- *Nouns*: game, critter, polygon, bitmap, animated loop, world, force, gravity, friction, controls, mouse-keyboard controls, bullets, view, graphics.

- *Actions*: move, draw, update, listen, shoot.

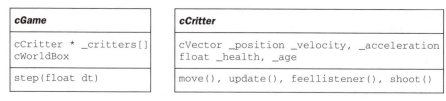

Figure 4.3   UML classes with members and methods

Once you have the two lists you can think about how best to group the nouns into classes, and about which class should be responsible for which action. Do be aware that often there will additional classes involved that aren't explicitly mentioned in the specification.

During this process you can draw a more detailed kind of UML picture of a class, wherein you list some of a class's members and methods inside the box that stands for the class. Two horizontal lines separate the class name, the class members, and the class methods. In these kinds of diagrams we often leave out the argument lists of the methods and the type declarations of the members.

Two of the classes you come up with for the game framework example might look as shown in Figure 4.3. Do note that not all of the members and methods are shown here. Also note that our final Pop Framework implementation of the **cGame** and **cCritter** will be a bit different from the preliminary design we've drawn here.

In UML diagrams we generally only show the things that are important for the point of the particular diagram being made. It's often better to draw two diagrams to make two different points than to have one diagram try to make two points.

Once you begin to get have a handle on which classes you might use, you can start to think about the UML class diagram. One part of becoming skilled with OOA is to draw a lot of UML class diagrams. Programmers often have a little trouble getting started with this process. Here are some pointers.

Dive right in

UML diagrams can be drawn at many levels, from the very simple to the very detailed. Usually a fairly simple diagram is all you need. Remember that UML class diagrams are supposed to be easy, so easy that anyone with a stake in the project can understand them. Don't approach them as if you're writing code that has to compile; the whole point of UML diagrams is that you should be able to get them done quickly and easily. They don't have to be perfect. To start with, the main thing is simply to get something down on paper.

Redraw many times

Typically you might start by drawing boxes with the names of all the main classes that you use (or plan to use) in the program. And then you add in the hollow-headed inheritance arrows, the diamond-tailed composition lines, and the solid-headed association-with-navigation arrows. Typically you'll end up with several lines crossing each other. Though there's nothing strictly 'wrong' about this (you can always erase a little space in one line to indicate the lines pass under or over each other), it doesn't look nice. It makes the diagram harder to read. So, really, you should redraw it. The process of redrawing the UML class diagram is not at all a waste of time. For while you're doing this, you'll begin thinking more concretely about your classes and the class instances as being definite entities that you are moving around. Drawing a UML diagram is as much about the process of drawing it as it is about the finished product. Since you're going to redraw it many times, its not a bad idea to do it with a pencil and a few sheets of paper to hand. It is possible to use special UML-drawing software that automatically generates a diagram from your code – in this case you'll usually get a diagram that has more detail than you want, and your revision process will involve pruning the thing down and rearranging the boxes. Try to avoid drawing your initial diagrams with an interface that's hard to use, and which discourages revision. If, for instance, you're drawing your UML diagram by inserting boxes and arrows with the Drawing Toolbar of Microsoft Word, it's a real pain to move things around, and you're not going to do it as much as you should. It's much better to always do a few first drafts with pencil, an eraser and a large, clean piece of paper.

Keep each diagram simple

Don't feel that you have to get every single class into one diagram, and don't feel you have draw every possible association line. A big program is like the Grand Canyon or the Rockies, you can't show all of it in one picture. Instead, you pick a telling vantage point and crop your frame to include only the features you are currently interested in. In order to give a fairly complete accounting of your classes, it's usually better to draw several UML class diagrams rather than one. Thus, when talking about the Pop Framework, we might use several different UML diagrams: one for the MFC framework classes having to do with document and view, one for the custom Pop Framework classes, one for the details of the various critter child classes, another for the sprite child classes, and so on.

Step through use cases

In order to tell if your UML diagram describes an architecture that will work you need to 'test out' the diagram. A good procedure is to step through the stages of various use case scenarios, thinking about which kinds of collaborator objects each object needs for the different steps of the scenario.

You'll find some examples of OOA problems to work on at the end of the chapter.

4.3   Encapsulation, inheritance, and polymorphism

The technique of putting data and methods inside a single object is called *encapsulation*. The two other words most commonly used when talking about OO are *inheritance* and *polymorphism*.

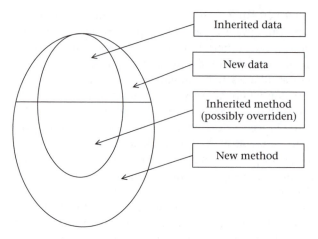

Figure 4.4   A class and a subclass

The idea behind inheritance is that if you already have a class that's almost like something you need, its a good idea to define a new class that is a child class of the existing class, recoding or *overriding* some of the new class methods so that they behave differently from the old class. We can draw a picture of inheritance as in Figure 4.4.

When an inherited method calls the code of the base method and then does something additional, we can say that it extends the method as well as saying that it overrides it. Thus, if ClassB inherits a foo() method from ClassB, we say that ClassB overrides foo so long as ClassB redefines the implementation code for foo in any way at all. And we can say that ClassB overrides and extends foo if the redefined code for foo has a form like ClassB::foo(){ClassA::foo(); doMore();}.

The MFC framework provides you with some key base classes called **CWinApp**, **CDocument**, and **CView**. Rather than reinvent the principles of Windows programming, we code our Pop program as a Windows application by implementing a **CPopApp**, **CPopDoc** and **CPopView** which are children of the standard MFC base classes. As we discussed in the last chapter, we draw pictures of inheritance relationships by drawing a hollow-headed arrow from the child to the parent class (see Figure 4.5). These kinds of drawings are the *UML class diagrams* that we mentioned before.

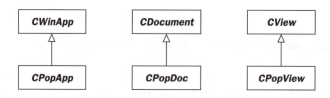

Figure 4.5   Inheritance diagram for basic MFC classes

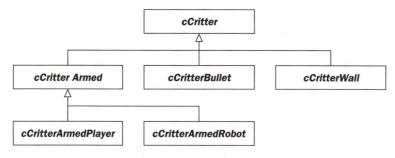

Figure 4.6 Class diagram for *cCritter* child classes

The notion of polymorphism is that an object 'knows' what class it belongs to, and when you have it call some method, it will be sure to use the version of the method that's coded up by its class. This takes on special significance when you have a collection of objects belonging to disparate classes.

As a concrete example of polymorphism, let's think about having some classes that inherit from a class called *cCritter*. The *cCritter* class has an **update()** method that changes a critter object's state according to the current situation of the game world. Now it might be that we have several different kinds of critters in our program. This is illustrated in Figure 4.6. (As before, to make the UML class diagram cleaner, we use horizontal bars to combine into one arrow what could otherwise be drawn as separate inheritance arrows.)

Now suppose we were to have an array called `biota` which is an array of N pointers to *cCritter* objects. The prototype might be something like `cCritter* biota[N]`. And then we'd be able to update all the critters at once with a line like `for(int i=0; i< N; i++) biota[i]->update()`. And each `biota[i]` *cCritter* pointer object would know exactly which kind of *cCritter* child it was pointing to, and would know to use the appropriate version of the *cCritter* move method.

> One annoying C++ gotcha is that in C++, *a variable that can have child class values assigned to it will only show polymorphic behavior if it is a pointer variable.*

That is, if the `biota` in the example just given were to be defined as `cCritter biota[N]` and the loop were to call `biota[i].update()`, then we would unhappily find that even if the various `biota[i]` objects were supposed to be differing kinds of `cCritterChild` classes, the base class *cCritter::update* would be executed for each of the `biota[i]` objects, with the actual child class information about these objects being totally ignored. The cause of this problem is that, in order to put a *cCritterChild* object `childcrit` into one of the `biota[i]` array slots, you'd actually need to 'upcast' it into a base *cCritter* object `(cCritter)childcrit`, thus losing its child class information. But a pointer variable works alright because a `cCritterChild *pchildcrit` pointer can be placed into a `cCritter * pointer` variable without having to change anything about the pointer.

This issue doesn't come up in Java, as all class object variables in Java are automatically pointers anyway. The moral is to use pointer-objects whenever you're planning to have them behave polymporphically. More information about this can be found in the reference Chapter 22: Topics in C++.

The two languages most used for OO these days are C++ and Java. This is not to say that there aren't others, such as Smalltalk and Ada 95. And Microsoft is currently promoting a new OO language called C# (pronounced 'C sharp'). Certainly most new applications are written with object-oriented code. This said, there are certainly a number of legacy applications that are in plain old C; this is particularly true for low-level programs such as device drivers.

Regarding Java and C++ for OOP, both have their pros and cons. At this moment in the history of computer science, a software engineer would do well to know both languages. C++ is a language of choice for stand-alone OO programs on a desktop machines, and Java is popular for distributed Web applications. By learning both languages you allow yourself a wider range of platform options. A less obvious point is that many aspects of OO only become really clear when you've learned more than one OO language. Learning Java has certainly increased this author's understanding of C++. And if you happen to know Java but not C++, learning C++ will undoubtedly increase your understanding of Java.

For a review of C++ and its OO features take a look at Chapter 22: Topics in C++ now. You may not want to read every detail of the chapter at this time, but at least skim through it, so that you'll know what information is there, and then you'll know where to look when you need it.

A little more terminology. The public methods for a class are sometimes called the class's *interface*. We often like to think of an object as a black box whose internals are hidden from the other objects. The interface to a black box like this is the methods you can use to make it do things.

A class normally has several different types of methods besides the constructors and the destructor. Specifically, *accessors* return information about an object's internal members, and *mutators* make changes to an object's members.

Occasionally we want to have a base class which doesn't actually have implementations of its methods. We can do this by giving the methods empty in-line code definitions, as in `void doSomething(){}`; or we can explicitly indicate that this method is not implemented at all with a line like `void doSomething() = 0;`. A method of the second type is called *abstract*, and a class with an abstract method is called abstract as well.

A base class with no data members and trivially defined or abstract methods is often called an interface. In the Java language there actually is an **interface** language construct that you can use in place of **class** to specify a base class with abstract methods.

Thus we can use the word interface in two senses. (a) If ClassB inherits from ClassA, then ClassB will have an interface (set of methods) that extends the interface (set of methods) of ClassA. (b) If ClassA really has nothing more than its set of methods, then we can simply speak of ClassA itself as being an interface.

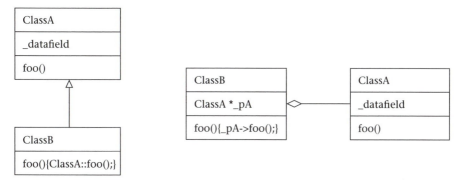

Figure 4.7 Inheritance and composition

4.4 Composition and delegation

We say that ClassB is composed with ClassA if ClassB has a ClassA or ClassA* member; for short we can say ClassB has a ClassA. And, as before, ClassB inherits from ClassA if ClassB is derived from ClassA as a child class; for short we say ClassB is a ClassA.

As it turns out, you can always replace an inheritance relationship by a composition relationship as indicated in Figure 4.7. If ClassB has a ClassA member object *_pA, then (a) a ClassB object gets a set of ClassA data fields wrapped up inside *_pA and, (b) ClassB can implement the same methods as ClassA simply by passing these method calls off to *_pA. When you pass method calls to a composed object, this is called *delegation*.

Note that you can also do composition and delegation by using a member object ClassA _mA, but we prefer pointer members because they permit polymorphic function calls.

Why would you want to use composition in place of inheritance? There are several reasons.

First, C++ code using multiple inheritance tends to be a bit difficult to maintain, and there are special MFC **CRuntimeClass** methods and macros that would need to be overridden if you want to use multiple inheritance. If you have a ClassB that you'd like to have inherit from both ClassA and ClassC, you can instead use composition for ClassA or ClassC. Figure 4.8 shows how this looks if we compose ClassB with ClassC.

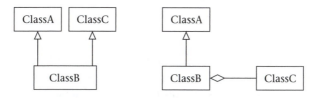

Figure 4.8 Use composition to avoid multiple inheritance

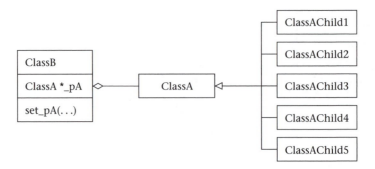

Figure 4.9 Composition makes dynamic change possible

Second, inheritance locks in a class's behavior at link time, while composition allows you to change the behavior of a class during runtime. This is illustrated in Figure 4.9. The ClassB has a set_pA member method to delete the old *_pA and install a new one. In the Pop Framework, when you use the Player menu to change the player's controls, you are actually changing the kind of cListener *_plistener member which the player **cCritter** is composed with.

Third, inheritance is sometimes called 'white box' code reuse, because when you inherit from a class its internals are visible to you. Composition, on the other hand, is called 'black box' code reuse because (unless you've unwisely used a **friend** statement) the internals of the class you compose with are hidden. A practical advantage of black box code reuse is that you're less likely to break things that are used by classes other than your own. A useful mental model when using composition is that you're making a class by snapping together pre-existing components.

A fourth and final reason why we often prefer composition to inheritance is that composition lets us avoid the 'combinatorial explosion' that we end up with if we try to separate out a class for every possible combination of the behaviors that we would otherwise delegate out to a composed member.

Of course there are still many situations where inheritance is the appropriate design method. Particularly if you're interested in having a polymorphic set of objects, it's good to have the objects inherit from a common base class. In the case of the Pop Framework, the **cCritter** base class plays this role. The individual **cCritter** child classes have constructors which compose specialized critters by 'snapping together' some component classes. And the individual **cCritter** update methods are usually overridden. We use inheritance so as to have a uniform list of **cCritter** child objects, and we use composition both to create new kinds of **cCritter** child classes and to possibly change the **cCritters** while the program is running.

Look, for instance, at the diagram of the critters and the classes they compose with (Figure 4.10). We see two kinds of critters, two kinds of sprites, two kinds of listeners, and two kinds of forces, eight classes in all. Now suppose that we wanted to avoid composition and put all of the behavior into the classes. Unless we use multiple inheritance, we'd end up with 18 classes: **cCritter** and

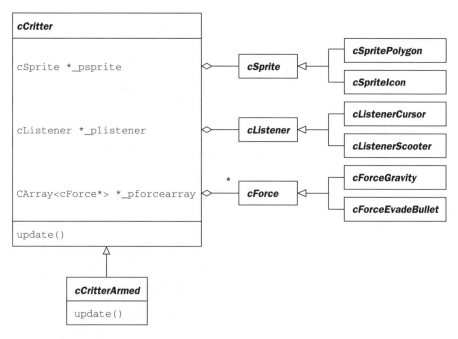

Figure 4.10 Critters and classes they are composed with

cCritterArmed, with eight child classes each, one child for each of the eight ways of choosing polygon/icon, cursor/fly, or gravity/evade. This is illustrated in Figure 4.11. But if we can use composition to farm out the choices to helper classes, then we end up with a smaller number of classes in all.

Now let's say a bit about the practicalities of composition and delegation. When you compose ClassB with a ClassA member _mA (or with a *_pA member) the owner ClassB will need to use ClassA accessors and mutators to get at the ClassA object's data. You can get around this by having ClassA declare ClassB as a friend, but generally we try to avoid friend statements as they break encapsulation.

When you use composition with delegation as illustrated in Figure 4.7, you need to explicitly declare and implement a ClassB function like foo() which is intended to pass off the call to the ClassA member method foo(). This is different from inheritance, where a child class automatically gets the methods of the parent class. In the case of composition, you of course don't have to give the ClassA method the same name as the ClassB method which it calls. In fact it is likely to make your code easier to understand if you give the ClassA method a name like 'feelfoo' or 'dofoo' or 'callfoo.'

A fairly trivial example of composition is that we give both our **cSprite** and our **cRealBox** classes a `cColorStyle*_pcolorstyle` member which holds things like the `fill color` to be used for the shape. The color-related mutators and accessors for **cSprite** and **cRealBox** pass the calls on to their `_pcolorstyle` members. This is shown in Figure 4.12.

Figure 4.11 Combinatorial explosion of classes

Figure 4.12 Simple composition

Why didn't we just make *cSprite* and *cRealBox* inherit from, say, a common *cUsesColorStyle* class? The reasons were that (a) other than being drawable with colors, the two classes really have nothing in common and, more importantly and (b) as we move from two-dimensional graphics to three-dimensional graphics, we'd like to allow the possibility of using richer and more complicated kinds of *cColorStyle* child classes to specify the colors and styles of our sprites and world boxes.

A less obvious point about delegation is that when ClassB delegates a method like foo(), you often want foo to be able to access and mutate the members of ClassB. If ClassB has a ClassA *_pA member, the correct way to delegate foo() so that it can access and mutate ClassB is the following.

```
ClassB::foo()
{
    _pA->foo(this);
}
ClassA::foo(ClassA *powner)
{
    /* Use ClassA accessors and mutators to read and change the fields
        of powner */
}
```

In the specific example of the *cCritter* and the cListener *_plistener that it's composed with, we have the following code.

```
void cCritter::listen(Real dt)
{
    _plistener->listen(this); /* We pass the pointer "this" to the
        listener so that it can change the fields of this calling
        cCritter as required. */
}
void cListenerScooter::listen(cCritter *pcritter)
{
    cController *pcontroller = pcritter->pgame()->pcontroller();/*The
        caller critter's pgame() holds the cController object that
        stores all of the keys and mouse actions you need to possibly
        listen to in here.*/
//Translate
    if (pcontroller->keyonplain(VK_UP))
        pcritter->setVelocity(pcritter->maxspeed()*
            pcritter->tangent());
            /* I want to move the critter position. But I don't just
                use a moveTo because I want to have a correct _velocity
                inside the critter so I can use it to hit things and
                bounce and so on. So I change the velocity. */
    //Etcetera....
}
```

In other cases it may be that the foo call does some setup code before passing the call off to the composed object. This is the situation where *cCritter* delegates some of its draw call to its cSprite *_psprite member. The matrix manipulations serve to translate and rotate the graphics frame of reference to match the critter's position and orientation.

```
void cCritter::draw(cGraphics *pgraphics, int drawflags)
{
    pgraphics->pushMatrix();
    pgraphics->multMatrix(attitude());
    _psprite->draw(pgraphics, drawflags);
    pgraphics->popMatrix();
}
```

4.5 Principles for OO design

In this section we list some principles for object-oriented software engineering. As kind of an intellectual game, we've made an effort to label each principle with an OOA, OOD, or OOP, according to at which stage of the software engineering process the principle is most likely to come into play. The idea is that principles marked OOA are things you can work out when you're doing the high-level design, the OOD are things that you'll get into when you work out the detailed design for the classes, while the principles marked OOP are design details that you're more likely to think of after you start coding. Don't take these labels too seriously!

- OOA: *An object is an organism*. Make class objects responsible for all their behavior. A class should own every method it needs to do things.

- OOA: *Let your classes multiply*. Freely derive classes from your base classes to implement variations on behavior. Remember, you want to start thinking of defining a class as something easy. Move as much code as possible up into helper functions that live in the base class; this makes deriving the children easier.

- OOA: *Use utility classes in place of primitives*. Most of your class members should be other classes, or pointers to other classes. Admittedly, somewhere you will need to have data that is of a primitive type such as **int**, **float** and **char**. But, so far as possible, you should wrap these primitives up inside of classes that are closer to the way you think. Thus we use the MFC **CString** objects instead of **char** arrays, and we use our *cVector* objects instead of pairs of float x, y. With practice, you can learn to think of creating a new class as something easy and helpful, rather than as something arcane and risky! Figure 4.13 illustrates the kind of class nesting that you might expect to see in an OOD.

- OOA: *Keep your classes light*. Don't make one single class do too much. You wouldn't want to have only one class called Main, with all of your program's data and methods in it! It makes the code easier to develop and maintain

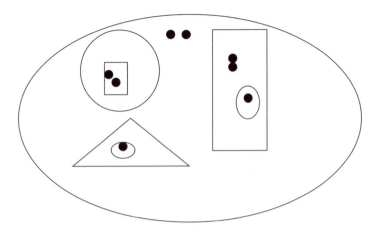

Figure 4.13   The dots are primitives, the shapes are classes

if each class has only a limited number of related responsibilities. Delegating a given functionality off into a separate class gives you the option of implementing it in some standard way in a base class with child classes for alternate behaviors.

- OOA: *Reuse classes.* When appropriate, inherit from or compose with other people's classes, or classes that you've used in other programs. Be aware of what classes are available for you in the MFC framework, for instance.

- OOA: *Prefer object composition to class inheritance.* If you use composition it makes it easier to have each class be focused on one kind of task. Composition also prevents a combinatorial explosion of classes.

- OOD: *Think like an object.* In trying to determine a class's methods, try and read through your code taking the viewpoint of one of your class objects.

- OOD: *Use pointer members rather than instance members.* When you give a ClassB a member object of ClassA, you can either declare it as ClassA _mA or as ClassA *_pA. The former is an instance member, the latter is a pointer member. Using pointer members is a bit more work because you need to remember to construct and destroy the object it points to. The virtue of a pointer member is that you can put child class variables into it without having to upcast them to the base class as you would with an instance member. This makes polymorphism possible; that is, if a pointer member is of type ChildA* instead of type ClassA*, then it will use the overridden methods of ChildA.

- OOD: *Program to an interface, not to an implementation.* When thoroughly carried out, this principle means that you have abstract, implementation-free classes at the top of your class hierarchies. This gives all of the derived classes identical interfaces. When less thoroughly done, this simply means that you try and think always in terms of what your classes have in common.

An example of this in action would be to have your object variables be given the highest base class type possible rather than a specific child class type. Thus, it would be better to have, say, a *cCritter** variable than to have a *cCritterSpaceWarGameAsteroid** variable. The reason is that if your code only mentions the base class *cCritter*, then the code is more reusable.

- OOP: *No forgery*. Avoid storing the same data in two different places. Any copy of a data object is a 'forgery' which may be corrupt. Thus, it would be a mistake to try and maintain an `int _crittercount` member in the *cGame* class, because the same information is already present in the `CArray<cCritter*> _pbiota` *cGame* member, and can be accessed as `_pbiota->GetSize()`. If we kept a separate `_crittercount` variable, we'd repeatedly have to worry about keeping the 'forged' `_crittercount` in synch with the 'genuine' `_pbiota->GetSize()`.

- OOP: *Don't write the same code twice*. Avoid writing the same code in two different places. If you have more than three or four lines of code that you use twice, put this code inside a method that you call in the different places. The reason for this is that if you have the same code in two places, then over time (bug-fixes, development) the two versions may drift apart and become different. Sometimes you will want to encapsulate the code inside a class that you can compose with.

- OOP: *Encapsulate methods*. If you use some piece of data as an explicit or implicit argument to function calls more than two lines in a row, think about giving the class that owns the data a method that accomplishes these lines with a single call. Thus, if we have a *cVector* v object, instead of writing `Real mag = sqrt(v.x()*v.x() + v.y()*v.y() + v.z()*v.z())`, we give *cVector* a *magnitude* method that does the calculation and allows us to just write `Real mag = v.magnitude()`.

- OOP: *Don't ask objects their class type*. If you're doing a switch on the type of a class, you should replace the switch with a polymorphic function call so you don't need to find out the class's type. This said, there are times when we will use the MFC **GetRuntimeClass** method to condition an action on the type of an argument object. But always think twice to see if it's really necessary.

- OOP: *Don't break encapsulation*. Avoid **friend** statements like the plague. Make most data private or at least protected. Conceal the actual implementation structure of your class, and reveal only the few basic public methods that others need to call. It takes only seconds to write in-line accessor and mutator methods like `Real age(){return _age;}; void setAge(Real age){age = _age;}`. If a method is in-line and non-virtual, there is no computational cost whatsoever in using it, because the preprocessor replaces each occurrence of, e.g., 'age()' by '_age'. So why bother? Because, with reference to the age example, at some point you may decide to associate another age-related variable with the _age variable, and then you may want to change the accessor, the mutator, or both.

4.6 The code interface

There's two ways of thinking of your body of code: the semantics and the syntax. The semantics of your code has to do with what it means, and the syntax has to do with what the text in your files actually looks like.

At the semantic level, your code is used to prototype and implement classes and to weave some class objects together into your program's run-cycle. That's what we've been talking about so far in this chapter.

In this section we'll say a little about your code syntax, and how you can make the syntax more 'object-oriented' – in the sense of being more like a black box with an interface of clearly accessible switches and settings.

Of course code is really more of a white box, since you can open up the files and read every bit of them. The point is that if you organize your code in a nice way, you can put something like an interface into it. Here we're not using 'code interface' in the sense of the class prototypes found in the header files – those are the class interfaces. By code interface we mean a collection of tricks and idioms that experienced programmers use to make their implementation files more tweakable.

C++ language features useful for creating a good code interface include the following.

- **#define** switches for **#ifdef** code blocks.
- **typedef** statements for renaming types.
- static variables.
- static methods.

Detailed information about **#define** and **#ifdef** can be found in the Pre-processor Directives section of the Part II Chapter 22: Topics in C++. Quite briefly, if you have two possible versions of some code, or a piece of code that you only want to turn on sometimes (for instance when debugging), it's a good idea to use a **#define** and an **#ifdef**. So you might have something like this example taken from critter.cpp.

```
//#define DRAWMOVINGTRIHEDRON
    /* This draws red, blue, yellow lines for each critter's
        _tangent, _normal, _binormal. It's useful in debugging motion
        problems. */
```

Intervening code . . .

```
void cCritter::draw(cGraphics *pgraphics, int drawflags)
{
    pgraphics->pushMatrix();  pgraphics->multMatrix(attitude());
    _psprite->draw(pgraphics, drawflags);
#ifdef DRAWMOVINGTRIHEDRON
    cColorStyle dummy;
    dummy.setLineColor(cColorStyle::CN_RED);
```

```
    pgraphics->line(cVector::ZEROVECTOR, 2.0 * cVector::XAXIS, &dummy);
    dummy.setLineColor(cColorStyle::CN_BLUE);
    pgraphics->line(cVector::ZEROVECTOR, cVector::YAXIS, &dummy);
    dummy.setLineColor(cColorStyle::CN_YELLOW);
    pgraphics->line(cVector::ZEROVECTOR, cVector::ZAXIS, &dummy);
#endif //DRAWMOVINGTRIHEDRON
    pgraphics->popMatrix();
}
```

When you have #define-controlled switches like this, be sure to put the #define line up at the top of the *.cpp (or *.h) file where it's used, and follow it by a long comment explaining the consequences of turning this switch off or on by, respectively, commenting it out or leaving it in.

Another type of code interface switch uses **typedef**. In the Pop Framework we use a lot of floating point real numbers. So as to avoid having to permanently commit to whether we want to use the faster **float** or the more accurate **double**, we have a file **realnumber.h** that includes these two lines.

```
//typedef double Real;
typedef float Real;
```

At present we're going for more speed and less accuracy, but if it ever seemed better to have more accuracy at the expense of speed, we would only need to edit those two lines. And everywhere in our files where we need a real number, we always use the defined type *Real*, rather than **float** or **double**. For this to work, of course, we have to have an #include realnumber.h in all of these files.

A simpler kind of code interface setting is a parameter whose value affects the way the program works. Always try and avoid putting raw 'magic numbers' in our code. Instead of a raw number you should either use a **#define** or, better, a static variable.

Using static variables is an example of a good OO practice that is more common in Java programming. In Java it's very easy to declare and initialize a static variable, you simply place it right into your class definition. In C++ it's a bit harder. You declare the static variable inside your class header, but you have to actually set the variable's value down inside one of your *.cpp files. As we show in Figure 4.14, a class will have multiple object instances, but all of these are thought of as showing the same static variables, and they all agree on the values of these variables.

Sometimes we make our static variables public; in this case they're the closest thing to a global variable that OOP allows. A static variable that you set once and for all is typed as a **const**. In Windows programming, a color is coded up as a 32-bit integer with the three right-most byte fields representing the red, green, and blue intensities, which can range from 0 to 255. An **RGB** macro assembles three intensities into a color-coding integer. To avoid having to remember all this, we can make **public static const int** variables in, say, a *cColorStyle* class. The **colorstyle.h** header would have code like this.

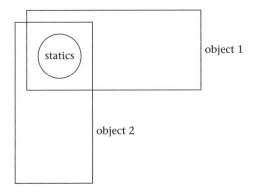

Figure 4.14   Objects share the static members of the class

```
class cColorStyle: public CObject
{
public:
//Color constants.
    static const int CN_RED;
//More code...
};
```

And the **colorstyle.cpp** would instantiate the static variable, giving it a place to 'live' by using a line like this.

```
const int cColorStyle::CN_RED = RGB(255, 0, 0);
```

The line does not appear inside any method, it's simply in the file as is. Note that when you instantiate a static you also are allowed to initialize it. Unlike Java, C++ won't let you initialize a static inside the class prototype in the header file. (Well, actually ANSI C++ *will* let you do this if it's a **const** static, but Microsoft C++ won't in any case.)

If a static variable is public, we can access it in any file of our code, assuming that file has included the header where the static's owner class is protoyped. A typical use of a static looks like this.

```
ppolygon->setFillColor(cColorStyle::CN_RED);
```

As a matter of good programming, we always prefix a reference to a static by its owner class name and the scope resolution operator '::'. You don't actually need this prefix if you are using the static within a method of the static's owner class, but it makes the code more uniform and easier to follow. It's also good practice to consistently use a different name style for statics; in the Pop Framework we always capitalize them.

We typically instantiate our statics in the *.cpp that matches the *.h file where they're declared. The statics specific to *cGameSpacewar* are initialized in **gamespacewar.cpp**, the statics specific to *cGamePicknpop* are initialized in **gamepicknpop.cpp** and so on.

The 'code interface' aspect of statics involves using them for parameters that we may wish to change during successive builds of the program – unlike a fixed constant like CN_RED. When you write a game, there are a lot of values that you may want to change repeatedly. If these are statics initialized (and well-commented) at the head of the *.cpp file, it's easy to keep adjusting them until you see the performance you like.

A few more facts about static variables. You can, if you like, instantiate a static in any *.cpp file you like. Generally it's easier to find them if they live in the file that goes with the header that declares them. But sometimes you may want to group a bunch of statics together, particularly if their initialization values depend upon each other. In the Pop Framework, for instance, we instantiate the 'mutation flag' statics all inside a file we created called **static.cpp**. The reason is so that we can make sure that these single-bit flag variables don't have conflicting values.

```
const int cCritter::MF_NUDGE = 0x00000001;
const int cCritter::MF_POSITION = 0x00000002;
const int cCritter::MF_VELOCITY = 0x00000004;
const int cSprite::MF_RADIUS = 0x00000008;
const int cSprite::MF_ROTATION = 0x00000010;
//Etc.
```

If a static has the **const** modifier, that means you aren't allowed to change its value anywhere in the code, other than in the line where you initialize it. Other statics can in fact be changed. One use of a non-**const** static might be a variable to keep track of whether any instance of a given class has been initialized yet. Thus we declare a static BOOL FIRSTTIME variable in **graphicsopengl.h**, instantiate it in the *.cpp as BOOL cGraphicsOpenGL::FIRSTTIME = TRUE, and have some code that, if FIRSTTIME is TRUE, sends some informational output and sets FIRSTTIME to FALSE. Or you might use a static **int** INSTANCECOUNT to track how many objects of a given type have been created, initializing INSTANCECOUNT to 0 and letting the class constructor and destructor respectively increment and decrement INSTANCECOUNT.

There are a number of reasons why it's better to use static variables rather than **#define** parameters.

- Type checking is performed on static variables, but not on **#define** parameters.

- Since the initialization of the statics is inside a ***.cpp** rather than inside a ***.h**, when you change the value of a static parameter, you don't need to recompile as much of your code.

- If you always put the class name and scope resolution operator in front of your static names, this adds a level of self-documentation to your code that **#define** names don't give you.

- Static variable names are less likely to cause namespace conflicts than **#define** names. That is, if you **#define** a name like CRITTERSPEED in two different files, your compiler won't like this. But if you have a cGameRunner::CRITTERSPEED and a cGameWalker::CRITTERSPEED there's no conflict.

- Using statics is a good habit to get into because it's useful for having OO-correct versions of things very much like global variables, such as the single `static cRandomizer cRandomizer::RANDOMIZER` object defined in our **randomizer.h** and **randomizer.cpp** files. This way, whenever we need a randomizer anywhere in our program, we just use `cRandomizer::RANDOMIZER`.

- Since a static is a variable, you can change it inside your code. Thus, for instance, many of our *cGame* child classes change the value of the static *Real* `cCritter::MAXRADIUS` as a way of altering the default maximum size of all the critters.

- Java doesn't allow the **#define** statement, so you might as well start learning to live without it.

Review questions

A What are OOA, OOD, and OOP? What are some outcomes of these processes?

B What are some basic principles for drawing UML diagrams?

C What are encapsulation, inheritance, and polymorphism?

D How can you replace inheritance with composition? Draw a UML diagram.

E What is meant by the interface of a class?

F What does it mean to delegate a method to another class? Draw a UML diagram.

G Why do you sometimes use the argument **this** when delegating a method?

H Why are pointer members preferable to instance members? What is the additional burden of having a pointer member?

I What do we mean by 'no forgery'?

J What is the combinatorial explosion of classes, and how can you prevent it?

K How do you use **#ifdef**?

L How do you declare and instantiate a static variable?

Exercises

Exercise 4.1: OOA for a concert ticket site

Let's revisit the ticket-site example that was mentioned in Exercise 2.1. Here's the specification again.

A client can visit the server and search a schedule for a concert. A concert specifies a performer, a venue and a date. After selecting a concert, the client sees a list of some available tickets, specifying seat and price. The client can view a map to see where the seats are located. The client can select tickets and add them to his or her order. The client can buy the order by filling in an address form and giving credit card information.

Figure out a set of classes based on some or all of the nouns in the description and arrange them into a UML diagram. Test the completeness of your diagram by tracing some use cases through it. Draw the diagram at least three times, improving it each time.

Exercise 4.2: OOA for a music sharing site like the old Napster

A couple of years ago the music-sharing site called Napster ran a 'share-server' that satisfied the following specification. A client can log into the share-server. The share-server maintains a 'share pair list' of 'share pairs,' where a share pair consists of a song name and a link to a client who has this song available. When a client logs in, the share-server adds share pairs for the client's songs to the share pair list. A client can request a song, and the share-server displays a sublist of the share pair list showing share pairs for that song. If a client selects a share pair, the song is transferred to this client from the client mentioned in the share pair.

Figure out a set of classes based on some or all of the nouns in the description and arrange them into a UML diagram. The diagram will primarily have composition lines connecting the boxes. Test the completeness of your diagram by tracing some use cases through it. Draw the diagram at least three times, improving it each time.

Exercise 4.3: OOA for a music sharing site like KaZaA

Napster was successfully sued by the record companies for maintaining a share-server like this. In 2001 a possibly legal work-around emerged. Companies like KaZaA added another layer to the architecture. Rather than maintaining a share-server, they maintain a meta-server which directs clients to other client machines that are acting as share-servers.

Show how to add a meta-server to the UML diagram you got in the last exercise.

Exercise 4.4: Writing a utility class

Write a few lines of code to implement a utility container **cCritterPair** class to hold two **cCritter** * pointers as private members. The class should have a constructor that takes a pair of pointers as arguments and two accessors to get at the member pointers. Don't bother with mutators. Assume that **cCritterPair** should not delete its members in its destructor.

Exercise 4.5: Tweaking static variable values in the Spacewar game

Here we make some changes to the initializations of the static variables in **gamespacewar.cpp** and see what happens. When you change a static, it's usually wise to leave the original value as a comment to the right so you can get it back if necessary.

Increase `cGameSpacewar::WORLDSIZE` and notice how much bigger the world gets relative to the critters.

Increase `cCritterAsteroid::DARTACCELERATION` and `cCritterAsteroid::DARTSPEEDUP` and notice that it becomes nearly impossible to shoot an asteroid.

Change `cGameSpacewar::ASTEROIDHEALTH` to four and notice how many times you have to shoot and split up an asteroid before finally getting rid of it.

Exercise 4.6: Composition and inheritance

Draw two pictures to represent the inheritance and composition relationships shown in Figure 4.8, but have your pictures represent classes by egg-shaped images as were used in Figure 4.5.

Software design patterns   5

Every year people's expectations of software get higher and every year the job of being a software engineer gets harder. The only way we can hope to keep our heads above water is to continually improve the tools of our discipline.

Software engineers are always looking for a higher-level way of working, a tower to climb to get some perspective. We go from low-level languages to high-level languages, we use object-oriented methods, and over time we learn a number of reusable idioms. And now there's a new route to higher ground: the use of software design patterns. Adding another layer to the UML dependency diagram (Figure 4.1) we now get Figure 5.1.

While object-oriented software engineering encourages us to think about encapsulating our data and methods into classes, software design patterns show us good ways to get our classes to collaborate with each other.

It turns out there are certain useful but non-obvious ways in which one can have classes interact with each other, and a certain limited number of these design patterns recur over and over again. The simpler kinds of patterns are simply idioms, but the more complicated ones are what we call software design patterns. In recent years, software engineers have taken to cataloging software design patterns.

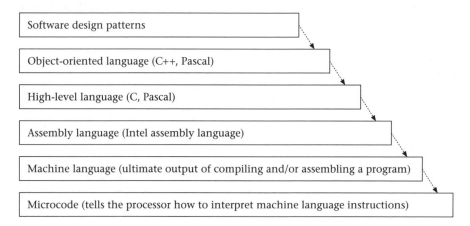

Figure 5.1 Levels of design

Repositories of these patterns can be found online and in textbooks such as Erich Gamma, Richard Helm, Ralph Johnson, and John Vlissides, *Design Patterns: Elements of Reusable Object-Oriented Software* (Addison-Wesley, 1995). The pattern names used in the *Design Patterns* book include Abstract Factory, Builder, Singleton, Adapter, Bridge, Composite, Decorator, Façade, Flyweight, Proxy, Chain of Responsibility, Command, Interpreter, Iterator, Mediator, Memento, Observer, State, Strategy, Template Method, and Visitor.

A software design pattern is usually described in terms of being a solution to a certain type of problem in a particular context. In this chapter's brief overviews, seven patterns are documented by describing the kind of *problem* the pattern is useful for, and giving a brief summary of the *solution* presented by the pattern followed by a mention of how the pattern is used in the Pop Framework.

5.1 Strategy

The Strategy pattern is an example of delegation, the general object-oriented idiom that was mentioned in the last chapter. Before starting, we should mention that in discussing implementations of patterns such as the Strategy pattern it will be helpful to use obvious, illustrative class names like **Context** and **Strategy**, as in Figure 5.2. But of course when you use the software patterns in your own code you can call your classes anything you like.

The *problem* addressed by the Strategy pattern is when we have a range of objects, all members of the same class called, let's say, **Context**, and we want to be able to change the behavior of the behave method of a **Context** object without having to change the class the object belongs to.

The *solution* is to create a **Strategy** class that holds a `behavealgorithm` method. The **Context** class will have a `Strategy *_pstrategy` member, and a `Context::behave(){_pstrategy->behavealgorithm(this)}`.

The reason you need to pass the 'this' to the `behavealgorithm` is so that the method can use the **Context** mutators and accessors to view and to alter the data of the **Context** object. Possibly `behavealgorithm` may call some other **Context** methods as well.

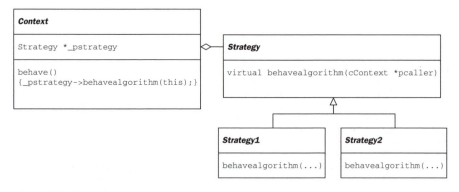

Figure 5.2 The Strategy pattern

If you find it useful, you can use the same name for the `Context::behave()` and `Strategy::behavealgorithm` methods.

The Strategy pattern plays a role similar to the role of function pointers in old-style C programming. One of the motivations for using the Strategy pattern is to avoid having a combinatorial explosion of classes. Rather than having to derive off new subclasses for new kinds of behavior, we use the Strategy pattern to let classes 'plug-in' whatever behavior they need.

In the Pop Framework, the `cCritter::`***feellistener()*** method calls a ***cListener::listen(cCritter *pcritter)*** method. In particular, we give each ***cCritter*** a ***cListener *_plistener***. The ***cCritter::feellistener()*** calls `_plistener->listen(this)`.

The ***cListener::listen(cCritter *pcritter)*** method takes input from the mouse or keyboard and affects the owner critter in different ways.

The fact that a ***Strategy*** object can be dynamically changed means that when you are running the Pop program, for instance, you can use the Player menu to select different kinds of controllers for the player. When you are doing this, you change the player's listening strategy.

5.2 Template Method

The *problem* arises when you have a range of different child classes with a common base class. You want each child class to execute some fixed sequence of methods in the same order, but you want to be able to vary what the individual calls of the sequence do.

The *solution*, as shown in Figure 5.3, is to place the sequence of method calls into a non-virtual ***templateMethod*** function that is not overridden by the child classes. The Template Method has calls to various virtual ***hookMethod*** calls that can be overridden.

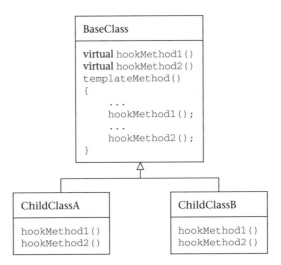

Figure 5.3 The Template Method pattern

In the Pop Framework, the *cGame::step* method is a template that holds a sequence of calls to *cGame* methods that update and show the critters in a certain order, with certain calls that you might override located at a certain positions within the sequence. In this case the methods you might override are *cGame::adjustGameParameters* and *cGame::gameOverMessage*.

The *cSprite::draw* method is another example of the Template Method pattern; it has some special 'don't touch me' code nested around the virtual method *cSprite::imagedraw* that the sprite child classes override.

5.3 Command

The *problem* is that you may want to ask an object to do something, but you don't know exactly when the object will carry out the request or exactly how it will do it.

The *solution*, as shown in Figure 5.4, is to create a **Command** object that represents which command you want executed, possibly with information about which target object is supposed to be affected by the command's execution.

Often the Command pattern is used in partnership with a **CommandProcessor** that holds the collection of commands that still need to be executed. The **CommandProcessor** can be derived from an array template or a linked list template.

The Windows operating system uses something like the Command pattern, although the pattern is not implemented in a fully object oriented way. In Windows all commands are stored as message structures that have an integer messageID specifying the type of command to be executed. Rather than individually implementing an execute method, the messages pass off the execution task to a big switch statement in the Windows code, with the switch looking at the value of the messageID.

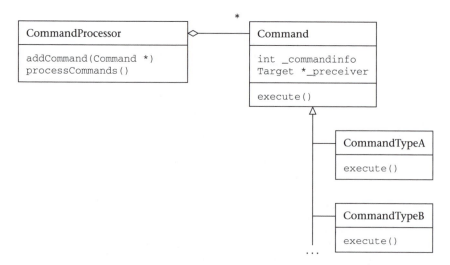

Figure 5.4 The Command pattern

In the Pop Framework, we do a similarly half-hearted implementation of the Command pattern; we use a ***cServiceRequest*** structure and pass the task of executing the command off to switch in the code of a cBiota object that holds our command queue.

A bit more detail. When we carry out an update of the game world, we walk through a list of critters and call an **update** method for each of them. When an object dies, it's not practical to remove it from the simulation until we're done updating all the other objects, otherwise one of the not-yet-updated objects may still need to finish interacting with the about-to-die object. What we do is maintain an array of ***cServiceRequest*** objects, where each ***cServiceRequest*** holds a cCritter *_pclient and CString _request field. And at a certain time specified by the ***cGame::step*** template, we make a call to the cBiota::***processServiceRequests*** method that carries out each of the pending commands.

5.4 Composite

The *problem* is that you may have a set of **Primitive** objects which you also group into **Composite** objects, and you want to be able to treat the primitive and the composite objects the same. You also want to be able to have composites made of mixtures of composites and primitives, and so on.

The *solution* is to have a base class called, say **Component**, with both the **Primitive** and **Composite** classes inheriting from it. **Composite** has a member, typically an array, which holds any number of **Component** objects.

When you use a Composite pattern the **Component** class usually has some virtual method **doSomething()** that you override in the child classes. Typically the primitive children of **Component** override **doSomething()** in various particular kinds of ways and the **Composite** child class overrides **doSomething()** to (a) walk through a loop to call **doSomething** for all of _pchildren[i] and (b) possibly do some additional step peculiar to the particular **Composite** class.

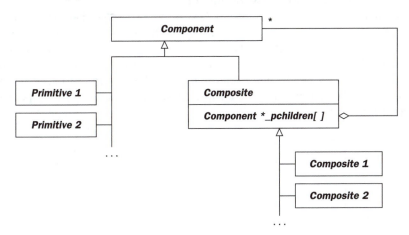

Figure 5.5 The Command pattern

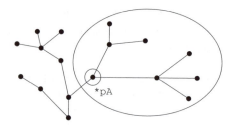

Figure 5.6   A Composite pattern tree

It's sometimes useful to think of a Composite pattern in terms of a tree. The **Primitive** objects are the leaves of the tree, and the **Composite** objects are the forks. When you call the **doSomething** at some fork, you end up working your way out to all the leaves above this fork. Thus, in Figure 5.6, if we supposed that *pA points to the object in the small circle, then the call pA->doSomething() will cascade down to all of the other objects included in the large oval.

In the Pop Framework we use the Composite pattern with our graphical sprite objects. That is, we have a base class **cSprite** with a some 'primitive' sprite child classes: **cSpriteBubble**, **cSpriteIcon**, and **cPolygon**. We also have a **cSprite** child class called **cSpriteComposite**, and this class has a CArray _ps
pritechild of **cSprite*** objects.

Java uses the Composite pattern for its graphics classes: there is a base **Component** class which has as child classes (a) **Primitive** classes such as **Button** and **Scrollbar**, and (b) a **Composite** class called **Container**, which holds an array of **Component** objects. In addition, the **Container** class has (c) child classes **Panel**, **Window**, **Frame**, **Dialog**, etc.

5.5   Singleton

The *problem* addressed here is that one may have a class that one only wants to have one single, easily accessible instance of.

The *solution*, as shown in Figure 5.7, is to give the **Singleton** class a single static Singleton *_pinstancncesingleton member. Initially this member is NULL. You give the **Singleton** class a public static accessor pinstance() that (a) initializes pinstancncesingleton if it's still NULL and (b) returns pinstancncesingleton. An additional wrinkle is that, in order to prevent the users of this class from making additional **Singleton** instances, you make the **Singleton** constructor private.

Singleton
private static Singleton *_pinstancesingleton;

private Singleton();
public static Singleton* pinstance();
public:
    //Useful Singleton methods...

Figure 5.7   The Singleton pattern

The static `Singleton *_pinstancesingleton` pointer instance resides in **singleton.cpp** and is initially set to NULL with a line like this.

```
Singleton* Singleton::_pinstancetancesingleton = NULL;
```

So when does `_pinstancesingleton` get initialized? The trick is to have **pinstance()** initialize it the first time it's called. That is, we use code like the following.

```
Singleton* Singleton::pinstance()
{
    if (_pinstancesingleton == NULL)
        _pinstancesingleton = new Singleton();
    return _pinstancesingleton;
}
```

In the Pop Framework, the **cRandomizer** class is a **Singleton** class. There are a large number of useful **cRandomizer** methods for returning random integers, reals, vectors, colors, and so on. In order to call these methods, we need a **cRandomizer** object to call them. The methods that return random values can't be static because the internal state of the **cRandomizer** object is changed by each of these calls. The internal state has to change so that the **cRandomizer** doesn't repeat itself any sooner than necessary.

An annoying but seemingly unavoidable side-effect of having a pointer singleton instance **Singleton *_pinstancesingleton** is that we need to have the app remember to delete this instance at exit. In the case of the **cRandomizer**, we have a static `cRandomizer::deleteSingleton()` method that we call in the **CPopApp** destructor. (In Java or C#, with automatic garbage collection, this isn't an issue you'd have to worry about.) In most cases, deleting this little **Singleton** object isn't really that important, since you are, after all, terminating the program, at which time any remaining memory is freed up anyway. But the Visual Studio debugger does give you a nagging warning if you fail to free all your memory, so it's just as well to do the right thing.

Why not just have the static **Singleton** member be an instance that we declare as `Singleton Singleton::_instancesingleton;`? And then go ahead and in-line the pinstance method as `Singleton::pinstance(){return &(Singleton::_instancesingleton);}`?

If we took this approach with **cRandomizer**, it would in fact work in most versions of the Pop Framework. But the approach is risky. The risk has to do with the fact that in a multi-file C++ project, the programmer has no sure control over the order in which the static objects declared in the various *.cpp modules get initialized. So it's possible that the constructor of some static object might call `Singleton::pinstance()` before the `Singleton::_instancesingleton` got initialized, and disaster would ensue.

By using the `Singleton::_pinstancesingleton`, we can make a fail-safe `pinstance()` that expressly initializes `_pinstancesingleton` the first time it's called.

5.6 Bridge

The Bridge pattern is a kind of super Strategy pattern, that is, it is a way of encapsulating alternate versions of a whole range of methods rather than encapsulating alternate versions of just one method.

The *problem* is that you may have a set of methods that you contemplate implementing in two or more completely different ways. You don't want to have to mess up the rest of your code with the details of the different implementations.

The *solution* is to write a base class **Interface** that includes more or less empty implementations of the methods you need, and then to derive off **Implementation** child classes that provide concrete implementations of these methods. In the rest of the program, you program towards the somewhat abstract interface of the **Interface** object without worrying about the details of the **Implementation** children.

The UML diagram (Figure 5.8) is very similar to that for the Strategy pattern.

Learning about the Bridge pattern was crucial for the development of the Pop Framework code. The author had initially targeted the code throughout for Windows graphics calls. But then the time came to try and support OpenGL graphics. How to port to OpenGL graphics without losing all the work done implementing for Windows graphics and without, God forbid, developing two alternate versions of the same program. The solution was to abstract out an interface of all the graphics calls needed for Windows graphics or OpenGL graphics and to form a **cGraphics** class with prototypes for all these methods. Derived from this class are the **cGraphicsMFC** class and the **cGraphicsOpenGL** class. The **CPopView** window object owns a cGraphics *_pgraphics member which can in fact be dynamically changed between being **cGraphicsMFC** or **cGraphicsOpenGL**. For each 'behave' graphics call inside **CPopView** the code is now passed to a virtual _pgraphics->behavealgorithm call. Depending on the type of _pgraphics, the behavealgorithm call is then dynamically shunted to the Windows graphics or to the OpenGL graphics code.

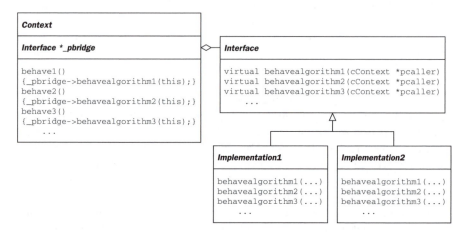

Figure 5.8 The Bridge pattern

Now that we have this instance of the Bridge pattern in place, a further port to DirectX graphics *should* be non-problematic (emphasis on *should* because one never knows with software engineering projects)!

5.7 Document-View

The Document-View pattern is also known as the *Document-View architecture*. In this section we'll discuss a refined version of the Document-View pattern that allows for an event notification mechanism. This refined version is sometimes called the Observable-Observer pattern, or the Publisher-Subscriber pattern.

The *problem* arises when you have a number of different representations of the same data. How do we keep the representations in synch with each other?

The *solution*, as shown in Figure 5.9, is to have one **Document** (or **Publisher**) class that holds the core data, and to have a range of **View** (or **Subscriber**) classes that display the data. To smooth out our exposition, we'll write 'document' or 'view' to mean, respectively, a **Document** object or a **View** object.

The document needs to be able to add and remove views from its active list. And it needs to have a **UpdateAllViews** method that tells all of the views that some of the data may have changed.

A view needs to have a **getDoc()** method that returns a pointer to the owner document. When the document calls **UpdateAllViews**, each view executes an **OnUpdate** method which checks the data in the document and updates the state of the view accordingly.

Another aspect of the Document-View architecture is that the view not only needs to be able to access the data in the document, it should also be able to mutate the data in the document. Part of the implementation of the document mutators must be that when document data is changed, the document calls **UpdateAllViews** so that all of the active views will show the new data. This acts as a roundabout way for the views to communicate with each other. We can represent this by a UML *sequence diagram* as shown in Figure 5.10.

As this is our first sequence diagram, we need to mention that UML sequence diagrams are used to show how the objects in a program interact over time. The diagram is set up as a series of columns, with one column for each object. Each column has a vertical lifeline showing the lifetime of the object. Arrows are drawn from lifeline to lifeline to symbolize the passing of messages via method calls. We normally label a message with the name of a method being called, and this method is expected to be a member method of the class column that the message points to. Use a dotted arrow line when the caller object is not shown. A call that an object makes to itself is drawn as an arrow that starts and

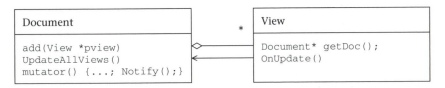

Figure 5.9 The Document-View pattern

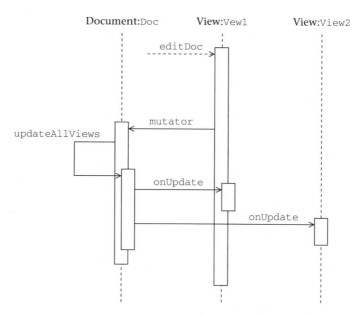

Figure 5.10 Sequence diagram of a view editing a document

ends on the object's own lifeline. The labels at the heads of the columns can either be class names or, if you want to distinguish among multiple instances of a class, you can use object names which are written in the format `Class:Object1`.

In this diagram, we see how the `View1` object can edit the `Doc` data and mutate it. The document mutator uses an ***UpdateAllViews*** call to 'publish' the changed data out to both `View1` and `View2`. Presumably there has been a call to `Document::updateAllViews` before the start of this sequence diagram, so that `View1` is in fact looking at a current view of the `Doc` before beginning to edit it.

Documents and views in Windows programs

Most Windows programs use variations of the Document-View pattern to simultaneously show multiple views of multiple documents. Putting this a bit differently, the Document-View architecture allows you to have different views of the same set of data, and it also allows you to display different views of different sets of data.

In a Windows Document-View architecture program you can get new views in two ways. (a) You can use a command with a name like **File | New** or **File | Open** to open an additional document, or (b) you can use a command with a name like **Window | New** to open an additional view of the currently active document. In case (a) what you have is a completely new set of data inside the new window, while in case (b) you get a different view of the data of one of the windows you already had open (the window which currently had the focus, i.e. the window that had the highlighted caption bar).

Each onscreen window view shows the data in an associated document. It is possible to have several view windows showing the same document, but it is not possible to have one view window showing more than one document.

One can imagine, say, a financial analysis program in which you might want to view the same numerical data both as a table and as a bar graph at the same time. These would be two different views of the same document, with the document being the set of numerical data. Or consider a computer game in which you want to show both a 3D rendered view of what virtual player sees, and a 2D overview map of the landscape. Here again, we'd have two views of the same document, where the document might have information like the game level, the positions of the players in the landscape, and the players' scores and strengths. In a word-processing program, the document is the text you're working on. If you use a splitter window, then the two subwindows represent two different views of the same document. In a paint or photo-retouching program, the document is the image you're working on, and you have a variety of possible views showing, for instance, different zoom levels, different layers of the image, and so on.

Having the different views show the same data is not something that you get for free. You have to write code to make it happen. It used to be fairly hard to write a Document-View architecture program, but now, thanks to MFC and the 'AppWizard' (the Visual Studio tool for creating projects), it's pretty easy. When you use the AppWizard to generate some starting code for a new project, its default choice is to use the Document-View architecture. The default program architecture chosen by the AppWizard is called MDI. This uses the Document-View architecture.

In Windows, Document-View architecture programs used to keep all of their views of all their documents inside a single-frame window. But now it's becoming the fashion to have a different frame window for each document. In the versions of Word starting with Word 2000, for instance, you'll find that the program pops up completely different frame windows when you open different documents. Some programs, such as Macromedia Dreamweaver, even pop up separate frame windows for each view, visually shattering the program into something like a sea of dialog boxes. But under the hood and on their menus, these are still Document-View architecture programs in which one executable manages a set of documents, each with its own set of views.

The app, the doc, and the view in MFC

Table 5.1 summarizes how MFC sets up the Document-View architecture for the Pop Framework.

As we discuss below, not *all* of your application's data is supposed to go into the **CDocument**. A flag saying whether or not you want to mute the speaker might go into your **CWinApp**. And a flag saying whether you want to show you graphical objects as solids or as wire-frames might go into your **CView**. It's only the data that relates to the description of what you're looking at that goes into the **CDocument**.

Table 5.1   The application, the document, and the view in MFC.

Colloquial name	Pop class	Inherits from	Code is in
Application	*CPopApp*	CWinApp	Pop.*
Document	*CPopDoc*	CDocument	PopDoc.*
View	*CPopView*	CView	PopView.*

This raises the point that you may want to be able to refer to one of the classes from inside one of the others. Suppose, for instance, that one of our *CPopView* methods wants to look at a _soundflag that lives inside *CPopApp*. And surely, our *CPopView* is going to need to find the data that's in the *CPopDoc*. If we're writing code inside a *CPopApp*, *CPopDoc*, or *CPopView* method, is there a way to talk about the other classes?

It turns out that in terms of navigating among the app, the docs, and the views there are four tasks that we normally care about.

- First, we need (but not very often) a way for any doc or view to get a pointer to the app that owns them.

- Second, we need a way for any view to get a pointer to its 'owner' doc.

- Third, we need a way for a doc to tell all of its views to update themselves, and we prefer to do this without having to individually list the views.

- Fourth, we need a way for a document to know which of its views, if any, is the active focus window of the user interface.

The first task is done by the global method **::AfxGetApp()**, as in:

```
CPopApp* papp = (CPopApp*)(::AfxGetApp());//cast CWinApp*
```

The second task is accomplished by the **CView::GetDocument()** method, as in:

```
CPopDoc* pdoc = GetDocument();
```

As it happens, you don't need the cast on **GetDocument**; because **GetDocument** is redefined for each child of **CView** to include the cast. (To make this clear, you can look at the definition of *CPopView::GetDocument()* in popview.h.)

The third task is accomplished by the **CDocument::UpdateAllViews** method, which cascades a call to **CView::OnUpdate** down to each of the doc's views.

The full prototype of this third method is **void UpdateAllViews(CView* pSender, LPARAM lHint = 0, CObject* pHint = NULL)**. The first argument isn't used very often. The second argument is used for a document to signal to its views if it is in some different-looking state, for instance if a game is over, the doc might put a number into lHint to tell the views to change color. The third argument is a catch-all where a doc can put pretty much anything it likes to pass to its views. That is, a doc can wrap some information up inside a class object and then pass the view a pointer to the class with the information.

As we mention in Chapter 23: Programming Windows with MFC in Part II, there actually is a way to individually step through a doc's views, but this is a technique that you should use only rarely. Using **UpdateAllViews** is a higher-level and cleaner way for your doc to pass information to its views.

The fourth task can be accomplished by a special *CPopDoc::getActiveView()* method that we wrote for our *CPopDoc* class; see the Levels of Windows section in Chapter 23 for details.

Documents and views in the Pop Framework

Using the Document-View architecture forces a programmer to think about where to declare his or her variables. In this subsection we talk about this issue in the Pop Framework.

Your program is normally going to have a number of variables that describe the data being displayed by the program as well as the current state of the program. These are the kinds of variables that you might once have made into global variables or into static variables living inside your **main** function. In MFC programming you will usually put these variables either into your **CDocument** class or into your **CView** class – well, actually they go into your app's specific children of these classes (which are called *CPopDoc* and *CPopView* in our example program). Once in a while you might store a particular variable in the **CWinApp** class or in your **CMainFrame** class instead; an example of this kind of variable might be a global switch that specifies whether or not to pause your program when another program is in the foreground. But the overwhelming majority of your variables will live in your **CDocument** and your **CView**. But in which one?

The **CDocument** variables tend to be either the kinds of file variables that you might want to save, or the kinds of temporary helper objects that you might want to share among several views. And variables whose values are specific to an individual view go into the **CView**.

Let's say more about the Document-View distinction in terms of a computer game program such as we'll be writing in this book. In a computer game you'll often have an array of 'critters' moving around on top of a bitmap background. Each of your critters will have a position, a velocity, a health-index, and so on. (Normally one of the critters will represent you, the player, and its actions will be controlled by your input rather than by the program code. But it's still just a critter.) As the user plays the game, he or she will see the critters moving inside a window. It may be that if the user wants the game to run faster, he or she will have the choice of showing the critters in simple outline instead of in colorful detail. The variable controlling this choice would probably be stored at view level rather than at document level. Another example of a situation where there might be a view-specific variable might be the user's 'point of view'. This would be a factor if the critters' world is larger than the window, and the user can scroll the view this way and that. Or perhaps the world has a lot of detail and the user can zoom in or out. Or perhaps the game is three-dimensional, and the user will have the option of changing the angle of view.

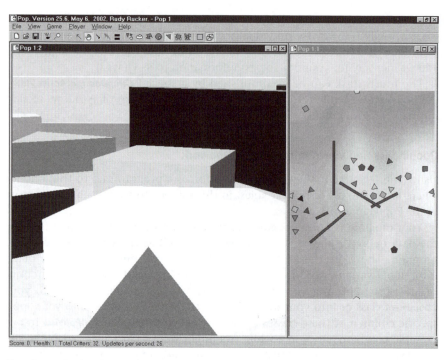

Two views of a Pop Dambuilder game document

In our computer games, we'd expect the critters and the background bitmap information to live in the **CDocument**. But, as mentioned, the switch that determines whether or not to show the critters in detail would live in the **CView**, as would the variable (perhaps a real-valued rectangle or a matrix) that specifies the user's point of view. If you were to 'save' your game, you'd normally only want to save the states of the critters, that is the document data. But it could happen that you might want to save some information about the view as well, e.g. the current location of the player's point of view.

It isn't always easy to decide whether to put a given variable into the document or into the view, but as we go along in our example programs the process should become a little clearer. Very often there is no one 'absolutely right' way to program something. (But there *are* plenty of things that are absolutely wrong!) For a beginning programmer, the number of choices is daunting, and it's easy to feel paralyzed with indecision. Well, the only real way to learn is by doing, so go ahead and program, but keep an open mind and be willing to go back and rewrite what you did before. Another way of putting this is that learning programming is a matter of first making every possible mistake, so the faster you make your mistakes the faster you're learning!

Here's how the *CPopDoc* updates the game. First, the *stepDoc* method calls _pgame->step, where the *cGame *_pgame* reference member object holds the data of the game document. And second, the *stepDoc* uses *UpdateAllViews* to update the views to display the newly updated _pgame data.

```
void CPopDoc::stepDoc(Real dt)
{
    CPopView *pview = getActiveView();
    _pgame->step(dt, pview); /* Move the critters for timestep dt.
        Maybe add or delete some critters. Critters might use the
        pview to sniff out the pixel colors near their current image
        locations (rarely used). */
    cTimeHint timehint(dt); //Wrap dt up so we can pass it to the views.
    UpdateAllViews(NULL, 0, &timehint); /* Redraw all the views and
        possibly animate their viewpoints with the dt inside
        timehint. */
}
```

As a sequence diagram, this looks like Figure 5.11. Since we only have one object of each class type in this picture, we just label the columns with the class names.

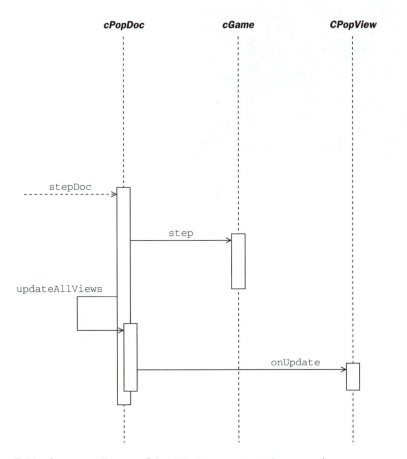

Figure 5.11   Sequence diagram of the *CPopDocument::stepDoc* cascade

Controlling multiple documents and views

How do you fit the Document-View pattern into your application if you want more than document? And how do you send messages to the various pieces of the program?

One solution is to have an *App* class that holds an array of *Document* objects, and to have *App*, *Document*, and *View* inherit from a base class *Target*. This is the architecture used by the MFC framework when you go for a MDI.

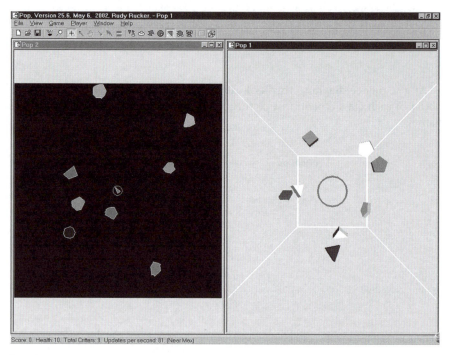

Pop showing two game documents

The idea is to use an *App* class in addition to a *Document* and a *View* class. In the MFC Application Framework, these classes are called **CWinApp**, **CDocument**, and **CView**.

What we have here is close to a pattern called 'model-view-controller.' In the model-view-controller pattern the 'model' plays the role of the *Document*, the 'view' is a *View* in the same sense we've already talked about, and the 'controller' is an abstraction of the user interface controls. Stretching things a bit, you might think of the controller as being the *App*, so that Document-View-App becomes a close analog of model-view-controller.

This analogy is, however, imperfect, because in the specific example of MFC we actually process user commands with any of the three Document-View-App components, which in MFC are the **CDocument** objects, the **CView** objects, and a **CWinApp** object. In an MFC program, all three of these classes can process messages and act like a 'controller'.

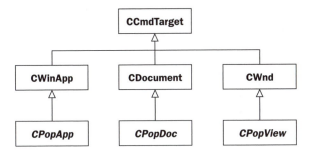

Figure 5.12 Inheritance diagram in a multiple document pattern

In any case, this is a good place to say a bit about how MFC processes user commands. In MFC there is a general base class called **CCmdTarget**. A **CCmdTarget** object is characterized as being an object that you can send Windows messages to. Put differently, a **CCmdTarget** is something that can process, say, menu item selection messages such as *OnCommandGamePlaySounds*. (As it so happens, in the Pop program this message was originally processed by the *CPopDoc*, and later we changed it so that the message is processed by the *CPopApp*.) Now we can send a message either to a document, to the application, or to a window, and Figure 5.12 expresses that notion. Just to make the diagram a little bigger, we've put in the three child classes *CPopDoc*, *CPopApp*, and *CPopView* as well.

This diagram shows inheritance; now let's talk about composition and navigation. As we've already said, the **CWinApp** class corresponds to the program as a whole, and the **CDocument** class corresponds to the files that the program currently has open. Although a **CWinApp** does not have a set of **CDocument** objects as explicit members, we certainly think of it as associating with the **CDocument** class. As for navigation, MFC happens to have a global ::AfxGetApp method that returns the current **CWinApp**, so we can navigate from **CDocument** to **CWinApp**. And, although it's not simple to describe, there is also an accessor-like process by which a **CWinApp** can walk through a list of its **CDocument** objects, so we can say that we can navigate from **CWinApp** to **CDocument**. (If you're curious about the details of Windows programs, see Chapter 23: Programming Windows with MFC). So we draw a composition line in one direction with a navigation line coming back the other way. A **CWinApp** can open as many views as we like (by using **Window | New**), but a **CDocument** has only one associated **CWinApp**. So we put a * by **CDocument** at the end of the composition line. This is shown in Figure 5.13.

This is entirely analogous to how a *Document* relates to a *View* (Figure 5.14).

Figure 5.13 App and documents

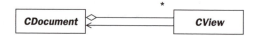

Figure 5.14   Document and views

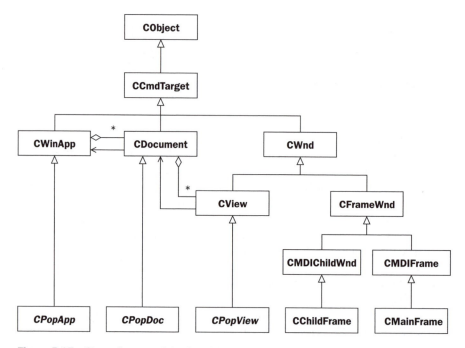

Figure 5.15   Class diagram of the Pop Framework MFC classes

For the sake of completeness, let's draw one more UML diagram (Figure 5.15) showing some of the relationships among our Pop Framework MFC classes.

You might say that this UML diagram is primarily about the Windows operating system, and the UML diagram of the Pop Framework classes in the last chapter was primarily about the Pop program. It make sense that *CPopDoc* and *CPopView* appear in both diagrams, because these classes are designed by MFC to contain, respectively, the application's data and the application's appearance. The *CPopView*, your app's onscreen image, is where it makes contact with the Windows operating system.

Review questions

A   What are software design patterns?

B   Give examples of the design patterns we discussed: the Strategy pattern, the Template Method pattern, the Command pattern, the Composite pattern, the Singleton pattern, the Bridge pattern, and the Document-View pattern.

C   For each pattern draw a relevant UML class diagram.

D   What are the standard Document and View classes called in MFC programs? What are some other basic classes used in MFC programs?

Exercises

Exercise 5.1: Strategy Pattern and sales chart display

Suppose that you have a *cSalesData* object with a *drawGraph()* method. Draw a UML including a few lines of code to show how you could use a Strategy Pattern to select at runtime between drawing a bar graph or a pie graph of the data.

Exercise 5.2: Template Method pattern and opening diverse file types

When you use Visual Studio you can open various sorts of files, edit them, and then save them. Text files are shown as text and bitmap files are shown as images. We might suppose that there is a **FileOpen(CString filename)** method. Some of this code will act the same no matter what kind of file you open, but part of the code will act differently depending on the kind of file. Describe how this might be accomplished by using the Template Method. Draw a UML diagram and write out some very rough code, simply using made-up names for the functions you use.

Exercise 5.3: Command pattern and a word-processor's Undo and Redo

Experiment a bit with the effect of **Ctrl+Z** (for Undo) and **Ctrl+Y** (for Redo) in your word-processor. What do you think might be a *WordProcessorCommand* in this context? What are the methods that *WordProcessorCommand* must implement? What kind of data structure might you need for holding the *WordProcessorCommand* objects? Draw a simple UML class diagram.

Exercise 5.4: Composite pattern and building a virtual city

Say that you want to develop a *cStructure* class for describing doors, walls, rooms, floors of buildings, buildings, city-blocks, cities, and so on. Draw a UML showing how to do this using the Composite pattern.

Exercise 5.5: Singleton pattern and preserving a connection

On many home computers you can to click some desktop icon to connect to the Net via a conventional modem or a broadband modem. Some email and browser software will try and make a connection even if one exists. Trying to make a connection when a connection is already open sometimes spoils the existing connection in such a way that it's impossible to reconnect without rebooting the machine. How might your operating system use the singleton pattern to avoid this problem? Draw a UML diagram.

Exercise 5.6: Bridge pattern and the look and feel of windows

In Java it's possible to change the 'look and feel' of your windows. This includes, for instance, how you draw a window frame, draw the caption bar, draw a button, and draw a scroll bar. You can select, for instance, a Windows, a Mac, or an XWindows look and feel. Draw a UML diagram showing how this can be done by using the Bridge pattern.

Exercise 5.7: Document-View pattern and guestbook conversation

Say that a number of clients are viewing a web page on a server. Suppose that the web page holds a guestbook that a client can update in real time by typing in characters and pressing a Send button. Draw a sequence diagram to show the steps by which Client1 can send a message to and get an answer from Client2 by using the server.

Animation

6

In this chapter we'll talk about how to write a program which continually updates itself onscreen. There are four tasks in an animation program.

- Place an animation update call in the app where you loop back indefinitely often.
- Calculate an appropriate timestep *dt* for each update.
- Cascade update calls from the app down to the individual data elements of the documents, passing them the current *dt*.
- Update the views after the data is updated.

In this chapter, we'll have one section on each of these four tasks.

6.1 The endless animation loop

In a game program like Pop, the images keep changing even when you're not giving it input. Things move. The program animates itself. Where is the point in the program that we can repeatedly loop back to for new updates?

Another characteristic thing about game programs is that the user can give input at any time, using the mouse or the keys to move the player icon. How do we synchronize these inputs with the game updates?

In any Windows program, the internal update processes and the user input processes are concurrent or parallel flows, that is, the updating is computed by the machine and the inputs are 'computed' by the player, with the two systems acting independently.

We'll draw a new kind of UML diagram to show how this fits together. Recall that UML has quite a range of diagrams. The use case diagrams are good for requirements gathering. Component diagrams are useful for mapping out the interdependencies of a project's source-code files. Class diagrams show how the classes inherit and associate. Sequence diagrams show the order in which program events happen. We're going to talk about more sequence diagrams in this chapter and also about one more kind of UML diagram: an activity diagram. Sequence and activity diagrams are for showing how a program runs. When you design a program you need to think not only about its classes but also about its run-cycle or work flow.

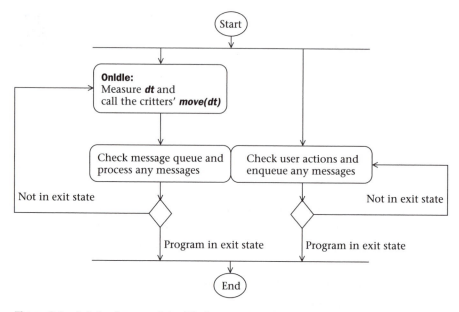

Figure 6.1   Activity diagram of the Windows program flow

A UML activity diagram is similar to a traditional flow-chart. We draw rounded rectangles around activities in the program and draw little diamonds to indicate test points. Arrows show the flow of the program control. What makes an activity diagram a bit more than a flow-chart is that it allows you to show concurrent processes. We use horizontal lines to indicate the 'forks' and 'joins' where parallel processes either split apart or join back together. Figure 6.1 is an activity diagram for the Pop program as a whole.

A Windows program maintains an internal structure called the message queue, which is basically an array of special **MSG** structures. A message is placed on the queue, or 'enqueued,' each time that the user does something – press a key, move the mouse, make a menu selection. And some Windows methods place messages on the queue themselves. A message can be placed on the queue at any time.

Rather than responding to each message immediately, a Windows program like Pop lets the messages wait in the queue until it is ready to deal with them. Pop works its way through the message queue, processing the messages in the order in which they arrived.

As we mentioned in Chapter 5: Software Design Patterns, this is an example of the Command pattern. Rather than executing a Windows message right away, we encapsulate the idea of the message into a command that we place into our message queue, to be executed when we have time.

When there are no more messages to process, Pop begins calling an internal method named **OnIdle**. When **OnIdle** returns, Pop checks if there are any new messages to process, and then it calls **OnIdle** again. When there are no messages at all, Pop's behavior is simply to call **OnIdle** over and over again. If you want to read more about the Windows execution flow see Chapter 23: Programming Windows with MFC.

Given that **OnIdle** gets called over and over, this is the spot to stick in the code to run your animation. The **CPopApp** class defined in the **pop.h** and **pop.cpp** files is a child of the MFC **CWinApp** class that owns the **OnIdle** method. So what we'll do to animate our program is to override and extend the code for *CPopApp::OnIdle* inside the **pop.cpp** file.

If you write an 'eternal-loop' program in the wrong way, you can find it impossible to terminate the program (short of using **Ctrl+Alt+Del** to get to the Task Manager). That's why it's a good idea to use the approach described here. By locating the eternal loop inside the **OnIdle** function, we're sure that all user messages to the program get properly processed. If a user message tells the program to terminate, then it never does get back to **OnIdle** and it exits smoothly.

Inside *CPopApp::OnIdle* we do two things: we compute an appropriate *Real dt* timestep, and we pass this *dt* to the documents with a *CPopApp:animateAllDocs(dt)* call. Before discussing these points, let's say a bit more about how we override **OnIdle**.

Using the OnIdle method to call *animateAllDocs*

We animate by overriding the **CWinApp::OnIdle** function. We want it to make calls to the **CDocument** objects that will cascade down to the *cGame* objects and the *CView* objects.

An application executes the **CWinApp::OnIdle** function at least once each time that it finishes processing its current messages. Normally the first two calls to **OnIdle** are used for maintaining the appearance of the user interface, that is, things like the toolbar buttons and the menu selections. Thus the first call to **OnIdle** will generate a call to, for instance, *OnUpdateGameSpacewar* to tell the menu whether or not the **Game | Spacewar** selection should have a checkmark next to it.

The return type of **OnIdle** is **BOOL**. If you want your application to keep calling **OnIdle** over and over again even if no messages are found, you have **OnIdle** keep returning TRUE. This is safe because **OnIdle** will continue checking for messages after each return in any case.

If you only want to call **OnIdle** once each time that you finish processing messages, then return FALSE. Here, a way to keep a program doing things 'forever' is to have its **OnIdle** function generate more messages. After the program processes these messages, it goes back to **OnIdle**, which produces more messages, and so on. We can think of either approach as an 'eternal-loop' program (see Exercise 6.5).

The simplest way to put an animation loop inside **OnIdle** might be to pick a target timestep of, say, 0.05 second (that is, 50 milliseconds, or 20 updates a second), and do something like this.

```
BOOL CPopApp::OnIdle(LONG lCount)
{
    CWinApp::OnIdle(lCount); //Do the base class WinApp processing.
    animateAllDocs(0.05);
        //Step through all the docs and feed this timestep.
    return TRUE; //Keep doing it over and over.
}
```

But we'll improve on this a bit.

- First of all, we'd like the timestep that we feed into *animateAllDocs* to reflect the actual time that it really takes the computer to do the update. To do this we need to get information from the computer about the system time. There is a C++ **clock** method which returns the time in milliseconds, but using the function is a bit messy. So we'll encapsulate our time-getting code within a class we'll call *cPerformanceTimer*, and give it a **tick** function which returns the time as a *Real* number of seconds. More about this in the following section.

- Secondly, we'd like to have a switch for turning the animation on and off.

- Thirdly, we'd like to avoid another problem with eternal-loop programs, which is that they can suck up every available machine computation cycle – a very bad situation if you minimize such a program, forget about it, and then try and run some other programs. If the minimized eternal-loop program is still running, you'll find that your other programs behave very poorly. Our standard practice for avoiding this is to have our eternal loop only be active when our eternal-loop program is the focus or foreground window, that is, only when it's the window whose caption bar is highlighted.

For full details about how to do this, see the *CPopApp::OnIdle* code in the **pop.cpp** file of the Pop Framework.

6.2 Processor-independent simulation speed

What value should we use for an animation's *dt*? We'd like to make it somewhat independent of the speed at which our program is running. The run speed can be influenced not only by your processor speed, but also by the size of your game window, and whether or not you have multiple views or documents open in your game. As far as possible, we'd like the apparent speed of our moving creatures to stay the same.

What exactly does this mean? As we discuss in Chapter 7: Simulating Physics, we give each simulation object a vector *_position* and a vector *_velocity*. For each update cycle, we compute an appropriate time step *dt*, we update our *_velocity*, and then we use the standard rule:

*_position = _position + dt * _velocity*

The issue at hand is this: what should *dt* be? One might imagine setting *dt* to some 'reasonable' fixed value like 0.1 that happens to look good on your own machine. But if your processor is running at 400 Mhz and your user's machine is running at 200 Mhz, your critters are going to move half as fast on the user's machine. If the user has a slow video card then your program is going to run even slower. And, on the other hand, when you get a 1.2 Gigahertz machine your critters are going to go three times as fast, and if they're part of a game this game is now going to be unplayable. (Gigahertz, or GHz, is of course a billion cycles per second, that is, a thousand Mhz. It took desktop machines something like 20 years to make it from MHz to GHz speeds. One of these days you'll see personal computers running at a terahertz or Thz speeds, where a terahertz is a trillion cycles per second.)

No, the trick is to let *dt* be *real time*. That is, we will measure the time length *dt* of each update cycle, and use that in our simulation. If the machine is slow, then the *dt* will be big, and the critter will move in a bigger step during each update cycle. If the machine is fast, the *dt* will be small, and the critter will move in smaller steps during each update cycle.

The way we implement this is to give our application a *cPerformanceTimer* object that has a *tick()* method which will return the elapsed time *dt* since the last time that *tick()* was called. And then we make our **OnIdle** method look like the following.

```
BOOL CPopApp::OnIdle(LONG lCount)
{
    CWinApp::OnIdle(lCount); //Do the base class WinApp processing.
    double dt = _timer.tick();
    animateAllDocs(dt);
        //Step through all the docs and feed this timestep.
    return TRUE; //Keep doing it over and over.
}
```

We'll say more about the *cPerformanceTimer* class in the next subsection. For now, let's analyze the effect of using a 'real time' *dt*. Suppose that we have a simulation running on two machines, at 25 updates per second on the slower machine and at 50 updates per second on the faster machine. If each machine computes a *dt* as the elapsed time between updates and updates a critter's position as pos+ = dt * vel, we'll get the figures shown in Table 6.1.

Table 6.1 The effect of basing **dt** on the updates per second.

Updates per second	Time between updates	Action during 0.04 second
25	0.04	pos + = 0.4 * vel;
50	0.02	pos + = 0.2 * vel;
		pos + = 0.2 * vel;

Compare the net action during 0.04 second on the machines. If the velocity is constant, the net observed motion is the same. It is possible to imagine a simulation in which the value of vel might change between the first and second updates; this would simply mean that the simulation on the faster machine would be more accurate, which is no surprise. But letting *dt* be real time elapsed makes the best of things.

Since we measure the *dt* in seconds, this means that the speed is in units-per-second. Another way of looking at this is to realize that the speed is the magnitude of the *_velocity*, and the velocity is (*new_position* – *_position*)/*dt*, which clearly has a units/sec magnitude.

In the Pop Framework we often give our critters a default speed of something like 2.0. What does this speed mean? The meaning emerges when you look at the size of the window world you are moving in. If you specify that the world is, say, ten units across, a speed of 2.0 means that a critter takes about five seconds to move across the window.

No matter what kind of computer you're using, and no matter how many or how few critters are running, no matter how big or how small the window is, the time for a critter to cross the screen should always be the same.

Measuring a timestep

We implement the timing of *dt* with a *cPerformanceTimer* class. The basic way that a timer works is to use a private double _currenttime member, a private double getsystemtime() method and a public double tick() method. The tick() call gets the system time, computes *dt* as the difference between the system time and the _currenttime, resets the _currenttime to match the system time, and returns *dt*. This is shown in Figure 6.2.

(Seasoned Windows programmers will be familiar with a special Windows object called a 'timer' that is created with a **CWnd::SetTimer** call. These timers are something like coarse beepers that can be set to send a window an **OnTimer** message at regular intervals, so long as the intervals aren't very short – a hundredth of a

---

cPerformanceTimer

```
double _currenttime
double _dt;

CPerformanceTimer(){_currenttime = getsystemtime();}
double getsystemtime();
double tick()
{
    double systemtime = getsystemtime();
    _dt = systemtime - _currenttime;
    _currenttime = systemtime;
    return _dt;
}
```

Figure 6.2   A *cPerformanceTimer* class

second is for instance a shorter interval than a Windows timer can handle. Instead of being a coarse beeper, our *cPerformanceTimer* is a highly accurate clock. It has no relationship whatsoever to the standard Windows timers.)

The Pop Framework implements the *cPerformanceTimer*. On newer machines the *cPerformanceTimer* computes the system time by using a so-called 'high-resolution performance counter.' On the latest machines this counter seems to run at the same clock cycle as the machine, that is, if a machine's processor runs at 400 Mhz, the high-resolution performance counter measures of 400,000,000 ticks per second. And then we figure out a time interval in seconds by taking the number of elapsed ticks divided by the number of ticks per second. On slightly older machines, the high-resolution performance counter runs at about 1 Mhz, or one million ticks per second. So, the counter frequency is not necessarily the same as the chip Mhz.

On very old machines, the *cPerformanceTimer* code has to use the old **clock()** function, which runs at about 50 ticks per second. The multimedia **timeGetTime** function seems to be essentially the same function as *clock*, by the way.

A minor point. When you pause, for instance by opening a modal dialog, reading a help file, or letting your mainframe lose the focus, a lot of time will elapse before you go back to the OnIdle. Before restarting the process, call _timer.tick(), otherwise the next _timer.tick() will return a *dt* that's too large, as it's been running while you were out of the AppUpdate. A good place to put this extra update call is inside the *CPopView::SetFocus* method, because that gets called by at least one view whenever your program gets its focus back and starts back up. We do put upper and lower bounds on the *dt* values that our *cPerformanceTimer::tick* is allowed to return.

First let's talk about very high *dt* values. A machine may run a program dreadfully slowly, maybe only at five updates per second, taking something like 0.2 second per update. If the *dt* step size gets too big, the motion starts to look jerky. The objects move too far with each step, and you lose the illusion of continuous motion. The critters look like they're hopping about instead of smoothly sliding. We have a brute force correction for this. If the *dt* turns out to be larger than some maximum size of a _maxdt value of, let's say, 0.1 second, we'll just 'lie' to the program and have **tick()** return the _maxdt.

Now let's talk about very small *dt* values. With a really fast processor it's possible for *dt* to get so small that the machine begins to act weird, with odd jumps in the motion. This is because now the *dt* is so short that it's less than the refresh rate of your video card. If you ask your video card to refresh itself, say, 120 times per second and the card hardware is only refreshing itself at 60 Hz, then you're going to be asking for invisible and useless graphics updates – worse than useless, actually, as the refresh requests can pile up and cause an odd-looking glitch when the message queue tries to process several of them in a row.

To avoid choking up the graphics pipeline, we set a _*mindt*, and make the **tick()** process spin in a **while** loop until at least _*mindt* seconds have passed. To compute an appropriate _*minddt* we find the graphics refresh rate by making a call to the global Windows method ::GetDeviceCaps(hdc, VREFRESH), and then we take the reciprocal of the refresh rate. The code looks roughly like the following.

```
int refreshrate = ::GetDeviceCaps(hdc, VREFRESH);
_timer.setMinDt(1.0/double(refreshrate));
    //Don't run faster than the card.
```

More details of this code can be viewed in the Pop Framework **mainfrm.cpp** file.

It's useful for the designer (and eventually the user) to be able to see how fast the simulation is running. A good place to show this information is in the status bar that appears at the bottom of your View window. Rather than displaying the timestep *dt*, it's more useful to show the reciprocal *1.0/dt*. The quantity *dt* is the seconds per update, and *1.0/dt* is the updates per second. Because Windows is always doing little tasks in the background, the actual value of the *dt* is going to vary somewhat from cycle to cycle. To keep our updates per second from jumping around a lot, and being hard to read in the status bar, we actually compute this number as a rolling average of the last 60 *1.0/dt* values. This means that when you make a change to your program, it takes a few seconds for the updates per second value to settle down.

Improving the animation speed

The speed at which a program like Pop runs depends on two factors: the amount of computation and the graphics overhead of putting images on the screen. If you have a large number of critters with complex update methods the computation will dominate. Remember that when you have N objects, the number of pairs of objects is proportional to N^2. If you are checking for collisions among each pair of critters, or using forces which involve evaluating all the critter-to-critter distances, your computational overhead will go up as the square of the number of critters.

More often it is the graphics overhead that dominates. The exact costs of the graphics depend on the kind of *cGraphics* that your program uses, that is, *cGraphicsMFC* or *cGraphicsOpenGL*.

Whatever kind of graphics you use, there is one basic cost that we may as well call the *pixel overhead*. For every frame of the animation that you show, you are doing some sequence of actions in order to set the color of each visible pixel in your program's onscreen window. There are three factors that affect this pixel overhead.

> *pixel overhead ≅ area of rectangle * colors per pixel * bus overhead*

The area of the rectangle is the number of pixels you are moving. Keep in mind that area grows as the *square* of the edge dimension. A 1600×1200 rectangle has *four times* as many pixels as a 800×600 rectangle. This means that if you develop your program while looking at a display with a 800×600 resolution, but some of your users run at a 1600×1200 resolution, then a full-screen animation program on their machine will run about four times as slow!

So one thing we do to help our animation programs run well on more machines is to start the main window out at moderate size of 800×600 rather than a full-screen size, because we have no control over how big 'full-screen' might be. Exercise 6.4 shows how to control the window size.

Table 6.2   The number of different bits per pixel in different color modes.

Number of colors	Bits per pixel
256	8
32,768	15
65,536	16
16,777,216	24
True Color	24 or 32

The importance of the number of colors per pixel is a little less obvious. Right-click on your desktop and select **Properties**... to bring up the Display Properties dialog. Go to the Settings sheet. The **Color Palette** control group has a dropdown select box with the options for the total number of colors. Some common options are listed in Table 6.2.

Many users tend to set the number of colors to a maximal value, although for many applications 256 colors are enough. The 256 limit is not as bad as it sounds, because a window is able to pick which particular 256 colors it uses. But programming for 256 color mode is a hassle, so our preferred choice is one of the next two higher selections, 32,768 or 65,536 colors.

The number of colors being used affects the speed of the pixel overhead because the more bits per pixel that you have, the more information your graphics implementation needs to move around. But this is not something that we can very easily change from within our program, nor should we, as it would be very poor Windows etiquette for your app to do something that affects all of the other apps on display. This said, it's actually quite common for commercial computer games to do this. In order to squeeze the most out of a system, commercial games usually bail out from Windows to a full-screen, single-task mode and adjust the graphics settings at will. But, in order to make our code as generally applicable as possible, we don't take that route in *Software Engineering and Computer Games*.

If you are using OpenGL graphics, then you sometimes must use the 16 bits per pixel mode, or 65,536 colors, as some graphics cards only provide hardware OpenGL acceleration for the 16-bit color mode. You can tell if you have hardware acceleration in the Pop Framework by consulting the **Help | Your System's OpenGL Graphics Support** dialog.

While we are on the topic of the Display Properties dialog, you may also be able to set the refresh rate of your graphics card on this dialog. A typical default speed is 60 Hz or 75 Hz, where, once again, 'Hz' means 'Hertz,' or 'updates per second.' Set this update speed as high as your card will allow for the pixel resolution you've chosen. You really shouldn't use a display running at only 60 Hz, as it will tire out your eyes. These days 90 Hz or higher is not uncommon. Upping this value gives your animation program the possibility of running faster; as was mentioned earlier in this chapter, you can't animate faster than your card's refresh rate.

A final thing to think about when you look at the Display Properties dialog is your pixel resolution. If your resolution is something like 1600×1400 and you try and run your game in a maximized window, the game is going to run slow, simply because of the enormous number of pixels in the window. If you want to run your game at a reasonable speed in a full-screen window, you need to reduce the pixel resolution. Alternately you can keep a high pixel resolution, but be aware that you shouldn't make your game window so large as to slow the update speed down too much.

We called the third pixel overhead factor 'bus overhead.' This is the time cost of moving the pixel information from one memory location to another. The reason we speak of 'moving the pixel information' is because normally one builds up a graphics image in some temporarily invisible offscreen memory location called a 'memory buffer', and then, when it's all ready, you move the image into a location called the 'frame buffer,' which is the information that the graphics card uses for painting the current image onscreen.

The bus overhead factor is very much dependent on the kind of graphics card you have, and whether you are running 2D MFC graphics or 3D OpenGL graphics. In the worst case, your graphics image is being stored in your system RAM and then being transferred to the frame buffer on the graphics card for each update. In a better kind of scenario, the memory image is on the graphics card 'near' the frame buffer. In the best possible situation, we don't actually have to move the memory image to the frame buffer; instead we use a trick called *page-flipping* to simply change the address that the graphic card uses as the location of the frame buffer.

In the past, graphics cards could only support page-flipping for an entire screen's worth of display. As mentioned above, you'll notice that most commercial computer game products do not in fact run in a windowed mode. They take over your whole screen. This is because (a) they want to use page-flipping for fast animation, sometimes (b) they want to set your screen resolution and colors per pixel down to lower values so that there's less pixels to have to set per image, and sometimes (c) they've written their code using brute pixel-count numbers and the code is not resolution-independent.

Perhaps wrong-headedly, we insist on having all our programs run inside windows on your desktop – it seems more modern and user-friendly, and it makes our code more usable for other kinds of applications. As it happens, OpenGL graphics will in fact page-flip for windowed apps. But in MFC graphics we have to move a screen-sized block of pixels for each update, using the **CDC::BitBlt** method. But this method is so fast on modern graphics cards that our animations can in fact run as fast as we want. For many years, you couldn't write such a computer game with the normal Windows API, but those days are truly over.

We haven't said anything yet about the graphics costs besides the pixel overhead. Generally bitmaps are more expensive to draw than are triangles and geometric objects. In OpenGL graphics a number of more specialized considerations arise. Smoothing objects costs computation, textures are expensive, lighting has its costs, and so on. We'll say more about these details in Chapter 26: OpenGL Graphics.

6.3 The animation cascade

This section discusses how the *CPopApp:animateAllDocs(dt)* cascades its calls down to the simulation objects of each open document.

Sequence diagram of the animation

In this subsection we'll give a description of the animation process and then we'll draw a UML sequence diagram of it.

First let's write out in words a description of how the animation process works.

- The *CPopApp::OnIdle* function makes a call to the *CPopApp:animateAllDocs(dt)*.
- The *cPerformanceTimer tick()* method returns the time *dt* elapsed since the prior update.
- *CPopApp:animateAllDocs(dt)* steps through the list of open *CPopDoc* documents and for each of these documents calls a *CPopDoc::stepDoc(dt)* function.
- Firstly, *CPopDoc::stepDoc(dt)* calls the *cGame::step(dt)* method for the game inside the *CPopDoc*.
- *cGame::step(dt)* updates the positions and appearances of an array of critters stored inside the game.
- Secondly, *CPopDoc::stepDoc* calls *CPopDoc::UpdateAllViews*.
- This sends down a *CPopView::OnUpdate* to each of the document's views, and each view generates a call to *CPopView::OnDraw*.
- The *OnDraw* methods use the *cGraphics *_pgraphics* member of the *CPopView* to draw an image of the game and to display it in the onscreen view window.
- Any remaining messages in the Windows message queue are processed.
- *CPopApp::OnIdle* is called again.

Let's draw a sequence diagram (Figure 6.3) showing some of these steps. As we mentioned in Chapter 5: Software Patterns, UML sequence diagrams are used to show how objects interact over time. The diagram is set up as a series of columns, with one column for each object. Each column has a vertical lifeline showing lifetime of the object. Arrows are drawn from lifeline to lifeline to symbolize the passing of messages via method calls. Use a dotted-line arrow if the caller isn't shown. We label a message with the name of a method being called, and this method is expected to be a member method of the class column that the message points to. A call that an object makes to itself is drawn as an arrow that starts and ends on the object's own lifeline.

We can draw activation boxes to symbolize the time during which a given method is active, although if it gets to be too messy we can leave out the activation boxes. These boxes are sometimes called 'candlesticks', because they're long and thin.

A sequence diagram is supposed to show the behavior of objects. Although there is a *class name* at the top of each lifeline, the line really refers to a particular *instance* of the class in question.

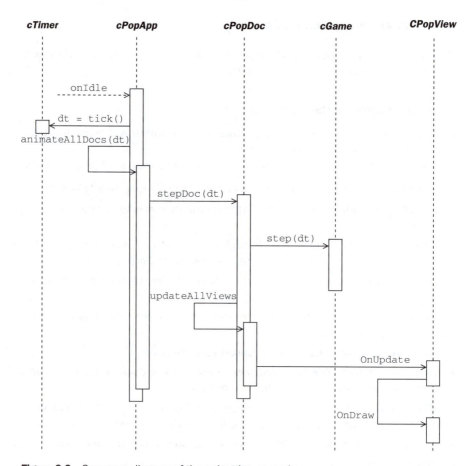

Figure 6.3   Sequence diagram of the animation cascade

Our sequence diagram leaves out details relating to the innards of *cGame::step* and *CPopView::OnDraw*.

One minor point about the diagram. Why does *OnDraw* appear down after the end of the *animateAllDocs* candlestick? This has to do with the way the Windows architecture works. When you want to redraw a view, as in the *OnUpdate* method, you place a message onto the Windows message queue that tells Windows to redraw the view whenever it's done doing whatever it's currently involved in. Thus Windows doesn't get around to executing the requested *OnDraw* until *animateAllDocs* is over.

The *stepDoc* method

The purpose of the *animateAllDocs(dt)* code is to find all the open documents and call their *stepDoc(dt)* methods. For details about how this works, you can look at Chapter 23: Programming Windows with MFC in Part II of this book.

The **stepDoc(dt)** method does two things: it tells the active game to update the critters, and it tells the views to draw a fresh image of the critters. Remember that in the Document-View architecture we separate out the values of the data from the view of the data. The document is a kind of bridge between the numbers being computed and the images used to represent them. In a nutshell, the **CPopDoc::stepDoc** looks like this.

```
void CPopDoc::stepDoc(Real dt)
{
    _pgame->step(dt); /* Move the critters and maybe add or
        delete some. */
    cTimeHint timehint(dt); /* Wrap dt up so we can pass it to the
        views. */
    UpdateAllViews(NULL, 0, &timehint); /* Redraw all the views and
        possibly move the views' _pcritterviewer according to the dt
        inside timehint. */
}
```

We'll discuss the details of **cGame::step(dt)** in Chapter 10: Games. And we'll talk about **UpdateAllViews** in the next section.

6.4   Updating the views

The **UpdateAllViews(CView* pSender, int lHint, CObject* pHint)** method generates calls to the **CPopView::OnUpdate(CView* pSender, int lHint, CObject* pHint)** method for each open view, passing on the same arguments.

A minimal version of the **OnUpdate** method could look like this.

```
void CPopView::OnUpdate(CView* pSender, LPARAM lHint, CObject* pHint)
{
    Invalidate(); /* Enqueue a message asking Windows to call OnDraw
        for this view. */
}
```

Invalidate produces a call to **OnDraw**, which is where the critters get drawn to the active window.

But what about the three arguments to **UpdateAllViews** and **OnUpdate**? It's possible for a view to initiate a call to **UpdateAllViews** with a line like this: GetDocument()->UpdateAllViews. This trick provides a path by which one view can contact the others. In some programs this mechanism is heavily used, and in programs like this you may want the other views to know which view initiated the **UpdateAllViews** call. This is what the psender argument is for. In the Pop Framework we don't make any use of the psender.

The second argument to the **OnUpdate** method is an *integer hint* field which lets the document feed in an integer to tell the view that some special action is called for here. In the normal run of things we just want *OnUpdate* to call **Invalidate** so the view will draw itself to the screen, but if you're in the process of starting up a new game you might need to do something additional, and in this case you'd have the call put in a hint integer to remind you. In the Pop Framework, the lHint will usually be 0, but in the case where we're starting up a new game, for instance, we use the PopDoc::VIEWHINT_STARTGAME hint value of 2.

Although *stepDoc* never produces an *UpdateAllViews* call with an lHint other than 0, there are other spots in the program where *UpdateAllViews* can be called. For instance the CPopDoc::setGameClass(..) method has a call to UpdateAllViews(NULL, CPopDoc::VIEWHINT_STARTGAME, 0).

The third argument to the *OnUpdate* method is a *pointer hint*, that is, it's a pointer to whatever kind of structure of additional information you want to pass to the view. In the Pop Framework, we pass the *Real dt* on to the view so that the view can appropriately move a viewer object that it owns, but we have to wrap it up inside a *cTimeHint* object with a single *Real* field so we can pass it.

Here are the steps taken by the *CPopView::OnUpdate(CView* pSender, int lHint, CObject* pHint)*.

- If lHint is CPopDoc::VIEWHINT_LOADINGARCHIVE, you're saving or loading a game, and you've placed a pointer to a *CArchive* file object inside the pHint field. Get the active *CArchive* from pHint and read or write the view parameters from or into the archive.

- If lHint is CPopDoc::VIEWHINT_STARTGAME, you're initializing a new game. In this case, use the *CGame* methods *initializeView* and *initializeCritterViewer* to prepare this view, and then return.

- If the lHint is the default value 0, we get the *dt* timestep out of the pHint.

- Use the *dt* to move and update the pviewpointcritter by the timestep *dt*.

- If this view is the active view, update the status bar, and pass any mouse or keyboard actions to the pviewpointcritter.

- Invalidate the view to force a call to *OnDraw*.

For further information, the commented source code for *CPopView::OnUpdate* can be consulted in **popview.cpp**.

The *OnDraw* method carries out these steps.

- Wake up the graphics.

- 'Garbage collect' any unused image resources.

- Graphically show the status of the game by adjusting the color of the window margins around the game.

- Clear the graphics background.

- Install the projection and view matrices.

- Draw the world, by default as a background and a foreground rectangle.

- Draw the critters.

- Send the graphics to your video display by a **BitBlt** or a page-flip.

More information about the action of *CPopView::OnDraw* can be found in Chapter 24: Two- and Three-Dimensional Graphics, or by looking at the source code for this method in **popview.cpp**.

Review questions

A   When is the **OnIdle** method called? Which class is it a method of?

B   How do we calculate the timestep *dt* between updates of our game?

C   How does a critter use *dt* and its velocity to get its new position?

D   What is the gain of having the *dt* we give our moving critters match the actual time between updates?

E   What are some factors that influence the frame rate of your animation?

F   How does the application pass the *dt* down to the individual critters in a game? Mention all the intervening classes.

G   How does the *stepDoc(dt)* call both update the critter positions and draw them on the screen? Draw a sequence diagram.

H   What is the relationship among *CDocument::UpdateAllViews*, *CView::OnUpdate*, *CView::Invalidate*, and *CView::OnDraw*? Draw a sequence diagram.

Exercises

Exercise 6.1: Timing the critter motions

	Min speed (units/sec)	Max speed (units/sec)	Avg speed (units/sec)	Approx. seconds to move ten units
Spacewar	0.5	3.0	1.75	About six
Defender3D	0.5	10.0	4.75	About two

Get a watch with a second hand, start up **Game | Defender3D**, and time how long it takes a critter to move across the screen. Is it about two seconds? Now make the window very small, and time again. Now make the window big, add more critters by selecting **Game | Large**, and time again. Do you still get about the same speeds? Now try with Spacewar. Time the critter motions again. Try editing the cGameDesign::CRITTERMAXSPEED value in **gamedesign.cpp** and try that game again.

Exercise 6.2: Estimating sizes

When you try and estimate the **BitBlt** overhead and its effect on a program's speed, it's nice to be able to carry out the calculations in your head or with a paper and pencil. Some key facts to remember are the following:

$2^{10} = 1$ K $\approx$ one thousand
$2^{20} = 1$ Meg $\approx$ one million
$2^{30} = 1$ Gig $\approx$ one billion
$2^{40} = 1$ Ter $\approx$ one trillion
$2^{50} = 1$ Pet $\approx$ one quadrillion
$2^{60} = 1$ Ex $\approx$ one quintillion

How do we use this knowledge? Suppose you want to estimate the number of bytes in an 800×600 pixel screen image in 16-bit color mode (64K colors per pixel)? $800 \times 600 \times 2$ is $480,000 \times 2$, which is about $1,000,000$, which is a Meg.

You can use the information another way around as well. If you see a number close to $32,000$, then you can think this is $2^5 * 1K$, which is $2^5 * 2^{10}$, or 2^{15}. So a mode in which you have about $32,000$ colors is a mode in which you use 15 bits per pixel.

How many bytes are used by an 800×600 display if you use the 'true color mode' of 24 bits per pixel? Give your answer in K or Meg.

How many bits per pixel are used if you are in what Windows calls $16,777,216$ color mode?

How many pixels are in a display of size 1024×768? or 869×1152? How many pixels in a 1024×1280 display? How many bytes are needed for each of these images if you are allowing $65,536$ colors per pixel? Give your answers in K, Meg or Gig.

Exercise 6.3: How to maximize the main frame

If you like, you can make your game program start out as a maximized window. As we mentioned above, this is actually unwise, because if someone is running their video card in a very high-resolution mode, then your runspeed is going to be unacceptably slow. But here's how to do it anyway. Try it out and see if it works.

Find the `BOOL CPopApp::InitInstance()` code in **Pop.cpp**, and comment in the first of the two code lines and comment out the second. Run the program. Note that now the window is maximized. But you can still bring it back to a default size by clicking the Restore icon box in the upper right corner of the frame.

```
//pMainFrame->ShowWindow(SW_SHOWMAXIMIZED | m_nCmdShow);
    //Use this version if you want main window maximized.
pMainFrame->ShowWindow(m_nCmdShow);
    //Use this version if you don't want main window maximized.
```

Exercise 6.4: How to set the main frame to a specific size

Here let's look at the spot where our default main window size is set. The numbers are set using some statics.

```
BOOL CMainFrame::PreCreateWindow(CREATESTRUCT& cs)
{
    if( !CMDIFrameWnd::PreCreateWindow(cs) )
        return FALSE;
    // TODO: Modify the Window class or styles here by modifying
    // the CREATESTRUCT cs
    cs.cx = CPopApp::STARTPIXELWIDTH; //800;
    cs.cy = CPopApp::STARTPIXELHEIGHT; //600;
    return TRUE;
}
```

Try changing the statics to 640 and 480, respectively.

Exercise 6.5: Why OnIdle returns TRUE for animation

Go into the *CPopApp::OnIdle* code and change the last line from `return TRUE;` to `return FALSE;`. Build and run the program. At first nothing moves, but then move the mouse around on the screen and look what happens. You're moving the whole world yourself! Each time the program processes some messages it calls **OnIdle** and generates a single call to `animateAllDocs(dt)`. As long as you keep moving the mouse, the motion proceeds smoothly. To make the program update continuously on its own, you can add a call to *OnIdlp* that "fakes" a key press: `PostMessageC::AfxgetMainWnd()->L getSafeHwnd(), WM_CHAR, ∅, ∅);`

Exercise 6.6: Why we clear the background for animation

Go into the *CPopView::OnDraw* code in **PopView.cpp** and comment out the line `_pgraphics ->clear(targetrect)`; This line erases the game area plus the rest of the game window at each update. Also comment out the `pDoc->pgame()->drawWorld(_pgraphics, _drawflags);`. This line fills the game area with the background color at each update. With these two lines out, your old sprites don't get erased. Run the program and look at the trails. Kind of nice at first, but after a while the screen gets too messy. If we *did* want to have critter trails a better way to do it would probably be to develop a *cSpriteTrail* class that inherited from *cSprite*, but which held an array of, say, a critter's most recent ten or twenty sprites, and then erased them.

Simulating physics 7

The physical world is the great teacher. A computer scientist is inclined to think of physics as the one supreme computation that has been running for billions of years. One can partially characterize the laws of physics as being (a) parallel, (b) homogeneous, and (c) local.

Regarding *parallelism*, the idea is that the world's computation isn't localized in some hidden controller chip, the computation is taking place everywhere at once. If you toss a rock into a pool of water, you see the ripples spread out in every direction. Each bit of water is computing the appropriate motion, and these computations add up to what we see as waves.

Homogeneity means that the same natural laws apply to all the objects in the system at every place and at every time. When objects seem to behave differently, these differences can be traced to special properties of the objects rather than to disturbances in the uniformity of physical law.

Locality expresses the notion that the state of an object or a region of the world will be updated solely on the basis of the immediately adjacent regions of the world. (What about gravity, like the pull of the Earth on the Moon? Isn't that action at a distance? Doesn't have to be. According to Einstein's General Theory of Relativity, Earth's mass warps the fabric of space-time, the warping propagates outward like a sag in a sheet, and the Moon moves in accord with the curvature of spacetime in its immediate neighborhood.) When we carry out the special types of physical simulations known as cellular automata or finite difference methods, we do implement locality. But in the case of the Pop Framework, we won't insist on locality. We'll feel free to have old-style 'actions at a distance' under which an object is attracted or repelled by an object that's nowhere near it.

In this chapter we'll focus first on implementing parallelism, and then on homogeneously applying Newton's laws of motion. That is, we allow a critter to access the positions and velocities of other critters, as if it could "see" them. Strictly speaking vision is local, by way of particle-photon interactions – but we won't simulate down to this low a level.

7.1   Parallelism

The most obvious way to implement parallelism would be to have a dedicated processor for each simulation object, and to have an operating system that keeps all these processors running in lockstep synchronization with each other.

At this stage in the history of computer science, of course, our computers are serial. At best you might have four processors running on your desktop machine. We simulate parallelism by keeping a master array of our 'physics objects' and trying to arrange our program so that the updates of the objects happen in a parallel fashion.

But why use an array? Why not give each object a concurrent execution thread, and let the threads execute in parallel? The fact is, by default, threads aren't really parallel. There's no way for them to get around the fundamental fact that your machine's computations are being carried out by, normally, a single processor that works its way down a long one-dimensional column of machine-code instructions, now and then jumping up and down the column, but never carrying out more than one instruction at once. The operating system gives first one thread a little execution time, then another, then another, with the actual scheduling being something that's fairly fluid and hard to control.

Indeed, if you give each of your objects its own thread, you'll find that the activities of the threads are far from parallel. One thread may get, say, two hundredths of a second in which to execute, the next thread may get three hundredths of a second, a third may get one hundredth of a second, and so on.

For certain kinds of simulations this disorder doesn't matter. But if you want your simulation to be as close to a parallel physical process as possible, you'll have more success if you keep the simulation objects in a single array and maintain a strict, logical control over the order in which the objects execute their individual simulation steps.

When we simulate physics objects, we an regard our objects as having two main simulation-related methods: (a) an *update()* method in which they look at all the objects around them, detecting forces, collisions, etc. and (b) a *move(dt)* method in which they change their positions. The *dt* argument is the current timestep that has been passed down from the application as described in Chapter 6: Animation.

A little more generally, if we think of our physics objects as active critters, we might say that (a) the *update* method incorporates looking, thinking, feeling, deciding and any other kind of individual behavior, while (b) the *move* method incorporates Newton's laws of motion.

In the Pop Framework, the programmer overrides the *update* method to individualize the critters. And the *move* method is a non-virtual method which we don't intend to override.

If we have a collection of objects numbered, say, from 0 to COUNT-1, there are various ways that we might systematically make an update and a move method call for each object.

On the one hand, we could do something like the following. This is an approach that we would consider wrong.

```
update 0
move 0
update 1
move 1
. . .
update COUNT-1
move COUNT-1
```

The problem with the approach just described is that, although object 0 sees the old position of object 1, object 1 will only see the new, moved position of object 0. Instead we could do something more parallel, something like this.

```
update 0
update 1
. . .
update COUNT-1

move 0
move 1
. . .
move COUNT-1
```

In this second approach, all of the objects look at and react to each other in the initial position. All the updates happen before anything moves. They don't actually carry out their motions until they've all had a look and decided what to do. This is a more parallel approach to the simulation.

To make these ideas clear, consider the following situation. Critter #0 is chasing critter #1. Critter #0's goal is to touch critter #1 as often as possible, critter #1's goal is to run away from critter #0. In Figure 7.1, we show the effects

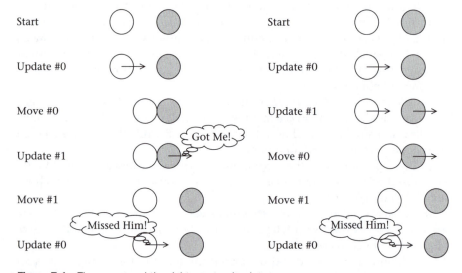

Figure 7.1 The wrong and the right way to simulate

of the two different ways of grouping the various update and move calls. In the figure, we draw an arrow to indicate the current 'intention' of a critter regarding its next move step, and we erase the arrow once the intended move has been carried out.

At the bottom of the left-hand column of events drawn in Figure 7.1, critter #0 does not think it has tagged critter #1, and critter #1 feels it's been tagged once. At the bottom of the right-hand column, critter #0 feels it hasn't tagged critter #1, and critter #1 feels it hasn't been tagged. The right-hand column shows a parallel simulation, the simulation in the left-hand column is not parallel. In thinking this over, remember that

> the critters only access the other critters' positions during their own update calls.

In terms of code, to say that we want to have a parallel simulation means that we don't want to have a runcycle like this:

```
for (i=0; i<COUNT; i++)
{
    physicsobject[i].update();
    physicsobject[i].move(dt);
}
```

Instead we want to do something more like this:

```
for (i=0; i<COUNT; i++)
    physicsobject[i].update();
for (i=0; i<COUNT; i++)
    physicsobject[i].move(dt);
```

Again, what's wrong with the first approach is that here the physicsobject[0] would already be at its new position before physicsobject[1] looks at it. So the behavior of the simulation would depend heavily on the order in which the physicsobject members happen to be listed in the array. We want to try and design our simulation so that the behavior is independent of the order in which the objects happen to be listed.

Now why exactly do we speak of this kind of simulation as 'parallel'? The idea is that we are emulating parallelism by repeatedly freezing and thawing the flow of simulated time. We freeze the flow of simulated time while our processor takes the time to let each critter look at the others and decide what to next. Then we thaw the simulated time and give a *dt* tick to each of the critters to move with. Then we freeze time again and let the critters evaluate the new state of affairs. And so on.

7.2 The laws of motion

As well as being parallel, physics is homogeneous. We implement the principle of homogeneity by making sure to derive all of our classes from a base class that has the necessary laws built into it. We give the base class a **move(dt)** method that encapsulates the laws of motion. And we ensure homogeneity by making **move(dt)** non-virtual so that the child classes can't override it.

What are the laws of physical motion that we need to use? Ordinarily we discuss motion in terms of a scalar *mass* quantity and four vector quantities: *position*, *velocity*, *acceleration*, and *force*. (Keep in mind that when we say, for instance, that *velocity* is a *vector*, we mean that *velocity* is a scalar *speed* times a unit *direction* vector.) The laws relating these are quite simple, where the **d/dt** operator is the derivative operator.

force = mass × acceleration
acceleration = d/dt velocity
velocity = d/dt position

If we suppose we are working in two or in three dimensions, then each line is really two or three scalar equations – for in a vector equation the corresponding components must match.

In our simulations, we want to think of the force as the given, and the position as the thing that we figure out. So we actually want to turn all of these equations around. It's clear how to turn the first equation around, but how do we 'turn around' an equation of the form *rate = d/dt quantity*? We do it in the following way.

rate = d/dt quantity
∴ *rate = dquantity / dt*

Taking a derivative is the same as evaluating the ratio of differentials.

dt × rate = dquantity

We can think of the differential *dt* as a normal number.

dt × rate = newquantity – oldquantity

The *dquantity* is the change in *quantity* from its old to its new value.

newquantity = oldquantity + dt × rate

We get this by moving the terms of the equation. Now drop the *new* and *old* to write a line that looks like computer code.

quantity = quantity + dt × rate

Think of the left side as the new value and right side as old value.

Now we can 'turn around' our three motion equations and come up with this.

(1)   *acceleration = force/mass*
(2)   *velocity = velocity + dt × acceleration*
(3)   *position = position + dt × velocity*

These are the equations we're going to use for the simulation of physics that we'll use in our Pop Framework. What characterizes this set of equations is that if you specify an object's *mass*, a *force* that acts on the object, a timestep *dt*, and an initial *position, velocity* and *acceleration*, equations (1), (2), and (3) will generate fresh values for *position, velocity* and *acceleration*.

In discussing simulations, by the way, it's a common practice to blur the line between the infinitesimal *dt* of a mathematical derivative and a *dt* that is instead thought of as very small real-number change. The fascinating subject of numerical analysis goes into the details of exactly when and how this can be done in a reasonable way so as to yield stable and accurate simulation equations. Suffice to say that what we're doing here is reasonably Kosher. [More precisely, we're doing 'Euler integration' of the motion path; for greater accuracy one can do 'Runge-Kutte integration' of the motion path. A good algorithm for Runge-Kutte can be found in the classic work *Numerical Recipes in C*, by W. Press, S. Teukolsky, W. Vetterling and B. Flamery (Cambridge University Press, 1992). *Numerical Recipes in C* can also be accessed for free online at www.nr.com]

Regarding the critters in the Pop Framework, let's mention how we compute their mass. The critters have a **Real** **_mass** field as well as a **_density**, and a **_radius**. The critter's internal mutators and accessor ensure that **_mass** is always the **_density** times the cube of the **_radius**. Making mass proportional to size gives behaviors that look more 'physical,' or realistic. The default **_density** is simply 1.0, but if we want a critter to be more resistant to the action of forces we set its density to a higher value. You can read more about this point in Chapter 8: Critters.

Both physics and computers like to do the same thing over and over. Physics works by continually reapplying the laws of motion to every object in the world. Our simulation will work by applying our three equations over and over.

We can state this a bit differently. It's common these days to speak of physics as a *dynamical system*. A dynamical system has some *state* and a *transform* operator that maps each state to a new state. In the case of motion, the *state* might be a triple consisting of

<acceleration, velocity, position>

and the *transform* would be specified by giving a mass and a force and three equations above. When we investigate (or play with!) a dynamical system we like to drop 'test particles' into it and watch what happens to them. This means that we specify a starting *state_0* and watch how it evolves under successive applications of the transform operator. That is, we look at sequences like this.

state_0
state_1 = transform(state_0)
state_2 = transform(state_1)
. . .
state_n+1 = transform(state_n)
. . .

That's essentially what we're doing when we run instances of the Pop program and repeatedly apply the **cGame::step**, which first calls an update loop and then a move loop. The **step** method as a whole is our *transform*.

Regarding our three equations for *position*, *velocity*, and *acceleration*, how do we divide these up between the 'update' and the 'move' phases? Changing the acceleration is more of an update thing because we are going to take into account the possibility of changes to an object's motion due to object–object collisions, possible forces among objects (including flight and pursuit), and possible user input. So we put the first equation into an **update** method and put the second two into a **move** method.

So we might imagine our physics objects as having methods like this.

```
update()
{
    acceleration = force/mass;
    /* Possibly make additional changes to acceleration and/or
        velocity due to collisions,
    object-to-object forces, or user input. */
}

move(dt)
{
    velocity = velocity + dt * acceleration;
    position = position + dt * velocity;
}
```

Our **cCritter::update** will use a **dt** argument in case the critter needs to do something to itself relating to the timestep; an example might be changing its size, as in a balloon leaking air. We feed a CPopView *pview into the **update** so that the critter can possibly 'sniff' at the graphical world of the **CPopView** to find out the pixel colors of some locations, perhaps reversing its velocity direction when approaching certain colors. In the examples given in this book, neither the dt nor the pview arguments are used by our critter **update** methods. But you will need to use these arguments for some of the exercises.

We'll say more about exactly how we represent our forces in the rest of this chapter.

7.3   Force and acceleration

We handle the question of the forces acting on our critters by using the Strategy pattern. That is, we let our critters be composed with `cForce *_pforce` objects, and we let a critter feel forces by calling `_pforce->force(this)`.

If we hadn't used the Strategy pattern, we might instead have given the **cCritter** class a virtual **cVector force()** method which would give the force acting on the critter at any location and time. But, we want to able to change the kinds of forces that act on a critter without having to derive a whole new child class for each combination of forces. For to derive off critter child classes for the different kinds of forces would lead to a combinatorial explosion of more and more kinds of critter child classes.

We want to allow for force fields such as gravity, friction, a whirlpool, etc. Rather than specifically defining gravity-influenced critters, whirlpool-influenced critters, friction-influenced critters, and so on, we take the notion of a force, and split it off into a separate class called **cForce**.

The main method of **cForce** is a **cVector force(cCritter *pcritter)**. The **cForce::force** method returns a vector that we think of as the force acting on the `pcritter`. Instead calling a **cCritter::force()** method, we'll have the critter call **_pforce->force(this)**.

Let's review from our discussions of composition and of the Strategy pattern the question of why we need the **this** argument. When we use a Strategy pattern, we usually want the delegated strategy function to have access to the calling critter. That is, in order to figure out the force acting on a critter, we may need to know where the critter is located, what its velocity is, etc. And it may also be that we want to have an 'impulsive' force that directly changes the critter's velocity. By passing **this** into the method call, we give the **cForce** object the ability to access the members of the calling critter by using the **cCritter** accessors and then mutate the calling critter with its mutators.

As it turns out, each of our **cCritter** objects has a **CTypedPtrArray<CObArray, cForce*> _forcearray**. This is an variant of the Strategy pattern; rather than strategizing out a single **force()** method we strategize out an arbitrarily sized array of such methods.

The basic **cCritter update** method feels the forces affecting the critter, and changes the acceleration of the critter accordingly.

```
void cCritter::update()
{
    feelforce();
}
```

The default **feelforce** method applies Newton's Law

*force = mass * acceleration*

or

acceleration = force/mass

That is, *feelforce* (a) sums up the vector forces acting on the critter, (b) divides the vector sum by the critter's mass, and (c) sets the critter's acceleration to this value. In code, these steps look as follows.

```
void cCritter::feelforce()
{
    cVector forcesum; /* Default cVector constructor sets this
        to (0,0) */
    for (int i=0; i<_forcearray.GetSize(); i++)
        forcesum += _forcearray.GetAt(i)->force(this);
    _acceleration = forcesum/mass(); /* From Newton's Law:
        Force = Mass * Acceleration. */
}
```

We make *cCritter::feelforce* virtual because in some situations you might not want to simply sum up the forces. This could happen if some of the forces were what the computer scientist Craig Reynolds calls 'steering forces' [Steering behaviors for antonomous characters', (www.red3d.com/cwr/steer/gdc99]. Suppose, for instance, that you had a steering force f1 that avoids bumping into obstacles and a steering force f2 that runs away from bullets. If you simply add the forces f1 and f2 it might sometimes happen that they cancel each other out and you end up hitting an obstacle and being hit by a bullet. A more sophisticated *feelforce* might prioritize your steering forces. Another possibility that might be used, if you are using several computationally expensive forces, is to 'dither' between them by doing first one force and then the other on alternating updates.

There's one other way that we change our critter's velocities and accelerations: via mouse and keyboard controls. Making another use of the Strategy pattern, we give each critter a *cListener* _plistener* object. *cListener* has a *listen(cCritter *pcritter)* method, and the *cCritter feellistener()* method calls *_plistener->listen*.

The Pop Framework provides several different kinds of built-in listener options, and some of them, such as the *cListenerCar* and *cListenerSpaceship*, act by adding in a vector value to the _acceleration of the calling `pcritter`. Other listeners, such as the *cListenerScooter*, act by directly changing the critter's velocity. You'll find more about listeners in Chapter 12: Listeners.

7.4   Implementing forces

The base class *cForce::force* returns a zero vector, but we have 'global' force classes *cForceGravity*, *cForceDrag*, and *cForceVortex* which return non-trivial values. We use them in the Ballworld and Dambuilder games, discussed in Chapter 18: Interesting Worlds. We also have 'relative' steering force classes liked *cForceObjectSeek*, *cForceClassEvade*, and *cForceEvadeBullet*.

Figure 7.2 is a class diagram of all the forces we provide with the Pop Framework.

The idea is that each *force(cCritter*)* method should return a force that the critter will divide by its mass and add into its acceleration. The magnitude of

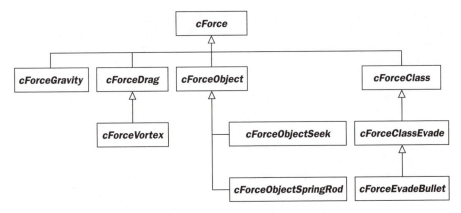

Figure 7.2 Class diagram of the *cForce* child classes

the force will depend on the critter's current situation in the world and on a
Real _intensity field that *cForce* has.

Gravity is proportional to mass – much as electrostatic attraction is proportional
to electric charge – and, again from Newton, we know that the gravitational
force (*F*) between two objects is a gravitational constant (*G*) times the product
of their masses (*m*1 and *m*2) divided by the square of the distances between
them (D²), to give a force like

$$F = G \times m_1 \times m_2/D^2$$

For simple simulations, we like to use a much simpler approximation to
gravitational force. It's characteristic of games to choose liveliness and speed of
execution over a 100% accurate emulation. For a small object near the surface of
the Earth, the distance to the Earth's center is so large that the object's motions
don't effectively change this distance. In a situation like this, we can lump
together the gravitational constant, the Earth's mass, the inverse square of the
distance to the Earth into a new constant (*g*), and then an object of mass (*m*)
will experience a gravitational force (*F*) of size

$$F = g \times m$$

It's useful to have the freedom to specify the direction of a 'global' gravity
like this, so we'll give our *cForceGravity* class a *_pulldirection* as well as its *_intensity*
constant.

```
cVector cForceGravity::force(cCritter *pcritter)
{
    return _intensity * pcritter->mass() * _pulldirection;
}
```

Remember that the *cCritter* maintains its mass as a quantity proportional to its
density times the cube of the critter's radius.

For simulating something like a solar system, we'd want to implement a more sophisticated kind of object-to-object gravity – this is left for Exercise 7.5.

We think of drag as being a force like friction. The effect of friction is to slow something to a stop. Normally friction increases with an object's speed, and acts in a direction opposite to the object's motion. Friction is also proportional to an object's area: think of a sliding puck or of an airship moving through the atmosphere pushed by the wind. More area means more drag.

To make our drag force more general, we allow for the possibility that it is a drag relative to some moving fluid. Either we think of objects sliding on a moving surface such as a conveyer belt, or we think of floating objects under the influence of air or water currents. We use a _**windvector** field to specify the speed and direction of the medium's motion. The effect of drag in a moving medium is to match the object's velocity to the velocity of the medium. If the _**windvector** is the zero vector, then our generalized drag force is the same as friction. The idea is to continually return a force that will act to accelerate the critter in such a way as to minimize the difference between the critter's velocity and the _**windvector**.

```
cVector cForceDrag::force(cCritter *pcritter)
{
    Real area = pcritter->radius()*pcritter->radius();
    return cVector(area * _intensity * (_windvector -
        pcritter->velocity())));
}
```

One caveat regarding *cForceDrag*. If you set the _**intensity** to a large value, there is a danger of overshooting the _**windvector** and oscillating back and forth. In terms of a simple frictional drag force with zero _**windvector**, if you define an overly large _**intensity** constant, then your simulated physics will cause a moving object to jerk backwards due to its counteracting friction force, and then, once it's going backwards, the drag will make the object jerk forwards again, and so on. Generally it's a good idea to keep the intensity of a *cForceDrag* between 0.0 and 1.0. (Do remember, however, that, in general, if you find some anomalous tweak of your values that enhances your game, go ahead and use the values even if they're not physically realistic.)

It might be fun to have some whirlpools, so we allow for a child of *cForceDrag* in which the windvector varies from point to point. We call our new force *cForceVortex*, and we set it up as shown in Figure 7.3. We specify a center of the vortex and, thinking of the eye of a hurricane, we call it _eyeposition. And we give a _spiralangle to determine which way the vortex is moving things: inward, outwards, or in a circular fashion.

The idea is that the drag force at a critter position is computed as follows: (a) take the vector that runs from the _**eyeposition** to the critter position; (b) imagine placing this vector with its tail at the critter position: and (c) rotate this vector couterclockwise by _**spiralangle** degrees. The further a critter gets from the eye position, the more powerful is the vortex force. Remember that in C++ angles are measured in radians, so we normally think of the angle as some

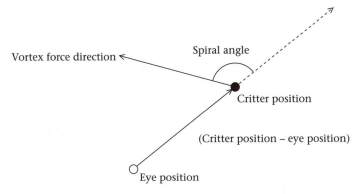

Figure 7.3 Vortex force

multiple of PI. (By the way, we #**define** PI in **realnumber.h**.) So if you want a circular motion, you set _spiralangle equal to PI/2.0. The *cForceVortex force* method gets implemented like this.

```
cVector cForceVortex::force(cCritter *pcritter)
{
    _windvector = (pcritter->position() - _eyeposition);
    _windvector.turn(_spiralangle);
    return cForceDrag::force(pcritter);
}
```

The next forces we look at are what might be called 'relative' forces as opposed to 'global' forces. Relative forces involve a critter's reaction to some other critter. We provide for two kinds of relative forces. In the *cForceObject*, we react to some one specific other critter that we're watching. The baseclass *cForceObject* holds a cCritter *_pnode reference field to a certain critter and its force(pcritter) method considers the pcritter situation relative to _pnode.

There are a variety of *cForceObject* forces like this that we might implement. Spring forces and relative gravitational forces come to mind. The Pop Framework provides a *cForceObjectSpringRod*, which is a force for attracting a critter to another critter by a 'spring' while using a 'rod' to keep them from getting too close. You can make amazing wobbly assemblages of things by hooking critters together with these. The *cForceObjectSpringRod:force(cCritter *pcritter)* does the following.

- If pcritter is closer than the desired _rodlength from the _pnode, we move pcritter out to _rodlength away from _pnode and return a zero force
- Otherwise return a force proportional to the distance between pcritter and _pnode.

The Worms game, described in Chapter 14: 2D Shooting Games, demonstrates a use of the *cForceObjectSpringRod*. Full code for all the forces can be found in **force.cpp**.

Another kind of relative *cForceObject* force is the *cForceObjectSeek*, which helps the pcritter pursue a _pnode critter. The simplest notion would be to have

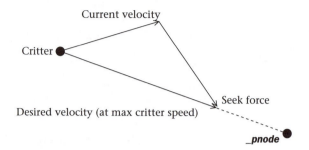

Figure 7.4 A seek force

cForceObjectSeek::force(pcritter) simply return a force along the vector direction from `pcritter` to the `_pnode` of the *cForceObject*.

The Pop Framework uses an improved seeking force suggested by Craig Reynolds (*op. cit.*, p. 154). Reynolds makes the point that rather than applying a force in the desired direction of motion, it's more effective to apply a force in the direction of the *difference* between the critter's desired motion and its current motion, as shown in Figure 7.4. We will also have the seek force set the critter's speed to its maximum.

There is a more general kind of relative force we can consider. This is a force in which a critter reacts to any and all members of a specified class of critters that we watch. We create a base class *cForceClass* for this and give it a *CRuntimeClass *_pnodeclass* member. As is discussed in Chapter 22: Topics in C++, a *CRuntimeClass* object keeps track of a class type, basically by storing a string with the name of the type along with some additional information.

One issue in interacting with objects of a certain class type K is whether we also want to interact with objects of class KChild, where KChild is a child class of K. We give the *cForceClass* a BOOL `_includechildclasses` field to let the programmer decide.

In the Pop Framework we provide a *cForceClassEvade* force for evading all objects of a given class, and we derive as child of this a *cForceEvadeBullet* to evade all *cCritterBullet* objects. Here's a summary of how *cForceEvadeBullet* acts.

- If there are no bullets to evade, return a zero force.
- Otherwise find the closest bullet.
- If the closest bullet is moving away from you, return a zero force.
- Set your evade direction to point away from the bullet.
- If this evade direction lies in the same direction the bullet is moving, you're in a 'rabbit running down a railroad track away from a locomotive' situation, which is no good. Rotate your evade direction by 90 degrees.
- Now, your desired evade velocity is your maximum speed times the evade direction.
- Return an evade force which is the vector difference between the evade velocity and your current velocity.

7.5   Preserving your physics

As a rule, once you have a *cCritter::move* that gives you a visually convincing simulation of some reasonably accurate physics, you shouldn't override it at all. If you ignore this rule, you run the risk of developing a game that runs great on your home machine, but which behaves badly when you bring the program in for a classroom demo – or, if you're working alone, when you try and show it off at a conference or at a friend's house. The critters may seem to be barely moving at all – or flying around the screen like neutrinos.

All the careful work in calculating a real time *dt* and passing it to your critters is going to make no difference if you make the *cCritter::move(dt)* method a virtual method and override it with a method that ignores *dt* and does something like `_position += _velocity`. Remember that it's only if you have the proper *move* code of `_position += dt * _velocity` that your program is going to adjust the motions of your critters to take into account the actual speed at which your game is running.

It should be possible to make all your changes to your critter motions by adding in forces to get used in the *update* call to *feelforce*, or by directly editing the update method.

- To apply a steady, ongoing force to a critter, give the critter a *cForce* that returns a non-zero vector.

- To apply a sharp impulse to a critter, such as when you hit it, change the critter's *_velocity* by using the *setVelocity* mutator to make the change. This call can be made from inside a *cForce::force* or directly within the *update* method or possibly some other method.

- To change a critter's position if you want to 'teleport' it from one spot to another, use the *moveTo* mutator.

We'll talk more about the user controls and the *cListener* class in Chapter 12: Listeners. For now though, we might as well mention some of the ways that some of our standard listeners change the main player critter's motion in response to an arrow key or a mouse action. Most of the time, a critter using a listener will ignore any acceleration due to forces. We ignore physics in order to have the player critter be fully responsive to the game's user.

- *Arrow key*. As long as an arrow key is pressed, set the velocity to the arrow key direction. If no arrow key is pressed, set the velocity to zero. Ignore any acceleration.

- *Scooter*. If the **Up Arrow** key is pressed, set the critter's velocity to be at the maximum speed in the critter's current direction. Pressing the **Down Arrow** key moves the critter in reverse. If neither the **Up** nor the **Down Arrow** key is depressed, the speed immediately drops to zero. The **Left** and **Right Arrow** keys rotate the critter's current direction. Ignore any acceleration.

- *Car*. As long as the **Up** key is pressed, add to the critter's forward acceleration. The **Left** and **Right Arrow** keys rotate the critter's current direction.

- *Cursor*. Move the critter to the current cursor position and give it a velocity that matches the motion from the old position to the new position. Ignore any acceleration.

Review questions

A   In what order must we call our `critter[i].move` and `critter[i].update` methods in order to make the simulation behave in a more 'parallel' fashion?

B   How do we justify converting the physical law *acceleration = d/dt velocity* into the computer code `velocity += dt * acceleration`?

C   How do we use Newton's law $F = m \times a$?

D   Draw a UML diagram and write a little code to explain how a **cCritter** object delegates its reactions to forces out to instances of the **cForce** class.

E   What is the code for the **cCritter::feelforce** method? Why is the argument `this` passed?

F   What are some of the kinds of forces implemented by the Pop Framework?

G   What's the difference between a **cForce**, a **cForceObject**, and a **cForceClass**?

Exercises

The use of forces is one of your most powerful tools for customizing your game. Here are a collection of problems to let you try this out. In doing these problems, don't forget that when you get into tweaking one particular game mode, it saves time to have the Pop program start up in the game mode that you want to play with. The way to control this is to edit the **CPopDoc** constructor in popdoc.cpp. Simply comment in exactly the one **setGameClass** line corresponding to the game you want to play. If you make a new game class, add a line for it.

Exercise 7.1: Changing the relative sizes of the critters and the world

The critters sometimes show forces better if you make them smaller. There are two ways you might make them smaller: (a) change the values of the statics `cCritter:: MINRADIUS` and `cCritter::MAXRADIUS` in your game constructor; (b) in your game constructor put a line `_border.set(newxsize, newysize);` with the `newxsize` and `newysize` larger than the default `cGame::WORLDWIDTH, cGame::WORLDHEIGHT` values defined in game.cpp and used in the **cGame** constructor. First try making the critters, say, three times as small and then put them back to the same size and try making the world three times as big. The relative sizes of the critter to the world should come out the same either way, that is, the screen sizes should come out the same. But something will be different: the critters will seem to move slower if you make the world bigger. This is because their speeds are set to some specific numerical values of units per second. Is it nicer to have the small critters move slower? Experiment with this a little and decide which way looks more playable.

Exercise 7.2: Making the world larger than the view

Many games are more interesting-seeming if they run across several view screens. You can do this by the following steps that we'll discuss in terms of, say, the `cGameStub` child class.

Go into your `cGameStub` constructor and add a line like `_border.set(100.0, 100.0)` (for a square world) or maybe `_border.set(100.0, 8.0)` (for a Mario-style side-scroller world).

In the `cGameStub` constructor after the `setPlayer` call, you can add a call like `pplayer()->moveTo(_border.locorner())`. This starts the player out at the corner of the world instead of in the center. This is something you may or may not want to do, depending on the game. In a side-scroller we like to start the player out at the left end of the world, but in an Asteroids-style game we might still want the player to start in the center.

In the `cGameStub::initializeViewpoint(cCritterViewer *pviewer)` method, replace the code with these lines.

```
pviewer->setViewpoint(cVector::ZAXIS, pplayer()->position());
pviewer->zoom(3.0);
pviewer->setTrackplayer(TRUE);
```

The exact value of the number you feed into the zoom call will depend on how zoomed-into the world you want to be. The call to `setTrackplayer(TRUE)` has the pleasant effect of automatically scrolling your screen to keep the player in view as it moves across the edges. The Ballworld game also overloads ***cgame::worldShape***.

Before doing the following exercises, make sure you've made the sizes of your critters smaller relative to the size of the world, otherwise the screen will be too crowded to see rich behavior.

Exercise 7.3: Adding forces

Get fresh (like original) copies of the **gamestub.*** files in case you changed them during the Space Invaders exercises (3.10.1–3.10.8). Change the ***cGameStub*** construcor to set `_rivalcount` to 0, and `_seedcount` to 20. Try using some of the different kinds of ***cForce*** constructors in the ***cCritterStubProp*** initializer. Try `cForceDrag(?, cVector(?, ?))` for a wind to the right. Try `cForceVortex(?)` for a spiraling-in vortex. One caution: if you make the first argument (which is 'friction' parameter) too big in `cForceDrag` or `cForceVortex`, the critters will have a bad kind of motion; rather than slowing them to a steady state, a too-large value of friction makes them overshoot and oscillate back and forth. Try `cForceDrag(300)` to see what we mean. Usually friction shouldn't be much bigger than 1 or 2.

Exercise 7.4: The spring and rod force

In the ***cGameWorms***, make a circular loop of the critters connected by spring and rod forces and push the loop around with the cursor. Adjust the force of the spring upward to make it fairly rigid. Try making a shape like an asterisk, with one critter at the center and four or five separate worms of connected critters coming out of the center. Try making a shape like a person. (You can find an interesting interactive website of rod and spring shapes by searching for 'sodaplay' or 'soda constructor.' The correct address was recently www.sodaplay.com, but this may change.)

Exercise 7.5: Planets

Now implement a **cForceObjectGravity** that gives a critter a gravitational attraction towards the _pnode of the **cForceObject**. Give it a **Real** _gravity field. The force ought to be something like `_gravity * pcritter->mass() * _pnode->mass() * pcritter->directionTo(_pnode)/(pcritter->distanceTo( pnode) *pcritter->distanceTo(_pnode))`, although you can speed up the computation a bit by prefixing the line with a call to `cDistanceAndDirection dnd = pcritter-> distanceAndDirectionTo(_pnode)`, and then in the next line getting the distance and direction out of `dnd` instead of doing three separate computations. In the **seedCritters** go ahead and walk through every possible (i,j) pair and connect every pair of critters with a **cForceObjectGravity**.

This is not the most computationally efficient way to do it, but first try it and see how it looks. You will need to tweak the gravity force and the speeds and the sizes for a while until you can start to get things like critters going into orbit around each other. Also you want to be doing this for a fairly large worldsize. Also, keep in mind that the mass of the objects depends on their density and size; if they're unresponsive, make them more massive.

Exercise 7.6: Brine shrimp

Try making a tide-pool world in which the critters move like brine shrimp. That is, whenever they slow down to a certain speed, they suddenly propel themselves forward in a slightly different direction.

Do this by having a `cForceDrag` to slow the critters down, and a new `cForceBrineshrimp` force to make them periodically dart forwards. The way the `cForceBrineshrimp` force ought to work is that if a critter's speed drops below a certain level, then the critter's speed is set to its maximum value. You must do a 'sudden impulse' change like this all at once by calling `pcritter->setSpeed` and *not* by returning an acceleration value, otherwise the critter will simply speed up a tiny amount to get faster than the trigger speed. When you apply the impulse, also wobble the critter a bit with a call to `pcritter->turn( ...small random argument...)`.

Exercise 7.7: Random linkages

This problem is suggested by a fascinating recent book, Stephen Wolfram, *A New Kind of Science* (Wolfram Media, 2002). Wolfram makes a case that all the seemingly complex behaviors and patterns we see in the world arise from the interactions of small simple programs. So let's see how well we can do with our simple drag, spring, ball-and-spring, seek and evade forces. Try a world in which each critter gets one or several randomly selected forces linking it to some randomly selected other critter. Arrange your program so that the behavior gets freshly randomized every time you reseed the world, and then press Enter a few times to look at the kinds of overall behaviors you get. Do you see anything that might be useful for making interestingly animated enemies or prey?

Exercise 7.8: Following waypoints

In adventure games and car racing games we often want to make some of the computer operated critters move along certain fixed paths. Thus you might want an enemy guard to patrol a certain route, or you might want a rival race car to drive around and around a track.

A good method to make this work is to set a series of 'waypoints' that you want the critter to follow. Implement a *cForceWaypoint* which has these fields.

```
CArray<cVector, CVector> _waypoint
int _currwpindex
Real _closeenough
```

You might also want to give *cForceWaypoint* an *add(cVector newwaypoint)* mutator method for adding points to be _waypoint array. Suppose that the constructor initializes _currwpindex to 0 and _closeenough to some reasonable (relative to your world size) value like perhaps 2.0.

If our waypoints are arranged in a circle, as on a race track, we might define the *cForceWaypoint* force method like this.

```
cVector cForceWaypoint ::force(cCritter *pcritter)
{
    if (distanceTo (_waypoint[_currwpindex]) <_closeenough)
    {
        _currwpindex ++;
        if (currwpindex >= _waypoint.GetSize())
            _currwpindex = 0;
    }
    setTangent(_waypoint[_currwpindex] - position()); /* setTangent
        will normalize the arg return cVector::ZEROVECTOR; */
}
```

Get this to work and then make a variation in which the critter moves back and forth along a curving line of waypoints. You can do this either by listing the inner points twice (once in each order), or by using a _currwpinc field that can be either +1 or −1 to determine the direction in which you traverse the waypoints.

Critters

8

8.1 Kinds of critters

In understanding the importance of the *cCritter* class for the Pop Framework, it will be useful to have a little overview of some of the *cCritter* child classes that we use. Let's put the UML class diagram (Figure 8.1) here of some (but not all) of our *cCritter* child classes.

We'll get into more details about various critter child classes later on. For now, note that in the Spacewar game, the player inherits from *cCritterArmedPlayer*, the asteroids inherit from *cCritter*, the UFOs inherit from *cCritterArmedRobot*, and the various kinds of bullets inherit from *cCritterBullet*. Children of the *cCritterWall* class are used in the Dambuilder and Airhockey games.

Typically you will define some special *cCritter* child classes for each new game that you write. The best practice is to put the prototype headers for your new critters in the same *.h* file as your game header, and to implement your over-ridden critter methods in the same *.cpp* file as your game implementation.

Which *cCritter* methods do you typically reimplement for child classes? Certainly you will write a child class constructor to change some of values of the critter fields set by the base class constructor. And you very often override the *cCritter::update* method. Other *cCritter* methods you might override are called *reset*, *touch*, *collide*, *die*, and *damage*. Table 8.1 on p. 180 lists the overrides.

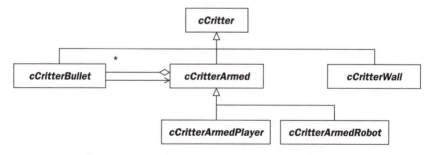

Figure 8.1   Some of the *cCritter* child classes

8.2 Overview of the critter class fields

Our critters will have a large number of primitive fields relating to their internal state, to the game they participate in, and to their motion. These primitive fields will mostly be **int**, *Real*, or *cVector* objects. Recall that *Real* is a type we typedef in realnumber.h to be **float**, although it could be changed to **double**.

Mixed in with the primitives, our *cCritter* objects will have pointer fields that hold references to a few other classes. The best way to get a quick idea of the class members is to look at the full *cCritter* prototype listing in the last section of this chapter.

In brief, the *cCritter* fields fall into these groupings.

- *State fields*, such as the *Real _age* and **int** *_health*.
- *Game fields*, such as the **int** *_score*, and the *cBiota* _pownerbiota*.
- *Position fields*, such as the *cVector _position*.
- *Velocity fields*, such as the *Real _speed* and the *cVector _velocity* and *_tangent*.
- *Acceleration*, *mass* and *force fields*, such as the *Real _acceleration* and *_density*, and a *_forcearray* of *cForce** objects.
- *Listener fields*, such as the *cListener* _plistener*.
- *Attitude* and *display fields*, such as the *cMatrix _attitude*, and the *cSprite *_psprite*.

Basic critter fields

In the coming pages, we'll see, step by step, how we to build up a *cCritter* class whose instances can serve as the all-purpose inhabitants of our computer games.

It's useful for every critter to know its age in seconds. How to measure this age? In keeping with our discussion in Chapter 6: Animation, we'll use real elapsed time for a critter's *_age*. Ten and a half seconds after the start of the game, all the critters should have an age of 10.5, and so on. When a critter is constructed, its age is set to 0.0, and we update the age within the code for the critter move(Real dt) method with a line like

```
_age += dt;
```

Another key state field is a critter's integer *_health*. By default the *_health* starts out at 1, and if the critter is damaged, for instance by a bullet, its health will drop. In the standard *cCritter::update* method, we have the critter die and get deleted if its health drops to 0 or below. We can also allow the possibility of giving a critter a *Real _fixedlifetime* and forcing it to die once its age passes this value.

These considerations lead to these fields.

```
protected:
    Real _age; /* Measure in seconds of time simulated, start at 0.0
        when constructed. */
    BOOL _usefixedlifetime; /* If TRUE, then die when _age >
        _fixedlifetime. */
    Real _fixedlifetime; /* Max lifetime in seconds, applies only if
        _usefixedlifetime. */
    int _health; /* Lose by being hit and taking damage(). Usually
        die when _health is 0. */
```

Since our critters are going to be part of a game, we're going to have some game-related fields as well. For one thing, a critter needs an integer *_score* field to track how well it's doing. So that a critter can 'see' the other critters in the game, we give it a pointer to a special kind of an array called a *cBiota*. In any given game, all of the active critters are stored in a common *cBiota* object. We'll say a bit more about this class in the next subsection.

In our repeated listings of the *cCritter* fields, we'll carry along some of the fields already mentioned, but not all of them lest our page gets too cluttered. Remember that the full listing can be found at the end of this chapter.

```
protected:
    Real _age;
    int _health;
    cBiota *_pownerbiota;
    int _score;
```

We want our critters to simulate a reasonable kind of motion like we discussed in Chapter 7: Simulating Physics. To start with, in the light of that chapter's discussion, it's clear that we want to have a vector *_position* and a vector *_velocity*.

The *cVector* class is defined in vectortransformation.h, with a switch that lets us make it either a two-dimensional or a three-dimensional vector throughout the program. Our current choice is to have all of our vectors be three-dimensional, so that really *cVector* stands for the class *cVector3*. In the case of the flat, two-dimensional games, the third vector component isn't really necessary, but carrying it along adds to generality and turns out to impose only a negligible penalty on speed.

In any case, to start with we'll give the *cCritter* two more fields. As mentioned above, we'll only relist the most important of the fields already mentioned.

```
protected:
    Real _age;
    int _health;
    cVector _position;
    cVector _velocity;
```

As we discussed in Chapter 7: Simulating Physics, the normal way that objects move can be approximated by repeated updates like this.

```
_position += dt * _velocity.
```

As we mentioned in Chapter 6: Animation, it's a good idea to let the time step **dt** be computed (by a *cTimer* object belonging to our *CPopApp*) to represent the actual time between program updates.

The *cCritter* has a *move(dt)* method for moving its position, with the assumption that dt is a real number measuring the time since the last update. Because we are going to construct this method rather carefully to embody the physical laws that apply to all of our objects, we are going to make it a non-virtual method that we can't override.

```
protected:
    Real _age;
    int _health;
    cVector _position;
    cVector _velocity;
public:
    int move(Real dt);
```

Whenever you run a simulation with moving objects, you have to worry about the objects moving off towards infinity and about the possibility of them speeding up and going unnaturally fast. To keep a *cCritter* from wandering off and getting lost, we'll need to give it a cRealBox _movebox to stay inside. The *cRealBox* class is a utility class of ours for holding real-valued rectangles or 3D boxes (as opposed to the MFC **CRect** which is for integer-valued rectangles).

A *cRealBox* is created by a constructor that takes two or three arguments. If there is no explicit third argument, it's assumed to be 0.0. The dimensions of a *cRealBox* are chosen so that it's centered on the origin (0.0, 0.0, 0.0), which is also known as *cVector::ZEROVECTOR*. This is illustrated in Figure 8.2.

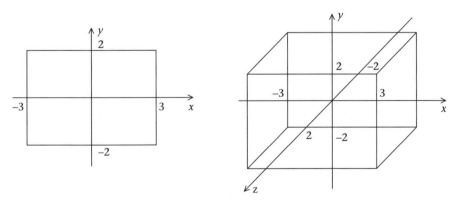

Figure 8.2   *cRealBox* (6, 4) and *cRealBox* (6, 4, 4)

Our **cGame** has a **cRealBox _border** that keeps the objects inside it. By default a critter has a **_movebox** that matches the **_border** of the game its added into. This setting happens because we normally give the **cCritter** constructor a `cGame *pownergame` argument.

When a critter hits a wall, we can do various kinds of things. We might just do something like `_movebox.clamp(_position)` to simply keep it inside the box, where the clamp function just forces a position to be inside the box. Or we might do something more subtle: we could make the **_position** 'bounce' off the walls of the **_movebox** like a rubber ball or, perhaps, let it 'wrap' from one edge of the box to the other. Conceivably we might want the critter to wrap across some walls but bounce off others. We'll use an **int _wrapflag** to decide which of the possible kinds of actions it does.

```
protected:
    Real _age;
    int _health;
    cVector _position;
    cRealBox _movebox;
    int _wrapflag;
    cVector _velocity;
```

To keep our **cCritter** class object from rushing around too rapidly, we'll give it a **_maxspeed** that bounds the magnitude of its **_velocity**. Since you're going to be computing this magnitude, it's convenient to keep it around as a **Real _speed** variable, and while you're at it, it's useful to maintain a unit-length vector **cVector _tangent**. We'll require that at all times `_velocity = _speed * _tangent`. You need to be a little careful with your mutators so as not to allow someone to change one of these three fields and not the other two: this is a classic example of a situation where you would not want your fields to be public, for otherwise someone might ignorantly change the `_speed` or the `_tangent` field without making the corresponding change to the `_velocity`.

```
protected:
    Real _age;
    int _health;
    cVector _position;
    cRealBox _movebox;
    int _wrapflag;
    cVector _velocity;
    Real _speed;
    Real _maxspeed;
    cVector _tangent;
```

By now our move method has become more a three-step process.

- Set _speed_ and _tangent_ to match the latest _velocity_. If _speed_ > _maxspeed_, reduce _speed_, and change the _velocity_ to match.
- `_position += dt * _velocity.`
- Make sure _position_ is not outside of _movebox_.

More complications arise when we put our critters into three-dimensional worlds. As well as tracking as the _tangent_ the direction the critter is moving in, we align a _normal_ with the direction the critter was most recently accelerating or turning in, and compute a _binormal_ perpendicular to _tangent_ and _normal_ (that is, we let _binormal_ be the vector cross product _tangent_ * _normal_).

```
protected:
    Real _age;
    int _health;
    cVector _position;
    cRealBox _movebox;
    int _wrapflag;
    cVector _velocity;
    Real _speed;
    Real _maxspeed;
    cVector _tangent;
    cVector _normal;
    cVector _binormal;
```

We'll also maintain a four column _cMatrix_ object called _attitude_. By default a critter will keep the four columns of _attitude_ equal to, respectively, the _tangent_, _normal_, _binormal_, and _position_. As it turns out, if we feed an _attitude_ like this into the graphics pipeline used in our display process, the critter will appear to be rotated so as to match the motion, using a bird-like or fish-like kind of way of holding its body. That is, we imagine that a critter's visual representation has three principal directions similar to, say, the long axis of a whale, the horizontal line of its flukes and the vertical line of its spout. And if we match the _attitude_ to the _tangent_, _normal_, _binormal_, and _position_, the 'whale' will 'heel over' in a natural kind of way when it makes a turn.

There are, however, situations where we want a critter's visible attitude not to match the motion; for instance, if our critter is a fighter that turns this way and that to shoot a gun. Here we have the option of freeing up the _attitude_ by setting an _attitudetomotionlock_ field to a FALSE value. In this kind of situation, we'd use some other method for setting the _attitude_, possibly controlling it with user key input, or possibly letting the critter tumble at some rate about an axis, with the spin rate and spin axis encapsulated inside a _cSpin_ _spin_ field.

```
protected:
    Real _age;
    int _health;
    cVector _position;
```

```
cVector _tangent;
cVector _normal;
cVector _binormal;
cMatrix _attitude;
BOOL _attitudetomotionlock;
cSpin _spin;
cVector _acceleration;
```

(Remember that for these illustrative listings of the *cCritter* fields, we don't keep showing every single field we've mentioned so far. A complete list of the *cCritter* fields appears in the code printed at the end of the chapter.)

Given our plan to have critters move like objects, we have an *_acceleration* vector as well. Leaving out the lines about checking against the *_movebox* and the *_maxspeed*, we would get something like this for our *move(dt)* method, just as described in Chapter 7: Simulating Physics.

```
_velocity += dt * _acceleration;
_position += dt*_velocity.
```

Of course if a critter is to do anything interesting, its motion should change over time. We can alter our motion in four ways: (a) use forces acting on the critter to change the velocity or acceleration, (b) make changes to the critter's position, velocity and/or acceleration based on user input, (c) use a *collide* method to bounce critters off each other, and (d) override the *cCritter::update()* method to make other changes to the velocity and acceleration, possibly related to the critter's age.

The details of how we carry out (a) and (b) depend on some class reference members in the *cCritter* class. Let's start a new subsection in which to discuss these kinds of members.

The *cCritter* reference fields

The associated classes are these: one owner *cBiota**, one display-delegate *cSprite**, and one listening-strategy *cListener** per critter. In addition, there is at most one target *cCritter**, and any number of *cForce** force-strategy objects. This is shown in Figure 8.3.

The *cBiota* class is an array-like container class based upon the MFC **CArray** template. *cBiota* acts as a helper class for the *cGame* class. Each *cGame* has a *cBiota* member that holds pointers to the active critters of the game.

We give each *cCritter* a *cBiota** *_pownerbiota* pointer which points to the array-like *cBiota* object that contains it. This 'back reference' provides a means for the critter to 'see' all the other critters in the simulation – by walking through the array of all the members of the *_pownerbiota* object.

The *cSprite** *_psprite* member specifies the critter's appearance on the screen. To make our code more modular, we don't want to tie ourselves to any one particular way of representing a *cCritter*. We'll work with several kinds of *cSprite*

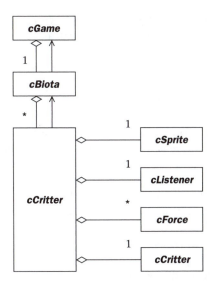

Figure 8.3   The reference members of the *cCritter* class

objects, the disk-like *cSpriteBubble* objects, the polygonal *cPolygon* objects, and the bitmap-based *cSpriteIcon* objects. The *cSprite* has a *draw* method that is called by the *cCritter:: draw* method. Note that before calling `_psprite->draw`, the *cCritter::draw* sends the current *_attitude* matrix into the graphics pipeline. We'll say more about *draw* below.

If critters hard-coded their display implementation, we'd be facing a combinatorial explosion of all possible critters times all possible sprites. Giving *cCritter* a *cSprite** member is an example of the object-oriented technique of delegation. More information about sprites appears in Chapter 9: Sprites.

The *cListener* _plistener* is another example of the delegation technique; more precisely it's an example of the Strategy pattern. Later, we're going to introduce a *cController* class which will hold current information about which keys or mouse buttons are being pressed. And we'd like critters to have the ability to 'listen' to this information. Most critters will ignore user input, so the default listening behavior will be to do nothing. Typically there will be at least one critter that represents the player and which responds to user input. And we might sometimes want more than one critter to be listening to user input. We might, for instance, want to write a two-player game. Or we might want a pinball game with two flipper critters that respond to user input. So we do need to have a listen method for every critter, and we want different critters to be able to listen in different ways. Even when we have only one player listening, we might want to choose between having the player be controlled like a PacMan that moves with arrow keys or having the player be controlled like a car or like a spaceship. Rather than calling a *cCritter::listen* method, we have a *cCritter::feellistener* method that calls *_plistener->listen*.

The *CTypedPtrArray<CObArray, cForce*> _forcearray* holds any number of force strategy objects that the critter accesses with a *feelforce* call made by the default *cCritter::update* method. The *CTypedPtrArray* is a variation on the MFC **CArray** template. As we discussed in Chapter 7: Simulating Physics, the *feelforce* makes calls to _forcearray[i]->force(this).

For the maximum of flexibility we allow for the critters to be subject to a variety of forces. To avoid a combinatorial explosion of classes, we don't specifically define gravity-influenced critters, whirlpool-influenced critters, lighter-than-air critters, and so on. Instead we use the Strategy pattern; that is, we take the notion of a force, and split it off into a separate class called *cForce*. The main method of *cForce* is a *cVector force(cCritter *pcritter)*. The *cForce::force* method computes a vector force for any critter with its concomitant location and velocity. The value of the returned force vector may be based on the critter's position, velocity, or other factors, and it's used to change the critter's acceleration. We also allow the possibility of a force directly changing a critter's position, velocity or acceleration.

We give each critter a *_forcearray* of *cForce* * pointers to force objects. As we already discussed in Chapter 7: Simulating Physics, we have a *cCritter::feelforce()* method which turns around Newton's law: $F = ma$ to have $a = F/m$.

```
_acceleration = (Sum over i of _forcearray[i]->force(this)) / mass()
```

We're going to estimate our critter masses by regarding them as three-dimensional spheres. That is, we'll maintain the equality _mass = _density * radius()^3. (Strictly speaking this is the formula for a cube's mass, but we can think of the necessary *4/3 * PI* multiplier for spherical mass as being part of the _density parameter.) Even though this is a two-dimensional simulation, the dynamics of bouncing looks better if you give things the masses of three-dimensional objects. Think in terms of balls rolling around on a pool table.

The *radius()* of a critter is going to be something that we get from the appearance of the critter, that is, *radius()* will get its value from the critter's *cSprite *_psprite* member, to which a critter delegates its display methods. That is, the *cCritter::radius()* simply returns _psprite->radius().

The *cCritter *_ptarget* member can be used when we want a critter to 'keep an eye' on one particular other critter. One example is the *cCritterArmedRobot* child critter class, which automatically aims and shoots at its *_ptarget*. Another example occurs in the Airhockey game, where each of the two *cCritterHockeyGoal* objects sets its *_ptarget* to the critter that's trying to knock the puck into that goal. This way the goal knows to whom to award a score point when the puck goes inside it.

Having a *cCritter** member of the *cCritter* class imposes a certain burden on us regarding destructors. That is, if a critter gets deleted somewhere in the game, any critter that has a *_ptarget* reference to the dead critter needs to be notified. The *cCritter* class has a virtual *fixPointerRefs* method that a critter calls in its destructor. The mission of *fixPointerRefs* is to go out and tell any other critters in the game to drop any references to the critter now being destroyed. Depending on how heavily referenced a given kind of critter might be by other critters, you may need to overload the *fixPointerRefs* in various ways.

Dropping a few fields from our growing list and adding in these new ones, we get something like this. Once again, if you want to see the full listing, it's at the end of the chapter.

```
protected:
    Real _age;
    int _health;
    cBiota *_pownerbiota;
    cVector _position;
    cVector _velocity;
    cMatrix _attitude;
    cSprite *_psprite;
    cVector _acceleration;
    CTypedPtrArray<CObArray, cForce*> _forcearray;
    Real _mass;
    cListener *_plistener;
    cCritter *_ptarget;
```

8.3   Critter methods

In order to run a game, we repeatedly call six methods for each critter, cycling through the calls over and over. The **cGame::step** method orchestrates the calls.

Figure 8.4 isn't any particular kind of official UML diagram, it's simply an informal way of showing the order in which a critter object is cycled through its main method calls, with time flowing in the clockwise direction.

The *Update*, *Feelforce*, and *Feellistener* methods

We give the **cCritter** a basic **update(CPopView *pactiveview, Real dt)** method. The argument isn't often used; a bit more about it appears below.

The basic **update** method feels the forces affecting the critter, and changes the acceleration of the critter accordingly. In addition, the basic update checks if the critter should die of old age.

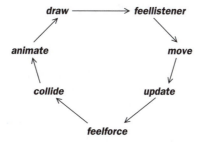

Figure 8.4   Critter methods called by the **cGame** step method

```
void cCritter::update(CPopView *pactiveview, Real dt)
{
    feelforce();
    if(_usefixedlifetime && _age > _fixedlifetime)
        dieOfOldAge(); /* I don't call die() because I like to use
            die for when a critter dies of unnatural causes, like
            getting shot. It's more likely that I override die()
            to do something dramatic than that I override
            dieOfOldAge(). */
}
```

The *pactiveview* arguments aren't used by any of our critters in the standard Pop Framework files; they're in place simply for possible use. Some students have in fact written two-dimensional games in which the *update* feeds the *pactiveview* into the method *COLORREF cCritter::sniff(const cVector &snifflocation, CPopView *pactiveview)*. The purpose of this is to let a critter adjust its behavior according to the colors of the nearby pixels as drawn in the active view; we've designed car-racing games in this way, for instance, by using the *sniff* method to let a critter know when it had driven off the track.

As we already discussed in Chapter 7: Simulating Physics, the *feelforce* method sums up the forces acting on the critter and applies Newton's Law to compute the acceleration.

```
void cCritter::feelforce()
{
    cVector forcesum; //Default constructor (0,0)
    for (int i=0; i<_forcearray.GetSize(); i++)
        forcesum += _forcearray.GetAt(i)->force(this);
    _acceleration = forcesum/mass(); /* From Newton's Law:
        Force = Mass * Acceleration. */
}
```

Recall that the base class *cForce::force* returns a zero vector, but we have 'physical' child classes *cForceGravity*, *cForceDrag*, and *cForceVortex* which return non-trivial values. We also have 'behavioral' force classes like *cForceObjectSeek*, *cForceClassEvade*, and *cForceEvadeBullet*

```
void cCritter::feellistener(Real dt)
{
    _plistener->listen(dt, this); /* We pass the pointer "this" to
        the listener so that it can change the fields of this calling
        cCritter as required. The caller critter's pgame() holds the
        cController object that stores all of the keys and mouse
        actions you need to process. */
}
```

Taken together, the sequence of actions involving the **update**, **feelforce**, and **feellistener** methods can be summarized as follows.

- Call **update** and, within **update**, call **feelforce()**.
- Call **feellistener(dt)** and possibly add in some more acceleration.
- Use the **_acceleration** in **move(dt)**.

The **Move** method

The **cCritter::move** method has a **dt** argument because we want the motion to adapt itself according to the speed of the processor running the program. A fast processor will pass very small **dt** to the **move** method, and we will want the critters to move only a slight amount with each update. A slow processor will pass larger **dt** timesteps to the **move** method, and in that case we need for the critters to move a larger amount with each update.

What we basically want from our **move(dt)** method is these two lines.

```
_velocity += dt * _acceleration;
_position += dt*_velocity.
```

But, as we mentioned in the last section, our **move(dt)** has to do a bit more.

- Age the critter by **dt** seconds.
- Add acceleration * **dt** to the velocity.
- Clamp the velocity's speed against maxspeed.
- Add velocity * **dt** to the position.
- Wrap, bounce, or clamp the new position relative to the border.
- Update the critter's normal and binormal to reflect the current state of motion.
- Set the critter's outcode according to which border edge, if any, it hit.

In terms of the special **cCritter** field names, this can be put a bit more precisely as follows.

- Increment the **_age** by **dt** seconds.
- Add **_acceleration * dt** to the **_velocity**, and recalculate **_speed** from **_velocity**.
- Clamp the **_speed** against **_maxspeed**, possibly redefining the **_velocity**.
- Add **_velocity*dt** to the **_position**.
- Wrap, bounce, or clamp the **_position** relative to the **_movebox**.
- Update the critter's **_tangent**, **_normal** and **_binormal** to reflect the current state of motion.
- Set the critter's **_outcode** according to which **_movebox** edge, if any, it hit.

As usual, for the fully complete and accurate version, look at the actual code in **critter.cpp**.

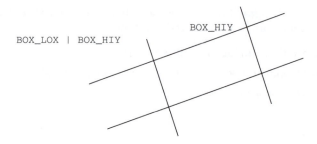

Figure 8.5 The nine outcode zones in two dimensions

Although it isn't really necessary, we happen to have implemented our *cCritter::move*, and some other critter-moving methods such as *clamp* and *moveTo*, so that they return the outcode. But the real use of the outcode is as the internal *cCritter* field *int _outcode*.

Let's say a few words about the meaning of the outcode. The word 'outcode' comes from computer graphics. The outcode value of the critter is set to reflect the relationship between the border box of the world and the last position the critter moved to (prior to having this position clamped or wrapped).

In two dimensions the outcode would distinguish among nine positions relative to a rectangle: inside the rectangle, to its right, to its top right, to its top, and so on. The idea is that we imagine extending the edges of the rectangle into infinite lines, and these lines cut space into nine regions. This is shown in Figure 8.5.

Relative to a box in three dimensions, an outcode can distinguish among 27 possible regions: think of a $3 \times 3 \times 3$ Rubik's cube of space regions built up around the central box. Rather than making up 27 different outcode names, it's more useful to OR together bitflags specifying a location's region relative to each axis.

The values we use for our outcodes are defined in **realbox.h** as follows. (These happen to be implemented as **define** values rather than **static int** constants.)

```
#define BOX_INSIDE 0
#define BOX_LOX 1
#define BOX_HIX 2
#define BOX_LOY 4
#define BOX_HIY 8
#define BOX_LOZ 16
#define BOX_HIZ 32
```

Thus in the plane, a critter located to the 'northwest' of a box would have an outcode of BOX_LOX | BOX_HIY. And to perform some action dosomething() only if a critter had touched the lower edge of a box, we could put a line like this into an overridden version of the critter's update method.

```
if(_outcode & BOX_LOX)
    dosomething();
```

Indeed, looking back at our Space Invaders Exercise 3.10 in Chapter 3: The Pop Framework, recall that we suggested a condition of just this form for use in the critter's **update** to detect if the critter had touched the bottom edge of the screen during its last **move**.

The *Draw* method

In order to draw a critter we need to have a pointer to a **cGraphics** object. Also we may have some drawflags to indicate some special aspects of how we want to draw the critter; generally, for instance, we draw a circle around the player critter, and we draw our critters as 'hollow' if they have been recently damaged.

So the **cCritter::draw** code looks essentially like the following, though the actual code you'll find in **critter.cpp** is a little more complicated.

```
void cCritter::draw(cGraphics *pgraphics, int drawflags)
{
    if (recentlyDamaged())
        drawflags |= CPopView::DF_WIREFRAME
    pgraphics->pushMatrix();
    pgraphics->multMatrix(_attitude);
    _psprite->draw(pgraphics, drawflags);
    pgraphics->popMatrix();
}
```

The draw code is an example of the Template Method pattern. We always want to multiply in the attitude matrix, doing the necessary set-up and clean-up to the pgraphics matrix stack. The part of the call that we override is separated out into the virtual **cSprite::draw** method.

We almost don't need to make **cCritter::draw** a virtual function, but the **cCritterArmed::draw** does override and extend the **cCritter::draw** to draw a short line segment to represent the gun.

The *Animate* method

Let's say a bit more about the critter's **_attitude** matrix. This specifies how we are to orient the sprite image that represents the critter. The place where the critter updates the **_attitude** is in its **cCritter::updateAttitude** call, which is called by the **cCritter::animate**.

```
void cCritter::animate(Real dt)
{
    updateAttitude(dt);
    _psprite->animate(dt, this);
}
```

If _attitudetomotionlock field is TRUE, the **updateAttitude** method matches the **_attitude** matrix to the motion matrix given by the tangent, normal, binormal, and position vectors. This is a good default behavior that makes the critters look lively. If _attitudetomotionlock is FALSE, we allow for the possibility that the critter is spinning.

```
void cCritter::updateAttitude(Real dt)
{
    _attitude.setLastColumn(_position); //always update position.
    if (_attitudetomotionlock)
        copyMotionMatrixToAttitudeMatrix();
    else //_attitudetomotionlock is FALSE
        rotateAttitude(dt*_spin);
}
```

As we'll see in Chapter 9: Sprites, the reason we pass this to the cSprite::animate() call is that the sprite may want to change itself depending on the direction or the health of its owner critter.

Randomizing and mutation methods

As well as the **randomizePosition** and **randomizeVelocity** methods, we can also change a critter by calling a **cCritter::mutate(int mutationflags, Real mutationstrength)** method.

The way this works is that we can feed in various combinations of the static **MF_** mutation flags, some of which are defined in **critter.h**, some in **sprite.h** and some in **spritepolygon.h**. The **cCritter::mutate** method changes a few critter values and then makes a call to the **cSprite::mutate** method. For randomizing purposes, these methods use the singleton **cRandomizer::pinstance()** object.

The *Die* and *Damage* methods

The default **cCritter::die** method is implemented in-line simply as virtual void die(){delete_me();}. This tells the owner game to delete the pointer and remove it from the **cBiota** array when the current round of critter updates is done. The reason we wait a bit is that it can cause trouble if you start adding and deleting critters to an array that you're in the process of updating.

Some critters override the die or the damage method to make a noise with a call of the form playSound("Bonk"). Both the **cCritter** and **cGame** classes have a **playSound** method. The string you feed into a **playSound** call needs to be defined in quotes as the ID of the relevant resource, for instance as 'BONK'. The names of resources are not case sensitive.

The standard **cCritter::damage(int hitstrength)** code reduces the _health by hitstrength, and if the _health is less than or equal to zero, the critter makes a call to die().

The *Collide* method

Collision is a tricky matter, and we'll give a more detailed discussion of it in Chapter 11: Collisions. Critters collide in pairs.

Each critter has the virtual **BOOL cCritter::collide(cCritter *pother)** method whose default behavior is to perform an elastic collision between the caller critter and the `pother` critter, changing their positions and velocities in a manner that would be physically natural if the critters were spheres.

We can override a critter's *collide* method to include a reaction to the critter that it's colliding with, possibly killing one of the critters, adding a score to one, or the like.

Sometimes we may have two `cCritter *pcritteri, *pcritterj` that belong to *cCritter* child classes that have different overrides of the *collide* method. In this case it makes a difference whether you call `pcritteri->collide(pcritterj)` or `pcritteri->collide(pcritterj)`. We generally don't want to call both *collide* methods as (a) this would waste computational time and (b) the *collide* methods are designed to have a symmetric effect on the critters, so it would be physically incorrect to call *collide* twice for one particular collision. As we discuss in Chapter 11: Collisions, we give the critters an *int _collidepriority* field and a virtual *int cCritter::collidesWith(cCritter *pcritterother)* method to resolve the question of which critter gets to control a given collision.

8.4 Critter method overrides

Table 8.1 gives you an overview of which critter methods we override to make the sample games provided with the Pop Framework.

8.5 The full *cCritter* prototype

Here's a full listing of the *cCritter* prototype from a recent **critter.h** header file. For the most current listing, you can examine the file itself inside Visual Studio.

```
////////////////////////////////////////////////////////////////////////
// Critter.h: interface for the cCritter class.
//
////////////////////////////////////////////////////////////////////////

#ifndef CRITTER_H
#define CRITTER_H
#include "randomizer.h"
#include "realbox.h"
#include "realpixelconverter.h"
#include "vectortransformation.h"
#include <mmsystem.h> //For PlaySound flags
class cGraphics;
```

```
#define USEBOUNCINESS /* Compile switch used in critter.cpp,
critterwall.cpp, realbox.cpp. */

    /* We don't need to include the headers for the following classes
    as we only mention them as pointers. In general, we only include a
    header in a header if we absolutely have to. Here we can get by
    with forward class declarations that simply say such and such a
    class exists. Of course we will need to include the headers in
    the critter.cpp which is where we actually use the properties of
    these classes. */
class cBiota; //For the *_pownerbiota member.
class cSprite; //For the *_psprite member.
class cListener; //For *_plistener member.
class cForce; //For _forcearray member.
class cDistanceAndDirection;
    // Return type of the distanceAndDirection function.
class CPopView; //Used as an argument to sniff.
class cGame; //For the return type of the pgame() method.
class cGraphics; //For the draw method.

class cCritter : public CObject
{
DECLARE_SERIAL(cCritter); /* An MFC macro used to enable
    CRuntimeClass reflection of class type, dynamic creation,
    and serialization. */
public:
// Statics =======================================
//Constant Statics ===============================
    //The MF_ statics are mutation flags used in the mutate methods.
    static const int MF_NUDGE;
    static const int MF_POSITION;
    static const int MF_VELOCITY;
    static const int MF_ALL; //MF_POSITION | MF_VELOCITY
    /* Wrapflag values specify possible behaviors when critter hits
        edge of world. */
    static const int BOUNCE;
    static const int WRAP;
    static const int CLAMP;
    /* special high density used for player or other immovable critter. */
    static const Real INFINITEDENSITY;
//Variable Statics ===============================
    //These might (rarely) be reset by a cGame constructor.
//Motion Statics ===============================
    static Real MINSPEED; //Used in randomizing critter _speed.
    static Real MAXSPEED; /* Used in randomizing, and to clamp _speed
        in move(dt). */
    static Real MINTWITCHTHRESHOLDSPEED;
        //Default for _mintwitchthresholdspeed
```

```
    static Real NEAREDGEPERCENT; // Default arg for moveToMoveboxEdge.
    static BOOL STARTWRAPFLAG;
    static Real DENSITY; //Default density.
//State Statics ===============================
    static Real MUTATIONSTRENGTH; //Default argument to mutate method.
    static Real MINRADIUS; //Used in randomizing
    static Real MAXRADIUS;
    static Real BULLETRADIUS; /* Gets set to cGame::BULLETRADIUS in
        cGame constructor. */
    static Real PLAYERRADIUS;
    static Real LISTENERACCELERATION;
        //Default for _listeneracceleration
    static int STARTHEALTH; //Default is 1.
    static Real SAFEWAIT; /* Time in seconds of invulnerability, use
        at start up and after damage, gives critters breathing room so
        they don't get damaged twice in a row, like by the same bullet
        volley. */
    static Real FIXEDLIFETIME; /* Default lifetime for critters with
        _usefixedlifetime TRUE. */
protected:
//==================================================
//State Fields. ====================================
//==================================================
    Real _age; /* Measure in seconds of time simulated, start at 0.0
        when constructed. */
    BOOL _usefixedlifetime;
        //If TRUE, then die when _age > _fixedlifetime.
    Real _fixedlifetime;
        //Max lifetime in seconds, applies only if _usefixedlifetime.
    int _health; /* Lose by being hit and taking damage(). Usually die
        when _health is 0. */
    BOOL _shieldflag; //Immunity to damage() calls.
    UINT _personality; /* Random bits to sometimes use for making
        critters have different behaviors, as when using evasion
        forces. */
    Real _mutationstrength; /* Number between 0.0 and 1.0 controlling
        how different a spawned copy will be. */
    cCritter *_ptarget;/* In case you are following or dragging or
        watching or aimed at someone else, use this field to track
        them. _ptarget is one of the only fields that is NOT
        serialized. We use the _targetindex with the _pownerbiota to
        copy or serialize _ptarget. */
//==================================================
//Game Fields ======================================
//==================================================
    cBiota *_pownerbiota; /* Used in makeServiceRequest and in other
        places. It allows the critter to be aware of all the other
```

```
        critters. Gets set by the cCritter(cGame *pownergame)
        constructor. _pownerbiota is NOT serialized. */
    int _score; //Usually gain by eating or shooting others.
    int _value; //Value to another critter shooting or eating this one.
    int _newlevelscorestep;
        //Step size between score levels that are rewarded.
    int _newlevelreward; //Health reward for new score level.
//=================================================
//Motion Fields. =================================
//=================================================
//Position Fields =================================
    cVector _position;
    cRealBox _movebox; //Keep critter inside _movebox.
    cRealBox _dragbox; /* Usually same as _movebox, but in
        cGamePickNPop, it's bigger, so can drag a critter outside of
        its _movebox. */
    int _wrapflag; //BOUNCE, WRAP, or CLAMP when you bump a wall.
    int _outcode; /* Flag info about which wall, if any, the last
        move bumped. */
//Velocity Fields =================================
    BOOL _fixedflag; //Refuse to move.
    cVector _velocity;
    Real _speed;
    cVector _tangent; /* We always keep _velocity = _speed * _tangent.
        It's useful to have _tangent around even when _speed goes to 0
        and _velocity is zero, this way we know what direction to
        start back up in. */
    cVector _normal; /* We maintain a _normal and _binormal vector to
        fully express themotion of the critter through 3D space. */
    cVector _binormal; //Always cVector::ZAXIS in 2D worlds.
    Real _maxspeed; //Clamp _speed below this in move().
    Real _maxspeedstandard;/* In case _maxspeed might be temporarily
        increased, for instance if the critter is allowed to move
        extra fast while fleeing or chasing another. */
//Acceleration Mass, and Force Fields =============================
    cVector _acceleration; /* _acceleration gets reset during every
        cycle, using the _forcearray and possibly the _plistener to
        change it. */
    Real _mass; /* Use fixMass() helper to maintain _mass = _density *
        radius()^3. */
    Real _density; /* Default is 1. We often assign the cCritterPlayer
        a very large _density so that it can whack others around. */
    CTypedPtrArray<CObArray, cForce*> _forcearray;
        //We serialize this array
//Listener Fields. =================================
    cListener *_plistener; //Never NULL. We serialize the plistener.
```

```
        Real _listeneracceleration; /* This is the acceleration used by
            listeners such as cListenerCar and cListenerSpaceship that
            "drive" the critter around. Like the critter's engine
            strength. */
//Collision Fields ===============================
        Real _collidepriority;
        /* These are default cCritter _collidepriority values, in
            increasing size for increasingly high priority, where in a
            pair of critters, the higher priority critter is the caller of
            the collide method, and the lower priority critter is the
            argument to the collide call. */
        Real _absorberflag; /* Don't change your own velocity after a
            collision. This siphons energy out of the system, cooling
            down the motions by absorbing it. */
        Real _bounciness; /* ranges from 0.0 to 1.0. Determines how
            elastically you bounce off of walls    or off of other
            critters.  1.0 is perfect bounce, 0.9 is pretty reasonable,
            0.0 don't bounce at all. */
        Real _mintwitchthresholdspeed; /* If we have
            _attitudetomotionlock, and we have some critters barely
            bouncing on a "floor" it looks bad if they keep twitching
            their orientation up and down. Don't change the _attitude
            to match the motion if the speed is less than
            _mintwitchtriggerspeed. */
//================================================
//Attitude and Display Fields ===========================
//================================================
        cSprite *_psprite; //Never NULL. We serialize the _psprite.
        BOOL _attitudetomotionlock; /* Shall I lock together the display
            sprite and the motion? By default the player has
            _attitudetomotionlock FALSE and all other critters have it
            TRUE. */
        cMatrix _attitude; /* The attitude expresses the way that the
            critter is situated for rendering. When _attitudetomotionlock
            is TRUE, _attitude has the columns   _tangent, _normal,
            _binormal, _position. If _attitudetomotionlock is FALSE,
            _attitude can be instead controlled by _spin or by the
            _plistener actions. */
        cSpin _spin; /* A cSpin holds the spinangle in radians per
            second and the spinaxis which is the axis to spin around
            (z by default). Presently used only when _attitudetomotionlock
            is OFF. */
        Real _defaultprismdz; /* We copy this into the psprite's _prismdz
            field in setSprite. If we are in 3D and if the sprite is, for
            instance, a polygon that makes use of the _prismdz field, then
            _prismdz will determine the z-thickness of the sprite. */
```

```
//===============================================
//Bookkeeping Fields =============================
//===============================================
//Serialized Bookkeeping Fields ==================================
    Real _lasthit_age; /* Age at last hit (or age at birth), use to
        time invulnerability. */
    BOOL _oldrecentlydamaged; /* Used in update() in connection with
        sprite display lists. */
    cVector _oldposition;
        //This is used by the cCritterWall::collide method.
    cVector _oldtangent;
        //This is used by the cCritter::fixNormalAndBinormal method.
    cVector _wrapposition1, _wrapposition2, _wrapposition3;
        //Use for showing wrap in 2D
    int _targetindex; /* _targetindex is a dummy used to copy and
        serialize the _ptarget pointer reference. */
//Nonserialized Bookkeeping Fields ===========================
    int _metrickey; /* Index into the _pownerbiota cBiota's _metric,
        can be used to look up metric values. _metrickey is NOT
        serialized. Uspd if #define USEMETRIC*/
public:
//===================================================
//Constructor and destructor and helpers =========================
//===================================================
    cCritter(cGame *pownergame = NULL); /* Initializes fields, adds
        to pownergame if not null. With the NULL default for the
        pownergame argument, this constructor doubles as a no-argument
        constructor. */
    virtual void copy(cCritter *pcritter); /* Helper function for copy
        constructor, and for clone method. */
    cCritter(cCritter *pcritter); //copy constructor
    cCritter* clone(); /* Returns a pointer to a cCritter of the same
        child class type, with the same info in it. */
    virtual ~cCritter(); /* deletes pointer members and calls
        cBiota::removeReferencesTo(this). The destructor is virtual
        so that child critter destructors can do extra cleanup before
        the baseclass destructor. */
    void removeReferencesTo(cCritter *pdeadcritter); /* Don't let
        pdeadcritter be the _ptarget or the pnode() of any
        cForceObject in the _forcearray. */
//===============================================
//Mutators =================================
//===============================================
//State Field Mutators ==============================
    void setValue(int value){_value = value;}
        /* The velocity, direction, and speed mutators always keep
            _velocity = _speed * _tangent. */
```

```
    void setShield(BOOL shield){_shieldflag = shield;}
    void setUseFixedLifetime(BOOL yesno){_usefixedlifetime = yesno;}
    void setFixedLifetime(Real lifetime){_fixedlifetime = lifetime;}
    void setMutationStrength(Real mutationstrength){_mutationstrength
        = mutationstrength;}
    virtual void setTarget(cCritter *pcritter){_ptarget = pcritter;}
        /* Comes in handy sometimes, though more often I'll use a
        cForceObject. */
    void setMetricKey(int i){_metrickey = i;}
    virtual void reset(); //can override to do special things.
    virtual void setAge(Real age){_age = age; _lasthit_age = _age -
        cCritter::SAFEWAIT;} //overridden by cCritterArmedRobot.
//Game Field Mutators ====================================
    void setOwner(cBiota* pownerbiota){_pownerbiota = pownerbiota;}
        //Used in Add and CBiota::Serialize
    virtual void addScore(int scorechange);
    void setHealth(int health){_health = health;
        if(_health<0)_health=0;} /* We can add health points at
        certain score levels. */
    void setNewlevelreward(int healthgain){_newlevelreward =
        healthgain;}
    void setNewlevelscorestep(int pointspread){_newlevelscorestep =
        pointspread;}
//================================================
//Motion Field Mutators ==============================
//================================================
//Position Field Mutators ==============================
    int setMoveBox(const cRealBox &box);
    void setDragBox(const cRealBox &box){_dragbox = box;}
    virtual void setWrapflag(int wrapflag);
        //We have a kludge override for cCritterWall
    virtual int moveTo(const cVector &newposition, BOOL
        treatascontinuousmotion = FALSE); /* Do the move,
        and then clamp against _movebox, return outcode of
        clamp. */
    virtual int moveToZ(Real z){return moveTo(cVector(_position.x(),
        _position.y(), z));} /* I use moveToZ in
        cGamePickNPop::seedCritters. */
    virtual int moveToProportional(const cVector &newposition,
        Real proportion, BOOL treatascontinuousmotion = FALSE);
        /* Proportion between 0.0 and 1.0 is how much of the way
        you want to move towards newposition. */
    virtual int dragTo(const cVector &newposition, Real dt);
        /* Move and clamp against _dragbox, return outcode. In
        addition, use dt to set critter velocity to match the drag
        velocity. I make it virtual so cCritterWall can override to
        NOT change the velocity. */
```

```
    void moveToMoveboxEdge(Real percent = cCritter::NEAREDGEPERCENT);
        /* Useful in some games, to start a critter near the _movebox
            edge. */
//Velocity Field Mutators ==============================
    void setFixedflag(BOOL flag){_fixedflag = flag;}
    void setVelocity(const cVector &velocity);
    void addVelocity(const cVector velocitychange)
        {setVelocity(_velocity + velocitychange);}
    void setTangent(const cVector &direction);
    void rotate(const cSpin &spin); /* cSpin is a way to express
        general 3D angles. */
    void yaw(Real turnangle); //Rotate around _binormal.
    void roll(Real turnangle); //Rotate around _tangent
    void pitch(Real turnangle); //Rotate around _normal
    void orthonormalize(); /* Make sure _tangent, _normal, _binormal
        are orthogonal units. */
    void setSpeed(Real speed);
    void setMaxspeed(Real maxspeed)
        {_maxspeed = _maxspeedstandard = maxspeed;}
    void setTempMaxspeed(Real maxspeed){_maxspeed = maxspeed;}
    void restoreMaxspeed(){_maxspeed = _maxspeedstandard;}
//Acceleration, Mass and Force Field Mutators ====================
    void setAcceleration(const cVector &acceleration)
        {_acceleration = acceleration;}
    void addAcceleration(const cVector &acceleration)
        {_acceleration += acceleration;}
    void setDensity(Real density){_density = density; fixMass();}
    void fixMass(); //Keep _mass = _density * _radius()^3.
    void addForce(cForce *pforce);
    void clearForcearray();
    void copyForcearray(cCritter *pcritter); /* This helper method
        will empty the existing force array and copy all of the forces
        in the pcritter force array. */
    virtual void copyPhysicsForces(cCritter *pcritter); /* A more
        modest kind of force copying. Here we don't wipeout the
        existing forces in the caller, and we only copy the "physics"
        forces like cForceGravity and cForceDrag from pcritter. Use
        the BOOL cForce::isGlobalPhysicsForce() to tell us which ones.
        We need this method so that bullets can copy the physics of
        their shooters but not their behavioral forces. */
//Listener Field Mutators ===============================
    void setListener(cListener *plistener);
    void setListenerAcceleration(Real la){_listeneracceleration = la;}
//Collision Field Mutators ==============================
    void setMinTwitchThresholdSpeed(Real twitchspeed)
        {_mintwitchthresholdspeed = twitchspeed;}
```

```
    void setBounciness(Real bounciness)
        {CLAMP(bounciness, 0.0, 1.0); _bounciness = bounciness;}
    void setAbsorberflag(BOOL flag)
        {_absorberflag = flag;
        _absorberflag?_bounciness=0.0:_bounciness=1.0;}
    void setCollidePriority(Real collidepriority);
        //Rebuild the pgame()->_pcollider just in case.
//===================================================
//Attitude and Display Field Mutators ================================
//===================================================
    void setSprite(cSprite *psprite);
    void setSpin(cVector3 spinvector){_spin = cSpin(spinvector);}
    void setAttitudeToMotionLock(int lockmode)
        {_attitudetomotionlock = lockmode;}
    void setSpin(Real spinangle, cVector3 spinaxis = cVector::ZAXIS)
        {_spin = cSpin(spinangle, spinaxis);}
    void rotateAttitude(Real angle);
        //{_attitude *= cMatrix::rotation(angle);}
    void rotateAttitude(cSpin &spin);
        //{_attitude *= cMatrix::rotation(spin);}
    void setAttitude(const cMatrix &attitude); /* This changes the
        orientation aspect of _attitude, but NOT the _position
        aspect, that is, it leaves the last column alone. */
    void resetAttitude(); /* Assume the identity orientation. */
    void setAttitudeTangent(const cVector &tangent); /* points
        _attitude in tangent direction. If _attitudetomotionlock is
        TRUE, we move _tangent to match. */
    void copyMotionMatrixToAttitudeMatrix();
    void copyAttitudeMatrixToMotionMatrix();
    BOOL lookAt(const cVector &targetpos); /* Aim attitudeTangent
        at targetpos, and try and perverse attitudeNormal while
        you're at it. Return FALSE if the targetpos is right on
        top of you, preventing you from looking at it, else return
        TRUE. */
    BOOL lookAtProportional(const cVector &targetpos, Real
        proportion); /* Proportion is between 0.0 and
        1.0 specifying how far towards targetpos you turn
        to look. */
    int setRadius(Real radius);
    void setPrismDz(Real prismdz); /* Sets _defaultprismdz and the
        current _psprite->_prismdz. */
//=============================================
//Randomizing mutators ===========================
//=============================================
    void randomizePosition( const cRealBox &startbox);
    void randomizePosition(){randomizePosition(_movebox);}
```

```
        void randomizeRadius(Real minradius, Real maxradius)
            {setRadius(cRandomizer::pinstance()->randomReal(minradius,
                maxradius));}
        void randomizeVelocity(Real speed);
        void randomizeVelocity(Real minspeed, Real maxspeed);
        void randomizeVelocity(){randomizeVelocity(MINSPEED, _maxspeed);}
        void randomizeSpin(Real minspeed, Real maxspeed);
        virtual void mutate(int mutationflags, Real mutationstrength);
            /* Mutate flagged position, velocity and sprite properties by
            an amount specified in mutationstrength. */
        void mutate(int mutationflags)
            {mutate(mutationflags, _mutationstrength);} /* Uses the member
            _mutationstrength, which defaults to 0.6. */
        void randomize(int mutationflags){mutate(mutationflags, 1.0);}
            //1.0 is maximum.
//================================================
//Accessors ======================================
//================================================
//State Field Accessors ==============================
    Real mutationStrength()const{return _mutationstrength;}
    int value()const{return _value;}
    unsigned long personality()const{return _personality;}
    BOOL shield()const{return _shieldflag;}
    BOOL usefixedlifetime(){return _usefixedlifetime;}
    Real fixedlifetime(){return _fixedlifetime;}
    Real age()const{return _age;}
    BOOL recentlyDamaged(){return (_age - _lasthit_age) < SAFEWAIT;}
//Game Field Accessors ===============================
    cBiota* pownerbiota()const;
    virtual cGame* pgame()const; /*Normally this will just return
        _pownerbiota->pgame(), but in the case of a cCritterViewer
        associated with a CPopView we use a different path to the
        cGame.*/
    cCritter* ptarget()const{return _ptarget;}
    cCritter* pplayer(); /* return pgame()->pplayer(), in other words
        the player of the game that this critter belongs to. */
    int score()const{return _score;}
    int health()const{return _health;}
//================================================
//Motion Field Accessors ============================
//================================================
//Position Field Accessors ===========================
    cVector position() const {return _position;}
    cVector oldposition() const {return _oldposition;}
    cPlane plane()const{return cPlane(_position, _binormal);}
    int wrapflag()const {return _wrapflag;}
    cRealBox moveBox()const{return _movebox;}
```

```
    cRealBox dragBox()const{return _dragbox;}
    cRealBox realBox(); //Smallest box holding the sprite.
    virtual BOOL draggable(){return TRUE;} /* Used to see if a critter
        is willing to be dragged in cGame::onLButtonDown. If you ever
        want a non-draggable critter child class, override draggable
        to return FALSE. */
    BOOL in3DWorld(); //Tells you if the owner game has a z-Thickness.
//Velocity Field Accessors ====================================
    BOOL fixedflag()const{return _fixedflag;}
    cVector velocity() const {return _velocity;}
    cVector tangent() const {return _tangent;}
    cVector normal() const{return _normal;}
    cVector binormal() const{return _binormal;}
    Real speed()const {return _speed;}
    Real maxspeed()const {return _maxspeed;}
    Real maxspeedstandard()const {return _maxspeedstandard;}
//Acceleration, Force and Mass Field Accessors ========================
    cVector acceleration() const {return _acceleration;}
    Real density()const{return _density;}
    CTypedPtrArray<CObArray, cForce*>* pforcearray()
        {return &_forcearray;}
//Listener Field Accessors ================================
    cListener* plistener()const{return _plistener;}
    Real listeneracceleration()const{return _listeneracceleration;}
//Collision Field Accessors ================================
    Real minTwitchThresholdSpeed(){return _mintwitchthresholdspeed;}
    Real bounciness(){return _bounciness;}
    BOOL absorberflag()const{return _absorberflag;}
    Real mass()const{return _mass;}
    Real collidePriority(){return _collidepriority;}
//=================================================
//Attitude and Display Field Accessors ==========================
//=================================================
    cSprite* psprite() const{return _psprite;}
    Real radius() const;
    cSpin spin()const{return _spin;}
    cMatrix attitude(){return _attitude;}
    cVector attitudeTangent()const {return _attitude.column(0);}
    cVector attitudeNormal()const {return _attitude.column(1);}
    cVector attitudeBinormal()const{return _attitude.column(2);}
    BOOL attitudetomotionlock() const{return _attitudetomotionlock;}
    Real defaultprismdz()const{return _defaultprismdz;}
//=================================================
//Bookkeeping Field Accessors =============================
//=================================================
    int metrickey()const{return _metrickey;}
//=================================================
```

```
// Serialize methods ==============================
//================================================
    virtual void Serialize(CArchive &ar);
//================================================
// Helper methods ==================================
//================================================
//Service Request Methods  ================================
    /* The point of these is that if a critter is do something that
        affects the set of critters as a whole, we want it to let the
        cBiota* _pownerbiota do it, so that all critter changes are
        coordinated. So critter just passes this request to its
        _pownerbiota, and later _pownerbiota calls
        cBiota::processServiceRequests. */
    void makeServiceRequest(CString request);
    void add_me(cBiota *pownerbiota, BOOL immediateadd = FALSE);
        /* Make a request to the pownerbiota to add yourself to its
        array, normally this doesn't happen until pownerbiota makes a
        periodic call to processServiceRequests, but you can force it
        to be immediate with immediateadd. */
    void delete_me(){_health = 0; makeServiceRequest("delete_me");}
    void spawn(){makeServiceRequest("spawn");}
    void zap(){makeServiceRequest("zap");}
    void replicate(){makeServiceRequest("replicate");}
        //copy yourself to all the others.
//Helper Methods for Move Methods ================================
    virtual int clamp();
        //Clamp against _movebox. cCritterWall treats differently.
    virtual int clamp(const cRealBox &border); //Clamp against border
    virtual void addvelocityandcheckedges(Real dt); /* do _position +=
        dt*_velocity, and clamp, wrap, or bounce the new position off
        the _movebox. Set _outcode to tell which edges. Called by
        move(). Need the dt to figure out a velocity bounce. */
    void synchSpeedAndDirectionToVelocity(); /* Enforces
        _speed*_tangent = _velocity and avoids having _speed less than
        SMALL_REAL */
    void fixNormalAndBinormal(); /* This is easy in 2D, subtler in 3D.
        Call this from inside move on every update. It also
        orthonormolizes _tangent, _normal, and _binormal. */
//Helper method for pointer references. ================================
    virtual void fixPointerRefs(); /* This helper is for fixing things
        like _ptarget after serialization, is also needed when we
        delete a critter.*/
//================================================
//Distance, touch, sniff, collide methods ================================
//================================================
    /* The first three methods' code depends whether USEMETRIC is
        #defined in metric.h */
```

```
    virtual cVector directionTo(cCritter *pcritter);
        //Use cMetricCritter or compute direct
    Real distanceTo(cCritter *pcritter);
        //Uses cBiota's cMetricCritter or computes direct
    Real distanceTo(const cLine &testline)
        {return testline.distanceTo(_position);}//Direct
    cDistanceAndDirection distanceAndDirectionTo(cCritter *pcritter);
        //ditto
    Real distanceTo(const cVector &vpoint); //Brute force.
    virtual BOOL touch(const cVector &vpoint);//Brute force.
    virtual BOOL touch(const cLine &sightline); /* In 3D, clicking the
        screen really picks a line of sight rather than a particular
        point in space. */
    virtual BOOL touch(cCritter *pcritter); /* TRUE if pcritter is
        different from this and the distance between the centers is
        less than the sum of the radii. Uses cBiota's cMetricCritter
        or just does the brute force distance checks. */
    virtual BOOL contains(cCritter *pcritter); /* TRUE if the disk of
        pcritter is inside the disk of the caller. */
    virtual COLORREF sniff(const cVector &snifflocation, CPopView
        *pactiveview); /* Can be used in update to check the current
        screen's pixel color at locations you're interested in. */
    virtual int collidesWith(cCritter *pcritterother); /* Returns
        cCollider::DONTCOLLIDE, ::COLLIDEASCALLER, or ::COLLIDEASARG
        to specify which of the pair, if either, gets to call for a
        collision. Default just checks _fixedflag and
        _collidepriority. */
    virtual BOOL collide(cCritter *pcritter); /* Does a physically
        natural collision and possibly overrides to make the critters
        react in some other way such as damage. */
//==========================================
//Game methods ============================
//==========================================
    virtual void die(){delete_me();} /* Can be overridden to add
        dying behavior. But should eventually produce a call to
        delete_me. */
    virtual void cCritter::dieOfOldAge(){delete_me();} /* dieOfOldAge
        is called in the update method if(_usefixedlifetime &&
        _age > _fixedlifetime). We distinguish between die() and
        dieOfOldAge() so die() can make a different sound for
        instance. */
    virtual int damage(int hitstrength); /* Deducts hitstrength from
        _health, calls die if this is below zero, returns _value as a
        reward to the damager. */
//==========================================
//Force and Listen methods ============================
//==========================================
```

```
    virtual void feellistener(Real dt); /* Call _plistener->listen,
        maybe more. */
    virtual void feelforce(); /* Do _acceleration =
        (sum of _forcearray[i]->force(this))/mass(). feelforce is
        virtual because you might possibly want to select which forces
        you feel, depending on the situation, like whether you're
        currently pursuing or fleeing. */
//=================================================
//Drawing methods ===================================
//=================================================
    void updateAttitude(Real dt, BOOL forceattitudeupdate = FALSE);
        /* This keeps graphical attitude matrix of the critter in
        synch with its motionmatrix. To prevent a too-busy look, we
        normally don't do the update if the _speed is less than
        _mintwitchthresholdspeed. But if we are controlling the
        critter with arrow key calls to, e.g. the yaw, pitch and roll
        methods, we do want to force the update of the appearance, and
        then you set the forceattitudeupdate argument to TRUE. */
    virtual void draw(cGraphics *pgraphics, int drawflags=0);
        /* Calls _psprite->draw. Has to be virtual because some child
        critters draw stuff (like guns) on top of sprite. */
    virtual void drawHighlight(cGraphics *pgraphics, Real
        highlightratio); /* Draw a highlighted XOR circle around the
        sprite with a size = highlightratio * radius(). */
//=================================================
//Sound methods ============================
//=================================================
    static void playSound(CString wavfileresourcename, int soundflags
        = SND_RESOURCE | SND_ASYNC);
        /* By default interrupts any current sounds to play this
            sound. wavfileresourcename has to be the resource name of
            a *.wav file that you added as a resource to your build. */
    static void stopSound(); //Turns off any currently playing sounds.
//=================================================
//Simulation methods ============================
//=================================================
    virtual void animate(Real dt); /* Calls _psprite->animate(dt,
        this). Can override to setAimVector. */
    virtual void update(CPopView *pactiveview, Real dt); /* Call force
        to set the _acceleration to zero or to the quantity determined
        by _pforce. The pactiveview argument can be used to sniff
        pixel colors. */
    int move(Real dt); /* You really should NOT change the delicately
        constructed move method, which is why its not virtual. */
};
#endif //CRITTER_H
```

Table 8.1 Special classes used in the Pop Framework.

Used in	Class name	Parent class	Overridden methods	New virtual methods
Basic classes	**cCritterArmed**	cCritter	animate, draw, fixPointerRefs, update	shoot
	cCritterArmedPlayer	cCritterArmed	collide, damage, draw, feellistener, shoot	
	cCritterArmedRobot	cCritterArmed	update	
	cCritterPlayer	cCritterArmedPlayer		initialize, isTarget
	cCritterBullet	cCritter	collide, collidesWith, fixPointerRefs, update	
	cCritterBulletRubber	cCritterBullet	collide, update	
	cCritterBulletSilver	cCritterBullet	damage	
	cCritterWall	cCritter	clamp, collide, collidesWith, distanceTo, dragTo	
Spacewar	cCritterAsteroid	cCritter	damage	
	cCritterUFO	cCritterArmedRobot	damage, update	
	cCritterUFOSmart	cCritterUFO		
Basketball	cCritterBasket	cCritter	collide	
	cCritterBallworld	cCritter	die	
	cCritterBallworldPlayer	cCritterArmedPlayer	die	
Dambuilder	cCritterDamFloat	cCritter		
	cCritterDamPlayer	cCritterArmedPlayer		
	cCritterDamBullet	cCritterBullet	isTarget	
	cCritterDamWall	cCritterWall		
Defender3D	cCritterDefender3D-Player	cCritterArmedPlayer	collide, damage, draw, reset, shoot, update	
	cCritterDefender3D-PlayerBullet	cCritterBullet		
	cCritterDefender3DProp	cCritter	collide, damage, die	
	cCritterDefender3D-PropFrag	cCritter	update, collidesWith	
	cCritterDefender3D-Rival	cCritterArmedRobot	collide, damage, update	
	cCritterDefender3D-Rivalbullet	cCritterBulletSilver	initialize	

Table 8.1 (Continued)

Used in	Class name	Parent class	Overridden methods	New virtual methods
Airhockey	cCritterHockeyGoal	cCritterWall	collide	
	cCritterHockeyPlayer	cCritter	reset	
	cCritterHockeyPuck	cCritter		
	cCritterHockeyRobot	cCritter	update	
Pick-N-Pop	cCritterJewel	cCritter	die, update	
	cCritterPeanut	cCritter	die	
	cCritterUnpackedJewel	cCritter	die	
Stub3D	cCritterStub3DPlayer	cCritterArmedPlayer	collide, damage, reset, update	
	cCritterStub3D-PlayerBullet	cCritterBullet		
	cCritterStub3DProp	cCritter	collide, damage, update	
	cCritterStub3DRival	cCritterArmedRobot	collide, damage, update	
	cCritterStub3D-RivalBullet	cCritterBulletSilver	initialize	
	cCritterStubPlayer	cCritterArmedPlayer	collide, damage, reset, shoot, update	
Stub	cCritterStubPlayerBullet	cCritterBullet		
	cCritterStubProp	cCritter	collide, damage, update	
	cCritterStubRival	cCritterArmedRobot	collide, damage, update	
	cCritterStubRivalBullet	cCritterBulletSilver	initialize	
Worms	cCritterWormSegment	cCritter	collide, damage, update	
	cCritterWormsPlayer	cCritterArmedPlayer	collide, damage, reset, update	
	cCritterWormsPlayer-Bullet	cCritterBullet		
	cCritterWormsRival	cCritterArmedRobot	collide, damage, update	
	cCritterWormsRival-Bullet	cCritterBulletSilver	initialize	

cCritter **initialization**

To complete this detailed code section, here's how the **cCritter** fields get initialized by the default constructor. Remember that when we define children of the critter class, like, say, **cCritterArmed**, when the **cCritterArmed** constructor is called the base class **cCritter** constructor gets called first. In other words, the **cCritter** constructor is code that all of our critters will execute at start up. Child classes may override some of these initialization values; they may also initialize additional variables that the child class may have.

We go ahead and list the full code of a recent version of the **cCritter** constructor here just to give you an idea of all the member fields actually used. A C++ usage worth noting here is that when we write a C++ constructor, it's common to set the values of fields by using initializer lines of the form _variable(value), rather than having a line of the form _variable = value; inside the curly brackets of the constructor. It makes the code easier to overview, and it's useful to see the allocation calls using **new** isolated inside the constructor's curly brackets, so that then it's easier to remember what you have to undo in the destructor. (If you happen to have any data fields that were declared as **const** you are in fact required to use initializer lines to set their values.)

Also note that if the pownergame argument isn't supplied, it will get the default NULL value, and the code involving it will be skipped over in the constructor.

```
cCritter::cCritter(cGame *pownergame):
    _pownerbiota(NULL),
    _age(0.0),
    _lasthit_age(- cCritter::SAFEWAIT), /* We do this so
        that critters don't start out thinking they were
        just hit. cCritter::SAFEWAIT is currently 0.3
        seconds. */
    _oldrecentlydamaged(FALSE), //Can use to notice when you need to
        change sprite.
    _health(cCritter::STARTHEALTH), //Default 1.
    _usefixedlifetime(FALSE),
    _fixedlifetime(cCritter::FIXEDLIFETIME),
    _shieldflag(FALSE),
    _outcode(0),
    _score(0),
    _newlevelscorestep(0),
    _newlevelreward(0),
    _value(1),
    _personality(cRandomizer::pinstance()->random()),
        //Use our static randomizing method.
    _movebox(cRealBox(4.0,3.0, 0.0)),
        //Dummy defaults to be reset with setMoveBox
```

```
_dragbox(cRealBox(_movebox)),
    //Dummy defaults to be reset with setDrag
_wrapflag(cCritter::STARTWRAPFLAG), //cCritter::BOUNCE
_defaultprismdz(cSprite::CRITTERPRISMDZ),
_density(cCritter::DENSITY),
    //This standard value is currently 1.0.
_mass(1.0), //Dummy default is reset by fixMass.
_collidepriority(cCollider::CP_CRITTER),
_absorberflag(FALSE),
_fixedflag(FALSE),
_position(cVector::ZEROVECTOR),
_oldposition(cVector::ZEROVECTOR),
_wrapposition1(cVector::ZEROVECTOR),
_wrapposition2(cVector::ZEROVECTOR),
_wrapposition3(cVector::ZEROVECTOR),
_velocity(cVector::ZEROVECTOR),
_speed(0.0), //Must match _velocity.magnitude().
_tangent(cVector(1.0, 0.0)),
    //We always want some unit vector _tangent.
_oldtangent(cVector(1.0, 0.0)),
_normal(cVector(0.0, 1.0)),
_binormal(cVector(0.0, 0.0, 1.0)),
_attitudetomotionlock(TRUE),
_acceleration(cVector::ZEROVECTOR),
_listeneracceleration(cCritter::LISTENERACCELERATION),
_spin(), /* _spin is initialized to 0 spinangle around ZAXIS by
    default constructor */
_maxspeed(cCritter::MAXSPEED), //Default 3.0
_maxspeedstandard(cCritter::MAXSPEED),
_mintwitchthresholdspeed(cCritter::MINTWITCHTHRESHOLDSPEED),
_bounciness(1.0),
_mutationstrength(cCritter::MUTATIONSTRENGTH),
    //Default 0.6 (out of 1.0 max)
_ptarget(NULL),
_metrickey(0)
{
    _psprite = new cSprite(); /* Let's always have a valid sprite.
        The default cSprite looks like a circle, by the way. */
    _plistener = new cListener(); /* For uniformity, always have a
        valid listener as well. The default listener does nothing.
        Don't call setListener(new cListener()) here as this call may
        have side-effects I don't want yet. */
    _attitude.setLastColumn(_position);
        /* The default _attitude constructor has set the matrix
        to the identity matrix, and it's more accurate to the
        make the fourth column match the position. */
```

```
    if (pownergame)
        pownergame->add(this, TRUE); /* This call will set _movebox
            and _dragbox to match pownergame->_border, and will set
            _wrapflag to match pownergame->wrapflag). The TRUE flag
            means to insert the critter into the game cBiota array
            right away. */
}
```

Review questions

A   What are some child classes of the *cCritter* class?

B   What are the *cCritter* methods most commonly overridden?

C   What are the three classes to which the *cCritter* delegates functionality?

D   In updating the critter's motion, what do we do to keep the critter from running off towards infinity or from acquiring an unrealistically large velocity?

E   What is the meaning of the information in the *cCritter*'s *_outcode* field?

F   Why is the *cCritter* draw method code an example of the Template Method pattern?

Exercises

Exercise 8.1: The importance of being virtual

If you don't explicitly label a method as virtual in the base class, then the child class overrides will ignore it. The Pop Framework has deliberately made *move* a non-virtual method, because it would be a bad idea for you to override it, like tinkering with the delicate innards of a watch. Even if you were to write a *move* method inside one of the child classes, your code would be ignored (unless you were to put `virtual` in front of the `move` prototype in **critter.h**).

Let's see what happens if we make *update* non-virtual. This will mean that all of the critters' specialized update methods will be ignored and they'll just use the base class update method, which in fact does very little.

Open up the Pop project file and remove the world '`virtual`' from the line `virtual void update(CPopView *pactiveview, Real dt)` at the bottom of the **critter.h** file. Build and run. You'll find that you're no longer able to shoot bullets in the Spacewar game. This is because the shooting behavior is part of the *cArmedCritter::update* code, which is now not being used.

Exercise 8.2: Tweaking the evolution process

Try changing the default *_mutationstrength* value, and make some changes to the *cPolygon* and *cPolyPolygon* mutate methods as well. See what kinds of interesting polypolygons you can come up with.

Sprites 9

9.1 Kinds of sprite

'Sprite' is a word traditionally used in computer game programming for the little character images that move around. Normally, computer game sprites are based on bitmaps, and we do indeed have a *cSpriteIcon* child of the *cSprite* class that uses bitmap images.

We also have some geometrical sprite objects. The *cSprite* child classes, *cPolygon* and *cSpriteCircle*, draw polygons and disks, respectively. Geometrical objects have the virtue of being scale-independent, crisp-looking, and lightweight in terms of memory use. Another good thing about them is that they can be easily rotated. Bitmaps can be rotated in OpenGL graphics, but not in Windows graphics.

Exercise 9.11 discusses how to create sprites of a variety of standard 3D shapes: sphere, cone, torus, tetrahedron, cube, octahedron, dodecahedron, icosahedron, and teapot.

The *cSpriteComposite* class uses the Composite software pattern to provide for sprites which are made up of component sprites. The *cSpriteBubble* is a composite holding a *cSpriteCircle* and a decorative *cPolygon* highlight. *cPolyPolygon* is a special kind of composite drawn as a polygon with polygons (or polypolygons) at its vertices.

The *cSpriteShowOneChild* of *cSpriteComposite* shows only one of the components rather than all of them. How might we choose which component to show? We might either look at the direction the sprite is currently moving in, getting the *cSpriteDirectional*, or we might track the passage of time and continually flip through an animation loop of sprites like the *cSpriteLoop* does.

Figure 9.1 is a UML class diagram of the *cSprite* classes used in the Pop Framework.

Students are usually most interested in the bitmap-based sprite *cSpriteIcon*; this is initialized from a *.bmp file that you add to your project resource. These work very well in Windows graphics, but in our three-dimensional OpenGL graphics, they run a bit slow. We presently implement the OpenGL bitmap sprites as texture maps that are applied to rectangles. In both the Windows and OpenGL graphics, we have the option of giving transparent backgrounds to our *cSpriteIcon* objects.

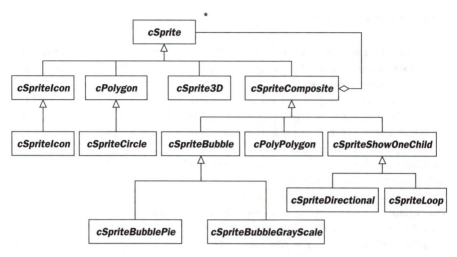

Figure 9.1 Our *cSprite* child classes

One can chain these constructions and have, for instance, a *cSpriteDirectional* that is an array of *cSpriteLoop* objects, so that one sees a different animation depending on the direction of the critter's motion. This is useful, for instance, for showing a running human form.

9.2 The *cSprite* class

Now let's look at what goes inside a *cSprite*. A sprite does not need to know the name of its owner *cCritter*. This is the way it should be, as a sprite is simply some geometry in space, possibly textured with a bitmap. This makes life easier as maintaining a *cCritter** pointer inside *cSprite* while maintaining an 'inverse' *cSprite** pointer inside *cCritter* would be a bit of a hassle, particularly when it came to writing the destructors for these objects.

A sprite is something that a critter uses to draw a picture of itself. We will think of the size of a critter as being the visual size of its sprite. So a sprite will have a *Real _radius* field. Our decision was to have the *_radius* belong to the sprite rather than the critter, by the way, because we want the radius to represent the visual radius that we see on the screen, and we'd like to have anything visual belong to the sprite.

The effective radius of a sprite may be affected by a scaling matrix, or by the fact that the sprite is a composite of several sprites, so it's not always going to be the case that the *virtual Real cSprite::radius()* method returns the same value as *_radius*.

Different sprites will override *radius()* in different ways. For purposes of collisions, a critter will regard its own *radius()* as being its `_psprite->radius()`.

The sprite also has a *cMatrix _spriteattitude* variable which is by default the identity matrix. This matrix is used in addition to the *cCritter* member *cMatrix _attitude*. We'll say more about the sprite attitude in the following sections.

The sprite *Draw* method

We'll give the *cSprite* a *draw* method with the same arguments as the *cCritter::draw*. The *cSprite::draw* manipulates the graphics matrices and calls a secondary helper method *cSprite::imagedraw*.

Our graphics pipeline is set up so that before drawing the sprite of a critter, the pipeline gets the critter's `_attitude` which moves the zero vector to the critter's current position. In addition the `_attitude` transformation rotates the sprite's spatial 'attitude' to match that of the critter. We only need to multiply a non-trivial `_spriteattitude` for cases where the sprite is to be positioned other than in the most natural way.

We implement the 'graphics pipeline' as a *cGraphics* object which maintains two *cMatrix* members. One of these matrices is called the projection matrix, and the other is called the modelview matrix. At the time when the *CPopView::OnDraw* calls on the *cGraphics* object to draw your sprite onto the screen, the modelview matrix MV will typically have the form $MV = V' * Mc * Ms$, where Ms is the `_spriteattitude`, Mc is the critter's `_attitude`, and V' is the inverse of the `_attitude` matrix of the *cCritterViewer* which views the scene. (See Chapter 24: 2D and 3D Graphics for a bit more about this.) A given vertex u of a sprite polygon will be drawn as being at the point $u' = P * MV * u$, where P is the projection matrix. In the case of a composite sprite the MV may incorporate subsidiary matrices for the individual sprite pieces and take on a form like $V' * Mc * Ms * Msa$, with Msa representing the location of a component of the sprite relative to the spirite as a whole. (Look for instance at the code for `cSpriteBubble::setAccentPoly()` in **spritebubble.cpp**.)

In order to right-multiply a matrix into the modelview matrix, we can use the *cGraphics::multMatrix* method as indicated in the sequence diagram of Figure 9.2. Note that in order to preserve the leading bits of the matrix for use by other critters and sprites, we use `pushMatrix` and `popMatrix` calls. The push call saves a copy of the current state of the modelview matrix in a stack, and the latter call copies the saved state back out of the stack.

In terms of our equation $MV = V' * Mc * Ms$, when we start at the top of Figure 9.2, MV is simply V'. The first `pushMatrix` call saves this value of MV, and the first call to `multMatrix` sets $MV = V' * $ `_attitude`. The second pushMatrix call saves this 'critter matrix' value, and the second `multMatrix` call sets $MV = V' * $ `_attitude` $ * $ `_spriteattitude`. The two succesive `popMatrix` calls restore MV back to the simple V' state.

As we mentioned in Chapter 8: Critters, a critter's call to `draw(pgraphics, drawflags)` uses a Template Method pattern to do the following.

- Push (that is, save) the graphics pipeline's current modelview matrix.
- Multiply the critter `_attitude` times the graphics pipeline's modelview matrix.
- Call `_psprite->draw` with the same arguments.
- Pop (that is, restore) the graphics pipeline's current modelview matrix.

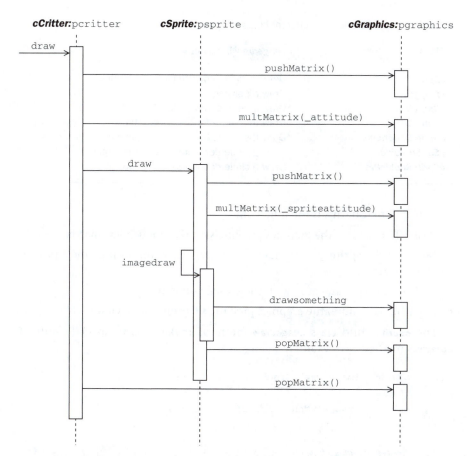

Figure 9.2   Sequence diagram of the *draw* cascade

The *cSprite::draw* method uses the same kind of Template Method pattern, again doing some standard things with matrices and passing the actual drawing off to a subsidiary method, this time the *cSprite imagedraw*.

```
void cSprite::draw(cGraphics *pgraphics, int drawflags)
{
    pgraphics->pushMatrix();
    pgraphics->multMatrix(_spriteattitude);
    imagedraw(pgraphics, drawflags);
    pgraphics->popMatrix();
    /* After the draw, tell the sprite that its current geometry has
        now been drawn once. */
    setNewgeometryflag(FALSE); /* This is for use by the
        cGraphicsOpenGL for knowing when it may need to change any
        display list id being used for the sprites.*/
}
```

Table 9.1   How we draw the different kinds of sprite.

Class	*imagedraw* behavior
cSprite	Default: draw a hollow circle and radius
cPolygon	Draw a polygon
cSpriteIcon	Draw a bitmap in a rectangle
cSpriteLoop	Draw the sprite for the current time
cSpriteDirectional	Draw the sprite for the current direction
cSpriteBubble	Draw a circle decorated with a rectangle
cSpriteBubblePie	Draw a circle decorated with a pie slice

In plain English, this is the following.

- Push (that is, save) the graphics pipeline's current modelview matrix.
- Multiply the sprite `_spriteattitude` times the graphics pipeline's modelview matrix.
- Call `_psprite->imagedraw` with the same arguments.
- Pop (that is, restore) the graphics pipeline's current modelview matrix.

The *cSprite* child class *imagedraw* methods make calls to special kinds of *cGraphics* methods. For example

```
void cPolygon::imagedraw(cGraphics *pgraphics, int drawflags)
{
    pgraphics->drawpolygon(this, drawflags);
}
```

The *cSpriteIcon::imagedraw* calls `pgraphics->drawbitmap(this, drawflags)`. The individual *cGraphics* child class can tell from the pointer argument `pgraphics` what kind of graphics it is. How the graphics class draws a polygon or a bitmap is up to the individual *cGraphics* child class. This is an example of the Bridge pattern; the *cGraphics* child classes have different implementations of the key drawing methods such as *drawpolygon* and *drawbitmap*.

The behaviors that we see when drawing the different kinds of sprites are shown in Table 9.1.

The *Animate* method

During every update of the game, each critter calls a *cCritter::animate(dt)* method that does two things.

- Make an *updateAttitude(dt)* call to
  - (a) match the critter's `_attitude` to the critter's current motion matrix if the critter's `_attitudetomotionlock` is TRUE, or, otherwise
  - (b) rotate the critter's `_attitude` by `dt*_spin` or
  - (c) leave the `_attitude` alone if `_spin` is zero.
- Call a *_psprite->animate(dt, this)*.

The default *cSprite::animate(Real dt, cCritter* powner)* doesn't do anything. But the *cSprite::animate* can be overridden to do various kinds of things. We might look at the `powner->recentlyDamaged()` value and set a sprite accordingly (see Exercise 9.10). Or you could use *dt* to increase and decrease the radius of the sprite to give a 'breathing' effect. If we have a polygon-based sprite, we might use *dt* to move some of the vertices of the polygon so as to make the image flex, perhaps opening and closing its 'mouth' (see Exercise 9.7).

When we use a bitmap based sprite in the *cGraphicsMFC*, we need to actually change the bitmap being used for different directions (because unlike *cGraphicsOpenGL*, *cGraphicsMFC* doesn't rotate bitmaps). And in any graphics implementation, you will need to flip through differing bitmaps if you want an animation effect for the sprite.

In these situations we use the *cSpriteShowOneChild* composite sprite and let the animate method set the `_showindex` used to determine the currently active component sprite.

The *cSpriteLoop::animate* method ages a time counter and adjusts the `_showindex` accordingly, while the *cSpriteDirectional::animate* adjusts the `_showindex` sprite according to the current `powner->tangent()`.

9.3 Polygons

Particularly in three dimensions, we very often want to represent our critters by colored polygons, perhaps by just one polygon, perhaps by a few, or perhaps by a whole mesh of them. Computer graphics systems draw polygons in an entirely different way from how they draw bitmaps. A bitmap is based on discrete pixel-by-pixel information, while a polygon is based on coordinates in continuous space. In drawing a polygon, we convert its space coordinates into pixel coordinates, use fill algorithms to color it in, and use line-drawing algorithms to draw its edges.

Windows has a built-in **CDC::Polygon(POINT * vertices, int vertexcount)** method which makes it easy to rapidly draw polygons on the screen. Our *cPolygon* class is designed to create polygon structures that can take advantage of this function call.

Initializing and decorating a polygon

We can create an empty polygon with the default polygon constructor *cPolygon()*, and then we can put some structure onto it by using one of our special mutators. Note that as usual you can leave out the trailing arguments which have default values defined.

```
void setRegularPolygon(int vertexcount);
void setStarPolygon(int vertexcount, int step);
void setRandomStarPolygon(int mincount, int maxcount);
void setRandomRegularPolygon(int mincount, int maxcount);
void setRandomAsteroidPolygon(int mincount = 5, int maxcount = 30,
    Real spikiness = 0.3);
```

The **setRegularPolygon** and **setStarPolygon** mutators produce polygons with a user-selected **vertexcount**. The **step** argument to the star polygon controls the kind of star that is drawn. In general, choosing a step smaller than the vertex count which has no divisors in common with the vertex count produces the nicest stars. At present the stars look good in **cGraphicsMFC**, but **cGraphicsOpenGL** still needs to be tweaked to draw them properly.

The **setRandomRegularPolygon** and the **setRandomStarPolygon** are methods for randomly making a regular or a star polygon with its vertex count and its radius within specified ranges.

The Spacewar game is something like the traditional Asteroids. So it will be useful to have some **setRandomAsteroidPolygon** to create random irregular polygons. To make the asteroid polygons look solid, we add their vertices in successive counterclockwise order – if we add them out of order we'll get something like a star. Stars look nice if they're regular, but an irregular star just looks like a scribble. We use the spikiness parameter to control the difference between minimum radius and maximum radius used for the various asteroid vertices.

Another approach, which we use when we want a particular shape, is to use the **cPolygon(n)** constructor and then use **n** calls to **setVertex (int n, cVector v)** to build up the polygon a step at a time. Note that by default, we assume we have a closed polygon in which the last point is automatically connected to the first point.

Once we have a polygon, we can adjust its interior with various mutators that you find in **polygon.h**. One easy way to vary a polygon sprite is to call the randomize method with the MF_ flags defined in **polygon.h**. For instance the `ppolygon->randomize(cPolygon::MF_COLOR)` will randomize the `ppolygon` fill color, and the **cPolygon::MF_ALL** flag will randomize everything.

We can adjust the lines around the edges of the polygon with the **_edged** and **_reallinewidth** fields. The **_reallinewidth** field controls the ratio of the thickness of the line to the polygon's radius. A value of, say, 0.2 will give a fat line. We state this quantity as a real number ratio rather than a pixel width so that the polygon will still have the same appearance when drawn at different size scales. But if the converted pixel width of the line would be less than one, we still draw a line of pixel width one, assuming that **_edged** is TRUE. Drawing lines of width greater than one slows the Windows **Polygon** function down inordinately, so we recommend sticking to the default **_reallinewidth** of 0.0, which will produce a line one pixel in width, which is what Windows really 'prefers' to draw. (**spritepolygon.h** also has a **#define** for a name for 0.0 to use in this 'line width' context: LW_ONEPIXEL.)

As a non-standard extra, we can also draw dots at our polygon vertices, using the **_dotted** and **_realdotradius** fields. The **_realdotradius** field controls the ratio of the radius of the vertex dots of the polygon's radius. A value of, say, 0.2 will give fat dots. We state this quantity as a real number ratio rather than a pixel width so that the polygon will still have the same appearance when drawn at different size scales. The dots look quite nice; they are drawn after the polygon so they seem to sit on top of it. We have the option of filling the dots or not, and of selecting their fill colors. Dots aren't implemented for **OpenGL**.

A related class is *cSpriteCircle*, which is simply a *cPolygon* with some static **int** cSpriteCircle::CIRCLESLICES number of sides. If you don't make the 'circles' too big, a reasonable value for CIRCLESLICES is 16.

We could have implemented *cSpriteCircle* to have an *imagedraw* that calls something like an ellipse method, but it was quicker and easier to just treat the circles as many-sided polygons.

Polygons in 3D

There are some differences between the implementations of *cGraphicsOpenGL* and *cGraphicsMFC::drawpolygon*. As of August, 2002, the dots only show up with *cGraphicsMFC*, and the star-shaped polygons aren't as nicely drawn in *cGraphicsOpenGL*. These are 'bad' differences that could be fixed.

A 'good' difference between the two graphics implementations of *drawpolygon* is that, to enhance the three-dimensionality of the view with OpenGL, the *cGraphicsOpenGL* actually draws a polygon as a thick prism, that is, as a base polygon with vertical sides extending upwards to an identical cap polygon. The exact thickness of the prism can be controlled via the *cSprite* field *Real _prismdz*, and this field can in turn be controlled either directly or by setting the *cCritter _defaultprismdz* field before adding the sprite. By default the various child critter classes use the following *_prismdz* values.

```
Real cSprite::WALLPRISMDZ = 0.75;
Real cSprite::PLAYERPRISMDZ = 0.5;
Real cSprite::CRITTERPRISMDZ = 0.3;
Real cSprite::BULLETPRISMDZ = 0.2;
Real cSprite::MAXPRISMDZ = 1.0;
```

Thus, if you open up Dambuilder in the 3D view, you'll see the walls as taller than the player, the player as taller than the other critters, and the bullets as the thinnest of all.

9.4 Composite sprites

The *cSpriteComposite* holds an array of *cSprite* pointers called *_childspriteptr*. The **default** *cSpriteComposite::draw* behavior is to walk the array and call *draw* for each of the child sprites.

```
for (int i=0; i< _childspriteptr.GetSize(); i++)
    _childspriteptr[i]->draw(pgraphics, drawflags);
```

We can make some nice shapes this way. We'll consider two examples in this section: the *cSpriteBubble* and the *cPolyPolygon*.

The *cSpriteBubble*

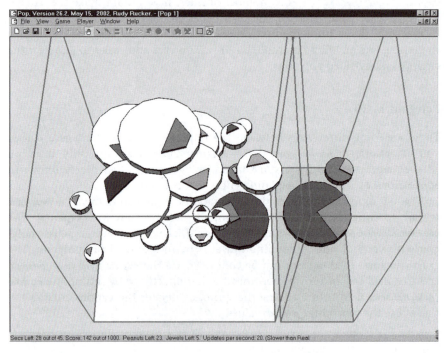

The PickNPoP game viewed in OpenGL 3D. On the left are **cSpriteBubble** and **cSpriteBubbleGrayScale**, on the right are **cSpriteBubblePie**

The **cSpriteBubble** consists of a disk with a rectangular highlight on it, meant to be mildly suggestive of the reflection of a window in the surface of a soap bubble. We implement **cSpriteBubble** as a **cSpriteComposite** with two members: a **cSpriteCircle** (that is, a many-sided polygon) and a **cPolygon** rectangle that we can access as the **cSpriteBubble::paccentpoly()**.

```
void cSpriteBubble::setAccentPoly()
{
    Real side = 0.33 * (pcirclepoly()->radius());
    cVector pverts[4] = {cVector(0.0, 0.0, 0.0),
        cVector(2*side, 0.0, 0.0),
        cVector(2*side, side, 0.0),
        cVector(0.0, side, 0.0)};
    cPolygon *prectpoly = new cPolygon(4, pverts);
    prectpoly->setSpriteAttitude(
        cMatrix::translation(cVector(side, 0.5*side, 0.1)));
    add(prectpoly); //Decoration rectangle.
    setFillColor(pcirclepoly()->fillColor()); /* Make the accent color
        match the circle. */
}
```

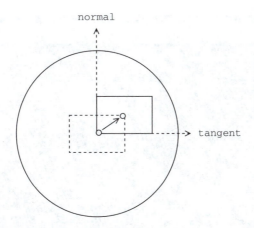

Figure 9.3 The **cSpriteBubble** composite sprite. Accent rectangle is translated away from origin.

Figure 9.3 is a picture of the construction.

The **cPolygon** constructor by default centers the rectangle on the origin, which is why we need to set the rectangular accent polygon's _spriteattitude to cMatrix::translation(cVector(side, 0.5*side, 0.1)). This moves the rectangle away from the origin and into the position shown. The 0.1 translation in the z slot is so that, when viewed in 3D, the accent rectangle sticks up a bit out of the disk of the circle. You need to be careful not to draw faces of polygons in the same plane in 3D as then they 'z-fight' with each other and flicker in an ugly fashion.

Polypolygons

Now let's say a bit about the **cPolyPolygon** class. A polypolygon is a **cSpriteComposite** which consists of a base polygon plus a secondary 'tipshape' polygon at each vertex.

The way we've implemented the polypolygons is to assume that a polypolygon will have the same tipshape at each of its vertices. We use the **cPolyPolygon** methods **setBasePoly(cPolygon* pppoly)** and **setTipShape(cSprite* pshape)** to set the base and the tipshape information.

You can view a bunch of these guys by opening up the Spacewar game and selecting **Game | Polypolygons**. Note that when the game reseeds itself, it reverts to asteroid sprites; if you want a game that sticks with polypolygon sprites, you need to code this fact into the constructors of the game's critters.

In order to make a more symmetric image, we design the **cPolyPolygon::draw** method so as to draw an image of the tipshape which is rotated slightly from vertex to vertex; more precisely, if a polygon has n vertices, then we draw the tipshape as is at the first vertex, and then rotate it by *2 * PI/n* for each of the successive vertices, rotating it back into starting position when we're done.

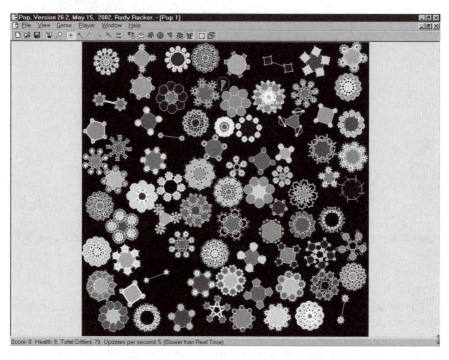

Score: 8. Health: 9. Total Critters: 79. Updates per second: 5. (Slower than Real Time)

Polyploygons in the Spacewar game

9.5 The *cSpriteIcon* class

The author did a lot of coding and encapsulating in order to come up with a
cSprite child class called *cSpriteIcon*. *cSpriteIcon* has a constructor *cSpriteIcon(int
resourceID)* which takes the ID of a bitmap resource as its argument. To make
things nicer, the *cSpriteIcon* will automatically make the background of the
image transparent. To give a critter a transparent-background sprite based on a
resource bitmap with an ID like, say, IDB_EARTH, we only need to add a single
line to the critter's constructor.

```
setSprite(new cSpriteIcon(IDB_EARTH));
```

We also have the option of not having a transparent background at all. The
full prototype of the *cSpriteIcon* constructor looks like this.

```
cSpriteIcon(int resourceID, BOOL transparent = TRUE,
    BOOL presetaspect = FALSE);
```

If we put a FALSE in the second argument to the constructor, we get a solid
bitmap.

The third *cSpriteIcon* constructor argument isn't often used. This presetaspect
field of *cSpriteIcon* relates primarily to the *cSpriteIconBackground*, which sets it to TRUE.
The purpose of *cSpriteIconBackground* is to make a solid big icon suitable for use
as a background in a game. Its constructor is of the form *cSpriteIconBackground(int*

Some transparent background bitmaps in an OpenGL Pop display. Note that OpenGL can rotate bitmaps to match the critter orientation. The Windows display doesn't rotate them

resourceID, const cRealBox2 &borderrect), where the *borderrect* is ordinarily going to be a wall of the 3D *cRealBox* that your game lives inside. When `presetaspect` has the normal *cSpriteIcon* default value of FALSE, the sprite is proportioned to match the shape of the resource bitmap specified by *resourceID*. When `presetaspect` is TRUE we want to cover some definite fixed shape like a border rectangle with our bitmap.

When you want to make a new bitmap of yours into a *cSpriteIcon* you need to be aware of the following points.

- First you have to save the bitmap in the *.**bmp** format. Most things you pull off the Web will be *.**gif** or *.**jpg**. In order to convert to the *.**bmp** format, you need to open the file in some reasonably powerful graphics tool such as a photo editor, and then save it in the *.**bmp** format.

- Before saving the *.**bmp**, you should resize the image so that it is not much larger than you expect it to be onscreen. It's pointless to save a screen-sized image of a face that you intend to use for a fingernail-sized icon. Not only is it a waste of memory to use a big source bitmap for a small target, if you leave it up to your system to dynamically squash your big bitmap down to a postage stamp, you have no control of the exact way in which the squashing is done. In the worst cases, the appearance of the small bitmap will seem to flicker and change as the critter moves about. Take the time to cleanly convert your bitmap into a size close to what you'll be viewing it in. If some important feature doesn't show up in the small size, edit the image to make it look right.

- In order to make OpenGL handle your bitmaps smoothly, it is important to adjust the pixel size of each source bitmap so that each each edge is a power of two, such as 16, 32, 64, 128, 256, 512, etc. The bitmap can be rectangular, that is, the edges don't need to be the same, but both edges should be a power of two. You can resize the bitmap in your image editor. In the case where resizing would distort the bitmap, as with a face, you simply need to add blank filler pixels along two edges; you can do this by copying the area you want to keep, making a new bitmap with the desired edge lengths and then pasting in the image area.

- There is one peculiarity of the *cSpriteIcon* constructor that you need to be aware of. When you make a transparent-background icon, the constructor will pick one color found in the resource bitmap and treat this color as if it is transparent. Which color should it use? You might say 'white,' but it might very well be that you want to have some white pixels inside your bitmap icon. The rule which *cSpriteIcon* uses is to look at the color of the pixel in the upper left corner of the bitmap resource and treat this color as transparent. Thus, if you want to have white in your bitmap, fill in the background that you don't care about with some other color, say purple, and make sure that the upper left hand corner pixel of your bitmap is purple. If you are using a complicated photo-based bitmap you need to make doubly sure that the upper left pixel is indeed the color which you want to have be transparent.

- In saving to the *.**bmp** format, you have the option of saving in '256 color mode' which is also known as '8 bit mode.' This is as opposed to a 'millions of color mode' or a 'true color mode.' The 256 color/8 bit mode will sometimes make your image look less good, but it has the virtue of making the image file smaller and allowing it to be put on the screen more rapidly. This is an issue either if you have a lot of bitmap images or if you have a bitmap image which is large (such as a background bitmap). Always try 256 color/8 bit first.

- Once you have the *.**bmp**, move it to the res subdirectory of the directory where your game's code lives. Now you can import this bitmap into your project as a new bitmap resource. Use **Project | Add Resource... | Import...** and then navigate to find your *.**bmp** file. The Resource Editor will open your imported bitmap. [With Version 6.0, import a bitmap by using **Insert | Resource | Bitmap | Import...** In Version 6.0, some bitmaps will not be viewable within the Resource Editor, but this doesn't mean they can't be added to the project.]

    It's helpful to give your bitmap an easy-to-remember resource ID name like IDB_HAPPYDOG instead of the machine-generated ID (like IDB_BITMAP1) it will have received. To call up the Bitmap Properties dialog you can **Alt+Enter** while the bitmap is open in the editor.

- Once you've done this, you can use the resource ID to make a new sprite with a line like new cSpriteIcon(IDB_HAPPYDOG).

- It is perfectly all right to have several different critters use the same bitmap and the same IDB_HAPPYDOG resource. But you must make a fresh *cSpriteIcon* for each of them. (If two critters share the same sprite, there will be trouble when the program ends, as the sprite will get deleted twice, which will cause a crash.) If you write your code properly and create and install the sprite inside the critter constructor this happens automatically.

- Don't worry about having lots and lots of critters with *cSpriteIcon* images, as our *cGraphics* implementations share resources among the *cSpriteIcon* objects in a memory-efficient way.

- In *OpenGL*, if you have a large view of a small *CSpriteIcon*, the speed drops. The *CSpriteIcon* is a texture pattern of squares derived from the bitmap pixels. Projecting large images of those squares is costly.

9.6 *cSpriteLoop* and *cSpriteDirectional*

The *cSpriteLoop* and *cSpriteDirectional* sprites are arrays of other sprites. As they inherit from *cSpriteComposite* they have an *add* method that adds new sprites into the array. You can feed *cSpriteComposite::add* method either a *cSprite** pointer as an argument or simply an integer resource ID number as an argument – in the latter case the add(resourceID) method constructs a new cSpriteIcon(resourceID) and then adds that sprite.

People often want to use sequences of bitmaps for their sprites. Suppose you have three successive bitmaps for a walking man and that you've saved them as resources with IDs of the form IDB_MAN1. To simplify things the Pop Framework lets you pass in a resource ID as the argument to add. A *cCritter* constructor could make and use such a sprite like this.

```
cSpriteLoop pmanwalk = new cSpriteLoop();
pmanwalk->add(IDB_MAN1);
pmanwalk->add(IDB_MAN2);
pmanwalk->add(IDB_MAN3);
setSprite(pmanwalk);
```

The *cSpriteLoop::animate* method ages a time counter and adjusts the active sprite accordingly. The effect is that *cSpriteLoop* flips from one image to the next. The default wait between images is a fifth of a second, or 0.2. You can change this wait time with the *cSpriteLoop::setFlipwait(Real flipwait)* method.

Note that the flipping is based on the real time elapsed and *not* on the number of updates you've done. This keeps our program appearance from being dependent on the speed of the processor. You never want to do anything on basis of cycle-counts. Always use the time.

The *cSpriteDirectional* is initialized much like the *cSpriteLoop*. We create a new *cSpriteDirectional* object and then use its *add* method, passing either *cSprite** pointers or bitmap resource ID numbers to the *add*.

The way the *cSpriteDirectional* picks which sprite to show is to look at the direction the critter that owns the sprite is pointing in. It distinguishes as many directions as the number of sprites that you added.

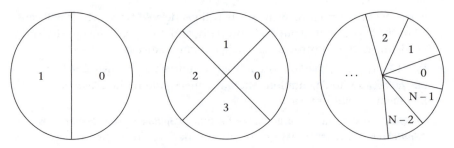

Figure 9.4 How the *cSpriteDirectional* picks the sprite with 2, 4, or N directions

The *cSpriteDirectional::animate* adjusts the active sprite according to the current `critterdirection`. It uses the animate method to select one among several directional bitmaps, as shown in Figure 9.4.

Use of the *cSpriteDirectional* gets around the fact that we can't rotate bitmaps on the fly in Windows graphics; a *cSpriteDirectional* can store various differently rotated versions of a bitmap. This is not an issue in OpenGL graphics, however the use of bitmaps does tend to slow OpenGL down more than is comfortable.

If you're ambitious, you can make a *cSpriteDirectional* whose members are *cSpriteLoop* animations. If you do this, don't forget that you need to create fresh sprite objects for each critter. It's fine to reuse the same resource ID, but you have to wrap them up in fresh sprites. To avoid having to write out the same code more than once, you should create and install the sprite inside your critter constructor. If you happen to have two different critters that will use the same complicated sprite, you might save code writing by making a new *cSprite* child class whose constructor carries out the complicated initialization.

As was mentioned above, the *cGraphicsMFC* and *cGraphicsOpenGL* allocate the *cSpriteIcon* resources in a memory-efficient way. Note also that they automatically rescale the size of your *cSpriteIcon* bitmaps when you resize the window.

Review questions

A   What is a *cSpriteComposite*?

B   What are some of methods we have for creating standard polygon sprites?

C   What are steps you take to load a *.jpg bitmap you've found into a *cSpriteIcon*?

D   What does the *cSpriteLoop::animate* method do?

E   What does the *cSpriteDirectional::animate* method do?

Exercises

Exercise 9.1: Making *cSprite::draw* non-virtual

If you don't explicitly label a method as 'virtual' in the base class, then the child class overrides will ignore it. Open up the Pop project file and remove the word 'virtual' from the line `virtual void draw(cGraphics *pgraphics, int drawflags);` at the bottom of the sprite.h file. Build and run. You'll see default base-class *imagedraw* methods for all the sprites. They'll be sprites that are drawn as hollow circles.

Exercise 9.2: What happens if you don't initialize the sprites?

By default every critter gets a base class sprite. If you forget to initialize the sprites you'll see the same default sprite as in the last exercise. You can test this by going into the gamestub.cpp file and commenting out the sprite initialization in the *cCritterStubProp* constructor.

Exercise 9.3: Making your own polygons

Sometimes you'll want to give a critter a sprite that has some particular polygonal shape that you like. In this exercise you'll make the player in the Game stub game be shaped like a slender rocket-like pentagon instead of like a slender triangle.

Here's an example of how we set a polygonal sprite shape taken from *cCritterBullet::initialize* method inside the critterarmed.cpp. The purpose of the code is to create a slender isosceles triangle and make this be the sprite for the *cCritterBullet* making the *initialize* call.

```
cPolygon *ppolygon = new cPolygon(3);
        /* Now make it a thin isosceles triangle, with the apex
            at the 0th vertex. All that matters at first is the
            tatops of the numbers, as we will use setRadius to
            make the thing the right size, and center it on the
            origin. */
    ppolygon->setVertex(0, cVector(3.0, 0.0));
    ppolygon->setVertex(1, cVector(0.0, 1.0));
    ppolygon->setVertex(2, cVector(0.0, -1.0));
    ppolygon->setRadius(cCritter::BULLETRADIUS); /* Call setRadius
        after adding all the vertices! */
    ppolygon->setFillColor(cColorStyle::CN_YELLOW);
    setSprite(ppolygon);
```

The idea is that if you want a polygon with N vertices, you create a new polygon with a **new** operator. Then give the new polygon as many vertices as you need with a call like `setRegularPolygon(N, cVector(0.0, 0.0), 1.0, 0.0)`, where only the first argument really matters. Then you go down the list of vertices and set them one by one, starting with 0 and ending with $N - 1$. Then you use a *setRadius* call to set the polygon shape to whatever size you like. (The *setRadius* call has the side effect of centering the polygon on the origin, so you may need to change the _spriteattitude if you want to move the object back to some other location. If you have your vertices just where you want, you don't necessarily need to call *setRadius* at all. When in doubt, call it, though.)

Now how do you figure out what numbers to use in the `setVertex` lines? Draw a little grid for yourself – or use some graph paper – and draw a picture of the shape you want. Write the coordinates of each point on your sheet of paper (if you try and do this in your head you're likely to mess it up). Then use these numbers in the `setVertex` calls. Make sure that the first vertex you put in – that is, the 0th vertex – is where you'd like the sprite to point when it moves. In the case of the rocket, this would be the pointed tip. And only put the starting vertex in once because you don't need to close the polygon back up by putting the starting vertex in twice. The *cPolygon* will take care of that on its own.

Your picture doesn't necessarily need to be centered on the origin; the *setRadius* call will take care of that, automatically storing the polygon in origin-centered form. (You can test this claim by putting the digits 10 in front of the x-coordinates in the code above to shift everything 100 units to the right.) The size of the number also doesn't matter, this is taken care of by the *setRadius* call. (You can test this by putting the digit 0 after each of the x and y coordinates to make the triangle ten times as big.) All that matters is the relative positions and ratios of the points you choose.

Now make your player be shaped like a biting mouth. Once that works, try making it be shaped like a fish. And then try a shape of your own invention. Remember that the polygon will move with the 0th vertex in the lead, so pick this one towards the front.

Exercise 9.4: Fish-shaped polygons

Suppose we'd like to have a lot of fish. What you can do is make a child *class cSpriteFish : public cPolygon*. Define the class in a file called polygonshapes.h. And then make a polygonshapes.cpp class that implements a constructor to make the thing be a polygon in the shape of a fish. The class doesn't have any additional data members, so its constructor is the only new piece of code you have to add. If we used a crude ten-point fish (see Figure 9.5), the *cSpriteFish* constructor would call `setRegularPolygon(10, ...)` and then make ten calls to `setVertex`. Don't forget to put in the DECLARE_SERIAL and IMPLEMENT_SERIAL macros; you can copy the way its done in the bubble.h and bubble.cpp files.

Make the class and test it in the PickNPop game by making the peanuts look like fish. So now it'll be an undersea treasure game! All you have to do is go into the gamepicknpop.cpp and change the single line of the `cCritterPeanut::cCritterPeanut()` constructor to read `setSprite(new cSpriteFish())`. Remember that for this to compile, you'll have to add an `#include "polygonshapes.h"` to the polygonshapes.cpp file, and the very first thing in the file has to be an `#include "stdafx.h"`.

Exercise 9.5: Composite polygon shapes

Looking back at our fish problem, shouldn't a fish have an eye? So maybe you better add an extra `cVector _vectoreyedot` and `cSpriteCircle *_pointeyedot` to the *cSpriteFish* definition and let the fish inherit from *cSpriteComposite*.

Think of some more shapes we might need and make more child classes that draw them. A *cSpriteRocket*, a *cSpriteBird*, a *cSpriteFootball*, and a *cSpriteUFO* might all be useful. Some of these would be better represented by several polygons – for a *cSpriteRocket*, for instance, you might want to have the rocket's fuselage (or fish's body) be a different color from its fins. Use the *cSpriteComposite* to have several polygons involved. Check the code in spritebubble.cpp for inspiration.

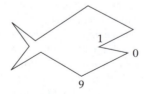

Figure 9.5 A fish with vertex numbers

Exercise 9.6: Other kinds of polypolygons

You can use any kind of sprite you like for the tipshape of a polygon; in fact you could nest and get polypolypolygons. Try to view some of these. You might look at the **cGame** code for generating random polypolygons for inspiration.

We've experimented with both the two-level and the three-level polypolygons, which are polypolygons whose tips are polygons whose tips are polygons. The runspeed gets pretty low with these guys, but they're interesting to look at once you tweak the various numbers good values.

Exercise 9.7: Flexing polygons

Make a **cPolygonFlex** child class with a drift method to make the vertices move when animate is called. Try and make a fish whose mouth opens and closes.

Exercise 9.8: Directional vs loop sprites

The Worms game is an example of how to use these multi sprites. By default the player uses a **cSpriteLoop**. Go into the **cCritterWormsPlayer::cCritterWormsPlayer()** constructor in **gameworms.cpp** and look at how this works. To see a directional sprite, go to the top of the file and comment out the line #define PLAYERSPRITELOOP. Once you see how both the kinds of sprite work, you might try changing the **cCritterWormsPlayer** constructor code to use something different for the different individual sprites. See how the loop and the directional sprite look with, say, four bitmaps.

Exercise 9.9: A loop sprite of polygons

If I wanted a critter's constructor code to have a ppolygons animated sprite that would cycle from triangle through hexagon, I could do it like this.

```
cSpriteLoop ppolygons = new cSpriteLoop();
ppolygons->add(new cPolygon(3));
ppolygons->add(new cPolygon(4));
ppolygons->add(new cPolygon(5));
ppolygons->add(new cPolygon(6));
setSprite(ppolygons); //Called by the cCritter whose constructor
    contains this code.
```

Try giving the Prop critters a sprite like this in the **cCritterStubProp** constructor in gamestub.cpp.

Exercise 9.10: A *HappySad* sprite

Suppose that you want to alternate between two kinds of sprites, depending on whether or not the critter was recently damaged.

Derive a **cSpriteHappySad** from the **cSpriteShowOneChild** sprite, and overload its animate method like this:

```
viod cSpriteHappySad::animate(Real dt, cCritter *powner)
{
    if (!powner->recentlyDamaged())
        setShowIndex(0);
    else
        setShowIndex(1);
    if (showindex != cBiota::NOINDEX)
            childspriteptr[ showindex]->animate(dt, powner);
}
```

When you use a **cSpriteHappySad**, you have to be sure to add at least two child sprites to it, the first added will be the 'happy' sprite, the second addded will be the 'sad' or 'recently damaged' sprite.

Note that we currently have a default method of showing a critter's damage by drawing polygons in wireframe mode. For this exercise, turn off this behavior by commenting out the `#define SHOWDAMAGE` line at the head of critter.cpp. (Also note that, in any case, the wireframe mode doesn't affect bitmap sprites.)

Now try giving the player in, say, the Worms game a **cSpriteHappySad**. You can use the current loop sprite (as it currently is) when the player is healthy, and add in a bitmap sprite for when the player is recently damaged.

Exercise 9.11: Three-dimensional sprites

The **glshapes**.* files in the Pop Framework provide some standard 'glut' methods for draw-ing three-dimensional shapes. 'Glut' stands for 'OpenGL Toolkit.' Although the glut library

The Gamestub3D showing OpenGL sphere, teapot, torus, and some polyhedra. The cog-like shapes are **cPolyPolygon**

includes a lot of useful high-level OpenGL methods, we only incorporate this one single glut file into the Pop Framework at present, in part because glut is based on a non-Windows framework that makes parts of it incompatible with MFC.

The **glshapes** files implement the following function calls, where **GLdouble** means the same as **double**, and **GLint** means **int**.

```
glutSolidSphere(GLdouble radius, GLint slices, GLint stacks);
glutSolidCone(GLdouble base, GLdouble height, GLint slices, GLint
    stacks);
glutSolidTorus(GLdouble innerRadius, GLdouble outerRadius, GLint
    sides, GLint rings);

glutSolidTetrahedron(void);
glutSolidCube(GLdouble size);
glutSolidOctahedron(void);
glutSolidDodecahedron(void);
glutSolidIcosahedron(void);

glutSolidTeapot(GLdouble scale);
```

For each 'Solid' function there is an analogous 'Wire' function, for instance, there is a `glutWireSphere(GLdouble radius, GLint slices, GLint stacks);`

The 'teapot,' by the way, is a standard test shape beloved of computer graphics programmers, and built up by using 'Bezier patches.' It's sometimes called the 'teapotahedron,' and is jokingly viewed as the sixth Platonic solid!

The `slices` and `stacks` parameters used for the circular shapes can be thought of as the number of north–south longitude and east–west latitude lines, respectively. That is, a sphere is drawn as a vertical pile of `stacks` many `slices`-sided polygons. You need values of at least 12 or so to make these shapes smooth-looking.

What you should do for this problem is to implement some or all of the classes **cSpriteSphere, cSpriteTeapot, cSpriteTorus, cSpriteCube**, and so on. First do one, and get it debugged, and then try a few more. You can try testing them out as sprites used by the critters in **cGameDefender3D**.

Each of the classes should have a constructor that takes a `Real` radius argument with a default value of 1.0. The circular sprites have additional `int` slices and `int` stacks arguments with default values of, say, 12, though these defaults ought to be statics. And the torus and cone each have an additional **Real** parameter: the torus should also have a `Real innerradius` argument and the cone also needs a `Real height` argument.

To draw the sprites, you could go one of two ways: many classes or one class.

Many classes

You could have each class emulate the behavior of **cPolygon** and **cSpriteIcon** and define, say,

```
void cSpriteSphere::imagedraw(cGraphics *pgraphics, int drawflags)
{
    pgraphics->drawsphere(this, drawflags);
}
```

And you'd have to add a new **drawsphere** method to **cGraphics**, giving it a void or trivial implementation for **cGraphicsMFC** and giving it an implementation in **cGraphicsOpenGL** that calls `glutSolidSphere` or `glutWireSphere` depending on whether `psphere->filled()` is `TRUE`.

```
virtual void drawsphere(cSpriteSphere *psphere, int drawflags )
```

You'd need to override *imagedraw* and implement a differently-argumented variant of *cGraphics::drawsomething* for each of the nine classes, which is a little boring to do.

One class

You could get by with slightly less typing by having all of these new classes inherit from a catch-all *cSprite3D* class. We could prototype *cSprite3D* something like this.

```
class cSprite3D : public cSprite
{
protected:
    int _slices, _stacks;
    int _shapecode;
    Real _extraparam;
public:
    cSprite3D(int type = cSprite3D::SPHERE, Real radius = 1.0,
        Real extraparam = 0.0, int slices = cSprite3D::SLICES,
        int stacks = cSprite3D::STACKS);
    virtual void imagedraw(cGraphics *pgraphics, int drawflags)
        {pgraphics->draw3Dshape(this, drawflags);}
};
```

And then you'd only need to prototype and code a single *cGraphics* method.

```
virtual void draw3Dshape(cSprite3D *pshape, int drawflags );
```

The *cGraphicsMFC* version of *draw3Dshape* can just draw a circle, while the *cGraphicsOpenGL* implementation will hold a big switch on pshape->shapecode(). Is the cost of the switch something worth worrying about?

No. Although we didn't raise this point earlier, the *cSprite::draw* method is constructed so that it will avoid the switch after the first call to a given draw method for a *cSprite3D* by using display lists.

You will need to do some work to implement a correct *radius()* method for these sprites, and to have the value returned by *radius()* match the radius argument that you feed in – and to match the visual appearance. If possible make *radius()* match the number in the _radius field, it may be that *cSprite3D* needs to maintain a supplemental Real _glutradius for the parameter that you actually feed into the glut call in cGraphicsOpenGL::draw(..), or for the parameter that you perhaps use in a scaling matrix. Compare our use of a Real _visualradius in the *cSpriteIcon* code.

The reason that radius is an issue is because you compute the distance from a cube's center to its corner one way, but you compute the distance from a tetrahedron or a cone's center to its furthest point another way. We care about the radius because in order for our cheap and dirty collision code to look right, the 'radius' of a sprite needs to match the radius of the smallest sphere that encloses it.

Games

10

A computer game, or other kind of simulated world, will contain a number of agents, or critters, each with its own sprite. It's natural to have a Game base class to hold the active array of critters. As well as being a container, the Game class should take on some additional duties. When the play begins, the Game object initializes the geometry of the world and adds in the critters. While the play continues, the Game object repeatedly updates the critters and shows them on the screen. At the same time, the Game object tracks the critters' status and decides when the world should be moved to a new level. And the play ends when the Game object decides that it's over.

We implement these design ideas as the *cGame* class that makes up the core of the Pop Framework.

Remember that in an MFC program like Pop, the data for the program lives in a *CPopDoc* document object, and the onscreen window display is controlled by a *CPopView* view object. Except for one little extra bookkeeping variable, the sole member that we put inside our *CPopDoc* class is a cGame* _pgame.

Why is it that we use a cGame* _pgame instead of a cGame _cgame? As we've mentioned before, we do this because we want polymorphism to work! In C++, a call like _pgame->seedCritters() will work polymorphically and figure out the correct version of the method depending on what kind of *cGame* child class object _pgame actually points to. But a call like _cgame.seedCritters() will always just use the base class *cGame::seedCritters*. Always remember, in C++ pointer variables behave polymorphically, but instance variables do not. See Chapter 22: Topics in C++ for more about this point.

10.1 The *cGame* class

The *cGame* and *cCritter* classes are the key classes for writing games using the Pop Framework. In using the Pop Framework to write a game you will typically define a few new child classes of *cCritter* and a new child class of *cGame*. Your *cGame* child will include some new members and will override some of the base class *cGame* methods.

The most significant member of the *cGame* is a *cBiota *_pbiota* object. The *cBiota* object is a collection of pointers to all of the game's active *cCritter* objects. The name of this class **cBiota** is based on the fact that the class is meant to hold the entire population, the 'biota' of the world of the game. This collection class is implemented as a type-safe, serializable **CArray**, and it has some array-walking methods: **draw, move, update, animate, feellistener.** Each of these methods calls the method of the same name for each member critter. Thus, for example, **update** acts like this.

```
void cBiota::update(CPopView *pactiveview, Real dt)
{
    for( int i=0; i<GetSize(); i++)
        GetAt(i)->update(pactiveview, dt);
}
```

There's more information about **cBiota** and its methods at the end of this chapter.

The **cGame** also has a distinguished **cCritter *_pplayer** that represents the player. In the Spacewar game, for instance, the _pplayer is the little ship shooting the asteroids. To make our code easier to maintain we always assume that _pplayer is some valid pointer (not NULL).

Usually _pplayer is a member of _pbiota, but in a few games, like the PickNPop Game, we don't have a visible player; in this case we use a default critter for _pplayer and don't add it to the _pbiota.

It may be that you'll want to add some other distinguished **cCritter** pointers to the **cGame**. Thus if, for instance, you want to have a goal to shoot at in the Airhockey game, you might want to define a **cCritterHockeyGoal** class and give your **cGameAirhockey** a **cCritterHockeyGoal *_pmygoal** member. We'll return to this idea later.

cGame also has a **cRealBox _border** member to specify the size of the game as a rectangle in the mathematical real-number plane or as a box in 3D space. We can choose to have a square flat game world as in Spacewar, or a long thin flat rectangle like in Ballworld. Alternately, **_border** can be like a solid aquarium as in the 3D Game Stub game, or like a hallway as in the 3D game Defender.

It's worth noting that the apparent sizes of the critters depends on the ratio of their sprites' radii to the size of the **_border.**

cGame has an integer **_wrapflag** to determine if the default behavior of its critters should be to wrap around the edges, bounce, or possibly just stop at the edges. (The codes for these three options are, respectively, cCritter::WRAP, cCritter::BOUNCE, and cCritter::CLAMP.) The individual **cCritter** have **_wrapflag** members as well, so this looks like an example of what we call a 'forgery,' that is, of keeping the same data in two different places. But we want to allow for the possibilities that different critters might have different wrap properties. The **cCritter(cGame *pownergame)** constructor sets the new critter's **_wrapflag** to match the game's **_wrapflag,** but then in the rest of the constructor you're free to set the critter's **_wrapflag** as you like. The **cCritterUFO** constructor does this for the Spacewar game, so that the **cCritterUFO** don't wrap even if the other critters do.

cGame has an integer **_seedcount** to specify how many critters to seed with, and it has an integer **_maxscore** that can be used to determine when a game is over. Normally the **cGame::score()** accessor will return the _pplayer->score().

Another *cGame* member that we like to adjust is the CArray<HCURSOR, HCURSOR> _arrayHCURSOR. This is used to specify which kinds of cursor tools the game will use. If you run the Pop program and switch among the games, you'll notice that for different games, different sets of cursor tool icons are active in the toolbar.

Another *cGame* member worth mentioning is the collection class *cCollider _pcollider*, which holds pairs of critters that we want to check for possible collisions. We'll discuss this class in Chapter 11: Collisions.

10.2   The game's timestep cycle

Probably the most important method in *cGame* is *step(Real dt)*. This is the method that controls the animation of the critters. First we'll outline the order in which *step* does things, then we'll explain why we use this order, and then we'll go over the outline again.

Updating a simulation of multiple objects is a delicate thing. You need to do things in the right order, and you need to try and have the objects being updated in parallel, but all at the same time. For this reason, *step* is not a virtual method of *cGame*; you are not supposed to override it. (All rules have exceptions, though. If you really want to override it, change it to a virtual!)

Here's what *step* does in brief.

- *Adjust.* Adjust game parameters. (Game over? Need to reseed? Change levels?)
- *Listen.* Pass recent user input to the critter *feellistener* methods, particularly to the onscreen player critter. (Use keypresses, mouse actions.)
- *Move.* Call the critters' *move* methods to keep physics working.
- *Update.* Call the critters' *update* methods to let the critters react to their environment.
- *Collide.* Check for and compute the collisions between pairs of critters which are sensitive to touching each other.
- *Clean up.* Remove any critters ready to die, and add any new ones that have been requested.
- *Animate.* Possibly animate the critters' sprites. (Flip-book, rotate, morph, etc.)
- *Draw.* After each call to *step*, all of the critters get drawn to the active views.

Why does the Pop Framework use this particular order of doing things?

Adjust comes first. It's reasonable to make any overall adjustments to the game at the start of each step, as there's no point continuing with a step if we're about the change the rules.

We want the onscreen player critter to have the most immediate possible response to the user's actions, so we do the *move* step right after the *listen* step.

After all the critters have moved, have them 'look around' and respond to their new positions. The looking-around process has two phases, the *update* phase and the *collide* phase.

The update and collide methods can be overridden to tell critters to die, and to tell critters to spawn off new critters. Once all these requests are in place, we process them right away with the *clean up* stage. Certainly if some critters are dead, we want to get rid of them right away before drawing them.

The *animate* step does some matrix work to bring the sprite's appearance into line with the critter's latest orientation. Clearly we want to do this before drawing, and we want to do it after having removed any dead critters and adding any newborn critters.

Now let's take a more detailed look at the sequence of events in the **cGame::step** process.

- *Adjust.* The game parameters are adjusted, usually on the basis of the score and the number of critters. Possibly the **_gameover** flag is turned on. Perhaps the critter population needs to be reseeded, or the game should be switched to a new 'level' mode.

- *Listen.* Before **step** was called, the **CPopView** passed any keyboard or mouse messages to the **cGame**. The **cGame** has reacted by putting these messages into a **cController _pcontroller** member. In addition, the timestep **dt** since the last full update is fed into the **step** as an argument.

  Any interested critters use **feellistener** to listen to any keyboard or mouse messages. This may change the critters' acceleration, velocity or position. Commonly the only visible critter that has a non-trivial listener is the player.

- *Move.* Each critter does a **move(dt)**. This changes the critters' age, velocity, position, and outcode.

- *Update.* Each critter updates itself by calling **feelforce** to react to its various **_pforcearray** members. It may react to the other critters' positions. The update may change the critters' acceleration or velocity. The critter may also make a 'service request' to be deleted or to create a new critter, as when a critter is shooting bullets from a gun.

- *Collide.* Each pair of touching critters that has been registered to the game's **cCollider** object generates a call to a **cCritter::collide(cCritter *pcritterother)** method which changes the position and velocity of the two critters involved.

- *Clean up.* The service requests from the *update* stage are processed, possibly deleting some critters and constructing some new ones. The method used is **cBiota::processServiceRequests**.

- *Animate.* Each critter and its sprite are optionally tumbled or animated in some other fashion.

- *Draw.* And then the **CPopView::OnDraw** is called to draw the critters on the screen.

Let's draw a sequence diagram (Figure 10.1) for some of this. Keep in mind that the **cBiota** is an array collection which holds some array walking methods. In addition, **cBiota** holds a queue of 'service requests' posted during the *update* phase. We don't really put in any details about the collide process yet.

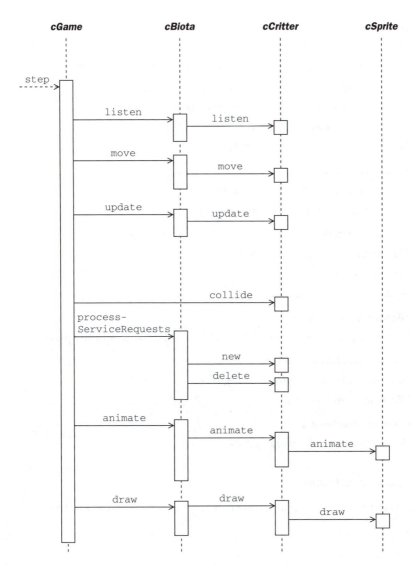

Figure 10.1 Sequence diagram of the *cGame::step* method

10.3   The virtual methods of *cGame*

Most of the coding you do involving the *cGame* class is going to involve extending the *cGame* constructor and overriding a few special methods called *seedCritters*, *initializeView*, *adjustGameParameters*, and *statusMessage*.

Here are the main things determined by these methods.

cGame::cGame

- The size of the game world.
- What colors to use for the edges and background of the world.
- What bitmaps, if any, to use for your backgrounds.
- Whether the world is wrapped or has edges.
- What class of player critter you'll use.
- What 'permanent' critters you'll use.

cGame::seedCritters

- What 'temporary' critters you have.
- Arrangement of the critters in the world.

cGame::initializeView

- The background image, if any, to use.
- The cursor tool to start with.
- Start in zoomed-in mode?

cGame::initializeViewpoint

- Where to place the viewer critter relative to the world and the player.

cGame::adjustGameParameters

- How the game is to change during play.
- When the game is over.

cGame::statusMessage

- What to write in the status bar line.

The *cGame* constructor

In a recent build, the default *cGame* constructor looks, in part, like this.

```
cGame::cGame() :
_seedcount(COUNTSTART),
_gameover(TRUE),
_maxscore(MAXSCORE),
_scorecorrection(0),
_wrapflag(cCritter::WRAP),
_cursorpos(0.0, 0.0),
_autoplay(0),
_level(1),
_newgame(TRUE)
{
//Allocate the pointer variables except for the player.
    _pbiota = new cBiota(this);
    _pcollider = new cCollider();
```

```
    _pcontroller = new cController(); /* This is a structure used to
        store key and mouse info. */
    _plightingmodel = new cLightingModel(); /* Can be used in 3D
        games to specify the lights. */
//Set the border size.
    _border.set(14.4, 9.6, 0.0); /* A flat rectangle that happens to
        seem good. */
//Set the border colors.
    _border.pcolorstyle()->setFillColor(cColorStyle::CN_WHITE);
    _border.pcolorstyle()->setLineColor(cColorStyle::CN_YELLOW);
    _border.pcolorstyle()->setLineWidthWeight(0.01);
//Set the background bitmap AFTER setting the size of the _border
    setBackgroundBitmap(IDB_BACKGROUND); /* Sets the
        _pbackgroundbitmap field. */
//Initialize the player AFTER setting the size of the _border.
    setPlayer(new cCritterPlayer(this)); /* Use the setPlayer accessor
        rather than setting _pplayer by hand. */
}
```

When you derive a game such as *cGameSpacewar* as a child of *cGame*, you write a *cGameSpacewar:: cGameSpacewar* constructor. Keep in mind that a child class constructor works by first calling the parent class constructor, and by then calling its own code. In other words, all of the code and initializations of the *cGame* constructor will have taken place by the time you get inside the first left bracket { of your *cGameSpacewar* constructor.

The *cGameSpacewar* needs to make the following changes (among others) to what the default constructor does.

- Change the dimensions of the *_border* to a square.
- Change the fillcolor of the *_border* to black. (This serves as the game's background color when no background bitmap is being shown.)
- Change the player by constructing a new *cCritterArmedPlayerSpacewar* and using the *cGame::setPlayer* mutator method to install it into the _pplayer field.

Here's the three lines you'd add to the *cGameSpacewar* constructor to do this.

```
_border.set(20.0, 20.0);
_border.pcolorstyle()->setFillColor(cColorStyle::CN_BLACK);
setPlayer(new cCritterArmedPlayerSpacewar);
```

We do allow the possibility for having a game in which the *_pplayer* is 'offscreen.' This means the player is not a member of the *_pbiota* array of the critters being moved and displayed. This is what you might do it if you were designing, say, a pinball game, a game in which the player is not represented as visible object on the screen. We do this in the PickNPop game for example. To add an offscreen player, use a line like the following.

```
setPlayer(new cCritter(), FALSE); /* Put dummy player offscreen, not
    in pbiota. */
```

Seeding the game

Once the constructor has been called and the view initialized, the *cGame* still needs to populate its *_pbiota* with more critters than just the *_pplayer*. This is what the *cGame::seedCritters* method does. And when we want to restart or reset a game, we call the *seedCritters* method again.

By the way, you can also create critters inside your overridden *cGame* constructor. The general rule of thumb is that any critter that you expect to have around for the whole game you can create inside the constructor. Any critters that will come and go should be defined in *seedCritters*. These include the critters that you would need to reseed when you reset the game or move to a new level.

Some examples.

- In the Spacewar game, the player gets added in the constructor, the asteroids get added in the *seedCritters* call, and the UFOs are added one at a time by the *adjustGameParameters* call.

- In Airhockey, the player, the puck, the goals, and the rival player are all added in the constructor. Nothing is added in the *seedCritters* call.

- In Ballworld, the player and the basket are added in the constructor. The balls are added in *seedCritters*.

- In Dambuilder, the player and the walls are added in the constructor. The other critters are added in *seedCritters*.

There are three different situations in which *seedCritters* is called.

Firstly, when you start the program or use the Game menu to select a new game type, the new game's *seedCritters* is called by the *cPopDoc::setGameClass(CRuntimeClass *pruntimeclass)* method. The argument to the *setGameClass* method is the 'name' of the game class we want. Thus, for instance, the *CPopDoc* constructor has a call to

```
setGameClass(RUNTIME_CLASS(cGameSpacewar)).
```

It's probably a good idea to pause here and mention that the **CRuntimeClass** holds a string with the name of the class, the size in bytes of the class objects, and information about the class's parent class, if any. There is more discussion of this in Chapter 22: Topics in C++. Now back to the discussion of the first way in which *seedCritters* can be called.

The purpose of the *setGameClass* call is to:

- construct a new game object of the required type and put it into the *_pgame* field of the *CPopDoc*;

- seed the new game;

- tell the documents' views to adjust their display for the new game.

Here's how the ***setGameClass*** code looks.

```
void CPopDoc::setGameClass(CRuntimeClass *pruntimeclass)
{
    /* Create a new pointer with the MFC CreateObject method. Even
       though we cast the new game into a cGame* pointer for the
       return, it "really" remains whatever kind of child class is
       described by the pruntimeclass variable, and will use the
       child class' overrides of any virtual methods. */
    delete _pgame; /* It's OK to delete a NULL, as happens at
       startup. */
    _pgame = (cGame*)(pruntimeclass->CreateObject());
    _pgame->seedCritters();
    UpdateAllViews(NULL, CPopDoc::VIEWHINT_STARTGAME, 0);
}
```

The only way we ever construct a ***cGame*** is via the ***setGameClass*** method which always calls ***seedCritters*** right after the constructor. This means that a game class constructor should *not* make a call to ***seedCritters***. If you call it yourself in the constructor, you'll actually be calling it twice, which can waste time or, worse, have the effect of giving you too many critters. The reason we separate out the ***seedCritters*** from the constructor is because you want to initialize the permanent members of your game in the constructor and only initialize the temporary members in ***seedCritters***.

The *second* situation where the Pop Framework calls ***seedCritters*** is when you press **Enter** to start a new game, either because you want a fresh start or because the current game session has ended. Pressing **Enter** generates a call to the ***cGame::reset*** method which calls ***seedCritters***.

On the subject of the ***reset*** method, we should mention that this call also resets the player's health and score to their starting values and returns the game's **_level** parameter to the starting value of 1. See Exercise 10.2 for an example of how to use the **_level**.

The *third* way to have a call for ***seedCritters*** is that a game may automatically call ***seedCritters*** from within its ***adjustGameParameters*** method. A game might do this to keep the number of onscreen critters from getting too low.

As an example, here's the ***seedCritters*** call from the Spacewar game.

```
void cGameSpacewar::seedCritters()
{
        /* Get rid of any asteroids and bullets, but if there are
           UFOs, leave them alone. */
    _pbiota->purgeCritters(RUNTIME_CLASS(cCritterBullet));
    _pbiota->purgeCritters(RUNTIME_CLASS(cCritterAsteroid));
    for (int i=0; i < _seedcount; i++)
        new cCritterAsteroid(this);
}
```

The **purgeCritters** calls are used to get rid of leftover critters you might want. The thing is, we allow the user to call for a restart at any time during game play. So it may be that there's some critters we need to get rid of. In the Spacewar game, the **adjustGameParameters** call may also call on **seedCritters**, in the event that it's time for a fresh wave of asteroids.

Inside the **seedCritters** method, we often use one or more loops to create new critters. We feed the current **cGame*** argument into the **cCritter** constructors as the **this** pointer. When you pass a game pointer to a critter constructor, the critter is automatically added into the game's **_pbiota** array, and the critter is then able to use its **pgame()** accessor to get information about the game, in particular, to get information about the size of the game world and whether its edges wrap. The critter constructors assign sprites to the critters, position them within the game world, and initialize their velocities.

How the game adjusts itself

The next method to discuss is **cGame::adjustGameParameters**. This method gets called once per game update (from within the **cGame::step** method). We don't necessarily make this method do much work. The default is for it to do nothing. The **cGameStub::adjustGameParameters** is fairly general.

```
void cGameStub::adjustGameParameters()
{
// (1) End the game if the player is dead------------------------
    if (!health() && !_gameover)
        //Player's been killed and game's not over.
    {
        _gameover = TRUE;
        pplayer()->addScore(_scorecorrection);
            // So user can reach _maxscore
        playSound("Tada");
        return;
    }
// (2) Perhaps reseed the screen if rivals and props are gone.------
    int othercrittercount = pbiota()->count(RUNTIME_CLASS(cCritter))
        - pbiota()->count(RUNTIME_CLASS(cCritterBullet)) - 1;
        /* Number of critters minus bullets minus player equals other
            critters. */
    if (!othercrittercount) //Player is alone with bullets
        seedCritters();
// (3) Maybe check some other conditions. -------------------------
}
```

See the description of the Spacewar game in Chapter 14: 2D Shooting Games for an example of a more complicated **adjustGameParameters** method.

Initializing the view

Depending on which game you're playing, there are all sorts of things you might want to adjust about your view. Does it use a background bitmap? Does it use the 2D *cGraphicsMFC* or the 3D *cGraphicsOpenGL*? What kind of cursor tool do you have? From what viewpoint do you look at the world? Is it zoomed in? And so on.

One initial point to make is how we think of our x-, y- and z-axes. We use the same default orientation in both our 2D and 3D computer games. We think of the x-axis as running from left to right across the screen, and we think of the y-axis as running vertically from bottom to top. And we often think of the origin of the axes as starting at the center of the screen. The z-axis is thought of as pointing out from the screen. Normally by default we would be looking down at the world from somewhere out on the positive z-axis, say at a point with coordinates (0.0, 0.0, 5,0), looking down at the origin point (0.0, 0.0, 0.0). Depending on the game, we may want to adjust which point we look at the world *from*, and which point of the world we are looking *at*.

The game itself is data that lives inside a document. When you start up a new game, how does the document manage to reach out and make changes to the view? Actually it's the other way around. The view reaches out and finds its document, gets the game out of the document, and then asks the game to initialize the view.

What prompts the view to do this? A *CPopView::OnUpdate* call with the integer code CPopDoc::VIEWHINT_STARTGAME in the *OnUpdate* call's lHint argument.

When you first start up the Pop program a direct *CPopView::OnUpdate* call is made by the *CPopView::OnCreate* method. And when the Pop program is running and you have a view already in place and you use the Game menu to select a new kind of game, the *CPopDoc::setGameClass* method document passes the static integer code CPopDoc::VIEWHINT_STARTGAME as the lHint to an *UpdateAllViews* call. As we discussed in both Chapter 5: Software Design Patterns and Chapter 6: Animation, the *CPopDoc::UpdateAllViews(CView* pSender, int lHint, CObject* pHint)* method generates calls to the *CPopView::OnUpdate(CView* pSender, int lHint, CObject* pHint)* method for each open view, passing on the same arguments.

However we call it, the relevant block of the *CPopView::OnUpdate* code looks like the following.

```
if (lHint == CPopDoc::VIEWHINT_STARTGAME)
{
    pgame()->initializeView(this);
    pgame()->initializeViewpoint(_pviewpointcritter);
    pgraphics()->installLightingModel(pgame()->plightingmodel());
    //And now go on and call Invalidate to show the game...
}
```

In these lines the *CPopView* uses its *pgame()* accessor to reach out and get a pointer to its game from its owner document. (The MFC framework provides a **CView::GetDocument()** method via which a view can always get a pointer to its owner document.) Once a Pop Framework view has a pointer to its owner game, the view asks the game to initialize it in three different ways.

- Initialize the view's settings with *initializeView*.
- Initialize the location and direction of the viewpoint with *initializeViewpoint*.
- Initialize the lighting model used by the view's graphics with *installLightingModel*.

At this point you might wonder why *initializeView* and *initializeViewpoint* are separate methods. Why have separate view and viewer initialization methods? The Pop Framework does it this way so the games will behave smoothly as you use the menu to switch on and off the various View menu options. If we were only writing one game with one kind of view this wouldn't be necessary; the complexity is a result of the code being usable as a flexible framework to build a variety of changeable games.

Here is the code in the base class *cGame* version of *initializeView*. As well as the standard calls, you'll notice a number of possible additional calls. The comments explain them pretty clearly.

```
void cGame::initializeView(CPopView *pview)
{
    pview->setCursor(((CPopApp*)::AfxGetApp())->_hCursorArrow);
    pview->setUseBackgroundBitmap(FALSE);
        //Default doesn't use bitmap background
    pview->setUseSolidBackground(TRUE);
        //Use a solid rect background.
    pview->setGraphicsClass(RUNTIME_CLASS(cGraphicsMFC));
    pview->pviewpointcritter()->setTrackplayer(TRUE);
        //Do not track player.
}
```

When you override *initializeView*, it's a good idea to put a call to the base class *cGame::initializeView(pview)* in the new method, lest you leave out some default call that the base class *initializeView* makes. A complicating factor in developing the Pop Framework demo program has been that the user is free to use menus to change the game type or the graphics mode or various other things without actually changing the identity of the view. So unless you are careful to reset everything in *initializeView*, there may be some left-over settings from the last game that you don't want.

Here's an example listing some ways you might override the method for an imaginary *cGameSomeChild* class.

```
void cGameSomeChild::initializeView(CPopView *pview)
{
    cGame::initializeView(pview); //Always call the baseclass method.
    //Some possible additional calls:
    pview->setUseSolidBackground(FALSE);
        //For no background at all, faster in 3D.
```

```
pview->setCursor(((CPopApp*)::AfxGetApp())->_hCursorPlay);
    /* To use the crosshair cursor for shooting with mouse
        clicks. */
pview->pviewpointcritter()->setTrackplayer(TRUE);
    /* To scroll after the player critter if it moves off
        screen. This can be confusing, but is useful if you plan
        to use a zoomed in view. */
pview->setGraphicsClass(RUNTIME_CLASS(cGraphicsOpenGL));
    //For 3D graphics
pview->pviewpointcritter()->setListener(
    new cListenerViewerRide());
    //To ride the player; this only works in 3D.
}
```

Now let's talk about the ***initializeViewpoint(cCritterViewer *_pviewpointcritter)*** method.

Initializing the viewpoint critter

Let's set the scene by printing the default ***cGame::initializeViewpoint*** code.

```
void cGame::initializeViewpoint(cCritterViewer *pviewer)
{
        /* The two args to setViewpoint are (directiontoviewer,
            lookatpoint). Note that directiontoviewer points FROM the
            origin TOWARDS the viewer. */
    if (pviewer->is3D())
        pviewer->setViewpoint(cVector3(0.0, -1.0, 2.0),
            _border.center());
            //Direction to viewer is down a bit
    else //2D case.
        pviewer->setViewpoint(cVector::ZAXIS, _border.center());
}
```

To get the point of this, you need to understand that each view of your game has an associated 'viewpoint critter.' More precisely, the ***CPopView*** class has a ***cCritterViewer *_pviewpointcritter*** member as well as a ***cGraphics *_pgraphics*** member. The viewpoint critter and the graphics object work together in the ***CPopView::OnDraw*** method, which includes these three steps.

- Use the viewpoint critter's zoom and perspective settings to set the projection method used by the graphics object.
- Use the viewpoint critter's position and orientation to set the view matrix used by graphics.
- Use the graphics to draw the world and the critters as seen by the viewpoint critter.

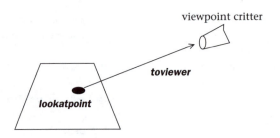

Figure 10.2   Setting the viewpoint

Clearly the view we see is going to depend upon the direction the viewpoint critter is looking in. A convenient way to set position and orient to the viewpoint critter is to use our ***cCritterViewer::setViewpoint(cVector toviewer, cVector lookatpoint)*** method, where we can think of `toviewer` and `lookatpoint` as illustrated in Figure 10.2.

In three dimensions you might ask how far out along the `toviewer` vector do we move the viewpoint critter? The ***setViewpoint*** call will position the viewpoint critter itself just far enough away from the world so that every corner of the world's ***_border*** box is visible.

In other words, a call to ***cCritterViewer::setViewpoint(cVector toviewer, cVector lookatpoint)*** computes an appropriate `seethewholeworld_distance` for the current zoom setting and then has the caller viewpoint critter execute lines to the following effect.

```
moveTo(lookatpoint + seethewholeworld * toviewer);
lookAt(lookatpoint);
```

If you would prefer to see a smaller part of the world, you follow the ***setViewpoint*** call with a call to the ***cCritterViewer::zoom(real zoomfactor)*** method.

In three dimensions we can think of the zoom as being a field of view angle that ranges from wide-angle to telephoto. With a call like `zoom(2.0)`, the critter will use a telephoto effect to see only half the world, or if we call `zoom(0.5)`, it will use a wide-angle effect to see a space twice as big as the world's border.

In two-dimensional worlds, all of this is simpler. The `toviewer` direction is always just the z-axis, as in a two-dimensional world you can always just imagine the viewer as hovering over the world staring straight down at it. But even in a flat world, we do need to think about which point we are to hover over, that is, the `lookatpoint` still matters. And in two dimensions we also need to think about how much we want to zoom in on – or away from – the world. The analogy to telephoto and wide-angle lenses doesn't make as much sense for the two-dimensional worlds; here it's easier to just think of a call like `zoom(2.0)` as making things look bigger and `zoom(0.5)` as making them look smaller.

In designing your game, rather than agonizing over the exact quantitative meaning of the `zoomfactor` numbers, it's easier to just experiment with a few till you get the look that works the best. Here's how we use zoom in the long, thin world of the Ballworld game for instance. At startup the player is positioned not at the `_border.center()` but rather near the `_border.locorner()`, that is, the lower left-hand corner of the long, thin game world. We want to position ourselves right over the critter, looking down at it, and we want to zoom in a bit rather than trying to fit the whole long, thin world onto the screen.

```
void cGameBallworld::initializeViewpoint(cCritterViewer *pviewer)
{
    if (!pviewer->is3D()) //2D case
    {
        pviewer->setViewpoint(cVector::ZAXIS, pplayer()->position());
        pviewer->zoom(1.5);
    }
    else
        //Do something slightly different in the 3D case...
}
```

By the way, how does the Pop Framework know when **CPopView::is3D** is TRUE? It looks at the kind of **cGraphics** currently being used by the view. If the graphics is **cGraphicsOpenGL** (or maybe, one of these days, **cGraphicsDirectX**) the view is 3D, and if it's **cGraphicsMFC**, the view isn't 3D. The dimensionality of the view is independent of the dimensionality of the game's **_border** box. Even though our Ballworld game is in a two-dimensional world, we can still fancy it up with a three-dimensional view. When we go to a three-dimensional view we actually enhance the sprites and give many of them a cosmetic z-axis thickness determined by the **cSprite::_prismdz** factor mentioned in Chapter 9: Sprites.

We can do fancy things with the viewpoint when we start thinking about three-dimensional views. Here's something we do for the three-dimensional viewpoint in the Airhockey game, so as to bring the viewer around behind the player's goal.

```
void cGameAirhockey::initializeViewpoint(cCritterViewer *pviewer)
{
    if (pviewer->is3D())
    {
        pviewer->setViewpoint(cVector3(-2.0, 0.0, 1.0),
            _border.center());
            //These args are the (directiontoviewer, lookatpoint);
        pviewer->roll(PI/2.0);
            //rolls the viewer to right orientation.
    }
    else //2D case just copies base class.
        pviewer->setViewpoint(cVector::ZAXIS, _border.center());
}
```

Still on the subject of three-dimensional views, there's an ***installLightingModel*** a call to initialize a new 3D graphics with the game's ***plightingmodel()***. But, at this point, we aren't doing much with this model other than using it to turn the lighting calculations on or off in ***cGraphicsOpenGL***. By default the lighting calculations are on in all the games except for PickNPop, simply because our default lights don't happen to look good on those particular shapes. Oddly enough, OpenGL graphics may run faster when you turn on the additional calculations of a lighting model! Perhaps this is because the OpenGL hardware on graphics cards is optimized to run best with lighting on.

The status message

The last method of the ***cGame*** which we'll discuss here is a method it has for generating a string to put into the status bar at the bottom of your Pop window. The active ***CPopView*** window repeatedly undergoes an MFC framework call named **OnUpdate**, and we have this method in turn use the active game's status message by a somewhat arcane line of the form `cMainFrame ->SetMessageText(pDoc->pgame()->statusMessage())`.

It's common to speak of methods that return useful objects as 'factory methods.' The ***statusMessage*** is a kind of factory method that creates a **CString** object. The default ***cGame*** behavior tailors the message to report the score and health of the player critter, the number of critters onscreen, and the number of cycles per second that the Pop program is currently running at. Recall that the Pop Framework is designed in such a way that it will never run at faster than the refresh rate of the graphics card, so if we're near that, we just say 'Near Max.'

Thanks to the richness of the MFC **CString** methods, it's pretty easy to make the status bar string. Here's a recent version of the default ***statusMessage*** code. Clearly this is something you want to override to give the most useful and relevant information for your particular game.

```
CString cGame::statusMessage()
{
    CString cStrStatusBar;
    int nUpdatesPerSecond;
    CString cStrUpdatespersecond;
    CString cStrHealth;
    CString cStrCount;
    CString cStrScore;
    CString cStrCollisionCount;
    if (!gamepaused())
    {
        nUpdatesPerSecond = int(((CPopApp*)::AfxGetApp())->
            _timer.updatesPerSecond());
        if (!nUpdatesPerSecond)
            cStrUpdatespersecond.Format(
                "Less than one update per second.");
```

```
        else
            cStrUpdatespersecond.Format("Updates per second: %d.",
                nUpdatesPerSecond);
        if (((CPopApp*)::AfxGetApp())->_timer.runningNearMaxSpeed())
            cStrUpdatespersecond += " (Near Max)";
    }
    else
            cStrUpdatespersecond.Format("Animation is paused.");
    cStrScore.Format("Score: %d.", score());
    cStrHealth.Format("Health: %d.", health());
    int crittercount = _pbiota->count(RUNTIME_CLASS(cCritter));
    int bulletcount = _pbiota->count(RUNTIME_CLASS(cCritterBullet));
    crittercount -= bulletcount;
    if (visibleplayer()) /*Subtract off 1 for player as well. */
        crittercount -= 1;
    cStrCount.Format("Other Critters: %d.", crittercount);
    cStrStatusBar = cStrScore + " " + cStrHealth + " " + cStrCount +
        " " + cStrUpdatespersecond;
    return cStrStatusBar;
}
```

In line with our usual policy of not keeping the same information in two
different places, we use a **cBiota::count** method to walk through the active critter
array and count up the kinds of objects on the spot – this is in place of trying to
maintain an integer that holds the count value in it. It costs a (very small) bit of
speed to walk through the array once to recompute the number each time you
need it, but the simplification to your code seems worth it.

The *randomSprite* factory method

Let's conclude by mentioning a factory method that **cGame** has. A factory
method constructs an object of a certain kind and returns a copy of it or, more
commonly, a pointer to it.

```
cSprite* randomSprite(int spritetypeindex);/* A factory method to
    return one of the various kinds of sprites. */
```

The kind of sprite that **randomSprite** returns depends on the argument you
give it. These are statics defined as follows.

```
const int cGame::ST_SPRITETYPENOTUSED = -1;
    //Indicates you will put in sprites by hand.
const int cGame::ST_SIMPLEPOLYGONS = 0;
    //Simple triangles, squares, pentagons.
const int cGame::ST_FANCYPOLYGONS = 1;
    //Diverse regular and star polygons.
```

```
const int cGame::ST_ASTEROIDPOLYGONS = 2;
    //Polypolygons that have polypolygons at their tips.
const int cGame::ST_POLYPOLYGONS = 3;
    //Polypolygons that have polygons at their tips.
const int cGame::ST_BITMAPS = 4; //cSpriteIcon bitmaps.
const int cGame::ST_BUBBLES = 5; //balls of various kinds.
const int cGame::ST_TRIPLEPOLYPOLYGONS = 6;
    //Polypolygons that have polypolygons at their tips.
```

When a *cCritter* child needs a random sprite of a certain type, we can get one with the *randomSprite* factory method like this.

```
cCritterAsteroid::cCritterAsteroid(cGame *pownergame)
{
    if (pownergame)
        setSprite(pownergame->randomSprite(cGame::ST_ASTEROIDPOLYGONS));
    //Etcetera
}
```

The *randomSprite* is a fairly generic method that hardly needs any members of the *cGame* class, but you might sometime want to override it. The *randomSprite* explicitly looks at another *cGame* member only when called with the `cGame::ST_BITMAPS` argument. In this case, the *cGame::randomSprite* chooses a resource ID for a bitmap from a *cGame* member array `_bitmapIDarray`. The `_bitmapIDarray` gets initialized in the *cGame* constructor, by the way. You can check the **game.cpp** file for details.

Also see Exercise 14.4: A Graphic Theme for Your Game for an example of how we might want to change `bitmapIDarray` in a game constructor override.

10.4 Arrays of critters: the *cBiota* class

One of the key members of the *cGame* class is a `cBiota *_pbiota` field. The *cBiota* class is a collection class that holds an array of pointers to *cCritter* objects. The *cBiota* object is based on an MFC array template, with a few special methods added. We encapsulate these methods into the *cBiota* rather than having them in *cGame* as part of the OOD strategy of not giving any one class too many responsibilities.

Some readers may be wondering why we have to use a collection of *cCritter** pointers. Beginning programmers have a fear of pointers and their burdensome requirements of being initialized with **new** and removed with **delete**. Why not just a collection of *cCritter* objects? Once again, this is because we want polymorphism to work. In C++, a call like `_pcritter->update(. . .)` will work polymorphically and figure out the correct version of the method depending on what kind of *cCritter** child class `_pcritter` actually is. But a call like `_ccritter.update (. . .)` will always just use the base class *cCritter::update*.

Now let's think about which kind of collection to use; an array or a linked list. This type of decision depends on what you plan to do with your collection, so let's think about what we'll do with the critters in a game.

Typically there will be 10–50 critters in action. As we step the game, we will repeatedly iterate through the collection of critters, updating them, moving them, drawing them, and so on. Now and then we will want to add new critters to the collection or delete old ones. Should we use a list or an array for our collection of critter pointers? Well, iterating through an array is faster than iterating through a list, but deleting objects is faster with a list than with an array. The cost of deleting something from the middle of an array is noticeable because then all of the higher-indexed array members need to be moved down one position in the array. On the whole, we expect more of our computation time to involve iterations than object deletions, so we'll use an array.

MFC provides a range of useful array templates. The particular template we use here is called **CTypedPtrArray**. This is what's known a serializable type-safe array. There's a bit about these templates in Chapter 22: Topics in C++, and Chapter 30: Serialization explains why the **CTypedPtrArray** is useful for saving and loading parameter files.

Because we may need arrays of critter pointers elsewhere in the program, we define a simple critter pointer array class *cCritterArray* and derive *cBiota* from that. We've drawn the diagram (Figure 10.3) so as to display the additional fact that our *cGame* class is going to hold a single *cBiota* object and we've also included some navigation arrows. Recall that we use the composition diamond symbol to indicate when an object (the object with the diamond) holds one or more objects of the class type at the other end of the line leading from the diamond.

A *cBiota* object is an array of *cCritter** pointers which also holds a `cGame *_pgame` pointer and a special bookkeeping array of simple objects called *cServiceRequest*. The member fields of *cBiota* can be seen in this partial listing of the prototype from **biota.h**.

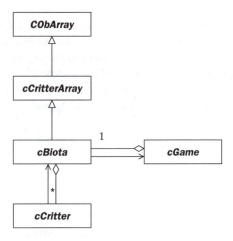

Figure 10.3 Class Diagram of the *cBiota*

```
class cBiota : private cCritterArray
{
public: //Statics
    static const int NOINDEX;
        // -1, impossible index, For use by cBiota::_index().
protected:
//Non-serialized helper members;
    cGame* _pgame;
    CArray<cServiceRequest, cServiceRequest> _servicerequestarray;
//Constructor
    cBiota(cGame *pownergame);
//Etcetera...
};
```

The **cBiota** uses its _pgame field to get to a particular **cGame** object, and the **cGame** uses its _pbiota field to get to a particular **cBiota** object. But the roles of the two pointers are different: the former is simply a navigational aid, the latter is an example of composition.

When a **cGame** object is deleted, its _pbiota object is deleted as well. This is knows as a 'cascading delete.' The _pbiota member of **cGame** is a composed object, and it is typical for a delete to cascade to a composed object.

When you delete a **cBiota** object you don't cascade the delete to the member _pgame. The _pgame member of **cBiota** is simply a navigational aid that is put in place by the **cBiota(cGame *pownergame)** constructor.

One reason why we want the **cBiota** to navigate to the **cGame** is so that the **cCritter** objects can go through the **cBiota** to get at **cGame** information. Thus, the **cCritter** class has a **pgame()** accessor that's defined as _pownerbiota->pgame().

We populate a **cBiota** by using its **Add** method, which is an override of the standard **CTypedPtrArray::Add**. We override the method so that it won't let you accidentally add the same thing twice; also it sets the added critter's **_pownerbiota** field.

A **cBiota** object is responsible for deleting all of its members. That is, the **cBiota** destructor calls the destructor for each of the critters in the array.

The most important methods of the **cBiota** class are its 'array-walking' methods. It has **draw, move, update, animate, render**, and **listen** methods, each of which simply walks its array and calls the corresponding method for each member of **cCritter**. Thus, for instance, the **cBiota::move** looks something like this.

```
void cBiota::move(Real dt)
{
    for( int i=0; i<GetSize(); i++)
        GetAt(i)->move(dt);
}
```

The place where almost all the **cBiota** array-walking methods get called is inside the **CGame::step** method, which is careful to call them in a certain order so as to make the program's behavior as parallel as possible. The **draw** method, however, gets called by **CPopView::draw**.

It's worth mentioning that the **cBiota::draw** walks the array in reverse order. This is because it's convenient to think of the critters early in the array as being visually on top of the others. But when you draw the critter sprites on the screen, the first drawn is going to have the other sprites drawn on top of it. The first shall be farthest, as it were. In graphics programming, this fact is called 'the painter's algorithm.' Usually our player is the first member of the **cBiota** array, and we like to have our player on top. So we walk the array in reverse order.

This consideration only matters in two-dimensional graphics, of course, as in three dimensions we would have the critters located at different depths, and use our current viewpoint to determine which order to draw them in.

Some of our games, such as PickNPop, or Dambuilder, allow us to use a pick or a drag cursor to select critters, and we store this information in the game by setting a cGame::_pfocus pointer to point to the critter being specially handled. One other special thing that **cBiota::draw** does is to put a highlight around the sprite of a critter that happens to be the 'focus critter' of the game. If you don't like this feature, either don't use the pick cursor or comment out the feature from the **cBiota::draw** code.

Service requests: the Command pattern in action

The **cBiota** class has a **CArray<cServiceRequest, cServiceRequest> _servicerequestarray**. The **cServiceRequest** class is a simple utility class that holds two fields, **cCritter *_pclient** and a **CString request**.

The purpose of the _servicerequestarray is to queue up requests from the critters. The reasoning goes like this. Suppose that during its update process a critter notices that its health is 0. Now the critter wants to do the right thing and die. If it's to die, then we should delete it from the simulation; if you're shooting hundreds of bullets it wouldn't do to keep all the bullets around after they hit something and 'die.' To get rid of a cCritter *pcritter we need to do at least two things:

- Call delete pcritter.
- Remove the invalid pcritter pointer from our **cBiota** array.

These are not actions that you'd want to take inside the middle of an i loop that's walking along a **cBiota** array. First of all it seems problematic to ask a **cCritter** to delete itself, and secondly it's not a good practice to change the size of an array you are currently walking through.

Our solution is to let a **cBiota** store up requests to do things: to delete critters, add critters, replicate critters, change the array location of critters, etc. And this is what we use the _servicerequestarray for.

One more point. It would mess up our **cGame** code if the current _pplayer ever actually got deleted. So if you were to look into the **cBiota** code, you'd find that even if a player makes a delete_me request, when the **cBiota** processes the service requests it doesn't actually call delete on the player.

Review questions

A   Name three important members of the *cGame* class.

B   What is the sequence of actions performed by the *cGame::step(dt)* method?

C   Which of the game's fields are normally set in the *cGame* constructor?

D   What is the *seedCritters* method used for, and when is it called?

E   What are two things that are typically checked for in *adjustGameParameters*?

F   What aspects of the game are set in *initializeView* and in *InitializeViewpoint*? Why are these methods separate?

G   What is the viewpoint critter?

H   How can you control the status bar message of a game?

I   What class does *cBiota* inherit from?

J   Why does the Pop Framework use the *cServiceRequest* class? What software pattern is this an example of?

Exercises

Exercise 10.1: Starting in a zoomed-in mode

Comment in the last line of the *cGameDambuilder::initializeView*, rebuild and run the Pop program, and switch to the **Game | Dambuilder**. Note that it is in a zoomed-in mode. Is it still zoomed-in if you switch back to Spacewar? Why not?

Exercise 10.2: A multi-level game

Often people like to write games which have more than one level. To get you started the Pop Framework provides an `int _level` member of *cGame* which is initialized to 1 in the constructor (not *everything* has start counting with 0!). The reset method returns `_level` to 1 in case it's changed.

To use level, in your `adjustGameParameters` you'd look for some trigger condition, such as score > 100, and have a block of code like this:

```
if (_level == 1 && score() > 100)
{
    _level = 2;
    setBackgroundBitmap(IDB_BACKGROUND_LEVEL2);
    seedCritters();
}
```

An alternate way in which you might switch to level 2 would be to have the player critter trigger the change inside its *update* method if some condition happened; for instance if the player were to reach the far right edge of a long Mario-style world.

If you're using levels, your `seedCritters` should have a switch on `_level` to change the way in which you seed the world.

If you change the bitmap when you go to the new level you need to remember to change it back when you call *reset* to return to level 1. This might best be managed by writing a new *setLevel* accessor for your game to not only set `_level` but to set the appropriate bitmap.

Collisions

11

By now you will have noticed that the critters in most of our games bounce off of each other. Collision-handling is a somewhat advanced technique used in coding computer games, or any other kind of physical simulation.

If the objects in your game or simulation have complicated shapes, getting them to collide properly can become exceedingly difficult. In games, of course, total physical accuracy isn't necessary, so we take some shortcuts to enhance our speed. One shortcut that we use in the Pop Framework is that, except for long thin wall critters, we collide our critters with each other as if they were little spheres. Another shortcut – that we didn't happen to implement here – is to cut the time spent on collisions by not calculating the collisions between objects that aren't presently in the field of view.

Let's start with how the individual critters collide, and then work our way up to how a game orchestrates all of the relevant collisions.

11.1 The critter *Collide* method

The *cCritter* class has a virtual *BOOL collide(cCritter *pcritter)* method. This method does the following: (a) check if pcritter is touching the caller, and if not, return FALSE, and (b) if pcritter is touching the caller, then execute a collision with pcritter, possibly changing the health, position, and velocity of both pcritter and the caller, and when you're done return TRUE.

There are three points to get straight right way.

- First of all, our *collide* might better be called *ifTouchingDoACollision*. But that seems a bit too unwieldy.

- Second, to avoid wasting time, and to keep our physics symmetric, we only want to call *collide* once for each pair <pcritteri, pcritterj>. That is, we intend for the collide code of a call pcritteri->collide(pcritterj) to have a physically symmetric effect affect on pcritteri and pcritterj.

- Third, as a result of the second consideration, given a pair <pcritteri, pcritterj> we're going to need some logical way of deciding whether to call pcritteri->collide(pcritterj) or to call pcritterj->collide(pcritteri).

The standard **cCritter::collide** method implements (a) the law of conservation of momentum, (b) the law of conservation of energy, and (c) the law that two objects can't be in the same place at the same time. The standard collision method is also based on the assumption that the critter behaves like a sphere. We'll say more about the physics later in this chapter.

We override the **collide** method for **cCritterWall**, as the narrow rectangular walls are not at all like disks. And other child critters may override **collide** by adding on additional refinements; bullets, for instance, may damage the other object and explode. A typical **collide** override like this can have the following form.

```
BOOL cCritterChild::collide(cCritter *pcritter)
{
    BOOL collided = cCritter::collide(pcritter);
    if (collided)
        //Do something additional to this caller and/or to the pcritter
    return collided;
}
```

So a typical override of **collide** might call the base class version of **collide** to handle the physics, and then do something extra if a collision took place. When we're done we return the **BOOL** that tells whether or not a collision took place.

Here are some examples of how **collide** gets overridden. First let's look at what we do with the **cCritterArmedPlayer** that we commonly use for the game player. In some games, such as our Spacewar game, we want to penalize the player critter each time that it bumps into an enemy critter, such as an asteroid. To enable this, the framework gives the **cCritterArmedPlayer** a **BOOL** _sensitive flag and codes the **collide** like this.

```
BOOL cCritterArmedPlayer::collide(cCritter *pcritter)
{
    BOOL collided = cCritter::collide(pcritter);
    if (collided && _sensitive &&
        !pcritter->IsKindOf(RUNTIME_CLASS(cCritterWall)))
    damage(1);
    return collided;
}
```

Let's look at a different way of extending **collide**, which is used by the basket in the Ballworld game. We want the basket to be like a black hole – things that fall into it disappear. Here we have the **collide** code and simply check if the argument pcritter is entirely inside the radius of the caller critter, as tested by a **contains** method.

```
BOOL cCritterBasket::collide(cCritter *pcritter)
{
    if (contains(pcritter))
        //disk of pcritter is wholly inside my disk
    {
        pcritter->die();
        return TRUE;
    }
    else
        return FALSE;
}
```

The *cCritterBullet* overrides *collide* to handle target critters in one way and other kinds of critters in the base class way. The method depends on the fact that we give our *cCritterBullet* class a *BOOL isTarget(cCritter *pcritter)* method which decides if a given *pcritter* is something that the bullet is willing to damage. We won't print the code for *BOOL cCritterBullet::collide(cCritter *pcritter)* here, but the basic idea is the following.

- If *pcritter* is one of your target critters and you're touching it, damage *pcritter* and die.
- If *pcritter* is a target and you're not touching it, do nothing.
- If *pcritter* isn't a target critter, collide with it normally.

As mentioned above, a *cCritterWall* overrides *collide* in a completely different fashion to reflect the fact that a wall isn't shaped like a sphere.

Clearly we're going to need a way to figure out which critter controls a given collision! We'll get to this soon. But first let's look at the broader issue of which pairs of critters we're going to test for collision at all.

11.2   Collision-handling

Here's an overview of how the Pop Framework handles collisions.

(1) Make a utility class for holding pairs of critters, and let this class specify which critter has the priority to control the behavior of a collision.

(2) Maintain a collection of all pairs of critters that might meaningfully collide.

(3) During each game step, iterate through this collection of candidate pairs.

(4) For each candidate pair, collide the critters by letting the higher priority critter call its *collide* method on the other.

(5) A critter's *collide(pcritter)* method checks if it's touching *pcritter*, and if so, changes the two critters' velocities and positions in a physically reasonable fashion. Child classes may override *collide* to alter the behavior.

We said a bit about (5) in the last section. In this section we'll figure out how to take care of steps (1) to (4).

The *N*-squared problem

If we have N critters, it would seem like there are N^2 pairs of critters we might consider. But we can easily cut this by a little more than half, down to $N *$ $(N - 1) / 2$. This is because, first of all, we don't have to worry about a critter colliding with itself, and, secondly, if we write our collision code symmetrically, then once A collides with B we don't need to turn around and carry out code for having B collide with A.

That is, if we think of listing the critter pairs in N rows of N columns each, we need only consider those (row, column) pairs for which the row number is strictly less than the column number. This way we cut down to a bit less than half of N^2. This is shown in Figure 11.1.

Of course half of N^2 is still too big for many simulations – remember that in the analysis of algorithms, any multiple of N^2 is viewed as 'order of N^2,' which is not considered to be a scalable kind of algorithm.

If we want to be able to run somewhat more complicated kinds of games, we need to find a way to prune down the collisions that we consider. Suppose, for instance, that you are running a PacMan-style game in which you have five active critters moving about in a maze made up of 45 walls. The possible collision pairs group like this.

- Active critter to active critter $(5 * 4) / 2 = 10$ pairs
- Active critter to wall $(5 * 45) = 225$ pairs
- Wall to wall $(45 * 44) / 2 = 990$ pairs

If you ignore the wall–wall pairs, you have a quite feasible 235 possible collision pairs to consider per update, otherwise you have a taxing 1225 pairs. Although 235 sounds like a lot, the Pop Framework does fine up to about 500 pairs, but if you get into the thousands of pairs, the performance suffers noticeably.

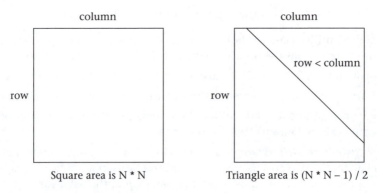

Figure 11.1   Halving the possible collision pairs

Our solution is to maintain a collection that holds only the pairs of critters whose collisions we actually want to check. To further speed things up, we'll structure these pairs so that they automatically tell us which critter is to control the collision.

A collision-handling architecture

In this section we'll talk about the two new classes the Pop Framework uses to limit our collision-checking to the pairs that matter to us. The new classes are *cColliderPair* and *cCollider*. Figure 11.2 is a UML class diagram of their relationship to *cGame* and *cCritter*.

And here's how these classes realize the first three steps of the collision-handling process we outlined above.

(1) The *cColliderPair* class has two *cCritter** members called *_pcrittercaller* and *_pcritterarg*. We have a *cColliderPair::collideThePair* method that calls `_pcrittercaller->collide(_pcritterarg)`.

(2) The *cCollider* class holds a collection of *cColliderPair* objects. The *cGame* has a *cCollider* `_pcollider` object. Whenever you add a *cCritter** `pcritternew` to the game, the *cCollider::smartAdd* method looks at all possible pairs that include the new `pcritter` and an existing critter in the game, creates appropriately ordered *cColliderPair* object for those pairs that matter, and adds the new *cColliderPair* objects to the `_pcollider` collection. Whenever a *cCritter** `pcritterdying` is deleted, its destructor calls `_pcollider->removeReferencesTo(pcritterdying)` to remove all pairs that mention `pcritterdying`.

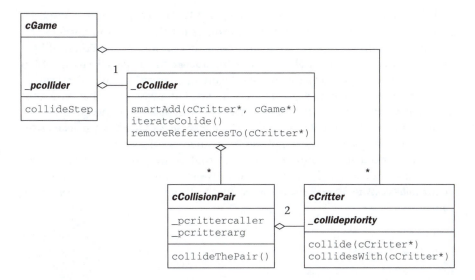

Figure 11.2 A collision-handling architecture

(3) In each update step, the **cGame::collideStep** method calls _pcollider->iterateCollide(). The **cCollider::iterateCollide()** method calls the **collideThePair** for each **cColliderPair**.

Note that we didn't explain yet how **smartAdd** decides which pairs matter and how it decides, for these pairs, which critter should be the caller and which should be the argument for an eventual **collide** call. This is the topic of the following subsection.

Collision priority

As already discussed, the individual **cCritter** child classes have their own virtual **collide(cCritter *pcritter)** methods to determine whether the pair is touching, and what to do if they are touching. Given a pair (pA, pB), should I call pA->collide(pB), or should I call pB->collide(pA)? Or should I not even try and collide the critters?

Our solution is to give the **cCritter** class a **Real _collidepriority** field and to give the **cCritter** class a **collidesWith(cCritter *pcritterother)** method that uses the **_collidepriority** information of the two critters involved. By 'priority' we mean that if pB has higher priority than pA, then, when we consider the pair (pA, pB), we will call pB->collide(pA) instead of the other way around.

The default **_collidepriority** values are real numbers that have default values that are set for the various kinds of critters in the following (descending) order.

- Walls
- Bullets
- Player
- Other critters

The reasons for our priorities are roughly this. The **cCritterWall** has a special **collide** method which correctly bounces things off the sides and corners of a rectangular wall. Ordinarily we would not expect a wall to be damaged by a bullet. As was mentioned above, the **cCritterBullet** has a special **collide** which checks if an object it touches is in the category of a target for the bullet. If it is a target object, the bullet damages it and then dies. Otherwise the bullet carries out a normal **cCritter::collide**. And the normal **cCritter::collide** is designed to correctly simulate the physics of colliding disks. The **cCritterArmedPlayer** has a special **collide** method that can call **damage** if a player is sensitive to collisions.

We also need to account for the fact that some pairs of critters aren't meant to collide at all. To handle all this, we give the **cCritter** class a **virtual int cCritter::collidesWith(cCritter *pcritterother)** method that can return the following values.

- `cCollider::DONTCOLLIDE = 2;`
- `cCollider::COLLIDEASCALLER = 1;`
- `cCollider::COLLIDEASARG = -1;`
- `cCollider::COLLIDEEITHERWAY = 0;`

The basic **cCritter::collidesWith** method compares the **_collidepriority** values and returns an appropriate code number. The **cCritterWall::collidesWith(cCritter *pcritterother)** is overridden to return DONTCOLLIDE if pcritterother happens to be a **cCritterWall**.

Finally, the **cCollider::smartAdd** method is implemented as follows.

```
void cCollider::smartAdd(cCritter *pcritter, cCritter* pcritterother)
{
    int collideswith = pcritter->collidesWith(pcritterother);
    int othercollideswith = pcritterother->collidesWith(pcritter);
    if (collideswith == cCollider::DONTCOLLIDE || othercollideswith
        == cCollider::DONTCOLLIDE)
    return; /* Don't collide if either
        one is unwilling, even if the other was willing. */
    if (collideswith == cCollider::COLLIDEASCALLER || collideswith
        == cCollider::COLLIDEEITHERWAY )
        AddTail(new cColliderPair(pcritter, pcritterother));
    else //(collideswith == cCollider::COLLIDEASARG)
        AddTail(new cColliderPair(pcritterother, pcritter));

    //ASSERT(collideswith == -othercollideswith);
        /* We chose the collision type codes to make this ASSERT
        likely at this point, but it might not always be true. Only
        comment it in for testing. Do note that we bail before we
        hit it if either type is DONTCOLLIDE. */
}
```

Note that **smartAdd** will only add the necessary pairs, and that it will add them ordered in the right way, with the caller first and the argument second.

Array or list? An N-cubed issue

It remains to discuss how we iterate though the collection of pairs in a **cCollider** collection. This depends on whether we implement the **cCollider** collection as an array or as a linked list. Which is to be preferred? As you will already have noticed if you looked enough to see the 'AddTail' in the block of code just above, we're going to use a list.

For most programmers, the natural inclination is to use arrays, simply because lists have a reputation for being hard to use. Some of us have acquired a lingering fear of lists and hash tables from a formative bad experience in a data structures course! But, thanks to templates and collection classes, the more sophisticated data structures are easy and safe to use, and we can afford to pick the correct data structure for any given situation.

As it turns out, you want to use a list and not an array for the collection that holds your set of possible collision pairs. Here's why. Say you have N critters – for purposes of discussion let's say N is 20 – and let's suppose that each critter wants to collide with all of the others, making roughly 200 collision pairs ($N^2 / 2$).

Now say you want to delete one of the critters. This means deleting roughly N member pairs from an array of $N^2/2$ members; that is, deleting 20 members from a 200 member array.

Now, when you delete something from the beginning of an array, you typically have to move down all of the higher-indexed elements. In other words, removing the first member of a 200 member array requires about 200 steps and removing the first member of an array of size $N^2/2$ takes about $N^2/2$ steps. Removing 20 members from a 200 member array could take roughly 4000 steps, and removing N members from an array of size $N^2/2$ takes on the order of $N^3/2$ steps.

You realize, of course, that an order-$N^3/2$ algorithm is very bad news! For 40 critters, you'd have an order of 32,000 steps – all this just to delete one single critter. Why, again, does it make so much work? Because you have to delete every pair the critter was involved in, and if the pairs are in an array, then every time you delete a pair from the array you have to move all of the higher-indexed array members.

With a list you don't get into this problem, because deleting a member from a list is an operation of a small, constant expense, no matter where in the list the member occurs. It's just a matter of fixing up a couple of 'next' and 'previous' pointers.

So we implement the *cCollider* as a linked list; specifically we let it inherit from the MFC class *CPtrList* – well, actually, we use a type-safe template variant of *CPtrList* called *CTypedPtrList<CObList, cColliderPair*>*. If you've ever implemented a linked list, you'll recall that you have to be a little careful about not corrupting the next and previous pointers – by using the built-in MFC List template we avoid having to worry about getting these details right. This is a good example of why, in object-oriented software engineering, we like to use classes that we don't have to write ourselves.

One last thought. We iterate through the entire *cCollider* list with every update, and iterating through an array is slightly faster than iterating through a list. Would it be better, after all, to have used an array? Well, no. The thing is, you want your game to run in a uniform fashion. You don't want it to race along and then suddenly slow down every time you shoot something. The (actually all but undetectable) slowdown of doing a single iteration sequence per update as a list instead of as an array is a fair price to pay for not having the game lag when a critter's destroyed.

11.3 Colliding spheres

Let's say a bit about how the standard *void cCritter::collide(cCritter *pother)* method should work. Before thinking about the code, we need to think about the physics. Consider the collision of two objects a and b with masses ma and mb and velocities va and vb which our collision is to convert into new velocities $newVa$ and $newVb$. According to physics, (a) the total momentum is conserved and (b) the total energy is conserved. This means the following two conditions should hold, where we write $|v|$ to mean the magnitude of a vector v.

(1) $Ma \times newVa + Mb \times newVb = Ma \times Va + Mb \times Vb$

and

(2) $(1/2) \times (Ma \times |newVa|^2 + Mb \times |newVb|^2) =$
      $(1/2) \times (Ma \times |Va|^2 + Mb \times |Vb|^2)$

The *newVa* and the *newVb* quantities are our unknowns, and the old *Va* and *Vb* are like constants fed into the equations. Geometrically speaking, condition (1) describes a 'line,' while condition (2) describes an 'ellipse.' The intersection of a line and an ellipse gives two solutions: the pre-collision and the post-collision solution.

To find them, you can replace (1) by two linear equations in the x and y components and replace equation (2) by a single quadratic equation in the x and y components. These equations can be solved by hand, though what the author did was feed them into the *Mathematica* symbolic computation program to come up with the two solutions, the pre-collision solution, *newVa* = *Va* and *newVb* = *Vb*, and the post-collision solution, in which some of the energy and momentum have been exchanged:

$newVa = (Ma \times Va - Mb \times Va + 2 \times Mb \times Vb) / (Ma + Mb)$
$newVb = (2 \times Ma \times Va - Ma \times Vb + Mb \times Vb) / (Ma + Mb)$

If we divide both numerators and denominators by *Ma*, and call *Mb/Ma* *massratio* we get

$newVa = (Va - massratio \times Va + 2 \times massratio \times Vb) / (1 + massratio)$
$newVb = (2 \times Va - Vb + massratio \times Vb)/ (1 + massratio)$

Simplifying a little more, we get

$newVa = [(1 - massratio) \times Va + 2 \times massratio \times Vb] / (1 + massratio)$
$newVb = [2 \times Va + (massratio - 1) \times Vb] / (1 + massratio)$

Note that if *massratio* is 1, then this is simply *newVa* = *Vb*; *newVb* = *Va*, which is the standard billiard-ball collision that one first thinks of. The case where the masses aren't the same is the less obvious case; this is the case we are doing all the work for. And if *a* has a huge (infinite) mass compared to *b*, then *massratio* is about 0 and we get *newVa* = *Va*; *newVb* = 2*Va* − *Vb*, which, if *a* is motionless, amounts to *b* simply bouncing off of *a*, which is another standard kind of collision example.

A third thing that needs to be taken into account is that we shouldn't have two objects in the same place at the same time. Usually when two critters are touching, they will actually be overlapping. We add code to our *cCritter::collide* so as to move the pair of critters apart along the line connecting their centers, moving them just far enough so they don't overlap.

Figure 11.3 Constructing a *cCritterWall*

A final issue in writing this algorithm is that we need to avoid having a collision move any critter that has its *_fixedflag* set to TRUE; such a critter might appear as a bumper in a pinball game or as an obstacle in a maze game. You can look at the full code in the critter.cpp file.

11.4 Colliding walls

One weak point in our standard c*Critter::touch* and *cCritter::collide* methods is that they always treat the critters as disks centered on the critter's position. This is only slightly problematic when we have, say, a triangular critter, but it is unworkable if we have a long thin critter such as one might use for a rectangular wall.

In more advanced kinds of game programs, collision detection usually uses a sphere-based collision detection to see if a collision is possible, and then switches to a slower and more detailed algorithm that looks at bounding boxes or individual vertices of the objects being tested for collision. In the Pop Framework we presently only do this for one particular kind of shape: a rectangular 'wall.'

So we have a special *cCritterWall* class. We normally create our walls with a call to the constructor: *cCritterWall::cCritterWall(const cVector &enda, const cVector &endb, Real thickness)*.

The *enda* and *endb* arguments in the constructor are the midpoints of what we consider to be the short ends of the wall (see Figure 11.3).

In the Dambuilder game, for instance, we add a bunch of walls in the constructor with lines of the following form. If you don't specify the *thickness*, the default cCritterWall::THICKNESS of 0.2 is used.

```
add(new cCritterDamWall( cVector(-4, 2), cVector(3, -2)));
add(new cCritterDamWall( cVector(1.5, -2), cVector(6, 0.3)));
```

If you play with the Dambuilder game, you'll notice you can drag the walls around and you can use the Copy cursor to copy them. You can 'build dams'! Our standard critter's behavior when being dragged is to keep the velocity of the drag; this lets us 'pick up and throw' critters if we like. But we normally don't want walls to drift around, so the *cCritter::dragTo* is overridden to prevent a wall from acquiring velocity by being dragged.

Ordinarily a critter thinks of its shape as being a disk. If a wall thinks of itself as a disk, then you are prevented from putting two vertical walls near each other, as the imaginary disks would seem to overlap. A similar issue can arise with trying to put a vertical wall near a vertical edge of the screen when the wall's wrap mode is set to *cCritter::BOUNCE*. Overriding the *clamp* method partly solves the problem. (We did a quick 'kludge' fix of the BOUNCE problem by overriding *cCritterWall::setWrapflag* to do nothing, so that in fact you can't put a *cCritterWall* into the BOUNCE mode. This is unimportant, but we note it here in case you are ever puzzled about why you can't get walls to bounce off the edges of the screen.)

The main effort in coding the *cCritterWall* went into the override for *collide*. One needs to consider eight cases; whether a colliding critter is impacting a wall on one of its four corners or on one of its four sides. Another complicating factor is to try and avoid the case where a rapidly moving critter might seem to move 'through' a thin wall by being on one side, and then at the next move step being on the other side, without ever overlapping the wall. We deal with this problem by looking at a critter's 'outcode' relative to the wall; where, as already mentioned in Chapter 8: Critters, an outcode is a flag value reflecting a position relative to a rectangle: inside, to the right, to the right and top, to the top, and so on.

Our *cCritterWall::collide(cCritter*pcritter)* compares the *pcritter*'s current outcode relative to the wall to its previous position's outcode relative to this wall, and in this way we can tell whether it jumped over the wall. And if it's hitting the wall, we can tell which region it came from. You can look at the gory details in critterwall.cpp if you're interested.

Review questions

A   What does the default *cCritter::collide* method do? Which quantities does it conserve?

B   How many pairs of critters can be found in a set of ten critters? In a set of 100 critters?

C   What is the meaning of the *cCritter* _collidepriority field? How is it used in the *cCritter::collidesWith* method? And, finally, where is the *collidesWith* method used?

D   Where does the Pop Framework keep a *cCollider *_pcollider* object? What is the purpose of this *cCollider* object?

E   Why does the Pop Framework choose to implement *cCollider* as a linked list instead of as an array?

F   How does the *cCritterWall::collide* differ from the normal *cCritter::collide*?

Exercises

Exercise 11.1: Turn off asteroid–asteroid collisions in Spacewar

Turn off the asteroid-to-asteroid collisions in the Spacewar game. To do this, override the *cCritterAsteroid::collidesWith(cCritter *pcritterother)* method. You'll need to prototype the method in gamespacewar.h and implement it in gamespacewar.cpp. The implementation code should have these two lines.

```
if(pcritterother->IsKindOf(RUNTIME_CLASS(cCritterAsteroid)))
    return cCollider::DONTCOLLIDE;
return cCritter::collidesWith(pcritterother);
```

Does this make the game run faster? Compare speeds before and after, using the Game popup menu to change the number of critters. When you compare the speeds of builds always make sure that both are Debug builds or both are Release builds.

Exercise 11.2: Compare performance of *cCollider* using list and array

(a) Run the Spacewar game on your machine and notice if it lurches when you shoot some critters. Note the updates per second with a huge number of critters. (b) Now go into collider.h, comment out the line #define USECOLLIDERLIST, to switch from a list to an array for the *cCollider*. Rebuild the program, making sure to use **Build | Set Active Configuration** to the Release build if the build you checked in step (a) was also a Release build. Compare performance. On some machines you won't notice a difference and on some you will. At one point a tester saw some freeze-ups of the program when using the array build, though maybe the bug was only a transient coincidence.

Exercise 11.3: Sequence diagrams for adding and deleting critters

Recall that a sequence diagram's column really represents one individual object's behavior. In the case where there's only one object of the type under consideration we only write the class name instead of the name of the object; in the case where we're discussing more than one object of a given type, we write a class name with a colon and an object name. In doing parts (a) and (b) we may want to check the Pop Framework code for details or, even better, use the debugger to step through the sequence of events when you add or delete a critter.

(a) Draw a sequence diagram with columns for *cGame, cColliderPair, cCritter:pa, cCritter:pb, cCollider* and possibly *cBiota* to map the functions called when you add pa to the game, assuming that pb is a critter already in the game that pa is interested in colliding with.

(b) Draw a sequence diagram with the same columns to show what happens when pa is deleted.

Listeners

12

In this chapter we talk about how we move our onscreen player sprite with the mouse and keyboard.

12.1   How the critters listen to the user input

The *cController* utility class

The Microsoft **void CView::OnKeyDown(UINT nChar, UINT nRepCnt, UINT nFlags)** method is triggered whenever a key is pressed. The nFlags argument is a collection of bitflags designed to tell you whether the **Ctrl**, **Alt**, and/or **Shift** keys are down, and whether this is a repeated typematic keypress. The nRepCnt is also supposed to hold the number of repeated typematic messages that a key press has generated, where 'typematic' refers to the feature that has most keys trigger additional **OnKeyDown** messages if you continue to hold them down. In point of fact, the nFlags and nRepCnt arguments don't reliably behave as Microsoft's documentation says they do, so we work around them, as you can see if you check the *CPopView* override of the **OnKeyDown** method.

To give clean access to the user input, we have a class called *cController* that serves to hold the current state of the keyboard and mouse and allow the programmer to access this information with some conveniently designed accessor methods. The various possible keys are represented by integer keycodes, ordinarily the keycode for any key has a name of the form VK_???, such as VK_A, VK_LEFT, VK_SPACE, and so on. Check Appendix A for a complete list of the VK_ code names used in the Pop Framework. Under the current versions of Windows, there are 166 distinct recognized keys; we #**define** this number to be VKKEYCOUNT.

The *cController* maintains an unsigned integer keystate for each key; the keystate uses bitflags to represent if the key is depressed, and whether the **Shift** or **Ctrl** keys were down when the key was first pressed. Also we maintain some bitflags that enable us to tell when a key has been down for more than one cycle of the *cGame::step* call. Here's a partial listing of its prototype.

```
class cController : public CObject
{
protected:
    UINT _keystate[VKKEYCOUNT];
    Real _keystateage[VKKEYCOUNT];
public:
    cController();
    virtual void update(Real dt); /* cController uses update to
        check for when keys are no longer depressed and for when
        keys have been made available to the listeners more than
        once. */
    BOOL keyon(int vkcode);
    BOOL keyonplain(int vkcode);
    BOOL keyoncontrol(int vkcode);
    BOOL keyonshift(int vkcode);
    BOOL keyoncontrolshift(int vkcode);
        /* The following *single accessors only return TRUE once per
            keypress, useful for impulse controls. */
    BOOL keyonsingle(int vkcode)
    BOOL keyonplainsingle(int vkcode);
    BOOL keyoncontrolsingle(int vkcode);
    BOOL keyonshiftsingle(int vkcode);
    BOOL keyoncontrolshiftsingle(int vkcode);
        /* Sometimes, as when using an arrow key to spin a player, it
            is useful to know how long a key has been depressed. */
    Real keystateage(int vkcode);
};
```

It's worth mentioning that there is a VK_LBUTTON as well; we use this to signal when the left mouse button is depressed. And the same is true for the right button. In other words, we can treat the mouse buttons like keyboard keys. A complicating factor with the mouse is that one often needs to know the mouse's current cursor position; we deal with this by having the **cGame** maintain a **cVector _cursorpos** that gets updated by the active view within its **CPopView::OnSetCursor** call. Windows forces an **OnSetCursor** call in the window underlying the current mouse cursor position during or before every call to **OnIdle**.

The sequence from keypress to critter

In order to play the game, we need for the player critter to be able to take input from the keyboard and/or the mouse. We get at the input in a somewhat indirect fashion.

- When you press a key, an **OnKeyDown** message goes to the active **CPopView**.
- The **CPopView::OnKeyDown** message handler sends a **cGame::onKeyDown** message to the active **cGame** object.

- The **cGame** object stores the key information in its cController *_pcontroller member.

- The **cGame::step** method calls **cCritter::feellistener** for the player.

- The player critter's cListener* _plistener member calls the **cListener::listen(Real dt, cCritter *pownercritter)** method.

- The **cListener::listen** uses the **pcritter->pgame()->pcontroller()** accessor to get at the cController *_pcontroller to see which keys are down, whether the **Ctrl** and **Shift** keys are also down, how long the keys have been down, whether the mouse buttons are down, and so on.

- Depending on the keystates, the **cListener::listen** may do something like using **cCritter::setAcceleration** to change the player's acceleration.

The reason the flow is so indirect is because we want for a given keystroke to be available to any critter in the game that has a listener – this would be a factor for two-person games, for instance. In addition, rather than processing keystrokes immediately as they happen, we want for the processing to happen at a certain predictable spot within the **cGame::step** cycle – otherwise we may have trouble keeping up the illusion that our critters are behaving in a parallel fashion.

We have a little more about the interaction between the keyboard and the controller in the Keyboard section of Chapter 28: Mouse, Cursors and Keyboard.

We can sketch the flow in a sequence diagram as shown in Figure 12.1.

If this complexity bothers you, don't worry about it; the whole point of all this framework coding was to give the programmer an unobtrusive and reliable interface to the user's keyboard and mouse input. In the next section, we'll talk about how the **cListener** objects use this interface.

12.2 The listeners

As we mentioned in Chapter 8: Critters, a critter uses the Strategy pattern to farm out the task of listening to its **cListener *_plistener** member with a call to **feellistener**.

```
void cCritter::feellistener(Real dt)
{
    _plistener->listen(dt, this);
}
```

We pass the pointer **this** to the listener so that it can change the fields of this calling **cCritter** as required. Because a **cListener** takes a **cGame*** argument to its **listen** method, we can say that the **cListener** can 'navigate' to a **cGame**. The caller critter's **pgame()** holds the **cController** object that stores all of the keys and mouse actions you need to process.

We pass a **dt** argument to the **plistener->feellistener** because the mouse-based listener **cListenerCursor** needs to know the **dt** so as to appropriately set the critter's velocity to match the critter's motion from one cursor position to the next.

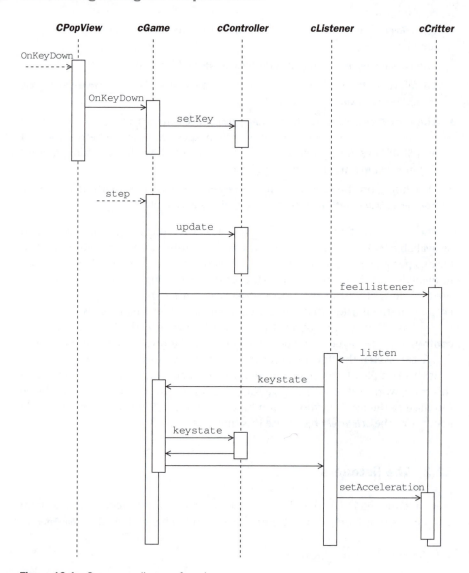

Figure 12.1 Sequence diagram for a key press

The **feellistener** method gets called inside the **cGame::step**. The successive calls to **cGame::step** generate calls to **feellistener()**, **move()**, **update()**, **feellistener()**, **move()**, **update()**, **feellistener()**, **move()**, and so on. In other words, after startup, the process for an individual critter is this.

- Call **update()** and, within **update**, call **feelforce()**.
- Call **feellistener()** and possibly add in some more acceleration.
- Use the _acceleration in **move()**.

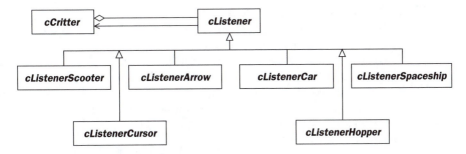

Figure 12.2 The *cListener* class diagram

Now let's start to look at what the different kinds of listeners do in their **listen** methods. To begin with, here's a class diagram of some of our listeners (Figure 12.2).

The **listen(Real dt, cCritter *pcritter)** method checks the current state of the keys as indicated by the `pcritter->pgame()->pcontroller()`. The **cListenerArrow::listen** code looks like the following.

```
void cListenerArrow::listen(Real dt, cCritter *pcritter)
{
    cController *pcontroller = pcritter->pgame()->pcontroller();
        /* Note that since I set the velocity to 0.0 when I'm not
        pressing an arrow key, this means that acceleration forces
        don't get to have accumulating effects on a critter with a
        cListenerScooter listener. So rather than having some very
        half-way kinds of acceleration effects, I go ahead and set
        acceleration to 0.0 in here. */
    pcritter->setAcceleration(cVector::ZEROVECTOR);
    if (!pcontroller->keyonplain(VK_LEFT) &&
        !pcontroller->keyonplain(VK_RIGHT) &&
        !pcontroller->keyonplain(VK_DOWN) &&
        !pcontroller->keyonplain(VK_UP) &&
        !pcontroller->keyonplain(VK_PAGEDOWN) &&
        !pcontroller->keyonplain(VK_PAGEUP)
        )
    {
        pcritter->setVelocity(cVector::ZEROVECTOR);
        return;
    }
        /* If you get here, you've pressed an arrow key. First match
            the velocity to the arrow key direction, and then match
            the attitude. */
    if (pcontroller->keyonplain(VK_LEFT))
        pcritter->setVelocity(- pcritter->maxspeed() *
            cVector::XAXIS);
```

```
if (pcontroller->keyonplain(VK_RIGHT))
    pcritter->setVelocity(pcritter->maxspeed() * cVector::XAXIS);
if (pcontroller->keyonplain(VK_DOWN))
    pcritter->setVelocity(-pcritter->maxspeed() *
        cVector::YAXIS);
if (pcontroller->keyonplain(VK_UP))
    pcritter->setVelocity(pcritter->maxspeed() * cVector::YAXIS);
if (pcontroller->keyonplain(VK_PAGEDOWN) &&
    pcritter->in3DWorld())
        pcritter->setVelocity(-pcritter->maxspeed() *
            cVector::ZAXIS);
if (pcontroller->keyonplain(VK_PAGEUP)&& pcritter->in3DWorld())
    pcritter->setVelocity(pcritter->maxspeed() * cVector::ZAXIS);
    //Now match the attitude to the motion, if locked.
if (pcritter->attitude to motion lock ())
pcritter->copyMotionMatrixToAttitudeMatrix();
    /* If pcritter is cCritterArmed*, its
        listen does more.
}
```

There are a couple of things to point out. The *cListenerArrow::listen* has its effects on the critter by setting the critter's velocity. Since I'm directly setting the velocity at each game step, the acceleration will not be able to have any significant effect on the velocity; a line of the form `_velocity += dt*_acceleration` will have a negligible effect since we keep resetting the velocity in each call of the *cListenerArrow::listen.* So we have this listener set the acceleration to the zero vector.

Another thing to notice is that we use the *cController::keyonplain* accessors to see which keys are pressed. This is so that we can use **Ctrl+Arrow** keys or **Ctrl+Shift+Arrow** keys for other purposes, such as moving the viewpoint.

A third thing to observe is that the *cListenerArrow::listen* will set the listening critter's attitude to match the current motion of the critter, if locked. This gives the expected effect of having the critter face left when you press the **Left Arrow**, and so on.

A final thing to notice is that *cListenerArrow::listen* is designed to work for critters in 3D worlds as well as for critters in 2D worlds. But we are careful not to impart 3D motion to a critter unless it satisfies the `is3D()` condition. This condition checks if the critter's `_movebox` has a non-zero z size.

The *cListenerScooter* also has an effect of directly setting the magnitude of a critter's velocity, so here we again set the acceleration to the zero vector. *cListenerScooter* changes the critter's motion vector in one of two ways; by changing the magnitude velocity, or by rotating the critter's motion vectors in various ways.

In order to fully describe the possible rotations in three dimensions, we need to think in terms of the critter as having a trihedron of three perpendicular unit vectors called the tangent, the normal, and the binormal. These three vectors make up the first three columns of the critter's 'motion matrix.' This is shown in Figure 12.3.

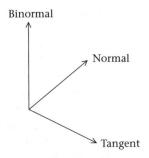

Figure 12.3 The trihedron of a critter

We can summarize the effect of **cListenerScooter::listen** as follows. In testing this, be aware that in the Pop program, the **cListenerScooter** is chosen with the **Player | Scooter Controls** selection. 'Scooter' makes sense as a name for this listener because, as with a scooter that only rolls while you kick it, **cListenerScooter** only moves a player as long as a key is held down.

- The **Up** key sets the critter's velocity to its maxspeed times its current tangent direction.

- The **Down** key sets the critter's velocity to the opposite, that is, the maxspeed times the negative of the critter's tangent direction. In this case we *do not* set the critter's attitude to match its motion, that is, we leave its tangent pointing in the same direction as before and let the critter be moving 'in reverse.'

- The **Left** and **Right Arrow** keys 'yaw' the critter by rotating its tangent around the z-axis or, in 3D, around the critter's binormal.

- In 3D, the **Pageup** and **Pagedown** keys 'pitch' the critter by rotating its tangent around its normal.

- In 3D, the **Home** and **End** keys 'roll' the critter by rotating its normal around its tangent.

- When we rotate a critter we *do* update its visible attitude to match the new orientation of the motion matrix.

In order to make the game more responsive, it's better to have two turn-speeds for your player, a fast turnspeed for whirling around to shoot something that's sneaking up on you, and a slow turnspeed for accurately aiming your fire so as to hit a small or distant object. We choose the correct rotation speed by using a helper **turnspeed** method inside the **cListenerScooter::listen** method. Our **cListener::turnspeed** function looks at the **cController::keyage** of a key to determine how large a rotation to return.

The **cListenerSpaceship** and the **cListenerCar** do not change the critter's speed directly. Instead they add or subtract from the critter's acceleration. The difference is that the **cListenerSpaceship** adds an acceleration whose direction is determined by the critter's current visual attitude, and the **cListenerCar** adds an acceleration whose direction is determined by the critter's current motion.

The *cListenerSpaceship* and the *cListenerCar* rotate the critter in the same way as the *cListenerScooter* controls. The difference is that the *cListenerSpaceship* rotates the critter's attitude, while the *cListenerCar* rotates the critter's motion.

Both of these listeners are compatible with having forces act upon the critter.

The *cListenerCursor* moves the critter with the mouse. This is done by setting the critter's acceleration to the zero vector and setting the critter's velocity to be whatever velocity is necessary to move the critter to the `pcritter->pgame()->cursorpos()` in the allotted *dt* time slice that is fed into the *cListenerCursor::listen(Real dt, cCritter *pcritter)* call. If you move the mouse rapidly this means that the critter will in fact move at an extremely high velocity; when a critter has a *cListenerCursor* we disable the customary condition that limits a critter to moving less rapidly than the value of its `maxspeed()`.

The reason we choose to have the *cListenerCursor* move the critter by changing its velocity rather than by simply calling a direct *moveTo* is that we want to be able to 'hit' things with a critter that we move with the mouse, and in order for a critter to collide properly with something, we need for its velocity to match its perceived motion.

Code for these listeners can be found in listener.cpp.

12.3 Shooting with the listeners

As well as moving our critters around, we also want to be able to make them shoot bullets or, if you will, eject objects. We will allow two shooting input methods: pressing the spacebar or clicking the left mouse button while the cursor is in a view that uses the `_hCursorPlay` cursor. You select this cursor by clicking on the crosshair button in the toolbar or by selecting **View | Shoot Cursor**.

The framework checks on the cursor type in the *CPopView::OnLButtonDown*. This method only stores a left click in the game *cController* object in the case where the cursor type is indeed the `_hCursorPlay`.

We derive any critter that shoots from the critter child class *cCritterArmedPlayer*. We'll discuss *cCritterArmedPlayer* in some detail in the next chapter; for now it suffices to know that this class has a *BOOL _bshooting* member, and when `bshooting` is `TRUE` the *cCritterArmedPlayer::update* method can shoot a bullet.

Rather than putting shooting code into each of our listeners, it's more efficient to put it into the *feellistener* method of the *cCritterArmedPlayer* itself. Leaving out a few complications, the method looks basically like this.

```
void cCritterArmedPlayer::feellistener(Real dt)
{
    cCritter::feellistener(dt);
    _bshooting = (pgame()->keystate(VK_SPACE) == cController::KEYON);
    if (pgame()->keystate(VK_LBUTTON) == cController::KEYON)
        /* shoot with left mouse click
        The controller will only have turned VK_LBUTTON on if you
        left clicked the Shoot Cursor; left clicks with other
        cursors will be ignored by controller. */
```

```
    {
        _bshooting = TRUE;
        aimAt(pgame()->cursorpos());
    }
}
```

Using the shooting cursor makes a nice interface for many games. As it turns out, users have trouble using complicated listeners to move the player. Much of the challenge of Asteroids (or our Spacewar) is that the **cListenerSpaceship** is so hard to use. The **cListenerCar** is in fact only practical for things like car races around an onscreen track. Ordinarily, users will prefer either the **cListenerScooter** or even the lowly **cListenerArrow**.

One of the drawbacks of a **cListenerArrow** for a shooting game is that the critter seemingly can only shoot in the cardinal directions: East, North, West, and South. But if you use a Shoot mode cursor, that is, the _hCursorPlay, with the **cListenerArrow**, then you can shoot in any direction by left clicking. An interesting side-effect (that you could of course code out if you don't like it) is that when you press the **Up Arrow** and hold down the left mouse button, a critter with the **cListenerArrow** will continuously move towards the cursor location.

12.4 Viewer listeners

Each **CPopView** has a **cCritterViewer *_pviewpointcritter** member that is used to set the projection matrix and the view matrix inside the **CPopView::OnDraw** call. We discuss the details of this process in Chapter 24: Two- and Three-dimensional Graphics. But the basic notion is simple: a view shows the game world as seen from the viewpoint of its _pviewpointcritter.

The user changes the appearance of the view by moving or rotating the _pviewpointcritter. It's also possible to change the magnification scale, or field of view angle, by making a pviewpointcritter->zoom(zoomfactor) call.

In order to let the user change the viewpoint, the **CPopView** code can attach a listener to the viewer with a call like _pviewpointcritter->setListener(new cListenerViewerOrtho()). The **cListenerViewerOrtho** is one of the three specialized **cListener** child classes that the Pop Framework provides for use with the viewers. Let's say a few words about the three kinds of viewer listeners.

- **cListenerViewerOrtho** is always used as the _pviewpointcritter listener for two-dimensional worlds. This listener reacts to **Ctrl+Arrow** key combinations to move the _pviewpointcritter back and forth parallel to the XY plane, and it causes the **Ins** and **Del** keys to generate zoom calls.

- Either **cListenerViewerFly** or **cListenerViewerRide** are always used as the _pviewpointcritter listener for three-dimensional worlds. **cListenerViewerFly** reacts to the **Ctrl+Arrow** key combinations to move the _pviewpointcritter along its intrinsic axes, that is along its tangent, normal, and binormal directions. The **Ctrl+Shift+Arrow** key combinations rotate the _pviewpointcritter around its intrinsic axes, and the **Ins** and **Del** keys zoom the viewpoint.

- **cListenerViewerRide** is used in three-dimensional worlds to let the viewer 'ride' upon the game's pplayer(). That is, this listener maintains a fixed **cVector** _offset_, keeps the _pviewpointcritter always at this offset from the player's position, and adjusts the _pviewpointcritter attitude to change along with the player's attitude. (Rather than exactly matching the player attitude to look parallel to the player, we have the rider tilt a bit to look at a point slightly ahead of the player.) The **Ctrl+Arrow** keys can be used to change the viewer's fixed offset from the player.

Here as an example is the **cListenerViewerOrtho::listen** code.

```
void cListenerViewerOrtho::listen(Real dt, cCritter *pcritter)
{
    cController *pcontroller = pcritter->pgame()->pcontroller();
// Use the Control + (Arrow keys, Insert or Delete) to translate.
    if (pcontroller->keyoncontrol(VK_LEFT))
        pcritter->setVelocity(pcritter->maxspeed() * cVector::XAXIS);
    if (pcontroller->keyoncontrol(VK_RIGHT))
        pcritter->setVelocity(- pcritter->maxspeed() *
            cVector::XAXIS);
    if (pcontroller->keyoncontrol(VK_DOWN))
        pcritter->setVelocity(pcritter->maxspeed() * cVector::YAXIS);
    if (pcontroller->keyoncontrol(VK_UP))
        pcritter->setVelocity(- pcritter->maxspeed() *
            cVector::YAXIS);
    if (!pcontroller->keyoncontrol(VK_LEFT) &&
        !pcontroller->keyoncontrol(VK_RIGHT) &&
        !pcontroller->keyoncontrol(VK_DOWN) &&
        !pcontroller->keyoncontrol(VK_UP) )
        pcritter->setVelocity(cVector::ZEROVECTOR);
// Use the Insert, Delete keys to zoom.
    cCritterViewer *pcritterv = (cCritterViewer*)(pcritter); /* Need
        the cast to use zoom
    ASSERT(pcritterv); //To make sure the cast didn't fail. */
    if (pcontroller->keyon(VK_INSERT))
        pcritterv->zoom(cCritterViewer::DEFAULTZOOMFACTOR);
    if (pcontroller->keyon(VK_DELETE))
        pcritterv->zoom(1.0/cCritterViewer::DEFAULTZOOMFACTOR);
}
```

Note that the **Ctrl+Left** combination moves the _pviewpointcritter to the right, which gives an effect of the visible world moving to the left. Users tend not to think in terms of there being a separate _pviewpointcritter (and why should they?), so it makes for a better interface to move the visible world in the direction of the arrows.

In most of our games both the player and the `_pviewpointcritter` will have a listener, and at every full update of the game, each of them gets a chance to 'listen' to the key information in the game's *cController* object.

12.5 How a listener initializes its owner critter

A final thing to mention about our *cListener* class is that it has a *virtual void install(cCritter *pcritter)* method. We attach a listener to a critter with the *cCritter::setListener(cListener *plistener)* method, and the *setListener* code calls `plistener->install(this)` to give the listener a chance to make any necessary adjustments to the critter that is going to start using it.

The default behavior of *cListener::install(cCritter *pcritter)* is simply to match the *pcritter*'s motion matrix to its attitude matrix to get things off to a good start – this match will not automatically be TRUE, as we normally do *not* lock the player critter's attitude to its motion. One other use for install is to temporarily set a critter's maximum speed to a very high value when it uses a *cListenerCursor*.

In the case of the viewer listeners, the *install* methods also set the *cCritterViewer _perspective* field to FALSE for the two-dimensional *cListenerViewerOrtho* and to TRUE for the three-dimensional *cListenerViewerFly* and *cListenerViewerRide*. A final wrinkle is that the *cListenerViewerFly* locks the viewer critter's attitude matrix to its motion matrix – as here we are effectively flying a camera around; while *cListenerViewerOrtho* does not lock the viewer critter attitude to its motion – because we want this viewer always to be staring down the z-axis at the world, even if we are moving it to the left and right. More details can be found in the listener.cpp file.

Review questions

A Given a `cController *pcontroller` object, how would you find out if the **Left Arrow** key is being pressed?

B What software pattern is embodied by the critter's use of a *cListener* object?

C How does the *cListener::listen* method get called?

D How does a critter respond to keys when it uses the Arrow listener? The scooter?

E What does the *cListenerCursor* do to a critter that uses it?

F What are the three kinds of viewer listeners the Pop Framework uses?

G What is the difference between a critter's attitude matrix and its motion matrix?

Exercises

Exercise 12.1: Spaceship listener with friction

Note that a player with the *cListenerSpaceship* is still able to feel forces such as gravity. Try giving the player friction in the Spacewar game and see if this makes it more pleasant to use the spaceship keys.

Exercise 12.2: Move the world or move the viewer?

Test out the effects of **Ctrl+Arrow** and **Ctrl+Shift+Arrow** in some 2D and 3D views. The visual effect of these keys is that you are moving the world. Now open the listener.cpp file and find the line `#define MOVEVIEW 1`. Read the comment on this line and change the line to `#define MOVEVIEW -1`. Now test the same **Arrow** keys in some 2D and 3D views. The visual effect of the keys is now to move the (invisible) viewer rather than the world. Which interface do you like better? Which do you think will be preferred by most users?

Shooters and bullets

13

We want for critters to be able to spawn off additional objects. The most common use of this is for shooting games in which the critters shoot at the player and the player shoots back. Do keep in mind that a game with this pattern can in fact be given a non-violent framing story. The critters might be dropping jewels that you want to pick up. Or you might be throwing food at them. Perhaps you're on a safari taking pictures, and you're firing flashbulbs. This said, let's go ahead and speak in terms of shooting bullets.

In order to prevent the player from drowning the screen in bullets and having the game be too easy, we will allow only some limited number of player bullets to be active at one time. Suppose you want to allow the player to have at most eight bullets active at one time. When there are already eight bullets present and the user presses the shoot control, what happens then?

There are two alternatives. One approach is to have the shoot control go dead until one of the eight active bullets hits something or dies of old age. This is not satisfying as then, if the player is menaced by some approaching enemy and all the bullets are in use, the player is left defenseless. A better approach is to have the shooting of a ninth bullet remove the oldest bullet from the screen. This specification-level decision will affect our design.

13.1 High-level design for *cCritterArmed* and *cCritterBullet*

We make a new class called *cCritterArmed* to encapsulate shooting behavior, and derive a *cCritterArmedPlayer* from it. We'll also have a *cCritterArmedRobot* that will have the feature of always automatically aiming at whatever *cCritter** is stored in its *_ptarget* field. This is illustrated by Figure 13.1.

Table 13.1 lists some of the key new methods and overrides of *cCritterBullet* and *cCritterArmed*.

And Figure 13.2 is a sequence diagram showing the flow of method calls involved in having an armed critter shoot a bullet at another critter.

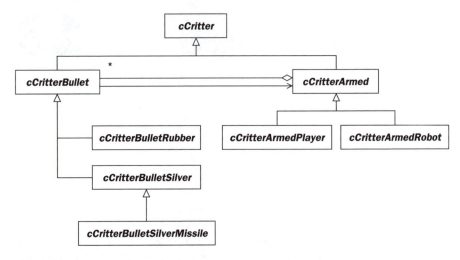

Figure 13.1 Diagram of the *cCritterArmed* and *cCritterBullet* classes

Table 13.1 The special classes used for shooting.

Class	New methods	Overrides
cCritterBullet	*initialize*	*update*
	isTarget	*collide*
		collidesWith
cCritterArmed	*aimAt*	*draw*
	shoot	*update*

13.2 The *cCritterArmed*

The *cCritterArmed* has the ability to shoot bullets; this is what its *shoot* method does.

To begin with, let's explain how the *cCritterArmed::shoot* gets called. The call is the responsibility of the *cCritterArmed::update* method, which checks if (a) the critter's *_armed* flag is on, meaning that it is allowed to shoot at all, and (b) the critter's *_bshooting* flag is on, meaning that it is supposed to shoot right now. When we use a *cCritterArmed* as a player, the *_bshooting* flag is something we normally turn on and off by pressing the space bar or the left mouse button. When we have a self-running 'robotic' *cCritterArmedRobot* child of the *cCritterArmed* class as a rival in our game, the *_bshooting* flag will often be continually on, with the *_waitshoot* time interval preventing the *cCritterArmedRobot* from shooting perpetually.

Here's a slightly simplified version of our *cCritterArmed::update* code.

```
void cCritterArmed::update(CPopView *pactiveview)
{
//(1) Call base class update to apply force.
    cCritter::update(pactiveview);
```

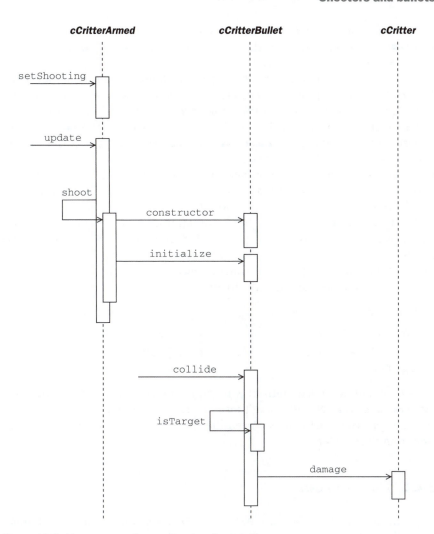

Figure 13.2 A sequence diagram for shooting a bullet

```
//(2) Align gun with move direction if necessary.
    if (_aimtoattitudelock)
        setAimVector(attitudeTangent()); /* Keep the gun pointed in
            the right direction. */
/* (3) Shoot if requested, and if enough time has elapsed since last
shot. */
    if (_armed && _bshooting && (_age - _ageshoot > _waitshoot))
    {
        shoot();
        _ageshoot = _age;
    }
}
```

To make the aim direction of the gun visible, we override and extend *cCritterArmed::draw* to draw a little line segment under *cCritterArmed's* sprite to represent the direction of the gun.

Now let's say something about what the *cCritterArmed::shoot* method does. We want to allow for different *cCritterArmed* child classes to use different kinds of bullets, so there is a *CRuntimeClass *_pbulletclass* variable to specify the kinds of bullets used. This means that we don't need to override the *shoot* method. Instead we just change the *_pbulletclass*. The *CRuntimeClass *_pbulletclass* variable is set by default in the constructor to RUNTIME_CLASS(cCritterBullet). You can find out more about the *CRuntimeClass* type in Chapter 22: Topics in C++. Basically it holds a string with a name of the class as well as an integer giving the size in bytes of the class instance objects.

The way *_bulletclass* gets used hinges on an interesting OOP feature, which allows us to create an instance of a class object from the name of the class. That is, there is a general *CRuntimeClass::CreateObject* method which will return an object of the type specified by the caller *CRuntimeClass* object.

The *cCritterArmed::shoot()* does the following.

- If the shooter has more than _maxbullets active, delete the oldest one.
- Create a pbullet with pbulletclass->CreateObject().
- Call pbullet->initialize(this), with a pointer to the shooter as an argument.

The reason we need both the second and the third step is that the **CRuntimeClass::CreateObject()** doesn't take an argument; in effect it always calls a no-argument constructor. So we need the extra *initialize* call to feed in information from the shooter.

13.3 The *cCritterBullet*

As mentioned in the last section, when a *cCritterArmed* fires a shot, its *shoot* method is called, and a new bullet gets initialized in two stages. First the bullet's no-argument constructor *cBullet()* is called. The constructor does the following.

- Sets the bullet's _collidepriority to the relatively high value cCollider::CP_BULLET. Since this value is higher than cCollider::CP_CRITTER, this means that when a bullet hits a normal critter, the bullet invokes the *collide* method as the caller instead of as the argument.
- Tells the bullet to have a limited lifetime by setting _usefixedlifetime to TRUE and setting the size of _fixedlifetime to cCritterBullet::FIXEDLIFETIME, which happens to be set to 3.0 seconds. (Note that you can do this for other critters, too if you like, although the default behavior is for critters to be 'immortal' with _usefixedlifetime set to FALSE.)
- Assigns the bullet a yellow isosceles triangle to be its default sprite.
- Sets the bullet's speed, its _maxspeed, and its _hitstrength.

In the second stage of a bullet's initialization, the *cCritterBullet:: initialize(cCritterArmed *pshooter)* is called with the shooting critter as the *pshooter* argument. The reference to *pshooter* allows the bullet to set its target according to the preferences of the *pshooter*.

The default *cCritterBullet* constructor gives the bullet a yellow isosceles triangle for its sprite. The default *cBullet::initialize* method does the following.

- Matches the bullet's attitude to the shooter's.
- Positions the bullet at the tip of the shooter's gun.
- Sets the direction of the bullet's velocity to match shooter's _aimvector, using the speed that the bullet acquired in its constructor. The result gives us what we might call a 'muzzle velocity.' It would be physically correct to then set the bullet velocity equal to this muzzle velocity plus the shooter's velocity – but in practice this gives unattractive game behavior. So we don't normally add in the shooter's velocity. We'll say more about this in the section on *cCritterArmedPlayer* below.
- Attaches copies of the shooter's physics forces such as gravity and friction to the bullet.
- Copies the shooter's _movebox to the bullet.
- Gives the bullet the same _ptarget as the shooter.

The *cBullet::update* method is written to call the base class *cCritter::update* and to kill off the bullet if it has touched an edge of the world and its *_dieatedges* flag is on. The way that *update* can tell if a critter has touched the edges of the world (wrapped or bounced from the edge on its last move) is to look in its *_outcode*, which is set by the *cCritter::move* method to be non-zero if the critter touches the border. The *cBullet::update* code looks like this.

```
void cCritterBullet::update(CPopView *pactiveview)
{
    cCritter::update(pactiveview); /* Feels force, also checks _age
        against _lifetime. */
    if (_outcode && _dieatedges)/* _outcode nonzero means near an
        edge. This keeps bullets from bouncing or wrapping, but it
        also makes the critters unable to fire when they are really
        near an edge. */
    {
    delete_me();
    return;
    }
}
```

The *_dieatedges* flag is TRUE by default for the *cCritterBullet* and the *cCritterBulletSilver*. The reason for having it normally be TRUE is that the game tends to look confusing if too many bullets wrap or bounce, so we normally kill them whenever they hit the edge. But you can optionally turn this behavior off by setting the _**dieatedges**_ flag to FALSE. The _**cCritterBulletRubber**_ constructor and the _**cCritterBulletSilverMissile**_ constructors both set _**dieatedges**_ to FALSE, in the first case because it's fun to watch the rubber bullets bounce around, and in the second case because we want to make the silver missiles particularly lethal and hard to escape.

Also remember that since a bullet has its _usefixedlifetime flag on, the base _**cCritter::update**_ call will kill off the bullet if it's older than the age _fixedlifetime, which is normally going to be three seconds.

The most characteristic part of a bullet's behavior is to damage things, and this code is in the _**cCritterBullet**_ override of the _**cCritter::collide(cCritter *pcritter)**_ method. We don't put the damage-other-critters-when-you-touch-them code into the _**cCritter::update**_ because bullets hitting things is about the interactions between _pairs_ of critters. It makes more sense – and is more time-efficient – to handle this inside the _**collide**_ method which is already in place to look at each pair of critters that you think you might be interested in.

The bullet _**collide**_ code goes like this.

```
BOOL cCritterBullet::collide(cCritter *pcritter)
{
    if (isTarget(pcritter)) //If you hit a target, damage it and die.
    {
        if (!touch(pcritter))
            return FALSE;
        int hitscore = pcritter->damage(_hitstrength);
        delete_me(); /* Make a service request, but you won't go
            away yet. */
        if (_pshooter) //Possible that _pshooter has died, is NULL.
            _pshooter->addScore(hitscore);
        return TRUE;
    }
    else //Bounce off other critters in a normal fashion.
        return cCritter::collide(pcritter); /* Bounce off non-target
            critters */
}
```

Given that the bullet's collision behavior is more complicated than a standard critter's collision behavior, the Pop Framework gives a bullet priority in calling the _**collide**_ method. As mentioned above, we do this by setting the bullet's _collidepriority to a higher value than ordinary critters have. In addition, we override the _**int cCritterBullet::collidesWith(cCritter *pcritter)**_ method to return cCollider::DONTCOLLIDE if pcritter is (a) the bullet's shooter or (b) another bullet from the same shooter. Condition (a) is fairly obvious. We need (b) because sometimes if you are moving in the direction that you're shooting, your bullets may be overlapping each other, and you don't want them to destroy or to bounce off of each other. You can check Chapter 11: Collisions to review the details about how *collidesWith* is used for adding collision pairs to the game's *cCollider* list of collision pairs.

The *BOOL cBullet::isTarget(cCritter *pcritter)* tells whether a given *pcritter* is something that the bullet wants to damage. The default *isTarget* method returns TRUE for every *pcritter* except for critters of the type *cCritterWall*.

The *cCritterBulletSilver* overrides the *isTarget* method to only target one particular critter. What makes these bullets 'silver' is that they are targeted for one thing and one thing only, in analogy to the silver bullets of legend with which one is supposed to be able to shoot a werewolf. For these guys, the *isTarget* method is simplicity itself.

```
BOOL cCritterBulletSilver::isTarget(cCritter* pcritter)
{
    return pcritter == _ptarget;
}
```

An example of a use of *cCritterBulletSilver* occurs in the Spacewar game, in which the enemy UFO critters are shooting silver bullets at the player. We want the player to be able to fend off these bullets by shooting at them. You might think the player's bullets would blow the silver bullets up in any case, as the default *cCritterBullet::isTarget* would return TRUE for these bullets. But remember that when we have a pair (pa, pb) we only call pa->collide(pb) or pb->collide(pa), but not both. If pa and pb are both bullets; we might be unsure about which one gets to control the collide; indeed this could simply depend on where they happen to be listed in the *_pbiota* array, which in turn depends on exactly when you pressed the spacebar to shoot your bullet relative to when the UFO shot its silver bullet. Seemingly it could happen that when your bullet hits a silver bullet, it is the silver bullet's *collide* method which is in control.

In order to avoid this bad state of affairs, we have the *cCritterBulletSilver* constructor set the silver bullet's _collidepriority to a value cCollider::CP_ SILVERBULLET which is slightly less than cCollider::CP_BULLET. This means that only correctly ordered bullet-to-silver-bullet collision pairs will be added to the game's collider list.

13.4 *damage* **and** *draw*

When a bullet hits a critter, it gets damaged. We have a *cCritter* method for this.

```
int cCritter::damage(int hitstrength)
{
        /* If we have our shield on, or were just hit, then don't
            allow a hit. */
```

```
    if ( _shieldflag || recentlyDamaged() )
        return 0;
    _lasthit_age = _age; /* Save age for use by the recentlyDamaged()
        accessor. */
    _health -= hitstrength;
    if (_health <= 0)
    {
        _health = 0; //Do not allow negative health.
        die(); /* Make a delete_me service request, possibly make
            noise or more. */
        return _value; //The reward for killing this critter.
    }
    return 0; //Not killed yet.
}
```

As you can see, *damage* does nothing if *_shieldflag* is on, or if you've been recently hit. By default `_shieldflag` is FALSE, and normally only the *cCritterArmedPlayer* sets the `_shieldflag` to TRUE. (This is done by the user making the **Player | Shield** menu selection.) I might mention here that commercial game designers almost always include a flag like *_shieldflag* to make their player invulnerable so that they can test out game scenarios without having to worry about the player getting killed. Many released games still have a secret 'cheat' switch for turning on your player's *_shieldflag*. The colorful expression '*God mode*' is often used for this state of player invulnerability.

Also note that a critter won't sustain damage if it was *recentlyDamaged()*. This inline *cCritter* method is defined in critter.h as BOOL recentlyDamaged(){return (_age - _lasthit_age) < cCritter::SAFEWAIT;}. The default size of SAFEWAIT is 0.3 second. The reason we use the *recentlyDamaged()* check is that it's not good if a critter can get damaged rapidly twice in a row. You don't want your player, for instance, to lose three health points simply from bumbling around near an enemy for a fraction of a second. And if you shoot a fusillade of bullets at an enemy, it's more reasonable to only let two nearby bullets manage to inflict one hit of damage.

In general, a single call to *cCritter::damage* can kill a critter, since the default *_health* is only 1. But the player usually starts higher.

The *cCritter::damage* is often overridden to make a sound as well. We could also override it to move the player critter to the center of the screen, as is done in some computer games.

In the Spacewar game, we start each *cCritterAsteroid* object's health out at 2, and we override *cCritterAsteroid::damage* to split a health-two critter into two smaller health-one critters.

As we mentioned above, we use the *recentlyDamaged()* method to prevent a critter from being damaged too rapidly twice in a row. It's useful to display this 'temporarily unavailable for damage' state. We do this with a line in *cCritter::draw* in **critter.cpp**. The DF_WIREFRAME flag causes polygons to be drawn unfilled, but it has no effect on bitmaps.

```
void cCritter::draw(cGraphics *pgraphics, int drawflags)
{
    if (recentlyDamaged())
        drawflags |= CPopView::DF_WIREFRAME;
            /* Draw yourself as a "shadow of yourself" if dead or
                recently damaged. */
    //More code...
}
```

13.5 Armed players and armed robots

In this section we discuss the *cCritterArmedPlayer* and *cCritterArmedRobot* child classes of *cCritterArmed*.

The *cCritterArmedPlayer* objects shoot when the user presses the spacebar or left-clicks the mouse. We implement this by deriving our players from the *cCritterArmedPlayer* class and letting *cCritterArmedPlayer* override the *feellistener(Real dt)* method so as use the left button or the spacebar to fire its gun. That is, as we already mentioned in Chapter 12: Listeners, we'll have an override something like this.

```
void cCritterArmedPlayer::feellistener(Real dt)
{
    cCritter::feellistener(dt);
    _bshooting = (pgame()->keystate(VK_SPACE) == cController::KEYON);
    if (pgame()->keystate(VK_LBUTTON) == cController::KEYON)
        /* shoot with left mouse click. The controller will only have
        turned VK_LBUTTON on if you left clicked the Shoot Cursor;
        left clicks with other cursors will be ignored by
        controller. */
    {
        _bshooting = TRUE;
        aimAt(pgame()->cursorpos());
    }
}
```

The *cCritterArmedRobot* objects, on the other hand, have their _bshooting flag permanently set to TRUE, so they shoot as often as they can, that is, whenever _waitshoot seconds have elapsed. To prevent a boring 'firing-squad effect' of having all the armed robots shoot in synchronization, we put a little age-randomizing trick into an override of the *cCritterArmedRobot::setWaitShoot(Real waitshoot)* method; you can check this and other details in **critterarmed.cpp**.

As we mentioned above, a bullet has a muzzle velocity given by the shooter's aim direction and the bullet's maximum speed. We normally take the bullet's velocity to simply be the muzzle velocity, without adding in the shooter's velocity. This is a good idea, in particular, for the moving *cCritterArmedRobot* critters, as we want to make it easy for them to aim and shoot directly at the player without having to worry about computing 'windage' compensation for their velocity relative to the player.

When it comes to the player, however, it makes the game feel a little more realistic if we do go at least part way towards adding the player velocity to the bullet muzzle velocity. Otherwise when you're moving forward and shooting, the bullets seem to pile up on each other. And, given that the player is controlled by a thinking human being instead of by two or three lines of computer code, it might be perfectly alright if the player's aiming process is made slightly more difficult.

But experimentation and beta-testing shows that directly adding the player velocity to the muzzle velocity gives effects that confuse some users. Remember that we aren't necessarily after complete physical accuracy here; the bottom line is to make an enjoyable game with controls that feel natural. So we actually only add in whatever component of the player's motion is in the direction the bullet is already moving. Provided that the bullet's default speed is less than its maximum allowable speed, this means that when a moving player shoots a bullet straight ahead it goes a little faster. We don't reciprocate by slowing down a bullet that the player shoots opposite to its direction of motion as this could lead to the visually confusing phenomenon of very slowly moving bullets.

```
cCritterBullet* cCritterArmedPlayer::shoot()
{
    cCritterBullet *pbullet = cCritterArmed::shoot();
#ifdef PLAYERBULLETSPEEDUP
    /* A simple pbullet->addVelocity(_velocity), gives unattractive
        results. Use dot product operator % */
    Real bulletspeedup = _velocity % pbullet->tangent();
    if (bulletspeedup > 0.0)
        pbullet->addVelocity(bulletspeedup * pbullet->tangent());
            //So bullets don't stack up.
#endif //PLAYERBULLETSPEEDUP
    return pbullet;
}
```

Some of the additional features of the *cCritterArmedPlayer* class are as follows.

- The constructor calls setAttitudeToMotionLock(FALSE) so the player can turn its sprite independently of its motion, and calls setAimToAttitudeLock(TRUE) so the player will align its gun with the attitude of its sprite.

- The constructor installs a default red isosceles triangle as the armed player's sprite.

- The class overrides *damage* to make a noise so the user knows something bad has happened.

- The class overrides *draw* to draw a circle around the player's sprite; this is to make it stand out from the other critters.

- The class adds a **BOOL _sensitive** field and overrides **collide** so that if _sensitive is TRUE, the armed player calls **damage** each time it touches another non-wall critter. This is useful for an Asteroids-style game. Since **cCritterArmedPlayer** has its own override of **collide**, the constructor sets its _collidepriority to cCollider::CP_PLAYER which is slightly higher than cCollider::CP_CRITTER, but less than cCollider::CP_BULLET.

13.6 The two-way *cCritterArmed/cCritterBullet* association

This optional subsection has some information about the somewhat tricky issue of how we maintain a two-way association between objects that can be deleted at any time.

As we mentioned at the start of the chapter, we will allow only some limited number of player bullets to be active at one time. If a player has shot, say, eight bullets and wants to shoot another, what we'll do is to remove the oldest of the bullets when we shoot a new one. (Of course the number doesn't have to be exactly eight; you can set it as cCritterArmed::MAXBULLETS.) This design means that the player needs to maintain an array of bullets. We choose an array rather than a list, because we traverse the collection a lot, and its not going to be big enough to make removing items from it a burden.

So a **cCritterArmed** object has an array holding pointers to the bullets that it has shot. And we do this for two reasons.

- If an armed critter wants to shoot more than some limited number of bullets, it should delete its oldest bullet in order to make space for a new one.
- When an armed critter is deleted it needs to tell its bullets that it's gone.

The reason the armed critter needs to tell its bullets when it's gone is because each bullet needs to know who shot it. That is, a **cCritterBullet** has a **cArmedCritter *_pshooter** pointer to the 'shooter' critter that fired it. This for the following three reasons.

- A bullet should not collide with or damage its shooter.
- When the bullet damages something it should award points to its shooter.
- When the bullet dies is it needs to tell its shooter that it's gone.

We often have a situation where an object A has a member pB which is a pointer to an object B. Now if B is not 'doing anything' independent of A, this is quite safe. We simply let A create and destroy the B in, respectively, its constructor and destructor. But if there is a chance that B might go off and get deleted 'on its own,' then we need to make sure that B tells A that its pB is no longer useable.

In the case of the bullets and the shooters, each of them is doing things on its own, and may be deleted while the other one is still alive. Since the shooter has pointers to its bullets, when a bullet dies, the bullet's destructor needs to tell the shooter to get rid of the soon-to-be invalid bullet pointer. Conversely, since a bullet has a pointer to its shooter, when the shooter dies, its destructor needs to tell each of the shooter's bullets to get rid of its soon-to-be invalid shooter pointer.

Let's take a look at the two relevant destructors, first the bullet's, and then the shooter's.

```
cCritterBullet::~cCritterBullet()
{
    if (_pshooter) /* The cCritteArmed destructor sets _pshooter to
        NULL in its destructor. So if _pshooter isn't NULL, then it's
        still a good pointer. */
        _pshooter->removeBullet(this);
}
```

The *removeBullet* method looks to see if the bullet is in fact in the `_bulletarray`, and if it is it takes out that entry from the array and shrinks the array by one, moving any higher positions down one slot.

And here's the *cCritterArmed* destructor.

```
cCritterArmed::~cCritterArmed()
{
    /* It could cause a crash if any surviving cCritterBullet still
        has a _pshooter pointer to this deleted cCritterArmed. So I
        set all the _bulletarray bullets' pshooters to NULL,
        and everywhere in the bullet code where I might use a
        pshooter, I always check that it isn't NULL. */
    for (int i=0; i<_bulletarray.GetSize(); i++)
        _bulletarray.GetAt(i)->_pshooter = NULL;
}
```

Review questions

A Draw a UML diagram to show the relation between the classes *cCritter*, *cCritterArmed*, and *cCritterBullet*.

B How does the *cCritterArmed::update* method know when to shoot a bullet, and how does it prevent you from shooting the bullets too close together?

C What steps take place when *cCritterArmed::shoot* is called?

D Why do we need a *cBullet::initialize* method in addition to the *cBullet* constructor?

E How does *cBullet::collide* make use of the *cBullet::isTarget* method?

F Why do bullets by default have a higher `_collidepriority` value than regular critters?

G How does the *cCritter::damage* method avoid having a critter getting damaged two times in a row by two nearby bullets?

H What causes a *cCritterArmedRobot* to keep shooting, and what controls how long it waits between shots?

I What are the default values for the *cCritterArmedPlayer* fields `_attitudetomotionlock` and `_aimtoattitudelock`? Why does the Pop Framework use these values?

Exercises

Exercise 13.1: Adding player velocity to the bullets

Open up the **critterarmed.cpp** file and find the `cCritterArmedPlayer::shoot` method. This shoot method is a compromise between adding in the player's velocity and not adding in the player's velocity; it only adds in velocity that's in the shooting direction. To see the effect of not adding in any velocity at all comment out the line `#define PLAYERBULLETSPEEDUP` at the start of the file. Run the program and look what happens in the Spacewar game if the player shoots while moving forward. Now, with the `#define` still switched off, check the effect of adding in the velocity by adding the line `pbullet->addVelocity(_velocity)` to the `cCritterArmedPlayer::shoot` method. (Be sure to type in this line outside the scope of the `#ifdef`.) Now look how the game behaves if you move the player around while shooting. Note that if you shoot perpendicular to the player's current motion, the bullets won't be aligned with the player, which is something most users find too confusing. And look what happens if you shoot in the reverse of the player's motion direction.

Exercise 13.2: Increasing the bullet velocity

Open up the **gamestub.cpp** file and edit the *cCritterStubRivalBullet* constructor to have the two lines `setMaxSpeed(100.0)`, `setSpeed(100.0)`. Then run the game and look how fast the enemy's bullets move.

2D shooting games   **14**

14.1 The Spacewar game

Let's write up a description of the Spacewar game with sections similar to what one might use for a presentation or homework project about a program's *specification* and about its *design*.

The name 'Spacewar' was chosen as an homage to the very first graphical computer game ever. The original SpaceWar was developed for the PDP-1 computer at MIT in 1962! If you do a web search you'll find that modern versions of the classic SpaceWar abound. The game that we are calling Spacewar in the Pop Framework actually resembles the old Asteroids rather than being like the classic SpaceWar, which is a two-player game taking place in the gravity field of a central star. We've left turning our Spacewar into a 'real' SpaceWar game as an open-ended exercise.

Specification

A specification should include (S1) a concept, (S2) a picture (hand-drawn is okay when you're starting out) of the game screen's appearance, (S3) a summary of the user controls, and (S4) an outline of the game play.

(S1) Concept
The concept behind this game is to make something similar to the traditional arcade and home game Asteroids. A ship on the screen tries to avoid polygonal asteroids and bullets and missiles fired by occasional UFOs. The ship can shoot back; some targets split in two and must be shot again.

To make the game a bit fresher, we make the asteroids run away from the bullets fired by the ship. To make the game more physically interesting, we have the asteroids bounce off each other.

(S2) Appearance

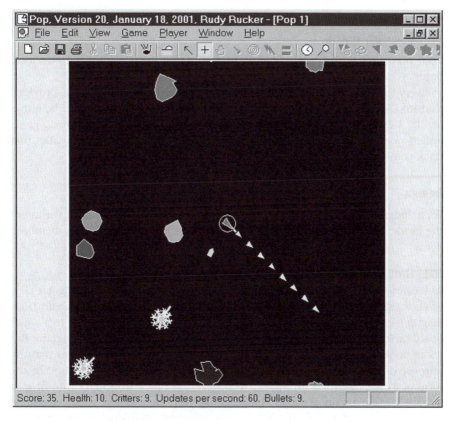

The Spacewar game with two UFOs attacking

(S3) Controls

We use the traditional Asteroids 'Spaceship' controls. The **Left** and **Right Arrow** keys rotate the ship, and the **Up** and **Down Arrow** keys accelerate the ship forward or backwards along its current direction. The spacebar fires bullets in the direction the ship points. We also allow the user to aim the ship and fire by left-clicking the mouse.

(S4) Game play

Whenever you kill all the asteroids, a fresh wave of them appears, and the new asteroids move faster than the last wave. You lose a health point whenever an asteroid bumps you or a UFO bullet hits you. Your own bullets can't hurt you.

You don't get any points when you first shoot an asteroid or a UFO and split it in two; you only get the score when you shoot the smaller pieces and remove them from the screen. Your score value for killing various creatures is the following.

- Asteroid   4
- UFO   6
- Green enemy bullet   4
- Blue enemy missile   8

Your player's health is improved by one point for every additional 100 score points you accumulate.

Every time you accumulate 40 more points, a new UFO will appear, provided that no UFO is currently present. The UFOs are randomly chosen to be either regular UFOs which have polypolygon sprites and shoot straight-moving green bullets or smart UFOs which have bitmap sprites and shoot smart missiles that track you. The UFO bullets will bounce off of asteroids they run into.

Design

For a design description we want (D1) a UML diagram and (D2) a draft version of the header file to show the method overrides and the additional class members, if any.

(D1) UML diagram

As it often turns out, our UML diagram will not in fact include every possible class or class relationship that we could mention. A characteristic thing about UML diagrams is that it's hard to fit them on a page! One can of course go to a white board or to a UML design program in order to draw a bigger UML diagram. But it can be self-defeating to make a UML too complete; always remember that the purpose of these images is to *communicate* the structure of the program in the form of a *comprehensible overview*. If you have too much information to fit into a single UML diagram, it's a good idea to use more than one of them. A general rule of thumb is that if your UML has any pairs of intersecting lines, then you should split it into more than one diagram.

Our UML class diagram for the Spacewar game appears in Figure 14.1. As is our custom, we use the diamond-ended composition line. Recall that the meaning of this line is that objects of the class type at the 'diamond' end have as members some objects of the class type at the other end of the line.

(D2) Draft of header file

Here's a simplified version of the Spacewar game header **spacewar.h** to show which method overrides and which additional members (in this case one) our classes have.

```
class cCritterArmedPlayerSpacewar : public cCritterArmedPlayer //Our
    player.
{
public:
    cCritterArmedPlayerSpacewar(cGame *pownergame = NULL);
    void reset();
};
```

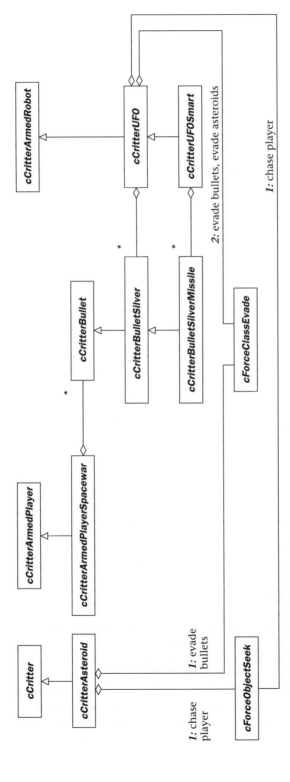

Figure 14.1   UML diagram for the Spacewar critters

```
class cCritterAsteroid : public cCritter
{
public:
    cCritterAsteroid(cGame *pownergame = NULL);
    virtual int damage(int hitstrength);
};

class cCritterUFO : public cCritterArmedRobot
{
public:
    cCritterUFO(cGame *pownergame = NULL);
    virtual int damage(int hitstrength);
    virtual void update(CPopView *pview); /* override to keep turning
        wrap flag off. */
};

class cCritterUFOSmart : public cCritterUFO
{
public:
    cCritterUFOSmart(cGame *pownergame = NULL);
};

class cGameSpacewar : public cGame
{
private:
    int _lastinvasion score;
public:
    cGameSpacewar();
    virtual void Serialize(CArchive& ar); /* Override for
        _lastinvasionscore. */
    virtual void reset();
    virtual void adjustGameParameters();
    virtual CString statusMessage();
    virtual void initializeView(CPopView *pview);
    virtual void seedCritters();
};
```

The Spacewar code

At this point, you may want to look at the **gamespacewar.cpp** code inside Visual
Studio. Let's discuss some of the highlights.

The ***cGameSpacewar*** constructor makes the `_border` square and gives it a black
background. A ***cCritterArmedPlayerSpacewar*** is used so that we can make special
adjustments to the player's ***_health***, ***_newlevelscorestep***, ***_newlevelreward***, and so on.
Also we want to make sure that our player's sprite uses white lines so as to show
up well against the game's black background. The ***_lastinvasionscore*** is initialized
to 0.

The **cGameSpacewar::seedCritters** gets rid of any asteroid or bullet critters, leaving any UFOs alone, and adds _seedcount **cCritterAsteroid** objects with this line.

```
for (int i=0; i < _seedcount; i++)
    new cCritterAsteroid(this);
```

The reason we made the decision to not have **seedCritters** remove the UFOs was as follows. Suppose you have two asteroids left and you kill one. Killing this asteroid raises your score enough to start up a UFO. If you kill the one remaining asteroid, the program will call the **seedCritters** method to start a new wave of asteroids. Should you at this time wipe out that one remaining UFO? Our design decision was to leave it, so as to make the game a bit harder for the player. As always, of course, any decision like this needs to be tested by user play.

The game is in the **cGameSpacewar::adjustGameParams**. The method does three things.

- Ends the game if the player's health is gone.
- Reseeds the screen with asteroids if all asteroids and UFOs are dead; also speed the game up when you do a reseed.
- Adds a new UFO each time the player gets a certain amount of additional score.

Here's the full code for how it works.

```
void cGameSpacewar::adjustGameParameters()
{
// (1) End the game if the player is dead
    if (!health() && !_gameover) //Player's been killed and game's
        not over.
    {
        _gameover = TRUE;
        pplayer()->addScore(_scorecorrection); // So user can reach
        _maxscore playSound("Tada");
        return;
    }
// (2) Reseed the screen if all the asteroids are gone (There may
//  still be UFOs present)
    if (_pbiota->count(RUNTIME_CLASS(cCritterAsteroid)) == 0 )
    { //If the crittercount - bulletcount = 1, then player's alone,
      //and the enemies are all gone.
        cCritter::MAXSPEED *= SPEEDMULTIPLIER;//Speed the critters up.
        if (cCritter::MAXSPEED >
                cGameSpacewar::CRITTERMAXSPEEDLIMIT)
            cCritter::MAXSPEED =
                cGameSpacewar::CRITTERMAXSPEEDLIMIT;
        seedCritters();
    }
```

```
// (3) Attack with a UFO if enough score has elapsed and there aren't
// any other UFOs
    if (score() - _lastinvasionscore > cGameSpacewar::UFOATTACKSCORE
        && //More score brings more UFOs
        !_pbiota->count(RUNTIME_CLASS(cCritterUFO)))
            //Don't start a new UFO till old ones are gone.
    {
        playSound("TaDa"); //Warning sound.
        if (cRandomizer::pinstance()->
            randomBOOL(cGameSpacewar::SMARTUFOPROBABILITY))
            new cCritterUFOSmart(this);
        else
            new cCritterUFO(this);
        _lastinvasionscore = score();
    }
}
```

One trick is that at each new level we generically allow all the critters to move more rapidly by changing the static cCritter::MAXSPEED value. This is about as close as object-oriented programming comes to using a global variable.

Now let's say a bit about the critters. The **cCritterArmedPlayerSpacewar** is almost the same as a **cCritterArmedPlayer**. We only have a special child class for it so that we can put some specific initialization code into the constructor (for instance of the _health).

The constructors for the **cCritterAsteroid**, the **cCritterUFO**, and the **cCritterUFOSmart** do more work. They select special sprites and they attach some forces so as to make the creatures into livelier opponents. The sprites used are, respectively, a **cPolygon**, a **cPolyPolygon**, and a **cSpriteIcon**. Here's what the **cCritterAsteroid** constructor looks like.

```
cCritterAsteroid::cCritterAsteroid(cGame *pownergame):
cCritter(pownergame)
{
    setHealth(cCritterAsteroid::HEALTH);
        /* One more than the number of times it splits. Splitting is
            also capped by the cCritterAsteroid::OVERPOPULATIONCOUNT,
            which might be about 10; if there are more than this many
            asteroids they don't split when you shoot them. */
    setValue(cCritterAsteroid::VALUE);
    if (pownergame) //Just to be safe.
        setSprite(pgame()->randomSprite(pownergame->spritetype()));
            /* Let the game pick the current default sprite. */
    randomize(cCritter::MF_VELOCITY | cSprite::MF_RADIUS);
    psprite()->setLineColor(cColorStyle::CN_WHITE); /* White edges as
        we use black background. */
    addForce(new cForceClassEvade(cCritterAsteroid::DARTACCELERATION,
        cCritterAsteroid::DARTSPEEDUP, RUNTIME_CLASS(cCritterBullet),
            FALSE));
```

```
        /* cForceClassEvade is an all purpose evading force used
            for evading any class I like.
            The third argument says which class to evade, and
            the fourth argument says whether to evade objects
            that are of classes that are child classes of the
            class to evade. Putting FALSE means I don't evade
            cCritterBulletSilver and CritterBulletSilverMissile
            (as that would be a waste of energy since these
            can't hurt me.)
        */
    moveToMoveboxEdge();
    if (pownergame) /* Then we know we added this to a game so
        pplayer() is valid. */
        addForce(new cForceObjectSeek(pplayer(),
            cCritterAsteroid::CHASEACCELERATION));
            /* Force for accelerating towards a critter. */
}
```

Although we really just want the asteroid sprite for this critter, we allow the user to set the game sprite type and have the asteroids use that kind of sprite. This feature is present partly because this lets you test out different versions of the game, and partly because it might be interesting later on to change the asteroid's sprites at different game levels.

The only differences between the **cCritterUFO** and the **cCritterUFOSmart** are that (a) they have different sprites, (b) a call to setMaxspeed(2*cCritter::MAXSPEED) lets Smart UFOs move twice as fast so they're harder to shoot, and (c) the Smart UFOs shoot **cCritterBulletSilverMissile** bullets that steer towards the player. The **cCritterBulletSilverMissile** type was defined in the **critterarmed.cpp** file; unlike other bullets, these **SilverMissiles** don't die when they hit the screen edges.

A new style of override for **cCritter::damage** is used by our enemy critters. The asteroids and the UFOs split in two when hit. The way we work this is to have the **damage** method shrink the critter and make a copy of it. It would be too confusing to split more than once, so we peg the splitting to the **_health** value of the critters and start their **_health** out at 2. Here's how it works for the asteroids.

```
int cCritterAsteroid::damage(int hitstrength)
{
    if ( _shieldflag || recentlyDamaged())
        return 0; /* Bail out right here if you were just damaged or
            if you were just replicated from a just-damaged guy.
            Otherwise a newly replicated critter hit by one of a
            fusillade of bullets that split its parent will get
            split as well. */
    int deathreward = cCritter::damage(hitstrength); /* This is
        _value (typically nonzero) you get for killing off the
        critter if you did that here. */
```

```
playSound("Ding"); //Signal the hit.
if (_health) /* If not dead yet, let's replicate unless there's
    too many cCritterAsteroid. */
{
    setRadius(radius()/sqrt(2.0));
    mutate(cCritter::MF_NUDGE); //Crude way to show a hit.
    if (pownerbiota()->count(RUNTIME_CLASS(cCritterAsteroid)) <
            cCritterAsteroid::OVERPOPULATIONCOUNT)
        replicate(); /* Ask cBiota to make a copy in next
            updateServiceRequests call. */
}
return deathreward;
}
```

The effect of the `replicate` call is to make a copy of the critter and, when the copy is made, to have it also call a `mutate(cCritter::MF_NUDGE)`, which has the effect of randomizing its angle, and of moving it a slight random amount.

14.2 The 2D Game Stub

The gamestub.* files are meant to be a possible starting point for your games. Alter the gamestub.* files freely. The basic idea is to have five kinds of critters: the player, the player's bullets, a rival armed critter, the rival's bullets, and a prop critter that can act as a kind of food or health-pack for the player. This means that six classes are prototyped in **gamestub.h: cGameStub, cCritterStubPlayer, cCritterStubPlayerBullet, cCritterStubRival, cCritterStubRivalBullet,** and **cCritterStubProp.** There's some more discussion of these classes and a UML diagram (Figure 3.11) of them in the last section of Chapter 3: The Pop Framework.

The **cGameStub** has an `int _rivalcount` field in addition to the `int _seedcount` field it inherits from **cGame**. These are used in the **seedCritters** method as follows.

```
void cGameStub::seedCritters()
{
    pbiota()->purgeNonPlayerNonWallCritters();
        /* Clean out any old non-player non-wall critters. Although
            we don't have walls yet, you might want to put some
            in. */
    /* Note that I can have some switch behavior in here depending
        on _level. */

    for (int i=0; i < _seedcount; i++)
        new cCritterStubProp(this);
    for (i=0; i<_rivalcount; i++)
        new cCritterStubRival(this);
}
```

The health-pack behavior of the ***cCritterStubProp*** is implemented by overriding the ***cCritterStubPlayer::collide*** method. The player controls the collision interaction since the default `_collidepriority` of a child of the ***cCritterArmedPlayer*** class is `cCollider::CP_PLAYER = 200.0` and the default `_collidepriority` of a child of ***cCritter*** class is `cCollider::CP_CRITTER = 100.0`.

```
BOOL cCritterStubPlayer::collide(cCritter *pcritter)
{
    BOOL collideflag = cCritter::collide(pcritter);
        /* We can sometimes do more stuff here if collideflag is
            TRUE. In the code below, for instance, we have the
            player "eat" cCritterStubProp critters, that is,
            increasing the cCritterStubPlayer health and killing the
            cCritterStubProp when they touch. */
    if (collideflag &&
        pcritter->IsKindOf(RUNTIME_CLASS(cCritterStubProp)))
    {
        setHealth(health() + 1);
        pcritter->die();
    }
    return collideflag;
}
```

Another feature of the 2D Game Stub game is that it uses a world that's larger than the screen. We talk about the details of how this is done in Exercise 14.2 below.

14.3   The Worms game

The Worms game isn't so much a game as it is a wacky-world testing ground for a bunch of tricks.

The most obvious new wrinkle is that, we have 'worms' that are made up by linking together ***cCritterWormSegment*** objects with ***cForceObjectSpringRod*** forces.

Another visually striking feature is that we're using a ***cSpriteLoop*** for the player's sprite; this means that the sprite changes appearance every third of a second. If you comment out the line `#define PLAYERSPRITELOOP` at the start of the **gameworms.cpp** file and recompile, the player sprite will now use a ***cSpriteDirectional*** that changes its color to match the direction it's pointing in.

The Worms code does some other things. The ***cCritterWormsRivalBullet*** objects run away from the player, and they don't view any critters as targets, so they never damage anyone. In fact we want them to act as health-packs, so we change the ***cCritterWormsPlayer::collide*** to get health from eating them.

In order to have the player control the collision with the rival bullets, we need to lower the `_collidepriority` of the rival bullets, so we add this line to the ***cCritterWormsRivalBullet*** constructor: `_collidepriority = cCollider::CP_CRITTER;`.

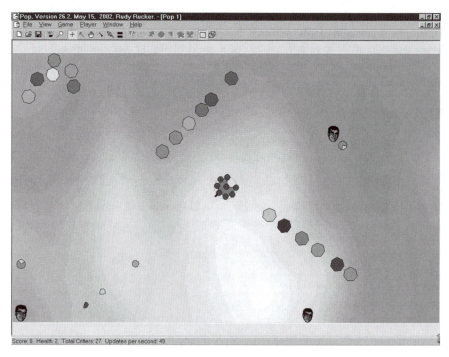

The Worms game

We play another trick with `collidepriority` here as well. We want the **cCritterWormsRival** objects to be reduced in size and possibly killed (when they get too small) by bumping into the **cCritterWormSegment** objects. So to let the **cCritterWormSegment** control the collisions, we give them a `_collidepriority` of `cCollider::CP_CRITTER + 1`, which is higher than the priority of the worm segments and the rival bullets, but lower than the priority of the player or the player's bullets.

In the Worms game we also manipulate the size of the **cCritterWormsRival** objects. The **cCritterWormsRival** critters grow when hit by the player's bullets, until they reach a certain size and sustain the standard base-class damage (which in fact kills them since their **_health** is only 1).

```
int cCritterWormsRival::damage(int hitstrength)
{
    setRadius(radius()*1.3);//Let's swell when hit by a bullet.
    if(radius() > 2.0) //Pop when you get too big!
    {
        playSound("Pop");
        return cCritter::damage(hitstrength); //Default behavior.
    }
    else
        return 0;
}
```

As yet another variation, in the Worms game, the **cCritterWormSegment::damage** method reduces the number of sides the polygonal sprite has until it runs out of sides and dies.

Exercises

Remember that, when tweaking one particular game mode, it saves time to have the Pop program start up in the game mode that you want to play with. The way to control this is to edit the **CPopDoc** constructor in **popdoc.cpp**. Do it now, it'll save you a lot of clicking later on.

Exercise 14.1: Put the sprites into the UML

Go ahead and complicate the Spacewar UML diagram (Figure 14.1) by adding in the sprite classes used by the various critters. This would include the **cPolygon**, **cPolyPolygon**, and **cSpriteIcon** classes. Can you find a way to do it without having any pairs of crossing lines? If not, then show these classes in a separate UML diagram. Are there any other important classes peculiar to the Spacewar game that we're leaving out?

Exercise 14.2: A larger world

You may have already noticed that the 2D Game Stub has a world larger than what you see on the screen. In this example we look at how to change Spacewar to use a larger world as well. You can check the **gamestub.cpp** file for code examples as well.

You can make the world of the Spacewar game larger by changing the initialization value of the `cGameSpacewar::WORLDSIZE` to a larger number, say 80.0 instead of 20.0. Alternately, and probably better, you can make the change directly to the arguments of the `_border.set(xsize, ysize)` call in the **cGameSpacewar** constructor.

One thing to keep in mind is that whenever you change the size of the `_border` you need to immediately call `setBackgroundBitmap(...)` so as to make sure that the game's **cSpriteIconBackground** bitmap object 'knows' the shape of the world whose background it is supposed to cover. Another point to mention here is that you will get better results if the visual aspect (that is, the y-size-to-x-size-ratio) of your background bitmap matches the aspect of the `_border`.

Okay, so now suppose you've changed the `_border` and alerted the background bitmap. By default the view will show the whole world, which isn't really what you want. The idea is to have a world that extends beyond your current view. To make the view smaller, edit the `cGameSpacewar::initializeViewpoint` code to include a line like `pviewer->zoom(3.0)`. The exact value of zoomfactor to use is something you have to experiment with.

What will happen now is that you see your player and part of the world, but if the player goes off one edge it disappears. Either you can require the user to use a **Ctrl + Arrow** keys to keep looking at the player or, which is more agreeable, you can make the view automatically track the player. To do this, find the `cGameSpacewar::initializeView` code and add the line `pview->pviewpointcritter()->setTrackplayer(TRUE);` `//Always look at the player.`

Exercise 14.3: Change the sprites with the level

Edit the **cGameSpacewar::adjustGameParameters()** so that it changes the game's `_spritetype` at certain score levels.

Exercise 14.4: A graphic theme for your game

You can fairly painlessly make an original-appearing game simply by taking the Gamestub game and giving it a uniform graphical theme. Select as a graphic theme some subject such as farming or hunting or ancient Egypt or the jungle or underwater diving or student life, etc. Now do the following steps. (a) Accumulate the bitmaps and get them into usable form. (b) Adjust their sizes and crop them as appropriate. (c) Import them into your project. (d) Set a large theme bitmap as your background. (e) Set some smallish theme bitmaps to be the sprites, the rivals and the props in this game.

(a) Get a theme and scout around for bitmaps. If you can't find bitmaps on a theme, change the theme. If your bitmaps are in a format other than *.**bmp**, such as *.**gif** or *.**jpg**, you will need to convert them to *.**bmp**. You can do this by loading the bitmap into some image-manipulation software like PhotoShop and then saving it as *.**bmp**. If they're already a *.**bmp**, you can manipulate it with the Windows **Accessory** | **Paint** program. If it doesn't degrade the color too much, try saving your bitmaps as 256-color bitmaps, as this makes the files considerably smaller. Save your bitmaps as *.**bmp** files in the **res** subdirectory of your project code directory.

(b) Looking ahead towards steps (d) and (e), adjust the sizes of the bitmaps. The size of the background bitmap you will use as your **cSpriteIconBackground** doesn't need to be as large as the screen; the Pop Framework code will stretch (or shrink) the bitmap to fit. It is important, however, that the proportions, or y-to-x-aspect, of the bitmap should approximately match the proportions of the world you plan to use it in.

The sizes of your critter icon bitmaps that you will use as **cSpriteIcon** for the critters should be about the same size in pixels as the critter images you expect to see. The critter images will adjust their shape to match the size of these bitmaps, so you don't really need to worry about these aspects. Do note these points: (a) crop the image so that there is not much extra blank space around it, (b) make sure the pixel in the upper left hand corner is the color that you wish to treat as transparent when you show this image on the screen, and (c) use powers of two.

(c) Now import the new *.bmp files into your code as bitmap resource. Use **Resource...** | **Insert...** and then navigate to find your *.bmp file. The Resource Editor will open your imported bitmap. [With Version 6.0, import a bitmap by using **Insert** | **Resource** | **Bitmap** | **Import...** In 6.0, some bitmaps will not be viewable within the Resource Editor, but this doesn't mean they can't be added to the project.]

It's helpful to give your bitmap an easy-to-remember resource ID name like `IDB_HAPPYDOG` instead of the machine-generated ID (like `IDB_BITMAP1`) it will have received. To call up the Bitmap Properties dialog you can **Alt+Enter** while the bitmap is open in the editor.

(d) Change your background by putting a line like `setBackgroundBitmap(IDB_UNDER-SEALEVEL1)` after the `_border.set(..)` call in your constructor.

(e) You can use specific character bitmaps by having lines like `setSprite(new cSpriteIcon(IDB_BLUEFISH))` in your critter constructors.

Alternately you can arrange things so that a critter constructor call to `setSprite(pgame()->randomSprite(cGame::ST_BITMAPS))` will automatically pick a random bitmap from some interesting new set of theme bitmaps you want to use. To do this, change the list of default bitmap IDs that your game keeps in the array `_bitmapIDarray`. You could do this by putting code like this into your game's constructor.

```
bitmapIDarray.RemoveAll();
bitmapIDarray.Add(IDB_BLUEFISH);
bitmapIDarray.Add(IDB_STINGRAY);
bitmapIDarray.Add(IDB_CUTTLEFISH);
bitmapIDarray.Add(IDB_HUMUHUMUNUKUNUKUAPUAA);
bitmapIDarray.Add(IDB_MAGURO);
```

Exercise 14.5: Walls

You can always enhance a shooting game by adding walls for the critters to hide behind and bounce off of. Look at the ***cGameDambuilder*** constructor code in gamedambuilder.cpp to see how to add walls into a world. We discuss walls some more in Chapter 18: Interesting Worlds.

Exercise 14.6: More levels

Look at Exercise 10.2: A Multi-Level Game that deals with using the game's `_level` parameter. Give some thought to a comprehensive series of level changes. Things that could change with the levels include the sprite type used by the critters (as mentioned in the last exercise), the background bitmap, the speeds of the critters, the sizes of the parameters in the forces the critters use to chase and avoid things, the radii of the critters, the size of the world, the number of critters, etc.

So as to facilitate tweaking, it's not a bad idea to store these level parameters in arrays, so that you have all the constants side by side for comparison. You'll probably want new members of your game class for these arrays. Also you ought to implement a ***setLevel*** method which will plug in all of the constants for you.

Exercise 14.7: A two-and-a-half dimensional game

Go to the `cGameSpacewar::initializeView(CPopView *pview)` implementation in gamespacewar.cpp and find these lines.

```
//   pview->setGraphicsClass(RUNTIME_CLASS(cGraphicsOpenGL));
     //Start in 3D
//   _plightingmodel->setEnableLighting(FALSE);
     //Try no light in 3D: ugly, slow.
```

If you comment in the first line, your game will start out in a 3D view. The default lighting model is to use lights, which is usually faster and better-looking. But you can try commenting in the second line as well to see how the world looks without lights.

2D games that are shown in a 3D view are sometimes called two-and-a-half dimensional games. You can beef up the effect here by making the critters have more thickness in the z-axis. This thickness is controlled by the sprite's `_prismdz` parameter. The best way to change this is with a call to the `cCritter::setPrismDz` method inside your critter constructors. Default values for the `prismdz` are specified by statics of the form `???PRISMDZ` in the **sprite.cpp** file.

Exercise 14.8: Make a better shoot method

In Spacewar, the **cCritterBulletSilver** that the **cCritterUFO** shoot at the player never hit the player as long as the player is moving. Give **cCritterUFO** an override of the `virtual void aimAt(cCritter *pcritter)` method that's a little smarter. Instead of aiming at where the **pcritter** is now, have the new method aim the gun at where the **pcritter** will be *when the bullet gets there*. Figuring out this algorithm is a non-trivial calculus problem. If you can't solve it, consider at least improving your `aimAt` with a rough guess. You might, for instance, estimate the `approxdt` time your bullet will travel to be the current distance to the target divided by the bullet speed, and then aim at where the **pcritter** will be after `approxdt` seconds. (Getting the `approxdt` estimate exactly right is where the calculus would come in!)

Exercise 14.9: Switching between different guns

Games often allow the player to have several different guns, which effectively means shooting different kinds of bullets. You might have a few high-test bullets that have a larger `_hitstrength`, for instance. Or missile or bomb bullets.

There are two things to do to give the player multiple guns. First we need an array of the allowable kinds of **CRuntimeClass** `*_pbulletclass` field, as well as a method for moving through this array. Second we need something to trigger the change to a different gun.

One option is to let the user change guns with the mousewheel or an accelerator key. This would mean changing the **OnMouseWheel** method of **CPopDoc** to act differently if the `_pgame()` is of your **cGameSpacewar** class. That is, the mousewheel should scroll among gun types instead of among cursor types. Alternately you might add a Bullet menu and then add some accelerator keys for the types of bullet in the menu. If you do this, use some accelerator keys that aren't currently taken, but try and make the keys easy to find and to remember.

So that the user doesn't always just use the best gun, you need some feature to limit the use of the 'good' bullets. Perhaps put a strict limit on how many times they can be used, and make the user pick up an ammo pack to replenish them.

Exercise 14.10: A round world

If you look at our online Java version of the Asteroids game at **www.mathcs.sjsu.edu/ faculty/rucker/asteroids/asteroids.htm**, you'll see that it uses a round game world border, with the objects able to bounce off this edge in a natural fashion (bouncing as if at each point on the circumference the edge were the same as its tangent line). Implement a round world for the Spacewar game. You can find hints in the source code of our Java asteroids online. Implementing the new world shape in a proper object-oriented way will involve some preliminary OOA and OOD. Think about what kind of base class you might use to serve as a container (if you use composition) or parent (if you use inheritance) for both a box world or a round world object.

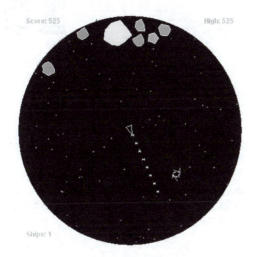

Wait, Click on Game, Press S.

S start game.
Left/Right Arrows rotate.
Up/Down Arrows thrust.
Spacebar fire.

B black or white.
C collide.
D details.
G godmode .
H hyperspace jump.
M mute sound.
P pause game.
R round or square.
W wrap or bounce.

A round Asteroids-style Java game

Exercise 14.11: The real SpaceWar

Do a little web research on the classic SpaceWar game. This is often played as a two-player game. See if you can implement it within the Pop Framework. You would need to have two player critters. And you'd need to write a new listener similar to the ***cListenerSpaceship***, but tune this second listener so that it is controlled by, say, the **D, E, S, X,** and **B** keys in place of **Right, Up, Left, Down,** and **Space**.

3D shooting games $\quad$ **15**

When you go into a 3D world it's very common to have the user's viewpoint be attached to a player who's immersed in that world. In this chapter we'll look at one particular game like this, our Defender3D.

15.1 The Defender3D specification and design

Specification

As in the section on the Spacewar game in Chapter 14: 2D Shooting Games, we describe: (S1) the concept, (S2) the appearance, (S3) the controls, and (S4) the game play.

(S1) Concept

Although the inspiration for the game was the old 2D Defender game, the current implementation is more like a 3D Space Invaders. Polygons rush at you, and you have to shoot them before they pass you and hit the back wall of your world.

(S2) Appearance

In the screen capture of Defender3D, the circle at the center is the player; the viewer rides directly behind the player and looks 'through' it. The marks near the middle of the player are bullets the player recently shot. The thick polygons are the onrushing flying critters the player is trying to shoot, while the disks on the bottom of the space are bouncing fragments resulting from the critters that have already been shot. The lines indicate the limits of the world. A sky bitmap covers the far wall.

The Defender3D game. Round objects are the 'prop frags'

(S3) Controls
The **Arrow** keys move the player **Left/Right** and **Up/Down**. The player can also move forward and backwards a bit with **PgUp/PgDn**. **Spacebar** fires bullets straight forward. It's also possible to play in more of a Doom mode by leaving the player in the middle of the screen and left-clicking or left-dragging the mouse to shoot in different directions. The **Arrow** keys mode seems to be more fun.

(S4) Behavior
You try to shoot all the polygons, each one that you hit adds ten points to your score; each one that gets past you costs you one health point. When you shoot a polygon it releases a shower of coins, that is, disks that bounce towards you along the bottom of the world. You can gain health points by bumping the player into a coin – a bump kills the coin and adds a point to player's health. The coins evaporate after three seconds, so you have to shoot a critter that's not too far off if you hope to eat its coins.

Design

UML diagram
The class design is fairly simple. Our *cGameDefender3D* class has a player, player bullets, props, and prop frags. Although we don't show it in Figure 15.1, the *cGameDefender3DProp* and *cGameDefender3DPropFrag* inherit from *cCritter*.

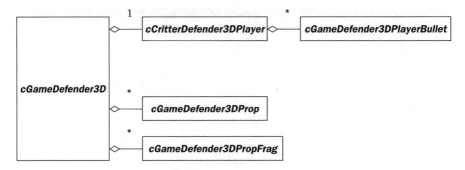

Figure 15.1   UML diagram of the Defender3D Classes

We won't bother printing any header file information here, as the headers are similar to what we already saw for the Spacewar game.

15.2   The Defender3D code

cGameDefender3D

The overrides for **cGameDefender3D** are fairly routine. In the constructor, we have `_border.set(19, 19.0, 41.0)` to give the world a z-thickness. We think of the z direction as running down into the screen. We give the game a **cCritterDefender3DPlayer**, and the **seedCritters** calls a simple loop to populate the world.

```
for (int i=0; i < _seedcount; i++)
    new cCritterDefender3DProp(this);
```

The **adjustGameParameters** code is also quite simple; if there are less than `_seedcount` props, it replenishes the count.

In order to have our games behave smoothly as we use the menu to switch on and off the various View menu options, we need to have two separate view and viewer initialization methods. If we were only writing one game with one kind of view this wouldn't be necessary; the complexity is a result of the code being usable as a flexible framework to build a variety of changeable games.

The **initializeView(CPopView *pview)** call sets the viewer (that is, the `pview->pviewpointcritter()`) to use a **cListenerViewerRide** listener. This means that the viewer is by default attached to the player.

The **initializeViewpoint(cCritterViewer *pviewer)** tweaks the viewer (that is, the `pviewer`) in various ways, depending on whether the viewer is using the default rider listener or whether you have possibly switched the viewer to use a Scooter type control that's not locked to the player. In the case where we are riding the player, this call positions the viewer directly behind the player so that we can look along the player's shooting direction.

Here you can see why the Pop Framework has separate view and viewer initialization methods? It's so the games will behave smoothly as you use the menu to switch on and off the various View menu options. If you turn off the Ride Player, then the code calls *initializeViewpoint* to reset the viewer to some reasonable position, and if you turn Ride Player back on, *initializeViewpoint* gets called again. We set the viewer to use the Ride Player option in *initializeView*, as this is the call that gets made when we start up a view.

Now let's discuss the overrides of the critters, which accounts for the bulk of the new defender game code.

cGameDefender3DPlayer

Let's talk about the *cGameDefender3DPlayer* constructor first. The constructor begins by giving the player a new kind of listener.

Since this is something like a Space Invaders game, we want to use some kind of **Arrow** key control. But rather than using a *cListenerArrow*, we use a *cListenerArrowAttitude*. The difference is that where the *cListenerArrow* uses **Left/ Right**, **Up/Down**, and **PgUp/PgDn** to move the critter along the *x*-, *y*-, and *z*-axes respectively, the *cListenerArrowAttitude* uses **Left/Right**, **Up/Down**, and **PgUp/PgDn** to move the critter along its normal, binormal, and tangent directions, respectively. The latter is more flexible for a wide range of orientations.

We want our player critter's sprite to maintain a fixed attitude, basically acting as a gun sight. Here's the code to do this from the *cGameDefender3DPlayer* constructor.

```
setAttitudeToMotionLock(FALSE); /* don't turn your sprite with the
    motions. */
setAimToAttitudeLock(FALSE); //Don't turn your attitude with the gun.
setAttitudeTangent(-cVector::ZAXIS); //point down into the world.
setAimVector(-cVector::ZAXIS);
setSprite(new cSpriteCircle());
psprite()->setFilled(FALSE); /* So I can see through the center of the
    disk. */
psprite()->setSpriteAttitude( cMatrix::yRotation(PI/2.0));
    //To face the user.
```

The purpose of the code above is to carry out these steps.

- Turn off any coupling between the attitude and the motion or the aim direction.
- Point the critter and its gun down the negative *z*-axis.
- Remove its filling so we can see through it.
- Rotate the sprite up out of the plane of the critter's tangent and normal.

The rotation step isn't quite obvious, and in fact the author got it by a little trial and error. In retrospect it seems right because the critter's intrinsic x-axis is its tangent, which now points towards the negative z-axis (into the screen) and the critter's intrinsic y-axis is its normal which points towards the negative x-axis (to the left of the screen), so the plane of these two is edge-on to the viewer. A 90° rotation about the y-axis is just what's needed!

It turns out to be pretty hard to effectively aim at a moving object in three-dimensional space. So we smarten-up our player's shooting skills by (a) having **cGameDefender3DPlayer::shoot** pick out the critter closest to the gun's current aiming line to be the target critter and (b) shoot at this chosen target critter by attaching to the bullet a **cForceObjectSeek** force that seeks this particular target.

```
cCritterBullet* cCritterDefender3DPlayer::shoot()
{
    playSound("Gunshot");
    cCritterBullet *pbullet = cCritterArmed::shoot();
    cCritter* paimtarget =
        pgame()->pbiota()->pickClosestAhead(cLine(position(),
        aimvector()), this);
        // Find critter closest to your aiming line but ahead
        // of you ("this").
    pbullet->addForce(new cForceObjectSeek(paimtarget, 20.0));
    return pbullet;
}
```

Another significant override of a player method is the **collide**. We want the player to view the coin-shaped **cCritterDefender3DPropFrag** as health food.

```
BOOL cCritterDefender3DPlayer::collide(cCritter *pcritter)
{
    BOOL collideflag = cCritter::collide(pcritter);
    if (collideflag && pcritter->
        IsKindOf(RUNTIME_CLASS(cCritterDefender3DPropFrag)))
    {
        playSound("Ding");
        setHealth(health() + 1);
        pcritter->die();
    }
    return collideflag;
}
```

In order to make sure that the player collides with these frags as the caller, but to avoid having to compute a prohibitively n-squared-type number of frag collisions, we override the **cCritterDefender3DPropFrag::collidesWith** so as to have frags only bother colliding with the player.

```
int cCritterDefender3DPropFrag::collidesWith(cCritter *pcritterother)
{
    if (pcritterother == pplayer())
        return cCollider::COLLIDEASARG; //so Player can eat them.
    else //to keep the speed up, don't do other collisions.
        return cCollider::DONTCOLLIDE;
}
```

cGameDefender3DProp

We want our props to be thick, tumbling polygonal prisms that fall towards the viewer. So that they can tumble, we unlock the attitude from the motion and set a spin. So that they move towards the viewer, we give them a gravitational force in the z direction. Here are some relevant lines from the **cGameDefender3DProp** constructor.

```
setAttitudeToMotionLock(FALSE); /* don't turn your sprite with the
    motions, instead let it tumble. */
randomizeSpin(1.0, 5.0);
addForce(new cForceGravity(30.0, cVector::ZAXIS));
```

Note that **cForceGravity** lets you specify the direction of the gravitational pull in the second argument.

Another issue with the **cGameDefender3DProp** is to start them out at the far end of the world, that is, at a location near the 'low corner' with the minimum z value. The constructor uses this line to pick a position in the far 20% of the _movebox. Note that since we fed the owner game in as an argument to the constructor, the critter's _movebox has already been set to match the game's _border.

```
randomizePosition(cRealBox(_movebox.locorner(),
    _movebox.hicorner() - (1.0 - 0.2)*
    _movebox.zsize()*cVector::ZAXIS));
```

Whenever a **cGameDefender3DProp** hits the closest wall of the world, we want to (a) penalize the player, and (b) kill off this prop critter. To accomplish this, we override the **cGameDefender3DProp::update** to check the condition (_outcode & BOX_HIZ), using a bitwise AND to check if the flag is set. Alternately, we could directly look at the position().z() value. If the condition holds, we have the prop critter penalize the player and disappear (see also Exercise 3.10.5).

```
void cCritterDefender3DProp::update(CPopView *pactiveview)
{
    cCritter::update(pactiveview); //Always call this first
    if (_outcode & BOX_HIZ) /* use bitwise AND to check if a flag is
        set. */
```

```
    {
        playSound("Bonk");
        pplayer()->damage(1); //punish the player
        delete_me(); //tell the game to remove yourself
        return;
    }
}
```

Finally there is the matter of having the prop burst into a shower of coins when you shoot it. We do this by overriding its *die* method, which carries out some exciting frills instead of immediately calling delete_me.

```
void cCritterDefender3DProp::die()
{
    playSound("Explosion");
//Make some new tumbling fragment critters.
    for (int i=0; i< cCritterDefender3DProp::FRAGCOUNT; i++)
        new cCritterDefender3DPropFrag(this); //custom constructor
//Change the prop sprite
    _age = 0.0; //Use age for a time of the "dying act"
    setUseFixedLifetime(TRUE);
    setFixedLifetime(cCritterDefender3DProp::EXPLOSIONDISPLAYTIME);
    setShield(TRUE); //so you don't die again.
    setAttitudeToMotionLock(FALSE); /* In case this happened to be
        on, turn it off here so you're free to set the attitude as
        you like. */
    setSpin(0.0); //Stop tumbling
    setVelocity(cVector::ZEROVECTOR); //Stop moving
    setAcceleration(cVector::ZEROVECTOR);
    clearForcearray(); //Stop falling
    psprite()->setFilled(FALSE);
    psprite()->setEdged(TRUE); //show as skeleton
    psprite()->setLineColor(psprite()->fillColor());
}
```

If you look at Exercise 15.1, you'll find that we have an alternate method of showing the prop damage by using a *cSpriteLoop* animation of an explosion. To finish off, let's print the *cCritterDefender3DPropFrag* constructor.

```
cCritterDefender3DPropFrag::cCritterDefender3DPropFrag(cCritter
    *pcritterprop)
{
    if (pcritterprop->pgame())
        pcritterprop->pgame()->add(this); //Sets moveBox.
    setSprite(new cSpriteCircle());
    psprite()->setEdged(FALSE);
```

```
psprite()->setFillColor(pcritterprop->psprite()->fillColor());
setRadius(pcritterprop->radius()/3.0);
setMaxspeed(10.0); //Very fast
randomizeVelocity(); //3D velocity
setAttitudeToMotionLock(FALSE);
    //don't turn your sprite with the motions.
randomizeSpin(1.0, 5.0); //Tumble
setShield(TRUE); // So you don't get shot.
setUseFixedLifetime(TRUE); //So you die off pretty quickly
setFixedLifetime(cCritterDefender3DPropFrag::FIXEDLIFETIME);
    //3 seconds
moveTo(pcritterprop->position());
addForce(new cForceGravity(100.0,
    0.05*cVector::ZAXIS-cVector::XAXIS));
    //Fall visually "down" but also towards the viewer.
addForce(new cForceDrag(0.1));
}
```

Exercises

Exercise 15.1: Bitmap loop sprites

Open the **gamedefender3d.cpp** file and comment in this line

```
//#define LOOPEXPLOSION
```

Also search down for LOOPEXPLOSION and take a look at the code to see what you're commenting in. Then recompile and shoot some props and see what happens. You get a nice *cSpriteLoop* that flips through three bitmaps.

Also watch what happens to your updates per second in the status bar when you shoot something. To check if this is due to the bitmaps or to the cascade of prop fragments, you can comment the LOOPEXPLOSION back out, run it again, shoot something and watch the updates per second.

It turns out that, at least the way the Pop Framework currently implements them, bitmap sprites are a little slow in the OpenGL graphics. The slowdown for bitmaps in the Pop Framework is especially strong if the bitmaps happen to be close to the viewer and take up a lot of the screen.

Exercise 15.2: A very long world

Let's change the game so it's a long world that you're moving through. Instead of the enemies coming at you, you are flying through them.

To do this, go to the cGameDefender3D constructor and change the third argument to the call _border.set(19, 19.0, 41.0); put in something big like 400. Then comment out the line in the cCritterDefender3DPlayer constructor that begins setMoveBox. Instead we'll be letting the player have its default movebox be the same as the _border.

If you run this version, you'll see that the prop critters are too far away. What we can do about this is to change the cCritterDefender3DProp constructor to position the new props at a random location ahead but not too far away – at a distance of, say, 30–40 units down the z-axis from the `player()->position()`. This means plugging in new locorner and hicorner arguments for the `randomizePosition` call based on `player()->position()`.

Another good change here would be to have the props die as soon as they are behind the player, rather than waiting for the BOX_HIZ flag to appear in a prop critter's `_outcode`.

It would also make more sense not to penalize the player when a prop gets by. Instead just penalize the player when a prop or a bullet hits the player. This move of course makes it too easy for the player, so we'd better put in some `cCritterDefender3DProp` critters to shoot at the player.

You might also want to put some kind of furniture on the 'floor' of the world, some fixed critters by which you can judge your motion. In addition, you could have the appearance of the sprite and rival critters change as you move further into the world.

Yet another change to consider would be to use some variation on **cListenerCar** or **cListenerSpaceship** so that you can 'drive' your player in a somewhat realistic fashion, with gravity having an effect upon it.

Sports games

16

There are plenty of games that don't involve shooting. Many of these games involve controlling the motions of balls or other objects. Tennis, airhockey, basketball, volleyball, golf, pinball, and Pachinko come to mind (Pachinko is a Japanese game similar to pinball but with dozens of balls at once).

In this chapter we'll talk about a ball game provided with the Pop sample code: Airhockey. And in the exercises, we'll show how to make it into a basketball game.

16.1   The Airhockey game

Specification

(S1) Concept
The Airhockey game is inspired by the table game of the same name. The user slides the player piece around and tries to knock the puck into the opponent's goal. The opponent, which is run by the computer program, tries to knock the puck into the player's goal. In order to make the game more challenging, neither the player nor the opponent can move across the center line of the playing field.

(S2) Appearance
We show a picture of it below. The ball with the triangular tail is the player, this critter is controlled by moving the mouse. The puck is the round critter, and the enemy is a robot player with an icon based on a photo of the author's face.

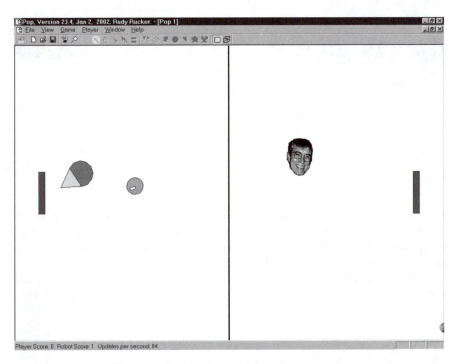

The Airhockey game. 'Robot' sprite is a picture of the author

(S3) Controls
Simplicity itself: the user moves the player piece with the mouse and uses the player piece to bump the puck. The faster you move the mouse the harder you can bump the puck.

(S4) Behavior
The robot is aware of the puck, and accelerates towards it. The user or the opponent gets a point for each goal. The game is over when the player or opponent reaches seven points.

Design

We represent the class design by the following UML diagram (Figure 16.1), which shows that the *cGameAirhockey* owns five special instances of the classes above it, that is, a *cCritterHockeyPlayer*, a *cCritterHockeyRobot*, a *cCritterHockeyPuck*, and two *cCritterHockeyGoal* instances.

A non-obvious trick we use is to have each goal be a critter that uses its _ptarget field to be aware of which of the two competing players wants to knock the puck into it, and it awards that player a point whenever a puck goes into it.

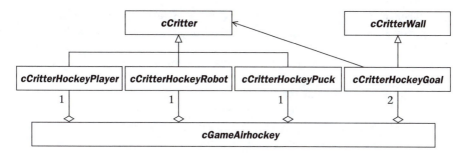

Figure 16.1   UML diagram for the Airhockey game

We could draw navigation lines from each critter class to the *cGameAirhockey*, but this would clutter the picture a little too much. We do, however, draw a navigation line from *cCritterHockeyGoal* to *cCritter* to emphasize the fact that each goal is going to use its _ptarget field to track the identity of the player who is shooting at it.

The Airhockey code

One special thing we do in this game is to set up all the game's critters inside the *cGameAirhockey* constructor. We construct the critters in a certain order, making the player first, as is our habit, and then being sure to make the puck *before* the hockey robot, and being sure not to define the goals until *after* the player and the hockey robot. The relevant part of *cGameAirhockey::cGameAirhockey* looks like this.

```
//Define _pplayer.
    setPlayer(new cCritterHockeyPlayer(this)); /* Sets the _pplayer
        field. */
//Define _ppuck
    _ppuck = new cCritterHockeyPuck(this);
//Define _phockeyrobot. Need to define _ppuck before _phockeyrobot.
    _phockeyrobot = new cCritterHockeyRobot(this);
//Define _pmygoal. Need to define _phockeyrobot before _pmygoal
    _pmygoal = new
        cCritterHockeyGoal(cVector(_border.lox()+GOALOFFSET,
            -GOALRADIUS), //Low point
        cVector(_border.lox()+GOALOFFSET, GOALRADIUS), //High point
        GOALTHICKNESS, this); //Thickness
    _pmygoal->setOpenside(BOX_LOY);/* cCritter wall views the two
        points you give it in the constructor as the neg and pos
        sides of the x axis, so it works out that "LOY" in this
        system is right on the screen. */
    _pmygoal->setTarget(_phockeyrobot);/* The guy who gets points when
        puck goes in pmygoal. */
```

```
//Define _probotgoal. Need to define _pplayer before _probotgoal
    _probotgoal = new cCritterHockeyGoal(cVector(_border.hix()
        -GOALOFFSET, -GOALRADIUS),
        cVector(_border.hix()-GOALOFFSET, GOALRADIUS), GOALTHICKNESS,
            this);
    _probotgoal->setOpenside(BOX_HIY); /* cCritter wall views the two
        points you give it in the constructor as the neg and pos
        sides of the x axis, so it works out that "HIY" in the this
        system is left on the screen. */
    _probotgoal->setTarget(pplayer());/* The guy who gets points when
        puck goes in probotgoal. */
```

cCritterHockeyRobot will be the computer-operated opponent for the Airhockey game. Most of its behavior will be produced by adding a cForceObjectSeek(_ppuck), but in its update we'll add another condition: that it move towards its own goal if the puck is between it and its goal.

The *cCritterHockeyGoal* will inherit from *cCritterWall* so as to bounce things off its corners and sides in a reasonable way. We will specify that one side of it is 'open'. In the *cCritterHockeyGoal::collide*, we call *cCritterWall::collide*, but also do something special if the colliding critter is the puck. If it's the puck we move the puck to the center with a reset call, and we also add a score to the player who is shooting for this goal. We use the _ptarget field of *cCritterHockeyGoal* to keep track of the identity of the team who is shooting for this goal.

The gameairhockey.h file has some fairly detailed comments on how the code is implemented, so you might want to read that for more information.

The Robot opponent

A key part of a sports game is having a computer-operated opponent that plays at an appropriate level. The robot player should be beatable, and it's better if it appears a bit erratic so that you can't easily predict and outsmart it.

In the Airhockey game, we have the *cCritterHockeyRobot* constructor give the hockey robot a basic urge to go towards the puck with this line.

```
addForce(new cForceObjectSeek(ppuck, ROBOTACCELERATION));
```

But this alone isn't enough. A robot that blindly charges the puck is (a) likely to knock the puck into its own goal, and (b) unlikely to accurately aim the puck at the opponent's goal. So the *cCritterHockeyRobot::update* has some more complicated tricks in it.

```
void cCritterHockeyRobot::update(CPopView *pactiveview)
{
    cCritter::update(pactiveview); /* This sets _acceleration on the
        basis of the cForceObjectSeek(_ppuck) you added in the
        constructor. We ALWAYS call the base class update. */
```

```
cGameAirhockey *phgame = (cGameAirhockey*)(pgame());
    /* This gives us access to all the fields of the game. Note
        that we need the cast, as pgame() returns a cGame*. */
cCritter *ppuck = phgame->ppuck();
cCritterHockeyGoal *probotgoal = phgame->probotgoal();
Real puckx = ppuck->position().x();
Real robotgoalx = probotgoal->position().x();
Real pucky = ppuck->position().y();
Real robotgoaly = probotgoal->position().y();
cVector togoal = directionTo(probotgoal);
cVector topuck = directionTo(ppuck);
/* If the puck is between robot and the goal go towards the goal,
    while avoiding hitting the puck into the goal yourself. */
    if (_position.x() < puckx && puckx < robotgoalx &&
            (_position.y() > pucky && pucky > robotgoaly ||
            _position.y() < pucky && pucky < robotgoaly)
        )
    {
        _acceleration = ROBOTACCELERATION * togoal;
            //Head for the goal
        if (togoal % topuck > COSINESMALLANGLE &&
            tangent() % topuck > COSINESMALLANGLE)
            _velocity.turn( (1 & _personality)?PI/2:-PI/2);
                /* If puck, my goal and me are in a line,
                and I'm moving towards the puck,
                then veer left or right. */
    }
}
```

This code represents only a second-level approximation to good play; with more thought you might think of some better strategies.

Exercises

Remember that, when tweaking one particular game mode, it saves time to have the Pop program start up in the game mode that you want to play with. The way to control this is to edit the ***CPopDoc*** constructor in **popdoc.cpp**. Do it now, it'll save you a lot of clicking later on. So make your startup game be cGameAirhockey or, if you've taken the trouble to make new files and change the names, cGameBasketball.

Exercise 16.1: Better hitting and other tweaks

It feels a bit cumbersome hitting the puck with the player. It would probably be easier if you make the player smaller. Try using a setRadius call in its constructor to make it smaller. In doing this you reduce the mass of the player (normally equal to the density times the radius cubed), so to keep this up, increase the density as well, using a setDensity call.

It would be nice have a sound effect when you hit the ball. You can do this by overriding the player's *collide* method similar to the way in which we override it in the Gamestub code, though here all we want to do is make a noise when colliding with the puck and not change health or score in the *collide*.

It might be better to have the game world a little bigger.

Make sure you have the maximum speeds and the frictions tweaked to good values.

Exercise 16.2: More players

How about giving your game another opponent, call it, say, *_phockeyrobot2. See how this works. You should initialize them to start at different positions, and to go to different positions in any reset calls, otherwise they may stay on top of each other.

Really it would be better to have the teammates' behaviors be quite different. One could guard the goal, say, while the other pressed forward. One way to do this would be to have the phockeyrobot2 be an instance of a different class called, say, *cCritterHockeyRobot2*, perhaps a child class of *cCritterHockeyRobot* and to give it a different update method. Another approach might be to make the robots' behavior depend on a nicely packaged set of parameters; rather than having several separate parameters, we could encapsulate them in a *cRobotParam* helper class.

In any case, as you add players, you will probably want to make the _border larger so the hockey robots have more room. Can you have more than two of them? How about adding some hockey robots to your own team?

Let's do a series of exercises to turn the Airhockey game into a Basketball game. You can either change the Airhockey game, or if you want to keep that one around, you can copy the gameairhockey.* files to gamebasketball.* files, adding the new files to the project, and then going through and changing the various capitalization forms of 'airhockey' to 'basketball' in the two files as was discussed in Exercise 3.7: Renaming a game.

For the purposes of the following exercises, we'll assume you took the easier route and are working directly on the Airhockey game.

Exercise 16.3: Position the goals like baskets

Change the *cGameAirhockey::cGameAirhockey* constructor code. Make _border have a larger *y* size than before. And position the two *cCritterHockeyGoal* objects so that they're higher up, horizontal, and with their open sides facing up.

Exercise 16.4: Another kind of basket

If the wall-type baskets are too hard to get a ball into, make a new kind of *Basket* class which overrides its *collide* method to use a contains(pcritter) call so as to only report a collision when the pcritter is entirely inside it. So as to let this *Basket* control the collisions, give it a higher _collidepriority than the puck or ball. Test to see which kind of basket makes for better game play, that is, play poised at the interesting border between too easy and too hard.

Exercise 16.5: Add gravity and friction

Now add gravity and friction so that it's harder to hit the ball up into the goals. See how the game works if you give your player a *cListenerCar* or *cListenerSpaceship*, so that it's sensitive to the gravity (the other kinds of listeners zero out any forces acting on the player). The following lines have been tested to good effect in another game.

```
setMaxspeed(40.0); /* For Scooter and Car to be able to WHACK the
    balls. */
setListener(new cListenerSpaceship()); //Or use ...Car());
setListenerAcceleration(80.0); /* So Car or Spaceship can overcome
    gravity. */
addForce(new cForceGravity()); /* Uses default gravity strength 25.
    Gravity won't affect player using cListenerCursor, but will with
    cListenerCar. */
addForce(new cForceDrag(2.5)); /* Stronger than default friction
    strength 0.5. Have such big friction to make player less hyper. */
setBounciness(0.9); /* Not 1.0 means it loses a bit of energy with
    each bounce. */
setRadius(cCritter::PLAYERRADIUS/2.0);
    /* Lets make radius half as big so it can dig under guys better.
    But then we better make the density 8 times as big, so that its
    volume mass stays the same. */
setDensity(8.0 * density());
```

Also be sure to use something like `setBounciness(0.9)` on the puck, otherwise it bounces around too much.

How does the robot player perform with gravity? Change its update method to make it play better.

Exercise 16.6: Basketball

Now try having more players as discussed in Exercise 16.2. You may find it frustrating to try and hit the basketball just with a spherical player. What if you have your player inherit from *cCritterWall*? You could then either always adjust the wall to be at right angles to the current direction of motion, or you could create a richer kind of listener that lets you rotate the wall. A good combination might be to use the mouse to move the player and to use the left and right mouse buttons or **Left** and **Right Arrow** keys to rotate the player.

Exercise 16.7: Make a tennis game

Make a player that is a child of *cCritterWall* and which hits things like a paddle. Give it a listener that makes it possible to rotate the paddle with the **Arrow** keys or with left/right mouse clicks. Put a short vertical wall in the middle for a net.

Selection games

17

A selection game is a game that you play by clicking and dragging on things. Memory is an example of this, that is, a game in which you try and click on covered-up icons that you've seen once. Many educational games are selection games, as when you try and click on the right word to complete a sentence. In this chapter we discuss the PickNPop game, which is a very easy selection game.

17.1   PickNPop specification and design

Specification

(S1) Concept
A race against the clock to unpack jewels from a box. We show a mixture of white bubbles and colored bubbles. Think of the colored bubbles as valuable *jewels*, with the white bubbles being disposable Styrofoam packing *peanuts*. The image of the Pop game is of someone unpacking a box filled with precious baubles packed in plastic peanuts. You want to pop the peanuts and keep the baubles. Another way of thinking of it, perhaps, is of an archaeologist digging up valuable relics. The idea is to get rid of all the dirt and not harm the treasure.

(S2) Appearance
Below is a screen capture of how the game looks.

(S3) Controls
We use the mouse control. The mouse uses one of two kinds of cursor tool, a popping tool and a dragging tool. Use the mouse wheel or the toolbar to select which cursor tool.

(S4) Behavior
There are two kinds of disks on the screen. Some are like bubbles that the user has to pop, and some are like jewels that the user wants to save. The screen is divided into two parts; at the start all the disks are on the left, and the user has to drag the jewels to the right.

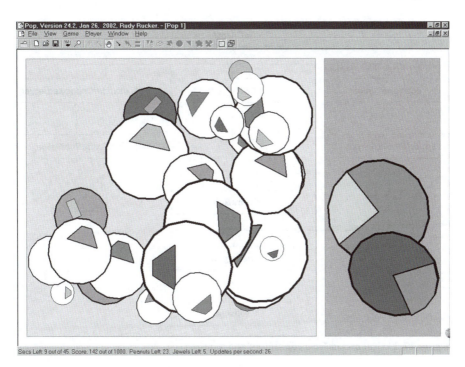

PickNPop in a 2D Windows graphics display. For a 3D view, see the plate on page 482

Assign the score so that a perfect game gives you 1000 points. You get a positive score for popping a bubble or for dragging a jewel to the right-hand box. You get a negative penalty if you pop a jewel.

Design

As usual, most of our design is inherited from the Pop Framework. The new design we do for PickNPop involves two things: add some new **cCritter** children, and add a new **cGamePicknpop**.

As this game doesn't have a visible player, we'll give the new game an off-screen player, which will be used as a place to accumulate the game score.

We'll also give the game two **cGraphicRealBox2** objects, a **_packingbox** and a **_targetbox**, with the peanuts and jewels starting in the **_packingbox**, and the player's task to move the jewels into the **_targetbox**.

We'll make a new kind of critter for each of the game elements: the peanuts, the jewels, and the promoted or 'unpacked' jewels.

Each critter will have a characteristic appearance that we set by picking a special kind of sprite in the critter constructor. In terms of a class diagram, we'll do it as shown in Figure 17.1.

We override the constructors of these critters so as to give them the appropriate sprites. We'll also set their _value fields.

In terms of methods to override, we'll override the **cCritter::die()** method for all three of these child critters. In each case, we'll have this method make a

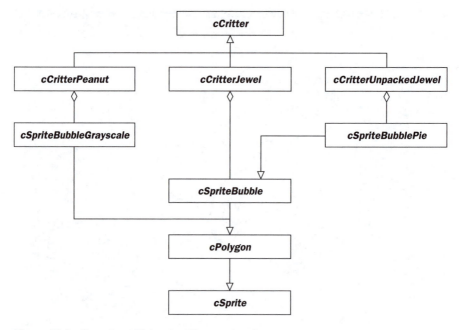

Figure 17.1 The *cGamePicknpop* critters and sprites

sound and add a number based on the _value to the game player, that is to
_pownerbiota->pgame()->pplayer().

One other method to override is the cCritterJewel::update. This method
will be responsible for noticing if the critter has been moved into the **targetbox**.
If so, the critter will have to replace itself with a cCritterGoodJewel.

Regarding the sprites, we'll have a *cSpriteBubble* sprite designed for drawing
circles, with the *cSpriteBubbleGrayscale* and *cSpriteBubblePie* inheriting from it. The
cSpriteBubble will in turn inherit from *cPolygon*, which is a child of *cSprite* to be
discussed in the next chapter. Although a circle really isn't a polygon, it's convenient to derive *cSpriteBubble* from *cPolygon*, because the polygon class already
has all the fields, mutators, and accessors for setting things like the colors and
the edgewidths. We will view a circle as a 'one-gon' polygon characterized by a
center and a single vertex, which lies on the circumference of the circle.

17.2 The PickNPop implementation

A lot of the work of designing software goes into improving the way that the
program looks onscreen. Software engineering is a little like theater, or like
stage-magic. Your goal is to give the user the illusion that your program is a
very solid, tangible kind of thing. Getting everything in place requires solid
design and a lot of tweaking.

One thing differentiating PickNPop from Spacewar and Airhockey is that we
chose to make the _border of the world have a non-zero *z* size so that the

shapes can pass above and below each other when we show the game in the OpenGL 3D mode.

Making the score come out even

Though not all games must have a numerical score, if you have one, then it should be easy to understand. On the one hand you might require that your game events have simple, round-number score values assigned to them. On the other hand you might require that your maximum possible game score total be a round easy number like 100, 1000, or even 1,000,000. If you are able to control the number of things that can happen in your game, then you can satisfy both conditions. If not, then you have to settle for one of the conditions: round-number values or round-number maximum score.

In PickNPop, we allow for varying sizes of worlds, and, since the game might still be developed further, we allow for recompiling the program with different values of JEWEL_PERCENT. So it's not possible both to have round-number values and to have a round-number max score.

Our decision here was to go for the round-number maximum score. In the CPopDoc::seedBubbles(int gametype, int count) method we figure out how many jewels and peanuts to make, and then we figure out how much they should be worth, and finally we calculate a *_scorecorrection* value that we add in at the game's end to make it possible for the user's score to exactly equal the nice round number MAX_SCORE.

In *cGamePickNPop::seedCritters()* we compute the peanutstoadd peanuts and jewelstoadd jewels needed, and then bury the jewels 'under' the peanuts by adding them in second. The default behavior of *cBiota* is to draw the earlier array members after the later array members. When using the two-dimensional *cGraphicsMFC*, this causes a 'painter's algorithm' effect of having the later-listed critters appear behind the earlier-listed ones. When using the three-dimensional *cGraphicsOpenGL*, the critters are actually sorted according to the z-value of their *_position* values. The cheap and dirty *cGame::zStackCritters()* call gives the critters different z-values, again arranging them so the earlier-listed critters have larger z-values than the later-listed critters' z-values and end up appearing on top in the default view from up on the positive side of the z-axis.

```
void cGamePickNPop::seedCritters()
{
    /* First we'll set the _bubble array to have room for count
        bubbles. Then we'll add jewels and peanuts, randomizing their
        radii, positions, and colors as we go along. In the case of
        PGT_3D, we go back and change the radii at the end. */
    int i;
    int jewelstoadd, peanutstoadd;
    Real jewelprobability = cGamePickNPop::JEWEL_WEIGHT;
    int jewelvalue(0), peanutvalue(0);
    cCritter *pcritternew;
```

```
        /* I use the jewelprobability to decide how many jewels and how
            many peanuts to have. These are the jewelstoadd and
            peanutstoadd numbers. We think of randomly drawing from this
            supply and adding them into the game. I want my standard game
            score to be MAX_SCORE, with JEWEL_GAME_WEIGHT portion of the
            score coming from the jewels and the rest and from the
            peanuts. The scores have to be integers, so it may be that the
            total isn't quite MAX_SCORE, so I will give the rest to the
            user as game-end bonus. */
//----------Get the counts and the scorevalues ready----------
        jewelstoadd = int(jewelprobability * _seedcount);
        peanutstoadd = _seedcount - jewelstoadd;
        jewelvalue =
int(_maxscore*cGamePickNPop::JEWEL_GAME_SCORE_WEIGHT)/
        (jewelstoadd?jewelstoadd:1);
        peanutvalue = (_maxscore -
            jewelvalue*jewelstoadd)/(peanutstoadd?peanutstoadd:1);
        _scorecorrection = _maxscore - (jewelstoadd*jewelvalue +
            peanutstoadd*peanutvalue);
            /* We'll add this in at the end, so that user's maximum
                score is the same as the targeted _maxscore). */
//--------------------Renew the _bubble contents ----------
        _pbiota->purgeNonPlayerNonWallCritters();
            // Need to delete any from last round
            /* Regarding the stacking, it's worth mentioning that
                cBiota::draw draws the critters in reverse order, last
                index to first, so the first-added members appear on top
                in 2D. We want the peanuts "on top", so we add them first.
                Of course in 3D, the zStackCritters is going to take care
                of this irregardless of what order the critters are drawn. */
        for(i=0; i<peanutstoadd; i++)
        {
            pcritternew = new cCritterPeanut(this); /* White bubble that
                we call a "Peanut", can't move out of _packingbox */
            pcritternew->setValue(peanutvalue);
        }
        for (i=0; i<jewelstoadd; i++)
        { /* Make a pcritternew and then add it into _bubble at the
            bottom of loop. */
            pcritternew = new cCritterJewel(this); /* Colored bubble
                that we call a "Jewel", can move all over within
                _border.*/
            pcritternew->setValue(jewelvalue);
        }
        zStackCritters();
}
```

The world rectangles

In PickNPop we want to try and fit our game as nicely as possible into our window. We give the *CDocument* a *cGraphicRealBox _packingbox* and *_targetbox* field. These are to be rectangles that fit nicely inside the *_border*. Rather than setting their values with brute numbers, we set their values as proportions of the *_border*. The *cRealBox::innerBox* function returns a *cRealBox* slightly inside the caller box. And we give them some nice colors and edges.

Converting a critter

One of the parts of the code the author initially had trouble with was in the *cCritterJewel* method where we react to moving the critter inside the *_targetbox*. Here we have to replace one class of object by a different class of object, while still having the object be in some ways the 'same.' It turns out that you can't do this with something so simple as a type-cast of the sort you'd use to turn an **int** into a **float**. Class instances carry too much baggage for that. What we do instead is to create a brand-new object which copies the desired properties of the object that you wanted to 'cast.' We do this by means of a *cCritterUnpackedJewel* copy constructor.

```
void cCritterJewel::update(CPopView *pactiveview)
{
    cGamePickNPop *pgamepnp = NULL;
//(1) Apply force if turned on.
    cCritter::update(pactiveview); //Always call this.
    cVector safevelocity(_velocity); /* To be safe, don't let any z
        get into velocity. */
    safevelocity.setZ(0.0);
    setVelocity(safevelocity);
//(2) Check if in targetbox, and if so, replace yourself with a good
//  jewel.
    if (pgame()->IsKindOf(RUNTIME_CLASS(cGamePickNPop)))
    /* We need to do the cast to access the targetbox field, and to
        be safe we check that the cast will work. */
        pgamepnp = (cGamePickNPop*)(pgame());
    else
        return;
    cRealBox effectivebox = pgamepnp-
>targetbox().innerBox(cGamePickNPop::JEWELBOXTOLERANCE*radius());
    if (!effectivebox.inside(_position))
        return;
    //Reaction to being inside _targetbox.
    playSound("Ding");
    cCritterUnpackedJewel *pcritternew =
        new cCritterUnpackedJewel(this); //Copy constructor
    pcritternew->setMoveBox(pgamepnp->targetbox());
```

```
pcritternew->setDragBox(pgamepnp->targetbox());
delete_me(); /* Just tell cBiota to just remove the old critter.
    Don't use the overridden cCritterJewel::die to make a noise
    and subtract _value from score.*/
pcritternew->add_me(_pownerbiota); //Tell cBiota add new
    critter.
pgamepnp->pplayer()->addScore(_value);
}
```

The delete_me makes a service request to the _pownerbiota **cBiota** object. The add_me makes a service request as well, but since **pcritternew** isn't yet a member of _pownerbiota, we need to pass this pointer into the add_me method.

17.3 Other selection games

A weakness in the PickNPop game is that playing it requires so little thought. A simple type of game that requires thought is the Memory style game. In this kind of game, the user tries to click on some desired shape that is hidden by some more generic shape. The classic Memory game uses a set of pairs of cards with pictures, with all cards turned face down, and the player turns over one card and then tries to turn over a card with a matching image. If two matching cards are found they're removed, a point is scored, and the player gets to continue the turn. If a non-matching card is found, the cards are turned face down again, and the player's turn ends. Either an opponent (possibly a robot) gets a turn then, or the original player gets a new turn, with the point of the game being to get all the cards with as few separate turns as possible. As the turns go by, the player learns the location of some of the cards, and presumably can remember these so as to do better on the following turns.

In a Memory game, you might use a **cCritterMemory** that has a BOOL _showcontents field and which has an extra sprite field cSprite *_pspritehide. You would need to take care of initializing this field in the constructor and deleting it in the destructor. The **draw** method could then be overridden like this, or see Exercise 9.10 for a more object-oriented solution.

```
void cCritterMemory ::draw(cGraphics *pgraphics, int drawflags)
{
    if (_showcontents)
        cCritter::draw(pgraphics, int drawflags)
    else
    {
        pgraphics->pushMatrix();
        pgraphics->multMatrix(_attitude);
        _pspritehide->draw(pgraphics, drawflags);
        pgraphics->popMatrix();
    }
}
```

There are many other selection game possibilities. One type is puzzles where one slides things around. For some good examples of puzzle games see the website of the master puzzler Scott Kim, **www.scottkim.com**.

Exercises

Remember that when you get into tweaking one particular game mode, it saves time to have the Pop program start up in the game mode that you want to play with. The way to control this is to edit the **CPopDoc** constructor in **popdoc.cpp**. Simply comment in exactly the one **setGameClass** line corresponding to the game you want to play. If you make a new game class, add a line for it.

Exercise 17.1: Have the popped bubbles shrink

A general principle in designing games is that things shouldn't happen abruptly. When an object is destroyed it shouldn't instantly disappear; instead it should show itself dying. Change Pop so that when you pop a bubble, it puts on a 'dying act.' You might do this by overriding the `die` methods by turning on a `BOOL` `_dying` flag instead of calling `delete_me` right away. And now override the `animate(dt)` method to shrink the bubbles. We might think of the bubbles as losing volume at some constant negative rate dV/dt called LEAKRATE. Since radius is proportional to the cube root of the volume, a little calculus reveals that dr/dt should be proportional to LEAKRATE/($r*r$). So we do something like `setRadius(radius() - dt*LEAKRATE/(radius()*radius()))` inside `animate(dt)`. And when a bubble's radius gets below 0.0, then you actually call its `delete_me` method, so do a check something like `if (radius() <= 0.0) delete_me`. Call the base `cCritter::animate (dt)` too.

Exercise 17.2: Use polyhedra

Show your jewels as spheres in the OpenGL graphics. Perhaps make the peanuts a 3D shape as well, maybe cubes. Do some OOA and OOD before you start coding, in particular, it would be a good idea to do Exercise 9.10: Three-dimensional sprites first.

Exercise 17.3: Add a jewel-popping deathstar

What if we had a fourth kind of critter in our game? Let's say we have a small, slow-moving deathstar critter that bursts any jewel that it gets close to, but doesn't harm the peanuts. Maybe the deathstar should have a sprite like a star-shaped polygon. The place to have it kill the jewels would be inside the `cGamePicknpop::collide` code. Maybe make the deathstar non-draggable by overriding its `draggable()` to return `FALSE`.

Exercise 17.4: Make the critters run away

Make the game more challenging by having the bubbles move away from the cursor. Do this by giving them a **cForceObjectSeek** with a negative acceleration. Add a static `Real` `cGamePickNPop::FLEECURSOR` multiplier to adjust the strength of the flight effect.

To keep them from getting too hyper you should probably use a **cForceDrag** as well.

Exercise 17.5: Memory

Complete a Memory game as outlined above. To make it more interesting, allow the separate **cCritterMemory** to have `_pspritehide` that look slightly different from each other, and have the critters slowly move about.

Exercise 17.6: Board games?

Can you make a checkers game? Laying out the board and putting on the men should be easy enough. A little work would let you drag a man only to a legal position. The tough thing here is figuring out code to make the computer play back. See if you can find some easier kinds of board games to try and program.

Interesting worlds

18

In this chapter we'll discuss some ways of enriching a game by changing the world. We'll discuss these four additions to a world.

- *Side-scroller*. Make the world long and thin and have your player move through it.
- *Gravity*. Put in gravitational forces.
- *Walls*. Put walls into the world.
- *Trails*. Use color to mark out a trail the player can move on.

18.1 The Ballworld side-scroller game

Specification

(S1) Concept
This is a game like the Mario side-scroller games. Your player moves to the right through a long world, that is, a world with a big x size and a small y size. Objects come towards you and you avoid letting them hit you.

(S2) Appearance
Below is a screen capture of how the game looks.

(S3) Controls
The player uses the Hopper Controls. The idea is to hop over the balls and maybe land on top of them. The Hopper Controls move the player left and right with the **Left** and **Right Arrow** keys. The **Up Arrow** key hops the player up into the air, but continuing to depress the **Up** key will not produce a continued hopping effect. You need to tap the **Up** key repeatedly if you want to add a hop to a hop.

(S4) Behavior
Your player starts at the left end of the world. Your goal is to use the **Arrow** keys to move your player to the right end of the screen and jump into a hoop you'll find there.

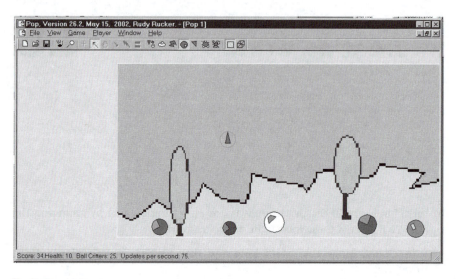

The Ballworld game

There are balls bouncing along the bottom of the world from right to left. When you collide with a ball, the effect on you depends on your height relative to the ball. If the player's low edge is higher than the ball's center, the player gets a score point. But, if the player's position is lower than the ball, the player loses a health point. In either case the ball is destroyed. Every time a ball is destroyed a new one is added to the world to the right of the player.

At the right end there is a hoop that gives you extra score when you jump into it. After you jump into the hoop, the player is moved back to the left end of the world.

Design

We call `_border.set(100.0, 12.0, 0.0)` in the constructor to make the world long and thin. In order to zoom in, we have a call to `pviewer->zoom(4.0)`; in `cGameBallworld::initializeViewpoint(cCritterViewer *pviewer)`. In order to keep the player in view, we have a call to `pview->pviewpointcritter() ->setTrackplayer(TRUE)` in `cGameBallworld::initializeView(CPopView *pview)`.

A final tweak regarding the view of a side-scroller world is that we add this line to the header of the ***cGameBallworld***.

```
virtual int worldShape(){return cGame::SHAPE_XSCROLLER;} /* Need this
    to signal the cCritterViewer to not wobble up and down when
    _trackplayer is on. */
```

If we were creating a long thin vertical world, we'd want to return `cGame::SHAPE_YSCROLLER`.

A fair amount of experimentation went into developing the *cListenerHopper* and tweaking the *cCritterBallworldPlayer* constructor so that the player has good hopping behavior with the *cListenerHopper*.

The *collide* methods of both *cCritterBallworldPlayer* and *cCritterTreasure* are overridden to control the interactions between the critters.

The method used to make the ball-shaped *cCritterBallProp* critters move to the left is to give them a gravity force that points slightly to the left, with this line in the *cCritterBallProp* constructor. `addForce(new cForceGravity(25.0, cVector(-0.03, -1, 0.0)));`. As always, more detail can be found in the source code: gameballworld.cpp.

An essential part of both the Ballworld and the Dambuilder games is that they use gravitational forces on the players. It's worth mentioning that when you have gravity, in general (a) you want drag or friction forces to keep the objects from speeding up too much; (b) don't have wrap, otherwise the objects go around and around the *y*-axis faster and faster; (c) if you don't want things to bounce too much off the bottom edge, you can use `setBounciness(0.9)` to make them lose energy with each bounce, alternately you can use `setWrapflag(cCritter::CLAMP)` to make them not bounce at all.

18.2   Games with walls

In many games, like PacMan, the critters are limited to move within the corridors of a maze. How can we implement this?

The simplest approach is to just put in a number of *cCritterWall* objects and let the critters bounce off the walls. Use as few walls as possible so as to keep down the number of pairs that you'll be processing in your collision-checking – that is, use one long wall in preference to two short walls butted together end to end.

The speed of the Pop Framework is indeed sufficient to handle worlds with little wall mazes such as PacMan.

The Dambuilder sample game isn't really a game, it's more of a starting point. We'll have a couple of exercises on it below (Exercises 18.1 and 18.2).

For a more Doom-like adventure game experience, you want a world with halls, doors, and rooms. It would be reasonable to make a slightly sophisticated *cMaze* object which contains some other classes (like perhaps *cRoom*) that use *cVector* points to specify a maze. To implement a particular maze, you'd first draw it on graph paper marked off to be the same size as your _border, and then you'd have your game constructor make a *cMaze* based on these numbers. And then in the *seedCritters* call you could perhaps call a *cMaze::install(cGame *game)* method that would place *cCritterWall* objects in place to match the coordinates of the maze. You might find a way to use the *cMaze* to cut down on the number of critter-to-wall collisions you worry about.

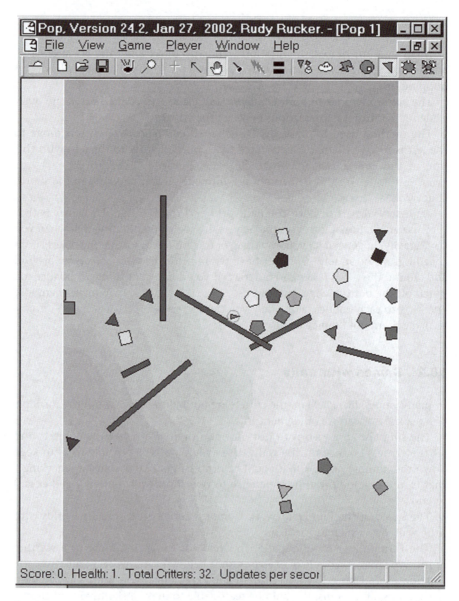

The Dambuilder game in 2D view

It's possible to make a completely different kind of wall game based on the traditional wooden game known as Labyrinth. In this game, you have a ball in a maze that has holes here and there in the floor. Your task is to gently roll the ball through the maze without falling into one of the holes. To design this game, you need a *cCritterHole* class and you need a new *cListenerTipper* listener for the player that lets you adjust the acceleration in the *x* or *y* directions by using the arrow keys. More about this in Exercise 18.8.

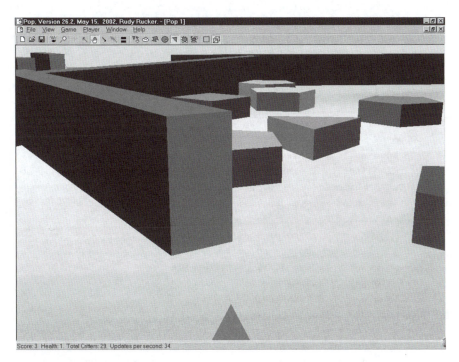

Dambuilder in 3D view and Ride the Player mode can serve as starting point for a first-person shooter game

18.3   Sniffing a trail

Suppose you want to program a car-racing game in which you look down at a track from above and use the controls to steer your car along the track. Lining the track with lots of little walls is an option, but in this section we'll talk about a different approach. The idea here is to lay down a trail that your critter can move along.

The *cCritter::update* method takes a CPopView *pactiveview argument. The reason we have this argument is so that the *update* can feed the pactiveview into the method *COLORREF cCritter::sniff(const cVector &snifflocation, CPopView *pactiveview)*. The sniff return value tells you the color of the pixel of the onscreen view corresponding to a given location.

The way to use sniff would be to make the track that you want your critter to stay on be some one particular color, say *cColorStyle::CN_WHITE*. And then, in that critter's update code, you could have it look ahead and see if it was about to move off the track, and if so, look for a better direction to move in.

A good strategy in looking for a better direction would be to successively try turning left or right by greater and greater amounts. Here's an untested example of how you might do it.

```
#define LOOKAHEAD 1.1 /* Maybe 1.1 is not the best value to use,
    maybe should depend on speed. */
#define SNIFFTURNSTEP PI/90.0 /* Radians for 2 degrees. Can make
    larger if this runs too slow. */
cCritterSnifferCar::update(cPopView *pactiveview, Real dt)
{
    cCritter::update(pactiveviewdt);
    COLORREF sniffcolor = sniff(_position + LOOKAHEAD * radius() *
        tangent(), pactiveview);
        //sniffcolor is the color of a pixel a just a bit ahead of me.
    COLORREF whitecolor = cColorStyle::CN_WHITE;
    if (sniffcolor == cColorStyle::CN_WHITE || //all clear ahead
        sniffcolor == -1)
            /* The "-1" color means your pixel is offscreen or not
                in clipping region */
    //Else you try to turn till you see a good spot.
    Real sign = 1.0;
    Real angle = SNIFFTURNSTEP;
    cVector originaltan = tangent();
    int whilecount = 0; /* Never go into a while loop without making
        sure you get out! */
    while(sniffcolor != cColorStyle::CN_WHITE) /* Waggle back and
        forth till you see a good spot */
    {
        setTangent(originaltan);
        yaw(sign * angle);
        sniffcolor = sniff(_position + LOOKAHEAD * radius() *
            tangent(), pactiveview);
        angle += SNIFFTURNSTEP;
        sign *= -1.0;
        if (++whilecount > 90) //Fuhgeddaboutit and bail
        {
            setTangent(originaltan);
            break;
        }
    }
}
```

All this said, sniffing pixels may not the best method to use to follow a trail. It won't work well if you switch to the OpenGL 3D view, although you could perhaps handle this by sniffing a 2D map of the world that you keep in a **cMemoryDC** instead of sniffing the screen.

In André LaMothe, *Tricks of the Windows Game Programming Gurus* (Sams, 2001), you will find a more robust trail-following technique called *waypoint pathfinding*.

Exercises

Exercise 18.1: Time the flow in Dambuilder

Let's go back to the original inspiration for Dambuilder. It has this name in memory of the childhood activity of making dams in little streams. The goal in building dams like this is to make the water move through the system as slowly as possible, but without the water getting stuck in any one place (and overflowing one of the dams).

You can use the cursor tools to make new walls and move them. Click with the Equals cursor to copy, prick with the Pin cursor to delete, drag with the Hand cursor to move. This is how you 'play the game'.

How do you tell how well you're doing in Dambuilder? We need to have a score that calculates the average time that it takes a critter to fall from the top to the bottom of the screen. We reset the critters' ages when they wrap bottom to top.

And we need some kind of penalty if a critter gets stuck for too long. Perhaps if a critter's age gets larger than some MUSTBESTUCK time value, then the critter explodes and destroys everything near it, including the dam that it's stuck behind. So your goal is to get the critters moving along as slowly as possible just short of being stuck and destroying the dams.

Exercise 18.2: Rotate the walls

Add a tool that lets you rotate the walls of the dams. The **cCritterWall** might need some special override of the **turn** code for this. An easy way to call this method would be to give the **cCritterWall** a scooter-style listener that turns it provided that the wall is currently the pfocus() of its owner.

If you feel more ambitious you could make a new cursor tool that uses the left click to rotate left and the right click to rotate right.

Exercise 18.3: Make a maze game

If you remove the gravity forces from the critters in Dambuilder and start with a **cGraphicsOpenGL** preference and set the critter viewer to ride the player, you get a fairly effective-looking first-person shooter game. But rather than changing Dambuilder, you might simply add walls to the GameStub game, which is already set up with enemies and health-packs. Note that this exercise is basically similar to Exercises 14.5 and 14.7 combined.

Exercise 18.4: Make a Pinball game

The hardest thing about pinball is making flippers. You would probably have **cCritterFlipper** be a child of **cCritterWall**. See if you can make a **cCritterFlipper** and put it into the Dambuilder game. You will also need to write a listener that uses the **Left Arrow** and **Right Arrow** to rotate the flipper around one of its ends.

Exercise 18.5: Make a Pachinko game

First get Pinball working, then find out what the popular Japanese arcade game Pachinko looks like and emulate that. Quite briefly, Pachinko is like a pinball game in which you have dozens of balls active at once. But there's more to it than that. Like pinball, many Pachinko machines are quite beautiful.

Exercise 18.6: PacMan

We all have a pretty clear idea of what PacMan looks like. Let your player be a *cCritterPacman* with a standard *cListenerArrow*. You can use *cCritterWall* objects.

Students have indeed written this game using the Pop Framework, and one issue is that in PacMan we have 100 or so *cCrittterPowerpellet* objects which are little yellow dots lining the maze paths. If you aren't careful, having so many critters can drastically slow down your program's execution speed. Make sure to set the `_fixedflag` to `TRUE` for these critters, and make sure that the various collision-controlling parameters are set so that the game's *cCollider* will ignore all *Powerpellet* collisions except those featuring a *cCritterPowerpellet* and a *cCritterPacman*. And in these collisions, have the *cCritterPowerpellet* get eaten: calling *delete_me* and adding some score to the *cCritterPacman*.

Another thing to keep in mind if you're worried about speed is that the Release build will run very noticeably faster than the Debug build. If the speed were still to be unacceptable, you could use a different approach for eating power pellets. Rather than having the PacMan check its distance from each and every power pellet at every update, you could use a sniff method and make the power pellets a distinctive color.

The biggest difficulty students find in making PacMan style games is in having the player's enemies be good at chasing the player or, if they are to be victims, be good at running away from the player. We discuss this in the next exercise.

Exercise 18.7: Smarter enemies for maze games

Suppose you write an adventure game in which the enemy critters use a *cForceObjectSeek* to run towards the player. Suppose also that your game has *cCritterWall* walls in it – think of something like a PacMan game in which the ghosts chase the player (or, if the player is powered-up, run away from the player).

If you use a simple *cForceObjectSeek*, the enemies will often get stuck pushing against a wall they can't get through. The easiest way out is simply to provide more enemies and expect that some of them will manage to be a threat.

But really you'd want to create a 'smarter' kind of seeking force. Let's discuss three increasingly sophisticated ways in which we can try and improve the situation.

(a)   A simple, but somewhat effective thing you could do instead is to create a *cForceObjectSeekImpatient*. The idea is that this is a seek force that will sometimes turn itself off in the hope that the enemy might then happen to bounce into a better location. We'll think of the default, non-seek-force motion as a 'cruise' motion. By a cruise motion we mean a force-free motion in which the critter simply moves along in straight lines bouncing off the walls.

Give the class these fields and initialize as suggested:

```
int _frustration;//Start at 0
int _maxfrustration;
    //Try 1 to start with and then try making it larger.
Real _oldsatisfaction;
    //Start at a large negative number like -1000000.0
Real _cruisetime; //Some time in seconds, like 3.0
BOOL _cruising; //Start FALSE
Real _resumeage //A scratch-paper field we can initialize to 0.0
```

Now use a *cForceObjectSeekImpatient* force coded something like this.

```
cVector cForceObjectSeekImpatient::force(cCritter *pcritter)
{
    if (_cruising)
    {
        pcritter->setSpeed(pcritter->maxspeed());
            //Keep moving fast
        if (pcritter->age() >_resumeage)
            _cruising = FALSE;
        else
            return cVector::ZEROVECTOR;
    }
    Real_newsatisfaction = -pcritter->distanceTo(_pnode); /* Use
        minus so the bigger the distance to the target, the lower
        your satisfaction is. */
    if (newsatisfaction <= oldsatisfaction)
        _frustration ++;
    else
        _frustration—-
    if (frustration <= 0)
        _frustration = 0;
    if (frustration > _maxfrustration)
    {
        _cruising = TRUE;
        _resumeage = pcritter->age() + cruisetime;
        _frustration = 0;
    }
    return cForceObjectSeek::force(pcritter);
}
```

(b) For a more sophisticated solution, you would want to use a *cMaze* class that inherits from CArray<cCritterWall *, cCritterWall*>. As we add the *cCritterWall* objects to our world, we also put them into the *cMaze*.

It will be useful to give the *cMaze* class a BOOL blocks(const cVector& start, const cVector& end) method, which walks through the array of member *cCritterWall*, checks the value of cCritterWall::blocks(start, end) for each wall, and returns **TRUE** if any of the member walls blocks the path.

In addition, we'd want to give the *cMaze* a CArray<cVector, cVector&>_waypoint member, and as we added in the *cCritterWall* objects to the maze, we'd want to fill _waypoint with points corresponding to significant points in the maze's passageways. In particular, you'd want to have a waypoint at each corner, and before and after each gap or doorway in the maze.

Once you have the *cMaze* in place, you could create a *cForceObjectSeekImpatientMaze* which has a cMaze *pmaze member. When 'frustrated' the force could direct the caller critter to proceed towards the nearest waypoint of the maze. We can measure frustration as before, or simply become frustrated right away if the *cMaze* blocks the path from the enemy position to the player position.

(c) The truly correct thing to do would be to use a *cMaze* as in (b), but to have a *cForceSolveMaze* which would determine the proper sequence of waypoints to follow in order to get to the critter being sought. This involves considering the tree of all non-repeating arrays of waypoints one might visit, starting with the nearest waypoint. We will only consider those waypoint sequences in which the maze doesn't block the path between any two successive waypoints. And our goal will be to reach a waypoint W such that the maze doesn't block the path from W to the target critter. If you know a little about AI, you would probably want to use a so-called A* search strategy; otherwise a simple breadth-first search will work well enough, provide your maze isn't too big.

To keep the speed of the program up it might suffice to only recompute the current path of *cForceSolveMaze* after every ten or twenty updates.

Exercise 18.8: A labyrinth game

There's a popular wooden maze game in which you move a ball by manipulating two knobs on the sides of the box. The knobs tilt the top surface of the game east/west or north/south. On the board is a ball-bearing, some little walls, and about 50 holes. There's a path drawn on the top, and your goal is to manipulate the knobs so that the ball rolls along the path from beginning to end, missing all 50 of the holes.

To implement this as a *cGameRollingMaze*, we'll have a *cCritterRollingball* as our player. We can use *cCritterWall* objects for the pieces of the maze. We should have some *cCritterHole* objects for the balls to fall into: make them fixed critters with perhaps a black *cBubble* for their sprite, and override their *collide* method so that when they collide with a *pcritter* they (a) add an acceleration to *pcritter* which points towards their center if the *pcritter* isn't fully inside (the way a ball speeds up towards a hole when it's partly over one edge) and (b) the call pcritter->delete_me() if the *pcritter* is inside. Well, actually doing a *delete_me* on a game's _pplayer has no effect (because all hell breaks loose if you have NULL player, and *cBiota* has a 'foolproofing' feature of ignoring delete requests on active players). But we'd like to keep the delete_me for the *cCritterHole* as we might sometime want to reuse the holes. What we really want to happen when the player falls in the hole is that the player goes back to the starting position. So you should override your *cCritterRollingball::delete_me* to call an overridden *reset()* which will indeed put the ball at the starting gate.

Whenever you have a lot of critters, you want to be careful not to try and compute unnecessary collisions as this will make the program run too slow. Regarding the many *cCritterHole* objects, the only kind of collisions we're interested in is between a hole and the player. And since we've overridden the *cCritterHole::collide* method for the special behavior, we want to call these collisions in the form phole->collide(pplayer). So set the relevant _collidepriority or collidesWith methods accordingly.

How about the knobs? Probably you can use a *cListenerTipper* listener that increments or decrements the acceleration in the *x* and *y* directions with the **Left/Right Up/Down** keys. You will want to put a good amount of friction on the ball's motions and/or give it a low _maxspeed so it doesn't get out of control.

How best to add all the *cCritterHole* and *cCritterWall* objects to the world? We might consider something like the *cMaze* object described in Exercise 18.7.b. Call it a *cRollerBoardlayout*. But, on second thought, maybe our class *cRollerBoardlayout* needn't hold critters as in 18.7b. Maybe it should just have geometrical information. It could store the coordinate information for the various walls and holes, and have a constructor like, perhaps, *cRollerBoardlayout(int wallcount, Real wallthickness, Real[] wallenda, Real[] wallendb, int holecount, Real holeradius, Real[] holecenter)*. And it could have an all-important *putBoardInGame(cGame *pgame)* method to create and add the desired *cCritterHole* and *cCritterWall* objects to *pgame*. So then our code could have some easily tweaked Real numbers WALLCOUNT, WALLTHICKNESS, HOLECOUNT, HOLERADIUS and three Real arrays WALLENDA, WALLENDB and HOLECENTER as statics or **#define** at the top of the cgamerollingmaze.cpp. And the *cGameRollingMaze* constructor would construct a temporary

```
cRollerBoardlayout layout(WALLCOUNT, WALLTHICKNESS, WALLENDA, WALLENDB,
HOLECOUNT, HOLERADIUS, HOLECENTER WALLENDS, HOLES)ü and then call
layout.putBoardInGame(this).
```

Exercise 18.9: Slot Car Racer

Use the trail-sniffing technique to make a car-racing game. Have your race course be a bitmap with a track marked in pure white pixels, give your player a *cListenerCar* listener, and make a robot car to race with you.

You can count on the update with the sniff method to keep the robot on the track, but how do you keep the robot going in the right direction? Assuming your track is roughly a closed curve around the origin you might try giving the robot a reasonably strong *cForceVortex* to keep it going in generally the right direction.

Rather than using sniffing, you may find it works better to keep your player on the track simply by lining the track by *cCritterWall*. If you are careful not to use too many walls (use a few long ones rather than a lot of short ones), the speed will be okay.

Whether or not you use use sniffing, you will need a reliable method to make your robot driver opponent do a good job. What works the best is to use a *cForceWaypoint* as described in Exercise 7.2.

Once you get this working you may want to tweak the listener controls to make the driving experience better. It should be possible to have a world larger than you see on the screen, provided you set the track player option so that the player is always on a visible part of the screen.

Try implementing a two-player mode, and have the other player car have a listener that's controlled by some letter keys, such as VK_S and so on.

Exercise 18.10: Feeding

Make a game in which you can feed the critters. One approach would be to have a player who scatters new *cCritterFood* when you press, say, the left mouse button. Basically the player could be like a *cCritterArmed* that shoots bullets that don't move. In fact *cCritterFood* could be a child of *cCritterBullet*. And maybe in your feeding process you are trying to lure the critters into a pen. Like catching chickens.

Exercise 18.11: Flocking

Make a *cCritterBoid* class and give its members a *cForceClassFlock* force which makes the 'boids' do the following.

- Collision avoidance: avoid collisions with walls and nearby flockmates.
- Velocity matching: attempt to match velocity with nearby flockmates.
- Flock centering: attempt to stay close to nearby flockmates.

Now for a few words on each of these behaviors.

- *Collision avoidance*: each boid keeps track of some optimal cruising distance that it would like to maintain between itself and its nearest flockmates. If a boid's nearest visible neighbor is at a distance less than this cruising distance, then the boid is in danger of colliding with its neighbor. The boid avoids the collision by slowing down if the too-near neighbor is in front of the boid, and by speeding up if the too-near neighbor is behind the boid.

As well as trying not to get too close to the nearest neighbor boid, a boid also tries not to get too far from the nearest visible boid. That is, if you're a boid and the nearest visible neighbor boid is farther than the optimal cruise distance, you speed up if that boid's in front of you, and slow down if it's behind you.

Note that these adjustments to cruising distance are done solely by changing the boids' speeds, rather than by changing their direction vectors. The phrases 'in front of' and 'behind' for boids are used to stand for computing the angle between a boid's direction and a given object and deciding if the angle is within a specified range.

- *Velocity matching*: each boid tries to fly parallel to its nearest neighbor. This is done by adjusting the boid's direction vector to match the direction vector of its nearest neighbor. This does not change the boid's speed.

- *Flock centering*: each boid tries to be surrounded by other boids on every side. This is done by having each boid compute the average position or centroid of the other boids, and try and move towards the centroid. To do this, a boid computes the unit vector that points towards the centroid, and then turns its own direction vector to match this unit vector. This does not change the boid's speed.

Here's some pseudocode for the process.

```
--------------------Boid Motion Algorithm--------------------
Boid Motion:
BEGIN
// Avoid the walls
    IF (The world is in walled mode and you are within
        NearWallDistance pixels of a wall)
        THEN (Add to Direction components of size VeerWeight
            pointing away from the walls that are too near);
// Copy your neighbor.
    Do Collision Avoidance and Velocity Matching with Nearest Boid;
// Head towards centroid of the Boid positions.
    Direction = Direction + CenterWeight * ToCentroid;
END
```

To make the process work, we actually need to compute some kind of weighted average of the four actions: avoid wall, avoid hitting closest neighbor, match neighbor, head towards flock center.

More information can be found off the page on the author's website dealing with his Artificial Life Lab program: **www.mathcs.sjsu.edu/faculty/rucker/boppers.htm.** And, above all, see Craig Reynolds's wonderful Java-based boids pages at **http://www.red3d.com/cwr/boids/**

More ideas for games

19

19.1 Commercial games

Once you start working on writing even a simple computer game, you get a new appreciation for what goes into commercial arcade games. Even the crudest, oldest games can have an incredible playability factor. It's not about animated texture-mapped three-dimensional characters, it's about game design. While your game is in the early design stages, spend some time playing a similar arcade game – and look at some arcade games again when you do your final tweaks.

It's not necessarily convenient to go out to a game arcade, and there aren't all that many of them left anymore, but many classic arcade games can be played at home.

Emulators

An emulator is a shareware software package that allows your computer to emulate old arcade video games. One of the best-known emulators is MAME, which stands for Multiple Arcade Machine Emulator. It's available for free download at **www.mame.net**.

In and of itself, MAME doesn't show video games, in order for it to show a specific game, you need to provide it with the code for the game. These code packages are called ROMs, and many arcade game ROMs can be found online.

A word of explanation about the name 'ROM.' Rather than having hard drives which contain their programs, arcade games have their program code on read-only memory chips, or ROMs. Although it looks like a piece of hardware, a ROM is really software. The code for a given video game is gotten by extracting the code from its ROM to get what's called a 'ROM image' or simply (by extending the meaning of the word) a ROM.

Although emulators such as MAME are legal, ROMs are illegal unless either you own the game program in question, or the ROM has been made public domain. The ROMs for most arcade games are copyrighted software still belonging to video game companies such as Williams, Midway, Bally, and CapCom. This means that most ROMs you can find on the web are in fact illegal, pirated code. So be careful only to download legal, public domain ROMs and, above all, don't get involved in redistributing illegal ROMs.

This said, all of the classic arcade computer games do exist as illegal ROMs. Having seen some of these ROMs running on the machines of less scrupulous individuals, the author can say that they're quite inspiring fodder for a game developer.

To run an arcade game emulation by using MAME follow these steps.

- Download the MAME emulator in zipped form from a site like www.mame.net.

- Unzip the emulator into a directory like c:\mame.

- Download some ROMs in zipped form, being sure only to get legal, public domain ROMs.

- Don't unzip the ROMs; simply copy them into the roms subdirectory which the MAME unzip will have put into its mame directory.

- Get a DOS prompt in the c:\mame directory. To load a ROM game, run a command of the form mame [ROMname], for instance mame somepublicdomaingamename.

- The game will run in a DOS full-screen mode.

- Usually the arrow keys move the player and the **Ctrl** and **Alt** keys act as the game buttons for actions like firing. You can get additional info about the controls by pressing **Tab**.

- **Esc** will exit a MAME game.

Game consoles

If you own a game console, take some time to closely study how your games work. Think about dimensionality, about viewpoint, about the listeners, and about the forces and the artificial intelligence that controls the game critters. Think about the graphics: about the background and foreground, about the resolution, and about the lighting. Now that you know a bit about programming games, you may well see things in a new light.

An inexpensive way to get to look at some reasonably low-level games is to get hold of one of the various Nintendo GameBoy machines with a cartridge of the classic arcade games.

Online games

A third way to look at arcade games is to search the web for online games, some of which are written in Java and some using alternate tools such as Shockwave. You might think these games wouldn't run fast enough, but many of them are quite good. Keep in mind that the actual computation is being done client-side on your machine by the downloaded Java applet or Shockwave code. The URLs of online games change so rapidly that it's not a good idea to try and list them here. As usual, using a search engine is the way to go.

19.2   The Pop Framework games hall of fame

Here are the names and concepts of some of the computer game projects that student teams have done using earlier versions of the Pop Framework in the author's software engineering class over the last few years. Almost all of these games are two-dimensional games, because only with Fall, 2001, did the Pop Framework begin to offer support for three-dimensional games. In the two-dimensional games, the user is normally looking down at a world from above, moving the player critter with the arrow keys or the mouse, similar to the games Asteroids or PacMan.

They're listed here in chronological order. Virus-checked executables and help files (but not the source code) for some of these are available online at the book website. If you make a game project with the Pop Framework that you're proud of, check on the book website to see about posting it there.

Fall, 1999

Body Defense. Germs fall down the screen shaped like an artery, and the player shoots them with an inoculation gun. Beautiful graphics, but a bit weak as a game, in that the player has only one degree of freedom in left/right motion. So it's a little too close to Space Invaders.

Brick Bugs. Player pounds a way out of an encircling wall of bricks, while little brick bugs shoot things. Numerous kinds of brick bugs; meaner ones are attracted by the 'noise' of the player pounding away bricks (which disappear after a few hits as in the arcade game Breakout). An original idea.

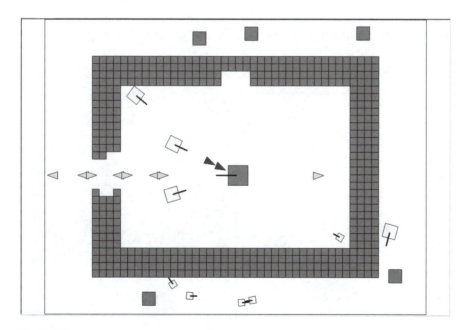

The Brickbugs game

Garden. Player feeds plants with water and tries to protect them with poison spray from attacking bugs. Water and poison sources are on ladders on either side of the screen. This was one of the first projects to use animated sprites.

The Garden game

Grammar. Player picks a floating disk with the correct word to complete a sample sentence. An effective educational game based on PickNPop.

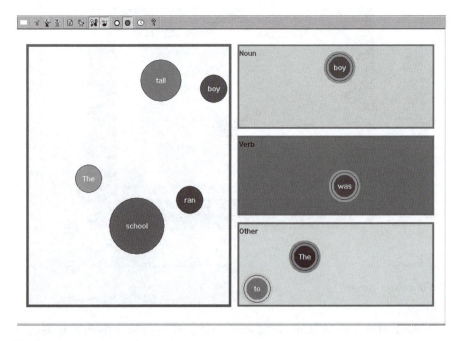

The Grammar game

Lunatic. One of many Spacewar-style shooting games. Player's vehicle takes on varying properties as different enemies attack.

Olympod. Car racing game in which cars go around on an oval track and the player needs to back up if a car runs off track. The cars use the 'sniff' method to look at the background pixel color at their location so as to detect when they have run off the track.

Paratrooper. Player jumps out of a helicopter moving across the screen, must shoot or avoid birds on the way down, tries to land in a rowboat at the bottom. Cleverly done.

Safari. Player rides in a jeep on a road going across the screen. Multiple screens. Player 'shoots' a camera to send light bulbs out to 'capture' critters that move by. A non-violent spin on a shooting-type game.

Shepherd Boy. Player herds sheep around, who are repelled by him, tries to herd them into a pen. Wolves come to eat the sheep, player can throw rocks at them. Good physics and playability in this one.

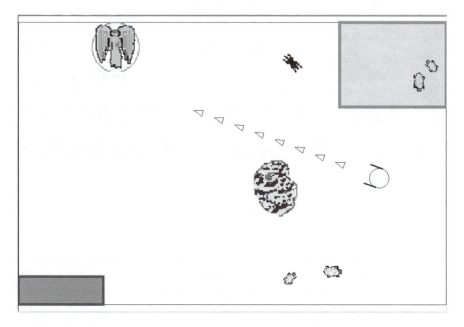

The Shepherd Boy game

Spring, 2000

Airstrike. A game like Spacewar, enhanced by having some moving clouds in the sky and by having critters explode into fragments when you shoot them. The bitmaps aren't handled very well here, that is, the background bitmaps are so intense that its hard to see the critters on top of them.

Amazing Mouse. A game like PacMan, with the player as a mouse eating pieces of cheese, and the enemies as cats. Each piece of cheese (or food-pellet) was a critter, the speed was kept high by not checking collisions for the cheese critters.

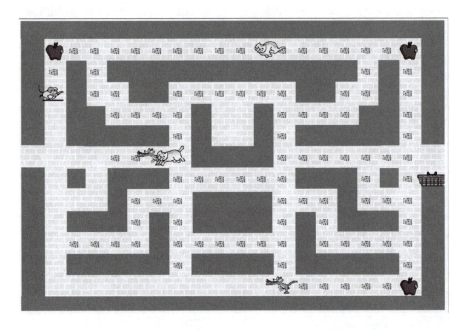

The Amazing Mouse game

BB Rampage. A game that's actually 'two- and a-half-dimensional,' that is, it's a two-dimensional game laid out to look three-dimensional. Player uses a variety of weapons to kill off cute dolls that have taken over their factory and run amok. Player must also press buttons in a certain order to turn the machinery off. Quite professional in execution.

Deer's Revenge. Player is an armed deer critter shooting at hunters. The world is larger than a single screen, and the background scrolls to keep the player in the center. Icons are animated, and they change appearance to match the motion direction of their critters. Both of these features were big achievements at the time, as player-tracking and animated icons weren't yet built into the Pop Framework.

Labyrinth Roller. Interesting game modeled on the wooden Labyrinth game in which player tilts the board this way and that to lead a heavy ball through a partially walled maze without falling into pitfall holes (see Exercise 18.8).

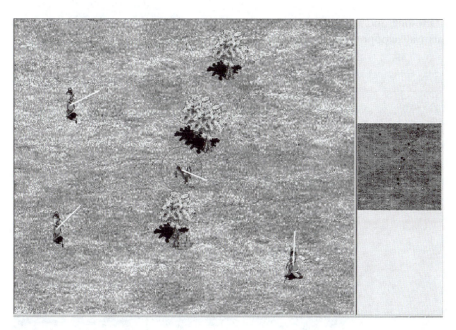

The Deer's Revenge game

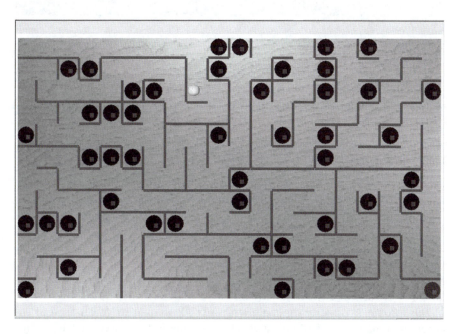

The Labyrinth Roller game

Pixie Quest. A three-level game based, like many other projects, on the Pop Framework Spacewar game. Beautiful background bitmaps make this game a stand-out, and rather than shooting bullets, the player is spreading pixie dust to neutralize opponents like wasps and bees.

The Pixie Quest game

Treasure Hunt. A multiple level game where player first gets past a wave of attacking fish, then lands on an island and avoids tigers by shooting them until a barrel of gold is found. Shooting an elephant by accident reduces player's score.

Fall, 2000

City Hunter. A world larger than one screen. Player moves around, looking for enemies to shoot, sometimes hiding behind tree and house critters when the enemies shoot back. There is a moving car critter the player can jump into and drive.

Climber. Player is climbing up an office building. The windows keep opening with critters throwing objects out. Player must avoid the open windows and the falling debris, which included typewriters and pianos! This is nice. It's really a kind of vertically oriented side-scroller.

Dash 2000. A car-driving game with a track shaped to go all around the border of a map of the United States. The sniff method was used to detect going off the track. There was some difficulty getting the view to zoom in, though this should be possible now with the latest Pop Framework.

Four Pieces of Fate. An Egyptian-themed game with four levels. On each level the player picks up a key, avoiding enemies and moving among walls.

The Climber game

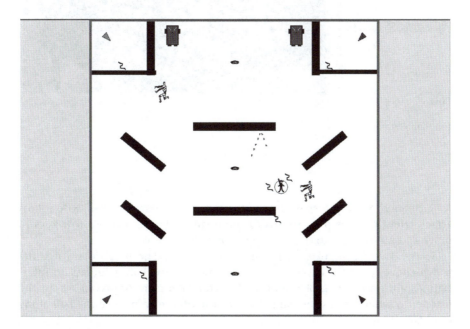

The Four Pieces of Fate game

LifeSaver. A tank game where player uses the arrow keys to drive a tank around a world you view from above. In the world are other tanks and walls. They shoot and player shoots back, aiming the gun with the mouse. There are health-packs and an imprisoned critter to be rescued. Second level player is in the water in a submarine, doing the same kind of thing.

Pinball. A pinball game with several levels. These students got the physics of the flippers to work correctly, which was a non-trivial task. The game still doesn't quite nail the problem of making a really good pinball game.

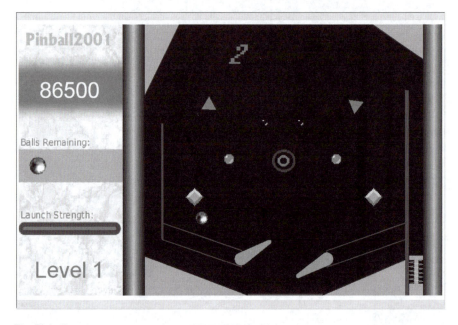

The Pinball game

Robonator. An impressive game with scads of animated icons. Little robots attack relentlessly as player moves from board to board, using arrow keys to move and mouse click to shoot. Inspired by Robotropolis.

Soccer. Two five-man soccer teams fight it out. The user's control shifts to whichever of the onscreen players is closest to the ball, which is an interesting solution to the problem of how to control a team of players – shift the listener to whoever has the ball! User has the option to dribble the ball along or to kick it.

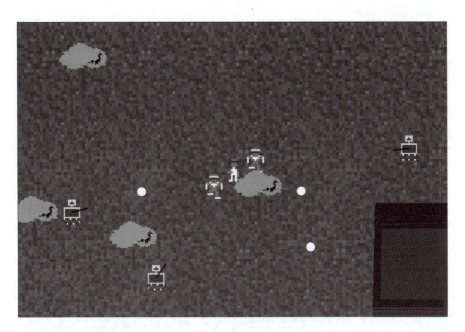

The Robonator game

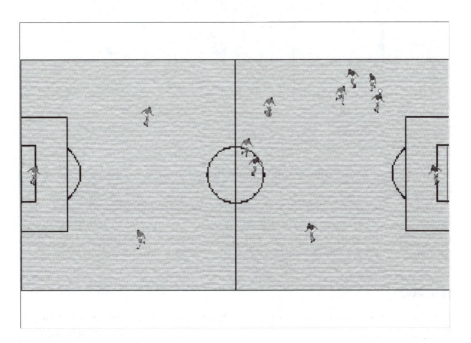

The Soccer game

Spring, 2001

Alien Invaders. A game similar to the arcade game Defender. Player is limited to the left half of the screen, and shoots to the right. Enemy critters stream in from the right. The game has a moving star-field background, regenerated by a series of little Line calls for each update.

Foosball. A nice game modeled on the physical Foosball game. This is a game with sliding rods and plastic soccermen mounted on them. Player moves the rods, trying to make the soccermen block a ball from going into the goal. A major weakness is that the player can't 'spin' his rod to make his players kick, they act only like blocks.

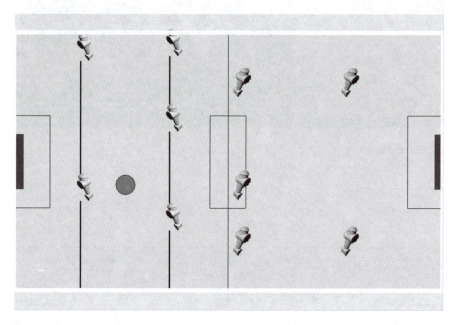

The Foosball game

Lost Crown. A nice side-scroller game in which player collects treasure and avoids monsters.

Triangle Stacker. A game similar to Tetris, using triangle-shaped pieces. Why not do real Tetris? Students are discouraged from doing the real Tetris game, as the code for this is so well known. This version isn't quite as solid as it could be, though.

Fall, 2001

3D Blaster. An enhancement of the Defender3D game. You fly your player forward for quite a long time, with waves of different kinds of enemies coming at you. In a way, the game is a kind of first-person-shooter sidescroller. Slightly rough in appearance, but runs at a good speed. An effective 3D experience.

The Lost Crown game

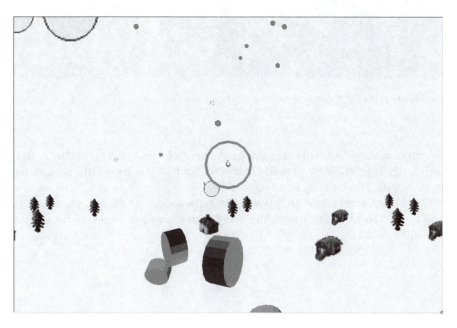

The 3D Blaster game

3D Jewel Hunter. An OpenGL view of a two-dimensional maze game, with three-dimensional creatures in it. The power-packs are spheres and, which is what makes this project impressive, the enemy critters are animated 3D mesh-shapes covered with graphical texture 'skins.' The shapes and skins are read in from standard Milkshape 3D files [a recent address for the shareware Milkshape 3D modeler's home page was http://www.swissquake.ch/chumbalum-soft/, and if this no longer works, search for 'Milkshape 3D.'] This is one of the few projects for which we'll place the source code on the book website.

The 3D Jewel Hunter game

AntiVirus. A well-crafted maze game where player tries to kill off enemy critters on a series of levels. Interest is added by the fact that you have different colored power-levels, selectable by an extra toolbar.

Bermuda. A basic Game Stub-type game with shooting enemies, power packs, and walls. World is larger than the visible screen, and is themed with marine bitmaps.

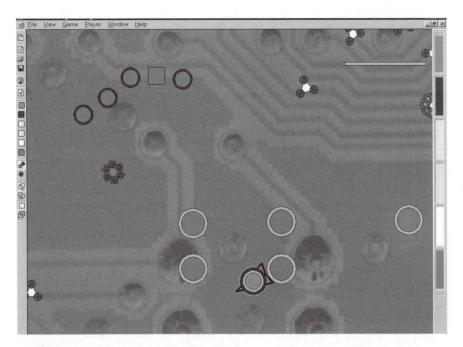

The AntiVirus game

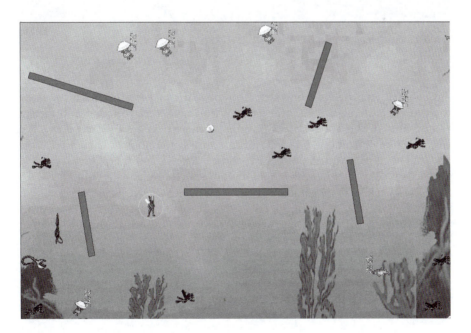

The Bermuda Triangle game

Ghostcastle. An excellent copy of the classic came Star Castle. Player shoots at a central mother ship that's surrounded by three rings of walls. Each of the wall-rings is an octagon made up of eight cCritterWall objects. The walls are kept rotating by a cForceVortex.

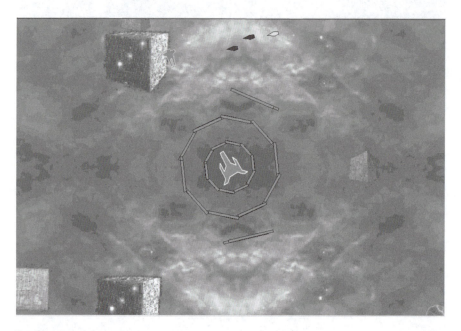

The Ghostcastle game

GoFishing. An original game idea. You move the player back and forth along the top edge of the screen, and use the **Up/Down** keys to lower and raise a fishing line. In the 'water' that fills most of the screen are fish and crabs. If a crab touches your line you lose a health point. If the hook at the end of your line touches a fish, you catch the fish and get a score point. Program has a bug that occasionally sets the crabs to multiplying uncontrollably.

TequilaWorm. A maze game inspired by Slithereens. Your player moves about in a maze trying to eat (from the tail-end first) some enemy worms. The worms are constructed as in the Pop program Worm game, as critters linked together by rod and spring forces. A good job.

The Go Fishing game

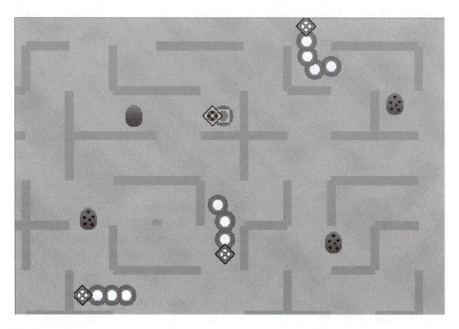

The Tequila Worm game

Spring, 2002

3D Bug. Based on Defender3D, but you aren't riding the player. You use a cross-bow to pop bubbles which contain bugs (bad) or butterflies (good). These flap over to a row of trees behind you, either eating the tree or producing fruit. Each critter has a 'brother' critter that acts as its shadow; the shadow critter copies its brother's (x,y,z) position, but sets y (which is 'up' in this world) to the low value of the border box.

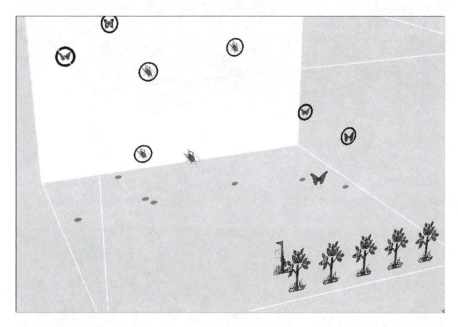

The 3D Bug game

3D Rat Race. Based on the GameStub with a *cGraphicsOpenGL* view to give a 3D effect. A maze-style game. The player has a nice-looking rat-like *cSpriteComposite* icon made up of circles and triangles. There are enemy birds that have their _spriteattitude set with a z-axis component that makes them appear to float above the board (even though their collisions are still computed as if they were down on the board with the other critters). The enemy birds have composite sprites consisting of a body and two wings, with the notable feature that the animate method adjusts the wing _spriteattitude matrices so as to make the wings flap.

The 3D Ratrace game

JumpSport. A side-scroller with moving platforms that your player hops onto. Nicely executed with attractive backgrounds.

The Jump Sport game

KillTime. A simple level-based 2D game with lots and lots of enemies chasing you. Tweaked for good playability.

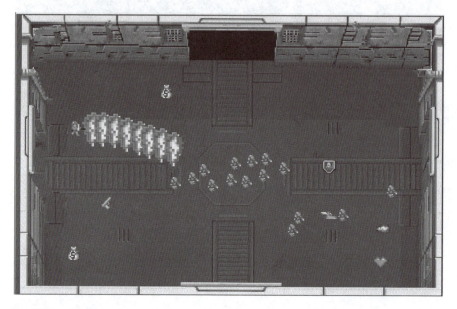

The KillTime game

Pop Rally. A car race game using the waypoint technique to enable the rival cars follow the track. (see Exercise 7.8) The player is kept on track by walls without having to use the sniff method.

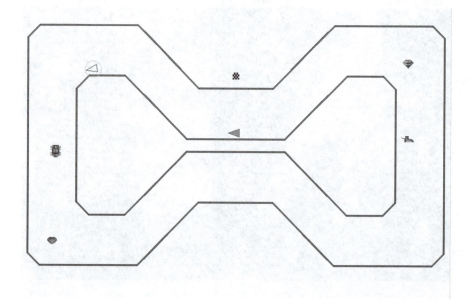

The Pop Rally racer game

Smart Cat. A maze-style game with dogs chasing the player cat which chases mice. Nice animated icons.

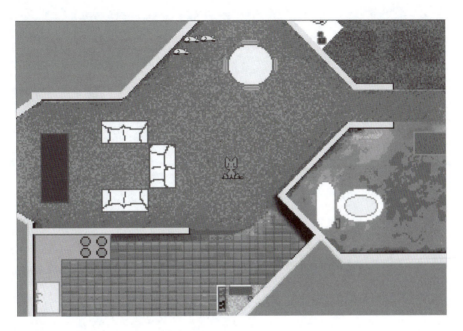

The Smart Cat game

Part II

Software Engineering and Computer Games Reference

Overview

This part of the book covers background topics that will be useful for working with the Pop Framework and for making your own projects. Look over the table of contents to get a general idea of what's in here, and then use the sections as you need them.

Using Microsoft Visual Studio

20

20.1 Navigating with Windows Explorer

In order to make this book as helpful and self-contained as possible, we're going to include some information that many readers will already be familiar with. This section is a prime example of something you may already know: it's about how to look at files and directories in Windows. Feel free to skip it.

Windows Explorer is a tool for exploring the files and directories on your hard disk and on your local network. It has nothing to do with the bundled web browser that Microsoft calls Internet Explorer. The similarity of the two names may well have been part of the Microsoft strategy to tie Internet Explorer to the Windows operating system and 'cut off Netscape's air-supply,' as one Microsoft exec put it in the 1990s. Note also that the exact name 'Windows Explorer' varies among the different versions of Windows.

Opening Windows Explorer

When you left-click the **Start** menu you find on your Windows taskbar, you get a structured menu that has a partial listing of the programs that are on your machine. The Windows Explorer utility can be found under the **Programs** selection of the Start button. A common way to talk about this is to write a vertical | to indicate a step down to a lower menu level. So what we're saying is that the utility we're looking for has a name like **Start | Programs | Windows Explorer**.

If you have a Microsoft-style keyboard with the special Windows Logo Key on it, you can very quickly open Windows Explorer by the key combination **Windows Logo Key + E.**

An alternate way to access Windows Explorer is to put a permanent shortcut for it on your desktop (or toolbar). You can do this by opening the **Start | Programs** menu and right-dragging **Windows Explorer** to the desktop (or to the toolbar) and then choosing **Create Shortcut Here** from the context menu that pops up.

Viewing and opening directories and files

Anyway, once you start Windows Explorer, it opens up a Windows Directory window which may either be in the **Classic Style** view or the **Web Style** view; you can select between these on the **View | Folder Options | General** controls. You can also choose a mix of the two called **Custom**, and adjust this using the Settings dialog. You can really customize the Explorer view quite extensively. It takes a certain amount of playing with it to find the settings you like the best. Some more of these are under **View | Folder Options | View** menu of the Windows Explorer.

In any case, Windows Explorer will show you two panes: in the left will be a list of directories; on the right will be a list of the directories and files in the directory that's currently selected on the left. You use the left pane to navigate to the directory you are interested in.

The right pane shows the files in the directory, when they were last changed, and what their size is. That is, it will show all this information assuming that you check the Windows Explorer menu option **View | Details**. You should also make sure that the box labeled **Hide File Extensions for Known Types** is *not* checked, as it is useful for a programmer to see the file extensions. This box will be in a submenu or dialog, depending on which version of Windows you have.

If you click on one of the files in the right window, Windows will try to 'open' the file. Traditionally a double-click was required. If you do a lot of programming, double-clicking can get quite tiring, even to the point of promoting repetitive stress disorder, so it's really worth avoiding having to do it. Explorer will be set so that a single-click activates a file or opens a directory if you are using the Web style view. If you are not using the Web style view, you can still open files with a single-click by selecting **View | Folder Options | Custom Style** and then clicking the Settings button to get to a dialog where you can choose single-click instead of double-click.

If the file is an executable, 'opening' it means running it, while if it is a text file it will be opened up in an application like WordPad. If the file is source code, Windows is likely to start a session of your compiler and open the file up inside of that. If Windows doesn't know what application to use to open the file, it will ask you what to do.

Copying directories and files

Windows Explorer is also useful for creating new directories. If you right-click in the right-hand part of the window you get a menu in which you can select **New**, and then you can select **Directory** and name the new directory. Or you can use the **File | New | Directory** selection from the Windows Explorer menu.

Note that you can repeatedly open Windows Explorer sessions (for instance by repeatedly pressing **Windows Logo Key + E**), so that you can have several of these windows open. Generally it's convenient to keep one or several Windows Explorer sessions open at all times. You can minimize them into your task bar when not using them.

You can use the Explorer windows to move or to copy files. You can move a file by dragging it from one Explorer window to another. If you want to copy a file without removing it from the source directory, hold down the **Ctrl** key while you do the drag. A less stressful method is to select the files to copy or move and to then use the keyboard shortcuts **Ctrl+C** for copy or **Ctrl+X** for cut in the source directory, followed by **Ctrl+V** for paste in the target directory.

There are other methods as well. For the sake of your body, you should try to learn to do what you want in the least physically stressful way.

Avoiding a Visual Studio gotcha

When you are working on a project, you should maintain an Explorer window that shows what is in the directory where you are keeping your source code. This is so you don't lose track of which files you are working on. Make sure you can see the time and date stamps for the files, and reassure yourself that these match the time and date when you are doing the changes.

In Microsoft Visual Studio the 'Solution Explorer' window (Workspace window in Version 6.0) does not show the directory paths of the files you are working on, so if you're not careful you can end up editing the wrong copy of a file, especially if there are several copies of the files with the same name.

If you open your files with the File | Open | File... dialog [which is just File | Open... in Version 6.0], you will in fact see a directory path name in the top of the dialog, but it's quite easy to overlook this information. And it sometimes happens that when you ask Visual Studio to open a file it will by default go to the most recently used directory rather than to the directory where your active project lives.

One bad thing that can happen is that you keep changing code and the project keeps building without errors, but the behavior never changes: this is because you are editing files in a different directory from the directory you are building from.

A different bad thing that can happen is that, after working in Visual Studio for a while and closing it, you may think that the files you just worked on are in, say, **C:\MyProject\Version1**, when in fact all along they were in **J:\Program Files\Hidden\Bogus\Version1**, and when you copy the files from the first directory to hand in for your homework or to share with a friend, you find you've copied the wrong thing.

As with most programming mistakes, everyone does this at least once. The secret of becoming an expert programmer is to grow and to learn, so that you don't make the same mistakes over and over again. And keeping an Explorer window open onto your project code helps make this error less likely.

20.2   Which version?

One key part of a project's software requirement is deciding which operating system you want to develop for, and which compiler you are going to use.

It is customary to develop any substantial program within a graphically interfaced environment where you select your compiler and linker settings from dialog boxes, edit your code with word-processing tools, and edit your resources with graphics tools. An IDE (Integrated Development Environment) is also expected to have online help and a full array of debugging tools. Sometimes people also call an IDE a compiler, though really it's more than that.

We are going to write code which can be used to build programs for the ever-more-numerous Microsoft Windows platforms: Windows 95, Windows 98, Windows NT, Windows 2000, Windows Millennium Edition, Windows XP, and so on.

Which compiler?

In order to build the kinds of Windows applications we're going to discuss, you need a C++ compiler which has libraries for implementing the many special Windows functions. These special functions are called the Windows API. The standard compiler for this purpose is the compiler from Microsoft, which their marketeers have variously called Visual C++, Visual Studio, and Visual Studio.NET. Visual Studio.NET can also be called Visual Studio, Version 7.0.

Various smaller companies give Microsoft some competition in this market, but the Microsoft compiler has overwhelmingly become the industry standard. If you're serious about wanting to write Microsoft Windows programs you should use the Microsoft compiler. Writing Windows programs is not the place for anti-monopolistic scruples. The competing compilers tend not to be so well tested and supported as is Visual Studio. And if you ever want a job as a Windows programmer, it's going to be Visual Studio your employer expects you to know. Time spent wrestling with other manufacturers' compilers for the Windows platform is time down the drain.

Visual Studio versions

Microsoft often releases different versions of Visual Studio at different price levels. Sometimes the less-expensive packages will in fact be an older release; you need to look at the fine print on the box to see what's actually in there. For the purposes of the code in the Pop Framework, any version from the older Version 6.0 or the newer Version 7.0 (also known as Visual Studio.NET) is acceptable. If you are working with a team, you will improve your code compatibility by all using the same release.

One issue to keep in mind is that Visual Studio.NET makes more hardware demands upon your machine than does Visual Studio, Version 6.0, so it may not be possible for you to run Visual Studio.NET until you eventually get a more powerful computer.

Visual Studio.NET is marketed in the following increasingly expensive editions: 'Academic,' 'Professional,' 'Enterprise Developer,' 'Enterprise Architect.' For the purposes of working with the C++ code of the Pop Framework we discuss in *Software Engineering and Computer Games*, all of these editions are equivalent. In particular, note that the Academic edition is exactly the same as the Professional edition, but with some additional sample code. The Enterprise Architect comes with some UML modeling tools that could be useful. The Academic version may only be readily available at college and university bookstores to students with valid student IDs.

[Visual Studio 6.0 was marketed in a 'Learning' version, a 'Professional' version, and an 'Enterprise' version. Here the Learning version was 'crippled,' that is, it lacked two commercially important features. (a) The Professional and Enterprise versions included more *code optimization* features, so that you could better instruct it to build a faster, or smaller, version of your program. And (b) the Professional and Enterprise versions allowed you to build programs with either the *static MFC library* or the *dynamic MFC library*, while the Learning version only offered the dynamic MFC library. The ability to use the static MFC library has the effect of making programs able to run on a wider range of Windows platforms. We'll explain more about this point later. Feature (a) is important if you write a program where you want to get as much speed as possible, and feature (b) is important if you plan to give (or sell!) your program to others, or plan to run it on a variety of machines. Note again, however, that in the case of Visual Studio.NET, the Academic edition *does* have both feature (a) and feature (b), in other words the Visual Studio.NET Academic edition is *not* crippled.]

All this varies from release to release and from year to year, so you may need to study the fine print on the box to be sure exactly what you're getting.

At commercial software stores there is a substantial (hundreds of dollars) price difference between the different versions of Visual Studio. It may not be worth the extra money to get anything other than the least expensive version if you're just starting to learn programming.

Another factor to be aware of is that, as mentioned above, many college and university bookstores sell lower cost versions of Visual Studio. The Academic version of Visual Studio.NET seems at this time to be a good choice in terms of being a complete and non-crippled package. But if your store has a higher-end version for the same or only a bit more money, you may want to get that.

Another option available at some college or university bookstores is for registered students to *rent* the install disks for some version of Visual Studio for a few days at some fairly low price, with the understanding that the rental gives them a Microsoft-authorized license to install and register the software on a computer.

Microsoft Foundation Classes

As well as being a C++ compiler, the Microsoft Visual Studio includes a special set of classes called the MFC. The purpose of using these classes is to make it easier to develop full-featured Windows programs. We're going to use MFC in all the programs in this book. In principle we could avoid using MFC, but MFC makes the programmer's life a bit easier and gives you a bit more leverage over the code. Code size is isn't as much of an issue as it used to be – at least not for personal computers. Of course if you were to write a game for a very small platform such as a cell phone, then you'd need to strip things down as much as possible. And some game companies prefer not using MFC because they perceive it as adding unnecessary complexity.

Speaking of MFC, note that Microsoft allows competing compiler manu-facturers to distribute the MFC libraries and documentation, so theoretically you can also make MFC Windows programs with a non-Microsoft compiler. But, as already mentioned above, this isn't a wise investment of your time and energy.

Dealing with change

Deciding which compiler and which libraries to use is something that can be debated very intensely at the beginning of a team software project. A reality is that people are usually going to push to use the compiler that *they* are familiar with. If you need to switch to a new compiler or a new version, do it quickly and quietly instead of wasting energy fighting the inevitable. It's not necessary to be the first to upgrade to the new version of Visual Studio as soon as it comes out, as it will be buggy. But some six months after the first release of the compiler, the customary Service Patch 1 will be out, and the worst bugs will be fixed. This is the time to upgrade and get it over with for a year or two. Always remember that change is a fact of life in software engineering. Being a software engineer is like being an athlete who has to continually train to stay in shape.

At some point in your programming career you will not only have to switch compiler packages, you'll have to switch to a completely new operating system as well – maybe Linux will take over next, or maybe something else. The best strategy is to get to work and just do it. When switching compilers or operating systems, try and find a person you can talk to face to face and ask the inevitable 'dumb questions' that somehow fail to be addressed in any of the available documentation. A fair amount of software engineering knowledge seems to be transmitted orally, rather than being communicated in any written form.

Remember that if you act enthused about the change rather than resentful or depressed, people will be more likely to help you. People who resist and grumble about change are correctly viewed as losers. The essence of being a software engineer is this: *grow or die*.

Visual Studio, Version 6 versus Visual Studio.NET, Version 7

The author has worked a fair amount with Visual Studio.NET, Version, 7.0 now, and would like to advise the reader that there is in fact no pressing need to switch to this product from Visual Studio, Version 6.0.

First and foremost, Version 6.0 is more stable. As of spring, 2002, one can expect any prolonged session with Visual Studio.NET to end in a crash. This is because Version 6.0 has been out for a long time and now has five service patches. Once enough service packs for Visual Studio.NET are available, it too will be stable.

Visual Studio.NET lacks some nice features that came with Version 6.0. In particular there is no Profiler. And, to the author's eyes, the .NET Properties dialogs for resources aren't as nicely designed, nor do they include as much useful help. But switching to .NET is inevitable.

A galling negative about Visual Studio.NET is the following gotcha. *Any executable built with Visual Studio.NET must be able to find the oleacc.dll file on the host computer, or it will not run.* And, unlike the situation with the MFC libraries that you can link in, linking in the oleacc.lib to your project file will *not* remove this problem! Older machines don't have oleacc.dll, and your executable won't run on them.

The oleacc.dll has to do with 'Object Linking and Embedding Access.' This file will be on computers with newer versions of Windows, and on computers with older versions of Windows that have appropriate upgrade patches installed. You won't have a problem on newer machines.

Given that the Pop framework doesn't *use* OLE, it's annoying to have the Visual Studio.NET compiler produce an executable that demands it. In a few years, this problem won't matter much, because by then there won't be many machines left with old, unpatched versions of Windows. But for now, if you want to distribute an executable that will painlessly run on everyone's Windows machines, build it with Version 6.0, and not with Visual Studio.NET.

20.3   The Visual Studio user interface

If you haven't done so yet, use Windows Explorer to find the Pop code, and click on the **pop.sln** file to start up Visual Studio if you are using Visual Studio.NET [or the **pop.dsw** file if you are using Version 6.0].

Note that Appendix C summarizes information about specific Visual Studio controls in Visual Studio.NET, Version 7.0, and Visual Studio, Version 6.0.

Appearance of the interface for Visual Studio.NET, Version 7.0

You'll see several windows inside the Visual Studio window, as illustrated in the screenshot. The largest window is a Document window for showing your code. There will eventually be tabs along the top of this window with one tab corresponding to each code file that you have open. We'll refer to a horizontal (or vertical) bar upon which tabs rest as a *tab group*.

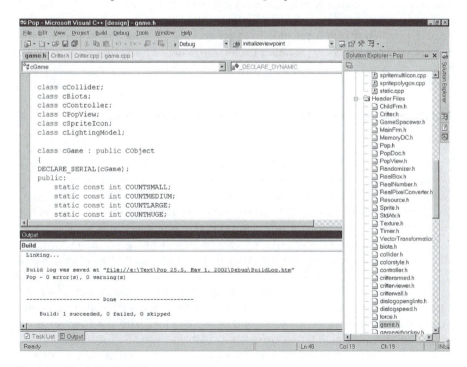

The new Visual Studio.NET

There will probably be an Output window near the bottom, where you can view such things as compiler and linker messages. If this window isn't immediately present, it will appear once you build your code. Or you can open it with **View | Other Windows | Output Window**.

Other windows may also appear near the bottom of the screen. And there will be a tab-select bar along the bottom of the screen with tabs in order to keep track of which of these windows is currently 'on top.'

There may also be a number of windows along the right- or left-hand side of the main window. The View menu will open up more of them.

The multiple windows along the edges are attached to *vertical* tab groups, one on the left and one on the right.

The tabs on the vertical tab groups shrink to button size when their associated window is not the active window. You can change the active window on a vertical tab group by moving your mouse over the buttons on the tab group.

On the horizontal tab groups at the bottom and top of the screen, you select a window by clicking on its tab rather than simply moving the mouse over the tab.

Each of the windows along the sides and bottom of the Visual Studio.NET interface has a 'pushpin' button that you can use to either make the window stay open (pin pointing down) or to have the window only appear when you move the mouse over the window's tab in the toolbar (pin pointing sideways). The document viewing windows don't have the pushpin feature.

One special window you generally want to have open is the Solution Explorer, which makes it possible to easily access your code and to change the project settings. Use **View | Solution Explorer** in order to open this window so we can investigate some of the files in the Pop framework.

[Appearance of the interface for Visual Studio, Version 6.0]

[You'll see two or maybe three windows inside the Visual Studio window. On the upper left will be the Workspace window, on the upper right will be a Document pane where you can view help files or source-code files, and on the bottom there may be an Output window where you can view such things as compiler and linker messages. You can also open and close these two windows by using the **View | Workspace** and **View | Output** menu selections.

The Workspace and Output windows are usually 'docking' windows, meaning that they stay stuck to the sides of your main window. (Windows that aren't docked are called 'floating.')

The Workspace window has three tabs at the bottom, so you can select the **Class View**, the **File View**, or the **Info View**. The first shows the structure of the classes used in your project, the second shows the files, and the third shows a list of the Microsoft help books currently available to you.

Click on the **File View** tab of the Workspace window so that we can investigate some of the files in the Pop Framework.]

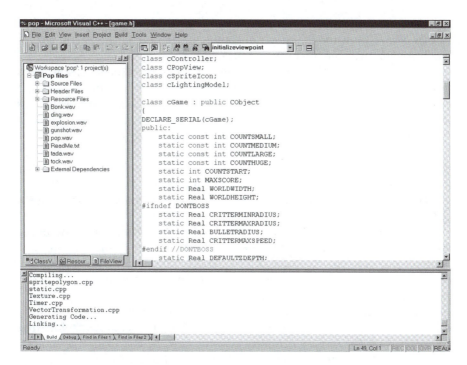

The tried and true Visual Studio, Version 6.0

Toolbars

There will be one or several toolbars at the top of the Visual Studio window. Sometimes Visual Studio may open up more toolbars than you want, thus eating up too much of your screen area, so you may want to close some of them down. You can control which toolbars are visible by right-clicking in the toolbar area and checking or unchecking various boxes.

Exploring the project files

Suppose now that you are looking at the Solution Explorer window in Visual Studio.NET [or at the File View of the Workspace (Version 6.0)].

Whenever you see an entry with a plus sign next to it, that means you can click it to see more. You'll see source files, header files, resource files and some free-standing *.wav sound files.

Look into the source and header files folders. Whoah! There's so many of them! How are you ever going to learn to use MFC and the Pop Framework?

Stay calm. Don't panic. In order to build on other people's code you need to be comfortable with a certain level of ignorance. You need to accept that the Pop Framework has given you this big stack of files and you may never get around to looking at all of them. This is a typical situation when you go to work at a company with an established code base. In the case of the Pop Framework, most of the files don't directly impinge on your near-term goal of building your own computer game project.

To get a quick overview of what the files are like, try double-clicking on a few of them. This opens them up in a text-editor in the document window, and you can scroll through them. One file worth looking at is ReadMe.txt, which has some short descriptions about what the special MFC files are all about. But at this point these short descriptions won't make much sense to you.

Sometimes you need to have *.obj or *.lib files as part of a project, for instance to support OpenGL or to support sound. We don't include these files in the File View. Instead we select the project and use the **View | Property Pages...** | **Linker | Input | Additional Dependencies** line [this is the **Project | Settings... | Link | Object/Library Modules** box in Version 6.0.]

One bad feature of the File View that you see in Solution Explorer [or in the File View of the Workspace pane (Version 6.0)] Studio Workspace window is that it doesn't state the directories where the files listed live. This can be dangerous if you have several versions of a file with the same name, as you can easily include a file from the wrong directory.

In Visual Studio.NET, you can check the directory for a file by highlighting it and using **View | Properties Window** to look at the Full Path field. Note that you don't want to use **View | Property Pages** to view the Full Path; the similarly named Properties Window and Property Pages are different dialogs.

[In Version 6.0, there is only one kind of Properties dialog for a file and it has a File Name field that shows the path. You can open this dialog by right-clicking the file and selecting **Properties** from the little menu that appears, or by pressing **Alt+Enter**. Note that in Visual Studio.NET, these actions will open Property Pages but not Properties.]

Output window messages

Once you've taken a look at some of the files which come with the Pop Framework, use the **Build | Build Pop.exe** selection to build Pop.exe. As the file builds you'll see a few messages down in the bottom of the screen in the Output pane that look something like the following. Depending on the processor speed of your machine and, more importantly, on how rapidly your machine can write intermediate files to its hard drive, the full build might take anywhere between a few seconds or several minutes.

Here's a copy of the output generated a while back, by building Pop version 21.

```
-----------------Configuration: Pop - Win32 Debug-----------------
Compiling resources...
Compiling...
StdAfx.cpp
Compiling...
biota.cpp
ChildFrm.cpp
```

```
colorstyle.cpp
[Lots more file names come here...]
Compiling...
VectorTransformation.cpp
Generating Code...
Linking...

Pop 21(Debug Build).exe - 0 error(s), 0 warning(s)
```

Yay! *0 errors, 0 warnings* is what you want to see.

If this doesn't work for you, look at the **Correcting Compiler and Linker Errors** subsection 20.5 below. If this *does* work for you, use the **Build | Execute Pop.exe** selection to get the program to run.

20.4   The Visual Studio help files

As well as special types, Windows MFC programming uses a lot of special classes, all of whose names start with uppercase C. There are scores of these classes, and they own perhaps thousands of function methods, and every time Windows is upgraded more of them are born.

A quick way to find help on some particular Windows expression such as a class or function name is to click on it in your code and then press **F1**. Another way is to select **Help | Index** and type it in. If you use **Help | Search** you will often get a lot more references than are practical to sift through, but if you need some really obscure kind of information, this is the way to go.

We should mention that, unless you have installed the documentation from your distribution CD onto your hard drive, you will only be able to access these reference books if the compiler package's distribution CD is in your CD ROM drive. If you have a lot of hard disk space and don't want to keep the CD in your drive, it's really worthwhile to install the help, also known as the 'Developer Library,' to your hard drive.

Visual Studio.NET comes with a nice help browser called Document Explorer. You'll find a shortcut to Document Explorer in the main Windows popup **Start | Programs | Visual Studio.NET**. The shortcut is a round blue circle with a question mark and is labelled Microsoft Visual Studio.NET Documentation. It's useful to drag or copy the shortcut to your desktop for easy access.

You can still open the help inside Visual Studio with the Help selection, but being able to access the help with a separate application is more convenient in terms of screen-space usage. Another issue is that (at least in early releases) the help system seems somewhat prone to crashing, so if you are running the help off in a separate application, you are less likely to drag down your session of Visual Studio as well.

Never try to do serious programming without having the help available.

Windows is so big and shaggy that nobody can possibly know it all. Get in the habit of using the help a *lot*. Every time you use it, you're likely to find out something you didn't know.

If you are on a network, the online help is only going to be available if your sysop has installed it on the server and has correctly tweaked your compiler's directory configuration. If the online help doesn't work, keep nagging your local authorities until it *does* work. Let's repeat it again:

> It's a brutal waste of time to try and program without having help available.

As mentioned above, the easiest way to find help on some particular class or function name is to highlight it and press **F1** or to type it into the **Help | Index** dialog. One word of caution here. When you do **Help | Search** for a function name, the bottom of the dialog will show several possible places to look for help. If you search for 'ellipse', for instance, you'll see two entries like this.

```
CDC::Ellipse    Microsoft Foundation Class Library and Templates
Ellipse    GDI : Platform SDK
```

And for some other keywords you'll see more kinds of entries. The various Microsoft Foundation Class entries are the ones we'll be interested in here.

20.5 Correcting compiler and linker errors

What if nothing seems to happen when you try to build and run your version of the Pop program? First make sure you can see the Output window, which is where your compiler errors are listed. If you can't find it, use a **Windows | Other Windows | Output** to open it [**Windows | Output** (Version 6.0)].

Then resize the Output window so you can see what's in there. Double-clicking on a compiler error will call up the Source-Code window with the cursor on the line where the error is. Locate the erroneous line and see if there's an obvious typo.

If not, go back and look at the error message. *Read all of the error message. Think about what it says.* Believe it or not, the message is trying to help you. In its own way, it's saying 'try this,' and not just, 'you're wrong.' If the message doesn't make sense to you, click on the error message and press **F1** to get information about it.

Go back to the Source-Code window and look at the line with the error again. If you're unsure about the usage of any of the API functions there, highlight them and press **F1** to get their documentation.

One thing that happens sometimes is that an error early in a code module causes a cascade of many more error messages further down. Generally, you should start trying to fix the errors from the beginning. If you fix a few errors and get to errors that don't seem to make sense, try to rebuild the program and/or recompile the module and see if some of them go away.

If you have an error that refuses to go away, skip over it and fix some of the later errors if you can. Maybe while you're working your subconscious will figure out what was wrong up above.

Let's repeat the key teaching we have to impart here:

> When fixing an error, READ the error message and THINK ABOUT what it says.

One tends to not want to read an error message, as it's bad news, but this is a mistake. The message is trying to help you! An error message is not your enemy, it's your friend. It's trying to save you from your own mistakes!

If you get a zillion error messages saying things aren't found, that means there are some files missing from your project file or from the directory where your project lives. Not being able to find windows.h, for instance makes a lot of errors. You may need to check that the directory setting is correct.

Sometimes when working in a lab with the compiler on a remote server, your machine can't find the place on the server where the standard include files live. This may be what's going on if you get the zillion 'file not found' messages.

Microsoft Visual Studio keeps the information about which directories it searches on the **Tools | Options... | Projects | VC++ Directories** sheet [this is the **Tools | Options... | Directories** sheet in Version 6.0]. These settings are not part of your project file, they are part of the individual compiler installation. The all-important Include directories setting is found by selecting **Include Files** in the **Show Directories** for combo box on this sheet. Make sure that one of the selections here corresponds to where your compiler has its include subdirectory. If you are working in a lab, your compiler may be on a remote drive with a funny letter name like K: or M:. You can use Windows Explorer to go out across the network and find where the Visual Studio Include directory lives.

Even if you have the directories right, you will get a 'not found' linker error if there is some function you prototyped but forgot to add the code for. Look at the error closely to figure out which function is missing. The function name will be in a 'mangled' format, so it can be a little hard to decipher.

Once in a while Visual Studio will get confused or lose track of what you've been doing, and even though you have properly defined all of your functions, it will say that it can't find one of them. This can happen if for some reason Visual Studio doesn't realize that it needs to recompile some files. The way to fix this situation is to use the **Build | Rebuild All** option to force a rebuild of all files.

Invoking **Build | Rebuild All** can also help if Visual Studio seems unable to find a resource that you're fairly sure you've put in place. If the rebuild doesn't fix things, then the problem is probably you; that is, you need to recheck what you think you've done.

20.6   Release and Debug builds

In Visual Studio, you have the option of building two different versions of your executables: the Debug or the Release version. You can switch between the one and the other using the combo box in the Build toolbar (if this toolbar is visible), or by using **Build | Configuration Manager** [this is **Build | Set Active Configuration** with Version 6.0]. The default setting is for Visual Studio to build the Debug version.

The difference between the Debug and the Release version is that the Debug executable includes debugging information, which makes the *.exe considerably larger.

What *is* debugging information anyway? Well, when you make the binary version of a program, things like the English names of variables get thrown away, not to mention the text of the source code. But you need to be able to get back all this stuff if you are debugging the program.

When you debug a program it actually runs inside another program, the debugger itself. If your program crashes, the debugger will normally highlight the line where the crash happened. Note that programs do run a bit slower inside the debugger. But while you are developing a program you never know when it will crash, so it is usually best to be inside the debugger.

Ordinarily you want to build the Debug version while you are developing the program, and once you start to distribute it to other people, you will want to use the Release version. The reason why you want to distribute the Release version is that (a) it will be a smaller file than the Debug version, and (b) the Release version will run faster, sometimes as much as 30% faster.

If you look in your source-code directory after a build, you'll notice that there will be some subdirectories in addition to the res subdirectory: the Debug subdirectory and/or the Release subdirectory. The res subdirectory, of course, has the necessary resource files and was part of the source code. The Debug subdirectory and/or the Release subdirectory are put there by Visual Studio when you build the Debug and/or Release versions. In building these executables, Visual Studio makes a number of intermediate files that are stored in the corresponding subdirectories.

By default, Visual Studio will put the Debug and Release executables in the corresponding Debug and Release subdirectories. But the author has edited the project file so as to put the executables in the same location as the source code.

You can control the name and location of your output file by first opening **View | Solution Explorer** and making sure the Pop project is highlighted and then editing the **View | Property Pages...** | **Linker | Output File** line. [In Version 6.0, this is the **Project | Settings | Link | Output File Name** edit box.] The default might be **Debug\Pop.exe**, but if you want the code for the Debug executable to be with your source, you might enter something like **Pop 25_5(Debug Build).exe**.

How would you change the name and location of the Release executable to, say, **Pop 25_5(Release).exe**? Look at the upper left-hand corner of the Property Pages dialog box you just opened [called the **Settings** dialog box in Visual 6.0]. There is a little **Configuration** combo box that you can set to **Debug**, **Release**, or **All Configurations**. [The combo box is called **Settings** for in Version 6.0.] When you switch this selection between the **Debug** and the **Release** selection, you'll notice that the entries in the dialog box change. Changing this combo box changes which configuration's settings are being shown and possibly altered by the project **Property Pages** dialog box [called **Settings** dialog box in Version 6.0.]

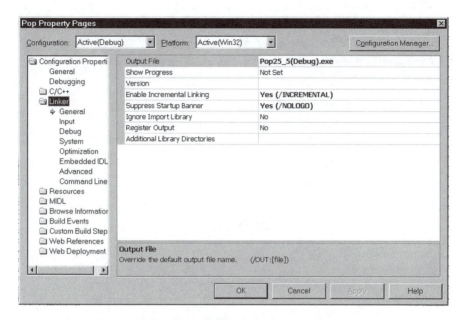

The Link project settings dialog in Visual Studio.NET

By the way, you might think that by changing the **active configuration** setting for the combo box, you might change which configuration was being built. This is not the case! The only way to change which version is being built is by using the completely separate dialog box **Build | Configuration Manager** [called **Build | Set Active Configuration** in Version 6.0].

20.7   Use MFC in static library or use MFC in shared DLL?

There are actually *four* different versions of the executable you might build. As well as choosing between the Debug and the Release build, you can either bind the ***.lib** version of the MFC code into your executable, or you can have your executable look for the ***.dll** version of the MFC code run time.

To control this, open **View | Solution Explorer** and make sure the Pop project is highlighted. Then select **View | Property Pages... | General**. [In Version 6.0, simply select **Project | Settings... | General**.] And then you can edit the **Use of MFC** field to be **Use MFC in a Static Library** or **Use MFC in a Shared DLL**. The DLL option is the Visual Studio default.

If you look at the Pop project settings, you'll notice that we've chosen to build the Release version with the static library option and the Debug version with the shared DLL option. What do these decisions mean, and why are they reasonable?

When you are using MFC, a lot of the code used by the program lives in external libraries. In Windows a library can have one of two forms, a *.lib file or a *.dll file. Code from a *.lib file gets linked into your executable, which makes

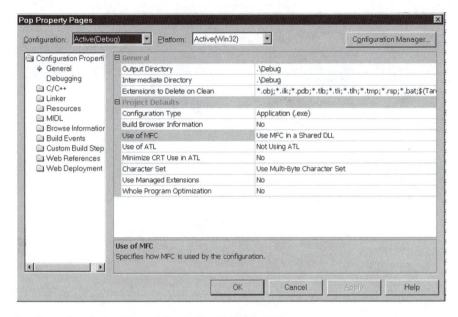

The General project settings dialog in Visual Studio.NET

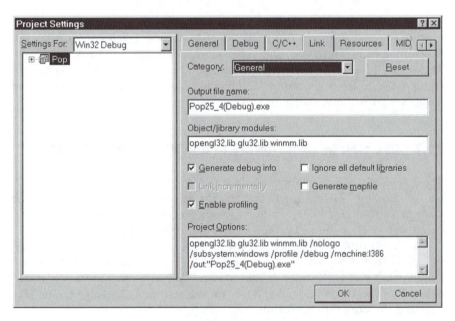

The Link project settings dialog in Visual Studio, Version 6.0

your executable bigger – about 1 Meg bigger in the case of an MFC program. Code from a *.dll file is left out of your executable, and when the executable starts up, it looks on the host computer's hard drive for a copy of the *.dll file it needs, and loads this code into RAM at that time.

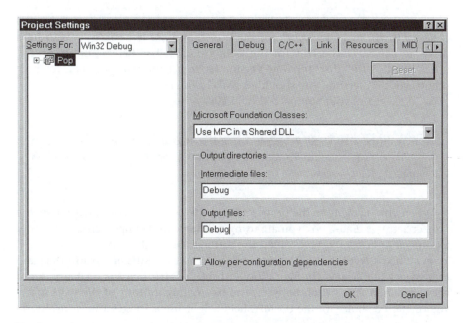

The General project settings dialog in Visual Studio, Version 6.0

If you have an MFC program that expects to find the MFC code in a DLL, when it tries to start up, it will be looking for a file with a name like MFC40.DLL or MFC42D.DLL or maybe MFC42.DLL. Now, Microsoft regularly changes the particular version of the MFC???.DLL distributed with Windows, so there is a very good chance that when you move your executable from your Windows machine to somebody else's Windows machine, your executable is not going to find the *.dll file it needs, and instead of running it's going to show the user a cryptic error message. And even if you give the user a copy of the missing *.dll file, you'll usually find that then there's yet *another* missing *.dll file that your program needs. And so on. Trying to distribute all the necessary *.dll is in fact too complicated to be practical.

It would seem, therefore, that you'd always want to use the MFC in a static library. But, as we already mentioned, using the static library makes the ***.exe** bigger. As an illustration, Table 20.1 shows the comparative sizes of the four different builds on the June 21, 2001, version of Pop code.

Table 20.1 Four ways to build an MFC executable.

Build configuration	Use MFC as	Size of exe
Debug	DLL	693 K
Debug	LIB	1917 K
Release	DLL	452 K
Release	LIB	744 K

You will be making lots of Debug builds on your machine as you develop the code, so it will make less work for the linker, and use less space on your hard drive, to use MFC as a DLL for the Debug builds. The Release build, on the other hand, is the 'distributable' version of your code that you plan to show others. For this version, you should use MFC as a LIB.

So, once again, your approach should always be

> Work with the *Debug configuration using the MFC as a DLL* while developing the product, and use the *Release configuration using the MFC as a LIB* when distributing the product.

When you navigate to the project's **Use of MFC** control as outlined above, the Project Settings dialog box you are using will have in its upper left-hand corner a **Configuration** combo box [called the **Settings For** combo box in Version 6.0]. You can first select the **Debug** configuration and set **Use MFC in a Shared DLL**, and then select the **Release** configuration and set **Use MFC in a Static Library**. From then on when you switch between the two configurations of the workspace, your preferred choice for the **Use MFC** field will be used. These settings are already in place for the Pop project.

[When using the Learning edition of Version 6.0, you don't have access to the **Use MFC in a Static Library** option. If you plan to distribute your ***.exe** to other people, you need to have either a 'Professional' or better edition of Version 6.0 or any version of Visual Studio.NET. Visual Studio.NET supports the **Static Library** feature across all of its editions.]

20.8 Cleanup

When you get through working on a program, you want to clean up the directories. The directory with your source code will have some files you don't need.

The *.opt, *.ncb and *.plg files (just to mention some examples) are what one might call 'mystery garbage files.' The Microsoft documentation doesn't seem to talk about the mystery garbage files. They reappear every time you compile the program. Bottom line is this: you can delete the *.opt, *.ncb and *.plg (and certain other garbage files) with impunity at the end of a day's programming. These files are just wasting disk space and will be automatically regenerated the next time you build the program. *Do* be sure to keep your source code, your *.dsw, and your *.dsp.

In addition, the Debug and/or Release directories in particular are going to have a lot of files in them that you don't need. First of all, they'll have a huge 'precompiled header' file with the *.pch extension, the intermediate *.obj files, and some additional junk files.

One way to clean up is to use the **Build | Clean** selection (its full name is **Build/Clean Solution** in Visual Studio.Net). If your configuration is set to **Debug**, this command will remove all the files in the Debug directory; If your configuration is set to **Release**, this command will remove all the files in the Release directory. But **Build | Clean** will not get rid of the various kinds of additional intermediate or support files that Visual Studio will write into your basic source-code directory.

Depending what kind of building, debugging, profiling, and so on you've been up to, there are a variety of these extraneous files that may be present. And you might as well delete the Debug and Release subdirectories once they're empty. Unfortunately, **Build | Clean** doesn't do all of this for you.

Instead of using the **Build | Clean** file selection, the author prefers to do a more thorough job of deleting things by using a batch file clean.bat that he keeps in the current project directory. You will find a copy of it in the Pop source-code directory.

If you double-click on this file in Windows Explorer it will run in 'console mode' (formerly known as DOS mode) and get rid of the extra files. Here's the contents of a typical version of the clean.bat file. You won't always have all of these kinds of files present, but depending on what you've been doing, any of them can occur.

```
REM Delete Garbage Files
del *.aps
del *.ilk
del *.map
del *.ncb
del *.opt
del *.plg
del *.pbi
del *.pbo
del *.pbt
del *.pdb
del *.tmp
del *._xe

REM Delete hidden archived garbage files, first changing their
REM attributes.
attrib -h -a *.gid
del *.gid

REM Optional: Delete Visual Studio Solution user options, which can be
REM useful to keep.
REM attrib -h -a *.suo
REM del *.suo

REM Delete Garbage Directories
del enc temp folder\*.*
rmdir enc temp folder
del DEBUG\*.*
rmdir DEBUG
```

```
del RELEASE\*.*
rmdir RELEASE

REM Optional: delete the executables that the project has written
REM to root.
REM del *.exe
```

In case you can reuse clean.bat for other projects, note that it's designed for the case where your *.exe files aren't saved in the Debug and the Release subdirectories (but are being saved in the source directory as pop.dsw is set to do).

Somewhat annoyingly, the del DEBUG*.* and del RELEASE*.* will pause and ask you in a DOS window if you really want to delete those files. You need to press y and **Enter**. Windows 98 has a **deltree** command that lets you do this in one step, but Windows NT doesn't support **deltree**.

Note that as the clean.bat paths are directory-relative, you need to put a copy of it into each of the new source-code directories that you work in.

The Pop project is set to put its ***.exe** builds into the same directory as the code. Although clean.bat could remove the executables with the del *.exe line, by default we comment this behavior out with the letters REM. The assumption is that you may want to cut and paste the *.exe to another location before zipping your directory.

20.9   Building blocks of a complete program

Now that we've talked about the mechanics of building a program, let's say a little more about the kinds of component files that go into making a Windows program.

First come the files which are involved in building the code of the main Windows executable.

- Project file: *.sln and *.vcproj [*.dsw and *.dsp in Version 6]
- Source-code files: *.cpp and *.c
- Header files: *.h
- Object code files: *.obj
- Static library files: *.lib
- Executable file: *.exe, and dynamic link library files: *.dll

Next come the files which are used for specifying the graphic user interface of the program.

- Resource files: *.rc, and compiled resource files: *.res

Finally we want to mention the files that are involved in creating the standard Windows help file.

- Help project files, source text files, and help files

Let's say a few words about each of these kinds of files.

Project files: *.sln **and** *.vcproj [*.dsw **and** *.dsp **(Version 6.0)]**

As we mentioned in Section 3.3, in order to build an executable file from a collection of source code and resource files, we need a *project* file to orchestrate how the files are to be combined. A Visual Studio project is described by two levels of files, a primary higher-level project file originally called a *workspace* file, and one or more secondary lower-level files simply called project files. Generically any or all of these kinds of files may occasionally be termed 'project files.'

Microsoft changed the standard file extensions for their project and workspace files when they replaced the Visual Studio, Version 6.0, by Visual Studio.NET, also known as Version 7.0. The older *.dsp and *.dsw are now *.vcproj and *.sln (see the table summarizing this in Section 3.3). Also Microsoft has replaced the word 'workspace' with 'solution.' But for the rest of this section, we will simply use 'workspace' file to mean either the older *.dsw file or the newer *.sln file.

Whenever you are building a program which uses more than one file, you need a project file to list the names of the various code modules that you will use. In addition to keeping a list of the component modules, a project file saves a rather large number of compiler and linker settings. These settings control such decisions as whether or not to include debugging information, whether to optimize the code for smaller size or for faster speed, how many kinds of warnings to display, and so on. The Microsoft project and solution [or workspace] files are in fact simple text files, and you can open them in your word-processor to see what's in there. Occasionally you can clear up a persistent problem more easily by a direct edit like this than by trying to get at the project files through the Visual Studio interface.

Source-code files: *.cpp **and** *.c

Source code files are ASCII text files which your C++ *code compiler* processes into binary object code.

Beginning programmers tend to want to put all of their code into one large module. It is in fact better to use many small modules. Generally you want to put all the functions of one type into one module together; this makes things easier to find. Another gain of using multiple modules is that, when you change something in your program, you only need to recompile the single, small module that you changed. Another reason not to use only one module is that, sooner or later, this module will get so big that the compiler will refuse to handle it.

The C++ language contains all of the C language. This means that any C code can also be regarded as C++ code. The convention is to use *.cpp (for 'C Plus Plus') as the file extension of C++ code modules. If you have a *.c module of C code, you can simply change the file's extension to *.cpp and then your file will be compiled as C++ code. In this book, we are only going to use C++ files, so from now on we'll assume that all of our source code files are *.cpp.

A peculiarity of MFC is that when you are doing an MFC build, every single *.cpp file must have as its very first line the line

```
#include "stdafx.h"
```

If you leave out this line, you will get a confusing error message.

Header files: *.h

A header file is a file which is included into another file by lines like this.

```
#include "types.h"
#include <windows.h>
```

If the file name after #include is in quotes, the compiler will look for the file in the directory where the project file lives; and if the include file is in pointy brackets, the compiler will look for the file in whatever directories the project file has set to be places to look for include files – typically the standard location for include files is the INCLUDE subdirectory of the directory where the compiler lives, but sometimes you will want to add other directories to the standard search path.

The #include directive is a preprocessor directive; it tells the compiler to do something before running. What the #include directive tells the compiler to do is to replace the #include "whatever.h" line with a full, exact copy of the Whatever.h file, just as if you had used your text editor to block copy the whole Whatever.h file and paste it in.

Note that the compiler is not sensitive to the case of the letters used in the names of the include files.

In general any line of C++ that starts with # is a preprocessor directive; we have more information about these in Chapter 22: Topics in C++.

In C++, we put the definitions of our classes in header files with extension *.h, and we put the code implementing the classes' methods in *.cpp files. Some programmers like to use the file extension *.hpp for these files, but this practice is discouraged by the Microsoft compiler and is not very common.

Another use for header files is to **#define** some macros or compiler switches in a header file, and to include this in many different files. We also sometimes **typedef** type variables in a header. And headers can also be used to **#define** labels for things such as buttons in dialog boxes.

Many headers include header files themselves. For each header file, we list the names of the header files which are included by a line like #include "critter.h" as well as the names of the classes that are declared by a forward class declaration like class cGame. The best practice is to only include a header in a header when we really have to, for instance if the header mentions an instance or method of a class that's defined in another header. If the header only mentions a pointer to a class instance, then just a forward declaration will do.

There are two problems you can get when we **#include** header files: the circular include and the double include.

The circular include happens like this. If A includes B and B includes A, then A includes A, so the compiler will go into an endless loop when it tries to compile A. Let's go over this again. Suppose you have a circular.h file whose first line is `#include "circular.h"`. When the preprocessor tries to handle this, it will get into an endless regress. It must replace the first line of the file with a copy of the file in which it must replace the first line by a copy in which, etc. Usually, of course, a circular include isn't quite this obvious. You might for instance have a chicken.h file that starts out with the line `#include "egg.h"` and an egg.h file that starts out with the line `#include "chicken.h"`. But the same infinite regress will arise. When you have a circular include the compiler will give you some odd error messages, but it won't flat-out tell you that a circular include is your problem.

The way to avoid circular includes is to be very stingy about putting include statements. Don't use them unless you really have to. If possible, put your include statements into the *.cpp files rather than into the *.h files. If all you need is a pointer to a class called, say, **SomeClass**, you can just put the line `class SomeClass;` into your header file rather than a full `#include "someclass.h"`. The line `class SomeClass;` alerts the compiler that you will eventually define a class with this name without specifying yet what it will look like. And you can put the `#include "someclass.h"` into the **.cpp** file where you actually need to use the inner details of **SomeClass**.

The double include happens if you happen to include the same header file twice. This can cause problems because if, for instance, a class is defined in the included header file, then including the file twice means you have two definitions of the same class, and the compiler won't allow this. To avoid double includes, we use the **#define** and **#ifdef** as discussed in Section 22.15.

If any *.cpp file happens to include some header file twice, you'll get a lot of error messages. The compiler will be upset because you are 'redefining' things that you've already defined. To prevent this from happening, you should make a habitual, automatic practice of including two standard lines at the start of each header file, and one standard line at the end. The lines to use in, for instance, ANYHEADER.H, should be as follows.

```
//--------------------ANYHEADER.H START------
#ifndef ANYHEADER_H
#define ANYHEADER_H
...
#endif //ANYHEADER_H
//--------------------ANYHEADER.H END------
```

The idea is that the first time you hit ANYHEADER.H it gets included, and if you try and include it again, ANYHEADER_H is already defined so then the code gets skipped over.

As a matter of interest, you may be wondering how it could happen that you would include the same *.h file twice. It could happen like this: your main module might use two classes, a *cWorld* class and a *cCritter* class, and it could be that there is a special *cVector* class which is used both in the definition of the *cCritter* class and in the definition of the *cWorld* class. You would put definitions for these classes in, respectively, a World.h, a Critter.h, and a Vector.h file. And your Critter.h and your World.h files might each have this line:

```
#include "Vector.h"
```

When the preprocessor goes over Critter.h or over World.h, it will actually replace that line by a full copy of the Vector.h file.

Meanwhile, your **View** or **Doc** module will have these lines:

```
#include "World.h"
#include "Critter.h"
```

Now, when the preprocessor works on theses two lines it replaces the first `#include` line by a copy of World.h, and replaces the second `#include` line by a copy of Critter.h. But, as mentioned above, the World.h file includes a full copy of the Vector.h file, and so does Critter.h. So your main module gets two full copies of Vector.h. And then the compiler complains because it looks as if your *cVector* class is getting defined twice. This is why the `#ifndef` trick is needed!

One specific header file which is used by every MFC program is called StdAfx.h. You might do well to open up and look at the StdAfx.h in the Pop Framework; there are some useful comments in there.

Any normal program is going to have lots of different files, and it's important to be including the same version of, say, afxwin.h in all of the different modules. It's a wise practice to have the `#include afxwin.h` line inside of a StdAfx.h file that everyone includes, so that everyone will have the same switch settings turned on before the `#include afxwin.h` and other include lines. As we mentioned above, when we use MFC, every single anyfile.cpp in the MFC is actually required to start with `#include "stdafx.h"`.

A note on precompiled header files

Many of your files include the same header files as other files. Visual Studio speeds up the build process by saving off a 'precompiled header file' with the *.pch extension, writing this to either the **Debug** or the **Release** subdirectory. Having the precompiled header file available avoids having to recompile code for each lines of the form, say, `#include stdafx.h`.

The *.pch file is quite large (on the order of ten megabytes), so it's important not to leave old *.pch files on your hard drive. Be sure and run our clean.bat file to remove it when you're done or use the **Build | Clean Solution** [which is **Build | Clean** in Version 6.0].

If you are running MFC over a network, be sure to copy your code and project files to the local machine's hard drive (perhaps the **C:\Temp** drive if you're in a lab). Build your program on the local hard drive only. When you are done for the day, close Visual Studio, clean your code, and copy it back up to your network drive.

The reason you want to build on the *local* drive is that doing an MFC build involves writing that ten megabyte precompiled header file someplace, and you don't want that place to be at the other end of a (possibly slow) network wire.

Object code files: *.obj

Your compiler package has a C++ Code compiler which converts your text *.cpp files into binary *.obj executable code files. Once all your modules have been compiled to make *.obj files, your *linker* combines these *.obj files and some *.lib files together to make an executable *.exe file.

There are three alternative ways you can ask your compiler to compile a file. You can **Compile**, **Build** or **Rebuild All**. You'll find these options on the **Build** menu for both Visual Studio .NET and Visual Studio Version 6.0.

We summarize these options below.

- **Compile current.cpp.** Compile only the file currently in the edit window. The Developer Studio helpfully puts the name of this file right into the menu selection; here we write 'current.cpp' to stand for the name.

- **Build current.exe.** Compile all *.cpp source code files whose *.obj files are out of date, and link these together into a new executable. Again, the Developer Studio fills in the name of the current target executable.

- **Rebuild All** Compile all *.cpp files in the project list, whether or not they are out of date, and link these together into a new executable.

To understand the distinction between the second two selections, you need to understand the idea of a *.obj file being 'out of date.' A compiled ***.obj** file is said to be out of date if (a) it doesn't exist yet, or (b) you have recently made any changes to the source code files used for this particular compiled file. The source-code files used to make, say, current.obj, will include not only current.cpp, but also any header file which current.cpp accesses by means of a #include. The #include relation is transitive; that is, if current.cpp has #include "critter.h" and Critter.h has #include "point.h", then both **Critter.h** *and* **Vector.h** are viewed as source-code files used to make current.obj. If you change **Vector.h**, then current.obj becomes out of date.

How exactly does the compiler package tell if a *.obj is out of date? The compiler's text editor affixes a fresh date and time stamp to a file every time you change it. In addition, the compiler affixes a date and time stamp to each compiled *.obj or *.res file. By comparing source code files like current.cpp, Critter.h, and Vector.h to the compiled object version current.obj, the compiler can see if the source code, or one of its include files, has a date and time later than the date and time of the compiled file of the same name. If this is the case, then the *.obj file is out of date and needs to be recreated by a compile operation.

When you ask for a compile or a build, the C++ compiler will save all open files, and check dates on the header `#include` files. It expects to find them either (a) in the directory where your current project file lives, or (b) in the INCLUDE subdirectory of the directory where your compiler lives.

A problem that most programmers will run into at least once a year is that somehow one of your source code files will get a bad date on it, a date which is off sometime in the future. Every time you go to build your program, the compiler will look at that file and say, 'This source file has a date stamp later than the date stamp on my most recent *.obj file based on it, therefore the source file must have changes in it, so I have to recompile and make a fresh *.obj.' If the file with the bad date happens to be a header file that's included in a lot of other files, then all of those files will be rebuilt as well. This is mystifying and time-consuming. When you work on a team, there will sometimes be one particular team member whose machine puts bad dates on your source files; this can be because this individual has carelessly let his or her machine's calendar get set to some crazy year date like 2100.

The fix for the bad date problem is, first of all, to get the right date onto your files by opening them, making a trivial change (such as typing a space and then deleting it) and then saving the file. (Or you can do this from the outside if you happen to have access to the Unix **touch** utility.) Second of all, try and eliminate the source of the bad date problem. Make sure that all your team members have computers set to the correct date, and check the time too, as a bad time can sometimes cause the same kinds of problems.

If your compiler can't find the include files you will get a lot of error messages at the compile stage; usually the first one will say something like 'windows.h not found.' This is might happen, for instance, if you are running your compiler over a network. To fix this problem, you need to explicitly tell your project where to find the **INCLUDE** subdirectory of the directory where the compiler lives.

In Microsoft Visual Studio, you can set the **INCLUDE** directory by opening the **Tools | Options** dialog and going to the **Directories** tab. On the **Show directories for...** drop-down box, select **Include files**. Then type in the correct drive and directory. If you're not sure what the correct directory is, minimize the compiler package and use Windows Explorer (File Manager in Windows 3.1) to find out where the compiler package lives.

Static library files: *.lib

Once your C++ compiler has turned your source code modules into *.obj files, these files need to be linked together to make up a full executable *.exe file. The tool that accomplishes this is called the *linker*, and it is part of your compiler package.

The linker needs more than what it will find in your *.obj files. It also needs the definitions of all the various standard C and Windows functions that you used without writing code for. These function definitions are found in *.lib files that come with your compiler package.

You don't need to specifically list the names of the necessary *.lib files in your project file listing; in fact usually you won't know these names by heart. The linker will go out and look for the *.lib files it needs on your hard drive. Ordinarily it expects to find them in the LIB subdirectory of the directory where your compiler lives.

If your linker can't find the libraries you will get a lot of "Unresolved external..." error messages at the link stage, saying that various functions are not defined. As with the INCLUDE directory, this is most likely to happen if you are running your compiler package over a network, for instance in a student lab. To fix this problem, you need to explicitly tell your project where to find the LIB subdirectory of the directory where the compiler lives.

Note, however, that if you only get one or two "Unresolved external..." message this probably just means that you forgot to put code for some of your methods.

In Microsoft Visual Studio, you can edit the directory paths as described in the table in Appendix C. Once you have the **Directories** dialog open, you can select **Library files**. On the **Show directories for...** drop-down box, select **Library files**. Then type in the correct drive and directory. As before, if you're not sure what the correct directory is, minimize the compiler package and use Windows Explorer to find out where the compiler package lives.

Executable files: *.exe, and dynamic link library files: *.dll

When you build a Windows project, there are actually two successive *.exe files that get made. First is the 'usual' kind of *.exe that is gotten by linking together the *.obj and *.lib files. Then a 'special' *.exe is made by adding in the resource code, as we describe in the next subsection.

Before doing that, let's say a little about *.dll files (for 'Dynamic Link Library'). Instead of putting shared function code into each *.exe file, you can leave it in a *.dll file on your hard drive and hope that your *.exe can find the *.dll whenever it needs one of the functions whose code is in them. It's common, for instance, for programs to use standard Windows *.dll code for managing the dialog boxes used to open and to save files. When all goes well, this is painless and invisible.

Ordinarily the *.dll files will be found in your Windows directory or in the System or System32 subdirectories of your Windows directory. But sometimes they are not found, and the program dies at start-up with something like a 'file not found' message.

When you use the MFC, there are a number of special function implementations which you can bind into your *.exe as *.lib files. An alternate approach is to let the *.exe dynamically look for the function code on the host computer at run time. In this alternate case, your *.exe will look for the missing code among the computer's various dynamic link libraries, which have the *.dll extension. It is not a good idea to distribute code that looks for MFC libraries in *.dll files. The reason is that many poeple will have the latest MFC *.dll files on their computer and an exe that depends on these dynamic link libraries will be unable to run.

For distribution, always bind in the *.lib files rather than expecting your users to have the right *.dll. Testing your release on a range of other machines will point out this issue if you've forgotten about it.

A completely different topic regarding *.dll files is that you can arrange it so that users of your package can create their own *.dll files so as to add on pieces of code to your program, and make your product more programmable. See the SJSU Capow code for an example of this, at http://www.mathcs.sjsu.edu/capow.

Resource description files: *.rc and compiled resource files *.res

Like a C++ file, a *.rc resource description file is an ASCII text file. The *resource compiler* turns a *.rc file into a binary file that represents such graphical user interface features as: menus, dialog boxes, bitmaps, and program icons.

The compiled version of a *.rc file is called a *.res file. This is analogous to the way in which the C++ compiler turns a *.cpp text file into a binary *.obj file of machine code.

Once you have the *.res file, the resource compiler can then be called again, and this time it performs a linker-like task and attaches the *.res file to the executable *.exe file to make a new *.exe file that includes the desired resources, the dialogs, menus, bitmaps, etc.

The resource compiler is called RC.EXE and it comes with your compiler package. Normally your *.rc file is part of your project file list, and the resource compiler gets called automatically when you build your program using, for instance, the **Build | Build** or **Build | Rebuild All** selections in the Visual Studio.

To design your *.rc file, you use a tool called a Resource Editor which comes with your compiler package. This tool is of the WYSIWYG (for 'What You See Is What You Get') variety – you create the dialog boxes and so on for your *.rc file by dragging around buttons, checkboxes, edit boxes, scroll-bars and the like.

If you open a *.rc file by double-clicking on it, the compiler package will run the *.rc file through the resource compiler and give you the WYSIWYG view. Once in a while you may want to edit a *.rc file as a text file. To do this, you need to use the **File | Open** dialog to open the *.rc file, and you have to select the **Text** option in the **Open As** combo box at the bottom of the box. This is a good idea if you want to check up on exactly how your resources are being defined, or if you want to quickly makes copies of a large number of items.

Your *.rc resource file will define a lot of buttons and menu items. Each of them has an identifier number that is associated with a mnemonic ID that normally starts with 'IDR_'. There are a lot of #define statements that associate the IDs with the integers, and these statements live in a header file which is usually called Resource.h. Rather than looking into the Resource.h file directly, you usually use **View | Resource Symbols...** to work with it. Due to the way MFC treats messages, you usually don't really need to worry too much about the ID symbols in any case. The reason is that you usually use MFC to add a 'message handler' function for each menu item or button without having to actually know the name or value of the associated ID.

Help project file: *.hpj, rich text files *.rtf, and help files *.hlp

As well as the C++ code compiler and the resource compiler, there is a third kind of compiler, the *help compiler*. The help compiler is used to build help files, which have the extension *.hlp. The help compiler is invoked through a Windows interface called the Help Workshop. The help compiler needs a help project file to work on. The result of a successful help project compilation is a help file Myprog.hlp.

In the Help Workshop, you can create, select and edit your *.hpj file. The help project file lists the names of the document files you are using to make the target *.hlp file. The help project file can also include special information relating to the hypertext structure of your help file.

The 'source-code' files used by the older help compiler are text files in the special *.rtf ('rich text format') format. A high-end word-processor such as Word Perfect or Microsoft Word for Windows can convert an ordinary formatted *.doc file into a *.rtf file. The newer HTML help files are based on *.html.

20.10   Profiling with Visual Studio, Version 6.0

Visual Studio, Version 6.0, came with a useful *profiler* tool for finding out how much time you are spending inside each of your functions. Unfortunately, Microsoft has removed this utility from the Visual Studio.NET, Version 7.0 release. It's almost worthwhile keeping a copy of Version 6.0 around just for the profiler! Otherwise you will need to get a third-party profiling tool to use with Visual Studio.NET.

In any case, let's briefly describe the use of the Visual Studio, Version 6.0, profiler. The Version 6.0 profiler is useful in figuring out how to make your program run faster. To get a dialog for starting the profiler, select **Build | Profile...**

- Because the profiler is basically a command-line utility, it will only work if the directory-name for your program has no spaces in it.

- The Version 6.0 profiler only works if the project is built in Version 6.0 with the **Project | Settings... | Link | Enable profiling** selection checked in the Version 6.0 project file. The default Pop Framework *.dsw settings for Version 6.0 have profiling enabled for the Debug build and not enabled for the Release build, but you may need to recheck that this selection is really turned on, particularly if you've used Visual Studio.NET first. [The Enable profiling selection doesn't exist in Visual Studio.NET.]

- The Profile dialog allows you to set the profiler to check various things such as speed and coverage. In order to check for speed, good settings to use are to select **Profile Type | Function Timing** and to type into the **Advanced settings:** box the parameters

```
/AT /STACK 1
```

- The program runs fairly slowly while in profiling mode. Let it run for a while so as not to have your data swamped by the statistics of the functions called during the (anomalous) startup period. Thus, if you don't wait very long, you'll see `CWinApp::DoMessageBox` as the most time-consuming call of a Pop program run – this originates from the message box that asks you to press **Enter**. When you've let the program run for a bit, terminate it normally.

- The output of the profiler appears in your Output window of Visual Studio. Scroll the window up to the top so you can see the more frequently called functions, which are the ones you care about. Don't wait for the output to finish listing all of its info before you scroll, otherwise the important information at the start may get truncated.

Check the Help menu in the Profile dialog for more suggestions.

Exercises

Exercise 20.1: Using Visual Studio help

Use help to look up the 'macro function' **COLORREF RGB(BYTE bRed, BYTE bGreen, BYTE bBlue)**. (A macro function is a global function that has a short inline code definition that is actually substituted for each call to the function.) Now use help to look up something more elaborate. Look at the documentation on **CDC**.

Exercise 20.2: Putting a version number into the name of the executable

Even though your successive versions of your program are going to live in separate directories, it's a good idea to put a number after the name of each executable, and to include the date. Change your Pop project settings so that the names of your Debug and Release output files will include today's date. For information about the controls to use, look at the table in Appendix C. (Although we already discussed this in Exercise 3.4, it's important enough to go over it again.)

Exercise 20.3: What happens if you forget some includes?

When you are making new class files you'll sometimes forget to put in a necessary include. In this exercise we look at the kinds of error messages you get so that when you see them again you may hopefully remember that the problem is a missing include file. First, try commenting out the line `#include "force.h"` in the critter.cpp file. If you build, you get error messages similar to `'cForce' : no appropriate default constructor available`. Put the line back in. Second, try commenting out the line `#include "game.h"` in the same file. This time you'll get messages like `use of undefined type 'cBiota'`. As it turns out, the game.h file has an `#include "biota.h"` in it, so when we lose `game.h`, we lose `biota.h` as well. Put the line back. Third, try commenting out the line `#include "randomizer.h"` at the start of the header file critter.h. When you try and build you get more than 80 error messages. Some of them say things like `left of '.randomReal' must have class/struct/union type`. This kind of line can be seem cryptic to a beginner. The compiler is trying to say that you are using an object that belongs to a class that you haven't defined by including the proper header file for it.

Exercise 20.4: Browsing in the afxwin.h include file

Use the **Start | Find** command to find **afxwin.h**. On the author's computer it lives in C:\Program Files\Microsoft Visual Studio\VC98\MFC\Include. Click on the file to open it inside of Visual Studio, and if this doesn't work, start a Visual Studio session and open the file using the **File | Open** command. Look through the file, and press **F1** on any words or symbols you wonder about. Note that **CPoint** is defined in here.

Tools for software engineering

21

Often when you encounter a new software engineering tool, you may feel like learning how to use the tool is more trouble than doing your task in some older and simpler way. Once in a while this is really true, but more often than not, the new tool is worth mastering. We're not out to make poor-but-honest, hand-pinched, wood-baked clay pots here. We're using incredibly powerful machines building cutting-edge, full-featured, high-technology computer programs and we need all the help we can get!

21.1   File names and directory structure

In this section we describe a manual method for keeping track of the version number of your code.

In general, you should change the output file name (as described in Exercise 3.4 or in the table in Appendix C) to put a version number to the name of your executable. It's also a good idea to put this information into the caption in the top bar of the program window, you might put both the current program version number and its build date there. Thus, the caption ought to say something like 'Your Name, MyApp, Version 2 – March 22, 1999.' The date is helpful because sometimes you'll be in a process of making minor changes to your program without assigning a fresh new version number to its directory, and then the date can keep you informed about which build of the version you're really looking at. There's nothing more frustrating than building a great new version and then having your co-workers mix it up with the old version!

Build directories

In terms of directories, a good way to organize things is to have a MyProject directory, and to have MyApp1, MyApp2, MyApp3, . . . subdirectories of MyApp. Although some files may in fact stay the same from version to version, the simplest approach is to go ahead and have *all* the files needed for building each version N inside each MyAppN directory, even if some files end up being duplicated. We will normally have our program's source code in MyAppN along with a res subdirectory with resource files and often a hlp subdirectory with the source for your help file.

Numbering and dating your build directories

With regard to numbering, you will also end up doing multiple revisions of the source-code modules that you write to implement special purpose classes of your own. These modules will go through numerous revisions. You need to log the revisions inside the code modules, putting your name and the date whenever you make a change. This is so other programmers can tell which version of the module they are using.

What would be so bad about using the wrong version of a code module? The worst thing that can happen is that you find a bug in, say, some class method, laboriously fix the bug, and then your fixed file gets replaced by an old unfixed file, and a few days or weeks later you notice that the bug you thought you fixed is still there.

If you always keep all your code modules inside the numbered project directory and hand off a full copy of it you are reasonably sure of getting the latest version of the module.

Don't use a common files directory

In a stable build situation where everyone is using the same directory structure, you might conceivably leave your common files out in some kind of a Common Files directory and tell your projects to look for some of their files out there. You can use the Visual Studio **Tools | Options | Directories** tab to set additional paths to use for Include files and for **Source** files. This seems like a good practice, because then as you improve your common files, each new build of all the versions of the program will use the improved versions.

But there is a big problem with having each project use paths to the same files in a Common Files directory, and this is that one tends to have difficulty in keeping the directory paths straight on a variety of machines. It makes the code less portable. If your directory names don't match mine, then when you build our project on your machine, Visual Studio may not be able to find all the files it's supposed to. This problem is particularly acute in a situation like distributing the Pop Framework, where each user is likely to have his or own particular file setup.

A second kind of problem with using a Common Files directory is that, as time goes by, you may change the common files, and you'd rather not have to go back and fix all the older builds if the new common files break the old builds.

So we will copy the necessary files from each build into each new project directory. This has the nice consequence that each of our project build directories will be completely self-contained, holding all the files necessary for a build.

Best practice for directory maintenance

The best practice is to do the following.

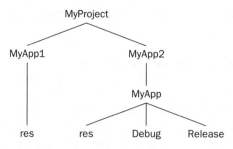

Figure 21.1   Directory structure

- Work in a numbered and/or dated directory till you like the code.
- Run clean.bat to get rid of the junk.
- Make a new numbered and dated directory, using no spaces in the directory name.
- Copy the old directory contents to the new directory.
- Start building your next release.

Recall that clean.bat is a batch file we supply with the Pop Framework; you should always keep a copy of it in your source-code directory. For clean.bat to work, the directory where it lives shouldn't have spaces in the directory name.

Your directory structure might look like Figure 21.1 after you've done working with MyApp1 and have started in on MyApp2. Since you've already run clean.bat in MyApp, you don't have the **Release** and Debug subdirectories under MyApp1.

Note that if you can start up a new directory even when you aren't ready to change version numbers, you can equally well put a date into the directory name. You might want to do this whenever you are about to make some risky series of changes that might ruin everything. That way, if you suddenly ruin the program in some mysterious way, you can still get back to the code that worked.

WinZip files

One final point is that its good to make *.zip compressed files containing all the code of successive builds. These files are good for giving to other people with whom you might be developing your code. They also serve a compact and more secure way of storing old builds. Always remember to (a) clean out the extra junk with clean.bat, and (b) include the res subdirectory in the *.zip so that the code is buildable.

To shrink the size of your source code, you can use the indispensible WinZip utility (available from www.winzip.com). Make your build directory into a Zip file as follows. Right-click on the directory with your code and select **WinZip** | **Add to Zip File**.

Choose **Maximum Compression** and don't check **Save Full Path Info**. When you zip a directory, WinZip will automatically include a directory's subdirectories, such as res and hlp, which is important, as you will need the res files in particular to be able to build the project. See the screenshot of WinZip version 8.1 below.

The Add dialog for WinZip, Version 8.1

21.2   Using the Visual Studio debugger

A typical debugging situation you face is that your program crashes. Your first problem is to find the line in your code which precipitates the crash.

First of all, make sure to press F5 so as to run the program in the debugger with all the debugging tools turned on. (In order to run outside the debugger to see how fast it can run, you use Ctrl+F5.) Breakpoints won't work, for instance, unless you are running a Debug build with the debugging tools turned on. Note that a simple **Build | Execute** will not invoke all the debugging tools, even if you are running the Debug build. You can use the F5 key to invoke the **Debug | Run** when you want to run your program and have it notice the breakpoints.

Finding the problem after a crash

When you are running the Debug version of your program and it crashes, the screen will sometimes – though not always – highlight the offending line that caused the crash, and you can fix your bug almost right away. But often the thing that causes your crash will be a small error that causes some complication later on, and then the 'crash line' your screen shows you may be some innocent-looking piece of code or, even less helpful, some assembly language from one of the Windows library functions.

In this case, the way to find the line of *your* code that caused the crash is to use the Call Stack window. This window will normally open automatically in Visual Studio.NET, and if you don't see it, look for its tab in the tab group at the bottom of the screen. [With Version 6.0, you may need to open the Call Stack window with **View | Debug Windows | Call Stack**.] The Calls Tack window will show a list of function calls, with the most recent call at the top, the previous call below that, and so on. As you work down the call stack list, you are working backwards through time. Often the first few calls in the call stack list will be mysteriously named functions that are internal to the MFC libraries. Scan down the list to find the first function name that you recognize as one of your own code's functions. Double-click on this name, and a window will open, highlighting the line of this function which set off the calls higher up in the stack. This is the line that is breaking your code.

Students never seem to remember this, so let's say it again in bold capitals!

> **WHEN YOUR PROGRAM CRASHES, OPEN THE CALL STACK WINDOW TO FIND THE LINE OF *YOUR* CODE THAT MADE IT CRASH.**

If you place the cursor over any variable in this line, a little onscreen window will show the value of the variable. You can get a more comprehensive view of the variable values by using a *Watch* window.

Visual Studio pops up some Watch windows automatically for you when you are in the debugger. There are several kinds of variable Watch windows, and possibly the variable you want to look at isn't showing up. If the variable you want isn't in the Watch window, look for the Watch window that has a tab at the bottom saying **Locals**. And let's repeat that, when execution is paused in the debugger, placing the mouse over a variable in the code near the current execution point will pop up (after a second or two) a tiny label stating the current value of that variable.

You won't always see the values for the watch variables you're interested in. Which variables are accessible depends on which function you are currently inside. Note also that you sometimes need to mouse around a little in order to see the fields and subfields of some complex object. Clicking on a pointer (such as **this**) will open up extra watch lines showing the values of the fields in the structure. You may need to click down through several levels before you find the variable you care about.

If you're lucky, you'll find an obviously bogus value in one of your variables. A bogus floating point number usually has an extremely large positive or negative exponent, so that it looks like, say, `1.234098009809809e-123`. A bogus pointer value will very often be the hexadecimal value `0000000c`; other times it may be `cdcdcdcd`. These bad pointer values are what happens to get put by default into an uninitialized pointer, and this will often be some noticeably regular pattern. Usually a good pointer will have a messy-looking value.

Having a bad pointer value is a very common kind of problem. This happens if there is some pointer in your program that you've forgotten to initialize. When an uninitialized pointer gets dereferenced by a call like `pbadpointer->x()`, the program typically crashes inside an MFC library function, and looking at the call stack leads you to a line holding `pbadpointer`. A good pointer value will be a more random-looking hexadecimal number. Chaos is health.

Breakpoints

Once you find a bad value in one of your variables you need to figure out how the bad value got there. Think about where this variable gets set or gets changed and find that spot in the code. It's useful now to get the program to run to this spot and stop. You can do this by setting a *breakpoint*. You set a breakpoint by right-clicking on a line of your code and using the context menu that pops up. Or you can just press F9 to set a breakpoint. A line with a breakpoint will have a special mark at its left end.

It's worth knowing that if you want to stop at the very end of a function to examine what happened inside it, you can set a breakpoint at the function's closing bracket }.

Remember that you can only set breakpoints and debug if you are working with the Debug build and not the Release build; you switch between this with the **Build | Set Active Configuration...** dialog. Also remember to use **Build | Debug | Run**, because if you simply use **Build | Execute**, the program won't stop at the breakpoints.

Now you can run the program up to the breakpoint. This means that the execution stops right before executing the line with the breakpoint. Usually it's a good idea to set the breakpoint before the troublesome bits of code and step through the code. When you are in the debugger, there are three ways to run your program: you can *step into*, *step over*, or *run to the next breakpoint*. The Visual Studio shortcut keys for these are F11, F10, and F5.

- To step into with F11 means to execute one line of code and stop, then the next line, then the next and so on. If you step into a loop, you will find yourself repeating the loop over and over, and you'll lose patience. The step out control gets you out – use the Visual Studio Shortcut key **Shift+F10**.

- If you use the step *over* with **F10** option, you go a line at a time, but you don't go into loops and you also don't go into the code of subfunctions that you call. This moves you forward faster, although sometimes you'll end up stepping over the piece of code you need to test.

- If you use the **F5** run to the next breakpoint option then you simply run to the next breakpoint, wherever it is. If you happen to be stuck tracing inside a loop or a subfunction, you can set a breakpoint past the loop code and use **F5** to run the debugger up to that breakpoint. Or you can step out. And, again, if you're interested in seeing what the end result of a function is, you can set a breakpoint at the function's closing bracket.

Getting familiar with a debugger takes some time, and of course the debugger interfaces change from release to release of the compilers. The basic things to understand are, as we just mentioned: call stack, watch variables, breakpoints, step into, step over, step out, and run.

TRACE statements

One other debugging technique that can be useful is a **TRACE** statement. **TRACE** uses exactly the same syntax as the C **printf** statement, but it dumps its output into the standard Debug output, which in Visual Studio will be one of the sheets in the little Output window at the bottom of your Visual Studio screen.

This is useful in a situation where some function gets called over and over, but only now and then does it encounter a bad value – not bad enough to crash the program, but bad enough to cause a malfunction of some kind. You're interested in figuring out exactly what triggers the malfunction, and you don't want to set a breakpoint and keep having to restart the program over and over. If, for instance, you were interested in comparing a local variable distance to, say, the radius value inside some structure pointed to by pshooter, you might have a line like the following.

```
TRACE('distance = %f, radius = %f \n", distance, pshooter->radius());
```

And then you'd press **F5** to run your program in Debug mode, adjust the sizes of your program and the Visual Studio window so that you could see them both onscreen, and do things in your program window while watching the values scrolling by inside the Visual Studio window.

When you build the Release version, all the **TRACE** commands are turned off, so you don't necessarily need to remove them, though you might as well remove or comment them out when you're done using them.

Finding memory leaks

Another useful feature of the debugger is that a fair amount of good information is output to the Debug sheet of the Output window. In particular, if you have any memory leaks, then messages about these will appear when you terminate a program that you've been running inside the debugger. Normally, leak information will not tell you where the leak came from, so it's not so helpful. There is, however, a not-too-well-known trick you can use to make Visual Studio tell you the origin of any memory leak. The trick is to add the following line to your stdafx.h file. See the Pop Framework stdafx.h file for a comment with more information about this.

```
#define new DEBUG_NEW
```

Testing

It's a good idea to let your program run for a time and see if anything bad happens to it. The **Player | Autorun** feature in Pop was designed with this in mind.

One point about testing to keep in mind is that you should test both the Release build and the Debug build after each new version of your program. The reason for this is that if you have broken the Release build, you need to find this out and fix it before developing any further.

Normally you are going to want to distribute the Release build of the program rather than the Debug build. Be sure and test the Release build as well as the Debug build. When the behaviour of your Release and Debug builds differs, this often means that you have some uninitialized variables inside your program. Why?

When you don't initialize a variable, whatever random bytes happened to be at that RAM location end up getting used for the correct data that you should have put there. If the bytes happen to be all zeroes, often things will run smoothly. But if your random crud happens to be there, the program will crash in an ugly way. A number that should be 0 will instead be something like 1.03 times ten to the 17th power. When you run a program over and over it may be that some uninitialized variable positions keep landing in a 'good' part of the RAM that happens to get wiped to all zeroes before each run. But when you switch from a Debug build to a Release build, the size of your program changes and it occupies a different 'footprint' on the RAM. So now maybe the unitialized variables are getting loaded with junk.

The catch with having a bug that only occurs in the Release build is that you can't pop up the debugger to see what's wrong! What you can sometimes do, however, is to save off the bad situation as a parameter file, start up the Debug build and load the misbehaving parameters, and now use the various Debugger windows to find the problem. If you come across a variable that has an odd value, this is where your trouble is coming from.

In order to find all the bugs in your program, you need to test it a lot. A testing trick that can be useful is to build a function into our program which randomizes all of our program's parameters upon request. This 'monkey on a typewriter' testing will often turn up bugs that might have escaped your notice.

In addition, you need to actually *use* your program a lot to find bugs – or to find bad aspects of your user interface. If you create, say, a game program, you should be willing to spend an hour playing with your program to see if it works!

Coding defensively

A basic principle for avoiding bugs is to code defensively. Be paranoid and take into account that some of the parameters fed into a routine might have bad values. Never, for instance, write a line like the following without first checking that x is not zero.

```
y = 1.0/x;
```

One way to check that x is not zero is to use the **assert** macro, and insert a line like the following before any line that tries to divide by x.

```
assert (x);
```

The advantage of using **assert** is that it's easy to do; the disadvantage is that if an **assert** statement fails while the program is running, then the program terminates with an error message which will frighten and mystify the user, something like this.

```
assertion failed in line 666 of trouble.cpp
```

By default **assert** always carries out the check (although you can turn it off, see the documentation on it). MFC has a version of the macro called **ASSERT** that we use more commonly in the Pop Framework. **ASSERT** only carries out the check in the Debug build of your program. This is a good thing if you plan to do plenty of testing before release, as it may be that checking the **ASSERT** condition takes up valuable time. If you want an assertion check that is also made in the Release build, you can use the standard C macro **assert**.

In the Debug mode, if an **ASSERT** line fails, the program halts with an error message. In the Release mode, an **ASSERT** line is ignored.

To make a solidly usable program, we test thoroughly for **ASSERT** failures in the Debug mode, and find ways to code in some reasonable non-program-terminating fallback course of action to take when an **ASSERT** might otherwise be triggered. If you really do want to check for the condition even in the Release version you can use the **assert** macro, but this is generally a fairly user-unfriendly thing to do. You really do want to find and work around any bad conditions while still coding.

By way of illustration, let's look at how you might avoid problems with division by zero. As a programmer you should *never ever* divide by something before making sure that it's not zero. Whenever you see a division in your program, do something about it. When you divide by zero the program crashes. To make life a little more confusing, a Windows program that crashes after division by zero will often as not give you an error message saying 'Square root of a negative number.' You don't want your users to see that.

So if, say, x and y are real numbers and n is an integer, instead of writing a line like x = y/n; you might write a line like

```
x = y/(n?n:1);
```

(**A?B:C** is the 'compactified C' question mark and colon syntax for an if-then-else statement. If **A** is true the value is **B**, otherwise the value is **C**.)

If the number you are dividing by is a real number u, then we need to avoid dividing by something very close to zero as well as dividing by zero. The problem is that dividing by something very close to zero can also produce a floating point error. To give a nice smooth fallback strategy, we might write something like the following in place of x = y/u.

```
#define SMALL_REAL 0.000001
if (fabs(x) < SMALL_REAL)
    x = (x>=0.0)?(SMALL_REAL):(-SMALL_REAL);
y = 1/x;
```

The **double fabs(double v)** is the floating point absolute value function. You should not accidentally use the **int abs(int n)** integer absolute value function instead, because calling this function will round off the argument to an integer; for instance, **abs(1.5)** is **1** and **abs(0.9)** is **0**.

Another technique for writing more bug-proof code is that you can handle bad parameter values with the more sophisticated C++ approach known as exception-handling, which uses the **try**, **catch**, and **throw** commands. But we won't cover exception handling in this book.

21.3 Windiff **and merging code**

In the old days it was customary to use the Unix **diff** or the DOS **fc** utilities for this. Now it is more common to use a graphically interfaced tool that comes with your compiler.

Windiff

Microsoft Visual Studio has a utility called Windiff which is pretty easy to use. The tool is still shipped with Visual Studio.NET, but in a default installation, Windiff will normally not be installed, so you may need to run through Visual Studio setup process to select this particular tool to be added onto your machine. It is part of the group of tools added by selecting **Visual C++ Tools | Win32 Platform SDK** in the Setup dialog.

As Windiff is an older program, it may not appear on your **Start | Programs | Microsoft Visual Studio | Tools** popup menu. If not, you can find it with Windows

Explorer or with the Windows Search utility. It will typically reside in the directory C:\Program Files\Microsoft Visual Studio\Common\Tools.

Once you open **Windiff**, you can ask it to compare two individual files or, which is usually more useful, all the files in two different directories. If you compare directories, **Windiff** gives you a list of the differing files, and then you can compare these pair by pair. When comparing two files, **Windiff** has a very nice and unique user interface. It's really a classic of good user interface design. A bar on the left shows a map of the two files with the differing places marked in red and yellow, with red meaning there's extra code in the one file, and yellow meaning there's differing code in the other file. Clicking on the bar jumps you to the location of the file in question. Practice with **Windiff** a little till you learn how to use it, and don't forget to take a look at the help file.

Once you have found the places where the programs differ, you need to merge the two together. This may work best if both programmers are present – although if they are prone to arguing (and many programmers are) this may not be such a good idea. Ideally the merge is being done by a person in authority, by the team leader or the chief engineer.

Suppose the two programmers are called Ann and Bob. To merge their files, make notes of where they differ (or leave them open in Windiff). And to edit the files open them up in Visual Studio as separate windows (you can't edit files within Windiff). If there are any windows open besides the two files to edit, close them. Select **Window | New Horizontal Tab Group** [or **Window | Tile Horizontal** in Version 6] so you can see both files. Decide which file you want to 'merge into,' Ann's or Bob's. The idea is that you should *merge into* the file that has the largest amount of new code in it. By talking about the files and/or by exploring them with Windiff, you can decide which has the most new code. Let's say that Ann's file has substantially more differences from the original commonly shared starting-point code than does Bob's. Fix in your mind which file is which in the editor window; you might for instance make sure that the file you are merging into is the upper file on the screen.

Now what you need to do is to scroll through the different files in **Windiff**, and look at all the places where Bob's code differs from Ann's. Where Bob's code is simply adding on a good feature or fixing something, you want to copy that piece of Bob's code into Ann's code, replacing Ann's code with Bob's. Where Bob's code has the old version which Ann has already changed, you want to just leave Ann's code as it is. If there are some places where Bob and Ann do the same thing in two different ways, you need to try and decide which approach is better. If you can't quickly agree, then use an #ifdef to incorporate both versions. That is, you can use a construction like this:

```
#define BOB_WAY
#ifdef BOB_WAY
//Put Bob's code here
#else //not BOB_WAY means Ann's way.
//Put Ann's code here
#endif //End of the Ann's way part of the BOB_WAY switch
```

Merging

Once you get the program to start building again, you can try turning the BOB_WAY switch on and off (by commenting it in or out), so that you can tell which *.exe runs better. At that point you would probably want to remove the less-good code, as keeping it in the file will make your file hard to read.

Often there is a temptation to make the merge process 'faster' by not bothering to use a file-comparing utility like **Windiff**. Can't Bob just *tell* Ann which pieces of the code he changed and have Ann copy those new pieces in? In practice this rarely works. Usually Bob will forget about some of his minor changes, and when he and Ann go to rebuild the code they will get a lot of error messages. If they're lucky, fixing these errors one by one ends up taking as much time as it would have taken to do the job right with Windiff in the first place. If they're unlucky, there will be some omitted change which doesn't generate a compiler error, but which does create a bug.

Revision control software

If you know that you are going to have to merge your code it's a good idea to try and localize your changes into one part of the document to make it easy to block-copy them. It can also be useful to flag your changes with comments that have your name.

There are advanced software engineering tools such as Microsoft SourceSafe that more or less automate the version control and merging process. Tools such as this are generally known as 'revision control software,' sometimes called RCS for short. An RCS package has several significant features.

The most basic feature of RCS is that it serves as a single centralized repository in which the source code lives. The RCS in fact saves every version of the code that you've given it, so that as well as having your current code in a centralized location, your team has access copies of your earlier builds as well.

RCS treats code files like books in a library. Only one user at a time can 'check out' a given file for editing. Until this user eventually 'checks in' the file, no other user will be able to change the file. You can always get a read-only copy of a file, but only one programmer at a time can check out a file for editing. This helps prevent difficult code-merge situations.

The RCS software normally requires a programmer to make some kind of log entry when he or she checks a file back in. The cumulative log entries help the team track when changes were made.

We're not going to discuss any specific RCS packages in this book, but if every member of your team has access to the same one, you would do well to spend a little time learning how to use it. If you are working in an environment where there is a shared directory (on the web or on a network) then it is definitely worthwhile to use some form of RCS to make it impossible for two people to work on the same file at the same time. As well as Microsoft SourceSafe, there is a well-known shareware Unix-based RCS tool called RCS. It's worth noting that the familiar Macromedia Dreamweaver web-site-building tool can in fact be used as an RCS system. Another option is to use a web-based collaboration tool, of which several exist. For that matter, it wouldn't be too hard to create a web page for your team that effectively acted as your RCS system.

Informally, you can achieve something like the effect of using RCS by being strict about not letting team members work on the same code at the same time. This is really worth doing, as merging code is such a hassle.

Once the group gets a new merged build that works, be sure to clean it, save off an archive copy of the code, make a *.zip of it, and distribute the *.zip to all team members. *Without exception*, each member of the development team should replace *all* of his or her source-code files with the new build's source-code files. This is to avoid having to repeatedly fix the same bugs or to merge the same code.

21.4   Counting lines of code

Often people like to measure the progress of a software project in terms of the number of lines of code in the project. One reason for doing this is that it may help you come up with a reasonable estimate for how long a project might take. That is, if you feel that project B is similar to project A, and you know that project A used nA lines of code, then you might guess that when you've written nB lines of code on project B, then project B is nB/nA of the way done.

Or, again, if you want to add some feature G to a project and you know that the feature G is similar to a feature F that was already added, then once again, you can gauge your progress on feature G by tracking the ratio of nG to nF, where nG would measure the lines of code related to feature G and your baseline nF would measure the lines of code related to feature F.

There are professional tools to track the number of lines of code, but here let's just mention a quick and dirty solution. It's a crude technique, but it's easy to use. It lets you come up with a painless, reasonably accurate estimate of how many lines of code you wrote.

To count the number of lines of code in all your project files, open up your main project file and use the **Edit | Find In Files** feature to search for the semicolon; in all the *.h and *.cpp files. If you want to count the lines of code in an individual file, you can change the **Edit | Find In Files** to only search in that file.

Other than the fact that **for** loops do introduce two extra semicolons apiece, there is a pretty close one-to-one correspondence between the number of semicolons in your project and the number of lines of code. This rough-and-ready metric can be thrown off a bit if you use a lot of semicolons in your comments. Another mild source of inaccuracy is that *.res files don't have semicolons, so your work on the interface doesn't get counted by the search-for-semicolons metric.

To be completely accurate, you can separate out the starting code that you didn't write yourself. In the case of a new Visual Studio project, this will be about 100 lines of code scattered across something like 12 small files.

Table 21.1 The number of lines of code in the Pop Framework.

Version	Total lines	New lines	Date	New days	New lines / New days ~
Starting code	99	0	July 4, 1999	0	
Pop 1	219	120	July 5, 1999	1	120
Pop 2	249	30	July 6, 1999	1	30
Pop 3	908	759	July 12, 1999	6	127
Pop 4	1431	523	July 13, 1999	1	523
Pop 5	1505	74	July 14, 1999	1	74
Pop 6	1755	250	July 26, 1999	12	21
Pop 7	1906	151	July 30, 1999	4	38
Pop 17	5036	3130	June 7, 2000	312	10
Pop 19	5380	344	Aug 15, 2000	73	5
Pop 20	5822	442	Jan 20, 2001	158	3
Pop 21	9135	3313	June 21, 2001	121	27
Pop 24	10067	872	March 11, 2002	203	4
Pop 25	10152	85	May 1, 2002	52	1

If you keep the source for your successive builds in different directories, and are careful to put the date of the build into the caption bar of your successive builds, you can work out a little table to get an idea of how fast you program. Table 21.1 gives some data on the progress of the author's Pop Framework over the last couple of years.

The 'Starting Code' represents the code that the Microsoft Visual Studio automatically generated when the author used the Visual Studio's 'AppWizard' to create a Document-View architecture (MDI) project named Pop.

The values of the rates in the last column are deceptively high for the earlier builds, because in those early builds the author was still adding in modules of 'tool class' code that he'd written before. Adding in some old code modules accounts for most of the new lines added between Pop 2 and Pop 4. The lower rates further down the column are more indicative of the actual speed the author programs, even when he's working quite hard. The jump from version 7 to 17 is a little anomalous, as it covers ten versions at once, and these versions were done over a year during which there were long periods when the author wasn't programming at all. Though, all along, he was still thinking about the program. Thinking is slower than typing. The rather substantial jump from Pop 20 to Pop 21 represents the introduction of three-dimensional vectors and OpenGL graphics.

As a program gets more developed and starts using high-level classes, you can actually make quite a large change to it with only a few lines. The hard thing, of course, is figuring out the lines. If they involve some tricky new concept like, say, a splitter window, just a dozen lines can take you all day, because most of that day you're reading up on splitter windows.

21.5 Help files without tears

Software Engineering and Computer Games is about software engineering and about games development. As part of the package, you need to learn how to make a fully complete program all on your own. This means you need some minimal knowledge about how to make a *help file*, that is a file that users can read from within your program.

We've already mentioned that from the earliest build on, your program should always include a User's Guide. And that it's crucial to discipline yourself to do this. Working on the User's Guide should go hand-in-hand with working on your project specification.

It turns out that you can use the very same text file as 'source' for both a print version of the User's Guide and a corresponding help file. So you might as well actually have a help file from quite early on. After all, as long as you have a User's Guide written, it makes sense to make it into a help file that your co-workers, professor, family, friends, etc. can look at when they test out your new build of the program. People are sometimes more willing to look at a help file than at written documentation. And written documentation can so easily be misplaced.

One might initially suspect that turning written documentation into a help file is so difficult that it's something you should put off for later. But this isn't true – if you keep things simple. If all you want is a vanilla, single-file help display with no table of contents, index, or hyperlinks, creating a help file is a snap. The fact is, the key thing about a help file is *what's written in it*. All the other stuff is just glitz that's only occasionally useful.

Help systems are often spoken of as having separate *topics*, and the topics are often kept in separate source-text files that are then compiled into a single, large help file. In order to keep our help development process as simple as possible we are going to only have one topic in our system, one topic in one big source-text file.

By limiting yourself to a single, large topic file, you can focus on making it a useful document. An additional benefit of working with a single topic file is that then you have a file you can print out as is for a hard-copy User's Guide.

Be aware that this is a somewhat non-standard approach. In a commercial program you would eventually want to break your help into separate topics, providing a table of contents and an index. But for now, we'll just keep it simple.

In defense of our approach, let it be said that if you have a limited amount of time to spend on the help, it's better to spend it on the writing than on electronic help features. One does encounter help systems in which the priorities have been skewed the other way. Thus, when the user wonders what a control like, say, **Clavier | Deviance** does, he or she has to navigate through a contents page that doesn't list it in the topics, use the search tool, follow a string of hyperlinks and end up with a single-sentence nugget of non-help such as, 'The Clavier Deviance Tool deviates the clavier.'

In the following subsections, we first have some notes about how best to create a User's Guide that's appropriate for converting into a help file. Then we discuss the troublesome fact that there are presently two possible kinds of help file: the newer HTML help and the old Windows help. Then we have a section about how to make each kind of help file. And finally we have a note about a mixed case that can arise for some developers.

Writing the User's Guide

Write the source documentation for your help as if it's something you might actually expect a human being to read. Don't fill up line after line with obvious and uninformative things like 'The **File | Save** command saves a file.'

It's good to break the guide into sections. You can use a format similar to what we used for the Pop User's Guide; this is the document that appears both as Appendix B of this book, and as the help file that comes with the Pop Framework. Start with a little introduction, describe what the user sees on the screen, including the cursor appearance, explain how the game is played and scored, explain all the non-standard menu items, tell about any other controls, explain any peculiar features of your program's interface, and add some tips for play. It's good to have a 'Getting Started' section at the beginning of the Guide to walk the user through the first few things he or she should try.

Let's stress again that when you're writing, you should always imagine that you're talking to a real person. Write as if you are explaining the game to a friend, not to a boss or to a professor. Be generous with the information. If there's some hint or suggestion or motivation that you always verbally tell someone when you watch them play your game, then this information should be part of your written documentation. Also be sure to put your name, the date, copyright info, and contact information at the end of your file.

Now for some remarks about the technicalities of word-processing.

Which word-processor?

Most people use a recent version of Microsoft Word, which is part of Microsoft Office. Word supports a variety of file formats; in particular you can use it to create the native *.doc (Word format) files, *.rtf (rich text format) files, or *.htm (HTML format) files. A nice feature of Word for this purpose is that you can format your text in any fashion you like, and when you save to *.rtf or *.htm, all of your fonts, spaces, indents, included bitmaps, figures, tables, and so on will be preserved – though you may want to double check the tables.

As we'll discuss in the following subsection, there are actually two different ways of making help files; you can make the old and nearly obsolete 'Windows' help files or you can make the newer HTML help files. If you plan to make Windows help files, you need to be able to save your files in the *.rtf format. If you plan to make HTML help files, you need to be able to save in the *.htm format.

If you don't have Microsoft Word, you can make *.rtf files with the WordPad accessory which comes free with Windows. If you don't have Word and wish to have a graphic HTML editor, you will need to find one; it may be that you have some Web design software that can help you create HTML.

Making an effective help file

There are a few key things you need to remember when you create a text file that's intended to be read onscreen.

- Make your file single-spaced. People are going to be reading it onscreen, where space is at a premium.

- Remember not to put a paragraph mark (an **Enter** key press) at the end of each line in a help file. This is because the help file text is going to be shown inside of a resizable window, and if you have 'hard' line breaks, then when the window is made narrow, the hard line breaks will appear at bad places. Only use **Enter** for the end of a paragraph or to skip a line.

- You can paste in bitmaps, but don't overdo it. Too many bitmaps will increase the size of your help file resulting in (a) a larger file to distribute with your program and (b) slower loading time of the help when the user calls for it.

- If using Word, format the lines at the heads of your sections with the styles Heading1, format the subsection lines with Heading2, and so on.

It's easier to avoid putting in unnecessary hard line breaks if you view your document in a mode where the breaks are visible. If you are using Microsoft Word, you can do this by putting a check into the **Tools | Options... | View | Paragraph marks** box. This will display paragraph marks in your text as you edit it, so that you can visually see the spots where you pressed **Enter** and put a hard break into a line.

The reason for formatting your section headings is that, first of all, this makes them visually stand out and, second of all, it allows you to automatically insert a Table of Contents, as we'll mention in the 'Creating and reading HTML help files' section further below.

The two kinds of help

Here's a bit of bad news. There are now two incompatible standards for help files: the older Windows help standard and the newer HTML help standard.

It would be easier for the author to advocate and explain only one of these approaches. But, in order to make the Pop Framework code as widely usable as possible, we're going to explain three approaches.

- Using HTML help with Visual Studio.NET, Version 7.0.
- Using Windows help with Visual Studio, Version 6.0.
- The mixed case: using HTML help with Visual Studio, Version 6.0.

The default behavior of the Pop Framework is to detect your compiler type and to use the first option if you have Visual Studio.NET, and use the second option if you have Visual Studio, Version 6.0.

The first approach is really the best, as this is where the future lies. And if you have Visual Studio.NET, it's the only way to go. If you plan to use this approach, you should now download the HTML Help Workshop from Microsoft. We have a link to the download site on our book's website www.rudyrucker.com/ computergames, or you can go to www.microsoft.com and enter `download htmlhelp` in the **Search** box at the top corner of the Microsoft home page. Once you've done this, you can pretty much ignore the rest of this subsection, though you might just skim over it so you know what's here.

If most or all of the people in your group are using Version 6.0, the second approach is probably the best for you for now. In this case you also can ignore the rest of this subsection, though again, a quick glance through it might be useful.

If you are in a mixed group, it's probably best if the people with Version 6.0 make the effort to switch over to the HTML help. In this mixed case, you'll need to read the rest of this section as well as the special Mixed Case subsection at the end of the chapter.

Let's get an overview of the distinctions between the two kinds of help. We summarize these in Table 21.2.

Up through and including Version 6.0, Visual Studio shipped with a hcw.exe, known as the *Help Workshop*. The Help Workshop's function was to convert *.rtf (rich text format) files into *.hlp *Windows help* files.

Now there is a new tool, hhw.exe, known as the *HTML Help Workshop*. The HTML Help Workshop's function is to convert *.htm (HTML) files into *.chm *HTML help* files.

Visual Studio, Version 6.0, shipped with the hcw.exe *Help Workshop*. The hcw.exe Help Workshop is now classed as obsolete and is not available as a download.

Visual Studio.NET, Version 7.0, ships with *neither* hcw.exe *nor* hhw.exe. As mentioned above, the hhw.exe HTML Help Workshop is available as a free download from Microsoft.

There are two different kinds of things a developer needs to do with help files.

- *Create* a help file using some sort of 'help workshop' tool.
- Add to the program code a function call which will *read* the help file.

  What's required to do these things?

- You need the HTML Help Workshop hhw.exe to create HTML help files.
- In order to have your program be able to read a *.chm HTML help file, your program must include the special header file htmlhelp.h, and it must link to the special library file htmlhelp.lib. These files are pre-installed by Visual Studio.NET in a place where the compiler can easily find them, and the Pop Framework code is set to, respectively, include and link the files with Visual Studio.NET.
- You need the Help Workshop hcw.exe to create Windows help files.
- In order to have your program be able to read a *.hlp Windows help file, you don't need to add anything more to your system.

When you install Visual Studio.NET, Version 7.0, it installs the support files htmlhelp.lib and htmlhelp.h into, respectively, the include and lib subdirectories of

Table 21.2 The new HTML help compared with the old Windows help.

	New HTML help	Old Windows help
Pop Framework default	Used for Visual Studio.NET, Version 7.0	Used for Visual Studio, Version 6.0
Authoring tool	hhw.exe (HTML Help Workshop)	hcw.exe (Help Workshop)
How to get the tool	Download from Microsoft	Shipped with Version 6.0. Not available as a download
Source files	*.htm (HTML files)	*.rtf (rich text format files)
Project file extension	*.hhp	*. hpj
Help file extension	*.chm	*.hlp
Window opens help file with a special call to	`::HtmlHelp` `(..."pop.chm"...)`	`::WinHelp` `(..."pop.hlp"...)`
Include file needed for this special call	`#include <htmlhelp.h>`	None
Library needed to be linked in for this special call	htmlhelp.lib	None
How to get the include file and library file	Ships with Version 7.0. And downloads from Microsoft with the HTML Help Workshop tool	None needed
Where to put the include file and library file	With Version 7.0: no action needed. With Version 6.0: either with your source code or in, respectively, Program Files\Microsoft Visual Studio\VC98\Include and Program Files\Microsoft Visual Studio\VC98\Lib	Doesn't apply

Visual Studio.NET\Vc7\PlatformSDK. This means that your compiler will easily be able to find these files.

Visual Studio, Version 6.0, doesn't install the support files htmlhelp.lib and htmlhelp.h, but if you are using the Help Workshop, you won't need them.

When you download the HTML Help Workshop package the package will also install htmlhelp.lib and htmlhelp.h onto your machine, by the way. By default, the download puts these files into, respectively, the include and lib subdirectories of Program Files\HTML Help Workshop. Note that Program Files\HTML Help Workshop will also contain the new HTML Help Workshop tool hhw.exe, along with a bunch of documentation about how to use the tool.

If you already have Visual Studio.NET on your machine, you won't need these new copies of htmlhelp.lib and htmlhelp.h, so you can delete them. If you are using Visual Studio, Version 6.0, you will want to use these files, as we discuss in the Mixed Case subsection at the end of this chapter.

Creating and reading HTML help files

This subsection tells you how to work with HTML help files using either version of Visual Studio. If you plan to use Visual Studio, Version 6.0, with Windows help files, skip this subsection and go to the next one.

(1) We'll keep our Windows help in the Help\HTML Help subdirectory of the project. Edit your source text and, if using Word, use the **File | Save As** selection to save as a web page (*.html, *.htm) file called, say, Myproject.htm. The HTML help will preserve any jumps or links that you put into your file. This is useful because Word has an **Insert | Index and Tables... | Table of Contents** feature that allows you to give your document a table of contents that's automatically generated by the heading styles used for your section headings (assuming that you used these styles). When you save a file with this kind of contents table in the *.htm format, the table of contents links will be preserved. (This is a shortcut that lets you postpone or avoid the more complex issue of making a standard HTML Help Table of Contents.)

(2) Find **HTML Help Workshop** under your main Windows **Start | Programs | HTML Help Workshop** and start it up. Or, if you already have a Myproject.hhp HTML Help Workshop project file, click on it to open it.

(3) To make a new HTML Help Workshop project, select **File | New... | Help Project file** inside HTML Help Workshop. When the dialog asks the name for your project file, choose the same name as your executable, say Myproject.hhp, and save it to the same subdirectory where you put your source-text file Myproject.htm. You also get the chance to choose the name and location for the completed Myproject.chm file. It's convenient to give it the same name as your executable and to write it up into the directory where you keep your source code and executables. (*Don't* call your help file Pop.chm!) Thus if you are making your help down in Help\HTML Help subsubdirectory of the source, you might want your target file to be ..\..\Myproject.chm. When, later on, your executable tries to open the help file, it will expect to find it in the directory where it lives.

(4) Use the HTML Help Workshop **Add/Remove Topic Files...** button to add the Myproject.htm user guide file from step (1) as a so-called topic file. You also have the option of using the **Add/Modify Window Definitions** button to control the appearance of the window in which your help file will appear. In the case of the default Pop.hhp project, we added a `PopHelp` window style which has the 'Navigation' panel closed (as we didn't make

a table of contents or an index to show in the panel), but which has Back, Forward, and Print buttons. Be sure to make the title of your window style match your project. There are other possible window style options you can explore.

(5) Click the **Save and Compile** button on the HTML Help Workshop window. It may show you one or two warnings, but it should in any case create your ..\..\Myproject.chm. Leave HTML Help Workshop open till after the next step.

(6) Find the newly built Myproject.chm help file in Windows Explorer and click on it to open (Windows can open any help file on its own). Before opening it, by the way, you might want to check its time and date in Explorer to be sure you're not opening an old version of the help file. If what you see in the file isn't satisfactory, open up your Myproject.htm in your word-processor and edit it. Then do a fresh save of the file, leaving the word-processor open if you like, go back into the HTML Help Workshop, and recompile. Repeat steps (5) and (6) till you're happy with the way your help file looks.

(7) Step (7) is already done for you in the Pop Framework, but we mention it for your future reference. Add a menu selection so the user can tell your app to open your help file, and link this menu selection to a handler in your code that will open the help file. To add the menu selection, use the Resource View to open up the project-specific IDR_POPTYPE menu, then add a selection named **User's Guide** to the Help popup. It gets the ID_HELP_USERSGUIDE. Add a handler for the selection; a good place to keep the handler is in the **CMainFrame** class, as when you open a help file, it must be linked to one of your onscreen windows. Your main frame window is the logical one to use. Thus the handler for the **Help | User's Guide** menu selection is **CMainFrame::OnHelpUsersguide**.

(8) Edit the handler code. The generic Pop handler code for HTML help is as follows. You will need to edit the code so that it looks for your own Myproject.chm file rather than for the Pop.chm file.

```
void CMainFrame::OnHelpUsersguide ()
{
    ::HtmlHelp (GetSafeHwnd (), "Pop.chm", HH_DISPLAY_TOPIC, 0);
}
```

(9) See if your project will build. It is possible that you will see an error message like this in your Output window when you reach the 'Linking' stage of the build.

```
Pop error LNK2019: unresolved external symbol _HtmlHelpA@16
    referenced in function "protected: void _thiscall
    CMainFrame::OnHelpUsersguide (void)"
    (?OnHelpUsersguide@CMainFrame@@IAEXXZ)
```

This message means that your project can't find the code for the **::HtmlHelp** method, and this means, in turn, that your project isn't linking in the necessary `htmlhelp.lib` library.

Open the Project Settings dialog and set the configurations being changed to **All Configurations** as described in Appendix C. Then edit the **Configuration Properties | Linker | Input | Additional Dependencies** edit box to include htmlhelp.lib. Now your program should build.

If you still have problems you may need to adjust the Visual Studio directory paths so that it can find htmlhelp.lib.

(10)   Build and run the program and select **Help | User's Guide**. There it is!

Creating and reading Windows help files

This subsection is only for those planning to use Windows Help with Visual Studio, Version 6.0. Do not bother with this subection if you use Visual Studio.NET.

(1)   We'll keep our Windows help in the Help\Windows Help subdirectory of the project. Edit your source text and, if using Word, use the **File | Save As** selection to save as a rich text format (*.rtf) file called, say, Myproject.rtf.

(2)   Find **Help Workshop** under your main Windows **Start | Programs | Microsoft Visual Studio | Microsoft Visual Studio Tools** and start it up. Or, if you already have a Myproject.hpj Help Workshop project file, click on it to open it.

(3)   To make a new Help Workshop project, select **File | New... | Help Project file** inside Help Workshop. When the dialog asks the name for your project file, choose the same name as your executable, say Myproject.hpj, and save it to the same subdirectory where you put your source-text file Myproject.rtf. You also get the chance to choose the name and location for the completed Myproject.hlp file. It's convenient to give it the same name as your executable and to write it up into the directory where you keep your source code and executables. (*Don't* call your help file Pop.hlp!) Thus if you are making your help down in Help\Windows Help subsubdirectory of the source, you might want your target file to be ..\..\Myproject.hlp. When, later on, your executable tries to open the help file, it will expect to find it in the directory where it lives.

(4)   Use the Help Workshop **Files... | Add** to add the Myproject.rtf user guide file from step (1) as a so-called topic file.

(5)   Click the Save and Compile button on the Help Workshop window. It may shows you one or two warnings, but it should in any case create your ..\..\Myproject.hlp. Leave Help Workshop open till after the next step.

(6)   Find the newly built Myproject.hlp help file in Windows Explorer and click on it to open (Windows can open any help file on its own). Before opening it, by the way, you might want to check its time and date in Explorer to be sure you're not opening an old version of the help file. If what you see in the file isn't satisfactory, open up your Myproject.rtf in your word-processor and edit it. Then do a fresh save of the file, leaving the word-processor

open if you like, go back into the Help Workshop, and recompile. Repeat steps (5) and (6) till you're happy with the way your help file looks.

(7) Step (7) is already done for you in the Pop Framework, but we mention it for your future reference. Add a menu selection so the user can tell your app to open your help file, and link this menu selection to a handler in your code that will open the help file. To add the menu selection, use the Resource View to open up the project-specific IDR_POPTYPE menu, then add a selection named **User's Guide** to the Help popup. It gets the ID_HELP_USERSGUIDE. Add a handler for the selection; a good place to keep the handler is in the **CMainFrame** class as, when you open a help file, it must be linked to one of your onscreen windows. Your main frame window is the logical one to use. Thus the handler for the **Help | User's Guide** menu selection is **CMainFrame::OnHelpUsersguide**.

(8) Edit the handler code. The generic Pop handler code for Windows help is as follows. You will need to edit the code so that it looks for your own Myproject.hlp file rather than for the Pop.hlp file.

```
void CMainFrame::OnHelpUsersguide ()
{
    ::WinHelp (GetSafeHwnd (), "Pop.hlp", HELP_CONTENTS, 0);
}
```

(9) Build and run the program and select **Help | User's Guide**. There it is!

The mixed case: reading HTML help files with a Version 6.0 build

Now let's talk about using HTML Help Workshop with Visual Studio, Version 6.0. First of all you need to read the subsection about HTML help. And in addition, you need to read this subsection about how to adjust your build so as to work with these files.

In order to build programs that can read HTML help files, each Version 6.0 team member needs to add a new library file htmlhelp.lib and header file htmlhelp.h to their build environment.

As we mentioned before, when you download the HTML Help Workshop package the package will also install htmlhelp.lib and htmlhelp.h onto your machine, by default putting them into, respectively, the include and lib subdirectories of Program Files\HTML Help Workshop. And, again, the Program Files\HTML Help Workshop will also contain the new HTML Help Workshop tool hhw.exe, along with a bunch of documentation about how to use the tool.

If you are using Visual Studio, Version 6.0, you will need to either (a) move these files to a spot where your Visual Studio can find them when it compiles and links your project, or (b) remember to prefix references to these files in your Visual Studio code or project with the path information about where the files are located, or (c) use the Version 6.0 dialog **Tools | Options | Directories** to add the appropriate paths to the lists of include and library directory paths searched.

If you are working with people who may easily get confused, the safest initial option is to (a) just put the two htmlhelp.* files in with your source code. Otherwise have them download the files themselves and either (b) put them in, respectively, their local directories Program Files\Microsoft Visual Studio\VC98\Include and Program Files\Microsoft Visual Studio\VC98\Lib, so that their Version 6.0 compiler can find them, or (c) change the include path list to have Program Files\HTML Help Workshop\Include and the compiler's library path list to have Program Files\HTML Help Workshop\Library.

In addition you will need to do two more things.

- Override the Pop Framework's default choice of Windows Help for Version 6.0.
- Add htmlhelp.lib to your Visual Studio, Version 6.0, *.dsw project file.

You do the first thing by commenting in a //#define POPHTMLHELP line in the mainfrm.cpp file. We print the line here and its comment, along with the preliminary code that detects which version of Visual Studio is being used and automatically defines or doesn't define POPHTMLHELP accordingly.

```
#if _MSC_VER >= 1300 /* Version abcd means your Visual C++ is
    version ab.cd. It turns out "Visual Studio.NET, Version 7.0"
    gives an _MSC_VER of 1300, or Build 13.00, and "Version 6.0"
    has _MSC_VER of 1200, or Build 12.00 for a _MSC_VER of 1200.
    We could also have distinguised the two by detecting the MFC
    version, with _MFC_VER. The _MFC_VER is, perversely, returned
    as a hexadecimal number. Version 6.0 uses MFC version 0x0060,
    while Version 7.0 uses 0x0070. */
#define POPHTMLHELP /* Normally don't use this with Version 6.0,
    though you can if you want, see the next comment down. */
#endif //End the _MSC_VER switch

//#define POPHTMLHELP //Comment in to force on for Version 6.0
    /* At this point POPHTMLHELP is turned on for Version 7.0 and
    off for Version 6.0. If you want to force it on anyway in
    Version 6.0, then comment in this #define POPHTMLHELP. Note that
    Version 7.0 puts two necessary files htmlhelp.h and htmlhelp.lib
    onto your machine in standard directories where the compiler can
    find them. If you are using Version 6.0, you have to get these
    files yourself, and put them in a place where the current
    Visual Studio Directories settings can find them. Note that
    for Version 6.0, you also need to add htmlhelp.lib to the list
    of Link files. Our Version 7.0 solution file already has the
    library in the link list, but the Version 6.0 workspace file
    does not.*/

#ifdef POPHTMLHELP
#include <htmlhelp.h>
#endif // POPHTMLHELP
```

To add htmlhelp.lib to your Version 6.0 project do the following. Open the **Project | Settings** dialog. Activate **Settings For | All Configurations** in the upper left corner of the Settings dialog. Now find the **Project | Settings | Link | General | Object/Library Modules** edit box, and type in htmlhelp.lib.

As we discussed above, you should have htmlhelp.lib in a place where the compiler's current directory settings can find it. Alternately you can put a path name in front of the htmlhelp.lib name, but this makes your project fairly non-portable.

By the way the POPHTMLHELP switch gets used as follows:

```
void CMainFrame::OnHelpUsersguide ()
{
#ifndef POPHTMLHELP
    //If not POPHTMLHELP do it the old way with a *.hlp
    ::WinHelp (GetSafeHwnd (), "Pop.hlp", HELP_CONTENTS, 0);
#else // POPHTMLHELP means use a *.chm.
    ::HtmlHelp (GetSafeHwnd (), "Pop.chm", HH_DISPLAY_TOPIC, 0);
#endif //End POPHTMLHELP switch
}
```

Exercise

Exercise 21.1: Counting semicolons

See what the semicolon count is for your version of the Pop Framework code. Make a note of this and then, as your project progresses, track your progress with a table similar to the one shown above. (Note that even if your version number appears in the table above, your line count may not exactly match the value in the table, as the author may have changed the Pop code in the meantime without giving it a whole new version number.)

Topics in C++

22

The Pop Framework and MFC use C++ very extensively. Here's a brief brush-up on C++, with emphasis on some of the trickier points. If you know C and/or Java but are new to C++ you should read this chapter carefully and refer back to it as the various topics come up.

22.1 Classes, objects and constructors

In object-oriented programming (OOP) we use a special kind of data structure called a class. A class is quite similar to an ordinary C **struct**. Particular instances of some class type are called objects. As well as having members which are data fields, a class also has members that are functions. If **SomeClass** were the name of a class and **SomeFunction(...)** happened to be the name of one of the class's member functions, then it would make sense to have two lines like:

```
SomeClass K;
K.SomeFunction(…);
```

The first line says that K is an object of the class type **SomeClass**. You can also say that 'K is a **SomeClass** object' or you can say 'K is an instance of the **SomeClass** class.' Supposing K has a bunch of data fields, what gets put into these fields when you make the '**SomeClass** K;' declaration? It turns out that when you define any class you also define a *constructor* function which serves to initialize new members of the class.

The second line says to let the object K call the class member function **SomeFunction**. **SomeFunction** might act on K's data members, do something to the **SomeFunction** arguments, possibly return a value, or do any combination of these three actions.

Sometimes a class's constructor function takes arguments. MFC includes, for instance, a **CPoint** class which has a constructor that can take two arguments, one for each of the point's coordinates. In this case you might have a declaration of the following form, creating a **CPoint** object with coordinates 3 and 7.

```
CPoint cpdot(3,7);
```

It is allowable for a class to have several kinds of constructors. The constructors can be thought of as functions that you can use to create objects of the class type.

We need to mention still another way of initializing an object. Suppose that you want to have, say, a global **SomeClass** variable, but that you won't know what numbers to initialize the **SomeClass** with until well into your code. One approach that you could use would be to use a global pointer to a **SomeClass**.

```
SomeClass *sc_ptr;
```

When you declare a pointer to a class like this, no initialization happens. No constructor gets called. Depending on the context, a junk value like **CDCDCDCD0x** or the NULL (zero) value gets put into the pointer, and no effort is made to create a legitimate class object for the pointer to point to.

The way that you make `*sc_ptr` correspond to a legitimate object is that later, down in the code when you find out what parameters, say x and y, you want to give to the **SomeClass** constructor, you put a line like the following.

```
sc_ptr = new SomeClass(x, y);
```

In C++, **new** is a special operator which (a) allocates space for a new object of the specified class, (b) calls the class's constructor on the indicated arguments in order to initialize the object, and then (c) returns a pointer to this newly constructed object.

When you create an object of a given class type the constructor gets called; the constructor encapsulates the initialization and the allocation code. You can 'create' an object either by declaring it as a variable or by using the **new** operator to create an object and return a pointer to it.

Note that in Java, all class instance variables are of the pointer type. Java doesn't explicitly use the * symbol to indicate pointers, but the variables for objects are indeed pointer variables. This is why in Java you need to call **new** whenever you want to initialize an object variable. Something that makes the situation a little confusing is that Java also has primitive type variables such as integers that are *not* pointers.

Saying the same thing again in a different way:

in the Java language *every class instance is a pointer.*

Sometimes beginning Java programmers have the impression that 'Java has no pointers.' But exactly the opposite is true. Everything in Java is a pointer, other than primitives like **int** and **char**. The Java compiler will remind you of this if you try and compile code with a line like `SomeClass nogood`. You'll get an error message saying something about a NULL pointer. Java requires you to rewrite the offending line as `SomeClass goodnow = new SomeClass()`.

22.2 Implicit arguments

Suppose that **SomeClass** is a class whose prototype includes a member `_val` and two functions **SomeFunction** and **SomeOtherFunction**.

```
class SomeClass
{
    int _val;
    int ValSquared(){return _val * _val;}
    int SomeFunction(int input);
    int SomeOtherFunction(int first, int second);
};
```

Now if K is an object of type **SomeClass**, then the value of, let us say, `K.SomeFunction(17)` will depend on (a) the argument 17, (b) the function definition of **SomeFunction**, and (c) the contents of the object K. K is an 'implicit argument' to this function call.

When you write out the code for **SomeFunction**, you play on the fact that you have an implicit argument to the function, even though you don't explicitly show it. Thus the code for **SomeFunction** might look like the following.

```
int SomeClass::SomeFunction(int input)
{
    return SomeOtherFunction(_val, ValSquared());
}
```

This means that `K.SomeFunction(17)` would be evaluated as `K.SomeOtherFunction(K._val, K.ValSquared())`, with `K.ValSquared()` being evaluated as `K._val * K._val`.

The initially bewildering C++ **this** is used inside a function as a way to refer to a pointer to the implicit calling object. The object itself is ***this**, that is, the object that **this** is pointing to. Remember that if `p` is a pointer, then `*p` 'dereferences' the pointer to stand for the actual object the pointer points to.

If we wanted to, we could have put `this->_val` or `*this._val` in place of `_val` inside the `SomeClass::SomeFunction` definition. But we don't want to, as this would be defeating the whole beauty of C++'s concise syntax.

In general, when you are looking at some unfamiliar code and you see a function call inside a class method definition, you can usually expect that any unfamiliar function you see being called 'naked' is in fact a member of the class. When we speak of a function being called 'naked,' we mean that it's being called without any explicit calling object in front of it, no `caller.` or `pcaller->` in other words. If you don't find the function listed as a method of the class, it may be that it's a method of the class's parent class.

Now and then we want to explicitly avoid using a class's own version of a member function, preferring to use a global function with the same name. In this case, we put the symbol :: in front of the function name. The name of this symbol, by the way, is the 'scope resolution operator.' We sometimes use it in

MFC programming, as most of our MFC class methods have the same names as some global method. In order to make the code easier to understand, when we use any global function at all we will habitually put the :: in front of its name just to remind ourselves that it isn't a member method of any class.

22.3   Defining a new class

Just to show that making a class doesn't need to be hard, let's do the absolute simplest implementation of, say, a *cDisk* that represents a circle. Suppose we assume that we specify the circle by a *cVector* center, a *Real* radius, and a **COLORREF** fillcolor.

For a class which has simple fields as members, C++ defines an appropriate default no-argument constructor, a default copy constructor, a default over-loaded **operator=**, and a default destructor. The default constructor allocates space for the data fields but doesn't initialize them, the default copy constructor and **operator=** copy the data from one object to another field by field, and the default destructor simply frees up the space used by a class object. (As an aid in debugging, when you do a Debug build of a program in Visual Studio, unitialized variables are filled with a distinctive bit pattern, commonly **0xCDCDCDCD**; so if you see a variable with a curiously regular value, it usually means you forgot to initialize it.)

For this very simple example, let's make all the class data members public so we don't have to think about mutators and accessors. So now we can define **cDisk** like the following.

```
class cDisk
{
public:
    cVector _center;
    Real _radius;
    COLORREF _fillcolor;
};
```

Is that painless, or what? Who says it's hard to use classes?

This is a time to remind you that

> when you write classes of your own, *you have to put a final semicolon at the end of the class declaration*. This is a possible slip-up that can lead to really confusing error messages from the compiler.

This is also a time to mention that in C++ we have the convention of starting all of our member variable names with an underscore. This makes your code more readable as then you can easily recognize when something is a member variable. Unfortunately this sound and useful convention was not carried over to Java. Do note that the code will compile just as well if you leave out all the underscores on the private field names; they are there only for the human programmer, the compiler doesn't care what you call the variables.

Where should we put the class definition? The clean thing to do is to put it into its own **disk.h** file that lives in the same directory as our Pop code. Since we don't have any *cDisk* methods to implement, we don't need a **disk.cpp** file.

How to make the **disk.h** file? There are several choices.

If your new class header file is similar to an existing class header file, simply make a fresh copy of the old class header file and change its name. Or use **File | New** to create the disk.h file in Visual Studio (or in any other text editor, provided you save it as a text only file).

In either case, you'll need to use the **Project | Add | Existing Item...** [**Project | Add | Files...** in Version 6.0] dialog to add the file to the Pop project.

You can create and add the file in one step with the **Project | Add New Item** dialog [**Project | Add to Project | New | Files tab** dialog in Version 6.0].

A final option, not highly recommended, is to use the Visual Studio menu selection **Add | Class...** (Note that this option is only visible if you have selected **View | Class View**.) [The control is **Insert | New Class...** in Version 6.0.]

The author doesn't recommend the last technique because it throws you into a dialog box situation with a lot of choices whose consequences aren't immediately clear; and when you're done, your files have some ugly machine-written code that you truly don't need.

One caveat; when you make your own header file, don't forget to bracket it with the following lines to prevent double header-file includes (as discussed in Chapter 20: Using Microsoft Visual Studio).

```
#define DISK_H
#ifndef DISK_H
... //The class prototype code goes here
#endif //DISK_H
```

However you end up making your new header file, you need to tell the files that want to use it about the class, by putting an `#include "disk.h"` into them. When you have classes with methods you need to implement, you need to make a file like disk.cpp to put the implementation into. You can make this new file in any of the ways mentioned above. Be sure that the first two lines of this file are these.

```
#include "stdafx.h"
#include "disk.h"
```

When working with an MFC project, if the `#include "stdafx.h"` isn't the very first (non-comment) line of your *.cpp, you will get a confusing error message when you try to compile.

22.4 Destructors

As well as a constructor, each class has a destructor method with a name like ~*SomeClass*. (On US keyboards, the '~' symbol is normally on the upper left-hand corner of your keyboard, but in other parts of the world you'll find it somewhere else.) We have no choice about the names of the constructor and destructor methods. For any class **SomeClass**, the constructor is called **SomeClass** and the destructor is called ~**SomeClass**.

When a variable goes out of scope its destructor is automatically called. Thus if your program has a global variable, the variable's destructor is called when your program terminates. If you have a function which has a local variable **sctemp** in it of type **SomeClass**, the **SomeClass** constructor is called when the code execution hits the line where the **SomeClass** variable is declared, and the **SomeClass** destructor code for **sctemp** is called when the execution hits the closing bracket of the function. More precisely, when you hit the closing bracket of a function, the destructors are called for all of the local variables that were declared inside the function. The destructors for local variables are called in the reverse order that the constructors were called.

In the case where you use the **new** operator to create a pointer to a **SomeClass** instance, you must explicitly call the **delete** operator on the pointer to call the destructor and free up the memory.

22.5 The const **function declaration**

When you look at documentation on classes, you see a lot of pesky **const**. What's all that about? Well, first off let's say that if they confuse you too much, it would in fact be OK to just leave them all out. But there is a reason for them. It's generally considered a good idea to put **const** after the declaration of any function with does not change the values of a class's private fields.

```
int Func(SomeClass input)const; //Doesn't change the caller class
int Func(SomeClass input); //May change the caller class
```

Meticulous programmers (and that's what we should all want to be!) use **const** as a way of telling the compiler to warn you if it finds anything in that function's code which changes a private class member. If you don't bother to put the **const** into your class and a meticulous programmer uses your class in another class definition where he or she has **const**, then there will in fact be trouble, as the compiler will be scared to use your non-**const** function in a **const** function definition.

There are some savage gotchas connected with the use of the **const** after a function prototype. These have to do with the fact that a C++ compiler internally 'name-mangles' function names so that a function has a completely different name according to whether it's a **const** or not. We could put the two Func prototypes above into a class and C++ would compile as if these were completely different functions.

This has two unpleasant consequences. First of all, whether the implementation of a function includes the word **const** or not depends upon the prototype. Otherwise you get a compiler error. That is, if either or both of the two different prototypes above were in a **cMyClass**, they'd be respectively implemented like this:

```
int cMyClass:Func(cSomeClass input)const{ .... }
int cMyClass:Func(cSomeClass input){ .... }
```

The second unpleasant consequence is much worse. Suppose you declare a virtual function in a base class and then redeclare it in a child class. (If you're hazy about what virtual functions are, look down at the description in Section 22.10.) If the const declarations of the two functions don't match, then the virtual base class function won't call the child class function. This happened to the author recently with some code like this.

```
class cSprite
{
    virtual void draw()const;
};
class cPolygon : public cSprite
{
    void draw();
};
```

When one sets a cSprite* psprite = new cPolygon() and calls psprite->draw(), one keeps getting the *cSprite::draw* instead of the *cPolygon::draw*. This is because C++ viewed our *draw()* in *cPolygon* as a new function completely different from the *draw()const* in *cSprite*.

Starting to use **const** is an all-or-nothing decision. That is, if you start using **const** in one file, then the compiler will make you use it in every related file. The reason for this is that if you try, say, to give a class *Careful* a **const** accessor method which uses the non-**const** accessor member of a *Casual* class member, then the compiler will balk. Here's an example:

```
class Casual
{
    int _val;
public
    int val(){return _val;}
};

class Careful
{
private:
    Casual _casual_member;
public:
    int val() const {return _casual_member.val();}
    /* Won't compile, will give error like "non-const function
    called on const object." */
};
```

Putting **const** declarations into your code is a bit of a hassle, but if you plan to have others use your code, you have to do it. Why? Because even if you like to be casual, your user may very well be careful, and, as just explained, when a careful class tries to use a casual class method there can be a conflict.

22.6   Pass by reference

The **&** symbol is a way of telling the compiler to pass an object by reference, that is, the compiler generates a pointer to the object and passes that, instead of copying out all the fields of the object. If you have a function with a prototype like the following, you can give it a ***cSomeClass*** argument input and ***Func*** can in fact change what's in the input.

```
int Func(cSomeClass &input);
```

One reason we do this is because we might actually want to change the fields of the object being passed. Recall that in C, you can't directly change the value of a variable being passed into a function. But the C++ trick of putting an **&** into the function prototype lets you have a function which *does* change the values of its input.

Another reason why we sometimes want to pass an object as a pointer instead of as a structure is that it's faster to pass a pointer to an object instead of copying the whole object. And there will be times you want this speed, but you definitely don't want to change what's in the input.

The troublesome **const** also arises in connection with the **&** symbol in function declarations. Here it relates to the argument of the function rather than to the caller. If you want the speed of passing an argument by reference, but you know you don't want to actually change what's in the object, then you use the **const** followed by the class name and the **&** to mean 'don't allow any change in this fields of this object, but do pass it as a pointer which you generate.' And you use a prototype like:

```
Func(const cSomeClass &input);
```

You can combine the **const** argument and the **const** function declarations in all the possible ways. C++ views all of these as different functions.

```
int Func(SomeClass &input)const;
int Func(SomeClass &input);
int Func(const SomeClass &input)const;
int Func(const SomeClass &input);
```

For full disclosure, we might as well mention four more possible ways that you might prototype a function in C++.

```
int Func(SomeClass input)const;
int Func(SomeClass input);
int Func(SomeClass *input)const;
int Func(SomeClass *input);
```

What a hassle, huh? A real nightmare! No wonder so many people want to abandon C++ for the calm of Java or C#. Bjarne Stroustrup, the inventor of C++, claims that the only reason that Java is simple is because it's a young language lacking all of C++'s features. He says that C++ is so complicated because it's mature.

But once you get some practice with using C++, you'll find that having eight possible ways to prototype a function isn't so bad as you might expect. The practice is always to make every function as **const** as you can, so you don't actually have to think about that so much. The different forms let you make sure your code is going to be as portable, safe, and fast as possible.

Remember to match the ***.cpp** implementation format to the ***.h** declaration format. And, above all, be careful that your derived classes use the same declarations as the parent classes.

22.7   Instance members and reference members

We often have members of classes which are themselves classes. Thus we might have something like this.

```
class MyClass
{
protected:
    ClassA aobject;
    ClassB *pbobject;
};
```

In this kind of situation, we say that `aobject` is an embedded or *instance* `ClassA` member, while `pbobject` is a pointer-based or *reference* `ClassB` member. We often prefer to use pointer-based members because then the methods of these members can be called polymorphically. When we talk about Serialization, Chapter 30, we'll see that there are some important issues relating to the difference between embedded and pointer-based members.

Generally you let primitive variables be instance members, and you let your object members be references. This is, in fact, the Java style of doing things. You should generally have in the back of your mind that you might need to port your C++ to Java (or C#) one of these days, or vice-versa, so, all things being equal, the more you can make your C++ code like Java and your Java code like C++ code the better.

A big win with having pointer-based reference members is that then polymorphism will work for these members – see Section 22.11: Polymorphism.

22.8   Parent and child class data

A parent class is a subset of a child class; that is, the child class includes all of the data members and methods as the parent. It's common also to speak of a parent class as a base class, and to speak of a child class as a derived class.

In order to allow the child class to have access to the private fields and methods of the parent class we need to declare those fields to be **protected** rather than **private**.

What about access to the public fields of the parent? The child can always access these, but these fields do not necessarily have to be public members of the child as well. A child can change a parent method from **protected** to **public** or from **public** to **protected** by redeclaring it.

In the declaration of a child class, you follow the child class's name by a colon, an access specifier, and the name of the parent class, like class cMyChild : public cMyParent.

We usually stick the word **public** in there because otherwise the access permissions will default to the default C++ value of **private**, which is not as commonly used. In particular, if you don't put in the **public**, then all of the parent's public methods are now private methods of the child.

Why would you ever want to use **private** inheritance anyway? This is appropriate when you have defined a class that is a specialization of a parent class that has some methods you don't want your code-users to be able to invoke.

Here's a specific example. We use a class called a *cBiota* which holds a bunch of *cCritter** pointers to lively little *cCritter* objects. Now *cBiota* actually inherits from a special kind of MFC class called **CObArray** which encapsulates the notion of an array of pointers to objects. The **CObArray** has standard array methods such as **GetSize()**, **operator[]**, and a method **Add()** for adding things to the end of the array. Now suppose that when you **Add** an element to the *cBiota*, you want to be sure to do some kind of branding on the element, like, say, giving it an internal pointer to the *cBiota* itself. So if we had a cBiota _biome and a cCritter* pcritter, we might write a line like _biome.Add(pcritter), but we might not want to be able to write a line like _biome[_biome.GetSize()-1] = pcritter;. Now if in this case you want to prevent yourself and the other programmers you work with from using all of the possible **CObArray** methods, you can declare class cBiota : private CObArray. And then down inside the *cBiota* definition, you can specify the Add method as public, and override it to do the critter-branding.

The author recently stumbled across an odd gotcha related to parent and child classes. C++ will let you declare a child class member with the same name as a parent class member. If you do this, your child class can be changing the value of this field, but when you use a parent class accessor to look at what you think is the same field, you'll get back the default value that lives in the parent class. In this situation, the parent field is said to 'shadow' (as in 'cover up') the child field. Here's an illustration.

```
class cSprite
{
    Real _radius; //Assume the constructor sets this to 0.0
    Real radius(){return _radius;}
};
class cPolygon : public cSprite
{
    Real _radius;
    Real makeRegularPolygon(int vertexcount, Real radius)
};
cPolygon poly;
poly.makeRegularPolygon(5, 2.0);//Changes cPolygon _radius to 2.0
Real polyradius = poly.radius(); //Makes polyradius 0.0, not 2.0!
```

22.9 Parent and child constructors and destructors

When a class object is constructed, the following sequence takes place.

(1) Memory storage for the object is allocated (e.g. enough bytes for the object's data fields are allocated in memory).

(2) The default constructor of the parent class (if any) is called, unless you explicitly request some other parent constructor in your initializer list.

(3) The constructors for each of the class member objects are executed (in the order of the member classes' declaration); if there is no initializer list the default constructors are called, but you can request special constructors in your initializer list.

(4) The class constructor code is executed.

When a class object is destroyed the following sequence takes place.

(1) The class destructor code is called.

(2) The destructor of each of the class member objects is executed.

(3) The destructor of the base class (if any) is executed.

(4) The memory storage for the object is recycled.

So the *cMyChild* constructor automatically calls the default *cMyParent* constructor before getting inside its own code. A handy way to think of this is to imagine that a *cMyChild* object has a *cMyParent* object as a member. The parent class and the members all get their constructors called.

Now, it may be that you want to feed some arguments into the base class or member constructors. To do this, you write out these constructors in an 'initializer list' that follows a colon after the constructor. Here's an example of a class definition.

```
cTeacherProgrammer : public cProgrammer
{
private:
    int _ugliness;
    cGollywog *_pimaginaryfriend;
public:
    cTeacherProgrammer(int flubba, float gleep);
    ~cTeacherProgrammer();
}
```

And here's a constructor using an initializer list.

```
cTeacherProgrammer::cTeacherProgrammer(int flubba, float gleep):
    cProgrammer(flubba, gleep),
    _ugliness(1000000)
{
    _pimaginaryfriend = new cGollywog(this);
}
```

And here's how the destructor would be defined.

```
cTeacherProgrammer::~cTeacherProgrammer(){delete _pimaginaryfriend);}
```

Note that the *cTeacherProgrammer* destructor *first* does the `delete _pimagi-naryfriend`, and *then* calls the parent *cProgrammer* destructor. You can remember the sequence by thinking in terms of working your way down the hierarchy at construction, and working your way back up at destruction.

When you need to code up several different forms of a constructor, it can be useful to have an initialization helper function that the different constructors in both the parent and the child class can call.

22.10   Virtual **methods**

The keyword **virtual** in front of a parent class method tells the C++ compiler that the class has a child class which has a method which has the same name but which acts differently in the child class. If (a) a method is declared as **virtual**, and (b) the object which calls the method is referred to via a pointer, then (c) the compiled program will, even while it is running, be able to decide which implementation of the **virtual** method to use. It is worth stressing that this 'runtime binding' only works if you the programmer fulfill both conditions: (a) you use **virtual** in your method declaration, and (b) you use a pointer to your object.

Except in the case of a destructor, corresponding virtual functions have the same name. You don't put the word **virtual** in front of the actual function implementation code in the *.cpp. You can put **virtual** in front of the child class function declaration in the child class's header file or not, as you like. In other words, to start with, you really only need to put **virtual** in one place: in front of the parent class's declaration of the function.

But, in order to make our code more readable, when we derive off child classes from a parent class with a virtual function, we usually *do* put **virtual** in front of the child method declaration as well as in the parent method declaration. The child does need to have a declaration for the method in order to override it in any case.

One slightly weird thing is that a parent class destructor like **~cProgrammer()** needs to be declared **virtual** even though a child class destructor like **~cTeacherProgrammer()** seems to have a different name. But you don't in fact call the destructor by name. In a program where we have a cProgrammer *_ptextbookauthor, we might be calling either the **cProgrammer** or the **cTeacher** destructor with a line like delete _ptextbookauthor;. The thing is, it's possible that _ptextbookauthor got initialized as new cTeacher, so we just don't know.

The **delete** operator calls the destructor without referring to the destructor method by name. So the compiled code needs to actually look at the type of the _textbookauthor pointer to find out whether it's really a **cProgrammer*** or a **cTeacherProgrammer***, so it knows which destructor to use. And unless you fulfilled the 'virtual condition' by making the destructor **virtual**, then the code won't know to do runtime binding and choose between using the parent or the child method as appropriate. The destructors are different here because the **cTeacherProgrammer** has more stuff to destroy, in particular, the cGollywog *_pimaginaryfriend.

Slogan for a class: *If your child is richer than you, you need a virtual destructor.*

One final point should be mentioned here. Ordinarily, when you have a method **virtual void somemethod()** in a base class called, say, **cParentClass**, then when you override the method in a child class called, say, **cChildClass**, the child class **somemethod()** will call the parent class method if we explicitly ask it to with code like this.

```
void cChildClass::somemethod()
{
    cParentClass::somemethod();
    //Your extra childclass code goes here....
}
```

But in the case of a **virtual** destructor, the parent class's destructor method will be *automatically* called when the object is deleted. This is in accord with the standard C++ execution order of constructors and destructors mentioned in the last subsection.

```
cChildClass::~cChildClass()
{
    //Your extra child class destructor code goes here...
...
    /* The cParentClass::~cParentClass destructor will be
        automatically called
            here at the end of the ~cChildClass destructor call. */
}
```

22.11 Polymorphism

Each Pop Framework game is based on a *cBiota* object which is a specialized kind of array of *cCritter** pointers. The program executes by walking through this array and letting each of the member critters call a method. At each step of the game's animation, for instance, we walk through the *cBiota* array and let each of the member *cCritter* pointers make a call to its **virtual** *update* method.

Rather than having to check which kind of critter we have in each slot, we're able to just let each critter call its own version of the *update* method. This is what polymorphism is for. In order to make a function behave polymorphically, we have to do two things. We already mentioned this in Section 22.10: Virtual Methods, but it's worth saying again.

The first step in making a method polymorphic is that the function has to be declared as **virtual** in the base class. As mentioned before, you don't need to put the word **virtual** in the child class declaration, though you can if you like.

The second step in making a method behave polymorphically is that it has to be stored in a pointer variable rather than in a base class instance variable. That is, consider the difference between these two declarations.

```
CArray<cCritter, cCritter &> _embeddedarray;
CArray<cCritter*, cCritter*> _pointerarray;
```

Suppose that, for the purposes of this discussion, the virtual *cCritter update* method is overridden by the *cCritterArmed* child class to do something different. Now, even if some of the objects in the _embeddedarray are 'really' *cCritterArmed* objects, when you placed them into the **CArray<cCritter, cCritter&>**, you had to upcast them into *cCritter* objects, so now if you walk through this array and call _embeddedarray[i].update(...), you will always end up just using the *cCritter::update* method.

But, if some of the *cCritter** pointers in the _pointerarray are actually *cCritterArmed** pointers, then when you walk through this array and call _pointerarray[i]->update(); you will get either the *cCritter::update* method or the *cCritterArmed::update* method, depending on the type of the pointer. Since a *cCritterArmed* class is a child of the *cCritter* class, a *cCritterArmed** can be thought of as a *cCritter**, so we are allowed to put it into the array. But a pointer 'remembers' what kind of class it really points to, and this information gets used when a possibly polymorphic method call is made.

This is why the Pop Framework uses an array of **cCritter*** pointers. It turns out, though, that for reasons having to do with writing the critter data to a file, it works better to use the less obvious array template **CTypedPtrArray<CObArray, cCritter*>** in place of the expected **CArray<cCritter*, cCritter*>**. More on this in Chapter 30: Serialization.

22.12   Runtime class information

When you have an array of polymorphic pointers, how do you tell what kind of class pointer you have? That is, after you set a cCritter* pcritter somewhere in your code, how can you tell if pcritter is just a **cCritter*** or whether it is perhaps a **cCritterBullet***? (For this discussion, assume that we have a **cCritterBullet** class that inherits from **cCritter**.) There are two ways to deal with this.

A hand-made way would be to keep a CString _classname field inside our **cCritter** class and set it to either cCritter or to cCritterBullet, depending on whether the object was constructed by the **cCritter** constructor or by the **cCritterBullet** constructor. And then you could find out if a **cCritter*** pcritter is really a **cCritterBullet*** by checking if pcritter->_classname is the same as the string cCritterBullet. People have written programs that way.

In MFC, however, we're encouraged to take advantage of the so-called **CRuntimeClass** structures. These objects have a **CString** field for the class name, just like the _classname field of the hand-made approach. They also keep track of how many bytes big one of our class objects might be.

The way that you associate an informational **CRuntimeClass** structure with one of your class objects? You have to do three things.

- First, declare your class as a child of the MFC **CObject** class, or as a child of another class that itself inherits from **CObject**. The essence of the **CObject** class is that it has a **CRuntimeClass** field for storing your class's name in it.

- Second you have to add a certain macro to the ***.h** class definition file, as described in the next paragraph.

- Third, you have to add another macro to the ***.cpp** class implementation file. There are a couple of different forms of these macro pairs, the DECLARE_DYNAMIC and IMPLEMENT_DYNAMIC pair, the DECLARE_DYNACREATE and IMPLEMENT_DYNACREATE pair, and the most powerful pair, the DECLARE_SERIAL and IMPLEMENT_SERIAL. Each takes a couple of arguments like class names and generates a few lines of code. More specifically, the DECLARE line declares a couple of functions, and the IMPLEMENT macro puts code for the methods. See Exercise 22.1 for fuller details.

MFC provides a couple of tools for working with the 'runtime class information' in a **CObject**-derived class. First of all, there is a macro called **RUNTIME_CLASS(classname)**, which generates a pointer to a **CRuntimeClass** description of a class if you feed it a class's name just written there without any quotation marks. This macro can only works if the class is **CObject** derived. Since **cCritter** inherits form **CObject**, we can indeed write RUNTIME_CLASS(cCritter) to produce a **CRuntimeClass*** reference to the kind of class that **cCritter** is.

The second main MFC tool involving **CRuntimeClass** information is the **BOOL CObject::IsKindOf(CRuntimeClass* pruntimeclass)** method. Thus, if you wanted to know if a **cCritter *pcritter** pointer is actually a **cCritterBullet*** pointer, you could evaluate pcritter->IsKindOf(RUNTIME_CLASS(cCritterBullet)).

Implementing the runtime class support is actually easier than thinking about it. Here are the three steps mentioned above.

- Declare **cCritter : public CObject**.
- Put this line inside the brackets of, the **cCritter** class definition.

```
DECLARE_SERIAL(cCritter);
```

Note that it can't just be anywhere in Critter, it has to be inside the **cCritter** class brackets.
- Put this line anywhere inside the **Critter.cpp** file after the **#include** lines.

```
IMPLEMENT_SERIAL( cCritter, CObject, 0 );
```

And we do the same steps for **cCritterBullet**, except that if **cCritterBullet** inherits from **cCritter**, it doesn't have to inherit from **CObject**. The inheritance relationship is transitive. The IMPLEMENT_SERIAL macro for **cCritterBullet** will mention the parent **cCritter**, rather than **cObject**, as follows.

```
IMPLEMENT_SERIAL(cCritterBullet, cCritter, 0);
```

A word of caution here. You have to be very disciplined about putting in the correct IMPLEMENT_SERIAL macro code into the *.cpp file when you add a new class that has the DECLARE_SERIAL macro in its *.h header. If you don't do it, or if you do it wrong in any way (for instance if you were to put **cObject** instead of **cCritter** in the IMPLEMENT_SERIAL macro for **cCritterBullet**), then your program will compile and build, but when you try and run it you will get a crash at startup accompanied by an inscrutable message. Try and remember this fact: if you ever do have code that seems to crash at startup 'for no reason,' then you should take a good look at all of your IMPLEMENT_SERIAL macro declarations and make sure that they're all in place and correct.

22.13   The scope resolution operator and global functions

In C++, the '::' is called the 'scope resolution operator.' If you put a class name like **MyClass** in front of the operator, this indicates that you want to use the version of the class method implemented by the **MyClass** code. If, for instance, you have a **ChildClass** and a **ParentClass**, then **ParentClass::Method()** and **ChildClass::Method()** could very well mean different things.

Some functions are 'global' functions that aren't a member of any class at all. We try to make a practice of always putting two colons with no class name in front of a global function to remind ourselves that this is a function that doesn't belong to any class. Ordinarily, putting the '::' in front of a global function doesn't add anything or change anything; the code compiles and runs equally well with or without it. It's just something you do make your code easier to read. Thus, when I want to refer to the global Windows API method **PlaySound**, I'll normally write **::PlaySound**.

The one time the '::' would really be *necessary* in front of a global function would be if you wrote a class method with the same name as a global function. If, for instance, you gave *CPopView* its own *PlaySound* method, then if you wanted to call the global *PlaySound* inside a *CPopView* method, you really would need to say *::PlaySound*, as a call to *PlaySound* would call the *CPopView::PlaySound* method.

22.14   Name-mangling

When a compiler processes C++ code it changes the names of functions to include information about the types of the function's arguments. This process, normally invisible, is called 'name-mangling'.

You most often notice the effects of name-mangling when you put a prototype of a class method in a header file, but then fail to implement the method in any of your project's ***.cpp** files. The project will compile all right, but at the very end, you will get a linker message. Thus, if you were to leave out the code for the *cCritter* method *int cCritter::move(Real dt)*, you would get a linker error like the following.

```
popview.obj : error LNK2001: unresolved external symbol "public: int
    __thiscall cCritter::move(float)" (?move@cCritter@@QAEHM@Z)
```

The string at the end at the end of the line is the name-mangled name of the method.

Remember how we talked about how having a **const** after the name of a function changes how C++ thinks of it? That's because the **const** goes into the name-mangled name.

Name-mangling can become an issue in advanced programming situations, for instance if (a) you want to link someone else's ***.c** module with your ***.cpp** modules, or (b) you want to locate a function by name inside a dynamic link library module. This is because although you may think the function's name is what you called it, say '**int MyFunction**(),' C++ will actually have assigned a different 'mangled' name for your function. You can turn off the name-mangling for a function name by specifically asking in its prototype that it be treated like a C function, using a line like the following.

```
extern "C" int MyFunction();
```

22.15   Preprocessor directives

Compiling a file is actually a multi-step process. Before actually compiling any code, a compiler uses something called a 'preprocessor' to look through the project files and carries out the instructions embodied in the various preprocessor directives. Any line of C++ that starts with **#** is a preprocessor directive. Some of them are **#include**, **#define**, **#ifdef**, **#endif**, and **#pragma**. Each preprocessor directive tells the compiler to do something before running. The instructions in the **#** directives are used to alter the contents of the file, which is only then passed on to the normal compilation process.

The #include directive

What the **#include** directive tells the compiler to do is to replace a line like `#include "whatever.h"` with a full, exact copy of the **Whatever.h** file, just as if you had used your text editor to block copy the whole **Whatever.h** file and paste it in.

If the filename after `#include` is in quotes, the compiler will look for the file in the directory where the project file lives; and if the include file is in pointy brackets, the compiler will look for the file in whatever directories the project file has set to be places to look for include files – typically the standard location for include files is the **INCLUDE** subdirectory of the directory where the compiler lives, but sometimes you will want to add other directories to the standard search path. Note that the compiler is not sensitive to the case of the letters used in the names of the include files.

The #define directive

The **#define** directive has this appearance.

```
#define ANYSTRING Any other string
```

The string between the first two blank spaces after the **#define** is replaced everywhere by the string which fills out the rest of the line after the second blank space. Who does the replacing? The preprocessor. It effectively does a search and replace, replacing each 'ANYSTRING' by 'Any other string.' It's good programming practice, but not formally necessary, to always use all capital letters for a quantity which you **#define**.

Another, non-obvious effect of a **#define** statement is that it adds the first string to a special 'symbol table' that the preprocessor constructs for the code being compiled; the symbol table being a private list of what strings have been used in a **#define**.

#ifdef and related directives

The next group of preprocessor directives have to do with control flow. Lines of the form **#ifdef**, **#ifndef**, **#else**, and **#endif** conditionally include or exclude parts of the file depending on whether some symbol has been placed into the preprocessor symbol table by a **#define**.

#ifdef, **#ifndef**, **#else**, and **#endif** are preprocessor directives to the compiler. The first two stand, respectively, for 'if defined' and 'if not defined.' If the expression (or 'token') after the **#ifdef** has been defined with a **#define**, then the block of code up until the **#endif** is included; if the token is not defined, then the code is not included. If the token after an **#ifndef** has been defined with a **#define**, then the block of code up until the **#endif** is not included; if the token is not defined, then the code is included.

As mentioned above, you can **#define** something without putting a 'replacement string' for it. That is, we can have this line.

```
#define ANYHEADER_H
```

This use of the **#define** directive adds the indicated string of letters to the preprocessor symbol table so as to possibly affect **#ifdef** or **#endif** statements.

There is also a **defined()** operator one can use in conjunction with a plain **#if** directive. So instead of `#ifdef WIN_H`, for instance, you can write `#if defined(WIN_H)`, and instead of `#ifndef WIN_H`, you can write `#if !defined(WIN_H)`.

The **#pragma** directive is used for miscellaneous kinds of special hints to the compiler. A common use is to turn off a warning that you don't care about. Thus the following line taken from our realnumber.h file turns off two warnings that result from treating a **double** as a **float**.

```
#pragma warning(disable: 4305 4244)
```

Sometimes you don't want to bother using a **pragma** to turn off a warning message of the form, say, "information lost in conversion from double to int". You can tell the compiler that in a particular case you really don't *mind* rounding, say, `sqrt(dx*dx + dy*dy)` off to the closest integer. In C we would have done this with a 'cast' by putting `(int)` in front of the number. In C++ it's more common to write a cast as a 'constructor' by putting `int(sqrt(dx*dx + dy*dy))`. In general, if you can get rid of a warning message by adding a little bit of code it's worth doing, so that then you know that any messages that do pop up in your compiler are important.

The typedef convention

Although **typedef** isn't a preprocessor directive, it has much the same force. typedef gives us a mechanism for defining a synonym for an existing type. The syntax is as follows:

```
typedef existing-type synonym;
```

If you want a synonym for a class name then its better to use **typedef** than **define**, as the compiler can then better check the consistency of what you're doing.

We might use a **typedef** in the case where a type name is very long and unwieldy. Thus we might do something like this (although actually we don't use this in the Pop Framework).

```
typedef CTypedPtrArray<CObArray, cCritter*> cCritterArray;
```

Another case where we use **typedef** is when we want to try out different builds of our code. The Pop Framework has two possible **typedef** for the *Real* type in realnumber.h, and in vectortransformation.h, it has a **typedef** based on whether we plan to use 2D or 3D graphics.

```
#define THREEDVECTORS
#ifndef THREEDVECTORS
    typedef class cVector2 cVector;
    typedef class cMatrix2 cMatrix;
#else //THREEDVECTORS
    typedef class cVector3 cVector;
    typedef class cMatrix3 cMatrix;
#endif //THREEDVECTORS
```

22.16   Resizable arrays

Suppose you want to have an array that holds, say, *cCritter* objects. There are really three options: maintain your own C-style array, use an array template from the ANSI C++ STL Standard Template Library, or use the Microsoft **CArray** template.

To maintain an array yourself means using a declaration like cCritter *_critter or cCritter _critter[]. (Note that C regards these two declarations as equivalent; in C an array *is* simply a pointer.) If you do this, you would also need an int _critter_count variable to keep track of the current number of points stored. And you'd either have to preallocate _critter to some generously large size (and worry about eventually writing off the end), or you'd have to keep reallocating the memory for the array as it grows.

That's a lot of work, and it's easy to make errors in doing it. Writing your own array code these days means reinventing the wheel. It's much better instead to use a presupplied array template. Here we have two choices: STL or MFC.

STL vector arrays

Every version of C++ comes with a platform-independent library of templates known as the STL or the Standard Template Library. This library was written at Hewlett-Packard around 1995 and is now part of the official ANSI C++ language standard, which means that all C++ compilers for every platform must support it. The STL library includes, among many other kinds of collection classes, an array template that's known as **vector**. The code for the STL template will

Table 22.1 A Standard Template Library (STL) array template compared to an MFC array.

Template usage for	STL	MFC
Include instructions needed in file.	#include <vector> using namespace std; This include should appear only in the files where <vector> is used, and it should be the last include listed at the head of these files.	#include <afxtempl.h>
Prototype of array of classes.	vector<cCritter> _critter;	CArray<cCritter, cCritter &> _critter;
Prototype of array of basic types.	vector<int> _radius;	CArray<int, int> _radius;
Adding element to end of array.	push_back(newpoint)	Add(newpoint)
Deleting the array member in the i slot.	erase(i)	RemoveAt(i)
Accessing size of the array.	size()	GetSize()
Setting the array size.	resize(newsize)	SetSize(newsize)
Accessing an element for reading or setting.	[i]	[i] ElementAt(i) GetAt(i), for read only

normally be found in a file in your Visual Studio include directory; the name of this include file is, a bit oddly, just plain **VECTOR**, with no file extension. For whatever reason, Visual Studio needs a bit of a nudge to let the STL work; whenever you include an STL file you need to follow it with a code line of the form using namespace std;. To create an STL array of some class type T, you use the new type vector<T>.

One plus of STL templates is that they're portable to all C++ platforms, so you can expect to be able to use them in more environments. But there are some annoying gotchas associated with the now fairly old STL templates – I won't go into them here. Certainly the Visual Studio documentation of the STL is not as easy to use as is their documentation of the **CArray**. And the **CArray** templates are tweaked so as to work smoothly with the MFC method of 'serializing' or saving and loading files. It's simpler to give in and do it the Microsoft way instead of trying to use STL. We're going to use the MFC **CArray** template in this book. Table 22.1 compares the template usage for STL arrays and MFC arrays.

MFC cArray arrays

The code for the **CArray** template is in a file called afxtempl.h. If you want to declare some **CArray** variables in a file, you need to add this line to the top of the file, so the compiler will know what we're talking about.

```
#include <afxtempl.h>
```

To create an array of objects of some type T, we normally declare our new type as

```
CArray<T, T&>.
```

The meaning of the second mention of T in the declaration is that this is the type used in some of **CArray's** internal functions that do things like add your elements to the **CArray**. The idea is that one normally uses the pass by reference for these types so as to marginally improve the speed of your code, by effectively passing pointers instead of copying whole structures. In the case where T is a primitive type like an **int**, we don't bother with the **&** for the second argument.

The default size of _critter in either case will be 0, and if you immediately try and execute a line that sets, say, _critter[1] to something, then your program will crash. Adding an element to an array will automatically grow it to a size large enough to hold the new element (i.e. it grows the size by one). But, if you are planning to read a lot of elements into your array using the [ ] operator, you need to set the array's size to be large enough before you start.

Another thing about array templates that it's important to be aware of is that when you add an element of type T to your array, it's a copy of your element which actually goes into the array rather than the element itself. So you need to be sure to have a good copy constructor and an overloaded **=operator** defined for any class of objects that you're going to put into an array template.

Actually we're going to be using a variation on the **CArray** template, and this is the **CTypedPtrArray<CObArray, _cMyClass_ *>** template. This is used for holding an array of pointers to instances of some class we've written called _cMyClass_. For this to work, the _cMyClass_ has to inherit from the MFC **CObject** class, which is a kind of universal base class in MFC. More on this below.

22.17 Real numbers

Simulations work better with real numbers, and there is a *Real* type and some macros we use in our programs, so we're going to have a file called RealNumber.h which we include in our files using real numbers. (If we didn't want to do all those includes, we could have put the #include "realnumber.h" somewhere inside of the StdAfx.h file, for instance right before the line that says //{{AFX_INSERT_LOCATION}}.)

In our code we use *Real* as another word for **double** or for **float**. To give ourselves the freedom to switch between **double** and **float**, depending on whether we have a greater need for accuracy or for speed, we have a line saying `typedef double Real` or `typedef float Real` inside RealNumber.h.

```
#ifndef REALNUMBER_H
#define REALNUMBER_H

/* Note that to use the Real type throughout my program, I have to
    always remember to include realnumber.h. */
#define USEFLOAT // float is slightly faster, slightly less accurate.
#ifdef USEFLOAT
    typedef float Real;
#else //not USEFLOAT
    typedef double Real;
#endif //USEFLOAT
/* When I use a float Real, I'll get warning messages generated by
    the fact that constants like 2.0 are viewed as doubles, so that
    if x is a float, the line x = x/2.0 would be viewed as converting
    a double to a float. These messages take this form: warning C4244:
    '=' : conversion from 'double' to 'float', possible loss of data
    warning C4305: '=' : truncation from 'const double' to 'float'
    I can disable these warning messages with a pragma stating the
    two warning numbers. */
#pragma warning(disable: 4305 4244)
#define PI 3.14159265358979
#define CLAMP(x,lo,hi) (x)=(((x)<(lo))?(lo):(((x)>(hi))?(hi):(x)))
#define SMALL_REAL 0.00001
#define BIG_REAL 1000000000.0

#endif //REALNUMBER_H
```

The point of the `typedef double Real` line is that if at some point you find that you want to squeeze a little more speed out of our program, you can come back here and replace **double** by **float**. We need PI because, although the ANSI C library is supposed to define an **M_PI** constant of this value in **math.h**, the Microsoft version of the **math.h** file doesn't seem to have any pi in it. (For sanity's sake, a software engineer learns not to obsess over things like this; simply fix them and move on.) The **CLAMP** macro is useful for forcing a variable x to lie between two values lo and hi. **SMALL_REAL** is convenient in code where you want to avoid dividing by numbers that are too close to 0. And **BIG_REAL** is useful to put in as a starting value in a search loop when we keep looking for a smaller number, as in the code for **cCritter* cBiota::pickClosest(const cVector &vclick)** in biota.cpp for instance.

22.18   A randomizer module

We are going to be randomizing our parameters a lot in this book. In most of our programs we'll want to have a bunch of different objects, and we will want to use randomization to keep the objects from all being the same. In our more advanced programs we may have our objects use randomization so as to give themselves an appearance of interesting behavior.

Even when there's only one object using a given set of parameters, it's not always clear which values to use. It may be that there are no 'best' values, and it's more interesting to look at a wide range of possibilities. In other cases, there may be a 'best' set of values, but the only way to try and find these values is to feel around the parameter space by trying lots of random possibilities.

The C library of standard functions supplies three relevant functions that are of significance here.

long int time(NULL)
srand(unsigned int seed)
short int rand()

Randomizing with the C library

Each call to **rand()** returns a 15-bit positive integer that lies between 0 and +32K. The way **rand** works is that the C library maintains a hidden 32-bit integer variable `holdrand`. When your program starts, `holdrand` has a default value of 1. Every time you call **rand()**, `holdrand` is replaced by `holdrand * 214013 + 2531011`, and `rand` returns the low 15 bits of the high word of `holdrand`. (That is, the return value is `(holdrand >> 16) & 0x7FFF`.)

If **rand** starts with the same value of `holdrand`, it's always going to give you the same sequence of values. So what we usually do is to use the **srand** function to initialize the randomizer to a fresh state. What `srand(seed)` does is simply sets the hidden `holdrand` variable equal to the `seed` argument.

But how can our deterministic program come up with a 'random' seed to feed into **srand**? What we usually do is to use the **time(NULL)** function. This function returns the number of seconds that have elapsed since midnight, January 1, 1970. For whatever reason, this is the official 'birth instant' of our computer era, a little like the anomalous moment when the Western calendar went from BC to 1AD.

The *cRandomizer* class

To make it easier to randomize things, we wrap the randomizing functions up inside a class called *cRandomizer*. Instead of having to use the % operator to bring numbers into range, the *cRandomizer* has a method *random(N)* that will give you a number between 0 and N – 1, a method *random(lo, hi)* that will give you a number from *lo* to *hi* inclusive, a *randomReal(loreal, hireal)* method to give you a real number between *loreal* and *hireal*, a *randomColor()* method, and so on. The *randomBOOL(double truthweight)* is a cute function that gives lets you specify a *truthweight* between 0.0 and 1.0. The *truthweight* is the probability of the *randomBOOL* returning a TRUE. So `randomBOOL(0.75)` would return TRUE three fourths of the time and would return FALSE one fourth of the time.

The default *cRandomizer* constructor seeds it with the **time** function. You also have the option of feeding a seed number into the constructor so as initialize your *cRandomizer* into some specific state. When you're debugging a program it's often a good idea to have the *cRandomizer* always set to the same state so that it's easier for you to reproduce the exact same behavior over and over.

```
#ifndef RANDOMIZER_H
#define RANDOMIZER_H

/* This is a set of 32-bit-based randomizing functions. The functions
use standard C library techniques. The code is written to be portable,
although there is one line you need to comment in or out at the head
of Randomizer.cpp according to whether or not you use Microsoft MFC.

    These randomizing functions are based on a modular scheme derived
from the Microsoft implementation of the C library randomizer. In the
Microsoft implementation, the C Library int rand() function works by
maintaining a _holdrand variable and iterating _holdrand * 214013 +
2531011. rand() returns (_holdrand >> 16) & 07FFF, which is a 15 bit
positive short integer. We use the same scheme, but tailor it to
return a 32 bit unsigned long integer. Returning _holdrand gives too
much correlation, so we actually execute the _holdrand update twice,
and use the high words of the two successive _holdrands as the upper
and lower words of the value we return.

    The Randomizer.cpp file includes a historical note at the end about
an unsuccessful attempt to base the randomizer on Wolfram's CA Rule 30.
*/

#include "realnumber.h"
    //For the Real typedef, which is double or float

class cRandomizer
{
private:
    static cRandomizer * _pinstancesingleton;
    unsigned long _seed; //Start value of _shiftregister
    unsigned long _shiftregister;
        //Used internally for the running compute process.
    unsigned long _thirtytwobits();
        // The internal pseudorandom function used.
    cRandomizer();
        //Uses the C Library randomizer and seeds it with the time.
    cRandomizer(unsigned long seednumber);
        //C Library randomizer seeded by seednumber.
public:
    static cRandomizer * _pinstance();
    static void delete singleton ();
```

```
unsigned long getSeed(){return _seed;}
void setSeed(unsigned long seednumber);
    //Start off in a specific state
unsigned long randomizeSeed(void);
    //Seed with the time in seconds
unsigned long random(); //Return an unsigned long int
unsigned long random(unsigned long n);
    //Return an int between 0 and n - 1
long random(long lon, long hin);
    //int between lon and hin inclusive
BOOL randomBOOL(Real truthweight = 0.5);
    // Return TRUE truthweight often.
unsigned char randomByte(void); //Return a byte between 0 and 255
unsigned short randomShort(unsigned short n);
    // Short between 0 and n-1
Real randomReal(void); //A real between 0.0 and 1.0
Real randomSignedReal(void); //A real between -1.0 and 1.0
Real randomReal(Real lo, Real hi); //A real between lo and hi
Real mutate(Real base, Real lo, Real hi, Real percent);
    //Mutate base by percent of size.
int mutate(int base, int lo, int hi, Real percent);
    //Mutate base by percent of size.
unsigned long mutateColor(unsigned long base, Real percent);
    //Mutate a color.
Real randomSign(void); //1.0 or -1.0
void randomUnitDiskPair(Real *x, Real *y);
    // Makes (x,y) a random point with distance <= 1 from (0,0)
void randomUnitPair(Real *x, Real *y);
    // Makes (x,y) a random point with distance 1 from (0,0)
unsigned long randomColor(); //A Windows COLORREF number.
};

#endif RANDOMIZER_H
```

Since we're going to use the *cRandomizer* a lot, you might wonder if, as time goes by, the *cRandomizer* will accumulate more and more functions. Later, for instance, we might have some *cMyClass* with parameters that we like to randomize, so will it make sense to add a *void cRandomizer::randomizeMyClass(cMyClass &myclassobject)*; method to the *cRandomizer* class?

No, this would be a bad idea, because then we'd always be coming back and changing the **Randomizer.h** and **Randomizer.cpp** files. For sanity's sake, it's much better to try and get your basic, general-purpose files working once and for all and not be continually going back and changing them. This is one of the reasons why we don't use **COLORREF** as a type in Randomizer.h (instead we use the equivalent **unsigned long**).

So how then can we write a method for randomizing a *cMyClass* with a *cRandomizer*? We'll put a randomizing method that's a member of *cMyClass*, that is, we'll have a void cMyClass::randomize(). And then inside the implementation for this method, we'll use standard *cRandomizer* calls to randomize the fields of *cMyClass*.

The static cRandomizer::Randomizer **object**

So as not keep having to create new *cRandomizer* objects to randomize things, we give the *cRandomizer* class a static *cRandomizer* member. This means that anywhere in our Pop program we can call, say, cRandomizer::RANDOMIZER.randomReal() to get a random real number. This is very much a Java-style thing to do; Java has lots of special members and methods that are statics of its standard classes. This is an example of what's called the 'Singleton pattern.'

In C++ a static such as *RANDOMIZER* has to be declared in a *.h file and it has to actually be instantiated, or 'live' as an instance, inside a *.cpp file. We put the instantiation inside randomizer.cpp.

```
cRandomizer* cRandomizer::pinstance()/* pinstance() allocates
    _pinstancesingleton if it's NULL, then returns it. */
{
    if (cRandomizer::_pinstancesingleton == NULL)
        //First time pinstance() is called
#ifndef _DEBUG //not _DEBUG means Release build
        cRandomizer::_pinstancesingleton = new cRandomizer();
    /* In Release build, the default constructor seeds
        with the time for variety. */
#else // _DEBUG means Debug build
        cRandomizer::_pinstancesingleton = new cRandomizer(1);
    // In Debug build, use a fixed seed to help replicate bugs.
#endif //End the _DEBUG switch
    return cRandomizer::_pinstancesingleton;
}
```

In understanding this code, you need to know that Visual Studio has a line #define DEBUG that gets preprocessed if and only if you are making the Debug build and not the Release build. Thus in our code, the compiler chooses between the two declarations depending on whether you are doing a Debug or a Release build.

We don't want the randomizer to be so random in Debug, because there we like to be able to start up a session over and over and keep seeing the same bug in the same spot.

Exercises

Exercise 22.1: Find the MFC code for DECLARE_SERIAL

Use **Edit | Find in Files** to search the **C:\Program Files\Microsoft Visual Studio\VC98** directory and subdirectories for DECLARE_DYNAMIC. The line you are looking for is the one that starts with `#define DECLARE_DYNAMIC`; it lived in **AFX.H**, last time the author checked. Look at this and the other macros mentioned in this section, especially `DECLARE_SERIAL` and `IMPLEMENT_SERIAL`. Note that a macro definition can extend over several lines if the lines keep ending with a backslash \.

Exercise 22.2: The second 4 Gig problem

Since **time** returns a 32-bit integer, we can expect a *Y2K* kind of problem some four billion seconds after 1970. (You might think of it as the *Second 4 Gig* problem.) This is when the **time** function will start repeating itself. Get out your calculator and figure out the date of this instant.

Exercise 22.3: Initializing the randomizer

Run Pop and use **File | New** to open a new document. Use **Window | Tile** so you can see them both. Do they look the same? Try this with both the Release and the Debug builds of the code. Why is the behaviour different?

Programming Windows with MFC

23

There's C, there's C++ and then there's *MFC*. 'MFC' stands for 'Microsoft Foundation Classes.' In this edition of the book, we won't get into Microsoft's new C# language at all.

The older style of Windows coding was called 'Win32.' Win32 code can in fact be incorporated into an MFC program, just like C code can be incorporated into any C++ program. So MFC is an extension of Win32 programming, just as C++ is an extension of C. MFC adds structure to Win32 at two levels: the low and the high. At the low level, MFC extends the Windows programming language by adding more types and more function names. At the high level, MFC makes it easy to automatically add a great many features to your programs by using the application frameworks, also known as AFX. In this subsection we'll talk primarily about MFC, and we'll talk about AFX below in Section 23.8: The MFC Program Flow.

23.1 Some Windows data structures

The COLORREF type

Windows represents colors as 32-bit numbers, of which eight bits each correspond to the red, green, and blue intensity. That is, the 'red' parameter ranges from 0 for *no red* up to 255 for *as much red as possible*, and likewise for 'green' and 'blue'. **RGB** is a macro that packs the three byte-sized numbers into a 32-bit number (the high eight bits are 'reserved').

These color-representing integers are treated as a type called **COLORREF**, where **COLORREF** is defined in the **windows.h** file to mean `unsigned long`. If you know 0 to 255 intensities r, g, and b of red, green and blue that you want, then you can use the Windows macro **RGB** to create a **COLORREF**:

```
COLORREF col = RGB(r,g,b);
```

The order of the bytes from left to right is reserved, blue, green, red. The high, reserved byte is usually set to 0, although when you use special Windows color palettes (as is necessary when in 256 color mode), you may put something else into the reserved byte, such as a flag indicating that the remaining three bytes contain an index into a special Windows palette object.

The RECT structure

There are few things to say about Windows rectangles. The **CRect** class discussed below is actually is a child of an older kind of Windows structure called a **RECT**.

A window's 'client rectangle' is the region, exclusive of the caption bar and frame, into which the user can write things. The **CWnd::GetClientRect(CRect box)** function puts the coordinates of the client rectangle into the **CRect** box object that you pass to the function as argument.

The coordinate system used by **GetClientRect** is said to be in terms of 'logical units' and by default the logical units are pixel units, with the upper left-hand corner of the Windows client rectangle being treated as the origin (0,0). The absolute screen pixel coordinates are *not* used here, although they *are* used by some other Windows functions.

When using the default logical pixel coordinates, a window measures the y-axis in the downward direction. So moving down the screen corresponds to increasing the value of y. Thus, the value of bottom is normally larger than that of top, unless the rectangle happens to have been deliberately or accidentally defined in a 'upside down' manner.

When working with Windows rectangles, we think of the (**left**, **top**) or **TopLeft**( ) corner as being 'inside' the rectangle, with the (**right**, **bottom**) or **BottomRight**( ) corner being 'outside the rectangle.' In other words, a rectangle can be thought of as having a closed boundary along its top and left edges, and an open boundary along its right and bottom edges. This is analogous to the calculus notion of a half-open interval like [0,1), which includes the left endpoint but not the right endpoint. In other words, the last lower-right-hand point actually inside the rectangle is (right-1, bottom-1).

Since the origin is in fact the (left, top) position of the client rectangle, after a call to GetClientRect(rect), rect.left is 0, rect.top is 0, rect.right is the width of the client area in pixels, and rect.bottom is the height of the client area in pixels. You can see that this is correct because, for instance, the pixels inside the rectangle have x-coordinates ranging from 0 up to rect.right - 1, which makes for rect.right pixels in all.

23.2   MFC utility classes

Unlike most classes, the handy utility classes, **CRect**, **CPoint**, and **CSize**, have public data members. That is because these classes are actually derived as child classes of the old Windows structures **RECT**, **POINT**, and **SIZE**, respectively. This is permissible in C++ because a structure can be thought of as a class all of whose members are public. The names of the data fields of these three classes are shown in Table 23.1.

Table 23.1 The fields of some simple MFC utility classes.

Class name	Public data fields
CRect	left, top, right, bottom
CPoint	x, y
CSize	cx, cy

These utility classes have some nice accessors and overloaded operators. For instance, we can get the CSize csmax of a CRect crbox by writing

```
CSize csmax = crbox.Size();
```

CString is a particularly useful MFC class. The **CString** takes the place of the char[] that you might otherwise use to store a string. A **CString** is a self-sizing array, so you don't need to preallocate memory space before you put characters into it. Using the **CString's** constructor we might instead write something like

```
CString cstrhello("Pop!");
```

Another thing worth noting is that the **operator==** is overloaded for **CString** so that stringa == stringb means that they have the same characters.

The MFC code for these utility classes is formulated in a sufficiently polymorphic way that you can usually pass these objects without an explicit **&** reference cast even if the calling function expects a pointer. In other words, MFC functions that are prototyped for a **CRect *** argument will also accept a **CRect** argument, passed by reference as a **CRect&**. A function that wants a data type with the kludgy old name **LPCTSTR** (for 'long pointer to a constant string') will accept a simple **CString** argument.

23.3   The MFC application framework

The really important MFC classes have to do with providing a Document-View architecture. Some of the most important of these classes are the **CWinApp**, the **CDocument**, the **CView**, and the **CDC**.

When you're running a program, there will be one **CWinApp** object, and this is the program itself. The **CWinApp** is responsible for things like routing the program messages, organizing the windows, and deciding what order to do things in. Later, when we want to make our programs do things like move images around even when there's no user input, it will be the **CWinApp** that does this for us.

In a particular program like Pop, your application is a *CPopApp* object. *CPopApp* is a class derived from **CWinApp**. It's defined in the Pop.* files.

When you're looking at a window, there are three ways of thinking of it. First of all, behind the scenes, there's a **CDocument** object in which you can store the data that the window displays. Second, the window itself is a **CView** (which is a specialized version of a general window class called a **CWnd**). Third, when you want to send graphics output to your window, you think of it as a **CDC**, where the 'DC' stands for 'Device Context.'

The **CView** contains the operating system's ID for keeping track of one window as opposed to another. The Windows operating systems uses the **CView** as a way of keeping track of which particular window is supposed to process a given message, such as a menu selection or a mouse-click.

A **CDC** is used whenever you want to write any text or graphics to the window. A window's **CDC** has information about the window's current location and appearance on the screen. As you resize the window, move it around, and possibly change its color palette, the appearance of the window will change, so usually you need to get a fresh **CDC** for the window right before you do a graphics call. Graphics functions such as **TextOut** and **Ellipse** are members of the **CDC** class.

Why does Windows have to make it so hard for us? Why do we have to have a **CWinApp**, **CView**s, and **CDC**s? Well, many programs have the ability to open up a number of different windows, so it stands to reason that, although there is only one **CWinApp**, your program may well have different **CView**. But, why must the **CDC** differ from the **CView**?

Well, it turns out that you can have a **CDC** which is not associated with an onscreen window. When you send text or graphics to your printer, you get a **CDC** for the printer, which is not a window at all. And we'll also find that we can have **CDC**s which contain invisible memory bitmaps rather than being actual windows. These 'virtual window' **CDC**s are essential for writing programs that have moving objects on the screen. The way Windows usually does animation is to prepare each new frame of the animation offscreen in a memory-based virtual window **CDC**, and then, once the new frame is ready, to use the rapid **BitBlt** operation to copy the image to the **CDC** of the visible onscreen **CView**.

As well as the **CWinApp**, **CView**, and **CDC** classes, there are MFC classes which represent graphics tools called pens, brushes, bitmaps, and more. These classes have names like **CPen**, **CBrush**, and **CBitmap**.

Take a look at the header files for some of the AppWizard-generated classes like **CPopDoc** as defined in popdoc.h and **CPopView** as defined in popview.h. Note that these machine-generated files are very messy-looking. It's a good practice to put all the things that *you* add down at the end of the class declarations so they're easy for you to find. In general the order in which things appear within a class declaration doesn't matter, so we put the human-written stuff at the bottom so it's easy to find. Generally, it's only the human-written code that you want to edit anyway. It's also a good idea to set off the human-written code with a comment line.

If you keep your code at the very bottom of the class it will be easy for you and other programmers to find. Although you can use the Class View to add variables, it is easier and safer to type in your variables by hand. There's no telling where Class View will put the variables inside the class. If you type them in by hand you can insist on keeping them all at the bottom of the class definition. By the way, it doesn't matter where any block of code appears inside a class definition.

23.4 Naming conventions

The naming conventions in MFC programs are that the MFC class names all start with a capital **C**, and the class member functions are all written as run-together phrases in which each word is capitalized. **FillSolidRect** is an example of such a function name.

We're free to give our variables any kinds of names we want, but since MFC programs are so big and cumbersome, we try and make the names as helpful as possible. A good variable name will give you (a) information about the type of the class the variable is an instance of, and (b) information about the meaning of your variable inside the program. A common convention is to give our variables names which start with some letters to remind us of the type of the variable, and to have the rest say something about what the variable does. A variable name should always start with a lower-case letter. If you like you can mix in some capitals later into the name, to indicate word breaks, as in bSoundFlag, for a **BOOL** variable. But all lower case for the variable names is easier to remember and faster to type.

Thus, we might give a **CString** variable the name cstrhello. Or we could use the names cstring_hello or cStrHello. In the cases where a variable is a pointer to a class, we like to start the variable name with a p. Thus a **CDC*** variable might be named pdc or perhaps pDC.

What about variables that are examples of general types rather than classes? It's common to use n as the prefix to indicate an integer variable. Sometimes, when an integer is a 'count' variable used to count something like the number of pixels in the screen's width, the c prefix is used. The letters f or b signal a variable which is a **BOOL** flag. As just mentioned, the letter p signals a pointer. The older Windows documentation sometimes raises the (no longer meaningful) distinction between a normal pointer type p and a 'long' or 'far' pointer lp. Win32 programming often uses a kind of pointer-like index object called a **HANDLE**, and the h prefix is used for variables of this type. In older Windows code we often see the prefix sz or lpsz to stand for a variable which represents a string of characters. Of course in MFC programming we will generally use **CString** variables instead.

You'll notice a bit of ambiguity in all this; the truth is that all of our naming conventions are a little flexible. The golden rule is to develop a few good conventions and stick to them in all of your code. As you learn more about programming, however, your ideas about the conventions will evolve, so don't feel duty-bound to forever stick to something dumb that you used to do when you were starting out.

Windows uses a lot of constants that are defined in its header files. These are always written in all capitals, with underscores separating the component parts. Often a defined constant has a prefix that reminds you of the context in which the constant is used. As a random example, the **DT_CENTER** and **DT_VCENTER** constants that can be used as arguments to the **CDC::DrawText** method have the **DT** prefix to remind you that these constants have to do with the **DrawText**.

As a rule you should never use one-letter names like u or x, unless it's immediately obvious what you mean, nor should you use meaningless names like foo or whatever. The one and only time it's definitely acceptable to use one-letter variable names is for the indices i, j, k used to index loops.

The AFX part of the MFC programming picture has to do with what's in those 30 or so files that the Visual Studio AppWizard creates for you when you make a new project. One thing worth mentioning here is that MFC has a few global functions with the prefix **Afx**. These functions are used for getting information about your program. An example of such a function is **CWnd* AfxGetMainWnd( );**. We'll look some more at AFX below. But first we'll have a little information for Win32 programmers, some information about documents and views, and another look at the Pop program code.

Later we'll also define a lot of classes of our own. To make clear that these are our classes, we'll start all their names with a *lower-case c*. Thus we will use a name like *cMyClass* rather than *MyClass*. We would absolutely never want to use a name like *CMyClass*, as that last format should be left only for use by MFC. The MFC class members generally start with **m_**, although the **CPoint** class members are just called **x** and **y** and the **CRect** members are **left**, **top**, **right**, and **bottom**. We'll always have our own class data members start with an underscore _. A general principle of naming members of your classes is to start the member names with an underscore, and then you have the possibility of using the name without the underscore as an accessor function name (although usually it's a better practice to start accessors with the word 'get'). It's a good idea to give your class's private or protected members 'ugly' names (by starting them with an underscore) to remind you that they are indeed not public.

When we define a special function as one of our class methods, we almost always use the convention of starting it with a lower-case letter and using capital letters at word breaks. Thus, we might have a *randomInt* method or a *setAutoRotate* method. You never want to start your methods with a capital letter because then they'll look like standard MFC functions, and next programmer to use your code will get confused when he or she tries to look up MFC documentation for these functions.

23.5 MFC classes are shallow wrappers

You might wonder what the members of the various kinds of MFC classes are. As it turns out, most of the classes have only one member, which is public. These members all have a name which starts with a lower-case m and an underscore: **m_**. Thus, for instance, the only data member of a **CWnd** is a public **HWND** called **m_hWnd**. What's an **HWND**, anyway? It means 'handle to a window.' In similar fashion, if you look inside a **CDC**, you'll find a public **HDC** field called **m_hDC**, where an **HDC** is a 'handle to a device context.'

Handles can be described as pointers to pointers. We can think of a handle as being like an index into a table of memory pointers. Saving an object's memory pointer at a second remove allows the operating system to move around the object's memory and change its memory pointer, while keeping the same handle pointer to locate the current value of the memory pointer.

As a practical matter, C++ really doesn't want you to worry about the data members of a class. You're supposed to use accessors to get information about what's in an object, use mutators to change an object's contents, and use the class methods to do things with the object. So usually we don't think too much about the **m_** fields inside our classes. But now and then we'll notice that the implementation of an MFC method refers to one of the class's **m_** data fields.

If you've ever worked with Win32 programming, you'll be familiar with the fact that Windows programming involves a number of special data whose names start with the letter **H**. An **HWND** is a type that represents a window, an **HDC** is a type that represents a 'device context,' an **HPEN** is a kind of virtual drawing object called a 'pen,' and so on. These types all start with the letter **H**, because rather than being visible data structures, they are handles for *hidden* Windows data structures.

The basic idea for MFC is instead of using handles to secret data structures, we should start using real pointers to real C++ objects. This means two things. For just about every **H***WHATEVER* type from Win32, MFC defines a corresponding **C***Whatever* class. Thus, **HWND** is replaced by **CWnd**, **HDC** by **CDC**, **HBRUSH** by **CBrush**, **HICON** by **CSpriteIcon**, **HBITMAP** by **CBitmap**, and so on.

In addition, most Win32 functions that had an H??? as the first argument type now become member functions of the corresponding C??? class. Thus **GetDC(HWND hwnd)** becomes **CWnd::GetDC()**. And all of the graphics design interface (GDI) functions that had an **HDC** as the first argument are now **CDC** member functions; for instance **Rectangle(HDC hdc, int left, int top, int right, int bottom)** is now **CDC::Rectangle(int left, int top, int right, int bottom)**. The formerly explicit **H***WHATEVER* argument is now an implicit **C***Whatever* argument that appears as the object calling the method. Where formerly we wrote Rectangle(hdc, 10, 20, 100, 200), we'll now write cdc.Rectangle(10, 20, 100, 200) or pDC->Rectangle(10, 20, 100, 200).

Many function arguments and function return values that used to be **H***WHAT-EVER* **HANDLE** types are now usually pointers to **C***Whatever* objects. Thus, for example we might see code like this in Win32.

```
myFunction(HWND hwnd)
{
    HDC hdc;
    hdc = GetDC(hwnd)
    TextOut(hdc, ...);
    ...
}
```

Converting all the H??? to C??? and changing from handles to pointers, we'd expect to see something like the following.

```
myFunction(CWnd *pWnd)
{
    CDC *pDC;
    pDC = pWnd->GetDC();
    pDC->TextOut(...);
    ...
}
```

Or what might happen is that *myFunction* is actually a member function of **CWnd** now, with code like the following. (Remember that the word 'this' refers to the calling object when used inside the code implementing a class method.)

```
void CWnd::myFunction()
{
    CDC *pDC;
    pDC = this->GetDC();
    pDC->TextOut(...);
    ...
}
```

What is actually inside these new classes like **CWnd**, **CDC**, and **CBrush**? What are their data members and what are their class methods? The answers are both a relief and an anticlimax.

Most of the *CWhatever* classes have only a single data member, which is a public field of type *HWHATEVER* named **m_h***Whatever*. Most of the *CWhatever* member methods are just modifications of regular old API functions that used to have a *CWhatever* as the first argument.

The MFC classes are in fact 'shallow wrappers' around regular old Win32 objects. Thus, the only data member of a **CWnd** is a public **HWND** called **m_hWnd**. A **CBrush's** single data member is a public **HANDLE** called **m_hObject**; normally this is in fact an **HBRUSH**. (The **CBrush** class is a child of the **CObject** class.) A **CDC** has two data members that are public **HDCs** called **m_hDC** and **m_hAttribDC**. (Normally these are equal to each other, but in the case where **m_hDC** represents a special metafile or is derived from a printer, **m_hAtrribDC** is derived from an onscreen window.)

The good news is that MFC is not very different from Win32, so if you already know Windows programming there's not all that much new to learn. The bad news is that if the Windows programming language was a confused, screwed-up mess, MFC is, if anything, even gnarlier. Like living organisms, real-world computer-languages evolve by successive mutations, rather than being written clean and fresh from the ground up. Every now and then there is a fresh new language, but eventually it too gets all crusty and frobby and tweaked after being out in the world, and (if it is lucky) being heavily used for a few years.

23.6 Navigating app, doc, and view

We've already discussed how MFC uses the Document-View architecture in Chapter 5: Software Design Patterns. This section fills in a little more information about how we can navigate among the app, the doc and the view.

In MFC you can always get there from here. But the pathways are a little oddly marked. Table 23.2 lists the code to use to get a pointer to the classes listed in the top row from inside a method belonging to class in the left column.

The **::AfxGetApp()** is a global MFC function, by the way; we write the '::' in front of it to remind ourselves that it's a global function rather than being a method of any particular class.

The access methods in the fine print look kind of unpleasant. In reality, however, they are just using a standard kind of pattern for iterating through a **CList**, or linked list, of objects. We use one of these odd-looking methods in the **CWinApp::animateAllDocs** method discussed in Chapter 6: Animation. We don't use them all that often, though. We only print them here so that you know they exist. And they are convenient for occasionally walking through all possible documents or all possible views, for instance if you want to count all the open views that you have.

If all you need is a pointer to the currently active view, there is an easier way to get to it from either **CWinApp** or **CDocument**; you can use the global **::AfxGetMainWnd()** method to get the main window, downcast the **CWnd*** return value into a **CMDIFrameWnd***, and then move down the window levels using the calls we'll discuss in the next section.

```
CView* activeview =
    ((CMDIFrameWnd *)::AfxGetMainWnd())->MDIGetActive()
        ->GetActiveView();
```

The exact way that you write the parentheses for the cast is important. To be more formal and possibly more readable, you can instead use the C++ dynamic_cast operator and write lines like the following. To help you catch errors, the **dynamic_cast** operator returns a NULL pointer if the cast is for some reason impossible.

```
CMDIFrameWnd *pframewnd =
    dynamic_cast<CMDIFrameWnd*>(::AfxGetMainWnd());
ASSERT(pframewnd); //Is NULL if the cast failed.
pframewnd ->MDIGetActive()->GetActiveView();
```

Walking through the open documents

In this subsection we'll give some details about how the **CPopApp::animateAllDocs** code is used to find all the open documents and call their **stepDoc(dt)** methods.

Windows uses 'MDI' to stand for 'multiple document interface'. A MDI program groups the open documents in terms of 'templates.' The way we find all

Table 23.2 How MFC app, doc, and view objects can access each other.

Get to? From?	CWinApp	CDocument	CView
CWinApp	**this**	`POSITION pos = GetFirstDocTemplatePosition(); CMultiDocTemplate *pTemplate = (CMultiDocTemplate *)GetNextDocTemplate(pos); pos = pTemplate->GetFirstDocPosition(); CDocument* doc = pTemplate->GetNextDoc(pos)`	`POSITION pos = GetFirstDocTemplatePosition(); CMultiDocTemplate *pTemplate = (CMultiDocTemplate *)GetNextDocTemplate(pos); pos = pTemplate->GetFirstDocPosition(); CDocument* doc = pTemplate->GetNextDoc(pos); pos = pDoc->GetFirstViewPosition(); CView *pTemplate = pDoc->GetNextView(pos);`
CDocument	**::AfxGetApp()**	**this**	`POSITION pos = GetFirstViewPosition(); CView *pTemplate = GetNextView(pos);`
CView	**::AfxGetApp()**	**GetDocument();**	**this**

open documents is to look at all the available templates, and look at all the associated documents for each of them.

You might wonder why we need to talk about templates at all? This is because it is possible for an MDI program to open different *kinds* of documents, and for each of these kinds there is a 'template' or, as MFC puts it, a **CMultiDocTemplate**. Your Visual Studio program, for instance, opens up *.cpp files in a text editor, but it opens up *.rc files with a two-pane view that has a tree view of the resources on the left and a WYSIWYG window of the currently selected resource on the right. And it opens up *.dsw workspace files in yet another way. So clearly the code for Visual Studio must involve several kinds of **CMultiDocTemplate** classes.

Our Pop programs don't do anything this sophisticated: they have only one kind of document template, a standard template which is constructed by the AppWizard-generated **CPopApp::InitInstance** code inside the **Pop.cpp** file. The documents of a given template type are stored as a linked list.

```
void CPopApp::animateAllDocs(Real dt)
{
    CMultiDocTemplate* pSelectedTemplate;
    CPopDoc* pDoc;
    POSITION docpos;
    POSITION pos = GetFirstDocTemplatePosition();
    if (pos == NULL)
        return; //No doc template exists yet.
    pSelectedTemplate = (CMultiDocTemplate*)GetNextDocTemplate(pos);
        //Only look at first template
    docpos = pSelectedTemplate->GetFirstDocPosition();
        //find first document
    while(docpos != NULL)
        //while there are documents left to process
    {
        pDoc = (CPopDoc*)pSelectedTemplate->GetNextDoc(docpos); /*
            This retrieves the document at position docpos and then
            increments docpos to the next position. */
        pDoc->stepDoc(dt); /* Will animate the *pDoc and
            call UpdateAllViews to update the *pDoc's views. */
    }
}
```

It's not important that you understand the iteration code, but it's worth glancing at. This type of code is common in MFC. The business about using a **POSITION** object to iterate through the collection is a standard technique used for iterating through **CList** template objects, which is how MFC implements linked lists.

We assume here that the first template we find is the only one to worry about. There's a similar sort of method for walking through all of a document's views, but we normally use the default **CDocument::UpdateAllViews** for that.

23.7   Levels of Windows

Very many of the rectangular areas on your screen are officially windows, more of them than you realize. A toolbar is a window, a button on the toolbar is a window, a scrollbar is a window, your main view is a window, and so on. When one window always lives inside some other window, we speak of them as a *child window* and a *parent window*. Thus a toolbar button is a child window of the parent toolbar window, and the toolbar is in turn a child window of the parent window running the application. When a parent window has the form of a frame around the child window, we often speak of the child window as the *client* of the parent frame.

One possible source of confusion here is that we also use the words 'parent' and 'child' about classes. Consider the situation where a class ClassB has a declaration like

```
class ClassB : public ClassA
{ . . . };
```

Here we say that class ClassB is a child of ClassA, or we say that ClassB inherits from ClassA. By the same token, we say that ClassA is a parent of ClassB, or that ClassB is derived from ClassA.

But when we talk about parent and child windows we mean something different. We are talking about the window positions in what is sometimes called the *windows tree*. As a window, the client area is a child of the frame. But as classes, the client window is perhaps a **CView** class, while the parent window is perhaps a **CFrameWnd** class or a **CMDIChild** class. As window class types, all three classes inherit from the basic **CWnd** class. But they are not in any class-type parent-child relationship to each other.

When we program an SDI (single document interface) or a MDI application in MFC, we usually speak of the window we are going to use for our input and output as the *view*. The view is an example of a **CView** object. Our code will include a special class to describe the behavior of our view; in the Pop program, for instance, this class will be called the *CPopView* class and is defined in the PopView.* files. The *CPopView* class is derived from a built-in MFC class called **CView**, which is in turn derived from a built-in MFC window class **CWnd**.

The outermost of your program's window rectangles is an object of your special type *CMainFrame*, and it's called the *main frame*. Your *CMainFrame* class is defined in your MainFrm.* files. As usual in this book, we focus on the MDI style of application, as opposed to the SDI. But it's worth mentioning that in an SDI app, your *CMainFrame* class is a child of the **CFrameWnd** class, and in an MDI program your *CMainFrame* class is a child of the **CMDIFrameWnd** class. Along with your underlying **CWinApp** program object, your *CMainFrame* main frame is 'mission control central'; it directs the shapes of the main window, the toolbar, the menu bar, the caption bar, and so on.

In a MDI program, you have the possibility of showing a variety of views. Each view has its own frame, which your program defines as a *CChildFrame*

Table 23.3 The 'window tree' for a view in the multiple document interface.

Colloquial name	Pop name	MDI inherits from	Code is in
Main frame	*CMainFrame*	CMDIFrameWnd	MainFrm.*
Child frame	*CChildFrame*	CMDIChildWnd	ChildFrm.*
User view	*CPopView*	CView	PopView.*

object. A MDI program's *CChildFrame* object inherits from the **CMDIChildWnd** class. And an actual view that you write in is the child or client of a **CMDIChildWnd** frame. We illustrate this 'window tree' in Table 23.3.

The child frame window is the caption bar and the frame and parent of your View window. In a MDI application, you can see the child frame particularly clearly when a view is not maximized. The caption bar of the child frame will usually have a three buttons in the upper right corner. One button is for closing the window, and the other two are for either minimizing, restoring (to a non-maximized and non-minimized size), or maximizing your window. Whichever two options are different from the window's current state are what is offered; for instance, if the window is maximized, you'll have the minimize and the restore options.

If you maximize a view in a MDI application, the view's child frame merges into the big main frame. And the child view's Minimize, Restore, and Close buttons move up onto the menu bar of the main frame. When seen this way, a MDI program closely resembles an SDI program, which is why sometimes one doesn't notice the difference. But the double set of Minimize, Restore, and Close buttons are a tip-off. The top set is for the main frame and MDI client; the lower set is for the child frame and view.

For the sake of completeness and full disclosure, we should mention that there is one extra intermediate-level in MDI. It's called the *MDI client window*. This is the gray background window that you see in an MDI application if you repeatedly use **File | Close** to close all the open views. You also see part of the MDI client window if you resize all of your active child windows so that none of them is maximized. The gray MDI background is sort of like a local 'desktop' that the MDI app uses. Ordinarily we don't customize it, so we don't use any kind of special class for it, and it's not mentioned in our standard code.

How about getting from one window to another? Here's how you would do it in MDI. Table 23.4 lists the code to use to get a pointer to the classes listed in the top row from inside a method belonging to class in the left column. This table is a useful piece of information to have; it can save you a lot of grief.

For the sake of completeness, we should also mention how to get to the gray MDI client window, should you want to do something to it. Like maybe you'd want to make it start being green. Get hold of one of the **CMDIChildWnd** objects, and then have that object call **GetParent()**. Although the main frame is the parent frame of the child frames, the immediate parent of the child frames is the skulking MDI client. A call to **GetParentFrame()** moves up the chain of parent windows until it finds one that is of the **CFrame** type.

Table 23.4 How the view and frame windows can access each other.

Get to? From?	CMDIFrameWnd (main frame)	CMDIChildWnd (child frame)	CView
CMDIFrameWnd (main frame)	this	MDIGetActive()	MDIGetActive() ->GetActiveView()
CMDIChildWnd (child frame)	GetParentFrame()	this	GetActiveView()
CView (client)	::AfxGetMainFrame()	GetParentFrame()	this

Our *CPopDoc* class defines a useful *getActiveView* method as follows.

```
CPopView* CPopDoc::getActiveView()
{
    CMDIFrameWnd *pFrame =(CMDIFrameWnd*)AfxGetMainWnd();
    if (!pFrame) //In case things aren't initialized yet.
        return NULL;
    CMDIChildWnd *pChild = pFrame->MDIGetActive();
    if (!pChild) //In case things aren't initialized yet.
        return NULL;
    CPopView *pView = (CPopView *) pChild->GetActiveView();
    return pView;
}
```

23.8 The MFC program flow

In this long section we're going to try and explain the execution of a Windows program built using the MFC framework (which is also called the AFX/MFC framework). The story is not all that clearly told in the Microsoft documentation, but one can check out the details by tracing function calls in the debugger.

The author has a lingering anxiety that he's made some mistakes in this account. On the other hand, he has a feeling of boredom and impatience about further examining the innards of MFC. One of the differences between science and computer science is that in science you are investigating things that are going to be around for a long time. In computer science, your objects of investigation are eternally moving targets, fleeting blossoms that bloom, shrivel, and blow away. Given that whatever knowledge one gets about Windows MFC programs is going to be worthless in ten years, it's hard to get super-motivated about getting every last detail right.

Even so, you do need a mental image of what any system is when you write programs for it. The 'system story' helps you organize your knowledge about what things work and what things don't work. Whether the story is correct in every detail doesn't really matter, just so long as it enables you to write good code.

Think of this The MFC Program Flow section, then, as a kind of 'creation myth' about the origins of your active MFC window. When you face other kinds of systems in the future, you'll need the ability to formulate creation myths of your own.

We'll give two versions of the creation myth, first a simple and practical one, and then a more complicated one.

All you really need to know

In simplest terms, here's the sequence of function calls that happen during the start of an MFC program.

- The *CPopApp* constructor.
- The *CPopApp* method InitInstance.
- The *CPopDoc* constructor.
- The *CPopView* constructor.
- The *CPopView* method OnCreate.

Now the program starts running. The following *CPopView* methods affect the view.

- OnDraw is automatically called when the view needs to be redrawn, because (a) it's new, or (b) it's been uncovered, or (c) it's been resized, or (d) it's had a call to Invalidate.
- OnSize is automatically called when the view is resized.

The various mouse, keyboard, toolbar, menu, and dialog control processing messages get called automatically. According to how the methods are coded, they can affect either the *CPopView* or the *CPopDoc*. When something is changed, we usually force an update of the view with a call to the *CPopView* method Invalidate. Or, more indirectly, we call the *CPopView* method OnUpdate and let it make the call to Invalidate. If you want the application to run on its own, you can put some code into the *CPopApp* method OnIdle.

When the program closes down the destructors are called in this order.

- The ~*CPopView* destructor.
- The ~*CPopDoc* destructor.
- The ~*CPopApp* destructor.

That's all you really need to know about the MFC program flow. But now, in case you're interested, we'll tell you a little more.

The invisible WinMain function

Any application, such as the Pop program, defines its own type of application as a child of the CWinApp. Pop uses a class called *CPopApp*, which is a child of the CWinApp class which is in turn a child of the CWinThread class. The *CPopApp* class has its prototype in Pop.h.

If we look in Pop.cpp we find the declaration of a static variable object of the type **CPopApp**. In general, your code is going to have exactly one object of the relevant kind of 'App' type. The AppWizard puts the code into Pop.cpp as follows. (By the way, your application object doesn't *have* to be called 'theApp,' you can call it anything you like; the crucial thing is that there be exactly *one* CPopApp object declared in your Pop.cpp.)

```
// The one and only CPopApp object
CPopApp theApp;
```

There is a **CPopApp()** constructor defined in **Pop.cpp** that carries out some of the initialization of theApp. And the rest of the initialization happens inside the program's **WinMain**, which is what we'll talk about next.

As you know, a C program always has a primary function called **main**. When the program starts, it starts running at the beginning of the **main** code, and when it gets to the end of the **main** code it exits. In a similar way, a Windows program always has a primary function called **WinMain** which starts, runs, and ends your program. In the older style of Windows coding, the programmer had to explicitly write out the **WinMain** code. But this code is almost the same from program to program, so the designers of the MFC have hidden the **WinMain** code from you. It's built-in as part of the AFX within which the MFC classes are patterned. The 'invisible' AFX **WinMain** function has a skeleton that looks like the following. To keep things simple, we've left out all the function arguments.

```
WinMain()
{
    pApp->InitApplication()
    pApp->InitInstance()
    pApp->Run() /* Calls the global ::DispatchMessage() or pApp->OnIdle
    pApp->ExitInstance() */
}
```

We describe our **WinMain** function in terms of a CWinApp *pApp pointer which is really just &theApp, that is, a pointer to the single **CPopApp** object, theApp.

This version of the **WinMain** code (including the comment) mentions six functions, and five of these are member functions of **CWinApp**. They are virtual members of **CWinApp**. They have their own default code, but since they are virtual functions, we are free to override them. We can change the code for the member functions of **CWinApp** by overriding their implementations for our **CPopApp** as defined in our Pop.cpp file.

InitInstance, Part 1: Initializing the *CMainFrame*

Here are the first two functions mentioned in our little outline of the hidden **WinMain** function.

- **CWinApp::InitApplication**

- **CWinApp::InitInstance**

Ordinarily you don't worry about overriding **InitApplication**, and you never even see the code for it.

By default, AppWizard expects you to override **InitInstance**, and AppWizard will put some code for it in your Project.cpp, file, whatever your 'project' name happens to be. A lot happens in here. We're going to be talking about this function for all of this and the next two subsections.

It turns out not to be a good idea to try and do any kind of heavy-duty initialization inside the *CPopApp()* constructor, as the program is in some sense not really ready yet at that stage. So this is one thing that we use **InitInstance** for, as a place to put initialization code. If you want to allocate something like a global memory bitmap resource at program startup, you would ordinarily put code for this at the start of our CPopApp::InitInstance; and when you then want to deallocate that memory, you would do it in the destructor CPopApp()::~CPopApp.

The default CPopApp::InitInstance code takes care of opening the main frame window. This is the place where the particular selections you made for the kind of program you want are implemented. The choices about your Document-View architecture go in here, for instance. The code looks (in part) like this; you can see the whole thing in Pop.cpp.

```
BOOL CPopApp::InitInstance()
{

    /* Register the application's document templates. Document
       templates
       serve as the connection between documents, frame windows and
       views. */

    CMultiDocTemplate* pDocTemplate;
    pDocTemplate = new CMultiDocTemplate(
        IDR_POPTYPE,
        RUNTIME_CLASS(CPopDoc), //your CDocument
        RUNTIME_CLASS(CChildFrame), // your CMDIChildWnd
        RUNTIME_CLASS(CPopView)); //your CView
    AddDocTemplate(pDocTemplate);

    // create main MDI Frame window
    CMainFrame* pMainFrame = new CMainFrame; //your CMDIFrameWnd
    if (!pMainFrame->LoadFrame(IDR_MAINFRAME))
        return FALSE;
    m_pMainWnd = pMainFrame;

    // Parse command line for standard shell commands, DDE, file open
    CCommandLineInfo cmdInfo; //Create a default cmdInfo object
    ParseCommandLine(cmdInfo); //Copy any command line params
```

```
// Now Dispatch commands specified on the command line.
// The default startup cmdInfo sends FileNew to your App,
// which creates a document, a child frame, and a view.
if (!ProcessShellCommand(cmdInfo))
    return FALSE;

// The main window has been initialized, so show and update it.
pMainFrame->ShowWindow(m_nCmdShow);
pMainFrame->UpdateWindow();

return TRUE;
}
```

The pDocTemplate is defined in terms of the *CPopDoc*, *CChildFrame*, and *CPopView* classes which are defined in, your project *.h and *.cpp files with the related names. Note that these specialized classes inherit from, respectively, the standard MFC classes **CDocument**, **CMDIChildWnd**, and **CView**. The template tells the application what kind of a document and view structure you have, answering questions like: are you using the SDI or the MDI; and is there more than one type of document you might open?

Once the app knows about your template structure, a main frame window is created by using **new** to call the *CMainFrame* constructor. Your *CMainFrame* class inherits from the MFC **CMDIFrameWnd** class and was defined by AppWizard in your project files MainFrm.*. If you have some global variables that will be used by all of your files, you might want to keep these variables in your *CMainFrame* class and initialize them in the constructor. And if you need to allocate and deallocate some kind of global pointer, you might want to do it in the *CMainFrame* constructor and destructor.

The call to LoadFrame(IDR_MAINFRAME) attaches whatever resources you've defined in your *.rc file for your main frame: things like menu bars and toolbars. Once we have a good pointer to a *CMainFrame* object, we store this in the **CWnd* m_pMainWnd** field of the **CWinApp** class, so the app can use it whenever it needs a pointer to its main window.

The next important group of calls use a **CCommandLineInfo** class that's basic-ally a data structure. We initialize a cmdInfo instance of the class with the default values set by the **CCommandLineInfo** constructor, and then we call the **CWinApp::ParseCommandLine** function to put any *command-line* arguments into the cmdInfo variable.

You might wonder how your app could receive command-line arguments anyway? After all, you're running Windows, not DOS or LINUX, and you never even see a command-line anymore! Well, you may have noticed in Windows Explorer that if you click on a file name, the file will often get opened by the application associated with it. Thus, clicking on a *.dsw file will typically start up a Visual Studio session, while clicking on a *.doc file may open up a session of Microsoft Word (if it's on your computer). When these apps are started up in this way, the Windows operating system passes them as *command-line parameters* saying, in effect, 'Do the File | **Open** command on the following file name . . .'

If there are no command-line parameters of this type, the default settings for a **CCommandLineInfo** object like `cmdInfo` will tell your app to start by processing a **File | New** command. And this is what happens when we hit the **CWinApp** method called **ProcessShellCommand** in the bit of code

```
if (!ProcessShellCommand(cmdInfo))
    return FALSE;
```

[If you haven't looked at much C code, this line may seem odd. But really it's just a cautious way of saying `ProcessShellCommand(cmdInfo)`. A typical programming trick is that when you call a function that conceivably might not work correctly, you have it return the Boolean value TRUE if all goes well, and return FALSE if there is a problem. That way the calling function can use this return value to pass on the bad news to the rest of the program. FALSE is really another name for the integer 0, with TRUE normally being 1, although any value other than 0 is normally also acceptable as TRUE.]

InitInstance, Part 2: Initializing the CDocument and CView

When your app hits the **ProcessShellCommand** call inside **InitInstance** (or when a user selects **File | New**) it needs to create a new **CDocument** and an attached **CView**. This sets off a whole cascade of MFC calls. In terms of initialization, the three key calls in the cascade are: (a) the **CDocument** constructor, (b) the **CView** constructor, and (c) the **CView::OnCreate** method.

Let's say a bit more about these three function calls.

Something you probably remember about C++ programming is that you're not allowed to initialize a variable as part of its class member declaration. If a variable isn't a member of a class – if it's a global variable, or a temporary variable inside a function, for instance – then you can declare and initialize it with a line like `int crittercount = 21;` or `int crittercount(21);`. But C++ does not allow you to initialize a variable inside a class definition. A variable which is a member of a class needs to be initialized in the class's constructor – or possibly somewhere else.

The **CDocument** constructor is the place to initialize and/or allocate any variables that belong to the **CDocument**. And if you have variables in your **CView**, you need to initialize these as well. Normally we initialize as many of these as possible in the **CView** constructor, but there will sometimes be **CView** variables that should be initialized a bit later: inside the **CView::OnCreate** method.

The reason why it's not always possible to initialize all the **CView** variables inside the **CView** constructor is that when this constructor is called, the **CView** window isn't really 'fully in existence.' When you're inside the *CPopView* constructor, for instance, if you try and use one of the **CView** methods it's likely not to work, because the special **HWND** window index called **m_hWnd** that's hidden inside the **CView** is still 0. And if you try and use the **CView::GetDocument()** function in here it'll crash because the document is still 0 as well. The only things that are safe to initialize inside the **CView::CView** constructor are things that don't use the **CDoc** and which don't in any way depend on the **CView** already existing as a graphical window object.

You need to wait until the follow-up **CView::OnCreate** function to do any initialization of **CView** that involves looking, say, at the size of the view, or looking at its owner document. You won't find the *CPopView::OnCreate* function listed in your CPopView.cpp file, but you can include it by adding a 'message handler for WM_CREATE.' More about message handlers in a bit.

InitInstance, Part 3: Putting the Windows on the screen

The last two function calls in **InitInstance** are the **CWnd** methods, **ShowWindow** and **UpdateWindow**. Note that they are called by the app's newly initialized **m_pMainWnd** field.

The **ShowWindow** function figures out the appropriate size for the main frame, and then draws the frame around that window on the screen. The **UpdateWindow** function fills in the internal 'client area' of the window. This will involve a cascade of function calls, as filling in the client area of the main frame involves first of all, creating and drawing a child frame window, and then creating and drawing a **CView** window inside the child. Another way of putting it is that when a **CView::UpdateWindow** is called, an **UpdateWindow** function gets called for all of that window's child windows.

Now of course before your view can appear on the screen, it has to have been initialized. But we're cool with that, it already happened when the **ProcessShellCommand** told our **WinApp** to behave as if it had received a **File | New** menu selection. We processed the **CDocument** constructor, the **CView** constructor, and the **CView::OnCreate** method.

So now the main window's call to **UpdateWindow** has generated a *CPopView::Update* window call. And what happens then? A call to **CView::UpdateWindow** generates a call to **CView::OnPaint**. If you look for *CPopView::OnPaint* in the Pop project files, you won't find it though. It turns out that **CView::OnPaint** in turn calls **CView::OnDraw**. And you will find the *CPopView::OnDraw* method in the CPopView.cpp file.

For most of our MFC programs, the **OnDraw** method of our view is where the rubber hits the road or, more accurately, where the pixels hit the screen. Let's look a little more closely now at the MFC run cycle.

The MFC run cycle

If you look back at our outline of the AFX 'hidden **WinMain**' function, you'll see that the following three functions are mentioned in it.

- **CWinApp::Run**
- **::DispatchMessage**
- **CWinApp::OnIdle**

Your app spends most of its time inside the **CWinApp::Run** function. What this function does is to repeatedly see if there are any 'messages' to process. If there is a message, then the global **::DispatchMessage** function is used to send the message to the piece of your code that is designed to handle it. When there is no message to process, then the **CWinApp::OnIdle** function is called until eventually there is another message to process. (Recall from Chapter 22: Topics in C++ that when we're doing MFC programming, we often put a :: in front of the names of global functions that are not the member of any class, just to remind ourselves that they're global.)

Talking about messages is going to take a long time, so let's put that off for the next section. Right here and now let's just say something else about **OnIdle**. As we discuss in Chapter 6: Animation, if we want to set in action a process which runs all the time, a good way to do this is to write a function *CPopApp::animateAllDocs* that executes whenever **OnIdle** is called. In the Pop Framework, we do this by replacing the base class **CWinApp::OnIdle** function with a *CPopApp::OnIdle* which calls the base class **CWinApp::OnIdle** and then calls a function we write as *animateAllDocs*. (As mentioned in Chapter 6: Animation, the *CPopApp::OnIdle* is actually slightly more complicated than what we show here.)

```
BOOL CPopApp::OnIdle(LONG lCount)
{
    CWinApp::OnIdle(lCount); //Do the base class WinApp processing.
    animateAllDocs(); /* Step through all the docs and update each
        doc and all its views. */
    return TRUE; //Keep doing it over and over.
}
```

The code for *animateAllDocs* is sort of ugly, so we printed it in Section 23.6. The net effect of the *animateAllDocs* function in our Pop program will be as follows.

- Step through the list of open *CPopDoc* objects and for each of these documents call a *CPopDoc::stepDoc* function which will
- call a *cGame::step* method to update the positions of a list of polygonal critters that are stored in the document.
- Make a call to **CDocument::UpdateAllViews** which will
- send down a call to a *CPopView::OnUpdate* for each of the document's views, and for each view this function call will
- use a **CView::Invalidate** call that generates a call to *CPopView::OnDraw*, which will
- use the current **cGraphics** to show an image on the screen.

But before we can start having that much fun, we will need to explain about Windows messages and the **::DispatchMessage** function.

Messages and message handlers

The Windows operating system maintains an internal message queue. Whenever you use the mouse or the keyboard a message is placed on the queue. Windows also puts a number of messages on the queue by itself. Windows works by continually taking messages off the queue and passing them to the window that they're intended for. The **AppWin::Run** function inside your hidden **WinMain** apportions the messages among the windows that belong to your app. The function that it uses to send off the messages is a global function called **::DispatchMessage**.

At the low level, Windows represents messages by a kind of structure called **MSG**. The Windows **MSG** structure can be written as follows.

```
struct MSG
{
    HWND    hwnd;
    UINT    message;
    WPARAM  wParam;
    LPARAM  lParam;
    DWORD   time;
    POINT   pt;
};
```

The first four of the special Windows variable types on the left are really all the same as 32-bit integers, while the last two are 64-bit integers, though a **POINT** can also be thought of as a pair of 32-bit integers. Even though it is customary to speak of the **MSG** structures themselves as *messages*, the **MSG** structure has a field whose name is 'message.'

The hwnd field of a **MSG** structure is an ID number which tells the Windows operating system which window (or which **CView**, in MFC terms) the message is intended for. If you press a key or take a mouse action, you will generate a **MSG** whose numerical hwnd ID value is equal to the numerical **HWND** index value for a currently active window.

The message field of a **MSG** structure is an integer code number describing what type of message this is. All of these message codes have names that start with WM_. You can look at a long list of them in Visual Studio by selecting the **Help | Index** dialog and typing in WM_. There are several hundred different WM_? messages, but most of them are rarely used.

It's common to blur the distinction between the **MSG** structure as a whole and the value of its message field. Thus it's common to speak of the operating system sending a window, say, a WM_CREATE message, even though strictly speaking, the window is really getting a **MSG** structure whose *message* field is WM_CREATE.

The wParam and lParam fields have extra information about the **MSG**. In the old-style Win32 programming, you need to learn what kind of information each message puts into these parameters. But in MFC programming, this is automatically done for you; the wParam and lParam information gets repackaged into an easier-to-use form. The *time* and *pt* fields of the **MSG** are rarely used.

In MFC, the code for processing a message takes the form of a 'message handler' function that lives in one of your **CWnd** classes, usually in your *CPopView*, but occasionally in your *CMainFrame* or *CChildFrame*.

Table 23.5 Windows messages and their MFC handler methods.

Message	Handler function	Comments
WM_CREATE	**OnCreate(LPCREATESTRUCT lpCreateStruct)**	Is called after the constructor. The best place to initialize your **CView** data
WM_SIZE	**OnSize(UINT nType, int cx, int cy)**	**nType** tells you if you've just Minimized or Maximized the window. (**cx, cy**) is the size of client area
WM_PAINT	**OnPaint()**	Is followed by a call to **OnDraw**, which is where we normally write our graphics
WM_LBUTTONDOWN	**OnLButtonDown(UINT nFlags, CPoint point)**	**nFlags** tells you which buttons are down. **point** is the cursor position in client-window coordinates
WM_MOUSEMOVE	**OnMouseMove(UINT nFlags, CPoint point)**	All mouse message handlers pass the same arguments as in **OnLButtonDown**
WM_VSCROLL	**OnVScroll(UINT nSBCode, UINT nPos, CScrollBar* pScrollBar)**	**nSBCode** tells what kind of scroll request, **nPos** holds the scroll bar position
WM_CHAR	**OnChar(UINT nChar, UINT nRepCnt, UINT nFlags)**	**nChar** is the ASCII code for the key if it's a letter key
WM_KEYDOWN	**OnKeyDown(UINT nChar, UINT nRepCnt, UINT nFlags)**	**nChar** is the Windows VK_ 'Virtual-key code' for the key
WM_DESTROY	**OnDestroy()**	Gets called right before the destructor at exit

Table 23.5 lists a few of the common Windows messages, along with the names of their MFC message handler functions and some information about the arguments that get passed to the message handler.

At this point, let's make a few remarks about the difference between **OnChar** and **OnKeyDown**. Generally speaking, you use the first function for doing word-processing and you use the second for using the keyboard as a control panel.

Although we can't seem to find them in the Microsoft online documentation, the virtual-key codes returned by **OnKeyDown** *are* all defined in the WINUSER.H file that lives in the INCLUDE subdirectory of your compiler. These codes have all have names starting with VK_ followed by a simple name for the key. The virtual-key code for the F1 key, for instance, is VK_F1, the virtual-key code for the Left Arrow key is VK_LEFT. The virtual-key code VK_A for a letter-key like A is in fact the same as the ASCII code 'A' for A.

If you press the A key alone, as opposed to pressing the A key with the **Shift** key, you'd really like to get the ASCII code for `'a'`, as opposed to the ASCII code `'A'`. How do we do this?

Well, when you press a letter key, your **CView** gets an **OnChar** message handler call as well as an **OnKeyDown** message handler call. (The **WinApp::Run** function makes this happen by using a global function called **::TranslateMessage**.)

So, if you care about the case of a letter key, then you look at the **OnChar** function input, as the **nChar** argument to this function will be the correct upper- or lower-case ASCII code for the letter that the user typed in by pressing a letter key and by possibly pressing the **Shift** key at the same time.

Usually we don't do anything with the other **OnChar** and **OnKeyDown** parameters, by the way. You might, for instance, be tempted to try and use the 'repeat count' variable **nRepCnt** in a game program to detect when the user is holding an **Arrow** key down, but this turns out not to work as reliably as does directly polling the key state with a repeated call from **WinApp::OnIdle** to the global **::GetAsyncKeyState(int vKey)** function.

Program termination

When you close down your file, either by ending the application or by using the **File | Close** menu selection, that means you are closing the view and the document, so the destructors will be called: first **~CView** and then **~CDocument**. If your program is closing, you'll then call the **~CMainFrame** destructor, and last of all the **~CWinApp** destructor gets called. In general, destructors always get called in the reverse order of the corresponding constructors.

Another spot where you might do some processing at program exit is in the **OnClose** or **OnDestroy** functions of **CView**. If you want code that asks the user whether or not he or she wants to save some file information, this call usually issues from inside the **OnClose** function, which is called after the **File | Close** menu selection is made, or when the view is killed by clicking on the 'X' or 'kill' box in the upper right corner.

Summing up, the sequence of function calls when you exit the program is as follows.

- **CView::OnClose**
- **CView::OnDestroy**
- **CView::~CView destructor**
- **CDocument::~CDocument destructor**
- **~CMainFrame destructor**

By the way, when you click the kill box at the upper right corner of your **CView**, it calls the **CWnd::OnSysCommand(UINT nID, LPARAM lParam)** message handler for your **CView**, with an **SC_CLOSE** in the **nID** parameter. **OnSysCommand** reacts by invoking your **CView::OnClose** message handler, if there is one. If your **CView** doesn't have an **OnClose** message handler (some hard-to-get-rid-of programs have an **OnClose** which puts up a message box asking 'Are you sure you want to exit?'), then the default **CWnd::OnClose** calls your **CView::OnDestroy** function and then passes control to the window's destructor.

23.9   Adjusting the program appearance

The caption bar and the About dialog

To start with, the caption bar for a project like Pop will say something like:

Pop – [Pop1]

The second name is the name of the View window that currently has the focus. If the child window is maximized, the name is in square brackets; otherwise it's not, and will say something like:

Pop – Pop1

The 'Pop1' is a program-generated name for the file (the 'document') that you currently have open. If you use the **File** | **Open** or the **File** | **Save As...** commands, this name will change to reflect your current choice of a file name. (At present, 'opening' or 'saving' a file will have no real effect except for changing the name in the caption bar. We'll show you how to properly save and open files later, when we'll have some data worth saving.)

The default first phrase, '**Pop**,' is the name of your project file. Particularly when you are working on a series of builds, as in a software project, you want this caption to have more information than your project file name, which you usually pick to be very short and generic. The easiest way to use the Pop Framework is just to leave the project name as it is, so your project file will still probably be Pop, no matter what your executable is. (It is possible to change the project name, but it's a little bit of trouble.)

You generally want your caption bar to also include your name and the date of the build. So if, for instance, you were calling your program, say, 'Skull Farmer,' you'd change the caption bar to say something like this, indicating that the program is showing the file number 1 opened by Version 7 of your Skull Farmer program.

Skull Farmer, Version 7, Your Name Here, July 5, 2010. – [Pop1]

The way to change the caption is to go to the Resource sheet of your Workspace pane in your compiler. Click on **Pop Resources** to show the resource categories and click on **String Table** to make a window open up listing your string resources. The first string will have the identifier IDR_MAINFRAME. This is the string that appears as your program name in the caption. Right-click on the text of this string to get a popup context menu, select **Properties** on this popup, and then you can edit the string to include the version number, your name, and the date.

It's also a good idea to put some information into the About dialog box. You can do this from the Resource view by clicking on **Dialogs** and then clicking on IDD_ABOUT. Right-click on the text area to get a context menu and select **Properties...** to get a dialog where you can change the text to have your name.

The program icons

It's a nice idea to use the Resource Editor to change the icons used by the your programs. Although this isn't immediately obvious, your program uses *four* icons, and to fully customize your program you need to change them all. The so-called IDR_MAINFRAME icon comes in two different sizes, and the IDR_POPTYPE icon comes in two sizes as well.

Under the Icons listing on the Resource sheet of the Workspace window, you'll find IDR_MAINFRAME and IDR_POPTYPE. IDR_MAINFRAME controls the icon that appears next to your *.exe in Windows Explorer and in the About dialog box; by default it shows three blocks with the letters MFC. You can change this icon in the Resource Editor, but at first you won't think it worked – because you'll still see the three blocks with MFC in your main menu bar. Why is that? Well, each icon is stored to actually hold images at two different resolutions. In the Resource Editor you'll find a **Device** dropdown with two choices: **Standard** (32 × 32) and **Small** (16 × 16). And you need to change the **Small** one of IDR_MAINFRAME to change what you see in the caption bar when the document window is maximized.

With IDR_POPTYPE, the **Standard** version will appear next to Pop documents if we eventually save any, while the **Small** version will appear in the menu bar when the document window is maximized.

The IDR_MAINFRAME and IDR_POPTYPE icons are saved in the current \res file as Pop.ico and PopDoc.ico respectively. Sometimes when you change the icons, the compiler seems not to pick up on the changes. This is particularly likely to happen if you drag new icons into the \res directory and simply assign them the names Pop.ico and PopDoc.ico. One way to 'jolt' the compiler and get it to notice that things have changed is to remove all icons from the \res directory, try and open the workspace file, and let the compiler complain that it can't find any icons. If you then put some icon files back in, the compiler will now use them.

Tweaking the File dialog

This is something you should do first of all when you start trying to serialize your program's documents. What we do here is find a way to give a distinctive file-name extension to our serialization files. Detailed discussion of the serialization process itself appears in Chapter 29 Serialization.

The reason it's a good thing to fix the File dialog before starting to implement serialization is that when you're testing out your code with repeated saves and opens, it's a lot easier to find the files you're testing if they have a distinctive kind of name.

Table 23.6   Where to edit the MFC document string to change your parameter file type.

Feuer's name	Default for Pop Project	Comments
App	\n	This is the text for the title bar by an SDI app, but an MDI app uses the IDR_MAINFRAME string instead
DocName	Pop\n	The default document caption, used with a number after it
DocType	Pop\n	Document type, used with the **File	New** command if your app has several types of docs
FileType	\n	A descriptive phrase shown by the **File	Open** and **File	Save** to filter for the app's types of documents
.ext	\n	The default file extension used for your file type
RegType	Pop.Document\n	Systemwide identifier used for the file type in the registry if the app registers itself
RegName	Pop Document	The user-readable name used for your type of file in Windows Explorer if the app is registered

If you use the Resource Editor to look inside the string table resource for your project, you'll find the second line has the label IDR_POPTYPE. By default, AppWizard sets it to the following string.

```
\nPop\nPop\n\n\nPop.Document\nPop Document
```

This kind of object is a kind of 'string of strings' because each of the \n symbols is a new-line symbol. Really we have seven substrings here, although by default three of them (the very first one, the fourth and the fifth) are empty strings of the form \n.

A good explanation for the Document String is in Alan Feuer's *MFC Programming* (Addison-Wesley, 1997), p. 218, where Feuer explains that the seven strings can be named like this and explained as in Table 23.6, where we've shaded the two lines that are important for us here.

```
App\nDocName\nDocType\nFileType\n.ext\nRegType\nRegName
```

Thus, when building, say, Pop21, you might want to use the extension .p21 for the files, and you might want to have the **File | Open** and **File | Save** dialogs refer to these files as having the type 'Pop 21 File.' To make this happen, all we would need to do is to use the Resource Editor to make two changes to the IDR_POPTYPE document string, so that it looks like this.

```
\nPop\nPop\nPop 21 File\n.p21\nPop.Document\nPop Document
```

23.10   The multiple document interface layouts

The MDI hierarchy

Now let's say some things about taking control of the MDI. Let's review some of the material from the Document-View section of Chapter 5: Software Design Patterns.

As the user's interface with the program, the **CView** has two different roles. On the one hand, it's the user's channel to the program's data. And on the other hand, the **CView** is a graphical Windows object that sits inside two levels of frame windows.

In terms of data, we have the hierarchy shown in Table 23.7. We include the *CMainFrame* here because we do sometimes keep program data in there.

Table 23.7   The application, the document, the frame, and the view in MFC.

Application class	MFC parent class	Defined in
CPopApp	**CWinApp**	**Pop.***
CMainFrame	**CMDIFrameWnd**	**MainFrm.***
CPopDoc	**CDocument**	**PopDoc.***
CPopView	**CView**	**PopView.***

And in terms of the window tree we have the hierarchy shown in Table 23.8. Note that the use of a **CSplitterWnd** adds an extra layer.

Table 23.8   The 'window tree' for a splitter window view in the multiple document interface.

Application class	MFC parent class	Defined in
CMainFrame	**CMDIFrameWnd**	**MainFrm.***
CChildFrame	**CMDIChildWnd**	**ChildFrm.***
CSplitterWnd	**CSplitterWnd**	**ChildFrm.***
CPopView	**CView**	**PopView.***

As we summarized it in Tables 23.2 and 23.4, there are a number of special MFC functions for getting a pointer to any one of these application classes from inside any of the other ones. Looking back at those tables you'll recall that the method for getting from the *CPopApp* down to the *CPopViews* is pretty ugly. But it's easier to move up the hierarchy of the window tree.

For reasons that we'll discuss shortly, we need a way for *CMainFrame* to count the number of open *CChildFrame* windows. So we write a *CPopApp::getMDIChildCount()* method that looks like this. Remember that a **CMDIChild** is what we call a child frame; in our program it's a *CChildFrame* object.

```
int CMainFrame::getMDIChildCount()
{
    int count = 0;
    CMDIChildWnd *next, *current = MDIGetActive();
        //Current focus child wnd.
    if (!current)
        return 0;
    while (TRUE)
        //We'll exit this endless loop with a return inside it.
    {
        count++;
        MDINext();
            //Move the child frame activation to the cyclically next one.
        next = MDIGetActive();
        if (next == current)
            return count;
    }
}
```

Automatic tiling and maximizing

To give our Pop Framework a good behavior, we don't want to ever waste screen space by showing the user the boring gray MDI client window that shows up when no views at all are open. What we want is the following.

- If there is only one child frame open, we want it to automatically maximize into the main frame.
- If there is more than one child frame open, we want them to automatically tile themselves into the main frame.
- If we resize the main frame, we want the child frames to retile so as to continue filling the frame.

You might think that a feature like this would be built into the MDI, but it isn't. This isn't necessarily a failing, this just doesn't happen to be something that the designers anticipated someone wanting to do. And, frankly, it isn't all that important a feature for the Pop Framework. It's developer gold-plating again. After all, why would we want to open more than one game document in the first place? And since we're using splitter windows anyway, we don't have much reason for opening a second view of a given doc either. Well, looking at how it works is a good way to gain a little more understanding of how MDI works. But if you're in a hurry, feel free to skip the rest of this section for now. You can always come back to it later.

What we've done here is to add a new **BOOL _autotile** variable to our **CMainFrame** class. We give it a default value of TRUE, and we put a menu item controlling it as **Windows | Autotile**. Our **CMainFrame** handles this menu item's messages.

The MFC call for tiling a window 'vertically' is **CMDIMainFrame::MDITile(MDITILE _VERTICAL)**. We need for our **CMainFrame** object to call this method whenever

Table 23.9   The function overrides needed for 'autotiling' a multiple document application.

Action	MFC method to override
Open a new child frame view of an open document with **Window | New**	**CMainFrame::OnWindowNew**
Open a new document with **File | New**	**CPopApp::OnFileNew**
Open a saved document with **File | Open**	**CPopApp::OnFileOpen**
Resize the main frame window	**CMainFrame::OnSize**
Close a child frame window	**CChildFrame::OnDestroy**

we do any of these five things listed in the first column of Table 23.9. In the second column we list the method that we need to override to make our autotiling work.

To make things more complicated, if there is only one open child frame, we don't want to call **MDITile**, because that puts our frame inside the client area of the main frame, and we have a wasteful extra caption bar. Instead, if we only have one child frame open, we need to make sure that this one view is maximized.

In order to distinguish between the case where we have one maximized view and the case where we have a number of views that we want to tile, we need a way to count how many views are open. And this is where we have to use that *CMainFrame::getMDIChildCount()* method.

As an example of the changes we had to make, we print our version of *CMainFrame::OnWindowNew* below. (In the Pop Framework the menu selection for invoking *OnWindowNew* is in fact labeled **Window \| Additional View of Current Game**, rather than with the more standard label **Window \| New**.)

```
void CMainFrame::OnWindowNew()
{
    CMDIFrameWnd::OnWindowNew(); //Call base class handler.
    //Our code. RR.
        /* Keep tiling so the child frames stay "stuck" to the outer
            window. The CMainFrame::getMDIChildCount() is a helper
            function I added. Gets the number of existing child
            frames, including this one. If there are more than one
            child, then I tile, otherwise I don't tile because
            whenever I have only one child, I've maximized it. You
            don't want to tile when a single window is maximized as
            this brings its caption bar back down into the MDI
            client area. */
    if (_autotile && getMDIChildCount() > 1) //
        MDITile(MDITILE_VERTICAL);
}
```

We make a similar change to the *CMainFrame::OnSize*, the *CPopApp::OnFileNew()*, *CPopApp::OnFileOpen()*, and the *CChildFrame::OnDestroy()*.

In the case of *CChildFrame::OnDestroy()* we have to work a little harder. This is the method that gets called when you kill off a child frame. Here it's possible that we had two open child frames and are now closing one of them. If only one child view is going to remain, then we need to maximize the single remaining child frame. If you're interested in how this works, you can look at the code in the Pop Framework's ChildFrame.cpp.

23.11   Splitter views

A splitter window holds two or more views of a document inside of it. There are two kinds of splitter windows, the *dynamic* splitter window and the *static* splitter window.

- A dynamic splitter window is a window such as you have in Microsoft Word or in Visual Studio that the user can choose to split or not to split. Usually a dynamic splitter window has the property that if you resize it, the pane on the right-hand side will change size, but the pane on the left stays the same width.

- A static splitter window is a window that is always split. With a static splitter window the programmer is better able to control the ratio of the size of the two panes. If you don't want to see the split, in a static splitter window, you can drag the split-divider over to one side, but if you go and click there, you'll find the divider bar is still waiting there.

The author designed the Pop Framework so you can build both. In the Adding a Static Splitter section below we show how to change from one build to the other. Our default build uses dynamic splitter, which you can activate with **Window | Split**.

In understanding the role of splitter windows we need to understand their place in the window tree. Ordinarily a **CView** is the immediate window child of its frame. In the case of MDI, which is what we're focusing on, the frame is a *ChildFrame* object (which is an instance of the **CMDIChildWnd** class). In the case of SDI, the frame would be a *MainFrame* object which is an instance of the **CFrameWnd** class. But in any case, the usual situation is that your view is right inside the frame, in terms of the windows tree.

When we add a splitter window, it gets in between the frame and view. Here's a picture showing the two kinds of window trees.

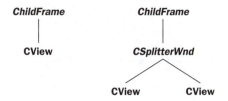

Let's describe how to add either kind of splitter. 'Dynamic' sounds more exciting and complicated than 'static,' but in some ways the static splitter windows are more powerful, and they're slightly harder to program. Let's explain the easier case first.

Adding a dynamic splitter

(1) Add a CSplitter _cSplitterWnd data field to **ChildFrame** in ChildFrm.h.

(2) Change the **CChildFrame::OnCreateClient** code in ChildFrm.cpp to have a single line as in the following.

```
BOOL CChildFrame::OnCreateClient(LPCREATESTRUCT lpcs, CCreateContext*
    pContext)
{
        /* When adding a splitter, be sure to comment out the base
            class code. */
        // CMDIChildWnd::OnCreateClient(lpcs, pContext);
        /* We pass the CSplitterWnd::Create call the "this" pointer,
            the max number of rows (1 or 2), the max number of
            columns (1 or 2), and an (x,y) size at which you want a
            pane to just disappear, the pContext variable, and a flags
            variable. */
    return _cSplitterWnd.Create(this, 1, 2, CSize(20, 20), pContext,
        WS_CHILD | WS_VISIBLE | SPLS_DYNAMIC_SPLIT); /* The default
            includes | WS_HSCROLL | WS_VSCROLL in the sixth
            argument, but I don't want scrollbars here. */
}
```

And that's it! If you rebuild now, you've got a working dynamic splitter window! If you use the **Window | Split** selection, you can split any of your views in two.

But there is one more consideration. It may be that you want the two panes of the split view to automatically be different. To do this, you could put some code like the following into your game's override of **initializeView(CPopView* pview)**, so as to make the views in the two panes be different. When the window is not split, your default behavior will be that of the 'left pane.'

```
CSplitterWnd* csplitter = (CSplitterWnd*)(pview->GetParent());
if (pview == csplitter->GetPane(0,0) ) //we're the left, main view.
{
    //Change the view settings the values you want in the left pane
}
else //we're the right, subsidiary view.
{
    /* Change the view settings to the values you want in the right
        pane. */
}
```

You might also want to override the *cGame* child's *initializeCritterViewer(cCritterViewer *pviewer)* with a similar kind of switch on `pviewer->_pownerview`.

Adding a static splitter

If you use a static splitter window, you have the ability to make your window keep a fixed layout no matter what size it is. The idea is to allocate some fixed proportion, like 0.75 of the window for the left pane and give the rest to the right pane. Of course the user can still move the splitter bar back and forth, but whenever we resize the frame window we'll go back to our standard proportions.

Look for the following block of code at the top of the Childfrm.h file. Comment STATIC_SPLITTER in, set the **Build | Set Active Configuration . . .** to select the **Release** option and rebuild.

```
/* Comment STATIC_SPLITTER out to have a dynamic (user selectable)
   splitter window rather than a static (automatically present)
   splitter window. If we have STATIC_SPLITTER, then we use
   LEFT_PANE_PERCENT to specify how much of the width of the child
   frame window is devoted to the left pane. The PERCENT macro is
   defined in stdafx.h to convert the 0 to 100 range to 0.0 to 1.0. */
//#define STATIC_SPLITTER
#define LEFT_PANE_PERCENT PERCENT(50)
```

Run the new *.exe and notice that when you resize the window, the left splitter pane always takes up 50 percent of the screen. Change the LEFT_PANE_PERCENT number to 75 and build again.

What makes this a little tricky is that a static splitter window is not fully initialized until you've *both* called **CSplitterWnd::CreateStatic** *and* repeatedly called **CSplitterWnd::CreateView** to put valid **CView** objects inside its panes. What with all the things the MDI framework does to initialize itself, you will hit the *ChildFrame::OnSize* method three or four times before you've managed to finish executing the *ChildFrame::OnCreateClient* code that initializes the *_cSplitterWnd*. So you need a **BOOL** *_splittercreated* field to keep you from trying to set the sizes of the *_cSplitterWnd*'s panes before they're fully ready.

If you look in the Pop **ChildFrm** code, you'll find the following two things.

- First, there is a `CSplitter _cSplitterWnd` data field of *ChildFrame* in ChildFrm.h, and a `BOOL _splittercreated` field as well. The **CChildFrame** constructor initializes `_splittercreated` to FALSE.

- Second, the **CChildFrame::OnCreateClient** method in ChildFrm.cpp is written to make a call to `_cSplitterWnd.CreateStatic`, three calls to `_cSplitterWnd.CreateView`, and a call to `_cSplitterWnd.RecalcLayout`. See the code in childfrm.cpp and its comments for details.

As in the case of the dynamic splitter, you may want to change your *CPopView::OnCreate* to initialize the views differently according to which pane of the splitter window they appear in.

Finally, if you want to change the behavior of the relative sizes of the panes when you resize the window, you can tweak the *CChildFrame::OnSize* method a bit further.

23.12   Portable classes

When you develop a general-purpose class like *cRandomizer*, *cVector*, *cRealBox*, *cRealPixelConverter*, or *cMemoryDC*, it's a good idea to try and keep the class as portable as possible. By 'portable,' we mean not having many dependencies upon other classes. A class that you develop as a programmer is like a tool that you build to help yourself do things. If you plan to keep programming for a number of years, you don't want to have to redesign your tools any more often than necessary. And, after all, C++ is a language meant to run on all kinds of machines, from Windows to Mac to Linux, so it would be nice to be able to take your tools with you if you happen to migrate.

One way to judge how independent a class is by looking at how many #include lines it has at the top of its definition *.h file and its implementation *.cpp file. Because of the demanding nature of MFC with the AFX application frameworks, we are forced to put the #include <stdafx.h> at the head of every *.cpp file that gets linked into our MFC project. So this one line's worth of linkage to MFC is unavoidable. But it could be unwise to bet the farm on MFC and, for instance, derive something as simple as *cVector* from the MFC base class **CObject**.

Let's look at the relationships among the special classes just mentioned. If you flip through the header files, you'll find that *cRandomizer*, *cVector*, and *cRealPixelConverter* use no other classes at all, although they do all use the *Real* type. But *Real* is simply a **typedef** we made in **realnumber.h** to stand for **double**, so it's use puts no crimp in portability.

The *cMemoryDC* class, on the other hand, is implemented in such a Windows-specific fashion that we don't worry about making it very MFC. The *cMemoryDC* is in fact a child of the **CDC**. Although the idea of a memory bitmap buffer is something you would want to use on any platform you work on, implementing something like this is so operating-system-specific that it's impossible to accomplish it in a portable manner. Actually, if you use the Swing graphics classes in Java, you don't need to implement double buffering, it happens automatically.

What about *cRealBox*? Well, thanks to having a *cVector randomVector(cRandomizer &rand)* method and a *draw(CDC *pDC, const cRealPixelConverter &rtop, BOOL bSolid)* method, the *cRealBox* uses all four of the other classes, not to mention the *Real* type and MFC. With *cRealBox* we're moving closer to the code for specific applications.

The Pop Framework classes are so far down into a specific kind of application that we don't worry quite as much about their generality. Even so, there is the possibility that we might someday port these classes to a different platform or even to a different OO language such as Java or C#. So we encapsulate as much of the Windows-specific things as we can. The various *cSprite* drawing methods use Windows graphics code.

One specifically MFC thing that we do with most of our classes is to make them inherit from the general MFC base class called **cObject**. Doing this allows us to include the DECLARE_SERIAL macros in the headers and the IMPLEMENT_SERIAL macros in the *.cpp files. The purpose of this declaration is twofold: (a) it makes the class support the MFC model for runtime class information, which involve such constructs as the macro **RUNTIME_CLASS(...)**, the **CObject** methods **GetRuntimeClass** and **IsKindOf**, and the **CRuntimeClass** method **CreateObject**; and (b) it makes it possible to use the **CObject::Serialize** method to save and load the objects' parameter information with external files.

Exercises

Exercise 23.1: Checking the **CRect** and **CString** documentation

Look up the documentation on **CRect**, **CSize**, **CString**, and **CPoint**. We're going to be using these classes from time to time. Be sure and get an idea of the different methods and constructors that these classes have.

Exercise 23.2: Checking the **WinMain** documentation

Look up **WinMain** in the Visual Studio Help and see what it says about **WinMain** in MFC.

Exercise 23.3: Using the debugger to look under the hood of MFC

How does one find out how the *CPopView::CView* constructor gets called from inside *CPopApp::InitInstance*? As a way of getting to know the debugger, let's work through some steps to figure it out.

First put a breakpoint inside the (empty brackets) code for the constructor in the CView.cpp file. Place the breakpoint by right-clicking at the spot where you want it and selecting **Insert/Remove Breakpoint** from the context menu. Then select **Build | Start Debug | Go** to run the program in the debugger until it hits the breakpoint. If the program stops too early, press F5 to make it run all the way to the breakpoint. Now select **View | Debug Windows | Call Stack** to see what functions were recently called. The window shows the most recent call at the top, the call before that one step down, and so on. Do any of these functions look familiar? Hmm, maybe not. This seems to be kind of a false start. Interesting, though, all those function calls. Do remember to use the Call Stack dialog later when your programs start crashing, and you want to try and step backwards from a given bug.

So now try something different to figure out how that constructor gets called. Put a breakpoint at the if (!ProcessShellCommand(cmdInfo)) line in CPopApp::InitInstance. Use the **Debug | Restart** selection to start over, press F5 if the debugger stops too soon, and when you get to the breakpoint, use the **Debug | Step Into** (or the F11 shortcut key for this, or the Step Into button on the Debug toolbar). You'll find yourself in a switch statement, and if you press F11 some more, you'll see you go into the case CCommandLineInfo::FileNew: of the switch. Aha! But why does the case value have that odd name? It turns out it's an **enum** value associated with the CCommandLineInfo class. To confirm this, place your cursor inside m_nShellCommand and press F1 for the help file information.

If you want to step further on, you may want to use the F10 or **Debug | Step Over** to avoid going into each function call.

Gnarly, huh? The moral is that you can get lots of information out of MFC and the Developer's Studio, but you have to feel around a bit to find it. There's so much more information than you can absorb, you need to be pretty quick and casual in the process – while remaining determined and implacable at the same time.

Exercise 23.4: Checking the message handling documentation

Look up the Help on the **CWnd::OnSysCommand** message handler. Aren't you glad you don't have to take care of all these situations yourself? The base class automatically handles these. For most messages, you will in fact be using the base class window behavior. And any message that doesn't happen to be handled either by your special **CView** or by the base class **CWnd** gets sent to a default message processing function. This default processor is the **CWnd::DefWindowProc** method. Look this method up in the Help.

Exercise 23.5: Changing the caption bar and the About dialog

Put your own name in the caption bar of Pop and in the About dialog box.

Exercise 23.6: Editing the icons

Change the appearance of the Pop 1 IDR_MAINFRAME icons. Be sure to change both sizes. Once you've opened the icon in the Visual Studio's Resource Editor, you can switch sizes with the Device: combo box, which has two options **Standard** (32 × 32) and **Small** (16 × 16). Figure out how to get these icons to appear in Windows Explorer and/or on your desktop.

Exercise 23.7: Changing the file extension

Try changing the file extension and file name for your version of Pop.

2D and 3D graphics   **24**

In this chapter and the following two chapters (on Windows Graphics and OpenGL Graphics), we talk about how the Pop Framework uses graphics to draw images. Rather than committing once and for all to one way of doing graphics, we've used the Bridge software pattern to abstract the common core of our graphics calls into an interface called **cGraphics**.

As of 2002, the Pop Framework had two implementations of **cGraphics**: **cGraphicsMFC** and **cGraphicsOpenGL**. A **cGraphicsDirectX** will probably be added at some point; check the book's web page for current information.

By way of review, Figure 24.1 is a UML class diagram of the Pop Framework, showing where the **cGraphics** class and its child classes fit in.

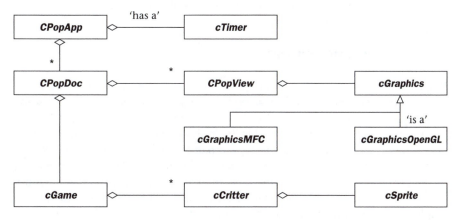

Figure 24.1 UML diagram of the Pop Framework with the **cGraphics** class

24.1 Vectors and matrices

The Pop Framework uses a **cVector** class to hold our critters' positions. Basing the **cVector** on real numbers helps to make our programs resolution-independent. Also the use of real numbers lets us give our simulated objects more interesting and physically realistic behaviors. We can use **cVector** for positions, velocities, and accelerations, and, because these vectors are based on real numbers, we can use some standard machinery from mathematics and physics.

We normally define the shape of an object by a collection of vectors near the origin, and then when we want to translate or rotate the object, we imagine transforming these 'shape vectors' into some new location. Without going into much detail, let's assume that you're vaguely familiar with the notion of a matrix from mathematics – you probably recall that a matrix is a square or rectangular array of numbers arranged as in a table, say as a four by four array. We have a certain way of 'multiplying' a matrix times a vector, and this proves useful in computer graphics for moving and rotating vectors. We will think of multiplying a chain of matrices on the left times a vector on the right.

In case you're a bit foggy on matrix multiplication, you can simply think of a matrix as a transformation that can be made up of translations, rotations, scalings, and/or shears. When you see a matrix-times-vector multiplication like `M*v`, you can think of it as meaning something like `M(v)`, that is, 'the result of letting `M` act on `v`.' If `View` and `Model` are matrices, a line like `Vertex = View * Model * Vertex` can be read as `Vertex = View(Model(Vertex))`, meaning that we are to apply first `Model` and then `View` to the `Vertex`.

As well as using matrices to move our objects into position, we also use matrices as a way to describe the position and attitude from which the user views the simulated world.

Our vector and matrix class headers and implementations live in files that are named VectorTransformation.h and VectorTransformation.cpp.

24.2   The graphics pipeline

In graphics the word 'render' means the process of converting information about geometric objects into a visual image on your computer screen. Rendering a scene is a multi-step process which is often described in terms of a *graphics pipeline*.

At one end of the pipeline we feed in polygon vertices, color information about the objects in our scene, bitmaps to paint onto some of the scene objects or use as backgrounds, and perhaps some locations of lights. At the other end of the polygon a rendered two-dimensional color image appears in a memory location called the *frame buffer*. The pipeline is rudimentary in two-dimensional graphics, and is shown in Figure 24.2.

In two dimensions the **Matrix Multiply** step converts the controlling vertices of our polygons, rectangles, ellipses, lines, etc. into locations that may be rotated or translated away from their standard positions. The *model* matrix expresses the motions caused by the objects associated with the given shapes, while the *view* matrix expresses the way in which the viewer may have moved relative to the world. We'll say more about this in the next section.

In the **Rasterization** step, we convert our vertices into pixel coordinates, and use basic graphics methods to draw the corresponding polygons, rectangles, ellipses, lines. The location into which we draw these pixels is the frame buffer.

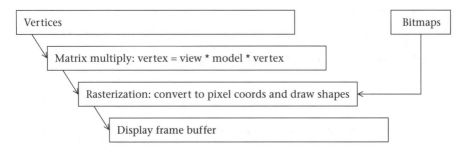

Figure 24.2   A 2D graphics pipeline

If we have some bitmaps that we want to use, say as backgrounds, we copy them into the frame buffer during rasterization.

Usually the frame buffer is an offscreen memory bitmap or a RAM region on the graphics card, as it is too visually disturbing to see the drawing happening bit by bit. Once the pipeline is done filling the frame buffer, the **Display Frame Buffer** step makes the frame buffer image appear in a visible window. This step is sometimes done by a so-called **BitBlt** operation, which (rapidly) moves the color information pixel by pixel. When the hardware allows it, the **Display Frame Buffer** can be accomplished by a more rapid technique called *page-flipping* or *buffer-swapping*.

The idea behind buffer swapping is that, rather than moving the pixel information from one region of memory to another, you simply change the address that the graphics card uses as the base location from which to refresh the visual information in your window. Doing buffer swap for an onscreen window is harder than doing it for an entire screen, but newer graphics cards and graphics libraries allow this.

Now let's talk about the three-dimensional graphics pipeline. The picture is considerably more complex, as shown by Figure 24.3. We'll say more about the **Matrix Multiply** step in the next section.

Two cases in which the **Per-Vertex** operations come into play are when your world has lights in it or when you plan to 'decal' or 'wallpaper' some image onto the surface of one of your three-dimensional objects. These glued-on images are called *textures*.

With regard to lighting, the color of a lit surface is going to vary depending on how the surface is oriented relative to the light source. With regard to texture, suppose, for instance, that you want to glue a bitmap of a circular logo onto the square wall of a house in 3D. If you look at the wall straight on, the logo appears as circle. But if you look at the wall from an angle, the bitmap image is going to have to be distorted into an elliptical shape. A texture-mapped square maintains an invisible grid of coordinates to use for pasting on the texture.

In the 2D **Rasterization** step, the graphics system draws directly into the frame buffer. But when rasterizing a 3D scene, the system can be thought of as drawing into an intermediate buffer called the *Z-buffer*. By using the Z-buffer we can automatically draw the closer shapes on top of the further shapes. Rather

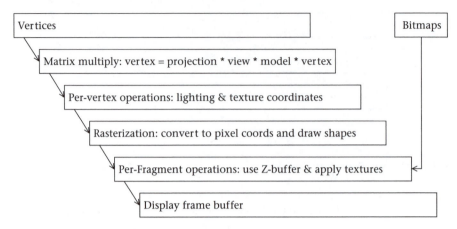

Figure 24.3 A simplified 3D graphics pipeline

than drawing 'pixels,' we speak of the 3D **Rasterization** as drawing 'fragments.' A fragment might hold a pixel location along with information about which colors you've tried to draw there at which depths.

In the **Per-Fragment** operations step the system picks the closest object's pixel for each fragment. This is also the place where bitmap textures can be applied in place of (or blended with) the lighting-adjusted fill colors.

As in the two-dimensional case, the **Display Frame Buffer** step abruptly transfers the image to a visible location on your computer screen.

24.3 Matrices in graphics

Attitude

Now let's take a more detailed look at the **Matrix Multiply** step of the graphics pipeline. We'll discuss the more general three-dimensional case.

In the **Matrix Multiply** step we right-multiply our input vertices by a series of three matrices, first the *model* matrix, second the *view* matrix, and third the *projection* matrix. Although we list the matrices from left to right in our formulas, and in fact feed them into the graphics pipeline in the left-to-right order, the matrices act on the vertices in the reverse right-to-left order. In other words, the matrix closest to the *vertex* in the ordering of the formula acts on the *vertex* first.

*vertex = projection * view * model * vertex*

The *model* matrix is frequently just the cMatrix _attitude member of the *cCritter* the *vertex* belongs to. The _attitude specifies a critter's orientation and its location. We think of each critter as having its own attitude *trihedron*, meaning a set of three mutually perpendicular unit vectors. As the critter pitches, yaws, and rolls, the vectors of its attitude trihedron move. At every step of the

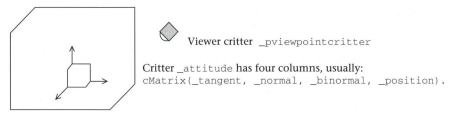

Viewer critter `_pviewpointcritter`

Critter `_attitude` has four columns, usually:
`cMatrix(_tangent, _normal, _binormal, _position).`

Figure 24.4 A critter's attitude

update we are careful to ensure that the trihedron vectors remain mutually perpendicular and of unit length. As the critter moves about, its position changes as
well. A critter's attitude embodies both its trihedron information and its position
information. In Figure 24.4 we show not only a critter with its attitude in a 3D
world, but also a viewer critter that will be used for projecting the 3D world to
2D plane that can be mapped to an onscreen window. We will take into
account the viewer critter's attitude as well.

In the Pop Framework, the *cVector* class represents three-dimensional vectors,
and the *cMatrix* class represents the matrices used for our graphics. We think of
our vectors as being column matrices of size three by one. Although you might
expect the matrices to be three rows by three columns, they are actually three by
four, that is, they have an extra column. This is a standard computer graphics
trick.

The matrices are three by four in size so that we can use the first three
columns to represent rotations and the fourth column to represent translations.
We might say that one of our 3D graphics matrices M is really a square three by
three matrix R and an extra column T, that is, we could informally say $M = (R, T)$.
If V is a vector, we compute $M * V$ as $R * V + T$, where the $R * V$ computation is
done in the same way that we would always multiply a square three by three
matrix times a three by one column matrix.

Mathematically we can make the computation seem consistent by imagining
that the matrix has a fourth row holding 0, 0, 0, 1, and that the vector has a
fourth row holding 1.

$$\begin{bmatrix} R11 & R12 & R13 & Tx \\ R21 & R22 & R23 & Ty \\ R31 & R32 & R33 & Tz \\ 0 & 0 & 0 & 1 \end{bmatrix} \begin{matrix} (Vx, \\ Vy, \\ Vz, \\ 1) \end{matrix}$$

$$(R11 * Vx + R12 * Vy + R13 * Vz + Tx,$$
$$R21 * Vx + R22 * Vy + R23 * Vz + Ty,$$
$$R31 * Vx + R32 * Vy + R33 * Vz + Tz,$$
$$1)$$

By default, we match the x-, y-, and z-axes of a critter's attitude matrix to,
respectively, the critter's *cVector _tangent*, *_normal*, and *_binormal* variables. The

tangent always points in the direction the critter is moving (or has most recently moved). The normal points in the direction in which the critter is turning (or has most recently turned). The binormal is the cross product (tangent * normal), a vector perpendicular to the first two. That is, by default we keep updating our critter's attitude matrix to have the following form.

$$\begin{bmatrix} \_tangent.\_x & \_normal.\_x & \_binormal.\_x & \_position.\_x \\ \_tangent.\_y & \_normal.\_y & \_binormal.\_y & \_position.\_y \\ \_tangent.\_z & \_normal.\_z & \_binormal.\_z & \_position.\_z \end{bmatrix}$$

Doing this makes the critters have a pleasing kind of motion, as they move about; they turn and roll like birds or fish. Sometimes, however, you may want to keep a strict control over your critter's attitude. In this case, you must use the **cCritter::setAttitudeToMotionLock** method to set the **cCritter _attitudetomotionlock** field to FALSE in place of the default TRUE.

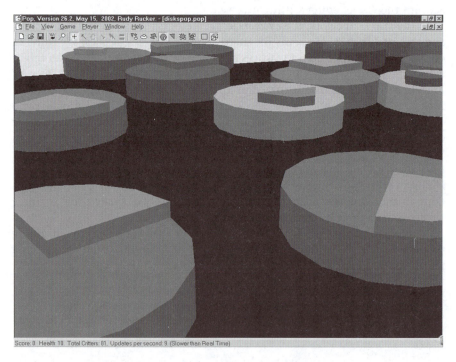

Spacewar game critters with their attitudes locked to their motions

A further complication arises in the case where the critter has a sprite that's offset or rotated from the critter's location and orientation. In order to manage this, we give the **cSprite** class a **_spriteattitude** field. When we feed a critter's *model* matrix into the graphics pipeline, we actually feed in attitude() * spriteattitude().

The view matrix

Let's look at our 3D graphics pipeline's Matrix Multiply step again.

vertex = projection * view * model * vertex

The purpose of the *view* transformation is to show the world as seen by the viewer critter. The original coordinates of the critter are given in terms of the world coordinate system. The view transformation is designed to change from the world coordinates to the viewer coordinates. Although the viewer is out at some arbitrary position, the viewer thinks of itself as being at the origin of its own coordinate system. Although the viewer may be pitched, yawed, and rolled relative to the world, the viewer imagines itself to be at the center of its own standard-oriented coordinate system. Although the world thinks of the critter as having a fairly arbitrary `viewpointcritterattitude`, the viewer thinks of its attitude as being the identity matrix `cMatrix::IDENTITY`. In Figure 24.5 we show the viewer critter's attitude. The viewer critter is going to think of its position as the origin of a coordinate system, and its attitude vectors as the *x*-, *y*-, and *z*-axes.

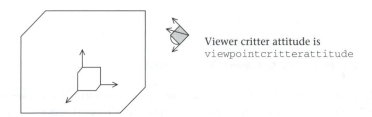

Viewer critter attitude is
`viewpointcritterattitude`

Figure 24.5 The viewer critter's attitude

The remarks about the viewer thinking it's at the center of things can be represented by an equation.

view * `viewpointcritterattitude` = `CMatrix::IDENTITY`

Assume that we have a `cMatrix::inverse()` operation to compute the multiplicative inverse of a matrix; this is analogous to the way that the multiplicative inverse of, say, 2 is 0.5. Then we can rewrite our equation like this.

view = `viewpointcritterattitude.inverse()`

This is one of the little miracles of computer graphics. The tedious matrix inverse operations have a use!

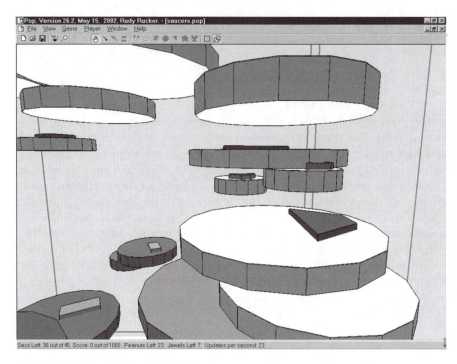

Secs Left: 36 out of 45. Score: 0 out of 1000. Peanuts Left: 23. Jewels Left: 7. Updates per second: 23.

An interesting viewpoint for the PickNPop game

24.4 Graphics in the Pop Framework

The data about the state of the game and its critters lives inside the **CGame** object in the **CPopDoc**. The individual **CPopView** is responsible for getting graphic onscreen representations of the sprite objects associated with the game's critters.

We allow the different views to use different kinds of graphics and to look at the world from different viewpoints. To this end, there are two key members of the **CPopView** class.

```
cGraphics *_pgraphics;
cCritterViewer *_pviewpointcritter;
```

Before continuing, let's redraw our Pop Framework UML class diagram another time (see Figure 24.6). In redrawing a UML diagram, you might think of the classes as little pieces of wood connected by strings, with the strings being the inheritance and composition lines. In redrawing the diagram, you can flip things around in order to bring out different features.

The *CPopView::OnDraw(CDC* pDC)*

The code of the **CPopView::OnDraw** is expressed using the **cGraphics** class with no reference to the details of any particular kind of graphics implementation. In the case of **cGraphicsMFC**, behind the scenes the child class uses a scratch-pad

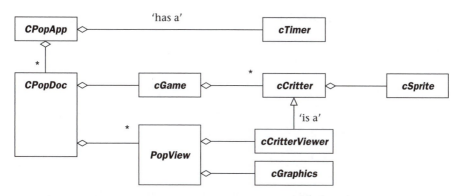

Figure 24.6 The Pop Framework classes

cMemoryDC to prepare the image by clearing it, and drawing the background and the critters on it. And then, still if our graphics is **cGraphicsMFC**, we use a rapid **BitBlt**-based copy operation to copy the bitmap to the screen.

If our graphics is **cGraphicsOpenGL**, the draw method activates an OpenGL context, writes the background and critters to an invisible 'graphics page,' and then 'flips' the page to make it visible.

The actual code goes like this. By the way, a **CDC** is an MFC class used to hold the device context of an onscreen window (or a printer).

```
void CPopView::OnDraw(CDC* pDC)
{
    if (pDC->IsPrinting())
        return; //Don't try to deal with printing case.
//Wake up the graphics.
    _pgraphics->activate();
//Tell the cGraphics to get rid of any extra unused image resources.
    _pgraphics->garbageCollect();
//Graphically show the status of the game.
    if (pgame()->gameover()) //Dim the lights
        _pgraphics->setClearColor(CPopView::GAMEOVEREDGECOLOR);
    else //turn the lights on
        _pgraphics->setClearColor(CPopView::GAMEACTIVEEDGECOLOR);
//Clear the graphics background.
    CRect targetrect;
    pDC->GetClipBox(&targetrect);
    _pgraphics->clear(targetrect);
//Install the projection and view matrices.
    _pviewpointcritter->loadProjectionMatrix(); /* Initializes the
        PROJECTION matrix or, in the case of cGraphicsMFC,
        initializes the cRealPixelConverter. */
    _pviewpointcritter->loadViewMatrix(); /* Initializes the MODELVIEW
        matrix */
```

```
//Draw the world, by default as a background and a foreground
//rectangle.
    pgame()->drawWorld(_pgraphics, _drawflags);

//Draw the critters.
    pgame()->drawCritters(_pgraphics, _drawflags);

//Send the graphics to your video display. cGraphicsMFC needs to draw
//foreground again in here.
    _pgraphics->display(this, pDC);
}
```

Finally let's make a sequence diagram for the drawing process. This is shown in Figure 24.7.

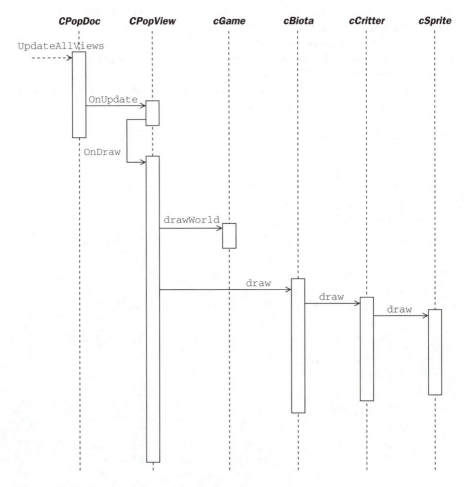

Figure 24.7 Sequence diagram for the Pop draw

Windows graphics

25

In this chapter we talk about Windows graphics. The *cGraphicsMFC* implements Windows graphics using standard methods that are in the Windows GDI. The good thing about the GDI graphics methods is that you can be sure they'll work on any Windows machine, no matter what libraries are installed and no matter what kind of graphics card it has.

A limitation of the *cGraphicsMFC* class is that we haven't bothered to implement three-dimensional methods for it, so if you want to show three-dimensional graphics you need to use *cGraphicsOpenGL* (or, should it become available, *cGraphicsDirectX*).

It would be nice to simply say that you should always use *cGraphicsMFC* for two-dimensional games and *cGraphicsOpenGL* for three-dimensional games. But on certain graphics cards, the *cGraphicsOpenGL* calls will actually run faster than the *cGraphicsMFC* calls. The Pop Framework leaves the choice up to the user, with controls to select one or the other kind of graphics.

Windows graphics can be made to run quite fast, thanks to double-buffering. In this chapter we'll discuss the basics of fast Windows graphics, and then we'll describe how the Pop Framework implements double-buffering for Windows graphics with a *cMemoryDC*, which is a memory-based device context.

25.1 The Windows sandwich

Windows graphics code typically has the form of a 'sandwich.' The top slice of bread is some preparation work, the filling is when you draw your graphics, and the bottom slice is cleanup work.

Assume that these variables get values set somewhere in your code.

```
COLORREF bubblecolor;
int intcenterx, intcentery, intradius;
```

Here's an example of Windows sandwich code that draws a circle of `bubble-color` with pixel `intradius` around the pixel (`intcenterx, intcentery`). The code uses two local **CBrush** variables, where a Windows **CBrush** is an object that Windows uses for filling in the insides of shapes. Note that one variable is a **CBrush** object, while the other is a **CBrush*** pointer.

```
CBrush cbrush, *pbrush_old;
```

- The preparatory 'top slice' of the sandwich looks like this.

```
cbrush.CreateSolidBrush(bubblecolor);
pbrush_old = pDC->SelectObject(&cbrush);
```

- The yummy sandwich filling might be as follows.

```
pDC->Ellipse(intcenterx - intradius, intcentery - intradius,
    intcenterx + intradius, intcentery + intradius);
```

- And the cleanup 'bottom slice' is this.

```
pDC->SelectObject(pbrush_old); //Need to unselect the brush before
deleting cbrush.DeleteObject(); //Delete the brush.
```

Whenever we need to write Windows sandwich code, we try and arrange the code so that we undo things in the reverse order to that we do them in.

When you first see Windows sandwich code, it's a little hard to believe how much trouble it is. But it's very versatile. And even though it looks like a lot of steps, it happens very fast.

At this point we need to say some more about Windows graphics tools, and how they relate to the MFC class used to hold the device context of an onscreen window (or a printer): **CDC**.

25.2   A CDC **is like a cranky six-legged ant**

MFC formulates graphics in terms of a **CDC** class which encapsulates a handle to a device context. A device context is simply something that accepts graphics calls. A **CDC** can correspond to an onscreen window, to a printer, or to a region in memory that's been tailored so as to behave like a virtual device context. The **CDC** class has one primary member, an old-style Windows **HDC** object holding a handle. The **CDC** class's state also includes certain active tool objects. In addition, the **CDC** class has a wide range of graphics methods.

For the purposes of this section, let's think of a **CDC** as a cranky six-legged ant. If you anger a **CDC**, it has the ability to kick up such a fuss that Windows will crash. (The author is attracted to the ant analogy because he once wrote a novel, *The Hacker and the Ants*, about ants in cyberspace.)

Each **CDC** ant is born with one each of six kinds of graphics tools which are instances of the classes derived from an abstract base class called **GDIObject**. The six tools are a **CPen**, a **CBrush**, a **CBitmap**, a **CPalette**, a **CFont**, and a clipping **CRegion**. Each of these graphics tool classes is a child of the **GDIObject** class. The **CDC** holds one of these in each of its six legs. It has a special pen-holding leg, a brush-holding leg, a bitmap-holding leg, and so on.

When a **CDC** is created, it is clutching default **GDIObject** tools in its six legs: a black solid width-one pen, a white brush, a default empty bitmap, an empty palette, a standard Windows font, and an empty clipping region.

These default **GDIObject** tools are so-called *stock objects*. Two common examples of stock objects are the fill brush and the drawing pen obtained as, respectively, `cbrush.CreateStockObject(WHITE_BRUSH)` and `cpen.CreateStockObject(BLACK_PEN)`.

A **CDC** is very possessive of its six tools. If you take one of them away, it spreads the alarm and Windows comes running to punish you! The **CDC** isn't particular about *which* tools it has, just so long as it has *some* tools. It just has to have one each of the six kinds of tool. The **CDC** can only hold *one* of each kind of tool. If you hand it a bitmap, it'll take the new bitmap with its 'bitmap leg,' but it'll have to drop the bitmap that it was holding before. So if we have a tool that we want to give the **CDC** ant for a while and then take back, there are two approaches we can use.

- Approach one: When we hand the **CDC** ant the good tool it will drop its old tool of the same type. So we just pick up the tool it dropped, and save it for giving back to the ant later on, when we need to get our good tool back.

- Approach two: Kill the ant before it can shriek. It drops all the tools it was holding and you can do whatever you want with them.

Generally we're going to use the first approach. This is because we will do almost all of our graphics calls inside of **CView::OnDraw(CDC* pDC)** methods. When the **OnDraw** method exits, the **CDC*** object is supposed to be still good; we don't have the option of killing it. Any temporary tool object that we create inside of **OnDraw** is going to be destroyed by its destructor at the termination of **OnDraw**; we need to make sure that the **pDC** isn't holding onto any of these soon-to-be-destroyed objects.

There's another reason why it's so important for us to be able to take tools back from the **CDC*** and destroy them. This has to do with the fact that Windows can only keep track of a limited number of **GDIObject** instances, and if you create too many of them the program will start acting badly. So the two key rules to remember are this:

- Don't delete **GDIObjects** while they are selected into a **CDC**.
- Delete all **GDIObjects** you create.

As we hinted at just above, the second of these rules will very often happen automatically, in the case that our tool is a local variable inside some function. This is because when a locally declared **GDIObject** instance goes out of scope it gets automatically deleted.

Whenever we want to draw graphics (or write text), we do this by using a method of the **CDC** class, using either a **CDC*** pointer or a **CDC** object to call the method. A properly designed Windows program normally does all of its graphics calls from inside the **CView::OnDraw(CDC* pDC)** function, in which case **pDC** is the **CDC*** object that makes the graphics calls.

One exception to this rule is that sometimes we use special *memory device context* **CDC** objects which can also make some graphics calls. More about this in Section 25.5.

We should also point out that if you really want to, you can get a **CDC*** and write some graphics from inside a **CView** method other than **OnDraw**. In this case you can get a **CDC*** by calling **GetDC()**, and you then need to free up this **CDC** with a call to **ReleaseDC(CDC* pDC)**. But let's repeat again that normally all of your graphics writing should take place inside **OnDraw**. The reason is that in this way you're able to make sure that your window's image is persistent.

Let's go over the Windows sandwich steps that we use in order to use a graphics tool such as a **CPen**, a **CBrush**, a **CBitmap**, a **CFont**.

- Create the **GDIObject**. We can do this in one step by using a constructor like in the line `CBrush cbrush(RGB(255,0,0))`. Or we can do it in two steps with lines like the following.

```
CBrush cbrush;
cbrush.CreateSolidBrush(RGB(255,0,0));
```

  Each kind of **GDIObject** has its own special constructors and initialization functions, such as **CreatePen**, **CreateFontIndirect**, and **CreateCompatibleBitmap**. Look in Help for the individual kind of object to find out more.

- Have your **CDC*** call the **SelectObject** method to select the tool. This call requires a pointer to a **GDIObject** class as an argument and returns a pointer to a **GDIObject** of the same class type. Save the 'old' tool in a temporary variable.

- Use your selected tool implicitly by having the **CDC*** make calls on its various graphical methods, such as **Ellipse**.

- Unselect the tool from the **CDC** by doing a **SelectObject** on the 'old' tool.

- Explicitly call the tool's **DeleteObject** method to destroy the tool. The Windows documentation implies that each kind of **GDIObject** destructor calls the **DeleteObject** method automatically when a tool goes out of scope, but *this may not be true* for every version of Visual Studio and the MFC. Do the **DeleteObject** yourself, or there is a real chance that your program will develop a 'resource leak.'

By the way, what does happen if **DeleteObject** doesn't get called for some **GDIObject** that you are repeatedly creating? The first few dozen or few hundred times this happens in a program, you won't notice any problem. But if the bug is inside a drawing function used in the animation loop of a program it can happen thousands of times. And then Windows runs out of the 'graphics handles' that it needs to create new pen and brush tools. Your calls to **CreateBrush** and the like start failing, and your pens and brushes always stay at their default values, which are, respectively, a thin black line and white filling. So if your colorful program suddenly turns black and white, this means you have a resource leak caused by the failure to call **DeleteObject** on some pen or brush that you are repeatedly creating.

Since an **CDC** always has some instance of each kind of tool pre-selected, it's customary to save a copy of this tool for reselecting back in when you want to 'unselect' the new tool before it gets destroyed by going out of scope. Say we have a CDC *pDC, and we want to draw a hollow circle with an edge that's int intedgewidth pixels thick and with color COLORREF edgecolor. Also assume that we have specified the center coordinates and radius as int intx, inty, intradius. We could write a block of code like this.

```
CPen cpen, *ppen_old;
CBrush cbrush, *pbrush_old;
cpen.CreatePen(PS_SOLID, intedgewidth, edgecolor);
ppen_old = pDC->SelectObject(&cpen);
cbrush.CreateStockObject(NULL_BRUSH);
pbrush_old = pDC->SelectObject(&cbrush);
pDC->Ellipse(intx - intradius, inty - intradius, intx + intradius,
    inty + intradius);
pDC->SelectObject(ppen_old); //Need to unselect the brush before
    deleting cpen.DeleteObject(); //Delete the pen.
    /* We don't really need to do these next two lines, but its just
    as well to be consistent in one's habits. The reason we don't need
    these steps is that we don't actually need to delete the cbrush
    because you don't need to delete stock objects. On the other hand,
    it doesn't cause any problems if you do happen to delete a stock
    object. And if I wanted to chain this code together with some
    further code that puts a new brush into cbrush, I would indeed
    need to have emptied it out like this so that I can indeed put
    something new inside it. Bottom line: Never pass up an opportunity
    to call DeleteObject! */
pDC->SelectObject(pbrush_old); //Need to unselect the brush before
deleting cbrush.DeleteObject(); //Delete the brush.
```

The trick is that whenever you call **CDC::SelectObject**, the operation returns the old tool or object of the appropriate type which was already in the **CDC**. Often as not this 'old' object will be a stock **GDIObject**, possibly with no real information in it (the default bitmap, for instance, is NULL). So why hang onto the 'old' object? Because there actually is no 'unselect' **CDC** function such as you would like to use in the 'Unselect the tool' step that we listed as the fourth bullet point in our description above. You accomplish an 'unselect' by selecting something else into the **CDC**.

Note that in order to have a circle or an ellipse drawn with an empty or 'transparent' interior, we need to select in a **CBrush** that's been set to the stock object NULL_BRUSH. By the same token, if you want to avoid outlining your shapes, you can select in a stock object NULL_PEN. Check the **Help | Index** on **CreateStockObject** to learn about the other kinds of stock objects.

25.3   Persistent display

It takes some work to make a Windows program have a persistent display that stays in place even if the window is resized or covered and then uncovered.

The OnDraw method

The standard practice is to have our Windows programs do all their writing to the screen within one single function, the **CView::OnDraw** method. When does your **CView** get an **OnDraw** message? Here are four important ways that this can happen.

- When the **CView** is first created, whether automatically at startup, by a **File | New** call or by a **Window | New** call. First there's a call to the constructor, then a call to **OnCreate**, and then a call to **OnDraw**.

- Whenever your **CView** gets resized, whether by dragging a corner using a command like **Window | Tile**, or by clicking the Maximize or Restore buttons in the upper right-hand window corner. First there's a call on **OnSize**, and then a call to **OnDraw**.

- When you uncover part of your window that has been covered by another window, whether by clicking on your window to bring it to the 'front' of onscreen windows, or by dragging a covering window to one side. Your **CView** gets an **OnDraw** call. If you put the line pDC->GetClipBox(rect) inside your **OnDraw** code, you'll find that the rect will receive the client window coordinates of the smallest rectangle that covers the part of the window that was just uncovered. This rectangle is known as the *clip box* of the **CDC**.

- When the **CView::Invalidate** function is called from within one of the other **CView** functions. This will queue up a message telling the **CView** to redraw itself as soon as there are no other messages for it to handle on its queue. If you want the redrawing operation to happen immediately and with no lapse in time, you sometimes follow a call to **Invalidate** by a call to **UpdateWindow**.

(By the way, if you try and do an **UpdateWindow** call without calling **Invalidate** first, the call may have no visible effect. **OnDraw** generally only redraws as much of the window as it 'thinks' needs to be done. A call to **Invalidate** tells the **OnDraw** that the whole window needs to be redrawn, but a naked **UpdateWindow** call on its own will generate an **OnDraw** call with a **CDC*** argument that 'thinks' that none of the window really needs redrawing.)

Bitmaps or display lists?

There are actually two possible approaches towards keeping a persistent appearance in our onscreen window, and we end up using both of them. These are sometimes called the *display list* approach and the *bitmap* approach.

The idea behind a display list approach is to set up code which will keep track of every time the user draws something on the screen and then 'replay' this during **OnDraw**. Because you have your items in a list, you can remove things from the list and add things, too. Keeping track of the display list takes a goodly amount of program machinery, especially if you write your own display list code. But thanks to the **CArray** template it's not so hard to do.

The display list approach embodies the insight that you can store a complicated graphics file rather compactly by getting a list of structures, with each structure including, say, a location and a description of what you wrote there. Any formatted word-processor file is a kind of display list. Instead of storing bitmap images of your pages, the file just stores the ASCII codes of the letters and information about their locations. The popular Adobe PostScript format extends this technique to files with lots of graphic information. There are two big wins with display lists. (1) They take up much less room than bitmaps. (2) They store the image in a format that is independent of the resolution. Printers typically have a much higher resolution than computer screens (a laser printer might have 600 dots per inch, while a typical monitor will show something more like 75 pixels per inch.)

Display lists usually use real-number-valued positions, where a 'real number' is a mathematician's expression for what a computer programmer calls a 'double' or a 'float.' We use our *cVector* class to hold pairs or triples of real numbers.

The idea behind the 'bitmap' approach is to keep a background bitmap as big as the window's largest possible size and do a pixel-for-pixel copy from this bitmap to the screen whenever you need to repair part of your window in an **OnDraw**. Windows has a powerful **BitBlt** function for moving blocks of pixels very rapidly. ('**Blt**' stands for '**bl**ock **t**ransfer,' and you pronounce 'blt' like 'blit.') There is also a **StretchBlt** function which can copy a block of pixels to an area of a different size. **StretchBlt** can help to make the 'bitmap' approach relatively resolution-independent, although one tries to avoid using **StretchBlt** whenever possible, both because it's slow and because its results aren't always pretty. Stretching a small bitmap to a large size introduces the 'jaggies,' while shrinking a large bitmap to a small size is done by rows and columns of pixels getting skipped, which can lead to a poor image.

Broadly speaking, paint programs or image-retouching programs tend to use a bitmap-based approach. What's being changed in these programs is primarily at the individual pixel level. A bitmap the size of a detailed photograph or image scan is quite large. It's easy for an image editor to run out of memory, and to start acting sluggishly as it pages memory from the RAM out to temporary files on the hard disk.

Computer drafting programs, mesh design programs like 3D Studio Max and libraries like OpenGL tend to use a display list approach. What's being done here is to compute things like the *cVector* coordinates of object positions. These programs are less memory-intensive, but they need to do a lot of computations in order to 'move' things around.

All professional programs will actually have some display list-like aspects and some bitmap-like aspects. Most 3D computer games use creatures that are based on display list meshes of polygons, with the polygons being filled in using pixel colors from bitmap skins.

Even in two dimensions, it's going to be worthwhile for our computer game programs to incorporate aspects of both the display list approach and the bitmap approach. The display list approach is an excellent way of achieving resolution-independence. And the bitmap method of refreshing the **OnDraw** method proves to be essential for preventing screen flicker. The bitmap approach is especially crucial for achieving the smooth real time animation effects you want in a program that shows rapidly moving objects. Our approach in designing our *cGraphicsMFC* class is that each of our views that is using Windows graphics will own a memory bitmap that's wrapped inside an instance of a new class called a *cMemoryDC.* (The situation works a bit differently with OpenGL graphics, as the OpenGL library automatically provides a kind of memory bitmap or *buffered graphics output.*) The array of moving game *cCritter* objects, on the other hand, acts a bit like a display list. In Windows graphics mode, a view's runcycle will go like this.

- Update the *cVector*-valued positions of the list of critters that are stored in the document.

- Convert the *cVector* positions into **CPoint** pixel positions relative to your **CView** client area. Blank out the old information in the *cMemoryDC*. Draw any desired background into the *cMemoryDC*. And then draw icons for the critters at the computed **CPoint** positions in your *cMemoryDC*.

- Use the **CDC::BitBlt** function to rapidly copy the *cMemoryDC* bitmap to the onscreen **CDC**.

25.4   Converting real coordinates to pixel positions

As mentioned before, many of the most interesting kinds of computer graphics are based on equations, drawn from mathematics, and physics. These equations are normally stated in terms of vectors and real numbers. In order to depict images and motions based on mathematics and physics we need to be able to translate back and forth between mathematical *cVector* positions and **CPoint** pixel locations in an onscreen window.

Windows has some GDI functions of the form **SetMapMode** and **SetViewport** that are useful in converting between different integer-valued sizes of windows. This is the kind of thing you need to do in, for instance, desktop-publishing when you want to control the physical sizes of printed versions of the images on the screen. But Windows does not have any built-in functions for converting between real numbers and pixels. The author has developed a *cRealPixelConverter* class for this purpose. By the way, Java comes with a somewhat similar class called **Transformation** built in, though not with all of our special methods supplied. And when you do OpenGL graphics, the transformation from real to pixel coordinates is something that the OpenGL graphics pipeline does for you automatically, with the settings being controlled by your calls to the ::**glViewport** method.

Here are the steps for using a *cRealPixelConverter*. If you want to see the details of the implementation, look in the realpixelconverter.h and realpixelconverter.cpp files.

- Declare a *cRealPixelConverter* object in a line like

```
cRealPixelConverter _realpixelconverter
```

Since our **View** windows are going to have different sizes, it makes sense to have a dedicated converter for each view.

- Tell your *cRealPixelConverter* the size of the Real window that you plan to use for the world in which your *cVector* values are going to live. This might be done in **CPopView::OnCreate**, with a line like

```
_realpixelconverter.setRealWindow(lox, loy, hix, hiy).
```

- Tell your *cRealPixelConverter* the size of the pixel window that you are going to be displaying your objects in. We always resize the *cRealPixelConverter*'s pixel window to match the current size of the onscreen window. This is done by adding a line of code to the view's **OnSize** message handler.

Your view's **OnSize(UINT nType, int cx, int cy)** method gets called (i) at startup, (ii) when you resize the view window by dragging on of its edges, and (iii) when you use the buttons at the View window's upper right-hand corner to minimize, maximize, or return to normal size. The **nType** variable tells you if the window's being maximized, minimized, or resized and the **cy** and **cy** tell you the size of the window's new client area. To tell _realpixelconverter to match its pixel window to the newly resized screen window, we use code like this. Note that we go ahead and call the base class **OnSize** function first; in general this is the correct and safe thing to do when you override the handling of a standard message.

```
void CView::OnSize(UINT nType, int cx, int cy)
{
    CView::OnSize(nType, cx, cy);
    // TODO: Add your message handler code here
    _realpixelconverter.setPixelWindow(cx, cy);
}
```

In the Pop framework, we allow for the different graphics implementations *cGraphicsMFC* and *cGraphicsOpenGL*, both derived from *cGraphics*. So our **CPopView** class has a cGraphics *_pgraphics member, and the actual Pop Framework **CPopView::OnSize** method calls _pgraphics->setViewport(cx, cy). A *cGraphicsMFC* object has a *cRealPixelConverter* member, and the *cGraphicsMFC::setViewport* code invokes this member's *cRealPixelConverter::setPixelWindow* method.

```
void CPopView::OnSize(UINT nType, int cx, int cy)
{
    CView::OnSize(nType, cx, cy); //Machine code.
    _pgraphics->setViewport(cx, cy);
    pviewpointcritter()->setAspect((Real)cx/(Real)cy);
        //width/height ratio
}
```

- For each object that you want to display, use your **cRealPixelConverter's** **realToPixel** function to convert the real number coordinates of the object into pixel coordinates. In the Pop Framework's graphicsmfc.h there are examples of this in lines like

```
_realpixelconverter.realToPixel(center.x(), center.y(),
    &intx, &inty);
```

- If you need to convert a real number length into a pixel window length use the **cRealPixelConverter::realToInt** method.
- If you need to turn a window coordinate such as a mouse click location into a real number location, use your **cRealPixelConverter::pixelToReal** method. In the Pop Framework's graphicsmfc.h, the **cGraphicsMFC::pixelToVector** does this with a line like

```
_realpixelconverter.pixelToRealintx, inty,
    &realx, &realy);
```

25.5 A memory-based device context

In order to keep our rapidly animated Windows displays from flickering, we use the **cMemoryDC** objects as virtual windows, or memory bitmaps. It is not a standard MFC class like **CPoint**, nor is it a well-known kind of user-written class like **cVector**. **cMemoryDC** is a special *memory device context* class that the author implemented here in order to make Windows programming easier.

The **cMemoryDC** class is a child of the standard **CDC** class. This means that we can write to a **cMemoryDC** with the same graphics methods that the **CDC** class uses to put graphics into an onscreen window or onto a printer page. And because **cMemoryDC** is a kind of **CDC**, we can use the powerful **CDC::BitBlt** method to do extremely fast copying from our **cMemoryDC** to a window-based **CDC**.

What makes the **cMemoryDC** special is that instead of being based on some actual device, its writing area is a bitmap that lives in memory. Ten or fifteen years ago, the **cMemoryDC** approach was not practical because it requires a goodly amount of RAM for the memory bitmap – and 10 or 15 years ago, computers didn't have very much RAM. Although nowadays using a memory bitmap is becoming a fairly standard kind of trick for professional programmers, many books on Windows programming don't mention it. One exception is *MFC Programming* *from the Ground Up*, by Herbert Schildt (Osborne, 1996). Though Schildt does not encapsulate the memory-bitmap-plus-HDC technique and make a class of it as we do here, he does informally refer to the assemblage as a *virtual window*. Charles Petzold's classic book *Programming Windows 95* (Microsoft Press, 1996) also has some discussion of the idea under the name of *memory device context*.

Our **Pop** program uses a **cMemoryDC** in order to achieve smooth-looking graphics updates. The idea is to assemble the pieces of the new image in an off-screen memory bitmap. We paint the **CPopView's** _cMemDC with our background color, and then we use the **cPolygon::draw** method to paste images of the polygons on top of the background. Once all this is done, _cMemDC uses its **copyTo** method to put the fresh image onto the visible screen.

Why not just do all this directly on the pDC that represents the onscreen window? Because it would be ugly and distracting to erase the critter bitmap images on the screen and then redraw them. You'd see drastic flicker. It's much nicer to use the _cMemDC as an offscreen drawing pad.

Another reason to use a **cMemoryDC** is that drawing to a memory bitmap device like _cMemDC is often much *faster* than drawing to an onscreen bitmap like the one embodied in the actual window's **CDC**. The reason is that when you write to screen, you have to go through your computer's graphics card, which is usually the biggest speed bottleneck of any graphics program. When we write to a memory bitmap, we're just letting our screaming-fast CPU processor chip move bytes around in our RAM.

So when you want to achieve a real time animation effect, the only way to go is to get your next frame ready in a **cMemoryDC**. The reasons are, again, that (a) it is prettier than having your users see the picture being assembled, and (b) it is faster.

You should use a **cMemoryDC** not only in animation programs but in any program at all where you are writing a bunch of graphics to the screen in **OnDraw**. The reason is that if you are writing a lot of graphics it takes some time, and if the user sees this happening it looks bad. The right way to do graphics is always to keep a **cMemoryDC** for your view, and inside your **OnDraw** put all the graphics into the **cMemoryDC** and then use the **cMemoryDC::copyTo** method to blast them into the user window.

Another use for **cMemoryDC** objects is to use one to hold an image of the background you want to use for your program. And, as we'll see below, there is a useful child class called **cTransparentMemoryDC** which is useful for holding small bitmaps to be used to represent movable objects such as game characters. A third trick is to use a large **cTransparentMemoryDC** as a foreground 'scrim' to put over your game pieces. But first we need to understand the basic use of a **cMemoryDC**.

The *cMemoryDC* class definition

Here's a partial, bare-bones listing of the **cMemoryDC** class definition. Because the author has worked with the **cMemoryDC** class for so long now, it's acquired a lot of bells and whistles, but we don't need to worry about those for now. See the memorydc.h code for a full listing.

```
class cMemoryDC : public CDC
{
protected:
    CBitmap _cBitmap;
    COLORREF _blankcolor;
    int _cx, _cy;
public:
//Constructors and destructor
    cMemoryDC();
    cMemoryDC(int nSize, COLORREF blankcol = RGB(255, 255, 255));
    virtual ~cMemoryDC(); /* The destructor is declared to be virtual
        because cMemoryDC has a child class cTransparentMemoryDC,
        and the child's destructor is different. The methods that
        differ between parent and child are also declared virtual. */
//Accessors
    int cx(){return _cx;}
    int cy(){return _cy;}
//Mutators
    void clear();
    void setBlankColor(COLORREF blankcol);
//Blt Methods
    virtual void copyTo(CDC *pDC, const CRect &rect);
};
```

The size of a class object

How much size might a *cMemoryDC* object take up? One might think that maybe a class object had to carry around pointers to its methods, and maybe a class object's size is larger than the sum of its data field sizes. But this is wrong. The C++ compiler keeps the names of a class's methods straight in some global class-method pointer tables that it builds. So a class object isn't responsible for keeping track of its function pointers, and a **class** is no larger than a **struct** with the same data.

So now our question is: how many bytes are used up by a *cMemoryDC* object's data fields?

Well, as a child of the **CDC** class, a *cMemoryDC* inherits the **CDC** data fields which happen to be two '**HDC** handles' called **m_hDC** and **m_hAttribDC**. (In all ordinary situations these two handles are the same, and we don't bother mentioning the second one.) Now a 'handle' is really just an **int** that the Windows operating system uses internally as a kind of half-baked pointer. So the size of the data inside a **CDC** is the same as the size of two integers. Since we're using 32-bit integers, this means four bytes per integer, so we have a total of eight bytes in a **CDC**.

Now we add in the size of the *cMemoryDC's* own data fields. How big is the **CBitmap** member? Like a **CDC**, a **CBitmap** is a 'shallow wrapper' around a Windows handle, in this case an '**HBITMAP** handle' that, once again, is really just an **int**. So we pick up four bytes here. The **COLORREF** is also an **int**-sized object, so here's another four bytes. And we get eight more bytes out of the two **int** _cx, _cy.

Adding it up, we get 24 bytes in all.

Is a *cMemoryDC* a lightweight object in terms of memory demands? Yes and no. Yes, there's a small amount of data in the fields of the *cMemoryDC*. But no, it isn't really lightweight because a *cMemoryDC's* **CBitmap** field is likely to hold the handle of an **HBITMAP** which represents a pixel for pixel copy of your whole screen. And as we'll see in Size of a Bitmap section below, this can run into several Meg of data.

Declaration and construction of a *cMemoryDC*

Usually we will want to have *cMemoryDC* for each of our views. Even if two views are showing the same data, we will normally want to size the data display to be an appropriate fit for the view's size. An exception to this would be a program in which we wish to work with a graphic image of some fixed size and simply let the views show different pieces of the image; in this case we'd put the *cMemoryDC* inside the document class. But for the rest of this preliminary discussion we'll assume we're putting it inside the view.

You can have your *cMemoryDC* be a simple class member or you can have it be a pointer member. If it's a simple member you declare it with a line like cMemoryDC _cMemDC and you construct it with a line like _memDC(CMEMDC_FULLSCREEN, blankcolor);. The CMEMDC_FULLSCREEN parameter tells the constructor to make the *cMemoryDC* have as many pixels as a full-screen window. The blankcolor parameter tells the *cMemoryDC* to use a background color of blankcolor. If you just want a white background you can leave out the blankcolor argument.

You can also give a CMEMDC_ONEPIXEL argument into the first slot of the constructor if you want a *cMemoryDC* that's only one pixel big. The default constructor with no arguments also makes a single-pixel *cMemoryDC*, by the way. The purpose of the single-pixel *cMemoryDC*s is that they are used for loading bitmaps to be used for background images or for character icons. When a *cMemoryDC* loads a bitmap it can dynamically resize itself to the size of the bitmap.

It's worth looking at what happens inside a call to the constructor *cMemoryDC(CMEMDC_FULLSCREEN, blankcol)* so we get an idea of how the *cMemoryDC* works. Keep in mind that the members of a *cMemoryDC* which need initialization are the CBitmap _cBitmap, the COLORREF _blankcolor, and the two int _cx, _cy. As we already mentioned above, every **CDC** has an **HDC m_hDC** member, so as a child of the **CDC** class, a *cMemoryDC* has an **HDC m_hDC** which must be initialized as well. This initialization is accomplished implicitly by a call to **CreateCompatibleDC**.

Here are the principal code blocks that are executed in the *cMemoryDC(CMEMDC_FULLSCREEN, blankcol)* call, with a short comment on each one.

```
CDC cDC_display;
cDC_display.CreateDC("DISPLAY", NULL, NULL, NULL);
```

The purpose of the temporary **CDC** object cDC_display is to provide a role model object of what a **CDC** should be like in the runtime environment where this *cMemoryDC* is going to be used. The cDC_display gets destroyed when it goes out of scope at the end of the constructor's code.

```
CreateCompatibleDC(&cDC_display);
```

This is the line that initializes our *cMemoryDC*'s 'shallowly wrapped' **HDC m_hDC** field. The call makes our *cMemoryDC* be a **CDC** compatible with the screen. Each **CDC** will have selected into it a **CBitmap** bitmap object of a certain area. The **CreateCompatibleDC** method only makes our *cMemoryDC* compatible with the screen, but does not give it a bitmap as large as the screen. It's worth noting that in Windows, a 'normal' device context such as one that you get from a window never has any interesting bitmap associated with it. These 'normal' **CDC** always have an empty bitmap, and they don't use it at all. But the **CreateCompatibleDC** call is designed for creating memory-based device contexts. Although the default **CDC** constructor gives a **CDC** an empty **CBitmap** tool, the **CreateCompatibleDC** call gives the **CDC** a **CBitmap** that is one pixel big. It's not much, but it's something. It's up to us to replace this bitmap with one the size of the screen. So now we figure out the size of the screen.

```
_cx = GetSystemMetrics(SM_CXFULLSCREEN);
_cy = GetSystemMetrics(SM_CYFULLSCREEN) - GetSystemMetrics(SM_CYMENU);
```

Calling **GetSystemMetrics** with the **SM_C?FULLSCREEN** arguments gives the actual size of a full screen client window's screen measured in pixels. This assumes the window has a caption. We subtract off the region for the menu. Now we make the bitmap that we need.

```
_cBitmap.CreateCompatibleBitmap(&cDC_display, _cx, _cy))
```

It is important to use the screen-based cDC_display as the argument to the **CreateCompatibleBitmap** call. (If you try and use your memory device context *this as the argument instead, you'll get a monochrome bitmap!) Another thing to note here is that **CreateCompatibleBitmap** is a kind of a memory allocation call, in that it's going to look for enough memory to hold a bitmap the size of _cx * _cy. Conceivably it might fail, so in our constructor code we're careful to check if this call is successful. Assuming it is, we now select the newly created _cBitmap into our *cMemoryDC*.

```
SelectObject(&_cBitmap);
```

And now our *cMemoryDC* is a screen-compatible **CDC** with an effective area as big as a full screen window. From now on, anything that we write to the *cMemoryDC* goes into the bitmap, and anything that we put into the bitmap appears in the *cMemoryDC*. (Although we don't mention this in the code printed here, we also need to do a **DeleteObject** on the single-pixel **CBitmap** that gets 'unselected' by the **SelectObject** call.)

Size of a bitmap

How much RAM memory is a bitmap like _cBitmap going to use? Software engineers frequently have to talk about memory usage, and it's good to get fast at estimating it.

If your computer is running graphics in the lowest resolution mode, it has 640×480 pixels which you can round off in your head to 600 * 500 pixels, which is 300,000 or 300 K. If you are using the common 256 color mode, then you're using one byte of data per pixel. So that means 300 K bytes for a low resolution 256 color bitmap. 300 K is only a third of a Meg, which is no sweat compared to the many Megs of RAM that you're likely to have.

A lot of people use the 800 × 600 with 256 colors mode; here the bitmap is 480 K, or about half a Meg, still no big deal. If you go up to 24-bit color in a 'megapixel' mode of 1200 × 1000 you might end up needing 4 Meg per bitmap, which is still okay on most modern machines. But if you push your resolution high enough and use a lot of bitmaps, you may find a point where your RAM starts to suffer.

When Windows can't find enough RAM for a bitmap it will usually store the bitmap on the hard drive rather than returning an error from the **CreateCompatibleBitmap** call. This is good in that it means your program doesn't crash, but it's bad in that your program's behavior turns ugly once it starts using disk-based bitmaps.

The reason is that using a disk-based bitmap means lots of thrashing of your hard disk every time you uncover or resize a window onscreen. If your program switches to disk-based bitmaps you will notice a disturbing grinding sound from your hard drive every time you move your windows around.

But even with a low amount of RAM, you can almost always afford two or three screen-sized bitmaps. And you can have lots of small, icon-sized bitmaps. You'll only tend to find yourself running out of RAM for the *cMemoryDC* if you open up, say 20 or 30 different documents and/or views at once.

Writing to the *cMemoryDC* in *OnDraw*

The general principle of using the *cMemoryDC* class is that whenever we want to write something to the screen, we instead write it to our *cMemoryDC _cMemDC*, and then use the *cMemoryDC::copyTo* method to send the image to the screen. The exception is when we're printing; in this case we don't worry about flicker and we write directly to the print **CDC** (which will either be the printer or an image inside the Print Preview window). As usual we can use the **CDC::IsPrinting()** method to distinguish between the two cases, and our **CView::OnDraw(CDC *pDC)** code could look something like this.

```
if (!pDC->IsPrinting()) //The standard onscreen window case
{
    //Put code here to draw your image into the _cMemDC... And then:
    _cMemDC.copyTo(pDC);
}
else //The Print or Print Preview case
    //Put code here to draw your image directly to the pDC...
```

When we are not involved in printing, we write to the screen in a two-step process. The *first step* is to assemble our image in the *cMemoryDC*, and the *second step* is to copy the *cMemoryDC* to the onscreen **CDC**.

The way we'll carry out our *first step* is that we'll write some kind of background image into our *cMemoryDC*, and then we'll write the images of our objects on top of it. In the case of the *Pop* program we use the simplest kind of background: we simply erase whatever was in the *cMemoryDC* and fill the image with the background color. This is encapsulated in our *cMemoryDC::clear()* method, which creates and selects a **CBrush** of color *_blankcolor* and then uses the **PatBlt** method to paint the whole *cMemoryDC* with the brush with the following line. (See the subsection below for information about **PatBlt**.)

```
PatBlt(0, 0, _cx, _cy, PATCOPY);
```

Once we've fixed our background, we put our graphics into the *cMemoryDC*.

And then we're ready for the *second step* of the *OnDraw* process, of copying the *cMemoryDC* to the screen. We do this in the line `_cMemDC.copyTo(pDC)`. This call to the *cMemoryDC::copyTo* function in turn calls the following line.

```
pDC->BitBlt(0, 0, _cx, _cy, &_cMemDC, SRCCOPY);
```

Note that in this **BitBlt** call, the 'target' `pDC` goes on the left and the 'source' `&_cMemDC` goes inside the **BitBlt** arguments. More about the **BitBlt** method is in the subsection below.

The **BitBlt** function

The **CDC::BitBlt** method is designed to move a rectangular block of pixel data from a source **CDC** to a target **CDC**. The **CDC** which calls the **BitBlt** method is the target; in effect, the caller **CDC** is saying 'copy a block of pixels to me.' You are allowed to specify the location and size of the target rectangle that you want to copy to, as well as the location of the source rectangle you're copying from. Since **BitBlt** does a one-pixel-to-one-pixel copy, the size of the source is the same as the size of the target. The prototype looks like this.

> **BOOL CDC::BitBlt(int** *x*, **int** *y*, **int** *nWidth*, **int** *nHeight*, **CDC*** *pSrcDC*, **int** *xSrc*,
> **int** *ySrc*, **int** *dwRop*);

The arguments represent: the left upper corner and the horizontal and vertical extent of the target rectangle within the target **HDC**, the source **CDC**, the upper left corner of the source rectangle in the source **CDC**, and the write method. There are 14 write methods called *ROP codes* for 'Raster OPeration', where 'raster' is a word meaning an orderly grid, such as the one pixels are arranged in. The most natural ROP method is called SRCCOPY. The other ROP methods form various logical combinations of the source pixels, the target pixels, and the active brush-pattern pixels.

In general the time it takes for a **BitBlt** to execute is directly proportional to the number of pixels moved, and this 'pixel area' is proportional to the product of the linear dimensions of the window. In other words, if you make your window twice as big, your **BitBlt** will run four times as slow. This is why one so often sees things like onscreen video being shown in very small windows.

The PatBlt function

PatBlt is a special kind of **BitBlt** function that doesn't use a source **CDC**. Its proto-type is like this.

BOOL PatBlt(int x, **int** y, **int** $nWidth$, **int** $nHeight$, **int** $dwRop$);

PatBlt takes the **CDC**'s currently selected **CBrush** and uses it to write over a specified target rectangle. Here the most commonly used ROP code is PATCOPY, which means to copy the brush pattern or color.

Let's take another look at our call to _cMemDC.copyTo(pDC) which gets turned into pDC->BitBlt(0, 0, _cx, _cy, &_cMemDC, SRCCOPY). The _cx and _cy are the size of a full screen, so mightn't this code be inefficient if our window is smaller than the screen? Actually it doesn't matter because the pDC that's fed into the **OnDraw** function has a clipping region set to the size of the 'damaged' rectangle that it needs to repaint. The **BitBlt** will actually only try and do the pixel copying for the points that lie within the pDC clipping rectangle.

In an animated program, at each step the entire window will need to be repainted, and that's how big the clipping rectangle will be. If all you've done is to uncover a small corner of the window in a non-animated program, then that corner will be the clipping rectangle.

Calling the OnDraw

There's one final thing to remember to do when you use a *cMemoryDC* inside your *OnDraw* function. You either need to use the Invalidate(FALSE) call instead of the Invalidate(), or, better, you need to override the **OnEraseBkgnd** to do nothing, like this.

```
BOOL CPopView::OnEraseBkgnd(CDC* pDC)
{
/* We normally don't want to erase the background because our onDraw
    will cover it up with the _cMemDC copyTo. If we did erase the
    background, we'd get flicker. This is also true with OpenGL. */
    return TRUE;
        //Don't call baseclass method, CView::OnEraseBkgnd(pDC);
}
```

The argument to the **CView::Invalidate(BOOL eraseflag)** method specifies whether or not you should call **OnEraseBkgnd**, which normally will erase the screen with a hidden Windows background brush before writing to the screen in the **OnDraw** function. When we are refreshing the screen with a **BitBlt** of a *cMemoryDC*, we don't need to erase it. The reason for this is that the copyTo(pDC) call is going to 'erase' the screen anyway; that is, it's going to cover the screen over with a copy of whatever image you've drawn into the *cMemoryDC*.

Now you might think it's harmless to go ahead and erase the screen anyway, but far from it. If you erase the screen, it's momentarily white, and your eye is going to pick up a flicker. And then all our work with the *cMemoryDC* is for nothing. But of course if we've overridden **OnEraseBkgnd** to do nothing, then calling it will do nothing. (If you didn't bother to override **OnEraseBkgnd**, you could partly avoid the flicker by feeding a FALSE argument into your **Invalidate** calls, but it turns out that resizing the screen would still call Invalidate(TRUE) and give you your flicker.)

Let's sum up the use of the *cMemoryDC*.

- Declare a cMemoryDC _cMemDC member of your *CView* class.
- Initialize _cMemDC with a call to cMemDC(CMEMDC_FULLSCREEN) in the *CView* constructor.
- In *CView::OnDraw* draw graphics into the _cMemDC, possibly using the _pMemDC->clear() to erase the old _cMemDC image.
- In *CView::OnDraw* use _cMemDC.copyTo(pDC) to copy the image to the onscreen **CDC**.
- Override *CView::OnEraseBkgnd(CDC *pDC)* to do nothing at all but return TRUE;. If you forget this, your view will flicker when you call Invalidate(), which by default calls Invalidate(TRUE). Also the view will flicker when you resize the window, as the resizing code automatically calls Invalidate(TRUE), which forces a call to **OnEraseBkgnd**.

Exercises

Exercise 25.1: What happens if you don't clear the *cMemoryDC*?

Comment out the line _pMemDC->clear(clearrect); from the cGraphicsMFC::clear(const CRect &clearrect) code in graphicsmfc.h and see what happens. Drag a corner of the window to resize it. Can you figure out what's going on?

Exercise 25.2: Invalidate and flicker

Change the *CPopView:: OnEraseBkgnd* method to call the default **CView** method. Look at the flicker.

Exercise 25.3: Writing your own memory **CDC** code

Occasionally students rebel at using the *cMemoryDC* class. 'I want to use my own code; if I have to do this at our job, I want to be able to do it myself.' But do keep in mind that the MemoryDC.* files (and all the other software in this book) are well-tested public domain freeware that you are explicitly authorized to reuse in any way, shape or form, with no acknowledgement necessary. But even so, there are individualistic souls who want to be sure they can do it unaided. And who can blame them? There is a sense, after all, in which you never completely understand code unless you have written it yourself, and then corrected your inevitable errors in the compiler, and then maybe even stepped through the code in the debugger. So this exercise asks you to write a screen-persistent version of Pop in which you *don't* use our *cMemoryDC* class. Here's how.

Put a static `CDC _memCDC` variable into **CPopView** followed by a `CBitmap _memBitmap` and a couple of `int _memcx, _memcy`. We can live without the **CBrush** variable. Imitate the **cMemoryDC** constructor code inside the **CPopView** constructor. The initialization is the trickiest thing about a **cMemoryDC**, so this will be the hardest part of your work. Do it like this after using the **GetSystemMetrics** to set `_memcx` and `_memcy` to match the screen measurements.

```
CDC cDC_display;
CBitmap pBitmap_old;
cDC_display.CreateDC("DISPLAY", NULL, NULL, NULL);
_memDC.CreateCompatibleDC(&cDC_display);
_memBitmap.CreateCompatibleBitmap(&cDC_display, _memcx, _memcy));
pBitmap_old = _memDC.SelectObject(&_memBitmap);
pBitmap_old->DeleteObject();
```

Copy this very exactly; resist the temptation to simplify things by leaving out the seemingly extra steps involving the temporary `cDC_display` variable. These steps are necessary. Now go to **CPopView::OnDraw**. Imitate the **cMemoryDC clear**, using **PatBlt** with the **WHITENESS** as the last argument. And use **BitBlt** to imitate the **copyTo** code.

You don't need to change the **CPopView** destructor, because the destructor will automatically call destructors on the **CPopView** data fields in the order they appear, which means `_memDC.DeleteDC()` will happen, and then `_memBitmap.DeleteObject()`. Of course if you'd created similar objects on a temporary basis somewhere, you might want to kill them off yourself, just to be sure that the **CDC** dies before the **CBitmap** (because if the **CBitmap** were to die first the **CDC** would have a cranky ant-fit!).

And don't forget to override **CView::OnEraseBkgnd(CDC *pDC)** to do nothing at all but `return TRUE;`. If you forget this, your screen can still flicker, as the default behavior of any call to **Invalidate()** is to first call **OnEraseBkgnd**, and that function's default behavior is to erase the view with the background brush.

OpenGL graphics $\qquad$ 26

Far from giving extensive coverage of OpenGL, this chapter simply provides a bare-bones outline of how the Pop Framework uses these libraries of C functions.

As mentioned in the introduction, there are three standard books on OpenGL, known as the *Blue Book*, the *Red Book*, and the *White Book*. The *Blue Book* is a reference manual, listing all the OpenGL functions, the *Red Book* is a programming guide explaining how to use the functions, and the *White Book* is a guide to integrating OpenGL into Windows programs. Turn to these books for more information.

26.1 Linking to OpenGL

To use OpenGL, you link your executable to the special OpenGL libraries and include some special OpenGL headers. Typically you do the 'linking' by adding these additional libraries to your project: opengl32.lib and glu32.lib. (You can see Appendix C for how to add libraries to a Visual Studio project.) And you do the 'including' by putting lines like the following into any files that mention the OpenGL functions. (In particular, the Pop framework has these lines in its graphicsopengl.h header.)

```
#include "gl\gl.h"
#include "gl\glu.h"
```

Once your code is linked up, you can make OpenGL function calls in your code. The OpenGL functions begin with one of the prefixes **gl** or **glu**. We usually put the scope resolution operator '::' in front of these functions names as a reminder that these are global functions, rather than being members of any class. In addition, Windows has some special functions designed for linking to OpenGL. Some, but not all, of these functions start with the prefix **wgl**.

The functions our code uses are found in the following libraries:

- **gl** functions from OpenGL (gl.h, opengl32.lib)
- **glu** functions from OpenGL Utilities (glu.h glu.lib)
- **wgl** functions from OpenGL Extension for Windows (windows.h, opengl32.lib)

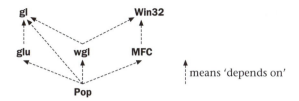

Figure 26.1 Component diagram for Pop's use of OpenGL libraries

And of course our code will, as usual, use special functions defined in the MFC libraries and in the basic Win32 libraries. Figure 26.1 shows how Pop and the various libraries depend upon each other.

26.2 The OpenGL state machine

It's useful to think of OpenGL as a state machine that has a special button on it to send images to the screen. The 'draw-the-picture' button represents the OpenGL function **::glFinish()**. Figure 26.2 illustrates the process.

Before calling **::glFinish()**, we prepare the state of the OpenGL machine by feeding in real number position coordinates, real number color triples or quadruples (with the fourth value α standing for transparency), and bitmap files. In addition, we can set the state by various **::gl...** functions that tell the state machine to combine the coordinates into a triangle, into a quadrilateral, or the like.

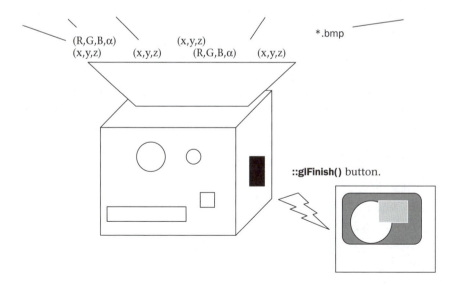

Figure 26.2 The OpenGL state machine

26.3   Generic OpenGL code

Let's look at an example of the kinds of calls that we feed into the OpenGL state-machine hopper so as to prepare to draw something. Specifically, let's see what it would take to draw a white square.

```
//Initialize the Window (Described in next subsection)
::glClearColor(0.0, 0.0, 0.0, 0.0);
::glClear(GL_COLOR_BUFFER_BIT);
::glColor3f(1.0, 1.0, 1.0);
::glOrtho(0.0, 1.0, 0.0, 1.0, -1.0, 1.0);
::glBegin(GL_POLYGON)
    ::glVertex(0.25, 0.25, 0.0);
    ::glVertex(0.75, 0.25, 0.0);
    ::glVertex(0.75, 0.75, 0.0);
    ::glVertex(0.25, 0.75, 0.0);
::glEnd();
::glFinish();
//Update the Window (Described in next subsection)
```

You can view a lot more code like this in the Pop Framework's graphicsopengl.cpp file.

26.4   OpenGL code in Windows

OpenGL is a platform-neutral library. It can run on operating systems such as X-Windows, the Macintosh, or Windows. In each of these systems you add a little extra code in order to interface your system to OpenGL.

The basic Win32 library includes a few built-in data types and functions to be used with OpenGL. Here's a block of code that shows how we initialize a window and update it. The data types PIXELFORMATDESCRIPTOR and HGLR are special built-in Windows types used for working with OpenGL. And **::ChoosePixelFormat**, **::SelectPixelFormat**, **::wglCreateContext**, and **::SwapBuffers** are built-in Windows methods for use with OpenGL.

```
PIXELFORMATDESCRIPTOR pixelformat;
int pixelformat_index;
HGLR openglrenderingcontext;
HDC hdc_view;

//Initialize the Window.
pixelformatindex = ::ChoosePixelFormat(hdc, &pixelFormat);
::SelectPixelFormat(hdc, pixelformatindex, &pixelFormat);
openglrenderingcontext = ::wglCreateContext(hdc_view);
::glMakeCurrent(hdc_view, openglrenderingcontext);
```

```
/* Use ::gl... and ::glu... calls to set GL states, add GL vertices,
    load GL textures,
//the example of a square was given in the previous subsection. */

//Update the Window
::glFinish()
::SwapBuffers(hdc_view);
```

Note that you don't need to re-initialize the window for every update. Each time you want to load the OpenGL state machine and send something new to the screen, it suffices to call **::glMakeCurrent** again, using the same openglrenderingcontext. In the Pop Framework, the call to **::glMakeCurrent** is encapsulated into our *cGraphicsOpenGL::activate()* method.

26.5   OpenGL in the Pop Framework

Look back at the code for *CPopView::OnDraw(CDC* pDC)* that we gave in Section 24.4: Graphics in the Pop Framework. Here is a bulleted list showing some of the corresponding OpenGL calls made by the _pgraphics member of *CPopView* if _pgraphics is of the type *cGraphicsOpenGL**.

- Wake up the graphics with

    ```
    _pgraphics->activate().
    ```

    This calls

    ```
    ::wglMakeCurrent( _pDC->GetSafeHdc(), _hRC )
    ```

- Clear the graphics background with

    ```
    _pgraphics->clear(targetrect).
    ```

    This calls

    ```
    ::glClear( GL_COLOR_BUFFER_BIT | GL_DEPTH_BUFFER_BIT );
    ```

- Install the projection and view matrices with these lines.

    ```
    _pviewpointcritter->loadProjectionMatrix();
    _pviewpointcritter->loadViewMatrix();
    ```

    These in turn call:

    ```
    ::glMatrixMode(GL_MODELVIEW)
    ::glLoadMatrixf(_pviewpointcritter->attitude().inverse());
    ```

```
::glMatrixMode(GL_PROJECTION)
::gluPerspective (fieldofviewangleindegrees, xtoyaspectratio,
    nearzclip, farzclip); //Values from _pviewpointcritter
```

- Draw your game world and then the critters with

```
pgame()->drawCritters(_pgraphics, _drawflags).
```

This generates a variety of **::gl** and **::glu** calls like, in the case of polygons

```
::glEnableClientState(GL_VERTEX_ARRAY);
::glVertexPointer(...);
::glDrawArrays(...);
```

- Send the graphics to your video display with

```
_pgraphics->display(this, pDC)
```

This calls

```
::glFinish();// Tell OpenGL to flush its pipeline
::SwapBuffers( _pDC->GetSafeHdc() ); // Now Swap the buffers
```

Menus and toolbars

27

One of the goals in *Software Engineering and Computer Games* is to show you how to put together all the necessary pieces for a complete program. This means we need to talk about some of the things we do to build user interfaces. In this chapter we'll talk about how to implement new menu selections and toolbar buttons.

27.1 Adding menu selections

To add menu selections, open the Resource View as described in Appendix C. Click on the boxed little + signs as necessary to navigate down into the display until you see the **Menu | IDR_POPTYPE** selection. Double-click on this to open the menu in the Resource Editor.

(By the way, you might wonder about the **Menu | IDR_MAINFRAME** selection. This menu is what appears when no game documents are open; you can see it by closing all active games in the Pop program. Normally we don't bother changing this menu.)

Once you open the IDR_POPTYPE menu in the Resource Editor, you see a picture of a menu bar resource in the Resource Editor window on the right; you can edit this menu bar in a graphical manner. You can also change the arrangement of the menu by dragging selections around inside the Resource Editor, which is fully WYSIWYG. There will be gray boxes with dotted outlines in various positions on the menu; these are the spots where you can add things.

Each of the menu items has properties associated with it. To change the properties you can open the menu item Properties dialog for an item by double-clicking it or by highlighting it and pressing **Alt+Enter**. If you are using Visual Studio.NET, you may need to resize the dialog so you can see all of it, or you can scroll through it to find the lines you need to change.

It's worth noting that the **Alt+Enter** key combination will open the Properties dialog for other kinds of resources as well. Visual Studio, Version 6.0, has a helpful question mark at the corner of the dialog box that you can select for specific information about the Properties entries. Visual Studio.NET instead has a more generic and less specific kind of help that you can access with **Help | Dynamic Help** or **Ctrl+F1**.

Anyway, once you get your menu item Properties dialog box open, your typing goes into the **Caption** field of this box and onto the menu bar resource. Usually you don't bother to fill in the **ID** field in this dialog, Visual Studio will put something reasonable based on the menu item's position and name. You can see what Visual Studio put you have to close the menu item Properties dialog box and then open again. Thus the **Game | Restart** selection gets the ID_GAME_RESTART as its identifier.

Note that menu selections usually have one of their letters underlined for the short-cut key. You set the shortcut key by putting an '&' in front of the desired letter in the **Caption** field of the menu item Properties dialog box for that item. Thus the caption for **Game | Restart** that we type in is &Restart. You shouldn't use the same shortcut letter for different controls on the same popup, as Windows will always just do the first of the two controls when you use this key.

Also note that in the menu item Properties dialog box we have the option of Setting to TRUE [or checking the box for (in Version 6.0)] the **Separator** or **Popup** selections. A *separator* is a horizontal dividing line. A *popup* selection leads off a menu bar or a popup to another popup. Generally you should avoid having popups go down more than two, or at most three, levels deep. If you have a lot of controls it's better to lay them all out on a dialog box.

A final thing to notice in the menu item Properties dialog box is a field at the bottom labeled **Prompt**. The string you put into this box supplies a user prompt that appears in the status bar when that particular menu selection is highlighted. It's a good idea to fill in a prompt for each of your menu items. Whenever possible try and include some really useful information that's not already contained in the caption of the menu item. For instance, it's better to have the **Game | Small** prompt be Show 20 critters than to have the prompt be Small. Don't be stingy with the user. Share what you know.

A second point about the **Prompt** is that it's common to actually have two strings inside the prompt, with the second string being a one or two word phrase that can be used for a 'tool tip' in the event that this menu selection becomes implemented as a toolbar button. The two strings are separated with a newline symbol \n. Usually a tool tip is little more than the name of the menu selection. Thus the full **Prompt** used for the **Game | Small** might be Show 20 critters\nSmall count. We'll talk more about toolbar buttons in the next section.

Handling and updating menu selections

For every menu item that your program has, MFC will let you add two 'message handler' methods to your **CView**. The first is a so-called **UPDATE** method, whose name usually starts with **On...** The second message handler is a so-called UPDATE_COMMAND_UI method, whose name normally starts with **OnUpdate...** By the way, UI stands for 'user interface.' And we're using '. . .' here to stand for a name which is normally based on the name of your menu selection. the default behavior of Visual Studio is indeed to give these methods names based on your menu item's name. In the case of the **Game | Small** selection, for instance, the corresponding **CView** methods are named **OnGameSmall** and **OnUpdateGameSmall**.

The **UPDATE** or *On...* method is where you specify what happens when the user clicks on the menu selection.

The UPDATE_COMMAND_UI or *OnUpdate...* method is where you specify the appearance of the menu selection. Is it grayed-out? Does it have a checkmark? etc. The *OnUpdate...* method for a menu selection gets always gets called automatically before you open a popup. You might think that you need to worry about calling *OnUpdate...* to fix your menus, but you don't. In fact the *OnUpdate...* method gets called every time your program has nothing else to do on its message queue. The reason it gets called so often is that it's possible to turn your menu selections into toolbar buttons, and Windows wants to make sure that the appearance of your toolbar buttons is always up to date.

In Visual Studio.NET we use something called the Event Handler Wizard to add the message handlers. You open the Event Handler Wizard by right-clicking on the menu item whose messages you wish to handle, and by then selecting **Add Event Handler...** from the context popup menu. You will see a wizard dialog with the Command Name filled filled in with the ID of your menu selection, suh as ID_GAME_SMALL.

[In Version 6.0, we use the so-called Class Wizard. To open the Class Wizard, right-click the item and select **Class Wizard....** You will see a multi-sheet Wizard dialog with the Message Maps sheet selected, and with the ID of your menu selection highlighted in the Object IDs box.]

You can now use the wizard to add the handler methods to your code. A box near the top middle says **Class list** [**Class Name** (Version 6.0)]. This is where we specify which class is going to be responsible for handling the menu selections. If a menu selection changes a parameter, it's most logical to have the class in which that parameter lives do the message handling. Our feeling regarding our new menu selections is that the **Game | Play Sound** should be handled by the *CPopApp*, the other **Game** selections should be handled by *CPopDoc*, and our new **View** selections should be handled by *CPopView*. By letting the classes that own the relevant parameters handle the menu-based changes of these parameters, we have to do a minimum of work in getting at the parameters.

Let's look at how we would add the handlers for the **Game | Small** selection. First we set the active field in **Class list** [or **Class Name** (Version 6.0)] to *CPopDoc* in the Wizard dialog. In the **Message type** box [**Messages** box (Version 6.0)] we see an UPDATE and an UPDATE_COMMAND_UI selection. One at a time, we highlight the selection. When you highlight a message selection, the wizard will suggest a default name for the message handler. You can edit this name in the wizard if you like. To actually put the handler into your code, you should click the wizard's Add and Edit button. Thus you can add, for instance, the prototypes and function bodies for the *CPopDoc::OnGameSmall* and *CPopDoc::OnUpdateGameSmall* methods.

Remember that menu selections will always need the UPDATE handler, and usually they will need the UPDATE_COMMAND_UI handler as well. In Visual Studio.NET, the wizard will close after you add one handler, so you will need to reopen it to add and edit the other handler.

[In Version 6.0, there is an Add button you can use to first add one handler before using the Add and Edit button to close the wizard and edit the handlers. Gotcha Alert! If you exit the Version 6.0 Class Wizard by just pressing the Esc key or by using the kill button in the corner of the dialog, the changes aren't saved. You need to exit the Version 6.0 Class Wizard either by pressing OK or by pressing **Add and Edit**, or **Edit Code**.]

[Once in a great while, in Version 6.0 you will start having trouble with the so-called Class Wizard *.clw file and Visual Studio will pop up warning messages about it. In this case you need to rebuild the *.clw file. To do this, close the project and delete the *.clw file. Then reopen the project, and select **View | ClassWizard**. Visual Studio will ask if you want to build a new Class Wizard file, say yes, and accept the defaults offered by the dialog.]

Now let's talk about the code for the handler methods. Remember that the **On...** method is for reacting to clicks on the menu selection. And the **OnUpdate...** method is for making the menu item's appearance reflect the current state of the program.

Remember that in handling our menu actions, we have the option of either affecting the underlying data in the document or of affecting the representation of the data in the view.

Let's look at an example involving a document variable.

```
void CPopDoc::OnGameSmall()
{
    _pgame->setSeedcount (cgame::COUNTSMALL);
}

void CPopDoc::OnUpdateGameSmall(CCmdUI* pCmdUI)
{
pCmdUI->SetCheck(_pgame->seedcount()==cgame::COUNTSMALL?1:0);
}
```

And here's an example involving a view variable.

```
void CPopView::OnViewKeepplayerinview()
{
    _pviewpointcritter->setTrackplayer
        (_pviewpointcritter->trackplayer()^TRUE);
        //Toggle the value.
}

void CPopView::OnUpdateViewKeepplayerinview(CCmdUI* pCmdUI)
{
    pCmdUI->SetCheck(_pviewpointcritter->trackplayer()?1:0);
}
```

The point of the *OnUpdate...* handlers is to put a checkmark by a menu item when it reflects the state of the program. Each time a popup is displayed, these handlers will automatically get called for *all* the menu items, so we can expect that only the desired ones of them will be checked.

An UPDATE_COMMAND_UI message handler like *OnUpdateGameSmall* takes a special MFC class **CCmdUI** as argument, this class can stand either for a menu selection or a toolbar button, and its most important methods are **Enable** and **SetCheck**. Enable takes a **BOOL** argument, and if this argument is TRUE, the effect is to gray a selection out. **SetCheck** takes an **int** argument which is 0 for unchecked and 1 for checked. The value of 2 is also used for toolbar buttons.

Yes, as we'll see in the next subsection, **SetCheck** can also be called by a toolbar buttons. SetCheck(0) leaves a toolbar button looking normal. SetCheck(1) makes the button's background a light gray, making it look as if it were in a pressed-down position. And SetCheck(2) sets a toolbar button to an 'indeterminate' grayed-out state, which is appropriate when the toolbar button doesn't apply to the current program state (for instance if no document windows are open).

27.2 Toolbar buttons

When we have a menu selection that we use a lot, it's nice to put a button on the toolbar so that you can do this action with one click. Although we can, in principle, have a toolbar button that does not correspond to an existing menu selection, it's considered good practice to always do it both ways. For this reason, even if you really just want a toolbar button for something, you ordinarily implement it first as a menu selection and then add toolbar button functionality for the menu selection.

You will notice that many of the Pop menu controls have toolbar buttons corresponding to them. According to which style of game is active, some of the buttons may be grayed out, or inactive.

Generally you want to put your most commonly used controls onto the toolbar to make the interface easier for the user. Any menu selection that you use more than two or three times during a typical play session should probably be a toolbar button. On the other hand, you don't want too crowded a toolbar as it then becomes confusing. The author makes no claim that the toolbar design for Pop is particularly good, the particular set of buttons on it got there by a slow process of accumulation, and should really be rethought. When you design your own computer game with Pop Framework, take a hard look at the toolbar, and make sure that you only have buttons that the users will need; you will want to remove some of the existing buttons and add others.

Let's look at the steps involved in adding a toolbar button for the **Game | Play Sound**. We open the Resource View window, click on **TOOLBAR** and double-click on IDR_MAINFRAME. The simplest practice is to use the same toolbar throughout your program; adding a new one yourself is quite a hassle. Rather than adding a new toolbar, we simply add buttons to the existing one.

The Resource Editor will show an image of your toolbar at the top, with an enlarged view of one of the buttons below. You can drag the buttons around on the toolbar as you like. To add a new button, highlight the blank button on the toolbar image. You can use the Resource Editor's graphics tools like a little paint program to draw something onto the button. If you don't see the graphics controls right-click on the Visual Studio menu bar and make sure that the Image Editor toolbar is checked. [In Version 6.0, make sure that the Graphics and Colors toolbars are checked.]

Once you've decorated the button to your liking, you need to connect the control to your program. To do this you need to open the toolbar button Properties dialog, which will look very similar to the menu item Properties dialog from before. Opening the toolbar button Properties dialog is a little harder though, because your mouse is busy acting like a graphics editor. You can't get to the toolbar botton Properties with a double-click or a right-click. The easiest way to open the Properties dialog for a highlighted button is to press **Alt+Enter**.

Once you've got your toolbar button Properties open, use the arrow on the ID field to scroll to the name of the ID of the menu item you want to imitate, in this case ID_GAME_PLAYSOUNDS. And make sure that the **Prompt** field ends with something like \nSounds to specify a 'tool tip' for Windows to show when your mouse pauses over the button.

At this point you're done! The **OnGamePlaySounds** and the **OnUpdateGamePlaySounds** message handlers we wrote earlier are already in place, and are already linked to all menu items and/or toolbar buttons that happen to have the ID_GAME_PLAYSOUNDS. And the **SetCheck** function will show the button as either in state 0 (looking normal) or in state 1 (pressed down).

If the message handler for a button lives inside the **CView** or the **CDoc** class, Windows knows to **SetCheck** that toolbar button to the 'indeterminate' state 2 when all the documents are closed. The nice thing about all this is that we the programmers don't need to worry about when to call the control update methods. Windows calls these all by itself; in fact each time your program has nothing else to do (no messages to process), Windows will call your program's control update methods.

By the way if you really did want to have a toolbar button that doesn't correspond to any menu selection, this would be perfectly fine. The only difference is that instead of scrolling through the existing ID_ values, you'd make up a new ID_ name for your toolbar button. And then you'd have to use Class Wizard to add handlers for the corresponding COMMAND and UPDATE_COMMAND_UI messages.

27.3 Accelerator keys

An accelerator key is different from a menu shortcut key. To use a View menu shortcut, you press **Alt+V** to open the View menu, and then press **P** or **C** to change the cursor. But an accelerator key is a single key or key combination that takes effect without opening any menu.

Adding an accelerator key for an existing menu item is easy. You go to the Resource View in the Visual Studio Workspace window, click on **Accelerators**, double-click on IDR_MAINFRAME to see the list of accelerator keys. Down at the bottom is a blank box with a dotted line around it. Double-click it or press **Alt+Enter** to open the accelerator key Properties dialog.

In the ID field you put the menu item selection that you want imitate. If you don't remember the name of the selection, pressing the **Arrow** key next to the ID field will show a list with all the existing selection IDs. In the **Letter** field you put the key that you want to use for the accelerator. There are three fields that you can turn on or off, according to whether you want to require a **Ctrl**, **Alt**, or **Shift** key with your key press.

It's often a convention to put the name of a menu item's accelerator key on the right side of the menu after the selection name. One thing to note about accelerator keys is that they *don't* work while a menu is open; unless of course the menu item shortcut happens to be the same key as the accelerator key.

27.4 Writing to the status bar

The ***CFrameWnd::SetMessageText*** method lets you write a string into the status bar. MFC provides us with a **CString** class that makes it very easy to create strings. In order to write the values of program parameters into a string, we use a **CString::Format** method, which behaves very much like the C language **printf** function. The **operator=** and **operator+** are overloaded for **CString**, with the **operator+** doing the logical thing of concatenating one string onto the end of another.

We write a little helper method called ***updateStatusBar*** for our ***CPopView*** class. As we mentioned before, we'll have our ***CPopView::OnSetCursor*** call ***updateStatusBar***, so that the status bar will reflect information about whichever window is currently under the cursor. In addition, we will need to call ***updateStatusBar*** at the bottom of our **OnLButtonDown** code because if you click the mouse without actually moving it, then your **CView** won't get an **OnSetCursor** call.

```
void CPopView::updateStatusBar()
{
    CMainFrame* cMainFrame = (CMainFrame*)::AfxGetMainWnd();
    cMainFrame->SetMessageText(pgame()->statusMessage());
        //Write to status bar
}
```

What goes into the actual statusMessage string is up to the individual game. You can look back to our section on the ***cGame*** class for the default game.cpp code for this method.

Exercises

Exercise 27.1: Add two game size buttons

We will probably use the Medium and Large game sizes the most. Add toolbar buttons for these two menu commands. Draw the buttons yourself.

Exercise 27.2: Add **Window | New** and **Window | Tile** buttons

The Pop menu labels the standard **Window | New** button as **Window | Additional View** of current game. Add a toolbar button for this menu command. Instead of drawing the button yourself see if you can find a way to copy it from somewhere else. One approach is to look for appropriate ***.bmp** images on your hard drive. Visual Studio, in particular, will have a lot of them in its subdirectories.

Exercise 27.3: Adding an accelerator key

Make the **Ctrl+A** combination be an accelerator for **Window | New**.

Exercise 27.4: Changing the caption

If you wanted to, you could write your information into the caption bar instead of into the status bar, using lines like the following. But there are reasons not to do this.

```
CPopDoc* pDoc = GetDocument();
ASSERT_VALID(pDoc);
pDoc->SetTitle(pgame()->statusMessage());
```

Try this and check what happens when you maximize a view. Check what happens when you use **File | New** to open an additional game document. Can you tell which view corresponds to which document?

Mouse, cursors, and keyboard

28

28.1 Mouse messages

Processing a mouse message

Windows generates a number of mouse-related messages, including WM_MOUSEMOVE and WM_ONLBUTTONDOWN. MFC handles these two with message handlers normally called **OnMouseMove** and **OnLButtonDown**.

The programmer is free to decide which class is to hold the handler methods. One way to do this is to open the Class View and to right click on the name of class that is supposed to handle the mouse message. In Visual Studio.NET you then select **Properties**... and click on the **Message** button in the Properties dialog. (In Version 6.0, you right click the class and select **Add Windows Message Handler**....)

In any case, the default message handler you'll get for WM_MOUSEMOVE will look like this.

```
void CPopView::OnMouseMove(UINT nFlags, CPoint point)
{
    // TODO: Add your message handler code here and/or call default
    CView::OnMouseMove(nFlags, point);
}
```

We override this as follows, telling the view to pass the mouse click right on to the game object.

```
void CPopView::OnLButtonDown(UINT nFlags, CPoint point)
{
//My Code. RR.
    SetCapture(); /* This is so that as long as the mouse button is
        down, this window gets messages from the mouse even when the
        mouse is outside the window. */
    pgame()->onLButtonDown(this, nFlags, point);
/* Don't need to figure out the game world pos, it's set as pgame()-
    >pbiota()->_cursorpos in OnSetCursor. */
}
```

Our special ***cGame::onLButtonDown*** (cPopView *pview, UINT nFlags, cPointpoint) code figures out which critter you should think of as being closest to the click with a line like this: cCritter* pTouched = _pbiota->pickClosest (pview->pgraphics()->pixelToSightLine(point.x, point.y));. And then, depending on the type of cursor currently active, the ***cGame*** does something to the pTouched critter. See the source later in this chapter for details.

We handle the ***OnMouseMove*** case in a different way. The cPopView::SetCursor has code to figure out the game world position closest to the pick point that also lies in the plane of the player critter.

```
void CPopView::OnMouseMove(UINT nFlags, CPoint point)
{
    /* Normally I track the cursor position in OnSetCursor, but this
        method doesn't get called during dragging, so I need to do it
        here */
    if ((nFlags & MK_LBUTTON) || (nFlags & MK_RBUTTON) ) //You're
        dragging.
        pgame()->setCursorPos(pixelToPlayerPlaneVector(point.x,
            point.y));
    pgame()->onMouseMove(this, nFlags, point);
}
```

Calling the OnDraw method

Often a mouse action changes the world in such a way that we need to redisplay it. This isn't an issue in our animated Pop framework, where the world is constantly being redisplayed. But in other programs it is an issue. The way to force a redisplay of all view windows from a given view's method is a line of the form pDoc->UpdateAllViews(NULL). You never try to call **OnDraw** directly, as this is a severe Windows no-no. One reason is that we'd have to do too much work in getting the right kind of CDC *pDC ready for the **OnDraw** argument, but there's some other considerations as well (which we won't go into).

No, the way to have, say, an **OnMouseMove** call **OnDraw** is to use an indirect approach. We call the **Invalidate()** function. But in order to keep our Document-View architecture smoothly functioning, we're not going to let ***OnMouseMove*** call **Invalidate** directly. Instead we're going to go all around Robin Hood's barn and do this.

- **CPopView::OnMouseMove** might kill off a critter say, and then call
- **CPopDoc::UpdateAllViews**, which calls
- **CPopView::OnUpdate**, which calls
- **CPopView::Invalidate**, which calls
- **CPopView::OnDraw** to draw the new state of affairs.

The pDoc->UpdateAllViews(NULL) line in the code has the default effect of telling the ***CPopDoc*** to send an **UpdateView** call to each of its views.

What about the **CPopView::OnUpdate** method? As it turns out, the default **CView** behavior for the method is just what you'd want; to call the **Invalidate()** method.

28.2 Cursor tools

Looking at the Pop Framework, you'll notice that the user can activate different kinds of cursors. When you have a program where users can change the tool action of the cursor, it's important to change the appearance of the cursor to match the mode. That is, the appearance of the cursor should inform the user about what the effects of mouse actions are likely to be.

We'll let the tool type depend on the view, so that it's possible to have two views open with a different tool being used in each one. This means that the data about which cursor to use should live in the *CPopView*. And the *CPopView* will be responsible for resetting the cursor whenever the cursor moves over the *CPopView's* window.

How does the *CPopView* keep track of which cursor type and tool type it is to use? A general principle of good program design is

> never to keep the same information in two different places.

The reason is that if a piece of data lives in two different places, then inevitably some change in your program will remember to change the data in one of its locations but not in the other. Now, since the *CPopView* is going to need to change the cursor's appearance, it might as well have an **HCURSOR** *_hCursor* variable that specifies the cursor's appearance – the **HCURSOR** type is a Windows handle used for this purpose. But since we're going to use the **HCURSOR** to change the cursor appearance, we might as well use it as the data to tell us which tool type is being used as well. That is, we do not need, or want, to have an *int _cursortype* variable in the *CPopView* in addition to the **HCURSOR** *_hcursor*.

Changing the cursor

A first thing to realize is that the cursor is a global resource; i.e. the cursor is not the property of any one window. The user is free to move the cursor away from your program's window and onto another window. So many of the Windows functions having to do with the cursor are global functions, i.e. functions that are not members of any class.

The global function used for changing the cursor's appearance is **::SetCursor(HCURSOR hCursor)**. It takes an **HCURSOR** handle to the new cursor resource as its argument. Remember a Windows handle is an indirect kind of pointer; it's a carry-over from the old Win32 programming that you don't see all that often in MFC. But, for whatever reason, the cursor functions are not wrapped up inside any MFC class. Remember also that, although strictly speaking we don't have to, we like to put the scope resolution operator :: in front of a global function with nothing to the left of the :: as a way of reminding ourselves that the function is not a member function of a class.

Now our **CView** is going to have an **HCURSOR _hCursor** variable, so this is probably what we want to feed into the ::**SetCursor** function. But where should we do this?

You might logically expect that we'd change the cursor only right after we change the **_hcursor** in the code that handles the menu or toolbar commands to change the active cursor type. Well, when do we change the cursor type in our program? Choosing the **View | Pin Cursor** and **View | Hand Cursor** menu selections calls the **CPopView::OnViewDraggerCursor** or the **CPopView::OnViewPinCursor** method. And inside these methods the value of the **_hcursor** does indeed change. So you might expect that in here would be the place to call **::SetCursor (_hCursor)**. But you'd be wrong.

This is because you can't just change your cursor once and be done with it. If you were to change the cursor to a pin only inside the **OnViewPinCursor** function, then as soon as you moved the mouse, your cursor would go back to being the default Windows arrow cursor IDC_ARROW. Windows resets the cursor *every time there is a mouse move*. The reason for this is that the cursor appearance needs to change as it moves across various windows and window-features on your program. Remember that the cursor is a global kind of thing. For instance, the cursor needs to turn into a double headed arrow if you place it over the corner of a window frame. And if a window has a special default cursor then that should be the cursor to show.

As it happens, every time the mouse makes a move over a **CWnd** window, the window gets a call to the **OnSetCursor** method for that window, so that's the place to put the code for changing the cursor. We use **View | Class Wizard** to open up the Class Wizard, and then tell it to add an **OnSetCursor** handler to our **CPopView**. And we edit the code to look something like the following partial listing of the Pop Framework code.

```
BOOL CPopView::OnSetCursor(CWnd* pWnd, UINT nHitTest, UINT message)
{
    /* This method get called whenever the cursor is over the client
       area of the view. Don't call the baseclass handler, that is,
       don't call: CView::OnSetCursor(pWnd, nHitTest, message).
       DON'T CALL THIS!!!! In particular, don't call base
       CView::OnSetCursor last because then you'll get the default
       IDC_ARROW cursor back!*/
//(1) Set the correct cursor for this view.
    ::SetCursor(_hCursor);

//(2) Use a special drag cursor if you are attached to the player.
    if (pgame()->playerListenerClass() ==
        RUNTIME CLASS (cListenerCursor))
        ::SetCursor(((CPopApp*)::AfxGetApp())->hCursorDragger);
```

```
//(3) Save the cursor position with cGame::setCursorPos if you're the
    active view
//if (isActiveView())
    {
    //First get the cursor position in a client area coordinates.
        CPoint point;
        ::GetCursorPos(&point);
            //Gets screen coordinates
        ScreenToClient(&point); //A CView conversion method
    //Then convert point to world coordinates and save with
    //setCursorPos
        if (pviewpointcritter->plistener()->
            IsKindOf(RUNTIME_CLASS(cListenerViewerRide)))
            pgame()->setCursorPos(pixelToPlayerYonWallVector(
                point.x, point.y,
                0.5 * pviewpointcritter->toFarZ()));
                /* If we are riding the critter, we want to pick a
                point on the "yon" wall, that is, the viewer's far
                clip plane. Given that we're on the critter, that
                distance from us will the viewpointcritter's toFarZ(),
                inlined as {return fabs(zfar - position.z());} */
        else
            pgame()->setCursorPos(pixelToPlayerPlaneVector(
                point.x, point.y));
                /* Otherwise we pick a point in the plane of the
                    player's body, that is, his tangent and normal
                    plane. */
    }

    return TRUE;
}
```

Notice that as well as setting the cursor here, we also tell the view's associated *cGame* object to update its current notion of where the cursor is. We do this update inside the *OnSetCursor* method because the method gets called essentially at every update.

Coming back to setting the cursor, how do we manage to put a valid **HCURSOR** value into the *CView _hCursor* variable?

Making a cursor in the Resource Editor

If we want to have special-looking cursors in our program, it's up to us to design their appearance. And then these cursor designs become part of our program's resources and get bound into the program executable where your application can find them at runtime.

It's pretty easy to add new resources to a program in Visual Studio. You just use the menu selection **Project | Add resource...** [**Insert | Resource | New...** in Version 6.0].

Either method pops up a dialog where you specify what kind of resource you want to insert. If you select **Cursor** you get a little Image Editing window. There are a few special things to know about cursor images.

- A cursor only uses the colors black and white.

- The cursor editor also uses pseudocolors that we might call 'transparent' and 'invert.' In the Visual Studio Resource Editor, these colors are represented by a grayish blue and by pink, respectively. Usually you want most of your cursor image to be 'transparent,' that is, you want the cursor to be a small shape that does not appear to have a white rectangular background.

- A cursor has an associated *hot spot* whose coordinates you can edit in the Resource Workshop. The hot spot is the location in the cursor image that is used to determine the pixel coordinates that are returned by mouse messages like **MouseMove** or **OnLButtonDown**. There are two considerations in picking the hot spot. (a) If possible, the hot spot should be near the upper edge of the cursor so that the cursor 'knows' as soon as you move it into the toolbar/menubar region at the top of your window. And (b) the hot spot's location should make sense relative to the visual appearance of the cursor, that is, it should be at the tip of a pencil, at the nozzle of a spraycan, etc. Sometimes you need to redesign your cursor image to satisfy both conditions. [In Version 6.0 you may need to close the Resource Editor's little Color and Tool windows before you can see the button that lets you pick the hot spot.]

As usual, when you create a resource you have the option of changing the name of the resource's ID mnemonic. By default, the Developer Studio will give a cursor resource a one-size-fits-all name like IDC_CURSOR1. You should change the name of the cursor resource to something that's easier for you to remember. To do this you need to get to the resource's Properties dialog. The easiest way to open the dialog is to press **Alt + Enter**. Or you can right-click on the IDC_CURSOR1 name of the cursor over on the Resource View and select **Properties** to see the cursor Properties box. You can either give your cursor an numerical ID mnemonic like IDC_PIN or, if you prefer, you can give it a string name like 'Pin,' being sure to put the string inside quotation marks. Remember to click on the little question mark at the corner of the dialog box for additional information.

The Resource Editor will save off a file with your cursor information. This file will have a generic name like Cursor1.cur and it will go into the .\res subdirectory of your build directory. It's fine for this file's name to be generic, because you normally don't need to directly access it, and if you did want to directly access it – say to quickly open it to edit it – you can tell what's in it by the appearance of the icon next to it in the Windows Explorer window. But if you really want, you can Rename the file in Windows Explorer and change its name to match inside the **File Name** field of the Visual Studio cursor Properties box. The first time you try and rebuild after doing a resource item file name change like this, you'll get an error message, but if you try a second rebuild, the Visual Studio will then accept your change.

If you aren't good at drawing, you can look for a cursor to copy. For the hand cursor, for instance, you might go through a process like this.

- Look on the distribution Visual Studio disk and find a lot of cursor files. Perhaps there's one called, say, **H_NW.CUR** that you like.
- Use Visual Studio **File | Open** to open this file inside the Resource Editor.
- Use **Edit | Copy** to copy the cursor image to the clipboard.
- Use **Insert | Resource... | New** to add a new cursor resource.
- Use **Edit | Paste** to paste the **H_NW.CUR** image from the clipboard onto the new cursor.
- And perhaps name the new resource IDC_DRAGHAND.

You might think you can copy the **H_NW.CUR** file to your **res** subdirectory and use **Insert | Resource... | Import** to add this resource. But when you do that and try to build, you may get a message saying 'Can't write H_NW.CUR, file is Read Only.' So that's why you need to use the **Edit | Copy** and **Edit | Paste** trick instead.

Getting a cursor resource

So alright, now we've talked about how to add an IDC_PIN and an IDC_DRAGHAND cursor to the project. How do we turn them into **HCURSOR** handles to feed into **::SetCursor**? It turns out that there is a **CWinApp::LoadCursor** method. So we add **HCURSOR _hCursorPin** and **_hCursorDragger** variables to the **CPopApp** class, and somewhere in the initialization phase of **CPopApp** inside the **Pop.cpp** file, we put these two lines.

```
_hCursorDragger = LoadCursor(IDC_HAND);
_hCursorPin = LoadCursor(IDC_PIN);
```

Where exactly 'in the initialization phase' do we put this? Well, you aren't supposed to try and do any serious initialization inside the **CPopApp::CPopApp** constructor, because when that constructor kicks in, the app isn't really fully ready to do anything. Instead you should do it right at the start of the code for **CPopApp::InitInstance()**. Do it at the start of the code block, mind you, and not at the end, because it's in the middle of the **InitInstance()** where ParseCommandLine(cmdInfo) is called to sneakily create your app's first **CDocument** and **CView**, and these guys may want to use something like the **CPopApp** information about the **HCURSOR**.

What a zoo, huh? But it's kind of exciting to figure MFC out and try to master it. In terms of sheer complexity and gnarl it beats the stuffing out of any computer game you'll ever see. And, let's face it, Windows programs are doing complicated things in a highly customizable fashion, so it's no surprise that they're so gnarly.

Another point to mention is that we need to make those **CPopApp** variables **_hCursorPin** and **_hCursorDragger** be public so that the **CPopView** can see them. Alternatively we can put a friend class CPopView declaration inside of **CPopApp**. (Note that you can do this without trying to #include "popview.h" inside **Pop.h**, which would be a risky thing to do, possibly leading to circular includes.)

The *CPopView* uses these variables when it changes the cursor. For instance we have this handler for **View | Pin Cursor**.

```
void CPopView::OnViewPincursor()
{
    _hCursor = ((CPopApp*)::AfxGetApp())->_hCursorPin;
}
```

Let's back up and take another look at the way we did this. Why don't we just do something like `_hCursor = ((CPopApp*)::AfxGetApp())->LoadCursor(IDC_PIN)` inside the `CPopView::OnViewPincursor()`?

Well, we have three reasons for not doing it this way.

- First of all, since **LoadCursor** is a **CWinApp** method, it seems like good object-oriented design to let the **CWinApp** be the one to call it from inside one of its methods.

- Second, if we load the cursors once at startup in the *CPopApp*, we then have the static fixed **HCURSOR _hCursorPin** and **_hCursorDragger** variables to use for distinguishing between the two cases of the *CView _hCursor* variable.

- Third, in a few chapters we're going to start loading bitmap resources that we want to use as icons for game objects, and then wrapping them up inside *cMemoryDC* objects to make it easy to **BitBlt** them into our game image. Often we'll have multiple game objects using the same bitmap, in which case it will make for a cleaner and more efficient design to have these identical bitmaps preloaded into static global *cMemoryDC* objects. So having our cursor object be a **CWinApp** member is good practice for later on.

What happens when you load a resource anyway? When you compile and link a Windows program, the resource code you've created is bound into your executable along with your compiled C++ source code. Your app finds the resource information by searching in the *.exe code that was loaded into RAM at the program's startup. You get at this resource information by various functions. **CWinApp::LoadCursor** and **CWinApp::LoadIcon** load cursors and icons. Later we'll see that **CDialog::DoModal** or **CDialog::Create** call up dialog box resources. You get at a resource-stored bitmap with a **CBitmap::LoadBitmap** call. If you have an alternate menu in your resources, you can get to it with a **CMenu::LoadMenu** function. **::PlaySound** can get a *.wav file out of your resources.

The first call to **LoadCursor** is in fact a slightly computation intensive operation, because at this call, the program has to find the resource somewhere inside the *.exe and convert it into a useable form in the RAM. You might think that successive calls to **LoadCursor** for the same resource would keep incurring the same computation cost, but in fact Windows is smart enough to not reload a resource if you've already loaded it once during a given program run. So our justification for only calling **LoadCursor** once has more to do with good object-oriented design than it does with execution speed.

While we're talking about loading resources, do recall that in all of these resource-loading calls the argument you give to the function is a name for the resource you want to get at. As we've mentioned before, the 'name' for your resource can either be a character string in quotes or it can be an ID_??? name that actually stands for an integer.

(Win32 programmers might possibly worry about whether or not you need to free up the resources involved in the **HCURSOR** handles you create. Although in Win32 you are responsible for calling **DeleteObject** for graphics-tool-handles like **HPEN** or **HBRUSH** you create, in the case of an **HCURSOR**, you *don't* have to delete the object. Windows will automatically get rid of it when your program terminates.)

In the Pop Framework, *cGame* has a *cArray_arrayHCURSOR* which is initialized in the game constructor to list the usable cursors.

Using the cursor tools

All the mouse message handlers take the same two arguments as in OnMouse Move (UINT nFlags, Cpoint point). The nFlags has information about which buttons are down, and the point gives the click location in client coordinates. Since the primary method used is going to be left-clicking, we put most of our code into the *cGame::onLButtonDown* function that we call from *CPopView::OnLButtonDown*.

So here, as an example of how we use the mouse, is what the base *cGame* class does with left mouse clicks.

```
void cGame::onLButtonDown(CPopView *pview, UINT nFlags, CPoint point)
{
    if (gameover() || gamepaused())
        return; /* Don't use mouse or keyborad messages until game
            starts. */
    if ((pview->hcursor() == ((CPopApp*)::AfxGetApp())->hCursorPlay)
        || playerListenerClass() == RUNTIME CLASS(cListenerCursor))
        pcontroller->onLButtonDown(nFlags);
        /* We put a left click into the pcontroller for the individual
            critters to see if either we have the hCursorPlay cursor,
            which is used for shooting, or if our player happens to be
            using a ListenerCursor. */
    if (playerListenerClass() == RUNTIME CLASS(cListenerCursor))
        return;
        /* Don't try and use the cursor as a tool if it's attached to
            the player. */
    cCritter* pTouched = NULL;
    pTouched = pbiota->pickTopTouched(pview->pgraphics()
        ->pixelToSightLine(point.x, point.y));
        /* the "pickTopTouched" method picks the top relative to a
            line. I need to define the sight line different ways for
            2D and 3D graphics, so I let cGraphics children overload
            pixelToSightLine. */
    if ((pview->hcursor() != ((CPopApp*)::AfxGetApp())-> hCursorPlay))
        setFocus(pTouched);
```

```
        /* Click any cursor except cursor play (shoot cursor) sets
        focus to a clicked critter, or to nothing if you missed 'em.
        Don't let playcursor setFocus. */
    if (!pTouched)
        return;
    pTouched->makeServiceRequest("move to front"); /* Only has visible
        effect in 2D worlds. */
//Click Hand case
    if (pview->hcursor() == ((CPopApp*)::AfxGetApp())->
        hCursorDragger)
    { /* The draggable condition checks if the critter is willing to be
        dragged. */
        if (pTouched->draggable())
        {
            bDragging = TRUE;
            onMouseMove(pview, nFlags, point); /* Move to the click
                point. */
        }
        return; /* Note that by bailing out here we leave
            the pfocus on the move critter, which has the
            side effect that cBiota::move doesn't move it,
            which is good. */
    }
//Click Pin case
    if (pview->hcursor() == ((CPopApp*)::AfxGetApp())-> hCursorPin &&
        pTouched != pplayer())
        pTouched->die(); /* makes "delete me" request, possibly does
            more */
//Click Zap case
    if (pview->hcursor() == ((CPopApp*)::AfxGetApp())-> hCursorZap)
        pTouched->zap();
/* makes "zap" request for this guy. */
//Click Replicate case
    if (pview->hcursor() == ((CPopApp*)::AfxGetApp())->
        hCursorReplicate)
    pTouched->replicate();
/* makes "replicate" request for this guy. */
//Clean up
    pbiota->processServiceRequests(); /* So you don't change
        critter twice. If you wait for the timer to trigger
        CPopDoc::stepDoc to call the processServiceRequest,
        you might possibly manage to click or drag the same
        critter again. The reason is that you may have several
        OnLButtonDown messages in the message queue, and when
        they are processed you will get several calls to
        onLButtonDown. */
```

setFocus(NULL); /* For all of the one-time actions, we release
    the pfocus after the action, because it's confusing to see
    the critter frozen in focus after you zap it for instance.
    (The freeze would be because cBiota::move doesn't move the
    pfocus.) We do leave in the freeze on the move cursor. */
}

And our ***cGame::onMouseMove*** code is as follows:

```
void cGame::onMouseMove(CPopView *pview, UINT nFlags, CPoint point)
{
    if (gameover() || gamepaused())
        return; /* Don't use mouse or keyborad messages until game
            starts. */
        pcontroller->onMouseMove(nFlags);
            /* We pass this on, but ordinarily the critters don't do
                anything with it. */
        if (playerListenerClass() == RUNTIME CLASS(cListenerCursor))
            /* Don't try and use the cursor as a tool if it's attached
                to the player. */
            return;
// No Drag Case
    if (!(nFlags & MK LBUTTON)
        return;
// Drag Hand Case, with (hcursor == ((CPopApp*)::AfxGetApp())->
    hCursorDragger)
    if (pFocus() && bDragging)
    {
        cVector cursorforcritter =
            pview->pixelToCritterPlaneVector(point.x, point.y,
                pFocus());
                /* It's going to be easier, at least to start with, to
                    drag only within the focus critter plane. */
        pFocus()->dragTo(cursorforcritter, pcontroller->dt());
            /* Feed the current dt to dragTo so as to set the
                critter's velocity to match the speed of the drag;
                this way you can "throw" a critter by dragging it. */
        pbiota->processServiceRequests(); /* In case critter
            reacts. If you wait for the timer to trigger
            CPopDoc::stepDoc to call the processServiceRequest, you
            might possibly manage to click or drag the same critter
            again. The reason is that you may have several OnMouseMove
            messages in the message queue, and when they are processed
            you will get several calls to cGame::onMouseMove. */
    }
}
```

A thing to point out here is the standard trick for dragging. The idea behind dragging is that you want your mouse move code to behave differently depending on whether or not the left button is down. The trick is to preface any dragging code with two lines like this.

```
if (!(nFlags & MK_LBUTTON)) //Bail unless the left button is down.
    return;
```

The Windows **MK_LBUTTON** constant is a single-bit binary number, like 1 or 2 or 4 or 8, and the nFlags will have this bit set if the left button was down at the time the mouse move took place. There are other **MK_** masks as well: **MK_RBUTTON, MK_MBUTTON, MK_CONTROL,** and **MK_SHIFT,** where the last two flags allow you to have the effect of a mouse drag depending on whether the Ctrl or Shift key is down.

A second thing to point out is that since we wanted the left drag with the Pin cursor to pop bubbles just like a left click does, we could do this by simply calling the *onLButtonDown* method. This is a far better practice than putting a copy of the relevant bubble-popping code inside the *onMouseMove*. This adheres to our general principle of good program design that you should never have copies of the same code in different places. (See game.cpp for details)

28.3   The mouse wheel

Though not everyone has a wheel mouse yet, they are becoming more popular. If you don't have one, you really should get one, as the wheel makes it a lot easier to scroll through all the files you have to look at when you're programming. An additional good feature of some wheel mice (such as Microsoft's high-end one) is that you can press down on the wheel to simulate a double click.

You can add a handler for WM_MOUSEWHEEL to add a method *BOOL CPopView::OnMouseWheel(UINT nFlags, short zDelta, CPoint pt)*. Check the Visual Studio help for the meaning of the arguments.

For our purposes, we only want the mouse wheel to scroll through the different tool types. In the Pop Framework build, the mouse wheel scrolls through all the available cursors for each game. Thanks to encapsulation and OOP, the mouse wheel code is particularly clean.

```
BOOL CPopView::OnMouseWheel(UINT nFlags, short zDelta, CPoint pt)
{
/* Swap the cursor functionality, depending which cursors the game
    uses. We just use the sign of zdelta, which will be some positive
    or negative number, depending on which way and how far you turned
    the wheel. */

    pgame()->nextHCURSOR(_hCursor, zDelta);
    return TRUE;
}
```

28.4   Focus and autofocus

A slight interface problem arises when we use the accelerator keys or the mouse wheel to change the cursor type. The problem is this. We might sometimes have two views open in a splitter window, one on the left and one on the right. Suppose that in the view on the left, the Pin cursor is selected and in the view on the right, the Hand cursor is selected. Since the *CPopView::OnSetCursor* gets called by a view whenever the cursor passes over it, the cursor changes from Pin to Hand as we move it from left to right, and changes back to Pin when we move back to the left. This happens automatically, without any clicking of the mouse.

In an MDI program with several views open, only one view will have what is called the *focus*. This is the view whose caption bar is highlighted. In an MDI program, you can change the focus by clicking on one of the views, by pressing the **Ctrl+F6** key combination, or by using the Window popup menu and selecting one of the views listed at the bottom. The focus view is the view which handles menu selections, toolbar buttons, and accelerator keys, and dialog information.

Now here's our problem. Suppose the left view has the focus. Its caption bar is highlighted. The cursor is over the left view and it shows the Pin cursor. Move the cursor over the right view, and the cursor changes to the Hand cursor. Now press 2 or rotate the mouse wheel. What happens?

The highlighted toolbar button showing the active cursor type changes. But the cursor doesn't change. And you're confused. You're an unhappy user. And then, to confuse you the more, if you move your cursor back over the left view, the cursor there is a hand instead of a pin.

The problem here is that the cursor's appearance is reflecting the toolstate of the view under the cursor. But the accelerator key and mouse wheel shortcuts are changing the toolstate of the focus view, which will not be the same as the view under the cursor *until you've clicked the cursor in that view*.

What to do? One option would be just to get rid of the confusing accelerator key and mouse wheel tool controls. Another option would be to use a context menu as described in Exercise 28.5. This option would work because once you right-click to open the context menu, you've clicked inside the underlying view and you've automatically made it your focus. An even easier option, that you can try in Exercise 28.7, is to let a right-click just swap the tool type without even showing you a context menu.

There is a more complicated solution, which is to have the focus change automatically to whatever view is currently under the cursor. The Pop Framework lets you choose this option by selecting **Window | Autofocus**. You can check the Pop Framework *CPopView::OnSetCursor* code in popview.cpp to see how it's implemented.

28.5   The keyboard

Let's talk about how we handle the keys in the Pop Framework. In order to process keys, your **CView** can either have an **OnChar** handler or an **OnKeyDown** handler.

But it turns out, the **OnChar** handler is only good for letter keys. So in order to process arrow keys we use VisualStudio to add to *CPopView* the **OnKeyDown** handler for the WM_KEYDOWN message.

When you press a key, the view that has the focus receives an **OnKeyDown** message. If you continue holding the key down, the focus view will continue receiving **OnKeyDown** messages (but it won't necessarily get repeated **OnChar** messages). The timing between these messages varies greatly from machine to machine, and you should never write code that depends on any assumptions about how often or how seldom the repeated **OnKeyDown** messages will come in when somebody holds down a key. One reason for the variation is that most computers have a BIOS setting for how often to generate 'autorepeat' or 'typematic' messages when a key is held down. Another reason for the variation is the behavior of Windows itself. If it matters to you if a key is being held down, it is up to you to keep track of this yourself rather than depend on repeated **OnKeyDown** messages.

When you release the key, the focus view receives an **OnKeyUp** message. One thing that can cause problems here is that if you press a key while a given view has focus, hold the key down, switch the focus (by selecting another view or by opening a menu popup or dialog), and then release the key, the initial view window will not receive the **OnKeyUp** message.

The UINT nChar argument to the key handlers is a keycode. For letter and number keys, this code is simply the ASCII code for that key. In C, C++ and Java we write an ASCII code for a character by putting the character in single quotes. Thus 'A' is the ASCII for the A key.

The keycodes for the non-ASCII keys are defined in a file called **winuser.h**. These codes have names that start with VK_. Thus VK_LEFT is the Left arrow key, VK_F2 is the F2 key, VK_SHIFT is the Shift key and so on. We list the keycodes in Appendix A; the numerical values of the keycodes should never make any difference to you, but it is good to have the listing just so as to know exactly what all the names are. (Without the list, you have to guess, for instance, whether the Control key, which has 'Ctrl' printed on it, is VK_CTRL or VK_CONTROL.) One gotcha in key programming is that you cannot automatically use a keycode like VK_A in place of the standard symbolism 'A'.

It can be useful to be able to tell if an **OnKeyDown** message is from the user's first press of a key or if it's from the user holding the key down. As mentioned above, most keyboards generate repeated **OnKeyDown** messages for any key you hold down. In the Pop Framework we won't actually care about this feature; what will matter to us more is whether the critters have already had a chance to detect a given keypress message.

As was mentioned in Chapter 12: Listeners, the Pop Framework has a special class called *cController* to encapsulate our key handling code, and each *cGame* object has a *cController* member. This means that in our *CPopView*, we do very little work inside the key handlers; we just have them pass the buck to the *cGame*. The game stores the key information in the controller, and then makes this information available to each critter. You could also override the methods so that the game did something extra for certain keypresses. The gain of having the key information in the controller is twofold: the controller organizes the keydown/keyup pairing and makes the key information available to any critter that needs it. In some games, you might well want to have more than one critter responding to the keys (e.g. left and right flippers in a pinball game).

Here's the code where the Pop Framework reads the keys:

```
void CPopView::OnKeyDown(UINT nChar, UINT nRepCnt, UINT nFlags)
{
        /* We will use the Windows-defined VK_??? symbols to stand
        for the various nChar values. Most of these are defined in
        the Visual C++ include file winuser.h. A few that should be
        defined are not, so we fix this by #defining them in the
        controller.h header file. */

        /*Although the documentation says nRepCnt gives you the
        number of repeated typematic messages from a keypress,
        this may not always to be true. Alternately, the doc says
        Bit number 14 of nFlags tells me if a prior OnKeyDown
        message has already been sent from this particular keypress.
        If this bit is on, the key is being held down. You access
        bit 14 via (fFlags & (1<<14)). But in any case we are not
        very interested in detecting repeated typematic OnKeyDown
        messages, instead we plan to make cController set a
        GOTTWICEBIT bitflag to signal when a given key press has
        been accessed more than once by the critters. This is more
        of an issue than whether we have a typematic repeat. */
    UINT control = (0x8000 &
        ::GetAsyncKeyState(VK_CONTROL))?cController::CONTROLBIT:0;
        /* Is control key down? The GetAsyncKeyState method returns
        a short unsigned int that has a one in its high bit if
        the key in question is down. I trust this more than using
        the nFlags.
            No matter how you detect Ctrl, on the Microsoft Natural
        Keyboard, the control key blocks the INSERT key, so we can't
        count on using the Ctrl+INSERT combination for anything. In
        the same critical vein, note that when the Alt key is down,
        you do not get any OnKeyDown messages at all. This contradicts
        the Microsoft doc that says the nFlags have a bit (#13) to
        tell you if the Alt key is down. */
    UINT shift = (0x8000 &
        ::GetAsyncKeyState(VK_SHIFT))?cController::SHIFTBIT:0;
        /* Is shift key down? Again, GetAsyncKeyState seems more
        reliable than nFlags. */
    nFlags = control | shift;
    pgame()->onKeyDown(this, nChar, nFlags);
}
```

The view reacts by passing the keydown messages to the *cController* which will detect on its own when a given key has been released. In its *update(dt)* method, *cController* uses the a global Windows method *SHORT* **GetAsyncKeyState (int vKey).**

We put the scope resolution operator in front of this method name with nothing to the left of it to remind ourselves that the method is indeed global and not a member of any class and call it **::GetAsyncKeyState**. The 16-bit signed integer variable returned sets 'the most significant bit' to tell you if the key is down or not, so we mask with 0X8000, which in binary is a one followed by 15 zeroes. This call works both with keys and with mouse buttons. (The left mouse button has key code VK_LBUTTON.) The **GetAsyncKeyState** method gets your key information regardless of which window currently has the focus. It's a direct hardware access method.

[A troubling issue with the keyboard in Windows is the behavior of the group of four **Arrow** keys, not the 'digital keypad' on the right, but the little group with **Up** and then below it **Left Down Right**. The **Left** key here fails to fire if the **Up** and **Space** are pressed. By 'failing to fire' we mean that the **Left** key passes a nChar value of 0 to the OnKeyDown. If you hold down **Space** and **Left**, the **Up** key is then blocked in the same way. What makes this especially puzzling is that the **Right** key *will* fire when the **Up** and **Space** are pressed. Also this blocking doesn't occur for the digital keypad **Left Arrow** keys, only for the keys on the extra little group of four **Arrow** keys.]

We use the *cController::onKeyDown* method to tell the controller when we press a key.

```
void cController::onKeyDown(UINT nChar, UINT nFlags)
{
    if (_keystate[nChar] == KEYOFF)
    {
        _keystateage[nChar] = 0.0;
        _keystate[nChar] = KEYON | nFlags;
    }
    else
        _keystate[nChar] |= TYPEMATICBIT;
            /* Notice when you get repeated keypresses by holding a
                key down */
}
```

The *cController::update* takes a *dt* argument for two reasons: first, *cController* remembers the last *dt* in case anyone needs it; and second, *cController* tracks how long each currently pressed key has been held down – this is useful for having, say, the rotation of a spaceship start out slow and then speed up a bit if you press, say, the **Left Arrow** key and continue holding it down.

Here's a simplified version of the code for *cController::update*. Note that since we have the *cController::onKeyDown* method to turn the keys 'on,' we use *cController::update* only to 'age' keys or to turn them off. Checking the key states 'by hand' with the ::**GetAsyncKeyState** method is safer than relying on the Windows **OnKeyUp** message, which may not get sent to the view you are currently in.

```
void cController::update(Real dt)
{
    for(int vkindex=0; vkindex< VKKEYCOUNT; vkindex++)
    {
        if (keystate[vkindex] & KEYON)
        {
            if (!(0x8000 & ::GetAsyncKeyState(vkindex)))
                //Key isn't down.
            {
                keystate[vkindex] = KEYOFF; //Turn off the keystate.
                    keystateage[vkindex] = 0.0;
            }
            else //Key is down.
            {
                keystateage[vkindex] += dt; //Age the keystate.
                if (keystate[vkindex] & GOTONCEBIT)
                    //keystate[vkindex] |= GOTTWICEBIT;
                else
                    keystate[vkindex] |= GOTONCEBIT;
            }
        }
    }
}
```

The place where the controller information may be used by the critters is this line of the *cGame::step(dt)* method: `_pbiota->listen(dt)`. These cascade down to *cListener* calls that have access to the game's *cController* object. Figure 12.1 in Chapter 12: Listeners is a sequence diagram of the process.

Exercises

Exercise 28.1: Viewing the *OnMouseMove* calls

Use a block like `#ifdef BOGUS` at the start and `#endif` at the end to temporarily comment out the *CPopView::onMouseMove* code inside the brackets and replace it with these three lines.

```
CDC *pDC = GetDC();
pDC->TextOut(point.x, point.y, "X");
ReleaseDC(pDC);
```

This way you'll see an X at each position where the mouse sends a an *OnMouseMove* call. Notice that if you move the mouse fast the X's are further apart. Also notice that if you resize the window after putting the X's in it they go away. Why is that?

The reason the three suggested lines look as they do is because you need to have a **CDC** object in order to call a 'graphics' function like **TextOut**. You can get a **CDC** from a **CView** using the **GetDC** function. The only requirement here is that when you get a **CDC** like this, you need to release it with a **ReleaseDC** call before leaving the block of code where you got the **CDC**.

Exercise 28.2: Using system-wide cursor resources

It turns out there are a few system-wide cursor resources you can use. The system-wide Windows cursors are called IDC_ARROW, IDC_CROSS, IDC_EXCLAMATION, and IDC_WAIT. You can get an **HCURSOR** for one of them by using the **CWinApp::LoadStandardCursor** method which takes one of these IDC_??? for a system-wide cursor name as argument. Change the Pop Framework code so that it uses the system-wide IDC_EXCLAMATION instead of our IDC_PIN.

Exercise 28.3: The grenade tool

In this problem, add a 'grenade' cursor tool which will remove all nearby critters when you click it. When you left-click with the grenade tool, you destroy all the critters whose center is within some fixed Real _grenadedistance of the *cVector* point corresponding to the cursor click. Or maybe it will be better to just destroy the first int _grenadekillpower count critters that you find within _grenadedistance, counting down from the closest ones. This way, if you have a really deep stack of critters, like the **Game | Huge** selection, you can have fun using repeated grenade hits to blast your way down. Try and think of a game where the grenade tool would serve a useful purpose.

Exercise 28.4: A Rotate tool

It would be nice in the Dambuilder game to have a rotating tool, that is, a cursor tool so that if you left-click with it, it will rotate a selected wall critter a bit counterclockwise. See if you can design and implement this.

Exercise 28.5: Creating floating popup menus

A lot of programs popup a context menu when you right-click. You can do this as follows. (a) Use the Resource View to add a new menu with an ID like ID_TOOLPOPUP. (b) Type any old character, which will add a top-level menu selection with a popup under it. Go down into the popup and add 'Pin' and 'Hand' selections with, respectively, the ID values ID_VIEW_PINCUSOR and ID_VIEW_DRAGGERCURSOR. (c) Class Wizard will ask which class to associate the new menu with. Associate it with *CPopView*. (d) Use Class Wizard to add a WM_CONTEXTMENU handler to *CPopView*. Code the handler like this.

```
void CPopView::OnContextMenu(CWnd* pWnd, CPoint point)
{
    CMenu menu;
    menu.LoadMenu(ID_TOOLPOPUP);
    menu.GetSubMenu(0)->
        TrackPopupMenu(TPM_LEFTALIGN | TPM_RIGHTBUTTON, point.x,
            point.y, this);
}
```

To make the popup really fast to use, make the easy keys 1 and 2 be the menu short-cuts on this little menu. That is, use these strings for our menu item names '&1 Pin' and '&2 Hand.'

Exercise 28.6: An accelerator key for autofocus

Open up about four windows and get an idea of what autofocus does. It would be a useful thing to have an accelerator key for **Window | Autofocus**. Use the **Ctrl+A** combination for this. The idea is that we might want to usually leave autofocus on, and only hit **Ctrl+A** to turn it off when we want to move our mouse away from a view and up into the menu bar and we don't want to worry about having the view get autofocused away from the view we want to change.

Exercise 28.7: Using the right mouse button

Give **CPopView** a message handler for WM_RBUTTONDOWN and have it change the cursor type. Or, if (a) you've done a right button popup and don't want to lose it and (b) your mouse has a middle button, use the WM_MBUTTONDOWN.

Serialization

29

In this chapter we're going to talk about how to save information about your current document's data, and how to read that kind of information back in. This process used to be called *file handling*, but these days it's called *serialization*. To serialize a document means either to write it to a file, or to read information into it from a file. The word 'serialize' is used to express the notion that we are converting a complicated data object into a simple *series*, or sequence, of 0s and 1s.

The MFC framework makes it exceedingly easy to open and save files. One good thing is that the work of finding the file names is already done for us. The presupplied File Open and File Save dialog boxes are examples of what are called Windows *common dialog boxes*. The Windows operating systems supplies us with a number of these.

Another good thing is that the place where we do our file loading and saving is easy to find; it's the **CPopDoc::Serialize** method in PopDoc.cpp. The AppWizard has put a skeleton of the code there with TODO comments indicating where to add your code.

Before undertaking serialization, you should adjust your File dialog so that it uses a reasonable default extension for the files you want to save and open (see Sections 23.9 and 29.9).

29.1 Serialization summary

Here's a summary of how to serialize the data in a **CDocument** class.

- Use the Resource Editor to change the document string to use a distinctive file extension for your files.

- If your document has any data members that are instances of a class **cMyClass** which you wrote, define the **cMyClass** as a child of **CObject** (or as a child of some other class which inherits from **CObject**) and add the DECLARE_SERIAL and IMPLEMENT_SERIAL macros to, respectively, the **cMyClass** definition in the *.h file and the **cMyClass** implementation in the *.cpp file.

- Override the **cMyClass::Serialize(CArchive &ar)** method so that it writes and reads the data members of **cMyClass**, according to whether or not ar.IsStoring()

is TRUE. Be sure to write and read the data members in the exact same order. Use the standard extraction and insertion operators to write and read simple types.

- If your document has an array member that holds an array of pointers to your *cMyClass* objects, declare the array type as *CTypedPtrArray<CObArray, cMyClass*>*.

- Override your *CDocument::Serialize*. First use overridden *Serialize* calls inside it to serialize embedded class objects or arrays, and follow this with code that uses ar.IsStoring()to decide whether to write or read, and which uses the standard extraction and insertion operators to write and read simple types.

29.2   Serialization in the Pop Framework

Serialization typically works by cascading downwards. Thus the *cPopDoc::Serialize* makes a call to the *cGame::Serialize* method which in turn calls *cBiota::Serialize* and so on. Figure 29.1 shows the cascade of some of the serialize calls that we use.

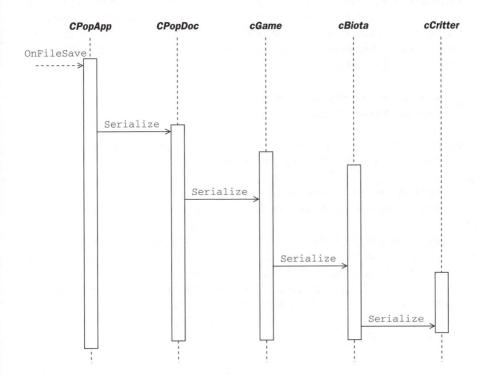

Figure 29.1   Sequence diagram of the Pop Framework serialize

29.3 Serialize, operator<<, **and** operator>>

Rather than working directly with files in MFC, we work with **CArchive** objects, which are friendly wrappers that have files buried down inside them. The general process of writing from or reading into a class such as *CPopDoc* or *cCritter* gets encapsulated into a method known as **Serialize**. **Serialize** is a polymorphic method that's declared way up inside **CObject** as **virtual void Serialize(CArchive& ar)**.

One of the useful things about a **CArchive** is that it 'knows' whether you're writing to it or reading from it. That is, if you have *SomeClass* which is perhaps a child of *ParentClass*, the *SomeClass::Serialize* function will normally have the form

```
void SomeClass::Serialize( CArchive& ar )
{
    if (ar.IsStoring()) //Writing data.
        // write to ar.
    else //Reading data.
        // read from ar.
}
```

How do we read and write data from a **CArchive**? If the data is a class that has its own **Serialize** method, you can call that. And for primitive data you use **operator<<** and **operator>>**. Only a class object can have a **Serialize** method. If you've worked with C++ file writing before, you're familiar with the overloaded 'extraction' **operator<<** and the 'insertion' **operator>>**. In MFC, these operators are friends of the **CArchive** class. For all the basic types like **int, float,** and **double**, and **CString**, there are operators like this.

> **CArchive& cArchive::operator <<(int i);**
> **CArchive& cArchive::operator >>(int i);**

For many MFC classes like **CString**, there are similar operators, though these are viewed as binary rather than unary operators. Examples are

> **CArchive& operator <<(CArchive& ar, const CString& string);**
> **CArchive& operator >>(CArchive& ar, CString& string);**

The << is called 'extraction' which means that you use it to extract data from your class and put it into a **CArchive**. The >> is called 'insertion' because you use it to get data from a **CArchive** and insert it into your class.

For a simple utility class like a 2D *cVector2*, we can overload the operators like this with these declarations inside the *cVector2* class definition.

```
friend CArchive& operator<<(CArchive& ar, const cVector2 &v);
friend CArchive& operator>>(CArchive& ar, cVector2 & v);
```

And then the *cVector2* implementations look like this.

```
CArchive& operator<<(CArchive& ar, const cVector2 &v)
{
    ar << v._x << v._y;
    return ar;
}
CArchive& operator>>(CArchive& ar, cVector2 & v)
{
    ar >> v._x >> v._y;
    return ar;
}
```

The reason that these operators return a **CArchive&** is so that you can chain them together, as we see in a line like ar << v._x << v._y. The C language associates expressions from the left, and parses this line as (ar << v._x) << v._y, so we need for the first **<<** call to return another **CArchive&** to use for the second **<<** call. The argument type is **CArchive&** rather than **CArchive**, because these calls change the state of the **CArchive**.

Just for completeness, we define a **Serialize** method for **cVector2** as well. As a general rule, we should, whenever possible, use **Serialize** rather than the overloaded operators << and >>. This is especially true for **CArray** objects, for which the overloaded operators << and >> don't work.

For a more complicated class like **cCritter** which we expect to use in serializing pointer-based **cCritter** objects from within other classes, we write the **Serialize** function first, and then add the special DECLARE_SERIAL and IMPLEMENT_SERIAL macros to tell the compiler to define **operator<<** and **operator>>** for the class. (This in fact might have been a good approach to use with the **cVector** class as well.)

The reason why we prefer to define **Serialize** and let the application framework generate the other operators is that, with a more complicated class, we really need two forms of the insertion and extraction operators. That is, we need the embedded forms:

> **operator<<(CArchive & ar, cCritter &critter).** Embedded extraction.
> **operator>>(CArchive & ar, cCritter &critter).** Embedded insertion.

And we need the pointer-based forms:

> **operator<<(CArchive & ar, const cCritter* pcritter).** Pointer-based extraction.
> **operator>>(CArchive & ar, cCritter *& pcritter).** Pointer-based insertion.

The idea behind the pointer-based forms is that we *don't* want to read and write the address that is the pointer. Instead we want the pointer-based extraction operator to extract data from a pointer-based object and write it to the archive. What we want the pointer-based insertion operator to do is more complex. We actually want it to turn the argument pointer into a pointer to a new object, and then to read the **CArchive** data into that.

If your class inherits from **CObject** and if the class definition and implementation use the DECLARE_SERIAL and IMPLEMENT_SERIAL macros, then you get all four of the special operators by writing one single function, the class's **Serialize** function.

How much of an object should we serialize? The best practice is not to worry about whether or not you really 'need' to serialize a variable. Perhaps it gets set by the constructor anyway? So maybe you don't have to serialize it? The best practice is to *serialize everything in sight*. Work your way down the list of declarations in the header file and serialize everything. Once you get the 'save' direction of the **Serialize** code written, block-copy it and turn all the << into >> to make sure you 'load' things in the same order.

Here's a small part of the **cCritter::Serialize**. A bit more of it is printed later in the chapter, and all of it's in critter.cpp of course.

```
void cCritter::Serialize(CArchive &ar)
{
    CObject::Serialize(ar);
        //Call the base class method to save the CRuntimeClass info.
    if (ar.IsStoring()) //Writing data.
    {
//Personal variables
    ar << _age << _lasthit_age<< _oldrecentlydamaged << _health <<
        _shieldflag <<
    //........ETCETERA..........
    }
    else //Reading data.
    {
//Personal variables
    ar >> _age >> _lasthit_age >> _oldrecentlydamaged >> _health >>
        _shieldflag >>
    //........ETCETERA..........
    }
}
```

For now, just focus on the fact that we write and read a sequence of things to ar in the same order.

The way we use the two SERIAL macros is that we start the **cCritter** class declaration like this in the file critter.h.

```
class cCritter : public CObject
{
DECLARE_SERIAL(cCritter);
```

And we put a line like this at the top of the critter.cpp file, right after the **#include** lines.

```
IMPLEMENT_SERIAL( cCritter, CObject, 0 );
```

Thanks to DECLARE_SERIAL and IMPLEMENT_SERIAL, using the *cCritter::Serialize*, MFC will automatically define four overloaded operators that work something like this. What we put here is not real code, it's the idea behind the code, or what's sometimes called *pseudocode*.

```
CArchive& operator<<(CArchive & ar, cCritter &critter)
    // Embedded extraction.
{       //=======CAUTION:PSEUDOCODE, NOT REAL CODE============
    //MFC sets ar so IsStoring() is TRUE
    critter.Serialize(ar);
    return ar;
}
CArchive& operator>>(CArchive & ar, cCritter &critter)
    // Embedded insertion.
{       //=======CAUTION:PSEUDOCODE, NOT REAL CODE============
    //MFC sets ar so IsStoring() is FALSE
    critter.Serialize(ar);
    return ar;
}

CArchive& operator<<(CArchive & ar, const cCritter* pcritter)
// Pointer-based extraction.
{       //=======CAUTION:PSEUDOCODE, NOT REAL CODE============
    //MFC sets ar so IsStoring() is TRUE
    pcritter->Serialize(ar);
    return ar;
}

CArchive& operator>>(CArchive & ar, cCritter *& pcritter).
    Pointer-based insertion.
{       //=======CAUTION:PSEUDOCODE, NOT REAL CODE============
    //MFC sets ar so IsStoring() is FALSE
    //MFC reads the CRuntimeClass information out of ar to get a
    //cCritterChild class type.
    pcritter = new cCritterChild();
    pcritter->Serialize(ar);
    return ar;
}
```

If you use **Edit | Find in Files** to root around in the MFC source code, you'll see that what the *operator>>(CArchive & ar, cCritter *& pcritter)* does is to make a call of the form pB = (cCritter *) ar.ReadObject(RUNTIME_CLASS(cCritter)), which (a) reads off the class name 'cCritterChild' and object size information for the next object in the archive, which makes it polymorphic, (b) calls pcritter = new cCritterChild(), and (c) calls pcritter->Serialize(ar) to copy the information from ar to *pcritter.

And what makes the critters get serialized in the first place? This results from the serialization of the _pbiota array in the *CGame::Serialize* method.

One gotcha to be aware of is that when you have as **CArray** type **_myarray**, you must serialize this object with calls to **Serialize** rather than trying to use **operator<<** and **operator>>**.

```
_myarray.Serialize(ar); //Yes, this works.
ar << _myarray; //No, this won't compile.
ar >> _myarray; //No, this won't compile.
```

The *& combination

The first time you see the *CArchive operator>>(CArchive & ar, cCritter *& pcritter)* declaration, you may perhaps be distressed by seeing the ***&** combination. Since you knew that ***** dereferences a pointer and that **&** generates a pointer reference to an object, you might have the feeling that the ***&** should cancel each other out. This would indeed be the case if you were to write something like this.

```
int x, y;
x = 1;
y = *&x;
```

The third line would indeed compile to exactly the same machine code as `y = x;`.

But when the **&** is used inside a function prototype's argument list it doesn't have the same meaning. Remember that if you write a prototype like `void someFunction(AnyType &mutable)`, what you mean is that you call `someFunction` with an `AnyType` argument and that `someFunction` is allowed to change the value of the `AnyType` argument.

```
AnyType mutable = whatever;
someFunction(mutable);
//mutable may no longer be equal to whatever.
```

So, logically, this means that if you write `void otherFunction(cAnyClass* &mutablepointer)`, what you mean is that you call `otherFunction` with a `cAnyClass*` argument, and that `otherFunction` can change the value of the `cAnyClass*` pointer that you feed into it.

```
cAnyClass* mutablepointer = whateverpointer;
otherFunction(mutablepointer);
//mutablepointer may no longer be equal to whateverpointer.
```

The reason that we want the **operator>>** to have a **cCritter* &pcritter** argument is that, typically, the **pcritter** argument we feed into it is going to be NULL, and we're going to be counting on the **operator>>** to construct a new **cCritter**, fill it with data, and set the value of **pcritter** equal to that nice new pointer.

Summing up, when you see a prototype like `otherFunction(cAnyClass*` `&mutablepointer)`, mentally insert some parentheses and read it as `otherFunction((cAnyClass*) &mutablepointer)`.

29.4 Serializing an array of pointers

The most important part about the Pop Framework's serialization code is one single line in the *cGame::Serialize* method:

```
_pbiota->Serialize(ar);
```

Getting that line to work was quite a task. Why? The `_pbiota` object is a *CTypedPtrArray<CObArray, cCritter*>* of pointers, some of which point to *cCritter* objects and some of which point to objects of child class types such as *cCritterBullet*, *cCritterArmed*, *cCritterArmedPlayer*, and the like. The array template type *CTypedPtrArray<CObArray, cCritter*>* is defined by MFC as an alternative to the simpler template type *CArray<cCritter*, cCritter*>*.

First of all, we need to tell the *cCritter* class and its subclasses how to write and read their data; we do that by implementing **Serialize** for the class and the subclasses.

Second of all, we need to arrange things so that we save and read the *contents* of the `_pbiota` array objects and not the values of the *pointer addresses*. This will happen partly because we used the DECLARE_SERIAL and IMPLEMENT_SERIAL macros and partly because we are using a *CTypedPtrArray<CObArray, cCritter*>* array rather than a vanilla *CArray<cCritter*, cCritter*>*.

Third of all, `_pbiota` is a *polymorphic* array of pointers, some of which are *cCritter** pointers and some of which are various child critter class object pointers, so we need some way to tell which is which when we are writing and reading their data. This, again, is taken care of by the fact that we used the SERIAL macros and the fact that we used the special complicated kind of **CArray** template *CTypedPtrArray<CObArray, cCritter*>* instead of the simpler *CArray<cCritter*, cCritter*>*.

It turns out that the default behavior of a standard **CArray** is in fact the wrong thing for arrays of pointers: it block copies whatever data is in the array. That is, it writes some information that you totally don't care about: the numerical values of the addresses where your data objects live. What you *want* to write is the data that lives in the objects. There are three ways of avoiding the inappropriate serialization behavior of **CArray**.

Serializing a CTypedPtrArray of CObject pointers

This is the most modern approach, the one we use in Pop Framework. If your class inherits from **CObject**, you can use a special kind of **CTypedPtrArray** instead of a **CArray** .

```
CTypedPtrArray<CObArray, cCritter*> *_pbiota;
```

(To be accurate we must immediately mention that _pbiota is actually a *cBiota** object; the *cBiota* class is a child of the class *CTypedPtrArray<CObArray, cCritter*>*.) The virtue of using the **CTypedPtrArray** is that a **CTypedPtrArray** 'knows' it's made of pointers so it will serialize your pointers by calling the proper kind of **operator>>** or **operator<<** for each pointer. This technique will *not* work if you use the CTypedPtrArray<CPtrArray, cCritter*> *_pbiota, in fact if you use an array like this, your serialization won't work at all.

The first modifying argument to a **CTypedPtrArray** definition can be either **CPtrArray** or **CObArray**. It's the second option that we must use here. The **CObArray** tells the **CTypedPtrArray** it is made of pointers to serializable **CObjects**. The effect of the first argument is to make *CTypedPtrArray<CObArray, cCritter*>* in fact be a special kind of **CObArray**.

[It would be more logical if the modifying argument used to specify the kind of **CTypedPtrArray** were **CObPtrArray**, and not **CObArray**, but, as we've said before, if MFC were fully consistent and logical, it wouldn't be true Windows programming! (Not that any other kinds of programming are perfectly logical either.)]

If you set a breakpoint at the line _pbiota.Serialize(ar) and step though a save or load in the debugger we find that the following MFC method gets called down in an MFC source-code file called Array_0.cpp. (In order to be able to step into MFC source code, you need to have set the options to install the source code when you installed Visual Studio.)

```
void CObArray::Serialize(CArchive& ar)
{
    if (ar.IsStoring())
    {
        ar.WriteCount(m_nSize);
        for (int i = 0; i < m_nSize; i++)
            ar << m_pData[i];
    }
    else
    {
        DWORD nOldSize = ar.ReadCount();
        SetSize(nOldSize);
        for (int i = 0; i < m_nSize; i++)
            ar >> m_pData[i];
    }
}
```

In looking at this code, understand that any kind of **CArray**, **CObArray**, or **CTypedPtr** array has two main private fields: its **m_nSize** that gives its size, and its **m_pData** that gives its array of elements. In the case of an array of *cCritter** pointers, **m_pData** will have the type *cCritter***.

As we described in the last subsection, we have a special overloaded pointer-based extraction *operator<<* and the special overloaded pointer-based *operator>>* to read the pointers intelligently. Rather than copying the address values of the pointers, the **CObArray** calls call these special overloaded extraction and insertion operators.

It's worth repeating that we don't explicitly define *operator<<(CArchive &, const cCritter*)* and *operator>>(CArchive &, cCritter *&)*. These are implicitly defined by (a) making *cCritter* a child of *cObject*, (b) putting the DECLARE_SERIAL and IMPLEMMENT_SERIAL macros in, respectively, **critter.h** and **Critter.cpp**, and (c) prototyping and implementing a *cCritter::Serialize(CArchive &ar)* method.

Serializing a CArray of CObject pointers by overloading ::SerializeElements

The second approach is to stick to the more familiar approach of defining CArray<cCritter*, cCritter*> _critters. The problem here will be, as mentioned above, that the default **CArray::Serialize** method will block copy the pointer addresses. So here we need override a certain global polymorphic the **SerializeElements** function. We would add some code like this to our **Popdoc.cpp** file.

```
void AFXAPI SerializeElements(CArchive &ar, cCritter **pcritterarray,
    int count)
{
    int i;
    if (ar.IsStoring())
        for (i=0; i<count; i++)
            ar << pcritterarray[i];
                // Uses operator<<(CArchive &, const c*)
    else
        for (i=0; i<count; i++)
            ar >> pcritterarray[i];
                //Uses operator>>(CArchive &, cCritter *&)
}
```

Note the peculiar prototype for the **SerializeElements** global function. Another tricky point here is that the linker will complain if you define this function in critter.h or Critter.cpp. Your override of **SerializeElements** has to be defined inside the document implementation file Popdoc.cpp. A good place to keep it is right before your override of the *CDocument::Serialize* function. You may be tempted to skip writing this odd little bit of code when using a standard **CArray** of pointers, but if you leave it out, then when you try and read in a file, your program will crash because you will read garbage values into your pointers.

Serializing a pointer array the hard way

We said there were three approaches, so what's the third? The third is to pigheadedly do it all yourself and not even derive *cCritter* from *CObject*. The price would be that we then need to keep a *CString _classname* field inside our *cCritter* and class to take the place of the **CRuntimeClass** information. It's enough to just have _*classname* be either *cCritter* or *cCritterBullet* or whatever. Note, by the way, that any child of the **CObject** class has a **CRuntimeClass** member, and one of the fields of **CRuntimeClass** is in fact a **CString** that holds the name of the class. So if you do this by hand, you're only copying what the MFC framework wants to do for you automatically.

The trick for serializing an object this third way would be to save off the name string before saving the object, and when you are reading it back in, you read in the name string and have a switch statement to construct the right kind of critter child class object pointer to read the object into. But there's no reason to work this hard. Save your energy for something other than reinventing the **CRuntimeClass**!

29.5 Serializing pointers

Serializing pointer members

CPopDoc has a `cGame*` `_pgame` object as its most important member. Serializing the `cGame *_pgame` pointer takes a bit of care.

Something to realize is that when you load into a *CPopDoc*, that *CPopDoc* object will already exist, so it will have been initialized by a constructor call. So the `_pgame` will in fact be a valid pointer. Whenever you load into a valid pointer variable `ptr`, you have to call **delete** on the pointer first, otherwise you'll have a memory leak caused by the 'orphaned' object that the pointer pointed to before you overwrote it with the load. For reasons we'll now explain, we must use an overloaded `ar >> ptr` operator to load into a pointer, rather than a call like `ptr->Serialize(ar)`.

To save and load the `_pgame` fields of *CPopDoc*, we use the autogenerated overloaded *operator<<(CArchive &ar, cgame *p)* and *operator>>(CArchive &ar, cGame *&p)*. MFC has 'written the code' for these operators automatically because the *cGame*

- inherits from **CObject**,
- has `DECLARE_SERIAL` and `IMPLEMENT_SERIAL`, and
- has its own *Serialize* defined

In the load case we want to make a new *cGame** and place it into the `_pgame` field, and this is exactly what `ar >> _pgame` does.

Now, as mentioned just above, in the load case, we `delete _pgame` before loading it. At first you might think you could load either with `_pgame->Serialize(ar)` or `ar >> _pgame`. But since you `delete _pgame` just before the load, it becomes an invalid pointer just before the load, and you would get a crash if you tried to call `_pgame->Serialize(ar)` for the load. We could actually use `_pgame->Serialize(ar)` in the save case, but for symmetry in the appearance of the read and write cases, we use `ar << _pgame` there.

Here's a partial listing of the *cPopDoc::Serialize*.

```
void CPopDoc::Serialize(CArchive& ar)
{
    CObject::Serialize(ar);
    if (ar.IsStoring()) // Save
        ar << _pgame;
    else //Load
    {
        delete _pgame; /*At CPopDoc construction a document creates a
            default cGame *_pgame. So if we're loading a game we need
            to delete the existing game first or there will be a
            memory leak.*/
        ar >> _pgame; /* Uses CreateObject to creates a new cGame*
            object of the correct child class, copies the new objects
            fields out of the file, and places the pointer to the new
            object in _pgame. */
        _pgame->setGameover(TRUE); /* So you can press ENTER to
            actually start it running. _brandnewgameflag will have
            been set to TRUE by the constructor call inside the ar >>
            call, so the first ENTER won't randomize things. */
        UpdateAllViews(NULL, CPopDoc::VIEWHINT_STARTGAME, 0);
    }
}
```

Serializing reference pointers

One exception to the principle of 'serialize everything in sight' is when your
objects have pointer members that are used as references to point to other
objects that may or may not be getting serialized as well. This is, in other words,
a case where our code actually has two or more copies of the same pointer in
two different locations. One of these copies is the 'member' and this copy gets
serialized as just described. But the other copies are meant only to echo the
address value of the member pointer object. In these cases we need to do
something a little tricky.

The **cGame** class, for instance, has a separate cCritter* _pplayer pointer
that is the same value as one of the **cCritter*** actually in the **cBiota** *_pbiota
member. We track the index of where it appears in the **cBiota** array, if it does
appear, and we save that. Here's some of the relevant code.

```
void cGame::Serialize(CArchive& ar)
{
    int playerindex;
    CObject::Serialize(ar);
        /*It's worth noting that when we call this next line in
            loading mode, the _pbiota will be pointing in a non-NULL
            cBiota that was created by the cGame constructor, so we'll
            need to have the cBiota::Serialize take care of deleting
            members of an existing cBiota before loading into it. */
```

```
    _pbiota->Serialize(ar);
    if (ar.IsStoring()) // Save
    {
        playerindex = _index(_pplayer);
        ar << _border << /* ETCETERA */ << playerindex;
    }
    else //Load
    {
        ar >> _border >> /* ETCETERA */ >> playerindex;
            /* _pplayer currently equals NULL or one of the old
                dummy pointers in the cBiota, either way we don't have
                to delete it. Remember it's only a reference
                copy. */
        _pplayer = _pbiota->GetAt(playerindex);
    }
}
```

29.6 The *cCritter* serialize

All the tricks we've discussed come into play with the ***cCritter::Serialize.*** A critter has a `cCritter* _ptarget` field that's a reference pointer, so when you save and reload the game file, which means saving and loading all of the critters, then the copy of the target critter is not going to be loaded into the exact same area of memory, and the old `_ptarget` pointer will no longer be correct. That's why we have the `_targetindex` field in the ***cCritter***.

This reference pointer problem comes back in even stronger form with the armed critters, who have pointers to their bullets. You can look at the **Serialize** code inside the `critterarmed.cpp` file to see one way to work things out. In particular look for the ***fixPointerRefs*** methods.

The ***cCritter*** also has member pointer fields. As we explained in the last section, in order to load the pointer `_psprite` and `_plistener` fields of ***cCritter***, we must first **delete** them and then use the overloaded **operator>>** to overwrite them with new pointers.

Note also that the **CArray** `_forcearray` has to be handled with **Serialize** and that, to avoid having a possible memory leak, you have to empty it out before you read into it. Here's some relevant code.

```
void cCritter::Serialize(CArchive &ar)
{
    CObject::Serialize(ar);
        //Call the base class method to save the CRuntimeClass info.
    if (ar.IsStoring()) //Writing data.
    {
        _forcearray.Serialize(ar);
            //Generally you cant use << with a CArray.
//Sprite
        ar << _psprite <<
```

```
//Listener
        _plistener <<
//Personal variables
        _age << _lasthit_age<< _oldrecentlydamaged << _health <<
           _shieldflag <<
        //........ETCETERA..........
//Pointer index variables.
        if (_pownerbiota)
           _targetindex = _pownerbiota->_index(_ptarget);
               //Prepare for a pointer reference.
        else
           _targetindex = cBiota::NOINDEX;
        ar << _targetindex;
}
else //Reading data.
{
        clearForcearray(); /* We have to empty out the array before
           reading into it or we'll have a memory leak in case
           something's in it. */
        delete _psprite;
           /* always delete a pointer before reading into it or you
               have a leak. */
        delete _plistener;
           /* always delete a pointer before reading into it or you
               have a leak. */
        _forcearray.Serialize(ar); /* Read in. You usually can't use >>
           with a CArray. */
//Sprite
        ar >> _psprite >> /* Uses CreateObject to creates a new
           cSprite* object of the correct child class, copies the new
           object's fields out of the file, and places the pointer to
           the new object in _psprite */
//Listener and force
        _plistener >> // See the comment just above.

//Personal variables
        _age >> _lasthit_age >> _oldrecentlydamaged >> _health >>
           _shieldflag >>
        //........ETCETERA..........
//Index for pointer reference variable.
        ar >> _targetindex; /* cBiota::Serialize will call
           cCritter::FixPointerRefs to replace this index
           by a pointer. */
    _ptarget = NULL; /* The cBiota::Serialize will call
        all pcritter->fixPointerRefs for each critter to fix the
        _ptarget, and also fix any pointer refs in the forces. */
    }
}
```

The **cCritter::fixPointerRefs** can only be called after all of the **cCritter** have been loaded and added to the **cBiota** array, with this array installed as the _powner-biota of each **cCritter**. The **fixPointerRefs** does the following, in part.

```
void cCritter::fixPointerRefs()
{
    if (!_pownerbiota)
        return;
    else
        _ptarget = _pownerbiota->GetAt(_targetindex);
}
```

29.7 Serializing child classes

If you have a child class of an existing class with a **Serialize** method, you will in fact inherit a serviceable **Serialize** method. And if you have put the correct DECLARE_SERIAL macro in your *.h and IMPLEMENT_SERIAL in your *.cpp, the inherited **Serialize** code will save and load the right kinds of child class objects.

If your child class has some new members then you need to override the **Serialize** method by adding this line to the class declaration: virtual void Serialize(CArchive& ar), and by then implementing the method in the code.

For instance our **cCritterBullet** class includes a new _hitstrength field, and a few other things, so we override its **Serialize** method to save and load this data. When overriding a **Serialize** method, you always call the parent class's **Serialize** method at the start of the code block like this.

```
void cCritterBullet::Serialize(CArchive &ar)
{
    cCritter::Serialize(ar);
    if (ar.IsStoring()) //Writing data.
    {
        if(_pownerbiota && _pshooter)
            _shooterindex = _pownerbiota->_index(_pshooter);
        ar << _hitstrength << _dieatedges << _shooterindex;
    }
    else //reading data
    {
        ar >> _hitstrength >> _dieatedges >> _shooterindex;
        _pshooter = NULL; //Gets fixed by the cBiota call to
            fixPointerRefs.
    }
}
```

Let's look at the relevant **fixPointerRefs** here, too.

```
void cCritterBullet::fixPointerRefs()
{
    cCritter::fixPointerRefs();
    if (_pownerbiota)
        _pshooter =
            (cCritterArmed*)(_pownerbiota->GetAt(_shooterindex));
}
```

As another example, **cGamePicknpop** uses two **cRealBox** rectangles, so we save and load them.

```
void cGamePickNPop::Serialize(CArchive &ar)
{
    cGame::Serialize(ar);
    if (ar.IsStoring()) //Writing data.
        ar << _packingbox << _targetbox;
    else //Reading data.
        ar >> _packingbox >> _targetbox;
}
```

It's really easy to mess up your **Serialize** code, and when you do, it's hard to debug it. The most common error is to fail to save and then load things in the same order. If this happens then, when you load, a lot of variables end up with garbage in them and the program crashes in some (usually) unenlightening way. When you have broken serialization code, the best practice is to back up to a point where it works, and then begin adding in the code bit by bit, being really obsessive about making things match.

One thing to keep in mind when testing your **Serialize** code is that the default MDI behavior is to not open a given file if a file of the same name is already open. So if you have saved a file as test.p17 and then leave it open and let it run for a while and then try to reopen it to get the old state back, nothing will happen. You need to close the current run of the game and then do a fresh open to get the old version back.

29.8 Serializing a *CRuntimeClass*

Here's a special bit of MFC arcana that took quite a while to figure out! How do we serialize a **CRuntimeClass**? Here's an example of how to do it from force.cpp file. The long comment explains why this was a difficult thing to do.

```
void cForceClassEvade::Serialize(CArchive &ar)
{
    cForce::Serialize(ar);
        /* I had a hard time figuring out how to serialize the
            CRuntimeClass *_pnodeclass.
```

```
             (1) You can't call _pnodeclass.Serialize(ar), as this is
                 not a method of CRuntimeClass.
             (2) Nor can you save off the CRuntimeClass m_lpszClassName
                 field and try and use RUNTIME_CLASS to reconstruct it,
                 as RUNTIME_CLASS requires a literal argument and not a
                 CString.
             (3) MFC provides a CArchive::SerializeClass(CRuntimeClass
                 *prtc). But it doesn't do the job either. It's
                 actually designed more for use as a compatibility
                 type-checker. If I put in
                 ar.SerializeClass(_pnodeclass), when I save and load,
                 I don't get anything read back into _pnodeclass
                 because SerializeClass treats its argument as a const
                 and won't change it in the load!
             (4) What DOES work is to save with
                 ar.WriteClass(_pnodeclass) and load with
                 _pnodeclass = ar.ReadClass(). */
    if (ar.IsStoring()) //Writing data.
    {
        ar.WriteClass(_pnodeclass);
        ar << _evadechildclasses << _dartacceleration << _dartspeedup;
    }
    else //reading data
    {
        _pnodeclass = ar.ReadClass();
        ar >> _evadechildclasses >> _dartacceleration >> _dartspeedup;
    }
}
```

29.9   Serializing the view and version

A difficulty in properly serializing a Pop Framework game is that we want to serialize the view information as well as the game information. If you've set your viewpoint to a certain location, direction, and zoom, you'd prefer to have it restored when you reload a saved game.

Since a document can have more than one view open, the default behavior for an MFC **CDocument** class is to not save any of the view information. The Pop Framework changes this by having a *CPopDoc* save the view information of the active view and, when loading, signal the active view to load its parameters from the archive being loaded.

Another point to worry about is versioning. When you make repeated builds of a program, you will occasionally change the number of fields in your key structures. If you then try and load an archive file from an earlier build, you'll get a hideous crash, because you'll be writing, say, 1003 bytes of file data onto, say, 998 or 1107 bytes of allocated RAM for the object you think you're reading in. So you'll end up by overwriting or non-initializing some bytes, and when the program goes to read those bytes there will be trouble.

MFC provides a method for versioning by putting an integer version number into the third argument of the IMPLEMENT_SERIAL macros. But changing these numbers is time-consuming and hard to remember to do, particularly as your code is going to have dozens of IMPLEMENT_SERIAL lines. So what we do in the Pop Framework is to treat the string in the program's caption bar as if it were a version name. In order to make this work for you, you need to remember to use the Resource Editor to change the IDR_MAINFRAME string each time you do a new build. You do this with the control sequence **View | Workspace | Resource View | String Table | IDR_MAINFRAME | Alt+Enter.**

Here's a copy of our code to both serialize the active view and do a version check based on the caption.

```
void CPopDoc::Serialize(CArchive& ar)
{
    /* So as to make sure that (a) I load and save my files with
        the same build and (b) I don't try and load non-Pop files,
        I'm going to write a version string at the head of each
        archive. */
    CString cStrAppVersion;
    VERIFY(cStrAppVersion.LoadString(IDR_MAINFRAME));
        /* VERIFY means always evaluate the expression, but if you
        are in the debug build and the expression is 0, then interrupt
        just like a failed assertion. */

    CObject::Serialize(ar);
    if (ar.IsStoring()) // Save
    {
        ar << cStrAppVersion;
        ar << _pgame;
        getActiveView()->Serialize(ar);
    }
    else //Load
    {
        CString cStrFileVersion;
        ar >> cStrFileVersion;
        if (cStrFileVersion.GetLength() > 256) //Then you opened some
            totally bogus file cStrFileVersion =
            cStrFileVersion.Left(16) + "..."; //Truncate
        if (cStrFileVersion != cStrAppVersion)
        {
            CString message = "File Version:\n" + cStrFileVersion +
            "\n\nDoesn't Match App Version:\n" + cStrAppVersion +
                "\n\nWill Abort the Load.";
            MessageBeep(MB_ICONEXCLAMATION);
```

```
        ::AfxMessageBox(message);
        ::AfxThrowArchiveException(0, NULL); /* This throws an
            exception which is caught inside the base class
            CDocument::OnOpenDocument call and then closes the
            badly opened document. */
        return;
    }
    delete _pgame; /*At CPopDoc construction a document creates a
        default cGame *_pgame. So if we're loading a game we need
        to delete the existing game first or there will be a
        memory leak.*/
    _pgame = NULL;
    ar >> _pgame; /* Uses CreateObject to creates a new cGame*
        object of the correct child class, copies the new objects
        fields out of the file, and places the pointer to the new
        object in _pgame. Constructor makes pnewgame->
        _gameisfreshlyinitialized be TRUE, so when you press ENTER
        it won't reseed. The CPopDoc constructor calls
        setGameClass. */
    _pgame->setGameover(TRUE); /* So you can press ENTER to
        actually start it running. _gameisfreshlyinitialized is
        true, as mentioned just above, so ENTER won't randomize
        things. */
        /* We used to not bother to try to load the CPopView info,
            and we just called UpdateAllViews(NULL,
            CPopDoc::VIEWHINT_STARTGAME, 0); But as of 9/2001,
            we wrap the CArchive in a cArchiveHint and pass it to
            the views. */
    cArchiveHint *parchivehint = new cArchiveHint(&ar);
    UpdateAllViews(NULL, CPopDoc::VIEWHINT_LOADINGARCHIVE,
        parchivehint); /* This call jumps right to
        CPopView::OnUpdate, so the ar information
        is still good. */
    delete parchivehint;
    parchivehint = NULL;
    }
}
```

The ***CPopView::OnUpdate*** code process the archive hint in the most obvious kind of way.

```
void CPopView::OnUpdate(CView* pSender, LPARAM lHint, CObject* pHint)
{
    //If you've just loaded a new game, use the game's initialization
    //code on this view.
    if (lHint == CPopDoc::VIEWHINT_LOADINGARCHIVE)
```

```
    {
        if (pHint && pHint->IsKindOf(RUNTIME_CLASS(cArchiveHint)))
        {
            CArchive *parchive = ((cArchiveHint*)pHint)->parchive();
            Serialize(*parchive);
        }
        return;
    }
    //More code for all the other lHint cases....
}
```

Since our **cPopDoc::Serialize** now does version-checking on its own, we don't really need to use numbered file extensions like *.p21 as was suggested in the tweaking the file Dialog subsection of 23.9. So the Pop framework just uses *.pop for its file extensions.

Exercise

Exercise 29.1: Binary or text file format?

Open one of the saved files in WordPad to see what it looks like. It's in binary form, so will be unreadable gibberish. Can you think of a way to save and load files that are written in readable text form? It can be done, though it takes some extra work. Figuring out how to do it is a good research project. The virtue of having files in readable text form is that you can edit them so as to change the nature of the objects being loaded; of course, there are risks to doing this as careless edits may make the file unreadable. But when developing a program, editable text files can provide a useful debugging tool as well as a kind of 'meta-interface' to the program.

Sound

30

30.1 Adding sound to your program

How do we get our program to make noise? The easiest way is to use the multimedia features of Windows to play so-called wave or *.wav files. A *wave* file is to sound as a bitmap is to graphics: it's a binary representation. Although Java code can also play files in the *.au format, the Visual C++ libraries don't supply this capability.

And what about music? What about playing *.mp3, or generating sounds with algorithms? Certainly a full-featured game ought to have some music and some more sophisticated sound-blending modes. Also you'd like to be able to use MIDI to avoid having to store a sound file in such a large format. But, in this chapter, we're only going to give you the bare minimum.

If you use the Windows **Start | Find** dialog you can look for *.wav files on your machine. Assuming that you have a sound card, and assuming that your speakers are turned on, you can 'play' these sounds by double-clicking on them. Before starting to work with sound programming, you should check that your system will indeed play sounds, otherwise you won't be able to tell if your program is working properly. Note that it often takes some fiddling to get sound to work, as there are usually several ways to turn it on and off, including both a control bar dialog and a physical knob on the speakers.

Let's take a look at an example of where the Pop Framework code makes a sound, the case where an asteroid is hit by a bullet in gamespacewar.cpp.

```
int cCritterAsteroid::damage(int hitstrength)
{
    int deathreward = cCritter::damage(hitstrength); /* This is _value
        (typically nonzero) you get
        for killing off the critter. */
    ((CPopApp*)::AfxGetApp())->playSound("Ding", SND_RESOURCE |
        SND_ASYNC); //Signal the hit.
    return deathreward;
}
```

The call to the **CPopApp::playSound** method simply wraps a call to the Windows multimedia API call **::PlaySound**. The reason we wrap it like this is so that we can check every call for sound against a 'global' _**soundflag**_ that belongs to **CPopApp**. Here's the code from **pop.cpp**.

```
void CPopApp::playSound(LPCSTR pszSound, DWORD fdwSound)
{
    if (_soundflag)
        ::PlaySound(pszSound, NULL, fdwSound);
}
```

Windows has an API function called **PlaySound(CString soundname, HINSTANCE programinstance, int flags)**. This function is not a member of any MFC class, and we put a **::** in front of it to remind ourselves of this fact.

The **soundname** is the name of some sound. There are three kinds of sound names you can use, with the type of sound indicated by a flag which is **OR**ed into the third argument. We'll come back to this in a minute.

The **HINSTANCE** argument in the second place is a throwback to the old Win32 programming and is not needed in MFC applications. In Win32 we need this argument when we want to use a sound that's stored as a program resource. But in MFC applications the second argument can always be NULL.

The **flags** in the third argument is made by combining various bitflags with the **OR** operation. A variety of **SND_** flags are defined in **C:\Program Files\Microsoft Visual Studio\VC98\Include\MMSYTEM.H**. Ordinarily we **OR** in a flag to tell **PlaySound** what kind of **soundname** you are giving it: SND_ALIAS, SND_RESOURCE, or SND_FILENAME.

Another flag which we almost always **OR** in is the SND_ASYNC. This tells the program to send the work of playing the sound off to the sound card and not to wait for the sound to finish playing before continuing program execution. If this flag is present in a first call of **PlaySound**, then this means that if a second sound wants to start up, the first sound will stop and let the second sound start. If the SND_ASYNC flag is *not* present in the first call of **PlaySound**, then the first sound insists on playing to conclusion before the second sound is allowed to start.

Usually it's better to use the SND_ASYNC flag when you are doing action-generated sounds, as otherwise the sounds can lag behind the actions. And you don't want to stop the action just for a sound. Better to cut a sound short than to have the next sound come too late.

Now let's talk about the three kinds of sound names we can use. The names usually have the form of a string in quotes. The string is not case-sensitive, by the way, so it doesn't really matter how it's capitalized.

- *System sound name.* You can use the name of some standard Windows event, and Windows will play whatever sound is associated with that event. In this case your call is of the form

  ```
  ::PlaySound("SystemExclamation", NULL, SND_ALIAS | SND_ASYNC);.
  ```

  Some of the system sound names you can use are: 'SystemExclamation,' 'SystemAsterisk,' 'SystemStart,' 'SystemExit,' and 'SystemDefault.' If you look at the sound dialog in your Windows **Start | Settings | Control Panel | Sounds** you can find other candidates. The names for system events are usually the obvious ones, consisting of the word 'System' run on with the name listed in the dialog.

- *External sound file*. You can use the name of some special *.wav file which holds a binary description of a sound. In this case your call is of the form

```
::PlaySound("Bonk.wav", NULL, SND_FILENAME | SND_ASYNC);
```

With a call like this, **PlaySound** looks in the same directory as the executable for the requested *.wav file. If it doesn't find the file it looks in the Windows and the Windows\System directory. If it still doesn't find the *.wav, it makes the default 'system ding' sound.

- *Resource sound file*. The third option is that you can have the sound file description bound into your executable as a resource. This is the one where Win32 requires something special for the second argument. But in MFC, NULL is still okay. Your call is of the form

```
PlaySound("Ding", NULL, SND_RESOURCE | SND_ASYNC);
```

You add a *.wav to your resource by placing the desired *.wav into the \res subdirectory under your source code and then using the **Project | Add resource...** | **Import...** dialog to import the file. [This is the **Insert | Resource...** | **Import...** dialog in Version 6.0.] Once you do this, the **Resource View** will show a 'WAVE' category. It will assign an integer-valued name like IDR_WAVE1 to your wave resource. Right-click on this name, select **Properties...** on the context menu and use the dialog to change the ID from IDR_WAVE1 to a string like 'Ding,' being sure to type in the quotation marks as well as the string. If **PlaySound** doesn't find a given resource it doesn't make any sound at all.

The benefit of the system sound approach is that you are fairly certain that the program will make *some* sound, as usually Windows has various sounds associated with different kinds of events. Also these sounds are user programmable. The drawback is that you have no control over which sound the user will hear. It depends on how he or she has configured the sounds on his or her system.

The benefit of the external sound file approach and the resource sound file approach is that you can control which sound the user hears.

In the external sound file approach, if the user wants to change the sound, he or she can rename a favorite *.wav file to match the one your program looks for. And at least **PlaySound** will make some kind of system sound even if it can't find the requested *.wav file. A drawback is that you need to distribute the necessary *.wav files along with your executable, and it's nicer to just be able to give someone a single *.exe that includes everything.

The benefit of the third approach is that you control which sound the user hears, and the sound is certain to be available in the *.exe. The drawback is that the *.exe will end up being a little larger than before: a small *.wav file is about 10 K, and they can be much larger.

The most professional approach might be to combine the second and third approaches. Include resource files, but allow the user to use File | Open to load external files if he or she likes. This would be an example of adding flexibility to the user interface.

Oh, one final point. Whenever your program includes sound, it *must* include a control for turning the sound off! Of course the user can turn sound off by using the Windows controls, but your program *must* be polite enough to be willing to turn its own sound off. That's, again, the reason that we pass all our sound call requests to *CPopApp*, and let it check against *_soundflag* before making noise.

Resource identifiers

Just as **PlaySound** with the SND_RESOURCE flag turned on loads sound files from the program resources, there is a **LoadBitmap** function that loads bitmap files from the resources, and a **LoadCursor** function to load cursor images from the resources. These functions take resource identifiers as arguments.

A resource identifier can be either an integer or a string. By default the Resource Editor assigns integers as identifiers for resources and then makes up mnemonic names like IDR_EDIT_UNDO or IDR_WAVE1 or IDR_BITMAP1 for them. But you can change the identifier to a string.

The MFC versions of **CBitmap::LoadBitmap** and **CWinApp::LoadCursor** are polymorphic; that is, they'll accept a resource identifier which is either an integer or a string.

The old-style Win32 non-MFC functions like **::PlaySound** will only accept resource identifiers which are strings. If you don't feel like replacing your resource's integer ID by a string you can fake it by using the Windows macro MAKEINTRESOURCE to convert the integer ID into a string ID which **::PlaySound** is willing to use. Thus you could call something like

```
::PlaySound(MAKEINTRESOURCE(IDR_WAVE1), NULL, SND_RESOURCE |
    SND_ASYNC);
```

If you want to dynamically select which resource to use it's sometimes handy to use integers to stand for them. If you need for the integer values to be consecutive numbers you can directly edit them in the resource.h file or indirectly in the View | Resource Symbols... dialog.

30.2   Adding libraries to your project file

If you're not using the Pop Framework, the first time you add the **::PlaySound** call to your code and try and compile the code, you'll get a compiler error that says something like PlaySound' : undeclared identifier'. To get rid of this, you need to add the line #include <mmsystem.h> to the top of your file.

And now after you get past the compile, you'll get a linker error, saying something like "PlaySound definition not found". Actually it will have a bunch of gibberish attached to the **PlaySound** name; this is because C++ does 'name-mangling' which means attaching symbols to a function name so as to specify what types the function expects as its arguments.

When you get a linker error of this kind, this means that you have used the name of some function without telling the compiler where to find the code that defines this function. The compiler is recognizing that **PlaySound** is a function, but the linker isn't able to find the code for it.

The response is to add more *.cpp or *.lib modules to your project file. If the function is one that you yourself have the code for, then the linker error means that you forgot to include the *.cpp file where your code lives. If the function is a Windows function, then the error means that this is some unusual function whose code is found in some Windows library other than the standard libraries.

How do you figure out which header and library to use for a function? Use **F1** or the **Help | Index** to find the documentation on **PlaySound**. This will include a **Quick Info** section that tells you what header file and import library the function uses. It turns out that the import library where **PlaySound** lives is winmm.lib, and the header file where its prototype lives is mmsystem.h.

So we want to tell the project file to include winmm.lib. The *wrong* way to do this is to use **Project | Add to Project | Files** to add the winmm.lib to your project files. This is not a good method because you need to tell the Add Files To Project dialog where winmm.lib lives, which means browsing around until you find it in, say, C:\Program Files\Developer Studio\VC\Libraries. Doing this takes a long time. Even worse, doing this has the effect of making your project file non-portable, because the path name you use becomes part of the name of the library file as stored by the project. This then means that if someone whose Developer Studio lives on his or her D: drive tries to use a project files that looks for winmm.lib in the C: drive, the project file won't be able to find winmm.lib.

The correct way to add a *.lib file to a project is to use the **Project | Settings** dialog. Open the dialog and change the **Settings For** dropdown to **All Configurations** in the upper left-hand corner of the dialog. Now click on the Link sheet of the dialog. Make sure the **General** selection is active at the top of the Link sheet. Now click on the **Object/Library Modules** edit box. The box may be empty, but if there are file names in it, use the **Arrow** key to move to the end of the list of *.lib files in this edit box. Type in winmm.lib, making sure there is a space between it and the previous file name. Don't put a path name in front of winmm.lib; the linker will look for the library in the Visual Studio's list of Library directories.

Let's reiterate that you should do this for **All Configurations**, so that you are making the change to both the Debug and the Release versions of your project. After making this change you need to do **Build | Rebuild All**.

From now on, the linker will look for winmm.lib in the list of **Library** directories maintained by the active installation of Visual Studio.

This list, by the way, is found under the **Tools | Options** dialog on the Directories sheet. To see the Library directories select **Libraries** in the box at the upper right of the sheet. Normally the correct library directory will be

among the options listed, but if it isn't you can type it in. Note that the **Tools |**
Options Directories settings are attached to the Visual Studio compiler when it is
installed on some specific machine. These settings are not part of your project
or workspace file.

30.3   An application-wide mute variable

The point of a mute variable is, as we mentioned above, to allow the user
to turn all the sound for the application off or on. Let's repeat that you should
never ever write a game that makes noise without giving the user an easily
usable control to turn the sound off. Why? Sooner or later a user might get
sick of the sounds. Or they might want to play the game without annoying the
person at the next desk. Or maybe they want to play it in a crowded airplane.
There has to be a way to tell the program to shut up.

What we need here is a **BOOL _soundflag** variable which we can set to either
TRUE or FALSE. Where should the variable live? Keep in mind that Pop is an
MDI application. It's capable of showing multiple views of multiple documents.
If you turn sound off in one view window of the Pop program, you don't want
it to suddenly come back on when you switch to another view or document
window. This means that we don't want the **_soundflag** variable to live down
inside the **CPopView** class. And by the same token, it won't do to put it inside
CPopDoc. No, we need for **_soundflag** to be something very much like a global
variable.

Well, what's the biggest scope object that an MDI program has? It turns out
that your program always has one single **CWinApp** object, which stands for the
program, or 'application' itself. We don't often put things into this class, but
when you do have some application-wide data, this is the place it should go.

So we opened up Pop.h, found **CPopApp**, and declared a private: BOOL
_soundflag; in the bottom of the class declaration. The variable doesn't need to
be public as only **CPopApp** will do things to it or look at it. And then we opened
Pop.cpp and initialized **_soundflag** to **TRUE** in the **CPopApp::CPopApp** constructor.

As we already discussed, we wrap the call to **::PlaySound** up inside a
CPopApp::playSound method, and we call this from anywhere in the program with
a line like

```
((CPopApp*)::AfxGetApp())->playSound("Ding", SND_RESOURCE |
    SND_ASYNC);
```

What is the first part of this line doing? MFC provides you a bunch of special
global functions for getting information about your application. These function
start with the letters **Afx**. The **AfxGetApp()** returns a pointer to the currently active
CWinApp object.

Alright, but why didn't we just write our code in a simple way like this?

```
(AfxGetApp()->playSound ...
```

Well, if it was simple, it wouldn't be Windows programming, would it? Look at the upside: if Windows programming was simple, you wouldn't be able to get such a good salary for knowing it!

The thing is, **AfxGetApp** returns a **CWinApp*** pointer. And the general **CWinApp** class of course doesn't have a *playSound* member function. Only the child class **CPopApp** has the *playSound()* method. And if we try and compile the code as written the 'simple' way, the compiler will give us an error message telling us the problem. So after we get the **AfxGetApp()** pointer to our application, we need to cast it into a **CPopApp*** pointer, a pointer to our modified child version of the **CWinApp** class.

By the way, since **AfxGetApp** isn't a member of any class, in consistency with our practice of signaling a non-class-member function by the :: symbol we put that in front of it. We actually write our code like this.

```
((CPopApp*)::AfxGetApp())->playSound ...
```

The exact way that you write the parentheses for the cast is important. That is, a C++ pointer cast has to have the form **(NewPointerType*)Pointer)**. As we mentioned earlier, you can instead use the C++ dynamic_cast operator and write lines like the following. Recall that, to help you catch errors, the **dynamic_cast** operator returns a NULL pointer if the cast is for some reason impossible.

```
CPopApp *ppopapp = dynamic_cast<CPopApp*>(::AfxGetApp());
ASSERT(ppopapp);
ppopapp -> playSound(...);
```

Exercises

Exercise 30.1: Changing the sounds of Spacewar

First of all, get sound working on your computer so that you can hear the Pop Framework sounds. (You need to have a sound card with speakers, and the speakers need to be plugged in. If you double-click the little speaker icon on the upper right of your Windows taskbar, the Mute button needs to not be checked. Also don't forget to see if your speaker has a manual, physical control.) Now try removing the SND_ASYNC from the *playSound* calls in the gamespacewar.cpp. Rebuild the program and see how it sounds. See what happens if you **OR** in SND_LOOP.

Now find some other *.wav file and incorporate it into the program. Where to find a *.wav file? First you can use **Start | Find** to look for them on your hard disk. Second, it's pretty easy to search the web for sites that have *.wav files for download. When picking sounds for effects in a game, avoid long sounds. For instance, once a student wrote a game where every time you shot something the game said 'Hasta la vista, baby,' and although that was funny the first few dozen times, it then got really old.

So get the *.wav, put it in the res subdirectory and add it to the resources. Give it a name like, say, 'Newsound.'

Now change the code so that when you shoot an asteroid it will make the 'Newsound' sound if the radius is bigger than some value, and it will make a 'Ding' sound if the radius is smaller than some value. What value? Look for some value that separates the big from the small asteroids.

Exercise 30.2: Using system sounds

Since the Ta-da sound usually lives in Windows\System directory you might get away with not including it as a resource and instead looking for the file externally with a call `playSound("Tada.wav", SND_ASYNC)`. See if this works.

Exercise 30.3: Encapsulating the *playSound* call

It's kind of a drag to have to write that stupid ***((CPopApp*)::AfxGetApp())->***. all the time. Assuming that it's normally a ***cCritter*** that's going to make a call to make a sound, try adding a ***cCritter::playSound(CString soundname)*** method to the ***cCritter*** class. Let the method do the tedious fetching of ***CPopApp*** and also let it stick in the standard flags `SND_RESOURCE | SND_ASYNC` as one of the arguments. Using this new method, add code to have the asteroids in the spacewar game make a little noise when they collide. Think of more sounds to add, too.

Bitmaps

31

In this chapter we talk about how we use bitmap background and bitmap sprites in the Pop Framework. First we'll talk about some common things about bitmap resources, then we'll talk about how we create bitmaps with transparent backgrounds in Windows graphics.

31.1 Bitmaps

For a professional-looking program you will often want to use bitmaps. We will talk about two uses for bitmaps. First we'll discuss using bitmaps as background images for your program. And second we'll talk about using small bitmaps as sprites to represent your moving critters. But first we need to say a bit about bitmaps in general.

A bitmap can be something that you draw inside a paint program, a photograph that you scan, or something that you grab off the web. In taking something off the web, however, be sure that it is public domain. If you use copyrighted images in your software, then you're not going to be able to legally distribute your program, and your work is effectively wasted.

Bitmaps come in various kinds of file formats, including *.gif, *.jpg, *.tif, and *.bmp. The Visual Studio, Version 6.0, compiler is only set up to easily deal with bitmaps in the *.bmp format. The MFC Version 7.0 supplied with Visual Studio.NET has a **CImage** class that does make it possible to handle the other formats. But we aren't presently using this class in the Pop Framework. If you have any kind of high-end image editor on your machine (such as a photograph editor) you can convert from one format to another by loading a bitmap from the existing format and saving it into the *.bmp format. Once you have something in *.bmp format you can, if you like, load it into the Windows Paint Accessory.

As we've discussed before, when you save something into the *.bmp format, you'll notice that you have several options for the kind of *.bmp you save. Typically the options will be labeled 16 Color, 256 Color, 24-bit Color, or True Color (which may use 32 bits per pixel). If your Image Editor doesn't show these options, you can load the *.bmp file inside the Windows Paint Accessory in order to see them.

The 256-color option is usually the best way to go. This gives you a richer palette than the 16-color option, but avoids the problems with 24-bit color and True Color bitmaps. And for a simple icon, 16 Color is okay.

What's wrong with 24-bit Color and True Color bitmaps? The problem is that bitmaps like this make for very large files because you are storing so much information per pixel. A 256-Color bitmap uses eight bits per pixel, rather than 24 bits. A large file can take up a lot of room on your disk, possibly making your *.exe be one or more Meg larger than it would be with 256-Color bitmaps. Another issue is that copying a 24-bit bitmap takes more time than copying a bitmap with a smaller 'color depth.'

Bitmap resources

Once you have a *.bmp file you want to use as a resource, copy it into the \res subdirectory of your code directory. Then use the Resource pane of your Workspace window, right-click on **Bitmap**, and select **Import**. In the dialog select the **All Files** option, find the *.bmp you want and click **Import**.

Give the bitmap an easy-to-remember ID name like IDB_BACKGROUND. This name will actually stand for some integer, but you don't care what the value of the integer is. If Visual Studio gives it a name you don't like remember that you can change the resource's properties by clicking on it and pressing **Alt+Enter**.

From now on, when you build your program, the binary code for the new resource bitmap will be bound into your *.exe file. If the bitmap is very large, then your *.exe is going to become very large. The nice thing about the having the bitmap inside your *.exe code is that now you can get at the bitmap by a couple of lines like

```
CBitmap cBitmap_new;
cBitmap.LoadBitmap(resource_ID)
```

To actually do anything with a bitmap, though, you need to load it into a **CDC**, and, in usual Windows fashion, this is a little trickier than any reasonable person might expect it to be. We've encapsulated the process into the **cMemoryDC** class as a method called **loadResourceBitmap** that can be found in the **memorydc.cpp** file.

> If you plan to use 3D graphics, it is extremely important to save your bitmaps so that all of their dimensions are powers of two.

31.2   Using a background bitmap

Suppose we want to use a background bitmap as a resource. The basic idea is that when we draw the view we want to do the following.

- Copy the background bitmap to a memory window.
- Write the critter sprites on top of the memory window as well.
- Copy the memory window to the screen.

What we need to do is to store our background bitmap in a ready-to-use form. At the high level, we wrap it up inside a **cSpriteIcon** object. In Windows graphics, we implement the image as a **cMemoryDC**, and in OpenGL we save it as a **cTexture** – both of which are classes invented for use in the Pop Framework.

A complication comes up. We want our program to be size-independent; that is, if we resize the window, we want the whole background bitmap to show. In Windows graphics, we could use a **StretchBlt** operation to keep stretching the background bitmap to fit the view's current size. But **StretchBlt** is a rather slow operation compared to **BitBlt**. So what we do is to equip the **cGraphicsMFC** object used for Windows graphics and the **cGraphicsOpenGL** object used for **OpenGL** graphics with methods for adjusting the size of a **cSpriteIcon** to fit the current window size. The author hardly even likes to think about the numb weeks of insane coding frenzy that it took to implement this. For the gory details, see the graphicsMFC.* and graphicsopengl.* files.

31.3 Transparent bitmaps

We have the option with the **cSpriteIcon** of giving it a 'transparent background.' The reason we'll be interested in transparent backgrounds is that we want to have a **cSpriteIcon** that shows a bitmap sliding around like a little live creature. If you have two normal bitmaps pasted on the screen close to each other, then the background region of one bitmap is likely to cut an unattractive white corner out of the other bitmap's central image.

How is this effect to be achieved? Since there is a simple way to make text and dotted line backgrounds transparent with the **CDC::SetBkMode(TRANSPARENT)** call, you might think it's easy to make bitmaps have transparent backgrounds. But this is not the case. Making bitmaps with transparent backgrounds is something we have to do by hand in two different ways, one for OpenGL, and one for Windows graphics.

- OpenGL has alpha blending methods which are in fact rich enough to produce transparent background bitmaps, and that's the route we use in the **cGraphicsOpenGL** implementation of the **cSpriteIcon** for which **transparent()** is TRUE.
- The Windows API includes methods called **AlphaBlend** and **TransparentBlt** that one might think would be useful here. But, prior to Visual Studio.NET, these methods have not seemed to give us what we need. What **AlphaBlend** (which is a generalization of **TransparentBlt**) does is mainly to overlay a full rectangle bitmap upon an existing image, but with the overlaid rectangle set to a certain level of transparency. Examples of this kind of graphic are the little station logos that one sees in the corners of many TV channels' images. But what we want is a way to write an image which is opaque in some parts (where our 'character' is) and transparent in other parts (where our 'background' is).

As mentioned earlier in this chapter, the MFC Version 7.0 supplied with Visual Studio.NET has a **CImage** class that improves the handling of bitmaps. In particular, you can use **CImage** to get transparent background bitmaps. However, the Pop Framework currently has its own, older way of doing transparent backgrounds.

In Windows graphics, we can get transparent bitmap backgrounds using a special trick based on something that the wonderful **BitBlt** function can do. **BitBlt** has nine arguments, and the last argument is an argument called a ROP code, where ROP stands for 'raster operation.' When you want your **BitBlt** to just copy the information from one **HDC** to another (which is most of the time), you use the SRCCOPY raster operation. But there is a wide range of other possible raster operation codes. The two we will be interested in here are SRCAND and SRCPAINT. The effect of these is to perform, respectively, a bitwise **AND** and a bitwise **OR** between the color codes of the target and source pixels.

Let's explain this in more detail. Suppose that at some pixel, the color in the target **HDC** is called *targetcolor*, and the color in the corresponding source **HDC** pixel is called *sourcecolor*. Finally, let *newtargetcolor* be the new color which ends up in the target pixel. The three different raster operations mentioned act like this:

- SRCCOPY: *newtargetcolor = sourcecolor;*
- SRCAND: *newtargetcolor = sourcecolor* **AND** *targetcolor;*
- SRCPAINT: *newtargetcolor = sourcecolor* **OR** *targetcolor;*

What exactly does it mean to combine two colors with **AND** or **OR**? Recall that in Windows a color is a **COLORREF** type, which is a block of 32 bits, of which the right-hand three bytes correspond to the intensities of red, green, and blue respectively. Combining the colors with **AND** or **OR** just means combining the corresponding bits pair by pair with **AND** or **OR**.

If we were to write *WHITE* to stand for the value RGB(255,255,255) which has three bytes of all 1s and write *BLACK* to stand for the **COLORREF** value RGB(0,0,0) with three bytes of all 0s, then it's not too hard to see that for any values of *targetcolor* and *sourcecolor*:

- *BLACK = targetcolor* **AND** *BLACK;*
- *targetcolor = targetcolor* **AND** *WHITE;*
- *WHITE = targetcolor* **OR** *WHITE;*
- *targetcolor = targetcolor* **OR** *BLACK;*

We are going to use these properties of **OR** and **AND** in order to create the illusion of a bitmap with a transparent background. Before going into the details, we should examine why this is necessary. Why can't we just put the image which we want on the screen and not paint any background at all? Well, the fast pixel-transfer operation called **BitBlt** only works on *rectangles* of pixels. This has to do with the fact that it takes very little calculation to single out a rectangle of pixels, as opposed to some irregular shape. Then why isn't there a transparent pixel color? Well, moving a pixel involves copying a color value to a memory location, which inevitably is going to change the value already there. The trick we use for getting transparent background bitmaps is not at all obvious: we use two bitmaps and two **BitBlts**, one with the SRCAND raster operation, and one with the SRCPAINT raster operation. A last point to mention here is that for the hardware on the graphics card, all three kinds of **BitBlts** are equally fast. Just as in assembly language the instruction **AND** AX BX is executed as fast as **MOV** AX BX, doing a SRCAND **BitBlt** happens as fast as doing a SRCCOPY **BitBlt**. You might think of a **BitBlt** as a 'super' assembly language instruction that is executed in parallel on many pixels at once.

So now let's look at how Windows bitmaps with transparent backgrounds work. Briefly, the way we're going to implement transparent background bitmaps is to use two bitmaps, a *mask* bitmap and an *image* bitmap. First you **AND** the mask bitmap with the target, and then you **OR** an image bitmap with the screen. The mask has *BLACK* pixels everywhere that the image is, and it has *WHITE* pixels everywhere that the image isn't. When you **AND** the mask with the target, you cut a black hole in the target just the shape of the image, and you leave the rest of the target alone. The pixels in the 'hole' all get set to black. The image bitmap has the image pixels set to the correct image color values, and the other background pixels of the image bitmap are set to *BLACK*. When you **OR** the image bitmap with the target you lay the image right into the waiting hole, and you don't change the other target pixels.

The *cTransportMemoryDC* class encapsulates this trick, automatically generating a source bitmap and mask bitmap in its constructor. See the memorydc.* files for details.

And that's about it for now. Happy programming!

Appendix A:
The Windows keycodes

It's important to know the keycodes if you want to make more sophisticated listeners. If you wanted to distinguish between the left and right versions of the **Shift**, **Control**, and **Alt** keys you would need to be actively checking these keys in each call to your *cController::update* method. You might write a *cControllerLeftRight* child class with an overridden *update* to do this.

This is taken from the file winuser.h. The default set-up for keycodes is that for normal letters and numbers like 0 or Z, you don't use VK_0 and VK_Z, instead you use the traditional ASCII code symbols '0', 'Z', etc.

```
/*
* Virtual Keys, Standard Set
*/
#define VK_LBUTTON        0x01
#define VK_RBUTTON        0x02
#define VK_CANCEL         0x03
#define VK_MBUTTON        0x04
      /* NOT contiguous with L & RBUTTON */

#define VK_BACK           0x08
#define VK_TAB            0x09

#define VK_CLEAR          0x0C
#define VK_RETURN         0x0D

#define VK_SHIFT          0x10
#define VK_CONTROL        0x11
#define VK_MENU           0x12
#define VK_PAUSE          0x13
#define VK_CAPITAL        0x14

#define VK_KANA           0x15
#define VK_HANGEUL        0x15  /* old name for compatibility */
#define VK_HANGUL         0x15
#define VK_JUNJA          0x17
#define VK_FINAL          0x18
```

```
#define VK_HANJA          0x19
#define VK_KANJI          0x19

#define VK_ESCAPE         0x1B

#define VK_CONVERT        0x1C
#define VK_NONCONVERT     0x1D
#define VK_ACCEPT         0x1E
#define VK_MODECHANGE     0x1F
#define VK_SPACE          0x20
#define VK_PRIOR          0x21
#define VK_NEXT           0x22
#define VK_END            0x23
#define VK_HOME           0x24
#define VK_LEFT           0x25
#define VK_UP             0x26
#define VK_RIGHT          0x27
#define VK_DOWN           0x28
#define VK_SELECT         0x29
#define VK_PRINT          0x2A
#define VK_EXECUTE        0x2B
#define VK_SNAPSHOT       0x2C
#define VK_INSERT         0x2D
#define VK_DELETE         0x2E
#define VK_HELP           0x2F

/* VK_0 thru VK_9 should be ASCII '0' thru '9' (0x30 - 0x39) */
/* VK_A thru VK_Z should be ASCII 'A' thru 'Z' (0x41 - 0x5A) */
/* Unless you define them yourself, you can't use symbols VK_0,
   VK_A, etc. in your code, and you must use '0', 'A', etc.
   instead. To correct this, The Pop framework defines the
   missing VK_0 through VK_9 and VK_A through VK_Z so you can in
   fact use these symbols if you include controller.h. */

#define VK_LWIN           0x5B
#define VK_RWIN           0x5C
#define VK_APPS           0x5D

#define VK_NUMPAD0        0x60
#define VK_NUMPAD1        0x61
#define VK_NUMPAD2        0x62
#define VK_NUMPAD3        0x63
#define VK_NUMPAD4        0x64
#define VK_NUMPAD5        0x65
#define VK_NUMPAD6        0x66
#define VK_NUMPAD7        0x67
#define VK_NUMPAD8        0x68
#define VK_NUMPAD9        0x69
```

```
#define VK_MULTIPLY       0x6A
#define VK_ADD            0x6B
#define VK_SEPARATOR      0x6C
#define VK_SUBTRACT       0x6D
#define VK_DECIMAL        0x6E
#define VK_DIVIDE         0x6F
#define VK_F1             0x70
#define VK_F2             0x71
#define VK_F3             0x72
#define VK_F4             0x73
#define VK_F5             0x74
#define VK_F6             0x75
#define VK_F7             0x76
#define VK_F8             0x77
#define VK_F9             0x78
#define VK_F10            0x79
#define VK_F11            0x7A
#define VK_F12            0x7B
#define VK_F13            0x7C
#define VK_F14            0x7D
#define VK_F15            0x7E
#define VK_F16            0x7F
#define VK_F17            0x80
#define VK_F18            0x81
#define VK_F19            0x82
#define VK_F20            0x83
#define VK_F21            0x84
#define VK_F22            0x85
#define VK_F23            0x86
#define VK_F24            0x87

#define VK_NUMLOCK        0x90
#define VK_SCROLL         0x91
/*
The following are left and right Alt, Ctrl and Shift virtual
    keys.Used only as parameters to GetAsyncKeyState() and
    GetKeyState(). No other API or message will distinguish left
    and right keys in this way.
*/
#define VK_LSHIFT         0xA0
#define VK_RSHIFT         0xA1
#define VK_LCONTROL       0xA2
#define VK_RCONTROL       0xA3
#define VK_LMENU          0xA4
#define VK_RMENU          0xA5
```

Appendix B:
The Pop help file

This appendix is a printout of a file that we saved both as pop.rtf and as pop.htm for making our Windows help file and our HTML help file. The Windows help file format doesn't support tables and has somewhat weak suport for bullets, so we don't use tables or bullets here. If were making only the HTML help file, we'd be able to use more elaborate formats.

As the Pop help file is primarily designed to be read on the screen in a help file window, it makes more use of bold fonts than does the rest of our text. Italic fonts don't stand out well on the screen.

This version of the help file matches Pop 27, September 2002.

About the Pop program

The Pop program was built using the Pop Framework classes for Rudy Rucker's textbook *Software Engineering and Computer Games*. Full source and executable for the Pop Framework are available from the book website www.rudyrucker.com/computergames

Normally developers build only one game at a time with the Pop Framework, but the Pop program includes nine games. Only four of these games are in a finished, playable state with a clear goal: Spacewar, PickNPop, Airhockey, and Defender3D. The others serve only to demonstrate features of the Pop Framework and to provide stubs for easy extension.

Since the Pop program is designed to let developers explore possibilities for their own games, there are more control options than one would want to have in a finished game.

Updates per second

When you first run the Pop program, you will see the startup game Spacewar, which resembles an Asteroids game. Look at the **Updates per second** figure in the status bar at the bottom of the Pop window. The number is a rolling average, so it takes a few seconds for it to respond to changes, and the value will sometimes dance between two or three nearby numbers. The highest rate the Pop Framework allows is the speed of your graphics card's updates per second; if you are at or near this rate the message will say '(Near Max).' If you are in a mode where the program is running slower than the real time that it simulates, the message will say '(Slower than Real Time).' Except in the '(Slower than Real Time)' case, one second of simulated game time equals one second of real-world time.

On most recent machines you should expect to see an **Updates per second** ranging from about 40 to whatever your graphics card's refresh rate is. Commonly used refresh rates are 60, 75, and 85. (For general ergonomic reasons, you should set your graphics card's refresh rate as high as is possible for the currently used resolution.) If you see a number below 15, your system is running the Pop program too slowly for effective play. You should remedy this before continuing, or use a different machine. Normally the cause of a low updates per second rate is an old or a low-quality graphics card.

Here are some steps you can try to improve your updates per second.

The updates per second is dependent on the number of pixels in the Pop window, so if you run your display at a very high resolution, large Pop windows will run slow. You can gain speed at any time by resizing the Pop window to make it smaller.

The updates per second is dependent on the number of critters in the game you are running. If you used the controls to create a very large number of critters, you can expect the speed to be slow, particularly if you also give the critters complicated sprites that are slow to draw.

Also note that there are both Release and Debug builds of the Pop program. A Release build always runs faster than a Debug build, sometimes even twice as fast, though this varies with the machine and with the nature of the game you are running. For better speed make sure you're running a Release build; you can tell which is which from the names of the executables.

Both the 2D and 3D graphics modes of Pop will often run faster if your monitor is set to use something like 64,000 colors rather than 'Millions of Colors' or True Color. To change the number of colors your display uses, right-click on your desktop, choose **Properties** from the floating popup menu, and then go to the **Display Properties** | **Settings** page. In this dialog you can also adjust your graphics card's refresh rate. (Note, however, that certain kinds of cards only support hardware OpenGl acceleration if you do set the number of colors to 24 Bit, 32 Bit or True Color.)

The Pop program has a View menu that allows you to run the games in the 2D Windows Graphics mode or in a 3D OpenGL mode. Different games default to different graphics, but all of the games except 3DStub and Defender3D work in either 2D or 3D view mode. On most systems the Windows Graphics mode is faster, but systems with certain types of 3D graphics acceleration may in fact run the 3D OpenGL mode faster.

If your games consistently run too slow when in the **View** | **3D OpenGL Graphics** mode, look into getting OpenGL hardware acceleration to work for your graphics card. Although most desktop machines have cards that support OpenGL hardware acceleration, the OpenGL drivers are often not put in place by the default install. You may need to download a driver from your graphics card manufacturer. The Web site `www.opengl.org/developers/faqs/technical/mswindows.htm` has further information about OpenGL hardware acceleration. Note, however, that some systems, including most laptops, have graphics cards that will not support OpenGL hardware acceleration.

Overview

The Pop display

Pop shows a border box with objects inside that that begin moving after the **Enter** key is pressed. The program's appearance and behavior are independent of the size of the window and, within certain limits, the speed of your processor.

Pop is a *multiple document interface* program, and it is possible to open up several Pop games or views of the games at once, with all the games and views running at the same time.

The way to open an additional view of a game session already open is to use **Window | Additional View of Current Game**. Opening an additional view of a game can be useful, as you can look at the game from two different viewpoints in the different views.

The way to open a window on a different game is to use the **File | New Game Window** control. There is in fact little point in opening more than one game at once, but we have this feature for the sake of completeness.

In practice, running multiple game windows makes the update speed quite low. The program limits you to opening at most four windows at once.

When the main Pop window is not the focus window on the Windows desktop, the animation of all the games and views is paused.

The moving objects in a Pop game are called *critters*. Each critter has an associated *sprite*, which is what you see. In some games you have the option of changing the kinds of sprites that are attached to the critters, so as to experiment with different design possibilities.

By default, the critters are oriented with their principal axes matching their current motion directions.

Except in the PickNPop game, there is always a distinguished critter called the player; this is usually represented as a small red triangle with a line indicating a gun, and with a circle around the triangle. If the player is dead or damaged, the filling of the triangle temporarily disappears. (Note that in Airhockey and in Worms the player has a different appearance.)

You normally move the player by using the **Arrow** keys, and you shoot the gun by pressing the spacebar. See the Keyboard and Mouse Controls section for more about the keyboard controls.

Some of the Pop games allow you to select different kinds of cursors, with the available cursors depending on the game. The cursors can act as tools that do things to the critters when you left-click. In particular if the Shoot, or Crosshairs, cursor is active, you can shoot by left-clicking the mouse.

If you prefer not to use the mouse button, or if you have a tracking device whose 'left-click' does not trigger the Pop program, you can press the Z key on your keyboard in place of left-clicking the mouse.

The games

The Pop program implements nine different games: Spacewar, PickNPop, Airhockey, Ballworld, Dambuilder, Worms, 2DStub, 3DStub, and Defender3D. The start-up game is the Spacewar game. Spacewar, PickNPop, Airhockey, and Defender3D are finished games. The others serve as starting points for games to program with the Pop Framework, or as demos of features of the framework.

All of the games except for 3DStub and Defender3D are essentially 2D. That is, in each of the games besides 3DStub and Defender3D, the critters are limited to move in fixed planes.

All of the games will take on a 3D *appearance* if you select **View | 3D OpenGL Graphics**. Critters that would be drawn as flat shapes are given a thickness for the 3D graphics mode.

Keyboard and mouse controls

There are five main kinds of keyboard controls.

First, there are controls to **move the player critter**, that is, to change its position, velocity, or orientation.

Second, you can often make the player **shoot**.

Third, there are controls to **change the view location**, that is, to move the world relative to your View window.

Fourth, you can reduce or increase the **zoom** or magnification of the 'lens' through which you view the world.

Fifth, when using 3D graphics, there are controls to **change the view direction** in which you look at the game.

To summarize let's use the phrase 'direction keys' to include the **Arrow** keys, the **PgUp/PgDn** keys and the **Home/End** keys.

These Controls	*Affect This*
Direction keys	**Player Critter's Motion**
Spacebar key	**Player Shooting**
Ctrl + direction keys	**View Location**
Ins/Del keys	**View Zoom**
Ctrl + Shift + direction keys	**View Direction (3D Only)**

Now for some details.

Player motion controls

The player controls include 2D and 3D controls. The 3D player controls apply only in the three-dimensional game worlds of 3DStub and Defender3D.

In using the player controls, remember to think of the direction the player's sprite points as 'forward.'

The rotations caused by the directional keys speed up if you hold these keys down longer than a fifth of a second. For delicate directional adjustments, just tap on the keys.

Something that complicates the situation is that the user has the option of using the Player menu to change which kind of controls the player uses. The player can use Arrow Key Controls, Scooter Controls, Car Controls, Spaceship Controls, Hopper Controls or Mouse Controls. At present the Hopper Controls selection is only enabled for the Ballworld game.

In describing the controls below, we first specify what the controls do in a 2D world, and then we describe the *additional* things the controls do in a 3D world.

Arrow key controls

2D: **Up/Down** arrows move the player up/down along the y-axis. **Left/Right** move the player left/right along the x-axis.

3D: **PgUp/PgDn** moves the player forward/backward along the z-axis (which by default points out of the computer screen).

2D & 3D: The Arrow Keys Controls are like classic PacMan. The player moves left, right, up, or down with the arrows, and points in these directions. If someone bumps into the player it will sometimes rotate a little. But normally the player is always aligned with the most recent direction of motion. This makes it hard to shoot in arbitrary directions.

A useful trick in a two-dimensional world is to use the Arrow Key Controls with the Shoot cursor. The Shoot cursor will aim the player and shoot in the direction where you left-click. Using the Shoot cursor makes up for the fact that the Arrow Key Controls always align the critter along the principal axes of the game world. This trick works to a lesser extent in a 3D world, as here the mouse click will always select points in the current plane of the player, and will not produce pitch or roll.

Scooter controls

2D: **Up/Down** arrows move the player forward/backward. Motion halts as soon as the key is released. Note that reverse motion is possible with the **Down** arrow. **Left/Right** yaws the player left or right.

3D: **PgUp/PgDn** pitch the player's tip up or down. **Home/End** rolls the player counterclockwise/clockwise around its direction of motion.

Car controls

2D: **Up** arrow accelerates the player forward up to a maximum speed. Player cruises along at the same speed until you slow it down. The **Down** arrow acts as a brake that can slow the player's speed down to zero. There is no 'reverse gear.' The **Left/Right** arrows yaw the player left or right, instantly changing its direction of motion.

3D: **PgUp/PgDn** pitch the player's tip up or down. **Home/End** rolls the player counterclockwise/clockwise around its direction of motion.

2D & 3D: You can think of Car Controls as Scooter Controls plus momentum. In Car Controls motion, you use **Up/Down** like accelerator/brake and use **Left/Right**, **PgUp/PgDn**, **Home/End** like a steering wheel.

Spaceship controls

2D only: with Spaceship Controls, the player's sprite doesn't have to point in the same direction as the player's motion. The **Up** key accelerates the player in the direction in which the sprite is pointing. The **Down** key gives the player a reverse acceleration, in the direction opposite to which it's pointing. If held down long enough, the **Down** key can make the player begin moving in reverse. The **Left/Right** keys rotate the player to the left and right.

Hopper controls

2D: the Hopper Controls move the player left and right with the **Left** and **Right** arrow keys. The **Up** arrow key hops the player up into the air, but continuing to depress the **Up** key will not produce a continued hopping effect. You need to tap the **Up** key repeatedly if you want to add a hop to a hop.

3D: **PgUp/PgDn** moves the player forward/backward along the z-axis (which by default points out of the computer screen).

Mouse controls

2D: the player effectively becomes the Mouse cursor and moves freely with the mouse. If you move the mouse outside of the game world, the current cursor icon reappears and the player 'waits' at the edge of the game world. The **Left/Right** arrow keys can also rotate the player.

3D: in a 3D world such as 3DStub, the mouse moves the player *within the current plane of the player's sprite*. You can use the **PgUp/PgDn** keys to pitch the player's attitude up or down, and the **Home/End** keys to roll the player counter-clockwise/clockwise.

2D & 3D: When moving the player with the Mouse Controls, the player's velocity matches the current velocity of the mouse motions. This means you can use the Mouse Controls to hit things with the player as if the player were a paddle. This feature is important for the Airhockey game.

Note that when the **Player | Mouse Controls** is being used, the cursor tools are disabled.

Player shooting controls

2D & 3D: The spacebar lets the player critter shoot bullets in the direction in which the player sprite is pointing. For realism, any forward component of the player's own motion in the shooting direction is added to the bullet motion. In 3D, the Pop Framework orients the bullets to have the same pitch, roll, and yaw as the shooter. Bullets are shot as long as the spacebar is held down.

In the case where the Shoot cursor is selected, the left mouse button or the Z key will also shoot. In addition, the left-click or Z key will aim the player in the direction of the current mouse position before shooting. Using the Shoot cursor you can fire at targets simply by left-clicking or Z-keying on them.

The Z key option has two purposes. First, it can be more ergonomic to use the Z key in place of the left mouse button. Second, you may need the Z key option if you have reassigned the meanings of the buttons on your tracking device, as in this case the Pop program may not recognize your current 'left button.'

A useful player control combination in a two-dimensional world is to use the Arrow Key Controls with the Shoot cursor. Using the Shoot cursor makes up for the fact that the Arrow Key Controls always align the critter along the principal axes of the game world. The Shoot cursor allows you to aim and shoot in any direction you like.

Standard view controls

The view controls include 2D and 3D controls, where the 3D controls apply if you are using 3D graphics such as **View | 3D OpenGL Graphics**. Unlike the player-controlling keys, the view key controls are not sensitive to how long the keys have been held down.

View location controls

2D or 3D: **Ctrl+Up/Down** arrow keys move the world up/down. **Up** slides the world up, **Down** slides it down. **Ctrl+Left/Right** arrow keys move the world left/right. **Left** slides it left, **Right** slides it right.

3D only: **PgUp/PgDn** move the world closer/further, that is, **PgUp/PgDn** move the viewpoint forward/backwards.

View direction

3D only: **Ctrl+Shift+Left/Right** yaws the world left/right. **Ctrl+Shift+Up/Down** pitches the world up/down. As with the View Location controls, **Ctrl+Shift+Left** swings the world to the left, **Ctrl+Shift+Right** swings the world to the right, and so on.

Ctrl+Shift+Home/End rolls the world counterclockwise/clockwise.

View zoom control

2D and 3D: **Ins/Del** magnify or shrink the image. The Zoom Controls change the field of view without changing the view position. You can think of them as smoothly transforming from a telephoto to a wide-angle lens. There are limits to how far in and out you can zoom.

To restore to a normal zoom, use **View | Reset Viewpoint** or the **Ctrl+R** shortcut.

View controls using Ride the Player

You can only choose the **Ride the Player** option in the 3D OpenGL view.

3D Only: when the **View | Ride the Player** option is selected, the viewpoint and view direction are controlled by the motions of the player critter. The viewpoint is perched upon a 'saddle' a bit behind and above the player, and the view direction is set to look out ahead of the player. When the **View | Ride the Player** option is in effect, the **Ctrl+Up/Down** keys affect the height above the player which the viewer rides.

When you Ride the Player, the View Direction controls have no effect. Instead, you change the view direction by turning the player. The **Ins** and **Del** keys still affect the zoom of the view.

A hardware Windows bug in the Arrowkey Controls

Unfortunately the combination of the standard Windows keyboard and Windows operating system has a minor bug that we can't seem to work around. This occurs when you use the Spacebar along with the small group of four **Arrow** keys that sits between the alphabetical keys and the rectangular block of numerical keys. We refer to the group of **Arrow** keys arranged like this near the bottom edge of the keyboard:

Up

Left   Down   Right

You cannot get this **Left** key, the **Space** key and any other of these **Arrow** keys to work at the same time. Barring a fix from Microsoft, the only way around this at present is to use the **Arrow** keys on the digital key pad to the right side of your keyboard, making sure that the **Num Lock** is off, so that these keys act like **Arrow** keys.

Spacewar

Getting started with Spacewar

You're in control of a little red triangle ship. Your goal? Avoid being bumped by asteroids and shoot the asteroids into pieces. When enemy UFOs appear, avoid being shot by their bullets and try to shoot them. In other words, shoot everything in sight before you get shot! Use the spacebar or left mouse clicks to shoot at the other creatures. (If you dislike shooting games, skip Spacewar and try PickNPop, Airhockey, Ballworld, 3DStub, or Dambuilder.)

The asteroids and UFOs in the Spacewar game have a primitive kind of intelligence. They run away from the bullets that the player shoots. And when they're not running away from bullets, the asteroids tend to move towards the player. Some users have described the Spacewar asteroids as 'cowardly and sneaky.'

You are only allowed to have eight of your bullets active at one time. When you try and shoot more than eight bullets, your oldest bullet is removed. This means that if you keep the spacebar down so as to be continuously shooting, you will see something that looks like a short stick of bullets coming out of your player. What's happening is that the furthest (oldest) bullet keeps being replaced by the next bullet that you're shooting out. In order to have your bullets travel some distance and hit the further away asteroids, you need to release the spacebar and give the bullets a chance to travel. Once a bullet is traveling, it will live for three seconds. A bullet will also die if hits an asteroid, a UFO, an enemy bullet, or the edges of the game world. Once a few of your bullets die off, you can shoot some more bullets.

Your player incurs damage if it is touched by one of the asteroids or by one of the enemy bullets; 'damage' means that the player's health is reduced by one point. If the player's health reaches 0, the game is over. The current health value is printed in the status bar below the game window.

Use your **Arrow** keys to run away from enemy bullets and missiles. At startup, your controls are in the Spaceship Controls mode; this means that the **Left** and **Right** arrows rotate the player's icon and shooting direction, while the **Up** and **Down** arrows add forward or reverse thrust in the direction that the player's icon is currently pointing. If you've never played an Asteroids-type game you will initially find these controls hard to use. The idea is that the player is supposed to be drifting in empty space and that you are steering it with blasts from its rocket. If you're not comfortable with the Spaceship Controls, you can use the Player menu to select a different control mode; Scooter Controls are particularly easy to use.

Shooting the asteroids, UFOs, enemy bullets, and enemy missiles increases your score. Note that you don't get a score reward for splitting an asteroid or UFO in two, you only get the score when you actually eliminate one. The current score value is printed in the status bar below the game window. Increasing your score by 40 brings on a new attack by a UFO.

When you kill all the asteroids and UFOs, a new wave of asteroids appears, and the maximum speed of the asteroids and UFOs is increased. Eventually they overwhelm the player and use up all of the health points.

When your player loses all of its health points, the region of your window outside the game world goes from gray to black. A message dialog appears. Click in the dialog or press **Enter** to restart the game. If you would prefer to play a different game, use the Game menu.

The status bar below the game window displays the player's score, the player's health, the total number of non-bullet critters on the screen (including the player critter), and the number of updates per second that your machine is currently doing for the animation.

Spacewar details

The critters collide with each other and rebound. The critters collide as if they were spheres with a mass proportional to their size. If two critters have an irregular shape this means that they will sometimes appear to collide before they visually touch each other.

When an object hits the edge of the game world it may either bounce, wrap around to the opposite edge, or die. At startup, the asteroids and the player wrap, the enemy UFOs bounce, the bullets die at the edge of the game world, and the enemy missiles bounce. You can force the asteroids to bounce off the edges by selecting **Game | Bounce** instead of **Game | Wrap**. This makes them a bit easier to shoot because then they can't run away as well. Note that the UFOs and blue enemy missiles will bounce off the game edges even if you have selected **Game | Wrap**, and that your bullets and the green enemy missiles or bullets will always die when they hit the game edges.

The starting number of asteroids is eight. When you shoot a larger asteroid, it will split in two as long as the resulting number of asteroids is not too large. At some point, if there are too many asteroids on the screen, shooting a large asteroid will shrink it to a small asteroid the first time you shoot it, without splitting. Shooting a smaller asteroid will always kill it.

When the player shoots a bullet, the velocity of the bullet is the vector sum of your own velocity in the bullet's direction plus the bullet's muzzle velocity.

To observe this feature, you can do as follows. Use **Player | Shield** to make the player invulnerable, press the **Up** arrow to get the player moving rapidly, use the **Left** arrow to rotate the player to point at right angles to the direction of motion, and then press the spacebar to shoot bullets. You'll notice that the bullets emerge and move off at an angle. Though this is physically correct, some users find it confusing.

The UFOs don't obey this 'bullet velocity = shooter velocity + muzzle velocity' rule; the game lets them ignore the physics so as to make it easier for them to reliably shoot right at the player. To sum up, a UFO's bullet goes exactly in the direction its gun is pointing, but the player's bullets go in a direction that's a sum of the gun direction and the player's motion. (If you really, really dislike this feature, get the Pop source, make the player critter shoot like a UFO critter, and rebuild the game!)

There are two kinds of UFOs, regular and smart. The smart UFOs can move twice as fast as the regular UFOs, which makes them harder to shoot. The regular UFOs split in two the first time you shoot them, no matter how many asteroids are present. The smart UFOs don't split. The regular UFOs have polypolygon sprites and shoot green bullets at you. The green bullets are aimed at you, but they can be deflected by asteroids. They will die if they hit the edge of the game world. The smart UFOs have a sprite that's a picture of a flying saucer; these guys shoot blue guided missiles at you. The missiles will follow you as you move, and they will bounce off the asteroids and off the edges of the game world.

Use the spacebar to shoot the bullets and missiles before they hit you, or use your **Arrow** keys to move out of the way of these bullets. Note that the UFOs never wrap around the edges of the game world; the best hope of hitting one is to first drive it into a corner.

Your score value for killing various creatures is the following. You don't get any points when you first shoot an asteroid or a UFO and split it in two, you only get the score when you shoot the smaller pieces and remove them from the screen.

- Asteroid   4
- UFO   6
- Green enemy bullet   4
- Blue enemy missile   8

Your player's health is improved by one point for every additional 100 score points you accumulate. Every time you accumulate 40 more points, a new UFO will appear, provided that no UFO is currently present.

More about shooting

As mentioned earlier in this help file, the spacebar causes the player to shoot bullets in the direction in which the player sprite is pointing. Bullets are shot as long as the spacebar is held down.

In the case where the Shoot cursor is selected, the left mouse button or the Z key will also shoot. In addition, the left-click or Z key will aim the player in the direction of the current mouse position before shooting. Using the Shoot cursor you can fire at targets simply by left-clicking or Z keying on them.

If your player (or an armed enemy) happens to be too near the edge of the world, it will not be able to shoot bullets, as any bullet near the edge gets removed.

Using the Player menu you can choose between **Deadly Bullets**, which split or destroy the asteroids and UFOs, and **Rubber Bullets**, which merely push them around. In a battle game like Spacewar, rubber bullets are of no use. They're here so that developers can consider using the feature in a non-violent game.

Rubber bullets are destroyed only when the screen is reseeded or you select **Game | Start or Restart Game**. But, as with deadly bullets, if you shoot a steady stream of rubber bullets, the older ones are repeatedly replaced by the newer ones. And if you have switched from rubber bullets to deadly bullets, the newly fired deadly bullets will replace the old rubber bullets. If a deadly bullet and rubber bullet collide, they both survive.

Other things to try in Spacewar

Try using the **Player | Shield** to make the player invulnerable so you don't have to keep restarting the game.

With the Shield mode on, use the **Game | Large Critter Count** selection to bring a large number of asteroids onto the screen. Use the **Arrow** keys to move the player around among them. Select **Player | Rubber Bullets** and shoot rubber bullets into the crowd. The way the rubber bullets work their way along is a model of particle diffusion. Try this both with **Game | Wrap** and with **Game | Bounce**. Use **Game | Medium** to get back to a reasonable number of sprites.

You can turn a background bitmap on or off from the View menu. And you can use **Game | Wrap** or **Game | Bounce** to turn a wrapping feature on and off for the player, the asteroids, and the rubber bullets. (The UFOs will always bounce and the deadly bullets will always die at the game world edge.)

Try turning **Wrap** on, setting **Player** to **Shield** and **Rubber Bullets**, and now use the rubber bullets to get all the critters moving in one direction. Then turn around and shoot rubber bullets till they move the other way. Turn off the **View | Background Bitmap** and use **View | Wireframe** to see the motions more clearly.

Set **Player | Auto Play** and sit back and watch the shapes zoom around.

Use **Window | Additional View of Current Game** to open a second view. Shoot some bullets. Notice how the action in the game is reflected in the second view.

PickNPop

Getting started with PickNPop

You've gotten a package in the mail! You set it down and open it; it's full of white disks and a few colored disks. We call the white disks *packing peanuts* and we call the colored disks *jewels*. Your goals are to pop the peanuts and to move the jewels out of the yellow packing box and into the pink target box. When a jewel is fully inside the target box it changes its appearance. If you don't drag it fully inside, it will fly back out.

In this game, the cursor tool can take the form of a *Pin* or a *Hand*. You can change cursor tools with the toolbar buttons, the mouse wheel, or with the accelerator keys 3 and 4.

You can click and drag the critters with the Hand (also called the Drag cursor). If you click on a critter with the Pin cursor, you kill it. Note that you have to click once for each kill action.

To get the maximum score, you must pop all the peanuts and drag all the jewels into the target area. A perfect game gives you a score of 1000 at the game end. You can save a bit of strain on your hand and forearm by using the Z key in place of the left mouse button when dragging.

The game lasts only 45 seconds. It ends when 45 seconds are over, or when all the peanuts are popped and all the jewels are popped or in the target box. At game's end, the white background changes to black.

To make the maximum possible score be exactly 1000, a correction term may be added on at the end.

Tips on PickNPop

If the game update rate is too slow, make sure to use **View | 2D Windows Graphics** rather than **View | 3D OpenGL Graphics**. PickNPop is essentially a 2D game, even though the program enhances the visual interest by spacing the critters along the z-axis in the 3D OpenGL Graphics mode.

If you are running the game in 3D, and you don't have a fast graphics card, it may be that PickNPop will be running at a rate slower than real time. A note in the status bar will alert you to this. In this case, the 45 seconds the program measures will in fact be longer than 45 real-world seconds.

You can go to the View menu and select Wireframe view in place of the Solid view so that you can see what lies under a given critter. Use **Window | Additional View of Current Game** to open a second window and then use **View | Wireframe** to change the second view to a Wireframe view.

Note that a left-click affects a critter if the click point is inside a visible part of the critter. You can't click on a critter if it is completely beneath other critters. A click only affects one critter at a time.

Left dragging the cursor means moving it while the left button or the Z key is held down. The Pop program allows you to use the Z key in place of the left mouse button when using cursor tools.

When you click a critter with the Drag cursor tool, the critter is visually moved to lie above the other critters. This is not the case in 3D OpenGL Graphics.

If your mouse has a wheel, you can switch between the Pin and the Dragger by turning your mouse wheel in either direction.

Airhockey

This is based on the familiar airhockey game in which you and a 'robot' opponent try and knock a sliding puck into each other's goals. Your opponent has the face of Professor Rucker, your player is shaped like a disk with a triangle tail.

Try and knock the puck into your opponent's goal, and to prevent the puck from being knocked into your goal. Each time the puck goes into your home goal, the robot gets a score point. Each time the puck goes into the robot's goal, you get a point.

The status bar shows your and the robot player's scores.

The game is set up so that you and the robot opponent each have to stay on your own side of the center line.

The game ends when either you or the robot opponent reaches a score of seven points.

You may enjoy using the **Player | Scooter Controls** instead of the default **Player | Mouse Controls**.

This game also looks very nice if you select **View | 3D OpenGL Graphics**, although on some machines it will then run too slow to be fun to play.

Your chances of getting the puck past the robot are better when you bank the puck off one of the side walls.

Defender3D

This is a nice 3D game, a little like Space Invaders. You are riding the player, which appears as a circle on the screen like a gun sight. You can move the player left/right, up/down and, to a limited extent, forward and backwards.

Falling towards you are polygonal slabs. Shooting the slabs adds to your score.

If the slabs get past you and hit the back of the world, you lose a health point. In order to give the player a little more of a chance, whenever the player has lost a health point, the player is immune to damage for the next half second or so. This means that if two slabs get past you at once, the first one will damage your player's health by hitting the back wall, but you will be immune to damage when the second slab hits – meaning that you'll only get one health point damage for the two closely-spaced slabs.

When you shoot a slab it releases a shower of coins that bounce along the floor. If you can maneuver your player to collide with a coin, it increases your health.

Try using **View | Ride the Player** to toggle off the default behavior of riding the player. This gives you a different view of the world.

Ballworld

This is a side-scroller game. Your player starts at the left end of the world. Your goal is to use the **Arrow** keys to move your player to the right end of the screen and jump into a hoop you'll find there.

There are balls bouncing along the bottom of the world from right to left. When you collide with a ball, the effect on you depends on your height relative to the ball. If the player's low edge is higher than the ball's center, the player gets a score point. But if the player's position is lower than this, the player loses a health point. In either case the ball is destroyed.

The player here uses the Hopper Controls. The idea is to hop over the balls and maybe land on top of them. The Hopper Controls move the player left and right with the **Left** and **Right** arrow keys. The **Up** arrow key hops the player up into the air, but continuing to depress the **Up** key will not produce a continued hopping effect. You need to tap the **Up** key repeatedly if you want to add a hop to a hop.

Every time a ball is destroyed a new one is added to the world to the right of the player.

At the right end there is a hoop that gives you extra score when you jump into it. After you jump into the hoop, the player is moved back to the left end of the world.

In the Ballworld game, the **View | Keep Player in View** is turned on at the game start. This means that when your player moves off an edge of the visible area, the window will automatically scroll to keep the player in view. To keep the Ballworld game from looking wobbly, the player tracking doesn't move the view up and down, it only moves the view left and right. If you were to zoom in a lot with **View | Keep Player in View** turned on, this means the player might be able to move out of sight above or below your view.

The game becomes trivial if you use the Mouse Controls. If you use the Mouse Controls or the Arrow or Scooter Control, the player is not subject to friction or gravity. Really the game only makes sense with the Hopper Controls, the other options are simply there so you can explore possibilities.

This game looks pretty nice in **View | 3D OpenGL Graphics**.

Ballworld is not a polished game. It's here for programmers to use as a starting point for a classic side-scroller-style game.

Dambuilder

This is a design for a game that has never quite been finished. The idea is to use the default Drag cursor to drag the dam walls around. Try and make the falling flow of the polygons as slow as you can without actually stopping the flow. You can use the Replicate cursor (the = sign) to make extra walls, and you can use the Pin cursor to remove them. Note that you can flip through different cursor types by using the mouse wheel. To work as a game, Dambuilder would need a clear goal and a mechanism for having advances and setbacks.

Most programmers instead use Dambuilder for a starting point for an adventure game. Typically they turn the gravity off, and arrange the walls in a more maze-like pattern. The player can then be hunting certain food or power-up critters, and avoiding certain rival critters.

We don't attach any gravity to the player in Dambuilder, so you can use Car Control without any confusion.

Dambuilder has an interesting appearance if you use **View | 3D OpenGL Graphics**. In order to have good speed, you should use **View | Solid Background** or **View | No Background** to turn off the background bitmap, which tends to be expensive in 3D. While in this mode, drive around the world, looking things over. You are riding the player. Try using **Ctrl+Up/Down** to alter your point of view. Even though this is essentially a 2D game, the program enhances the visual interest by making the walls higher than the critters in the 3D mode. While still in 3D mode, use **View | Ride the Player** to turn off Ride the Player so you can see the whole world from above. Now try zooming in on the world with **Ins**, and select **View | Keep Player in View** so the player is always visible.

Worms

The player has an animated sprite that cycles through a series of colors. There are other critters with face icons and 'worms' made up of worm segments, which are polygon-shaped critters that tag after each other as if playing follow the leader.

If the player touches a worm segment, it reduces the player's health by 1.

The player's bullets are small polypolygons.

When a player bullet hits one of the worm segments, the number of sides in the worm segment's polygon decreases, down to a minimum of three, after which the segment disappears, effectively splitting the worm in two.

The face critters shoot out 'food' bubbles at a right angle to the direction towards the player, and the food bubbles avoid the player. The player gains score points by running into the bubbles, effectively eating them. The value of the food bubble goes up with the square of its size. The bigger the bubble the better. The bigger the face, the bigger the food bubbles it shoots out.

When a player bullet hits one of the faces, the face will grow, up to a certain size upon which it pops and disappears. So you should shoot each face until it's just short of popping and then eat its bubbles.

Meanwhile, whenever a worm segment bumps a face, it makes it smaller, so you need to try and keep the faces away from the worms. This is tricky, as the faces run away from you.

You can use the **Game | Large Critter Count** to make longer worms.

2DStub

The 2DStub is close to being a game, though it's primarily meant to be a piece of code for the developer to improve.

In the 2DStub game, besides the player, there are two kinds of critters: *rivals* and *props*. The rivals have bitmap sprites, and the props have polygonal sprites.

The rivals shoot bullets at the player. They run away from the player bullets so fast that your only hope of killing them is to chase them down.

Chasing them down is made harder by the fact that they wrap around the world, but your player doesn't.

The props run away from the bullets of the rivals and from the player bullets. If the player runs over a prop, the player's health is improved by one point. The props are like health-packs.

Unlike the Spacewar game, the player needs to move around a lot to do well in 2DStub. Trying to sit in the middle of the screen and shoot is a losing strategy, as the rivals are so evasive and since the props need to be chased down.

The player's default controller is the Scooter Controls.

The game world is larger than a single screen, and we start with a zoomed-in view.

3DStub

This is not a game at all, simply a little demo to show some possibilities. You can look at the view in this game, trying out the various Viewpoint and View direction controls, looking at the appearance and running speed you get with different kinds of sprites, flying the player around, and testing out the Ride the Player option.

With the Ride the Player on, try using Home to roll your player and shoot rubber bullets while you are rolling.

The world is equipped with some non-critter furniture objects. The critters do not interact with these shapes. It's sort of interesting to fly the viewpoint to the inside of the teapot and look around.

The cursor tools

The cursor on a Pop Framework view takes on a different appearance according to which cursor tool is active for that view. Left-clicking on a critter has an effect that depends on the currently active cursor tool. Do note that not all of the games have all of the cursor tools enabled. If a cursor tool isn't enabled, it's corresponding toolbar button will be grayed out.

Note that if you have currently selected the **Player** | **Mouse Controls**, you can't use any cursor tools, as the cursor is busy controlling your player.

If your mouse has a wheel, you can switch among the active cursor tools by turning your mouse wheel in either direction. Otherwise you can select a cursor tool with the toolbar buttons, with View menu selections, or with accelerator keys.

For purposes of detecting a click, critters are treated as circles. That is, a cursor tool affects a critter if the click lies within a circle around the center of the critter's sprite with a radius equal to the outermost point of the sprite.

Whenever you click on a critter it becomes the *focus critter*. All views of a game have the same focus critter. The focus critter is drawn with a circle around it, and its motion across the screen is paused. The size of the focus critter circle is slightly larger (10%) than the size which the critter is regarded as having. Sometimes you'll barely notice the circle, but for the wall critters in the Dambuilder game, the focus circle will look surprisingly large.

There does not necessarily have to be a focus critter. If you click on an unoccupied part of the game world, then there will be no focus critter, and all the critters for that game will move about freely.

The Pop Framework allows you to use the Z key in place of the left mouse button when using cursor tools.

In 3D worlds, the cursor tool click is thought of as acting on the line that runs from the viewpoint to the cursor. This means that clicking on a critter will affect it, just as in the 2D case.

Shoot cursor (crosshairs icon)

Clicking with this cursor aims the player in the direction of the click and makes the player fire a bullet. You can use the Z key instead of the left-click. In 3D, the default is to pick the aiming point to lie in the same plane as the player, that is, it is the point where your line of sight to the cursor cuts the player's plane. However, in 3D if you are using the **View | Ride Player**, the aiming point is picked to be the spot on the far wall in the direction you are looking in, that is, it is the point where your line of sight to the cursor cuts a vertical wall parallel to the screen.

Pick cursor (arrow icon)

The Pick cursor is a default cursor that has no effect on the games.

Drag cursor (hand icon)

The Drag cursor is used to drag critters to new locations on the game world.

In a 3D game world such as 3DStub, you can drag a critter only in the plane of its body.

In 2D or in 3D, if you drag a critter against a boundary such as a wall or the edge of the world, the critter will slide along the boundary, using whatever component of the drag motion lies parallel to the surface of the obstacle.

In the 2D Windows Graphics view, when you click a critter with the Drag cursor tool, the critter is visually moved to lie above the other critters. In 3D OpenGL Graphics, the critter's relative depth location is not changed like this by the Drag cursor.

Pin cursor (pin icon)

The Pin cursor kills a critter when you click on it. If you kill off some of your critters and restart the game (for instance by pressing **Enter**) the same number of critters are created as the current count. You need to make a separate left-click for each kill action, that is, dragging the Pin cursor has no additional effect.

Zap cursor (lightning bolt icon)

The Zap cursor mutates the critter that you click on. It can be used on the player as well as on the other critters.

The active hot spot of the Zap cursor is the upper left tip of the lightning bolt icon.

To 'mutate' a critter means to change its size, and possibly the appearance of its sprite.

Replicate cursor (equals sign icon)

This makes an exact copy of the clicked critter at a location near to the clicked critter. You are not allowed to replicate the player critter. Note that if you go wild and replicate dozens and dozens of critters, your updates per second will drop down, eventually making the game run too slow.

The menu controls

Here are the names of all the Pop menu controls and the toolbar controls that are visible when a game is open. The menu controls which have a corresponding toolbar button have an asterisk after them.

File popup

Start or Restart Game
New Game Window * Open...*, Close, Save...*, Save As...
Recent File
Mute *
Pause *, Motion Smoothness...
Exit

View popup

3D OpenGL Graphics*, 2D Windows Graphics*
Reset Viewpoint
Keep Player in View, Ride the Player
No Background, Solid Background, Bitmap Background
Solid Objects, Wireframe Objects

Shoot cursor *, Pick cursor *, Drag cursor *, Pin cursor *, Zap cursor *, Replicate cursor *

Toolbar, Status Bar

Game popup

Wrap, Bounce

Spacewar, PickNPop, Airhockey, Ballworld, Dambuilder, Worms, 2DStub, 3DStub, Defender3D

Small Critter Count, Medium Critter Count, Large Critter Count, Huge Critter Count

Mixed Sprites *, Bitmaps *, Asteroids *, Bubbles *, Simple Polygons *, Fancy Polygons *, Polypolygons *

Player popup

Shield

Arrow Key Controls, Scooter Controls, Car Controls, Spaceship Controls, Hopper Controls, Mouse Controls

Deadly Bullets, Rubber Bullets

Auto Play

Window popup

Additional View of Current Game, Cascade, Tile, Arrange Icons, Split

Autotile, Autofocus

Help popup

About The Pop Framework..., Your System's OpenGL Graphics Support, Pop Program User's Guide

The toolbar controls

Each toolbar button has the same effect as selecting the corresponding menu control. From left to right, the buttons of the Pop toolbar correspond to these menu selections:

New Game Window, Open..., Save...,

Mute, Pause

Pick Cursor, Shoot Cursor, Drag Cursor, Pin Cursor, Replicate Cursor, Zap Cursor

Mixed Sprites, Bitmaps, Simple Polygons, Asteroids, Bubbles, Fancy Polygons, Polypolygons

2D Windows Graphics, 3D OpenGL Graphics

The status bar

The standard status bar displays the player's score, the player's health, the total number of non-bullet critters in the game (including the player critter if one is present), and the number of updates per second that your machine is currently doing for the animation.

For some games such as Airhockey, the player health information is not useful, as in those games the player's health is always the same.

As was mentioned in the Updates Per Second section, the updates per second number is a rolling average over a period of time, so it will take a while for this number to stabilize when you do some change to the current game – such as changing the number or the types of the critters. The program is designed not to demand more than your graphic card's current updates per second, so you will never see an update number higher than that value.

As discussed in the Motion Smoothness Dialog section below, the program is geared to match the size of the critters' simulation time steps so that the critters take the same time to cross the game world irregardless of how fast your computer runs.

When you open a menu, the status bar shows a tip about the currently highlighted menu selection.

Using the menu and toolbar controls

File menu controls

File | Start or Restart Game starts the animation of the game. If the game has already been run once, this control re-initializes the game and resets the player.

The **File | New Game Window** control creates a default Spacewar game.

The **Open...**, **Save** and **Save As...** opens or saves all of the currently active Pop game, critter, and sprite information. The Pop Framework does not save or reload the particular View menu settings such as viewpoint, view direction, using solid or wireframe sprites, using a background bitmap, etc.

A somewhat annoying feature of the Pop Framework is that you can't open a given file if a file of the same name is already open. So if you have saved a file as **test.p20** and then leave it open and let it run for awhile and then try to reopen it to get the old state back, nothing will happen. You need to close the current run of the game and then do a fresh open to get the saved **test.p20** version back.

When you load a saved game, the game waits for you to press **Enter** to make it start running.

Mute toggles the sounds of the games on and off.

Pause toggles the motion of the critters on and off.

The **Motion Smoothness...** selection opens the Motion Smoothness dialog. The dialog is documented below.

View menu controls

The **3D OpenGL Graphics** and **2D Windows Graphics** options select between a visually interesting, slower-running 3D view and a crisp, flat, rapidly running 2D view.

Reset Viewpoint moves the viewpoint and view direction back to a standard location. It also sets the zoom back to the standard size. This is useful if you've gotten lost and can no longer see any of the game world.

Keep Player in View toggles an option whereby the view will adjust itself so that the player always shows. This is useful in a large world or in a zoomed-in view where the player can easily slide off the edge of the screen. When this option is in effect you cannot set the viewpoint and view direction so as to look away from the player.

Ride the Player attaches the viewpoint to a 'saddle' a bit behind and above the player, and the view direction is set to look out ahead of the player. When this option is in effect, the **Ctrl+Up/Down** keys affect the height above the player which the viewer rides, and the View Direction controls have no effect. Instead, you change the view direction by turning the player.

The **No Background**, **Solid Background**, and **Use Bitmap Background** controls let you have a neutral wireframe background, a solid rectangle of color for the background, or a rectangular bitmap for the background. The background resizes itself along with the window and adjusts itself to match the view. In 3D worlds, the background is viewed as one face of the world box.

The **Solid Objects** and **Wireframe Objects** selections toggle between a normal view of the sprites and a wireframe view. In wireframe mode, the polygons are drawn with no filling, and the bitmaps are drawn as rectangular bounding boxes surrounded by circles sized to match the sprite radius.

Depending on the game, you can select among some of these five different cursor tools: **Pick**, **Shoot**, **Drag**, **Pin**, **Zap** and **Replicate**. See the Cursor Tools section for more information about the actions of these tools.

Game menu controls

The **Wrap** control causes the critters to wrap around the border box from left to right and top to bottom as they move. Note that the wrapped sprites are clipped by the border box. Note also that when a sprite moves off an edge or corner, it is simultaneously drawn as coming in from the other side or sides.

The **Bounce** control makes the critters bounce off the edges of the game world. **Wrap** and **Bounce** are mutually exclusive.

The **Spacewar**, **PickNPop**, **Airhockey**, **Ballworld**, **Dambuilder**, **Worms**, **2DStub**, **3DStub**, and **Defender3D** selections switch the Game mode. Note that making one of these selections may also affect the current cursor, the background, the available cursor tools, and other settings.

Small, **Medium**, **Large**, and **Huge Critter Count** set the number of critters to, respectively, 4, 8, 25, and 80. You can further tune the number of critters by killing off unwanted critters. Note that if you have a huge number of critters, your program will run slowly. Check the updates per second in the status bar.

Although the critter count controls have no effect in the Airhockey game, they aren't disabled for this game.

Mixed Sprites, Bitmaps, Asteroids, Bubbles, Simple Polygons, Fancy Polygons, and **Polypolygons** set the sprites to various kinds of shapes. All of the sprites align themselves with the critters' motion, with the exception of the bitmaps in the 2D Windows Graphics. There's no easy way to rotate bitmaps in Windows graphics, but it is in fact possible to turn them in 3D OpenGL Graphics.

The sprite change controls are disabled for some of the games. In Dambuilder selecting a sprite change control doesn't change the sprites of the walls.

The **Mixed Sprites** control selects a mixture of the following kinds of sprites.

The **Bitmaps** are a variety of bitmaps stored as resources in the program. The bitmaps present are variously based on resource workshop drawings, on a computer-generated fractal graphic, and on a scanned photograph. The bitmap sprites have transparent backgrounds like cursor icons.

The **Asteroids** are irregular and spiky. They are drawn filled, and they can have thick or thin edge lines.

The **Bubbles** are circles which may be drawn with rectangular highlights or with pie-slice highlights.

The **Simple Polygons** are filled triangles, squares and pentagons.

The **Fancy Polygons** are regular and star polygons, with the regular polygon having between two and nine vertices, and the star polygons having between five and 14 vertices. (A polygon of two vertices is simply a line segment.) In addition, the fancy polygons have the possibility of having thick lines for their edges and the possibility of having dots, or small circles, at their vertices.

The **Polypolygons** are fancy polygons which have a copy of a *tip polygon* at each vertex. The tip polygons are fancy polygons as well. The tip polygons rotate in a symmetric synchronization with each other, but independently of the main polygon.

Player menu controls

The **Shield** switch makes the player invulnerable; that is, in Shield mode the player is unaffected by collisions with enemy critters. Even though the Shield control has no purpose in games like Airhockey, it may still be enabled for some of these games.

Arrow Keys, Scooter Controls, Car Controls, Spaceship Controls, Hopper Controls, and **Mouse Controls** allow six different ways of having the player respond to the arrow keys. See the keyboard and mouse controls section for details about this.

The player can shoot two kinds of bullets: **Deadly Bullets** and **Rubber Bullets.** In a battle game like Spacewar, rubber bullets are of no use. But the rubber bullets might be useful in a world where you use them to herd critters around.

The **Auto Play** switch is mainly for use in doing demos or for testing the program. It makes the program behave as if you are holding down the **Up** key, the **Left** key, and the spacebar, except that the player will be turning at the slower of the two possible turn speeds. The Auto Play is geared for use in the Spacewar program, but could be implemented for other games.

Window menu controls

Additional View of Current Game and **Split**. These controls open up new views of the same game. You can have different View menu settings in the different views. When you resize a split window, the size of the left pane will stay fixed, and the size of the right pane will vary depending on the window's size. If there is no room left for a right pane while preserving the size of the left pane, the right pane is eliminated.

Cascade and **Tile**. These are standard Windows controls. Cascade arranges the open windows like a stack of file cards. Tile arranges them like a grid of cells in a table.

Autotile. This feature automatically maximizes any single child window, and automatically tiles multiple child windows into the outer frame. When Autotile is active, opening a new view or a new file will retile the window so that all the windows show. It's a useful feature added to the Pop Framework that doesn't happen to be standard for Windows programs. This is on by default.

Autofocus. When this feature is on, the focus will move to whatever window the cursor is over. Ordinarily one has to click on a window to select it, but Autofocus selects a window automatically. This is convenient if you are using the cursor tools in several different windows. If you have many windows open, this feature can be inconvenient, as the focus will change if you move your mouse up to the menu bar or toolbar to make a selection. This is another useful non-standard feature added to the Pop Framework, but as it can be confusing, it's turned off by default.

Help menu controls

The **About The Pop Framework** dialog displays some contact information. The **Pop Program User's Guide** selection shows this document. Rather than being a multiple-topic help file, the Pop help file is a single long document suitable for printing.

The motion smoothness dialog

This dialog is opened from the File menu. It has an informational Updates Per Second field and a Motion Smoothness field that you can edit. The Motion Smoothness index number changes how smoothly and slowly your critters seem to move. A high value of the Motion Smoothness is like running in slow motion, a low value is like running in fast forward.

The informational Updates Per Second field on the Motion Smoothness dialog shows the current number of game updates per second. This should be the same number that you see in your status bar. The Motion Smoothness dialog can't change the updates per second; the only way to change the updates per second is to change the size of the game window or the settings of your system graphics.

The Motion Smoothness control has a number that you can set between 1 and 10. These are artificial index numbers that have nothing to do with the numerical value of the Updates per Second. Lower smoothness values produce faster, jerkier motion. Higher smoothness values produce smoother, slower motion.

The default Motion Smoothness value is 5. At the default Motion Smoothness of 5, the simulation time per processing step matches the actual real time that elapses between updates. The games based on the Pop Framework are designed to function best with Motion Smoothness 5.

The reason for having a Motion Smoothness control at all is that if you have a slow machine, then there will be a long time step per update, which entails a longer simulation time step, which entails a greater distance step in each critter's update. This will produce unpleasant, jerky-looking motion. Therefore, if you have a slow machine, it is advisable to select a higher Motion Smoothness index.

Another time you might want to increase the Motion Smoothness is if a game seems to run too fast for you. If you have a fast machine and would like to see the critters acting very hyper, you can select a lower Motion Smoothness.

If you change the Motion Smoothness setting, this new setting stays in effect even if you use the Game menu to select a different game.

Accelerator keys

Start or Restart Game	**Enter**
Open Game Param file	**Ctrl+O**
Close Game Window	**Ctrl+F4**
Save Game Param file	**Ctrl+S**
New Game Window	**Ctrl+N**
Mute	**Ctrl+M**
Pause/Unpause	**Ctrl+P**
Close Pop Program	**Alt+F4**
Reset Viewpoint	**Ctrl+R**
Shoot Cursor	1
Pick Cursor	2
Drag Cursor	3
Pin Cursor	4
Zap Cursor	5
Replicate Cursor	6

There are also a few standard Windows accelerator keys that aren't listed here.

Contact information

The Pop program is shareware by Rudy Rucker, Copyright © 2002 all rights reserved. Contact rucker@rudyrucker.com for further information.

Appendix C:
Summary of the controls for Visual Studio

Action	Visual Studio, Version 6.0	Visual Studio.NET, Version 7.0
Open the Pop project	Click **pop.dsw** in Explorer or use **File	Open workspace...**	Click **pop.sln** in Explorer or use **File	Open solution...**
Edit Visual Studio directory paths for include and library files (usually not necessary)	**Tools	Options... |Directories**	**Tools	Options...	Projects	VC++ Directories**
Open the File View	**View	Workspace	File View** tab	**View	Solution Explorer**
Open the Class View	**View	Workspace	ClassView** tab	**View	Class View**
Open the Resource View	**View	Workspace	Resource View** tab	**View	Resource View**
Open the Output window	**View	Output**	**View	Other Windows	Output**
Open a view of the Call Stack	**View	Debug Windows	Call Stack**	**Debug	Windows	Call Stack**, or select **Stack Frame** on the **Debug Location** toolbar
Open a file for editing	**File	Open . . .** or double-click the file name in the File View	**File	Open	File...** or double-click the file name in the File View
Determine the directory of a file in the project	Open the File View, right-click the file, select **Properties**	Open the File View, highlight the file, select **View	Properties Window**
Add a file to the project	**Project	Add to Project	Files...**	**Project	Add Existing Item...**

Action	Visual Studio, Version 6.0	Visual Studio.NET, Version 7.0
Add event handlers for a menu item	Right-click the item and select **Class Wizard...**	Right-click the item and select **Add Event Handler...**
Import a bitmap	**Insert | Resource | Bitmap | Import...**	**Project | Add Resource... | Import...**
Set the active configuration to build	**Build | Set Active Configuration**	**Build | Configuration Manager** and scroll the **Active Solution Configuration** box
Open the Project Settings dialog	**Project | Settings...**	Open **View | Solution Explorer** and highlight the **Pop** project (not the solution), then select **View | Property Pages...** or press **Shift+F4**
Select which configuration's settings are being viewed in the Project Settings dialog	Open the Project Settings dialog and use the **Settings for** combo box	Open the Project Settings dialog and use the **Configuration** combo box
Set the output file name and directory	Open the Project Settings dialog, select which configuration to change, and edit **Link | General | Output File Name**	Open the Project Settings dialog, select which configuration to change, and edit **Configuration Properties | Linker | General | Output File**
Select how to use MFC (dll or lib)	Open the Project Settings dialog, select which configuration to change, and edit **General | Microsoft Foundation Classes**	Open the Project Settings dialog, select which configuration to change, and edit **Configuration Properties | General | Use of MFC**
Add an additonal library to the project	Open the Project Settings dialog, select all configurations, and edit **Project | Settings | Link | General | Object/Library Modules**	Open the Project Settings dialog, select all configurations, and edit **Configuration Properties | Linker | Input | Additional Dependencies**
Run the program in the debugger	If necessary, use **Build | Set Active Configuration** to select the Debug Configuration, then select **Build | Start Debug | Go**, or press the shortcut key F5	If necessary, use **Build | Configuration** Manager to select the Debug configuration, then select **Debug | Start**, or press the shortcut key F5

Action	Visual Studio, Version 6.0	Visual Studio.NET, Version 7.0
Run the program in without debugging	**Build | Execute**, or the shortcut key combo **Ctrl+F5**	**Debug | Start Without Degugging**, or the shortcut key combo **Ctrl+F5**
Key shortcut to build the program	**F7**	**Ctrl+Shift+B**
Key shortcut to build only the active file	**Ctrl+F7**	**Ctrl+F7**

Index